Handbook of Culture and Economic Behavior

Volume 1

Handbook of Culture and Economic Behavior
Volume 1

Edited by

Benjamin Enke

Paola Giuliano

Nathan Nunn

Leonard Wantchekon

ELSEVIER

N·H

North-Holland

An imprint of Elsevier

North-Holland is an imprint of Elsevier
Radarweg 29, PO Box 211, 1000 AE Amsterdam, Netherlands
125 London Wall, London EC2Y 5AS, United Kingdom

ISBN: 978-0-443-47184-1
ISSN: 3051-1682

Publisher: Zoe Kruze
Acquisitions Editor: Jason Mitchell
Editorial Project Manager: Sneha Apar
Production Project Manager: Bharatwaj Varatharajan
Cover Designer: Muthukumaran Thangaraj

Typeset by VTeX

Introduction to the series

The aim of the *Handbooks in Economics* series is to produce a definitive source, reference, and teaching supplement in different branches of the subject for use by professional researchers and graduate students. The series continues to bring out new handbooks in core areas and also seeks to expand into new areas that reflect modern developments in the methodology and the practice of economics.

Steven Durlauf
Sanjeev Goyal
Rosa Matzkin

Contents

4. The global variation in risk and time preferences

Anke Becker, Christina Borner, Thomas Dohmen, Armin Falk, David Huffman, and Uwe Sunde

Part II
Theories of culture

5. The nature of culture

Robert Boyd and Peter J. Richerson

11. A stairway to success: how parenting shapes culture and social stratification

Francesco Agostinelli, Matthias Doepke, Giuseppe Sorrenti, and Fabrizio Zilibotti

Contributors

Francesco Agostinelli, University of Pennsylvania, Philadelphia, PA, United States

George Akerlof, McCourt School of Public Policy, Georgetown University, Washington, DC, United States

Anke Becker, Harvard Business School, Boston, MA, United States

Alberto Bisin, Department of Economics, New York University, New York, NY, United States
NBER, Cambridge, MA, United States
CEPR, London, United Kingdom

Christina Borner, LMU Munich, Munich, Germany

Samuel Bowles, Santa Fe Institute, Santa Fe, NM, United States
CORE Econ, University College London, London, United Kingdom

Robert Boyd, School of Human Evolution and Social Change, Institute of Human Origins, Arizona State University, Tempe, AZ, United States

Jean-Paul Carvalho, Department of Economics, University of Oxford, Oxford, United Kingdom

Klaus Desmet, SMU, NBER, and CEPR, Department of Economics and Cox School of Business, Southern Methodist University, Dallas, TX, United States

Matthias Doepke, London School of Economics, London, United Kingdom

Thomas Dohmen, University of Bonn, Bonn, Germany
Maastricht University, Maastricht, Netherlands

Armin Falk, University of Bonn, Bonn, Germany

Steven J. Heine, University of British Columbia, Vancouver, BC, Canada

David Huffman, Cornell University, Ithaca, NY, United States

Rachel Kranton, Department of Economics, Duke University, Durham, NC, United States

Stelios Michalopoulos, Brown University, CEPR, and NBER, Providence, RI, United States

Ignacio Ortuño-Ortín, UC3M, Department of Economics, Universidad Carlos III de Madrid, Getafe, Madrid, Spain

Peter J. Richerson, Department of Environmental Science and Policy, University of California, Davis, CA, United States

Nikolaus Robalino, Department of Economics, Rochester Institute of Technology, Rochester, NY, United States

Arthur J. Robson, Department of Economics, Simon Fraser University, Burnaby, BC, Canada

Katrin Schmelz, Santa Fe Institute, Santa Fe, NM, United States
Technical University of Denmark, Kongens Lyngby, Denmark

Giuseppe Sorrenti, University of Lausanne, Lausanne, Switzerland

Uwe Sunde, LMU Munich, Munich, Germany

Thierry Verdier, Paris School of Economics and Ecole des Ponts-Paris Tech, Paris, France
PUC-Rio, Rio de Janeiro, Brazil
CEPR, London, United Kingdom

Romain Wacziarg, UCLA and NBER, UCLA Anderson School of Management, Los Angeles CA, United States

Fabrizio Zilibotti, Yale University, New Haven, CT, United States

Preface

Recent decades have seen the emergence of a large and rapidly growing body of research that seeks to understand human behavior by taking seriously the influence of values, beliefs, norms, identities, and moral commitments. These forces are central to economic and social life, yet they have often been difficult to incorporate into conventional theoretical and conceptual models of behavior.

The *Handbook of Culture and Economic Behavior* is organized around the concept of culture, defined as socially transmitted information that influences human behavior. Culture encompasses, for example, the values held by a society; the norms and identities its members are expected to adopt; beliefs about the afterlife; and understandings of the relationships among the human, physical, and spiritual worlds. Cultural traits may be transmitted vertically from parents to children, obliquely across generations, or horizontally among members of the same generation.

A central question in this literature is how cultural values and beliefs shape human behavior, and most chapters in this Handbook address some aspect of this question. At the same time, researchers have sought to understand the dynamic processes through which cultural traits emerge, persist, and change. Considerable theoretical and empirical progress has been made on both fronts. We now know much more about the determinants of the diverse cultural traits observed around the world, as well as the conditions under which societies exhibit cultural continuity or, instead, rapid cultural change.

As editors, we have sought to assemble a set of contributions that is broadly representative of the field and attentive to its intellectual foundations. The economics of culture has emerged from several areas within economics, particularly economic history, political economy, cultural evolution, and experimental economics. It is also deeply rooted in influential literatures outside economics, especially evolutionary anthropology and social psychology. Seminal contributions from these fields have become foundational for economists studying culture, and several leading scholars from these disciplines outside of economics have contributed chapters.

Research on culture is distinguished within economics by the remarkable diversity of its approaches, tools, and methods. The work represented in these volumes includes theoretical modeling, ethnographic and archival research, historical case studies, text analysis, laboratory and field experiments, surveys, reduced-form empirical analysis, and structural estimation. One of the field's important accomplishments has been its ability not only to accommodate this methodological diversity but to celebrate and draw strength from it.

This intellectual and methodological breadth is reflected in the contributions across the three volumes, which can be organized around six broad themes: theoretical models of the formation, transmission, evolution, and consequences of culture; the contemporary and historical measurement of culture; the deep historical origins of cultural traits; the short-run economic, institutional, and social forces that shape culture; the effects of culture on individual economic behavior and outcomes; and the relationship between culture and aggregate economic, political, and institutional outcomes.

The Handbook is structured as follows. Volume I focuses on measurement and theory, examining how cultural differences can be quantified and presenting the models of cultural evolution, transmission, identity, and norms that underpin the field. Volume II turns to the evidence on the deep origins of cultural variation and its consequences for institutions, economic growth, gender, religion, finance, and health. Volume III examines cultural change and its interactions with politics and public policy, covering topics ranging from migration and market interactions to political preferences, economic development, and nation-building.

Although the study of culture within economics has advanced substantially, many fundamental questions remain unresolved. We hope that these volumes will serve both as a synthesis of the field's achievements and as a foundation for future research on the role of culture in economic and social life.

Benjamin Enke
Paola Giuliano
Nathan Nunn
Leonard Wantchekon

Part I

Measuring and quantifying cultural heterogeneity

Chapter 1

Understanding the cultural foundation of psychology

Steven J. Heine
University of British Columbia, Vancouver, BC, Canada

A growing number of psychologists and economists are concerned with the ways that culture shapes human behavior, and the two fields stand to learn much from each other. In this chapter, I offer the perspective from a cultural psychologist on our understanding of how culture is implicated in the ways that people think, feel, and behave which I hope will be of utility for economists interested in culture. I first consider how psychology came to terms with the study of culture, and how culture can be seen as a fundamental part of human nature. I explore how cultures come to be, and how they change and persist across time. As members of a cultural species, people come to internalize many meanings from their cultures into their self-concepts, which facilitates their functioning, and I'll discuss how people tend to thrive when their self-concepts are better aligned with their cultures. I then review some of the most commonly studied aspects of culture that have been examined by cultural psychologists.

1 The role of culture in past psychological research

The study of culture has not always been much of a concern for the field of psychology. In the first century of the field's existence, with a few notable exceptions (e.g., Berry, 1969; Triandis, 1972; Vygotsky, 1929; Wundt, 1921), researchers gave relatively little regard to the topic. Rather, researchers commonly relied upon the assumption, often implicit (but occasionally explicit; e.g., Miller, 2003; Shepard, 2004), that the phenomena that they were studying reflected an underlying universal human nature. The particular psychological phenomena that were identified, such as cognitive dissonance, noun biases, or particular visual illusions, were assumed to be characteristics of the human species. There seemed to be a consensus in the field that one could draw conclusions about human nature by studying any healthy individual's mind, because all people were assumed to share the same underlying brain circuitry. There were the occasional dissenting voices to this consensus about assumed universality (e.g., Bruner, 1990; Cole et al., 1971; Gergen, 1973), but the vast

Handbook of Culture and Economic Behavior, Volume 1, ISSN 3051-1682
https://doi.org/10.1016/bs.hceb.2026.01.001

majority of researchers did not appear to view culture as particularly relevant for understanding the mind.

This universal orientation among psychology may have arisen from the field having inherited a theoretical framework guided by Newtonian principles (Kroupin et al., 2024), which some feel has left psychologists suffering from physics envy in their desire to identify phenomena that transcended any particular histories or contexts (e.g., Rozin, 2001). Moreover, during the cognitive revolution of the 1950s and 1960s, much research in the field was guided by a metaphor that the mind was like a computer (e.g., Gardner, 1985; Newell et al., 1959). As a computer, the hardware remains separate from the information that it is processing – it is independent of the content that it processes and the context that it is operating within. Applying this metaphor to the human mind suggests that researchers should try to describe the operations of the mind in terms that transcend matters of content and context – participants should be presented with identical content in a standardized context to best reveal the inner workings of this imagined underlying central processor (Shweder, 1990). With such a perspective of a universal and context-independent brain, there was not much incentive for researchers to compare the thinking styles of people in different cultures. Cross-cultural experiments introduce a lot of extraneous noise into the investigations, in that participants often speak different languages, have different norms about how individuals might interact with an experimenter, and have different degrees of familiarity with completing surveys, all of which would interfere with researchers' ability to observe the functioning of this assumed universal mind (Greenfield, 1997; Shweder, 1990).

The assumption of universality has had a significant impact on the ways that psychological research has traditionally been conducted. To the extent that the field believed that any one person's mind was viewed to be as good as any other's for revealing truths about human nature, it followed that researchers should focus on studying the minds that were most convenient for them to access. Rather than launching costly expeditions to measure the psychological processes in minds of participants from far-flung places, researchers instead tended to study the minds of the people who were more accessible, typically students from their own classes. A tendency to rely on convenience sampling came to be *de rigueur* in the field – for example, one review found that between 67 and 80% of the studies published in the top psychology journals had been conducted with university students (Arnett, 2008). Moreover, it was rare for researchers to consider their findings with respect to the samples that they had studied; indeed, the details about their samples, aside from gender and age, were often not even mentioned in the method sections, suggesting that the authors didn't consider this information to be relevant for understanding what they had identified (Henrich et al., 2010a). The participants who made up the psychological database seemed to be viewed as though they had been randomly sampled from a universal pool of humans.

Another factor that likely contributed to psychology's long period of neglecting culture was that the field had largely been a Western enterprise through much of its history. Most psychologists were from Western countries – an analysis of the first authors of papers that were published in the top psychology journals revealed that 73% were at American universities, and 99% were at universities in Western countries (Arnett, 2008). Likewise, another analysis revealed that 70% of citations in psychology come from authors located in the US, which was the highest proportion among the 20 different academic fields that were examined – for example, the percentage of American citations in chemistry was only 37% (May, 1997). Moreover, after the US the countries that had the next most psychology citations were also from English-speaking nations: the United Kingdom, Canada, and Australia, respectively. With so much of psychological research coming from researchers at Western English-speaking countries who tended to study convenience samples of the people around them, researchers would have had relatively few occasions to notice how findings from samples in other countries compared. The question of how psychology came to be so dominated by Western research has yet to be adequately addressed in the literature, although I suspect it may have something to do with the relatively greater salience of the self and inner psychological experiences among people from individualistic cultures, a topic that we'll return to later.

This peculiar Western fascination with psychology, alongside common practices to study convenience samples, has had one striking consequence for the field: it has resulted in a database of psychological research that is largely made up of participants from Western, Educated, Industrialized, Rich and Democratic (WEIRD) societies (Henrich et al., 2010b). For example, one investigation found that 96% of the samples in the top journals in the field came from WEIRD samples (Arnett, 2008), meaning that psychological research has had relatively little to say about the psychological processes of the bulk of the world's population. Despite increasing attention to this issue, more recent assessments of the representativeness of the psychological database have found that the field's relative neglect of non-Western samples largely continues (Nielsen et al., 2017; Rad et al., 2018; Thalmayer et al., 2021; Williamson et al., 2022).

Despite this historical inattention to concerns with the nature of samples in research, there have been some signs that the field of psychology has started to recognize the role of culture in shaping the human mind. First, there has been a growing appreciation of the limitations of a computer metaphor for characterizing the human mind. While there are certainly useful parallels between computers and brains that have facilitated psychological research, a key limitation with a computer metaphor is that brains do not remain detached from content and context. As much research over the past few decades has revealed, brains are rewired on the basis of people's experiences. For example, cab-drivers in London, before the onset of GPS navigation devices, had to represent a complicated map of possible routes which resulted in them developing larger posterior regions of the hippocampus – a region of the brain which facilitates spatial memory in navigation; the longer an individual had been driving a cab, the larger was this region of their hippocampus (Maguire et al., 2000). Another example reflects the ways brains are rewired when people learn how to read: the brains of literate and illiterate individuals differ from each other in a variety of complex ways, as the efforts involved in learning to read effectively rewired parts of the left ventral occipito-temporal region, the corpus callosum, and Broca's area (Dehaene, 2009; Henrich, 2020). This growing realization that our brains are shaped by experiences points to the key role that culture must play in psychology. Across cultures people have very different experiences, so it follows that their brains have been shaped accordingly (Chiao et al., 2013; Kitayama and Salvador, 2017).

In the past decade, psychology journals have made efforts to encourage more cultural research (e.g., editorials by Cooper, 2016; Kitayama, 2017). For example, some journals now ask authors to explicitly specify any constraints on generalizations that they are offering, challenging the implicit assumption that one's findings reflect a universal human nature (Simons et al., 2017). In addition, some coordinated efforts, such as the Psychological Science Accelerator (Moshontz et al., 2018), have strived to facilitate the collection of data from many countries at a time. With an increasing effort to study people from a variety of cultures, the field has identified a large number of psychological phenomena that vary across cultures in pronounced ways (e.g., Heine and Lehman, 1997a; Heine et al., 1999; Kim, 2002; Nisbett et al., 2001; Ryder et al., 2008; Tsai, 2007). Moreover, findings that reveal that many psychological phenomena show changes alongside the amount of time that immigrants have spent in a new cultural environment (e.g., De Leersnyder et al., 2011; Heine and Lehman, 2004; Tsai et al., 2004), provide further support to the notion that many psychological phenomena are shaped by the context that individuals are raised in. This growing appreciation of the role that culture plays in psychological phenomena is reflected in the increasing proportion of psychological research targeting questions about culture over recent decades (Kashima, 2016).

2 Humans are a cultural species

To explore the role of culture in the human mind we first need to be clear what we mean by culture. A variety of different definitions of culture have been relied upon by different fields (e.g., Geertz, 1973; Hall, 1980; Schein, 2004), which differ subtly in their points of emphasis. Cultural psychology largely relies on two different definitions of culture which have guided research, which we will consider in order: culture as information, and culture as social groups. First, culture is commonly used to refer to a particular kind of *information*. Richerson and Boyd (2005, p. 5) define it as "information capable of affecting individuals' behavior that they acquire from other members of their species through teaching, imitation, and other means of social transmission." We can see evidence for this kind of culture in many species throughout the animal kingdom where individuals acquire information from other conspecifics (Whiten, 2021), including some species with modest nervous systems, such as guppies (Lachlan et al., 1998) and fruit flies (Danchin et al., 2018).

In particular, much research has explored the cultural learning capacities in our closest animal relatives, chimpanzees, which sheds much light on the central role of culture in human lives. Like humans, chimpanzees are large-brained primates who live in complex social groups (De Waal, 1982; Dunbar, 1993), and they demonstrate some striking mental capacities (e.g., strategic competitive skills, working memory capacity) that rival those of humans (Inoue and Matsuzawa, 2007; Martin et al., 2014). Chimpanzees show clear evidence for cultural learning, yet the most comprehensive analysis of chimpanzee culture identified only 7 habitual behaviors (such as whether they would use a leaf as a sponge to retrieve water, or whether they would shake branches to attract attention from others) which reliably distinguished members of different chimpanzee populations, and another 32 behaviors that were observed by some members of each population (Whiten et al., 1999), although the role of cultural learning in these abilities continues to be debated (Acerbi et al., 2022; Vaesen et al., 2021). This cultural repertoire is far more limited than that of humans, for whom there is a vast number of culturally-learned behaviors and practices, many of which, such as dialects, some cultural practices, and specific tools, are accessible to virtually every member of a population.

In the roughly 6 million years since humans last shared a common ancestor with chimpanzees (Suddendorf, 2013), humans have evolved several adaptations that have facilitated their ability to acquire and depend upon cultural information. For example, the human eye evolved a white sclera and a wider shape that makes it easier to detect the direction of an individual's gaze; something that stands in contrast to the more than 200 other species of primates (Kano et al., 2022; Kobayashi and Kohshima, 2001). This suggests that it was adaptive for humans to have their gaze seen by others, likely because it provided some clues as to what they were considering. Humans also evolved complex languages that far outstrip the capacities of other species which enabled them to effectively communicate and share meanings with each other (Deacon, 1997; Lieberman and McCarthy, 2013). Moreover, humans evolved a neural system that rewards them when they share information about themselves with others. For example, one experiment found that when people are sharing their experiences with others they show increased activation of the reward centers of the brain (Tamir and Mitchell, 2012). Perhaps this is why so much of human conversation is based on people sharing their experiences with others (estimates of 30–40% of utterances; Dunbar et al., 1997; Emler, 1994), and why this content dominates what people post on social media (e.g., Naaman et al., 2010). This strong desire to share one's experiences suggests that it was adaptive for humans when others had a richer understanding of what they were thinking. These adaptations facilitated humans' abilities to engage in joint attention with others, and to achieve a sense of common ground, where they are aware that they and their interlocutors are attending to the same event (Tomasello, 2014). In contrast chimpanzees appear to show little interest in what others are thinking about (Engelmann et al., 2012; Silk et al., 2005), and they rarely achieve a sense of common ground (e.g., Tomasello et al., 2005). By being motivated to share their thoughts with others, and having the means to communicate them with others, humans evolved the capacities for engaging in cultural learning.

A second definition of culture that guides research in cultural psychology is that culture refers to a group of individuals. I have defined culture as "a group of people who are existing within some kind of shared context" (Heine, 2020, p. 5). Within a given context, people regularly communicate with each other, transmitting their ideas and perspectives, and these accumulate into edifices of commonly understood meanings that create shared realities (Baumeister, 2022; Bourdieu, 1977; Heine et al., 2024). These shared meanings lead to the formation of norms that guide people's behaviors and are often distinguished from the norms that emerge from people who live in other contexts (Ricart-Huguet and Paluck, 2023). These norms frequently come to dictate what kinds of behaviors are valued, encouraged, tolerated, or shunned.

The shared contexts that constitute cultures occur at a number of different levels, such that individuals belong to numerous overlapping cultures. At the broadest level, we can refer to cultures that cut across wide swaths of the globe, such as "Western culture", in which people are exposed to similar values, institutions, and preferences for particular kinds of art, music, and cuisine that are shared among people living in Europe and the places that were colonized by Europeans (with European-descent individuals becoming the majority, such as Australia and the US). One step down and we can consider cultures as nations, the most common level of culture studied by psychologists, in which their members typically share a common history, language, media, various cultural practices, and government. Cultures can also be distinguished at regional levels, such as differences between the cultures of New York and Boston, or between Tuscany and Sicily. But culture is not just coterminous with geography, as people who share the same geography may nonetheless be part of distinctive social networks which determine who they are communicating with. In particular, religions are highly influential cultural groups (White et al., 2021), but any regularly interacting networks of individuals may create their own cultures. So we may speak of Harvard culture, LGBTQ culture, Gen-Z culture, African-American culture, Apple culture, or pickle-ball culture. Any individual belongs to an overlapping set of cultural contexts, and depending on which context is salient at any given time, they may alternate between different sets of cultural norms (e.g., Anderson, 1999; Hong et al., 2000).

3 Cultural evolution and persistence

As influential as cultures may be on people's thoughts and behaviors, they do not take long to emerge. For example, one study compared the attitudes of university students who were randomly assigned to live in particular college residence houses (Cullum and Harton, 2007). Shortly after moving into dorms the students were surveyed about their attitudes on various topics, and then 3 months later, they were again asked to complete the same list of attitudes. Over that rather brief period of time, there was evidence for a significant clustering of attitudes; students came to have more similar attitudes to people living within their dorms, and rather distinct attitudes from those living in other dorms; in sum, new subcultures were beginning to form. Other research has similarly found that new cultures with distinctive norms can emerge in relatively brief periods of time (Ricart-Huguet, 2022; Ricart-Huguet and Paluck, 2023; Talhelm and Dong, 2024).

As the speed with which new cultures can emerge attests, cultures are dynamic systems. They continue to change as new information is incorporated into existing cultural practices and norms, which can occur as a function of such things as technological innovations, climatic change, war, mass migrations, and international trade (Giuliano and Nunn, 2021; Henrich et al., 2019; Putnam, 2000). The rate of cultural change is a product of how many individual minds are linked together (Derex et al., 2013; Muthukrishna et al., 2014). Some kinds of cultural contexts are hypothesized to be more likely to undergo rapid cultural change, such as collectivistic cultures, or cultures with tight social norms (Muthukrishna and Schaller, 2020; Schaller and Muthukrishna, 2021). The dynamic nature of cultures means that the study of psychology is necessarily historical, as any observations of a culture are but a snapshot in time (Muthukrishna et al., 2021).

Cultures continue to evolve over time, and even though there are many common experiences and innovations that may be shared across different cultures, each culture is somewhat path-dependent and on its own unique trajectory, evolving from earlier conditions by interweaving new cultural innovations into its distinctive history. Even in the present, during a period when the world is vastly interconnected and facing numerous globalizing forces, national cultures have been found to be diverging further apart from each other in some respects (Barber, 1995; Jackson and Medvedev, 2024). One recently developed method that is commonly used for calculating the magnitude of cultural difference between any pairs of cultures (whether they be nations, generations, genders, religions, etc.) is the cultural fixation index (Muthukrishna et al., 2020), which compares how different responses are to a large set of values from the World Values Survey (Inglehart et al., 2014).

Although cultures are dynamic and are capable of rapid change, somewhat paradoxically, cultures often demonstrate remarkable persistence over long periods of time. Cultures tend to be self-perpetuating, as all new cultural members, either those who are born into the culture or those who have migrated to it, are exposed to, and shaped by, the cultures' norms and practices, thereby reproducing those norms and practices themselves. Much like the processes of biological evolution, where new mutations are constrained by the existing structures, any new cultural innovation must be woven into the web of extant cultural meanings, and in this manner serves to preserve much of the cultural norms. Moreover, cultures tend to be slower to change because of forces of pluralistic ignorance, where individuals tend to collectively misinterpret the private views of others based on their public actions, which are often misleading because people tend to act in ways that they assume will be perceived favorably by others (Prentice and Miller, 1996; Van Boven, 2000; Brown et al., 2022). These collective errors can preserve cultural traditions even in cases where majorities of cultural members may privately disapprove of those traditions (Cohen, 2001).

There are many documented instances of striking cultural persistence across centuries. For example, Putnam et al. (1993) demonstrated that the relatively egalitarian institutions of the northern regions of medieval Italy contrasted with some of the corruption and lawlessness of the southern regions in ways that parallel the current regional differences in Italian governance, social capital, and average income, despite the emergence of a central national government and the passage of more than 8 centuries (Guiso et al., 2016). Likewise, regional differences in anti-Semitism across Germany during the time of the Bubonic Plague in the 14th century (as evidenced by pogroms) were paralleled by similar regional differences in anti-Semitism during the rise of National Socialism in the 1920s (Voigtländer and Voth, 2012). Another discouraging example of cultural persistence comes from the Atlantic slave trade. The centuries of slave-raiding spawned pronounced feelings of mistrust towards others in Africa. Tellingly, the regions of the continent where more slaves had been captured prior to the 19th century continue in the 21st century to have far less trust towards others compared with regions where fewer slaves were taken, which has undermined economic development (Nunn, 2008; Nunn and Wantchekon, 2011). It is because of the forces of cultural persistence that we can often recognize familiar cultural themes when reading historical accounts of the past from around the world.

Humans are thus strongly shaped by their cultures, which continue to evolve over time. Moreover, as with all other species, we are also the product of genetic evolution. However, humans may be largely unique in the animal kingdom in that our genetic evolution has endowed us with a brain that is dependent upon cultural learning in order to survive. Moreover, these dual inheritance systems can interact, through a process termed gene-culture coevolution (Henrich, 2016). For example, some ancient cultural inventions, such as cooking and dairy-farming, may have shaped the genetic evolution of our digestive systems (Beja-Pereira et al., 2003; Wrangham, 2009). Likewise, it was through genetic evolution that humans are endowed with adaptations such as a visible gaze, the ability to communicate with language, and a drive to share one's experiences, that facilitated the evolution of our cultures. Culture is thus implicated not just in the environments that humans exist within, but it has also played a role in shaping our species' genome.

4 Different cultures beget different selves

As a product of gene-culture co-evolution, culture is inextricably linked to human functioning, and to a degree far greater than that of other species. So dependent are humans on their culture, that their ecology importantly includes particular cultural meanings (Heine et al., 2024). That is, unlike the ecologies of other animal species that consist of a physical and sometimes a social environment, human ecologies are also importantly constituted by the cultural meanings that have accumulated across human history. These cultural meanings include specific practices, technological innovations, norms, habits, and institutions – core features of cultures that people may rarely think about how they emerged, but are nonetheless dependent upon. Cultural meanings have evolved and accumulated within all human cultures, and they determine how people lead their lives, such as dictating what one should have for dinner, what kinds of careers one may pursue, which gods they will worship, and how one should strive to attract and maintain a mate. These accumulated frameworks of cultural meanings determine the kinds of behaviors that are valued, shunned, tolerated, and encouraged in a society.

While cultural meaning frameworks can vary tremendously across societies, humans all share a set of species-wide basic needs that they need to fulfill. These include needs for physiological resources, self-protection, belongingness, status, mate acquisition and retention, and parenting (Kenrick et al., 2010). However, the ways that people pursue these needs are directed in particular ways that are shaped by their cultures. For example, humans are a pair-bonding species which means that they typically strive to retain their mates which is adaptive because of the extended period that their offspring are dependent on their care and cultural teachings. Yet the ways that people enter and maintain pair-bonding relationships are guided by norms that can vary substantially across cultures. In some societies marriages are arranged by relatives; some allow husbands to have multiple wives; in others, wives may have multiple husbands; some allow people to marry their cousins, or children, or people of the same sex as themselves. These different ways that people ultimately satisfy their needs to retain their mates and parent their children are not just differences in what is familiar or preferred; a kind of marriage that is commonplace in one culture may be explicitly forbidden, and subject to harsh penalties, in another.

Humans pursue all of their basic needs in culturally-guided ways, and they are thus dependent upon their abilities to understand and master local cultural meanings in order to survive. This deep dependence on cultural meanings requires that these meanings are highly accessible to individuals, such that their default reactions in any situation would largely be aligned with local cultural norms. Baumeister et al. (2018) propose that the human self evolved as a means to make these meanings more accessible. People's selves internalize cultural meanings, which ensure that individuals interpret any events in ways that are consistent with the surrounding cultural meanings (Heine, 2005). Selves organize and consolidate cultural meanings to facilitate people's abilities to act in ways that are aligned well with local cultural meanings. They enable people to act promptly and consistently in ways that are in accordance with cultural meanings, so that their actions are more likely to be successful. As Baumeister (2022, p. 4) put it, "The self exists at the interface between the human animal body and the complicated social structures that we call society and culture." Cultures and selves are deeply entangled, such that cultural meanings come to shape the self, while at the same time the interaction of selves comes to direct the evolution of cultures. This notion of the mutual constitution of self and culture is one of the key premises in the field of cultural psychology (Heine, 2020; Markus and Kitayama, 2010; Shweder, 1990).

The self is a central feature of human psychology, as people's selves serve as the lens through which they perceive and understand their worlds, and thus are central to people's psychological experiences (Baumeister, 2022; Markus and Kitayama, 1991). People with different kinds of selves have associated psychological processes that also vary importantly from each other, such as maintaining different kinds of relationships with others (e.g., Adams, 2005; Thomson et al., 2018), experiencing emotions differently (e.g., Mesquita, 2022; Tsai et al., 2006a), being motivated by different concerns (e.g., Heine et al., 1999; Kim and Markus, 1999; Savani et al., 2008), and reasoning in different ways (e.g., Nisbett et al., 2001; Peng and Nisbett, 1999). Much research has found striking differences in the kinds of selves that are common across cultures (e.g., Krys et al., 2022; Ma and Schoeneman, 1997; Talhelm et al., 2014; Uskul et al., 2023). Correspondingly, cross-cultural findings commonly reveal that people from different cultures often react in strikingly different ways to the same situation or set of stimuli (e.g., Grossmann and Kross, 2010; Miller, 1984; Heine et al., 2001; Masuda and Nisbett, 2001; Segall et al., 1963). The key ways that selves have internalized cultural values highlight the limitations with assuming that individuals can be used interchangeably in studies or models; each individual is guided by a set of cultural values that may vary substantially from one another.

While cultures shape people's selves and associated psychological processes, it is important to recognize that people participate in multiple overlapping cultures, such as those from their country, their ethnicity, their religion, their local community, and so on. Accordingly, people tend to develop multiple self-concepts which are associated with the different cultures that they belong to (Anderson, 1999; LaFromboise et al., 1993). People navigate between their different cultures by these different selves becoming more accessible whenever they move between cultural contexts through a process known as frame-switching (Benet-Martinez et al., 2002; Gardner et al., 2004). Much research has been conducted to investigate people's reactions when aspects of their different cultures have been made salient to them. This has been achieved through a variety of means, such as presenting participants with photos from their cultures (e.g., Hong et al., 2000), comparing the responses of bilinguals when the task is presented in different languages (e.g., Lee et al., 2010; Ross et al., 2002), or priming collectivistic vs. individualistic aspects of the self (Oyserman and Lee, 2008; Trafimow et al., 1991). Commonly, these studies reveal that people respond to these situations in ways that are consistent with the cultures that have been made most salient to them.

5 Alignment of culture and self facilitates health and well-being

Though selves and cultures are mutually constituted, this does not imply that people who share the same culture will largely share the same selves. Cultures emerge from the interactions of their individual members who may differ from each other in countless ways, such as having different genomes, life histories, and memberships in different sets of subcultures. These many individual differences among cultural members mean that although people in a given culture will largely be exposed to many of the same cultural meanings, they may respond to those meanings in quite different ways, with some people strongly embracing particular cultural meanings, others actively resisting them, and others neglecting them. This individual diversity within cultures is important not just for the course of cultural evolution, but in the ways that cultures affect their members.

The diversity of individuals that exist within any cultural context means that there is variation in terms of how closely a given individual's self is in alignment with the dominant cultural meanings in a given context. The extent to which an individual's unique characteristics align with the prototypes of their cultures is termed "cultural fit" (e.g., Levine et al., 2016). To the extent that the self is functional because it makes cultural meanings more accessible to individuals, selves that fit better with a dominant culture's meanings should be more efficacious in their actions. The reflexive thoughts and behaviors of individuals with greater cultural fit should be in better alignment with the ways that the culture encourages, whereas the reactions of "cultural misfits" may often be at odds with cultural norms.

In recent years, a burgeoning body of literature has demonstrated that people who have greater cultural fit are more likely to experience a variety of positive outcomes. For example, cultural fit has been found to facilitate acculturation (Cross, 1995; De Leersnyder et al., 2011) and more satisfying relationships with others (De Leersnyder et al., 2014; Friedman et al., 2010). Likewise, students who have better cultural fit with their university tend to earn higher grades in their coursework (Phillips et al., 2020); people whose religious views are more similar to the dominant religion within a country enjoy better psychological adjustment (Gebauer et al., 2012); wealthier people tend to be happier in more affluent countries than in poorer ones (Tay et al., 2014), people who act in ways that deviate from social norms tend to be lonelier (Heu, 2023), and people whose personality profile is more similar to the prototypical personality within a culture tend to enjoy better well-being (Fulmer et al., 2010; Götz et al., 2018). This research finds that having a self that fits well with the surrounding cultural context brings many psychological benefits. Curiously, the benefits of cultural fit extend to people's physical health as well. For example, people whose selves align better with the surrounding cultures have been found to eat healthier diets (Levine et al., 2016); people whose sleep durations are more similar to local cultural norms tend to have fewer chronic health conditions (Ou et al., 2025); people whose political views (Ebert et al., 2023) and religious beliefs (Ebert et al., 2020) are more similar to those around them tend to live longer, and obesity is associated with more harmful health outcomes in contexts where fewer people are overweight (Berkessel et al., 2024). In sum, in many ways fitting in with the surrounding culture tends to make life a little easier. These benefits of cultural fit underscore just how much cultures and selves are intertwined and suggest that researchers should attend both to the culture and an individual's fit with that culture in predicting their well-being.

6 Some key culturally-shaped traits

Because cultural norms arise in any shared context of individuals, there would seem to be a nearly endless variety of ways that cultures differ from each other. However, there are a few key culturally-shaped traits that have been identified in several different populations that have been found to have a strong influence on people's thinking styles. While economists have studied some features that differ across cultures, such as patience, risk aversion, and a long-term orientation (Falk et al., 2018; Galor and Özak, 2016; l'Haridon and Vieider, 2019), these traits have received less attention among cultural psychologists. Below I consider some of the cultural traits that have attracted the most research attention among psychologists.

6.1 Collectivism-individualism

For the most part, the different cultural traits that have been identified by cultural psychologists have been explored in separate lines of research, and little is known about how they may relate to each other. An exception to this pattern is that a number of key cultural traits share in common a concern with how individuals relate to those around them (i.e., collectivism-individualism, relational mobility, analytic vs. holistic thinking, honor, and tightness-looseness). The trait underlying this that has received, by far, the most research attention is the dimension of collectivism-individualism. Collectivism has been defined as "a social pattern consisting of closely linked individuals who see themselves as parts of one or more collectives (family, co-workers, tribe, nation); are primarily motivated by the norms of, and duties imposed by, those collectives; are willing to give priority to the goals of these collectives over their own personal goals; and emphasize their connectedness to members of those collectives" (Triandis, 1995, p. 2). Collectivism is commonly contrasted against individualism which has been defined as "a social pattern that consists of loosely linked individuals who view themselves as independent of collectives; are primarily motivated by their own preferences, needs, rights, and the contracts they have established with others; give priority to their personal goals over the goals of others; and emphasize rational analyses of the advantages and disadvantages of associating with others" (Triandis, 1995, p. 2). Individualism and collectivism are often assessed through a number of self-report scales that assess the degree to which people prioritize individual vs. collective goals (e.g., Hofstede, 2001; Triandis, 1996), or by comparisons of demographic and culture-level measures (e.g., Pelham et al., 2022; Vandello and Cohen, 1999).

Cultural differences in collectivism and individualism can lead to some strikingly different behavioral patterns. A real life example of the prioritization of collective goals over individual ones that is a defining characteristic of collectivist societies could be seen in the COVID-19 pandemic, where more collectivistic regions of countries had higher rates of mask-wearing (English et al., 2022), and better health outcomes than more individualistic regions of those same countries (Talhelm et al., 2023); and parallel findings emerged between countries as well (Feng et al., 2023; Lu et al., 2021). Collectivist practices may have beneficial trade-offs for collective-action problems such as pandemics, however, they do bear some other costs. For example, the prioritization of one's own group over another group can facilitate corruption, and several investigations have identified more corruption among more collectivist cultures (e.g., Jha and Panda, 2017; Judge et al., 2011; Zheng et al., 2013). The large body of research on collectivism-individualism has revealed a number of psychological tendencies that are associated with it, which we'll explore below.

People living in more collectivistic societies commonly develop an interdependent self-concept, which can be contrasted with an independent self-concept, which is more common among individualistic societies (Markus and Kitayama, 1991). These self-concepts are typically assessed through a variety of self-report measures (e.g., Kitayama et al., 2009; Kuhn and McPartland, 1954; Singelis, 1994). Interdependent selves are especially prevalent across several East Asian societies (e.g., Heine, 2001), where a large proportion of cross-cultural research has been conducted. More generally, though, interdependent selves are also relatively more common in South Asia (e.g., Kitayama et al., 2022), Latin America (Krys et al., 2022), Arabic cultures (e.g., San Martin et al., 2018), among some Native American tribes (e.g., Fryberg and Markus, 2003), parts of Africa (e.g., Ma and Schoeneman, 1997), and among many Mediterranean societies (e.g., Uskul et al., 2023). While the specifics of the ways that interdependence is expressed in particular cultures can vary substantially in the details (e.g., Vignoles et al., 2016), a number of characteristics have been identified in various research programs. For example, people with more interdependent selves tend to understand themselves as a relational entity who is deeply connected and sustained by their close relationships (Markus and Kitayama, 1991). They tend to define themselves relatively more in terms of the groups that they belong to, the roles that they have with others, and the relationships that they have with ingroup members – they focus less on themselves as individual agents and more as someone participating in a larger social unit (Cousins, 1989; Heine, 2001). They are also relatively detached from outgroup members, to whom they have far fewer obligations and tend to trust less, which means that they maintain a more pronounced boundary between in-group and out-group relationships (Heine, 2020; Yamagishi and Yamagishi, 1994). People with interdependent selves are also likely to attend closely to what they think others are thinking of them, and this is an important guide to their behavior (e.g., Cohen et al., 2007; Kim et al., 2010). This attention to others and to the context leads people with interdependent selves to feel relatively more different when they are in different contexts (e.g., Kanagawa et al., 2001; Suh, 2002), and to maintain relatively greater beliefs that their self is malleable and can change across time (e.g., Heine et al., 2001; Lockhart et al., 2009; Rattan et al., 2012). Nonetheless, despite that people with more interdependent selves feel such strong ties to ingroup relationships, they may often be in competition with ingroup members, and remain vigilant of each other's behaviors (Liu et al., 2019; Yamagishi, 1988).

In contrast to the interdependent self, people from much of Western Europe and in places colonized by Western Europeans (Markus and Kitayama, 1991; Triandis, 1994), are more likely to possess independent self-concepts. In contrast to those with more interdependent self-concepts, people with independent selves are more likely to understand themselves as an autonomous entity, and they focus on their psychological characteristics, such as their personality traits, attitudes, emotions, and abilities, which serve as important guides for their behavior (e.g., Heine, 2001; Mesquita, 2022). People with independent selves tend to have more open relational networks, and maintain a less pronounced distinction between ingroup and outgroup relationships (Heine, 2020; Thomson et al., 2018). And independent selves tend to feel more fixed, feeling as though they change relatively little across contexts and across time (e.g., Heine et al., 2001; Suh, 2002). It is important to emphasize that there is much variation in ways that interdependence and independence are experienced across cultures and across individuals within cultures, however, these kinds of broad cultural differences have been identified using a variety of kinds of methods including questionnaires (e.g., Ma and Schoeneman, 1997; Triandis et al., 1990), behavioral experiments (e.g., Kim et al., 2010; Talhelm et al., 2019), assessments of cultural products (e.g., Kim and Markus, 1999; Tsai et al., 2006b), and brain imaging (e.g., Kitayama et al., 2017; Zhu et al., 2007).

As the self-concept is so central to psychological experience (Baumeister, 2022), these differences between independent and interdependent selves are paralleled by cultural differences in a broad suite of psychological tendencies. For example, people with more interdependent selves have a relatively stronger motivation to fit in, compared with those with more independent selves (Markus and Kitayama, 1991). Correspondingly, conformity tends to be valued more (Clegg et al., 2017; Kinias et al., 2014; Tian and Bian, 2023), and guides people's behaviors more in collectivist societies where interdependent selves are more common (Bond and Smith, 1996). Similarly, people's preferences for distinctive objects, as opposed to common objects, are more pronounced in individualistic societies (e.g., Ishii et al., 2014; Kim and Markus, 1999). Another way that psychological experiences differ across people with different views of self is that emotions tend to be experienced more collectively, and are guided more by relational concerns, among those with more interdependent views of self (Kitayama et al., 2000; Mesquita, 2001; 2022; Savani et al., 2013; Uchida et al., 2022). More generally, because people with interdependent selves tend to be looking more to cues from others and from the environment to guide their behavior, they are less likely to closely attend to their emotional experiences. Some evidence for this is that people with interdependent selves report feeling their emotions less intensely and less frequently (Dzokoto, 2010; Kitayama et al., 2000; Ma-Kellams et al., 2012; Mesquita and Karasawa, 2002), and have less difficulty in suppressing them in contrast to those with more independent views of self (Butler et al., 2009; Schunk et al., 2022; Tamir et al., 2024). Another example of how the self-concept is associated with different ways of thinking, is that people with more interdependent selves tend to be guided more by moral concerns of community, and view their obligations towards others in their social networks in full moral terms, as opposed to matters of personal choice (Buchtel et al., 2018; Miller and Bersoff, 1992; Miller et al., 2017; Vauclair et al., 2014).

6.2 Relational mobility

Another psychological construct which covaries somewhat with collectivism/individualism is termed relational mobility (Thomson et al., 2018; Yuki et al., 2007). This refers to the extent that people view others that they encounter as those who they could potentially form relationships with, as opposed to being seen as someone who is bound to their other social networks. In cultural contexts with high relational mobility, people have much freedom in moving between relationships. They are existing in a relatively open relationship market and have plenty of opportunities to form new relationships rather than being bound by their existing ones, and they tend to maintain larger social networks (Seth et al., 2023). In these contexts people seem to view their relationships as choices, and they may dissolve ties with relationships that do not seem particularly satisfying or rewarding to themselves. Their default view towards any other individual is that they do not have a relationship with them unless both parties feel that it is in their interests to act in ways to form and maintain the relationship. Hence, people in high relationally mobile contexts need to make efforts to both attract new relationship partners, and to keep the ones that they value. Any traits or behaviors that signal that one may be a desirable relationship partner are particularly valued and cultivated. High mobility contexts are more common in individualistic cultures, such as North America, and Western Europe, but they are also especially pronounced in Latin America. They are also more common in urban regions, and among herding communities, where there is less reliance on neighbors, than in farming regions (Plaut et al., 2009; Thomson et al., 2018). Relational mobility is most commonly assessed with a self-report measure (Thomson et al., 2018).

In contrast, in contexts with low relational mobility, people have relatively few opportunities to form new relationships. They exist in a more closed relationship market, and their relationships can be seen as being somewhat assigned to them; they include their family members, the people in their neighborhoods, classmates, and co-workers. These relationships are viewed as stable, often lifelong connections to whom they have obligations towards, and can receive benefits from. Their default view towards those in their network is that they have a relationship, whether they make efforts to maintain them or not. Traits that may be useful for attracting new relationship partners tend to be of relatively lesser value compared with more mobile contexts. These low mobility contexts are more commonly found in collectivistic regions, such as East and Southeast Asia, North and West Africa, and the Middle East (Adams, 2005; Thomson et al., 2018). Farming communities tend to have relatively lower relational mobility because people have few opportunities to move. Moreover, places which are prone to natural disasters or high pathogen prevalence tend to form tight close-knit communities and show little trust towards outsiders (Thomson et al., 2018).

An appreciation of the dynamics of relational mobility can help to shed light on a number of psychological phenomena. For example, friendships tend to be viewed in more ambivalent terms in places with low relational mobility. Friendships not only entail sharing good times and offering social support, but they also come with costly obligations (Adams and Plaut, 2003; Li et al., 2015), and they may sometimes be in competition with the self (cf., Liu et al., 2019). In contexts where an individual is largely bound to their relationships, they are not easily able to avoid those relationships which elicit bad feelings, and over time, these protracted negative exchanges may develop into enemyships (Adams, 2005). For example, people in Ghana, a low relational mobility society, not only report having far greater numbers of enemies than do Americans, a high relational mobility society, they are more likely than Americans to report that the enemies that they do have are members of their ingroups (Adams et al., 2004; also see Li et al., 2018). In contrast, people from more mobile societies are more likely to avoid people that they don't view as desirable, and enemyships are less likely to develop. Rather, they tend to choose to spend time with those people that offer the most beneficial exchanges, and they make efforts to be a rewarding partner to their friends.

In high relational mobility contexts, people stand to gain by forming relationships with partners who will benefit them the most. This breeds much competition among potential relational partners and people need to find ways to attract and maintain the most desirable partners. In such a context, any trait or attribute that advertises one's desirability should be especially important. For example, people who are more physically attractive tend to enjoy various benefits in their lives, such as being evaluated more positively by their teachers (Clifford and Walster, 1973), earning higher wages (Johnston, 2010), being assumed to be more moral (Klebl et al., 2023), and being more successful as a politician (Stockemer and Praino, 2015). Yet, in less relationally mobile societies, where people are not seeking new relationships, these kinds of benefits of physical attractiveness are not as evident (Anderson et al., 2008; Lee and Adams, 2021; Plaut et al., 2009). Another characteristic which has been found to play a key role in attracting others in more relationally mobile societies is similarity. On average, people in these societies tend to like those who are similar to themselves in terms of personality (Griffitt, 1966), attitudes (Newcomb, 1961), interests (Hogan et al., 1971), and background (Buss, 1985) – a phenomenon that is known as the similarity attraction effect (Byrne, 1971). Yet, similarity to oneself is not viewed as positively in societies that have lower relational mobility (Bahns et al., 2019; Heine et al., 2009; Schug et al., 2009). There is less benefit associated with being perceived as having similar characteristics to someone if they are in a closed relationship market and have fewer opportunities to form new relationships or to leave existing ones.

Relational mobility also plays a role in the nature of romantic relationships. In high relational mobility societies, individuals recognize that their partners may be tempted away from them by more desirable competitors, so they are incentivized to make more efforts to be a generous partner. For example, they may routinely emphasize how much they love their partner, they may self-disclose more, and they may show more passion towards their partners. These behaviors are less evident in low relational mobility contexts (Kito et al., 2017; Schug et al., 2010; Yamada et al., 2017). In contrast, in less mobile contexts, couples are less likely to get divorced (Thomson et al., 2018), and relationship satisfaction tends to be more predicted by levels of commitment (Ng and Cheng, 2010).

Similar to relational mobility is the construct of residential mobility, which refers to the frequency with which individuals change their residences over the course of their lifetime (Oishi and Tsang, 2022). When people move their home, they also need to establish a social network in their new community, so this also requires the creation of new relationships. Residential mobility varies both among individuals (some move more often than others), and among communities (some communities have more people coming and going). The

US has historically been noted for having high rates of residential mobility (see De Tocqueville, 1835/2003), although in recent decades this has been decreasing (Buttrick and Oishi, 2021). Residential mobility is associated with various psychological correlates: for example, studies with American college students find that those who have moved more tend to show more conditional loyalty to their colleges (Oishi et al., 2009), continue to acquire more Facebook friends over time (Seder and Oishi, 2008), view their group memberships as less of a part of their identity, instead emphasizing their personality traits more (Oishi et al., 2007), and seek familiarity, for example, by preferring to shop at large national chain stores over local regional stores (Oishi et al., 2012). These moves can cause some distress, particularly among adolescents (Li et al., 2019), but they do bring better job opportunities, which can accumulate over generations, and families with a history of higher residential mobility tend to have higher incomes (Alesina et al., 2015). Likewise, American communities that have higher degrees of residential mobility have been found to have more fair-weather sports fans (Oishi et al., 2007), higher crime rates and less pro-community action (Oishi et al., 2007; Sampson et al., 1997), and more large national chain stores per capita (Oishi et al., 2012).

6.3 Analytic vs. holistic thinking styles

The ways that people relate to others also come to shape how they think about the physical world (Nisbett, 2003; Nisbett et al., 2001). People with interdependent selves tend to closely monitor each other's behaviors to keep track of their reciprocal obligations, and this is associated with a tendency to pay close attention to the social environment (San Martin et al., 2019). They are likely to conceive of other people in terms of the social networks that they belong to, and they thus view relationships as key predictors of the behavior of individuals. This is contrasted with people with more independent selves, who tend to think of others as distinct individuals, who can be best understood by considering their inner psychological characteristics. Likewise, when attending to objects in the physical world, people with more interdependent selves tend to consider how individual objects are related to other objects, and to the surrounding context. They show a more *holistic* perceptual style, where they are likely to attend to a scene as though all of the elements are bound together as an inseparable whole (Swallow and Wang, 2020; cf., Witkin, 1969). In contrast, people with more independent selves tend to demonstrate more of an *analytic* perceptual style, and view the physical world as a collection of discrete objects, whose behavior can be predicted by inner characteristics of those objects. Some evidence for this distinction in perceptual styles can be observed when people view scenes in which elements of the scenes have been changed. Americans tend to show a more analytic perceptual style and their perception of the foreground tends not to be affected by any changes to the background, whereas the performance of East Asians tends to be more affected by any changes in the scene (Masuda and Nisbett, 2001; also see Chua et al., 2005; Gutchess et al., 2006; Masuda et al., 2008a, 2022; Miyamoto et al., 2006). These differences in perceptual styles have been linked to differences in artistic traditions (Masuda et al., 2008b; Savani and Markus, 2012), and people's abilities to identify objects in busy scenes (Wang et al., 2012). Holistic and analytic thinking styles are commonly assessed with a variety of cognitive tasks (e.g., Ji et al., 2004; Masuda and Nisbett, 2001) or by self-report measures (e.g., Choi et al., 2007).

Holistic and analytic thinking styles have also been observed with respect to how people reason about events in the world. Holistic thinkers are more likely to conceive of the world in terms of the relations among objects, and are thus more likely to categorize objects in terms of their relations with each other (e.g., hammers go with nails). In contrast, analytic thinkers understand objects in terms of their component parts, and thus tend to categorize objects in terms of their shared attributes (e.g., hammers go with wrenches; Ji et al., 2004; cf., Luria, 1976). Analytic thinkers are more likely to base their reasoning on abstract rules, whereas holistic thinkers are more likely to reason by family resemblance and similarities (Norenzayan et al., 2002b). Moreover, holistic thinkers, in perceiving that everything in the world is bound by relationships, consider a far broader range of causes as being potentially relevant in understanding what is happening in the world (Choi et al., 2003).

Holistic vs. analytic thinking styles can also help to make sense of how people explain the behaviors of others around them. Analytic reasoners tend to explain events by referring to internal properties of the object, and they likewise are more prone to explain the behavior of other people in terms of their inner attributes: that is, their dispositions. So an individual who is seen acting angrily may be understood as having a short temper and a disagreeable personality. In contrast, holistic reasoners tend to explain events by referring to interactions between objects and the surrounding field, and they are more likely to explain other people's behaviors as a function of the situation that they're in. So the same individual who is acting angrily may be understood as someone who has just been treated unfairly. A long tradition of person perception in psychology, which was initially based on studies conducted almost exclusively with Western participants, has found that when asked to explain the behavior of others, people tended to largely attend to the person's disposition as a means for explaining the behavior, even when there were compelling situational constraints available (Jones and Harris, 1967; Ross et al., 1977) – a tendency robust enough that it has been termed the "fundamental attribution error" (Ross et al., 1977). However, research conducted in non-Western cultures often reveals a somewhat different pattern. For example, Shweder and Bourne (1982) found that Indians tended to eschew traits for explaining others' behaviors but rather would explain their behaviors in descriptive terms. Building upon this idea, Miller (1984) found that Indian adults tended to favor situational information over dispositional accounts. Several studies conducted with East Asians and Americans reveal that whereas Americans attend to dispositions first, regardless of how compelling the situational information may be (Gilbert and Malone, 1995), East Asians are more likely than Americans to infer that behaviors are controlled by the situation (Norenzayan et al., 2002a), and to attend to situational information (Miyamoto and Kitayama, 2002; see Church et al., 2006, for comparable findings with other cultural groups). These differences suggest that anti-social behavior may be understood quite differently across cultures (e.g., Morris and Peng, 1994), and this has implications for inferring criminal responsibility. Similarly, East Asians are less likely than Americans to use trait adjectives when describing someone's behaviors (Maass et al., 2006; Na and Kitayama, 2011), and they spend less time scrutinizing people's faces when trying to explain their behaviors (Shimizu and Uleman, 2021). All in all, the tendency to understand and predict others' behaviors by focusing on their imagined dispositions is less common among cultures where holistic thinking is more common.

These holistic thinking styles are widespread around the world, having been identified as more common among Turkish farmers and fishermen than among Turkish herders (Uskul et al., 2008), among Arabs, Brazilians, and Russians (De Oliveira and Nisbett, 2017; Grossmann and Varnum, 2011; Norenzayan et al., 2007); among Europeans in regions with stronger kinship ties and less historical exposure to the Western church (Schulz et al., 2019), among politically conservative Americans and Chinese in contrast to their liberal counterparts (Talhelm, 2018; Talhelm et al., 2015), among working class Americans and Russians in comparison with their middle-class compatriots (Grossmann and Varnum, 2011), among people in rice-growing regions as opposed to wheat-growing regions of China (Talhelm et al., 2014), and among people from other Judeo-Christian faiths in contrast with Protestants (Colzato et al., 2010, 2008). In the context of the world's cultures, analytic thinking styles are relatively unusual, as they are most pronounced among people who have had contact with Western society or education systems (Varnum et al., 2010).

6.4 Honor

Another key cultural trait that is shaped by how people relate with others is honor. Honor cultures around the world vary in some details, but what they tend to share in common is a willingness to retaliate violently in order to defend their reputations (Nisbett and Cohen, 1996; Peristiany, 1965). Cultures of honor are found around the world where the local rule of law is weaker, and often where people's livelihoods are based on herding livestock (see below for more discussion on why herding and honor tend to go together). In particular, much research on cultures of honor has been conducted in Turkey (Uskul and Cross, 2019), Brazil (Vandello and Cohen, 2003), parts of Africa (Galaty and Bonte, 1991), Spain (Mosquera et al., 2002), the Middle East (Maitner et al., 2017), and in the US South (Cohen, 1996; Cohen and Nisbett, 1994), where larger percentages of the population first immigrated to the country from herding regions of Scotland and Ireland (Fischer, 1989). More generally, research from ethnographic records, historical folklore information, large-scale surveys, and global data on contemporary conflicts confirms that around the world and across history, places where herding was practiced tend to have more of a culture of honor (Cao et al., 2021). Moreover, cultures of honor can also form in other contexts where people can't readily turn to a formal police force to protect them, such as in the inner city (Stewart and Simons, 2006), or among organized criminal gangs (Travaglino et al., 2014). These individuals similarly strive to cultivate a reputation as someone who will retaliate with violence to any perceived slight.

Cultures of honor are focused on an individual's reputation for negative reciprocity, and because reputations are about how one is viewed in the mind of others, which individuals have to infer for themselves with some uncertainty, they are especially prone to the forces of pluralistic ignorance (Cohen, 2001). This leads cultures of honor to be remarkably persistent (Cao et al., 2021). For example, consider the case of the American South. Despite that relatively small percentages of Americans currently have occupations that involve herding livestock, norms for honor are still nonetheless commonplace in regions that historically had more herding or had more immigrants from herding regions. One analysis found that the homicide rates in individual counties in the US South in the 21st century could be predicted by the percentage of the population that had emigrated from Scotland or Ireland in the 1790 census (Grosjean, 2014). Likewise, even among contemporary American university students studying in the same institution (i.e., the University of Michigan), students from southern states were more likely to respond aggressively to insults than those from the North (Cohen et al., 1996, 1999). This cultural persistence is all the more striking because of the many harms that tend to co-occur with honor cultures. For example, rates of intimate partner violence tend to be higher in honor societies (Brown et al., 2018; Vandello and Cohen, 2003), as do other kinds of violence, such as school shootings (Brown et al., 2009) and armed conflict (Cao et al., 2021). We also see a greater reluctance of to seek mental health care (Brown et al., 2014; Gul et al., 2021). Herding regions also tend to have norms that place greater restrictions on female sexuality, especially regarding premarital sex, and women may be prevented from going out without their husband's permission, perhaps the product of male herders often being away from their families for long periods of time (Becker, 2019). Honor is commonly assessed via self-report measures (e.g., Uskul et al., 2012) or by a variety of behavioral measures (e.g., Cohen et al., 1996).

6.5 Tightness-looseness

Norms emerge whenever people are participating in a shared context, as people's interactions and behaviors mutually influence each other. These norms are highly influential in guiding how people will act themselves. However, cultures vary importantly in terms of how strong these norms may be. Cultures that have strong norms and have low tolerance for anyone violating them are described as "tight," and these are contrasted with "loose" societies where the norms are weaker, and there is more acceptance of behaviors that aren't in alignment with them (Gelfand, 2019; Gelfand et al., 2011; Stamkou et al., 2019). Often collectivist cultures are tighter than individualistic cultures, but there are exceptions of tight individualistic societies such as Germany and Switzerland, and loose collectivistic societies such as Brazil and the Philippines. The strength of a culture's norms is not a constant, and the degree of tightness in a society can change over time (Jackson et al., 2019). Tightness has been calculated via self-report surveys about the perception of social norms (Gelfand et al., 2011), the amount of variance in people's responses within populations (Uz, 2015), or the presence of tight or loose words in publications (Jackson et al., 2019).

Tight societies differ from loose ones in a number of ways. For example, tight societies tend to have more vengeful gods, where people express beliefs that any counter-normative behavior may be met with much divine punishment (Jackson et al., 2021). People in tighter societies prefer that their leaders also follow the rules (Stamkou et al., 2019), yet at the same time also value autonomous leaders (Aktas et al., 2016). Tight societies appear to maintain stronger control over the outbreak of infectious diseases. This was particularly evident during the COVID pandemic. Governments around the world imposed various rules to curb the spread of the disease, such as lockdowns, mask-wearing, and vaccine mandates, yet people's tendencies to cooperate with these rules varied alongside a country's tightness-looseness. On average, countries and regions with higher levels of tightness had greater degrees of mask-wearing, and lower rates of cases and deaths from COVID (Gelfand et al., 2021; Talhelm et al., 2023; Wei et al., 2023).

Tightness-looseness is also associated with creativity. On average, cultures which have tighter norms place more constraints on people's behaviors and these restrictions tend to be associated with lower levels of creativity. For example, countries which are more accepting of norm violations have been found to produce more innovations and are rated higher in creativity (Bonetto et al., 2022). Likewise, it has been found in the US that states which have higher levels of tightness tend to have fewer patents per capita, as well as fewer artists (Harrington and Gelfand, 2014). Moreover, rates of tightness change over time, and in the US norms have been loosening over the past couple of centuries, which has been associated with heightened levels of national markers of creativity, such as the number of feature films produced and the number of trademarks (Jackson et al., 2019). However, the links between cultural tightness and creativity are nuanced, especially when people are presented with norms from multiple cultures (Chua et al., 2015). Moreover, in contrast to the positive relations between looseness and creativity in the US, an investigation of tightness-looseness across 31 provinces in China revealed that tighter provinces in China had higher rates of incremental innovations (although not with breakthrough innovations), which may reflect that the central government's efforts to encourage companies to generate more innovations are more effective where norms are tighter (Chua et al., 2019).

6.6 Motivations to enhance self-esteem vs. to maintain face

Several other cultural traits have been studied that are not as easily categorized in terms of relationships with others. For example, much research has compared cultures in people's motivations to *self-enhance*, that is, a desire to view oneself positively. Many studies have found that Westerners apparently have a strong need to view themselves in positive terms. For example, the vast majority of North Americans score above the theoretical midpoint of self-esteem scales (Baumeister et al., 1989), show much evidence for unrealistically positive views of themselves (e.g., Greenwald, 1980; Taylor and Brown, 1988), and engage in various compensatory self-protective responses when they encounter threats to their self-esteem (e.g., Steele, 1988; Tesser et al., 2000; Wills, 1981). These positive self-views among Westerners generalize beyond assessments of the individual self to also include other things that are connected to the individual, including one's relationships, groups, or even possessions (Brown, 1986; Chatterjee et al., 2013; Gawronski et al., 2007; Tajfel and Turner, 1986). Moreover, the extent to which Americans view themselves positively, as measured by self-esteem, has been on the rise in recent decades. A meta-analysis from 1965 to 1995 of studies using the Rosenberg (1965) self-esteem scale with American college students found that self-esteem scores had increased substantially over that time ($d = .6$; Twenge and Campbell, 2001), and more recent studies find that the increase has continued to the point that there are problems with ceiling effects, as the modal self-esteem score of American college students is now the maximum score on the scale (Gentile et al., 2010).

However, research has identified pronounced cultural differences in motivations to enhance self-esteem, with the most extreme differences being found in contrasts of East Asians and North Americans. A meta-analysis found that the difference in self-enhancement motivations between East Asians and Westerners was large ($d = .84$), and emerged across a diverse array of methods (Heine and Hamamura, 2007). For example, in measures of self-enhancing biases, East Asians (as compared to North Americans) evaluate themselves in a lower percentile relative to other students within the same culture on a number of positive traits (Heine and Lehman, 1997b), attribute fewer positive attributes to themselves than to their peers (Heine and Renshaw, 2002), show less evidence to take credit for their successes while externalizing blame for their failures (Mezulis et al., 2004), and are less likely to think that positive events will happen to them than others from their culture (Heine and Lehman, 1995). Moreover, East Asians also maintain less positive views of their relationships and possessions compared to Westerners (Heine and Lehman, 1997b; Maddux et al., 2010).

Motivations to enhance one's self-esteem can be understood as one way that people can view themselves as a good person, and these motivations are particularly pronounced in Western cultures. In contrast, in hierarchical Confucian societies such as East Asia, the key currency for becoming a good person is maintaining "face" (e.g., Chang and Holt, 1994; Heine, 2005). Face has been defined as "the respectability and/or deference which a person can claim for himself from others by virtue of the relative position he (sic) occupies in his social network and the degree to which he is judged to have functioned adequately in that position" (p. 883, Ho, 1976). In such a context, succeeding is not so much the product of individuals' beliefs that they are good, but by having significant others believe that they are meeting the consensual standards associated with their roles. One key difference between self-esteem and face is that face requires an attention to how one believes that others are evaluating oneself, and much research finds that East Asians are especially attentive to the judgments of others (Kim et al., 2010; Liu et al., 2017; Seo et al., 2016). A second difference between self-esteem and face is that face is more easily lost than it is gained, because the amount of face that one has is largely determined by the role that one occupies. It takes time and effort to rise in the hierarchy, yet one bad behavior can cause one to lose face. East Asians appear to be relatively more attentive to negative information about themselves than Westerners, and show more pronounced prevention orientations (Elliot et al., 2001; Kung et al., 2016; Lockwood et al., 2005). The pursuit of face appears to be facilitated by self-improving motivations in which individuals aspire to identify where others might think they are falling short of expectations, in order to work at correcting them. Much work has identified that East Asians are more likely than Westerners to possess self-critical views, sometimes even overestimating how poorly they are doing (Heine et al., 2000; Kitayama et al., 1997). These self-critical views appear to be particularly motivating for East Asians, as studies find that when East Asian students have received negative feedback they respond by working harder, in contrast to findings that North Americans work harder following positive feedback (Heine et al., 2001; Oishi and Diener, 2003; Shu and Lam, 2016).

6.7 Valuing choice as a means of self-expression

Cultures also differ from each other in the extent of personal choices that they have to make. There are many key decisions that people face in their lives, such as what career one should pursue, who one should marry, whether one should have children, where one should live, etc. It has become somewhat normative for middle class people in individualistic cultures to make these choices for themselves and to desire to make individual choices whenever they can. But in many cultures today, as well as in much of the world in the past, key life decisions like this have often been made by others, especially by families. One salient example of this is the prevalence of arranged marriages. Historically, marriages around the world have commonly been arranged by families, rather than by the couples themselves (Broude and Greene, 1983; Skolnick, 1987), and this became the norm in many parts of the world following the development of agriculture (Jankowiak and Nelson, 2021). However, the percentage of arranged marriages has been dropping in many cultures, including China, India, Japan, and Turkey, and among orthodox Jews (Hortacsu, 1999; Sprecher and Chandak, 1992; Xu and Whyte, 1990). The notion of someone else having a say in who one selects as a life partner may seem puzzling to many people living in individualistic societies, who tend to see individual choice of partners as necessary for a lasting and happy marriage. Strikingly, though, some past studies contrasting love marriages and arranged marriages that have been conducted in several countries often find that the arranged marriages are at least as happy as the marriages based on love; Israel (Shachar, 1991); India (Gupta and Singh, 1982; Jaiswal, 2014); among American members of the Unification Church (Galanter, 1986); China and Japan (but only for men; Blood, 1967; Xu and Whyte, 1990). A study in Turkey found arranged marriages to be as successful as love marriages (Hortacsu, 1999), but a more recent Turkish study found love marriages to be more successful so perhaps the success of arranged marriages may be dropping as individualistic norms are taking firmer hold (Imamoğlu et al., 2019). But the normativity and success of arranged marriages in the past reminds us that it's not necessarily the case that choices made by individuals necessarily lead to the most desired outcomes.

Attitudes towards choices vary around the world. In particular, Americans seem to value having the freedom to make choices (Inglehart et al., 1998). One way we can see the value of choice is in terms of the number of options that people prefer to select from. In one study, participants from France, Germany, Italy, Switzerland, the United Kingdom, and the US were asked whether they would prefer a choice of 10 ice cream flavors or 50 ice cream flavors. It was only in the US that a majority of people said they would prefer to make a choice from 50 flavors (Americans also preferred more choices on menus from upscale restaurants; Rozin et al., 2006). Much research finds that making choices is not as desired to the same extent in other cultural contexts (Bao and Lam, 2008; Iyengar, 2010; Iyengar and Lepper, 1999; Rudy et al., 2015), in part, because Americans appear more likely to view their choices as an act of self-expression (Kim and Sherman, 2007), and they tend to place particularly high value on the outcome of their choices (Roets et al., 2012). Variation in preferences for choices is not just found between countries, as middle-class Americans are more likely to seek and defend their choices (Snibbe and Markus, 2005), and are less influenced by the choices of others (Na et al., 2016), compared with working-class Americans.

In particular, much research has contrasted how people make choices between India and the US. Making choices appears to be a less frequent experience for Indians than Americans as when given a list of choices to make Indians take longer than Americans, and Indians didn't respond as negatively when they were deprived of the opportunity to choose (Savani et al., 2008). Indians are more likely than Americans to defer to the views of others with more expertise when making choices (Savani et al., 2012), and they trust that others have more altruistic reasons in helping them with their choices (Savani et al., 2011). More generally, Americans are more likely than Indians to construe their actions as personal choices – when engaged in the identical sets of behaviors, Americans claimed that they had made more choices than Indians, and this was especially the case for actions that were viewed to be especially important (Savani et al., 2010). These cultural differences in the valuation of choice raise questions about whether more choice is always better, particularly because research finds that choices entail psychological costs of cognitive effort and perceived responsibility (Heine, 2005; Iyengar and Lepper, 2000; Schwartz, 2004; Vohs et al., 2008).

6.8 The pursuit of happiness

People from different cultures reliably differ in the likelihood that they report that they are feeling happy. While there has been some debate about the validity of national scores of happiness (Kahneman and Krueger, 2006; Mathews, 2012), the fairly consistent cross-cultural differences in average scores of various kinds of measures of happiness have raised interest in the possibility that these national scores reflect the success of a society (Choi et al., 2022). In 2011, following the lead of Bhutan, the UN General Assembly passed a resolution to urge countries to measure the happiness and well-being of societies, the so-called Gross National Happiness, in order to consider non-economic aspects of well-being.

A number of reliable trends have emerged in national rankings of happiness, although the rank orderings of countries vary somewhat by year and also by the ways that happiness is operationalized (e.g., questions about happiness, subjective well-being, or frequency of positive emotions). The countries that tend to cluster at the top are Scandinavian and Nordic countries, some former British colonies, and much of Western Europe. In contrast, countries that tend to score the lowest are former Soviet republics and some of the poorest countries in Africa and South Asia (Diener and Tay, 2015; Helliwell et al., 2023; Veenhoven, 2014). Other ways of operationalizing happiness have also pointed to fairly similar cultural differences, such as frequency of smiling, negative content in tweets, and interdependent happiness (Hsu et al., 2021; Krys et al., 2023; Senft et al., 2021; Talhelm et al., 2019). However, when countries are compared with respect to the frequency that they have positive experiences (rather than happiness per se) then countries in Latin America and Southeast Asia emerge near the top (Gallup, 2023).

There are a few features of societies that reliably predict rankings on happiness. On average people who are wealthier tend to be happier, and this trend holds both within societies (Killingsworth, 2021) and between them (Lawless and Lucas, 2011), however, the strength of the relation between income and happiness varies somewhat across societies (Lomas, 2024), and appears stronger among the poorest and most unequal countries (Biswas-Diener and Diener, 2002; Oishi et al., 2022). Moreover, people living in small-scale societies, who tend to have low incomes, commonly report high levels of happiness (Galbraith et al., 2024). People also tend to be happier in countries where human rights are protected, and the rule of law is followed (Helliwell et al., 2014). Yet some countries score differently than one would predict on the basis of these trends. For example, several Latin American countries tend to be happier than what would be predicted by their income level, equality, or human rights, whereas countries in East Asia, especially rice-farming regions, tend to be less happy than would be predicted by these same factors (Diener et al., 1995; Lee et al., 2023). These exceptions to the general patterns suggest that there are aspects of cultures that may influence the degree to which people report being happy.

Much research has explored some cultural considerations that relate to people's feelings of happiness. First, it's informative to note that prior to the Enlightenment, there was scant discussion of the notion of the pursuit of happiness (Carlyle, 1843). Following the Enlightenment, Westerners began to see the world as an increasingly rational and predictable place, such that an individual may feel that if they planned their lives carefully and acted responsibly they could expect better outcomes in their lives, and would enjoy more happiness. This contrasts with a view of happiness that it was largely a matter of good luck. In support of this notion, Oishi et al. (2013) studied dictionary definitions of happiness in several countries. In the US, dictionary definitions of happiness included luck as part of the definition of happiness until 1961, indicating that happiness has become viewed more as something that is under one's control. Moreover, a survey of dictionaries from 30 countries found that good luck was part of the definition of happiness in 24 of those countries pointing to some cultural variability in how happiness is conceived. In addition, an analysis of the phrases "happy nation" and "happy person" in a Google Ngram database of American books found that the term "happy" used to be far more likely to refer to nations than individuals prior to 1920, when happy became more commonly used to refer to individuals. Similarly, research finds that people living in individualistic countries tend to have a more individual-centered approach to happiness compared with those in more collectivistic countries (Gardiner et al., 2020; Krys et al., 2023; Lu and Gilmour, 2004).

The pursuit of happiness appears to vary across cultures in that people from different cultures differ in the extent that they wish to experience positive emotions, such as happiness. When describing their ideal life, Westerners are more likely than East Asians to envisage a life that is dominated by feelings of happiness (Hornsey et al., 2018), and East Asians are less likely to emphasize their positive emotions (Ma et al., 2018). Cultural differences in people's desires for positive emotional experiences may result in people making different kinds of choices in their lives. For example, one study contrasted the choices that Asian-Americans and Euro-Americans made between computer games and university courses when their descriptions varied in terms of how enjoyable or useful they were. The prospect of future positive emotional experiences seemed to matter more for Euro-Americans as they were more likely to select options that were described as enjoyable in contrast to the Asian-Americans (Falk et al., 2010). Relatedly, cultures vary in terms of how much people's feelings of passion drive their achievement. On average, people who live in more individualistic cultures tend to have a stronger relation between their passion for a subject at school and their performance in it in comparison with people who live in more collectivistic cultures (Li et al., 2021). Cultures thus seem to vary in terms of how much people are driven to follow that which they are passionate about.

Perhaps this relative hesitance towards positive emotions among people in some collectivistic cultures is a product of emotions being less correlated with well-being outside of the West. For example, whereas European-Americans and Hispanic Americans who report more positive emotions are less susceptible to depression, this same relation doesn't hold for East Asians (Choi and Chentsova-Dutton, 2017; Leu et al., 2011), and happiness-boosting activities don't seem to be as effective among East Asians as they are among Westerners (Layous et al., 2013). On the converse side, negative emotional states are not viewed as problematic among East Asian samples as they are among Western ones (An et al., 2017; Yoo et al., 2022). Likewise, whereas ruminating on the travails of life reliably predicts depression among Americans, it does not seem to among Russians or East Asians (Choi and Miyamoto, 2023; Grossmann and Kross, 2010; Schunk et al., 2022). Cultures have different norms for reflecting on negative emotions, and Russian children's books have more references to negative emotions such as sadness, fear, and anger in comparison with American books (Chentsova-Dutton et al., 2021). Even among Western cultures there are differences in how people approach negative emotions. For example, when comforting someone who is struggling, Americans are more likely than Germans to try to cheer them up, whereas Germans tend to emphasize more that they are sharing their pain (Koopmann-Holm et al., 2021).

The kinds of emotions that people experience across cultures vary in a number of ways. More generally, people from more collectivistic cultures tend to report experiencing and perceiving mixed emotions more readily than people from individualistic cultures (Fang et al., 2018; Grossmann et al., 2016); indeed, some research finds that East Asians tend to have rather dialectical emotional experiences, feeling both positive and negative emotions simultaneously (Miyamoto et al., 2010; Sims et al., 2015). Even within the category of positive emotions, cultures vary in terms of the specific emotions that they prefer. Relative to Canadians, Americans and Mexicans, East Asians tend to prefer positive emotions that are lower in arousal, such as relaxation, and feeling at peace; in contrast, people from Western cultures tend to prefer high arousal positive emotions, such as excitement, and elation (Ruby et al., 2012; Tsai et al., 2006a). Accordingly, Westerners tend to engage in more kinds of activities that tend to heighten the experience of high arousal positive emotions, whereas East Asians pursue activities that lead to more low arousal positive emotions (see Tsai, 2007, for a review). In sum, the kinds of emotional states that people are pursuing vary in important ways across cultures.

The above review covers many of the cultural traits that have received the most attention by cultural psychologists thus far. I should note, though, that in recent years many scientific fields (e.g., Begley and Ellis, 2012; Prinz et al., 2011), especially psychology (e.g., Youyou et al., 2023), have suffered from a replication crisis, where the field has come to recognize that many widely used analytic habits and a reliance on smaller sample sizes have increased the likelihood that false positives have been published (Simmons et al., 2011). Thus far, I don't know of any of these false positives being reliably identified in the cultural psychology literature, and many of the effects reported here have been replicated multiple times. However, perhaps because of the cost and difficulty involved in securing cross-cultural samples, it may be the case that researchers have yet to attempt to replicate as many cross-cultural studies as in other areas of psychology. Moreover, an additional challenge in considering replications of cross-cultural research is that because cultures are dynamic and always evolving there may well be some phenomena that have been identified in the past that might not replicate with more recent samples due to cultural change (Greenfield, 2017). Readers are thus advised to consider all research findings with a grain of salt, particularly if the findings are limited to just a few published studies.

7 Many cultural traits have roots in the ecology and in institutions

Understanding how these cultural traits came to be is a challenging enterprise, as the path dependence of cultures means that they are often on their own trajectory, evolving from previous conditions. Moreover, cultures are situated in particular ecologies, which are shaped by their local geography and climate, and these afford the kinds of lifestyles that people can live. For example, ecologies which require courage and physical prowess to obtain food (such as large-game hunting, or deep-sea fishing), tend to have cultures that prize masculinity, whereas more benign environments with plentiful food tend to have more androgynous gender norms (Gilmore, 1990). Similarly, cultures which have had a higher historical prevalence of pathogens, more frequent natural disasters, resource scarcity, and higher population density tend to be tighter, as survival in these contexts is more dependent on coordinated collective action (Gelfand et al., 2011; Harrington and Gelfand, 2014; Roos et al., 2015). People facing these kinds of environmental challenges would be incentivized to follow strict norms to have the greatest likelihood of surviving. Likewise, people who live in ecologies where water is in chronically short supply have been found to emphasize moderation and engage in more long-term planning, as a strategy for confronting this ecological challenge (Harati and Talhelm, 2023).

Some features of the ecology, such as coastlines, navigable rivers, an east-west continental axis, and the presence of easily domesticable species of grain and livestock can have significant long-term consequences for the cultures, as these can afford the birth of agriculture, labor specialization, and trade (see Diamond, 1997, for a provocative review of the broad cultural influences of geography). Geography thus has a substantial impact on cultural evolution, with one analysis estimating that approximately 20% of the cultural variation in people's thinking styles is due to the surrounding ecology (Wormley et al., 2023). Nonetheless, because of the key role of path dependence in cultural evolution, even cultures that share the same ecology continue to have pronounced differences from each other (Richerson and Boyd, 2005).

In particular, the ecology affords different kinds of subsistence systems, which may facilitate different kinds of lifestyles, and incentivize different kinds of habits. One mode of subsistence that is common in many parts of the world is open range livestock herding, such as herding cows, pigs, goats, and sheep. Often this kind of herding is practiced in regions where the land is too dry or rocky for most agricultural crops, yielding fewer calories per acre, and thus they commonly do not support large communities (Nisbett and Cohen, 1996). The herds are often managed by single families with relatively little dependence on neighbors. The key challenge with livestock herding is that much of a family's wealth is concentrated in the animals that one owns, yet these are often quite vulnerable to theft. If a herder is not attending to their herds, it is not that difficult for a thief to capture one or more of the animals – a family could wake up in the morning to discover that their herds have been absconded with. Making matters even more challenging, because herding regions tend to be sparsely populated, institutions such as police and courtrooms are relatively ineffective as they tend to be located far away. Herders are thus in a precarious position as they need to protect their own herds from rustlers with relatively little support from others. As discussed above, a common solution for herding cultures is to cultivate a culture of honor, in which people (especially men), strive to develop a reputation for vengeance and aggression. If one is known to respond to any affront with violence, any potential thieves may conclude that it is too risky to attempt to steal their herds. But for one's reputation to be an effective deterrent, it's important to develop it long before actually encountering any potential rustlers. The ethnographer, J.K. Campbell (1965), who lived with the Sarakatsani shepherds in Greece, noted that "The critical moment in the development of the young shepherd's reputation is his first quarrel. Quarrels are necessarily public. They may occur in the coffee shop, the village square, or most frequently on a grazing boundary where a curse or a stone aimed at one of his straying sheep by another shepherd is an insult which inevitably requires a violent response." In a culture of honor one is incentivized to be vigilant to cultivating a reputation as someone who will always pay back against slights, because only if one has such a reputation will they be able to ensure that their family's wealth is relatively secure. The absence of effective institutions to regulate matters, which is common in the sparsely populated herding regions, behooves individuals to take matters into their own hands to develop a fearful reputation. These reputations for violence can be seen as a type of costly signaling (Thrasher and Handfield, 2018), and modeling studies reveal that when institutions are lacking, an aggressive honor culture can be adaptive (Nowak et al., 2016).

Whereas herding tends to occur in sparsely populated regions where individuals develop minimal cooperative ties with their neighbors, on the far other end of the spectrum, the cultivation of rice tends to be associated with a great deal of cooperation and coordination with neighbors. Much research has contrasted the different kinds of psychological traits that are associated with rice-growing and wheat-growing regions of China (e.g., Lee et al., 2023; Talhelm et al., 2014). At first glance, the particular crops that a farmer cultivates may not seem to be much of a distinction – isn't it all just farming? But these crops require very different behaviors in order to cultivate them, which has an impact on people's psychology. First, rice farming is far more labor intensive. Premodern rice farming takes more than twice as many hours of labor as does wheat farming (Buck, 1935). The extreme labor demands for farming rice required farmers to exchange labor with that of neighboring farmers, which has led to strong norms of reciprocity among farmers (Bray, 1986). Moreover, because rice farmers were exchanging labor with each other, they also had to coordinate to plant their fields at different times, so that they wouldn't all be ready to harvest at the same time. Rice farming thus requires that farmers cooperate with their neighbors and coordinate their labor with that of their neighbors (Talhelm and English, 2020). Moreover, unlike wheat, rice is grown in a paddy in standing water, which means that irrigation is necessary to manage the water levels in each paddy. The irrigation systems that were developed required much collective labor that had to be coordinated, and to ensure that everyone contributed their share, rice farmers often set up systems to assign chores and monitor compliance (Fei, 1983). The irrigation systems required farmers to coordinate their efforts so that all fields could be flooded and drained at the same time (also see Buggle, 2020). In contrast, wheat farmers have historically relied upon the rain that falls on their fields rather than depending on irrigation networks, and they are more likely to take care of all of their planting and harvesting themselves, rather than relying on neighbors (see Talhelm and English, 2020). This reasoning suggests that places where rice was cultivated should have incentivized people to cooperate with their neighbors, resulting in more collectivistic norms. Talhelm and his colleagues (Dong et al., 2019; Talhelm and Dong, 2024; Talhelm and English, 2020; Talhelm et al., 2014) have found that when they compare farming regions in China they find a striking pattern. Despite that some of these regions are in close proximity, straddling the Yangtze River, people living in the rice-growing regions are more likely than those in the wheat-growing regions to show a number of traits that are consistent with collectivism.

Whereas cultural practices that emerge from collective actions such as rice-farming cultivate interdependent selves, the kinds of cultural practices that have been identified which have facilitated the emergence of individualism and more independent selves appear to stem from particular religious institutions. Henrich and colleagues (Henrich, 2020; Schulz et al., 2019) maintain that, starting around the 6th century CE, the Western Church (which evolved to what is known today as the Roman Catholic Church) began enacting and enforcing a number of religious laws regarding the nature of families that shaped the self-concepts of people who were under its influence. These laws included prohibitions against marriage to blood relatives (up to one's sixth cousin, at the most extreme), suppressions of arranged marriages, and encouraged newly married couples to set up independent households that were separate from their parents. These laws served to weaken the intensity of kinship ties, diluting the obligations that people felt towards large clans and families. As a consequence, Henrich argues that people no longer showed a default preference to align with and trust those who they were connected to by blood relations, but instead these new laws incentivized people to go about creating their social networks by themselves. This led people to attend to the attributes of others, as opposed to their kinship ties, to identify who would be trustworthy and competent, thereby making a beneficial relationship. This orientation towards the characteristics of a person over their relationships cultivated the traits associated with independent selves. In support of this reasoning, countries which have had a longer exposure to the medieval Western Church have been found to have more independent self-concepts (Schulz et al., 2019).

Moreover, as the Western Church continued to evolve and splinter into competing sects, newer religious ideas further spurred the evolution of individualism and independent selves, in particular, Protestantism. A key tenet of Protestantism was that individuals could communicate with God directly, sidestepping the role of the priest, and they were encouraged to learn how to read the Bible for themselves, thereby establishing an individual relationship between God and each person. Martin Luther proposed that everyone has a calling – a unique God-given purpose to fulfill during their lifetime, and it was up to people to discover what their own unique calling was. Perhaps as a result of these ideas, places with more Protestants became more individualistic. For example, according to one of the most cited rankings of national individualism (Hofstede, 2001), the six most individualistic countries in the world are largely Protestant, and the least individualistic Western countries are predominantly Catholic. In comparison with Catholics, Protestants also show more impersonal trust, are less likely to conform, are less tied to their families, and view people's private thoughts to indicate their moral standing (Arrunada, 2010; Cohen and Rozin, 2001; Henrich, 2020). In sum, the ways that cultures come to be are influenced by a variety of factors, including religious traditions, geography, and modes of subsistence.

8 Conclusion

The many ways that aspects of people's psychology differ across cultures underscore the notion that our species is a cultural one. We are born into a world with a brain that evolved to acquire cultural information, and our survival is dependent upon our mastery of this information. As members of the same species, we all share the same basic needs, such as needs for physiological resources, belongingness, status, and so on (Kenrick et al., 2010), however we go about satisfying these needs in culturally particular ways, which can often significantly differ between societies. This means that researchers may be led astray by assuming that people pursue their needs in universal, context-independent ways. Rather, to better understand human nature we need to have a rich understanding of the cultural meanings that they are draped in.

Our cultural nature means that participants in psychology studies are not all interchangeable. Each participant has been shaped by a lifetime of prior experiences within particular cultural environments, that have shaped the ways that they relate to others, the practices that they engage in, the goals that they have, how they understand themselves and others, and ultimately how their brains are wired. Cultural psychology has revealed that cultures and selves are mutually constituted and this means that the cultural part of people's psychology cannot easily be separated from a hypothesized underlying universal human nature.

In recent decades there has been growing recognition in psychology of the necessity of cross-cultural research for understanding how and why people think in the ways that they do. An increasing number of psychological phenomena are being studied across diverse cultural samples, and many of these efforts reveal some striking differences across populations. It would seem that economists might benefit by attending to these kinds of differences between societies. For example, much research has studied the many downstream consequences that are associated with people who tend to prioritize the individual vs. those who prioritize the collective, suggesting that people may be incentivized to pursue different actions across cultures. Relatedly, people who live in an environment where they see many opportunities to form new relationships tend to invest more in efforts to attract and maintain their relationships than those who see their relationship opportunities as limited, and these differences may help to understand differences in people's openness to engage with new trading partners. People who participate in honor cultures have more exposure to norms regarding negative reciprocity, and these should shape people's motivations to cooperate with others. We can also understand cultures in terms of the strengths of their norms, and the ways that people respond to the tightness of norms may help us to understand when people are more likely to innovate. This chapter reviewed numerous examples of cross-cultural research, yet there still remain many aspects of psychology that have yet to be thoroughly explored across cultures. We still have much work to do to better understand the cultural foundation of how people think, feel, and behave, and this research is likely to also be relevant for shaping economic theories as well.

References

Acerbi, A., Snyder, W.D., Tennie, C., 2022. The method of exclusion (still) cannot identify specific mechanisms of cultural inheritance. Scientific Reports 12, 21680.

Adams, G., 2005. The cultural grounding of personal relationship: enemyship in West African worlds. Journal of Personality and Social Psychology 88, 948–968.

Adams, G., Anderson, S.L., Adonu, J.K., 2004. The cultural grounding of closeness and intimacy. In: Mashek, D., Aron, A. (Eds.), The Handbook of Closeness and Intimacy. Erlbaum, Mahwah, NJ, pp. 321–339.

Adams, G., Plaut, V.C., 2003. The cultural grounding of personal relationship: friendship in North American and West African worlds. Personal Relationships 10, 333–348.

Aktas, M., Gelfand, M.J., Hanges, P.J., 2016. Cultural tightness-looseness and perceptions of effective leadership. Journal of Cross-Cultural Psychology 47, 294–309.

Alesina, A., Algan, Y., Cahuc, P., Giuliano, P., 2015. Family values and the regulation of labor. Journal of the European Economic Association 13, 599–630.

An, S., Ji, L.-J., Marks, M., Zhang, Z., 2017. Two sides of emotion: exploring positivity and negativity in six basic emotions across cultures. Frontiers in Psychology 8.

Anderson, E., 1999. Code of the Street: Decency, Violence, and the Moral Life of the Inner City. Norton, New York.

Anderson, S.L., Adams, G., Plaut, V.C., 2008. The cultural grounding of personal relationship: the importance of attractiveness in everyday life. Journal of Personality and Social Psychology 95, 352–368.

Arnett, J., 2008. The neglected 95%: why American psychology needs to become less American. The American Psychologist 63, 602–614.

Arrunada, B., 2010. Protestants and catholics: similar work ethic, different social ethic. The Economic Journal 120, 890–918.

Bahns, A.J., Lee, J., Crandall, C.S., 2019. Culture and mobility determine the importance of similarity in friendship. Journal of Cross-Cultural Psychology 50, 731–750.

Bao, X.-H., Lam, S.-F., 2008. Who makes the choice? Rethinking the role of autonomy and relatedness in Chinese children's motivation. Child Development 79, 269–283.

Barber, B.R., 1995. Jihad vs. McWorld: Terrorism's Challenge to Democracy. Ballantine Books, New York.

Baumeister, R.F., 2022. The Self Explained. Guilford Press, New York.

Baumeister, R.F., Maranges, H.M., Vohs, K.D., 2018. Human self as information agent: functioning in a social environment based on shared meanings. Review of General Psychology 22, 36–47.

Baumeister, R.F., Tice, D.M., Hutton, D.G., 1989. Self-presentational motivations and personality differences in self-esteem. Journal of Personality 57, 547–579.

Becker, A., 2019. On the Economic Origins of Restrictions on Women's Sexuality. Working Paper. Harvard University.

Begley, C.G., Ellis, L.M., 2012. Raise standards for preclinical cancer research. Nature 483, 531–533.

Beja-Pereira, A., Luikart, G., England, P.R., Bradley, D.G., Jann, O.C., et al., 2003. Gene-culture coevolution between cattle milk protein genes and human lactase genes. Nature Genetics 35, 311–313.

Benet-Martinez, V., Leu, J., Lee, F., Morris, M.W., 2002. Negotiating biculturalism: cultural frame switching in biculturals with oppositional versus compatible cultural identities. Journal of Cross-Cultural Psychology 33, 492–516.

Berkessel, J., Ebert, T., Gebauer, J.E., Rentfrow, P.J., 2024. On the unequal burden of obesity: obesity's adverse consequences are contingent on regional obesity prevalence. Psychological Science 35, 1260–1277.

Berry, J., 1969. On cross-cultural comparability. International Journal of Psychology 4, 119–128.

Biswas-Diener, R., Diener, E., 2002. Making the best of a bad situation: satisfaction in the slums of Calcutta. Social Indicators Research 55, 329–352.

Blood, R.O., 1967. Love Match and Arranged Marriage. Free Press, New York.

Bond, R., Smith, P.B., 1996. Culture and conformity: a meta-analysis of studies using Asch's (1952b, 1956) line judgment task. Psychological Bulletin 119, 111–137.

Bonetto, E., Pichot, N., Adam-Troïan, J., 2022. The role of cultural values in national-level innovation: evidence from 106 countries. Cross-Cultural Research 56, 307–322.

Bourdieu, P., 1977. Outline of a Theory of Practice. Cambridge University Press, Cambridge (translated by R. Nice).

Bray, F., 1986. The Rice Economies: Technology and Development in Asian Societies. Blackwell, Oxford, UK.

Broude, G.J., Greene, S.J., 1983. Cross-cultural codes on husband-wife relationships. Ethnology 22, 263–280.

Brown, G.D.A., Lewandowsky, S., Huang, Z., 2022. Social sampling and expressed attitudes: authenticity preference and social extremeness aversion lead to social norm effects and polarization. Psychological Review 129, 18–48.

Brown, J.D., 1986. Evaluations of self and others: self-enhancement biases in social judgments. Social Cognition 4, 353–376.

Brown, R.P., Baughman, K., Carvallo, M., 2018. Culture, masculine honor, and violence toward women. Personality & Social Psychology Bulletin 44, 538–549.

Brown, R.P., Imura, M., Mayeux, L., 2014. Honor and the stigma of mental healthcare. Personality & Social Psychology Bulletin 40, 1119–1131.

Brown, R.P., Osterman, L.L., Barnes, C.D., 2009. School violence and the culture of honor. Psychological Science 20, 1400–1405.

Bruner, J., 1990. Acts of Meaning. Harvard University Press, Cambridge, MA.

Buchtel, E.E., Ng, C.Y., Norenzayan, A., Heine, S.J., Biesanz, J.C., Chen, S.X., Bond, M.H., Peng, Q., Su, Y., 2018. How much do you want to do what you have to do? Cultural differences in the experience of obligation. Personality & Social Psychology Bulletin 44, 1545–1566.

Buck, J.L., 1935. Land Utilization in China. University of Chicago Press, Chicago, IL.

Buggle, J.C., 2020. Growing collectivism: irrigation, group conformity, and technological divergence. Journal of Economic Growth 25, 147–193.

Buss, D., 1985. Human mate selection. American Scientist 73, 47–51.

Butler, E.A., Lee, T.L., Gross, J.J., 2009. Does expressing your emotions raise or lower your blood pressure? The answer depends on cultural context. Journal of Cross-Cultural Psychology 40, 510–517.

Buttrick, N., Oishi, S., 2021. The cultural dynamics of declining residential mobility. The American Psychologist 76, 904–916.

Byrne, D., 1971. The Attraction Paradigm. Academic Press, New York.

Campbell, J.K., 1965. Honour and the devil. In: Peristiany, J.G. (Ed.), Honor and Shame: The Values of Mediterranean Society. Weidenfeld and Nicolson, London.

Cao, Y., Enke, B., Falk, A., Giuliano, P., Nunn, N., 2021. Herding, warfare, and a culture of honor: Global evidence. NBER Working Paper Series.

Carlyle, T., 1843. Past and Present. Chapman & Hall, London.

Chang, H.-C., Holt, G.R., 1994. A Chinese perspective on face as inter-relational concern. In: Ting-Toomey, S. (Ed.), The Challenge of Facework: Cross-Cultural and Interpersonal Issues. SUNY Press, Albany, NY, pp. 95–132.

Chatterjee, P., Irmak, C., Rose, R.L., 2013. The endowment effect as self-enhancement in response to threat. Journal of Consumer Research 40, 460–476.

Chentsova-Dutton, Y., Leontyeva, A., Halberstadt, A.G., Adams, A.M., 2021. And they all lived unhappily ever after: positive and negative emotions in American and Russian picture books. Emotion 21, 1585–1598.

Chiao, J.Y., Cheon, B.K., Pompattananangkul, N., Mrazek, A.J., Blizinsky, K.D., 2013. Cultural neuroscience: progress and promise. Psychological Inquiry 24, 1–19.

Choi, E., Chentsova-Dutton, Y.E., 2017. The relationship between momentary emotions and well-being across European Americans, Hispanic Americans, and Asian Americans. Cognition and Emotion 31, 1277–1285.

Choi, H., Diener, E., Sim, J.H., Oishi, S., 2022. Happiness is associated with successful living across cultures. The Journal of Positive Psychology 18, 958–977.

Choi, I., Dalal, R., Kim-Prieto, C., Park, H., 2003. Culture and judgement of causal relevance. Journal of Personality and Social Psychology 84, 46–59.

Choi, I., Koo, M., Choi, J.A., 2007. Individual differences in analytic and holistic thinking. Personality & Social Psychology Bulletin 33, 691–705.

Choi, J.H., Miyamoto, Y., 2023. Cultural differences in rumination and psychological correlates: the role of attribution. Personality & Social Psychology Bulletin 49, 1213–1230.

Chua, H.F., Boland, J.E., Nisbett, R.E., 2005. Cultural variation in eye movements during scene perception. Proceedings of the National Academy of Sciences 102, 12629–12633.

Chua, R.Y.J., Huang, K.G., Jin, M., 2019. Mapping cultural tightness and its links to innovation, urbanization, and happiness across 31 provinces in China. Proceedings of the National Academy of Sciences 116, 6720–6725.

Chua, R.Y.J., Roth, Y., Lemoine, J.-F., 2015. The impact of culture on creativity: how cultural tightness and cultural distance affect global innovation crowdsourcing work. Administrative Science Quarterly 60, 189–227.

Church, A.T., Katigbak, M.S., Del Prado, A.M., Ortiz, F.A., Mastor, K.A., Harumi, Y., et al., 2006. Implicit theories and self-perceptions of traitedness across cultures: toward integration of cultural and trait psychology perspectives. Journal of Cross-Cultural Psychology 37 (6), 694–716.

Clegg, J.M., Wen, N.J., Legare, C.H., 2017. Is non-conformity WEIRD? Cultural variation in adults' beliefs about children's competency and conformity. Journal of Experimental Psychology 146, 428–441.

Clifford, M.M., Walster, E., 1973. The effect of physical attractiveness on teacher expectations. Sociology of Education 46, 248–258.

Cohen, A.B., Rozin, P., 2001. Religion and the morality of mentality. Journal of Personality and Social Psychology 81, 697–710.

Cohen, D., 1996. Law, social policy, and violence: the impact of regional cultures. Journal of Personality and Social Psychology 70, 961–978.

Cohen, D., 2001. Cultural variation: considerations and implications. Psychological Bulletin 127, 451–471.

Cohen, D., Hoshino-Browne, E., Leung, A., 2007. Culture and the structure of personal experience: insider and outsider phenomenologies of the self and social world. In: Zanna, M.P. (Ed.), Advances in Experimental Social Psychology, vol. 39. Academic Press, San Diego.

Cohen, D., Nisbett, R.E., 1994. Self-protection and the culture of honor: explaining southern homicide. Personality & Social Psychology Bulletin 20, 551–567.

Cohen, D., Nisbett, R.E., Bowdle, B.F., Schwarz, N., 1996. Insult, aggression, and the southern culture of honor: an "experimental ethnography". Journal of Personality and Social Psychology 70, 945–960.

Cohen, D., Vandello, J., Puente, S., Rantilla, A., 1999. "When you call me that, smile!": How norms for politeness, interaction styles, and aggression work together in Southern culture. Social Psychology Quarterly 62, 257–275.

Cole, M., Gay, J., Glick, J., Sharp, D.W., 1971. The Cultural Context of Learning and Thinking: An Exploration in Experimental Anthropology. Basic Books, New York.

Colzato, L.S., van Beest, I., van den Wildenberg, W.P.M., Scorolli, C., Dorchin, S., Meiran, N., Borghi, A.J., Hommel, B., 2010. God: Do I have your attention? Cognition 117, 87–94.
Colzato, L.S., van den Wildenberg, W.P., Hommel, B., 2008. Losing the big picture: how religion controls visual attention. PLoS ONE 3, e3679.
Cooper, M.L., 2016. Editorial. Journal of Personality and Social Psychology 110, 431–434.
Cousins, S.D., 1989. Culture and selfhood in Japan and the U.S. Journal of Personality and Social Psychology 56, 124–131.
Cross, S.E., 1995. Self-construals, coping, and stress in cross-cultural adaptation. Journal of Cross-Cultural Psychology 26, 673–697.
Cullum, J.G., Harton, H.C., 2007. Cultural evolution: interpersonal influence, issue importance, and the development of shared attitudes in college residence halls. Personality & Social Psychology Bulletin 33, 1327–1339.
Danchin, E., Nobel, S., Pocheville, A., Dagaeff, A.-C., Demay, L., Isabel, G., 2018. Cultural flies: conformist social learning in fruitflies predicts long-lasting mate-choice traditions. Science 362, 1025–1030.
De Leersnyder, J., Mesquita, B., Kim, H.S., 2011. Where do my emotions belong? A study of immigrants' emotional acculturation. Personality & Social Psychology Bulletin 37, 451–463.
De Leersnyder, J., Mesquita, B., Kim, H., Eom, K., Choi, H., 2014. Emotional fit with culture: a predictor of individual differences in relational well-being. Emotion 14, 241–245.
De Oliveira, S., Nisbett, R.E., 2017. Beyond East and West: cognitive style in Latin America. Journal of Cross-Cultural Psychology 48, 1554–1577.
De Waal, F., 1982. Chimpanzee Politics. Johns Hopkins University Press, Baltimore, MD.
Deacon, T.W., 1997. The Symbolic Species. Norton, New York.
Dehaene, S., 2009. Reading in the Brain: The Science and Evolution of a Human Invention. Viking, New York.
Derex, M., Beugin, M., Godelle, B., Raymond, M., 2013. Experimental evidence for the influence of group size on cultural complexity. Nature 503, 389–391.
De Tocqueville, A., 1835/2003. Democracy in America. Penguin Books, New York.
Diamond, J., 1997. Guns, Germs and Steel: The Fates of Human Societies. Norton, New York.
Diener, E., Suh, E.M., Smith, H., Shao, L., 1995. National differences in reported subjective well-being: why do they occur? Social Indicators Research 34, 7–32.
Diener, E., Tay, L., 2015. Subjective well-being and human welfare around the world as reflected in the Gallup World Poll. International Journal of Psychology 50, 135–149.
Dong, X., Talhelm, T., Ren, X., 2019. Teens in rice county are more interdependent and think more holistically than nearby wheat county. Social Psychological and Personality Science 10, 966–976.
Dunbar, R.I.M., 1993. The co-evolution of neocortical size, group size and language in humans. Behavioral and Brain Sciences 16, 681–735.
Dunbar, R.I.M., Duncan, N.D.C., Marriott, A.M., 1997. Human conversational behavior. Human Nature 8 (3), 231–246.
Dzokoto, V., 2010. Different ways of feeling: emotion and somatic awareness in Ghanaians and Euro-Americans. Journal of Social, Evolutionary, and Cultural Psychology 4, 68–78.
Ebert, T., Berkessel, J.B., Jonsson, T., 2023. Political person-culture match and longevity: the partisanship-mortality link depends on the cultural context. Psychological Science 34, 1192–1205.
Ebert, T., Gebauer, J.E., Talman, J.R., Rentfrow, P.J., 2020. Religious people only live longer in religious cultural contexts: a gravestone analysis. Journal of Personality and Social Psychology 119, 1–6.
Elliot, A.J., Chirkov, V.I., Kim, Y., Sheldon, K.M., 2001. A cross-cultural analysis of avoidance (relative to approach) personal goals. Psychological Science 12, 505–510.
Emler, N., 1994. Gossip, reputation, and social adaptation. In: Goodman, R., Ben-Ze'ev, A. (Eds.), Good Gossip. Kansas University Press, Lawrence, KS, pp. 117–133.

Engelmann, J.M., Herrmann, E., Tomasello, M., 2012. Five-year olds, but not chimpanzees, attempt to manage their reputations. PLoS ONE 7 (10), e48433.

English, A.S., Talhelm, T., Tong, R., Li, X., Su, Y., 2022. Historical rice farming explains faster mask use during early days of China's COVID-19 outbreak. Current Research in Ecological and Social Psychology 3, 100034.

Falk, A., Becker, A., Dohmen, T., Enke, B., Huffman, D., Sunde, U., 2018. Global evidence on economic preferences. The Quarterly Journal of Economics 133, 1645–1692.

Falk, C.F., Dunn, E.W., Norenzayan, A., 2010. Cultural variation in the importance of expected enjoyment for decision making. Social Cognition 28, 609–629.

Fang, X., Sauter, D.A., Van Kleef, G.A., 2018. Seeing mixed emotions: the specificity of emotion perception from static and dynamic facial expressions across cultures. Journal of Cross-Cultural Psychology 49, 130–148.

Fei, X., 1983. Chinese Village Close-Up. New World Press, Beijing, China.

Feng, Z., Zou, K., Savani, K., 2023. Cultural antecedents of virus transmission: individualism is associated with lower compliance with social distancing rules during the COVID-19 pandemic. Journal of Personality and Social Psychology 124, 461–482.

Fischer, D.H., 1989. Albion's Seed: Four British Folkways in America. Oxford University Press, New York.

Friedman, M., Rholes, W.S., Simpson, J., Bond, M., Diaz-Loving, R., Chan, C., 2010. Attachment avoidance and the cultural fit hypothesis: a cross-cultural investigation. Personal Relationships 17 (1), 107–126.

Fryberg, S.A., Markus, H.R., 2003. On being American Indian: current and possible selves. Self and Identity 2, 325–344.

Fulmer, C.A., Gelfand, M.J., Kruglanski, A.W., Kim-Prieto, C., Diener, E., Pierro, A., et al., 2010. On "feeling right" in cultural contexts: how person-culture match affects self-esteem and subjective well-being. Psychological Science 21, 1563–1569.

Galanter, M., 1986. "Moonies" get married: a psychiatric follow-up study of a charismatic religious sect. American Journal of Psychiatry 143, 1245–1249.

Galaty, J.G., Bonte, P. (Eds.), 1991. Herders, Warriors, and Traders: Pastoralism in Africa. Westview Press, Boulder, CO.

Galbraith, E.D., Barrington-Leigh, C., Minarro, S., Alvarez-Fernandez, S., Attoh, E.M.N.A.N., Benyei, P., et al., 2024. High life satisfaction reported among small-scale societies with low incomes. Proceedings of the National Academy of Sciences 121, e2311703121.

Gallup, 2023. Global emotions report. Retrieved from https://www.gallup.com/analytics/349280/gallup-global-emotions-report.aspx.

Galor, O., Özak, O., 2016. The agricultural origins of time preference. American Economic Review 106, 3064–3103.

Gardiner, G., Lee, D., Baranski, E., Funder, D., 2020. Happiness around the world: a combined etic-emic approach across 63 countries. PLoS ONE 15 (12), e0242718.

Gardner, H., 1985. The Mind's New Science: A History of the Cognitive Revolution. Basic Books.

Gardner, W.L., Gabriel, S., Dean, K.K., 2004. The individual as "melting pot": the flexibility of bicultural self-construals. Cahiers de Psychologie Cognitive/Current Psychology of Cognition 22, 181–201.

Gawronski, B., Bodenhausen, G.V., Becker, A.P., 2007. I like it, because I like myself: associative self-anchoring and post-decisional change of implicit evaluations. Journal of Experimental Social Psychology 43, 221–232.

Gebauer, J.E., Sedikides, C., Neberich, W., 2012. Religiosity, social self-esteem, and psychological adjustment: on the cross-cultural specificity of the psychological benefits of religiosity. Psychological Science 23, 158–160.

Geertz, C., 1973. The Interpretation of Cultures. Basic Books, New York.

Gelfand, M., 2019. Rule Makers, Rule Breakers: Tight and Loose Cultures and the Secret Signals That Direct Our Lives. Scribner, New York.

Gelfand, M.J., Jackson, J.C., Pan, X., Nau, D., Pieper, D., et al., 2021. The relationship between cultural tightness-looseness and COVID-19 cases and deaths: a global analysis. The Lancet Planetary Health 5, e135–e144.
Gelfand, M.J., Raver, J.L., Nishii, L., Leslie, L.M., Lun, J., Lim, B.C., et al., 2011. Differences between tight and loose cultures: a 33-nation study. Science 332, 1100–1104.
Gentile, B., Twenge, J.M., Campbell, W.K., 2010. Birth cohort differences in self-esteem, 1988–2008: a cross-temporal meta-analysis. Review of General Psychology 14, 261–268.
Gergen, K.J., 1973. Social psychology as history. Journal of Personality and Social Psychology 26, 309–320.
Gilbert, D.T., Malone, P.S., 1995. The correspondence bias. Psychological Bulletin 117, 21–38.
Gilmore, D.D., 1990. Manhood in the Making. Yale University Press, New Haven, CT.
Giuliano, P., Nunn, N., 2021. Understanding cultural persistence and change. The Review of Economic Studies 88, 1541–1581.
Götz, F.M., Ebert, T., Rentfrow, P.J., 2018. Regional cultures and the psychological geography of Switzerland: person-environment-fit in personality predicts subjective well-being. Frontiers in Psychology 9, 517.
Greenfield, P.M., 1997. Culture as process: empirical methods for cultural psychology. In: Berry, J.W., Poortinga, Y.H., Pandey, J. (Eds.), Handbook of Cross-Cultural Psychology, vol. 1. Allyn & Bacon, Boston, pp. 301–346.
Greenfield, P.M., 2017. Cultural change over time: why replicability should not be the gold standard in psychological science. Perspectives on Psychological Science 12, 762–771.
Greenwald, A.G., 1980. The totalitarian ego: fabrication and revision of personal history. The American Psychologist 35, 603–618.
Griffitt, W.B., 1966. Interpersonal attraction as a function of self-concept and personality similarity-dissimilarity. Journal of Personality and Social Psychology 4, 581–584.
Grosjean, P., 2014. A history of violence: the culture of honor and homicide in the US south. Journal of the European Economic Association 12, 1285–1316.
Grossmann, I., Huynh, A.C., Ellsworth, P.C., 2016. Emotional complexity: clarifying definitions and cultural correlates. Journal of Personality and Social Psychology 111, 895–916.
Grossmann, I., Kross, E., 2010. The impact of culture on adaptive versus maladaptive self-reflection. Psychological Science 21, 1150–1157.
Grossmann, I., Varnum, M.E.W., 2011. Social class, culture, and cognition. Social Psychological and Personality Science 2, 81–89.
Guiso, L., Sapienza, P., Zingales, L., 2016. Long-term persistence. Journal of the European Economic Association 14 (6), 1401–1436.
Gul, P., Cross, S.E., Uskul, A.K., 2021. Implications of culture of honor theory and research for practitioners and prevention researchers. The American Psychologist 76, 502–515.
Gupta, U., Singh, P., 1982. Exploratory study of love and liking and type of marriages. Indian Journal of Applied Psychology 19, 92–97.
Gutchess, A.H., Welsh, R.C., Boduroglu, A., Park, D.C., 2006. Cultural differences in neural function associated with object processing. Cognitive, Affective & Behavioral Neuroscience 6, 102–109.
Hall, S., 1980. Cultural studies: two paradigms. In: Bennett, T., Martin, G., Mercer, C., Woollacott, J. (Eds.), Culture, Ideology and Social Process. Open University Press/Batsford, London.
Harati, H., Talhelm, T., 2023. Cultures in water-scarce environments are more long-term oriented. Psychological Science 34, 754–770.
Harrington, J.R., Gelfand, M.J., 2014. Tightness-looseness across the 50 United States. Proceedings of the National Academy of Sciences 111, 7990–7995.
Heine, S.J., 2001. Self as cultural product: an examination of East Asian and North American selves. Journal of Personality 69, 881–906.
Heine, S.J., 2005. Constructing good selves in Japan and North America. In: Sorrentino, R.M., Cohen, D., Olson, J.M., Zanna, M.P. (Eds.), Culture and Social Behavior: The Tenth Ontario Symposium. Lawrence Erlbaum, Hillsdale, NJ, pp. 95–116.

Heine, S.J., 2020. Cultural Psychology, 4th edition. Norton, New York, NY.
Heine, S.J., Folk, D.P., Guan, K.W., Benjamin, R., Bahng, J.M., Proulx, T., 2024. An ecology of meaning: an integrative framework for understanding human motivations. Advances in Motivation Science.
Heine, S.J., Foster, J.A., Spina, R., 2009. Do birds of a feather universally flock together? Cultural variation in the similarity-attraction effect. Asian Journal of Social Psychology 12, 247–258.
Heine, S.J., Hamamura, T., 2007. In search of East Asian self-enhancement. Personality and Social Psychology Review 11, 4–27.
Heine, S.J., Kitayama, S., Lehman, D.R., Takata, T., Ide, E., Leung, C., Matsumoto, H., 2001. Divergent consequences of success and failure in Japan and North America: an investigation of self-improving motivations and malleable selves. Journal of Personality and Social Psychology 81, 599–615.
Heine, S.J., Lehman, D.R., 1995. Cultural variation in unrealistic optimism: does the West feel more invulnerable than the East? Journal of Personality and Social Psychology 68, 595–607.
Heine, S.J., Lehman, D.R., 1997a. Culture, dissonance, and self-affirmation. Personality & Social Psychology Bulletin 23, 389–400.
Heine, S.J., Lehman, D.R., 1997b. The cultural construction of self-enhancement: an examination of group-serving biases. Journal of Personality and Social Psychology 72, 1268–1283.
Heine, S.J., Lehman, D.R., 2004. Move the body, change the self: acculturative effects on the self-concept. In: Schaller, M., Crandall, C. (Eds.), Psychological Foundations of Culture. Erlbaum, Mahwah, NJ, pp. 305–331.
Heine, S.J., Lehman, D.R., Markus, H.R., Kitayama, S., 1999. Is there a universal need for positive self-regard? Psychological Review 106, 766–794.
Heine, S.J., Renshaw, K., 2002. Interjudge agreement, self-enhancement, and liking: cross-cultural divergences. Personality & Social Psychology Bulletin 28, 578–587.
Heine, S.J., Takata, T., Lehman, D.R., 2000. Beyond self-presentation: evidence for self-criticism among Japanese. Personality & Social Psychology Bulletin 26, 71–78.
Helliwell, J.F., Huang, H., Grover, S., Wang, S., 2014. Good governance and national well-being: What are the linkages? OECD Working Papers on Public Governance, No. 25. OECD, Paris.
Helliwell, J.F., Layard, R., Sachs, J.D., De Neve, J.-E., Aknin, L.B., Wang, S., 2023. World happiness report. Retrieved from https://happiness-report.s3.amazonaws.com/2023/WHR+23.pdf.
Henrich, J., 2016. The Secret of Our Success. Princeton University Press, Princeton, NJ.
Henrich, J., 2020. The Weirdest People in the World. Farrar, Straus, and Giroux, New York.
Henrich, J., Bauer, M., Cassar, A., Chytilova, J., Purzycki, B.G., 2019. War increases religiosity. Nature Human Behaviour 3, 129–135.
Henrich, J., Ensminger, J., McElreath, R., Barr, A., Barrett, C., Bolyanatz, A., et al., 2010a. Markets, religion, community size, and the evolution of fairness and punishment. Science 327, 1480–1484.
Henrich, J., Heine, S.J., Norenzayan, A., 2010b. The weirdest people in the world? Behavioral and Brain Sciences 33, 61–135.
Heu, L.C., 2023. The loneliness of the odd one out: how deviations from social norms can help explain loneliness across cultures. Perspectives on Psychological Science 20 (2), 199–218.
Ho, D.Y.F., 1976. On the concept of face. American Journal of Sociology 81, 867–884.
Hofstede, G., 2001. Culture's Consequences: Comparing Values, Behaviors, Institutions, and Organizations Across Nations, 2nd ed. Sage, Thousand Oaks, CA.
Hogan, R., Hall, R., Blank, E., 1971. An extension of the similarity-attraction hypothesis to the study of vocational behavior. Center for Social Organization of Schools Report, Johns Hopkins University, 105 p. 8.
Hong, Y., Morris, M.W., Chiu, C., Benet-Martinez, V., 2000. Multicultural minds: a dynamic constructivist approach to culture and cognition. The American Psychologist 55, 705–720.
Hornsey, M.J., Bain, P.G., Harris, E.A., Lebedeva, N., Kashima, E.S., Guan, Y., et al., 2018. How much is enough in a perfect world? Cultural variation in ideal levels of happiness, pleasure, freedom, health, self-esteem, longevity, and intelligence. Psychological Science 29, 1393–1404.

Hortacsu, N., 1999. The first year of family- and couple-initiated marriages of a Turkish sample: a longitudinal investigation. International Journal of Psychology 34, 29–41.
Hsu, T.W., Niiya, Y., Thelwall, N., Ko, N., Knutson, B., Tsai, J.L., 2021. Social media users produce more affect that supports cultural values, but are more influenced by affect that violates cultural values. Journal of Personality and Social Psychology 121, 969–983.
Imamoğlu, E.O., Ads, M., Weisfeld, C.C., 2019. What is the impact of choosing one's spouse on marital satisfaction of wives and husbands? The case of arranged and self-choice Turkish marriages. Journal of Family Issues 40, 1270–1298.
Inglehart, R., Basanez, M., Moreno, A., 1998. Human Values and Beliefs: A Cross-Cultural Sourcebook. University of Michigan Press, Ann Arbor.
Inglehart, R., Haerpfer, C., Moreno, A., Welzel, C., Kizilova, K., Diez-Medrano, J., et al., 2014. World values survey: all rounds – country-pooled datafile 1981–2014. Retrieved from http://www.worldvaluessurvey.org/WVSDocumentationWVL.jsp.
Inoue, S., Matsuzawa, T., 2007. Working memory of numerals in chimpanzees. Current Biology 17, R1004–R1005.
Ishii, K., Miyamoto, Y., Rule, N.O., Toriyama, R., 2014. Physical objects as vehicles of cultural transmission: maintaining harmony and uniqueness through colored geometric patterns. Personality & Social Psychology Bulletin 40, 175–188.
Iyengar, S.S., 2010. The Art of Choosing. Hachette, New York, NY.
Iyengar, S.S., Lepper, M.R., 1999. Rethinking the value of choice: a cultural perspective on intrinsic motivation. Journal of Personality and Social Psychology 76, 349–366.
Iyengar, S.S., Lepper, M.R., 2000. When choice is demotivating: can one desire too much of a good thing? Journal of Personality and Social Psychology 79, 995–1006.
Jackson, J.C., Caluori, N., Abrams, S., Beckman, E., Gelfand, M., Gray, K., 2021. Tight cultures and vengeful gods: how culture shapes religious belief. Journal of Experimental Psychology. General 150, 2057–2077.
Jackson, J.C., Gelfand, M., De, S., Fox, A., 2019. The loosening of American culture over 200 years is associated with a creativity-order trade-off. Nature Human Behaviour 3, 244–250.
Jackson, J.C., Medvedev, D., 2024. Worldwide divergence of values. Nature Communications 15, 2650.
Jaiswal, T., 2014. Indian Arranged Marriages: A Social Psychological Perspective. Routledge, London.
Jankowiak, W., Nelson, A., 2021. Does love always come before marriage?. Sapiens. Retrieved from https://www.sapiens.org/culture/love-and-marriage/?utm_source=SAPIENS.org+Subscribers&utm_campaign=629e307a5a-EMAIL_CAMPAIGN_2021_12_2&utm_medium=email&utm_term=0_18b7e41cd8-629e307a5a-227292151&ct=t.
Jha, C., Panda, B., 2017. Individualism and corruption: a cross-country analysis. Economic Papers 36, 60–74.
Ji, L.J., Zhang, Z., Nisbett, R.E., 2004. Is it culture or is it language? Examination of language effects in cross-cultural research on categorization. Journal of Personality and Social Psychology 87, 57–65.
Johnston, D., 2010. Physical appearance and wages: do blondes have more fun? Economics Letters 108, 10–12.
Jones, E.E., Harris, V.A., 1967. The attribution of attitudes. Journal of Experimental Social Psychology 3, 1–24.
Judge, W.Q., McNatt, D.B., Xu, W., 2011. The antecedents and effects of national corruption: a meta-analysis. Journal of World Business 46, 93–103.
Kahneman, D., Krueger, A.B., 2006. Developments in the measurement of subjective well-being. The Journal of Economic Perspectives 20, 3–24.
Kanagawa, C., Cross, S.E., Markus, H.R., 2001. "Who am I?": the cultural psychology of the conceptual self. Personality & Social Psychology Bulletin 27, 90–103.
Kano, F., Furuichi, T., Hashimoto, C., Krupenye, C., Leinwand, J.G., Hopper, L.M., et al., 2022. What is unique about the human eye? Comparative image analysis on the external eye morphology of human and nonhuman great apes. Evolution and Human Behavior 43, 169–180.

Kashima, Y., 2016. Culture and psychology in the 21st century: conceptions of culture and person for psychology revisited. Journal of Cross-Cultural Psychology 47, 4–20.
Kenrick, D.T., Griskevicius, V., Neuberg, S.L., Schaller, M., 2010. Renovating the pyramid of needs: contemporary extensions built upon ancient foundations. Perspectives on Psychological Science 5, 292–314.
Killingsworth, M.A., 2021. Experienced well-being rises with income, even above $75,000 per year. Proceedings of the National Academy of Sciences 118, e2016976118.
Kim, H.S., 2002. We talk, therefore we think? A cultural analysis of the effect of talking on thinking. Journal of Personality and Social Psychology 83, 828–842.
Kim, H.S., Markus, H.R., 1999. Deviance or uniqueness, harmony or conformity? A cultural analysis. Journal of Personality and Social Psychology 77, 785–800.
Kim, H.S., Sherman, D.K., 2007. "Express yourself": culture and the effect of self-expression on choice. Journal of Personality and Social Psychology 92, 1–11.
Kim, Y., Cohen, D., Au, W., 2010. The jury and abjury of my peers: the self in face and dignity cultures. Journal of Personality and Social Psychology 98, 904–916.
Kinias, Z., Kim, H.S., Hafenbrack, A.C., Lee, J.J., 2014. Standing out as a signal to selfishness: culture and devaluation of non-normative characteristics. Organizational Behavior and Human Decision Processes 124, 190–203.
Kitayama, S., 2017. Editorial. Journal of Personality and Social Psychology 112, 357–360.
Kitayama, S., Markus, H.R., Kurokawa, M., 2000. Culture, emotion, and well-being: good feelings in Japan and the United States. Cognition and Emotion 14, 93–124.
Kitayama, S., Markus, H.R., Matsumoto, H., Norasakkunkit, V., 1997. Individual and collective processes in the construction of the self: self-enhancement in the United States and self-criticism in Japan. Journal of Personality and Social Psychology 72, 1245–1267.
Kitayama, S., Park, H., Sevincer, A.T., Karasawa, M., Uskul, A.K., 2009. A cultural task analysis of implicit independence: comparing North America, Western Europe, and East Asia. Journal of Personality and Social Psychology 97, 236–255.
Kitayama, S., Salvador, C.E., 2017. Culture embrained: going beyond the nature-nurture dichotomy. Perspectives on Psychological Science 12, 841–854.
Kitayama, S., Salvador, C.E., Nanakdewa, K., Rossmaier, A., San Martin, A., Savani, K., 2022. Varieties of interdependence and the emergence of the modern West: toward the globalizing of psychology. The American Psychologist 77, 991–1006.
Kitayama, S., Yanagisawa, K., Ito, A., Ueda, R., Uchida, Y., Abe, N., 2017. Reduced orbitofrontal cortical volume is associated with interdependent self-construal. Proceedings of the National Academy of Sciences 114, 7969–7974.
Kito, M., Yuki, M., Thomson, R., 2017. Relational mobility and close relationships: a socioecological approach to explain cross-cultural differences. Personal Relationships 24, 114–130.
Klebl, C., Rhee, J.J.S., Greenaway, K.H., Luo, Y., Bastian, B., 2023. Physical attractiveness biases judgments pertaining to the moral domain of beauty. Personality & Social Psychology Bulletin 49, 282–295.
Kobayashi, H., Kohshima, S., 2001. Unique morphology of the human eye and its adaptive meaning: comparative studies on external morphology of the primate eye. Journal of Human Evolution 40, 419–435.
Koopmann-Holm, B., Bruchmann, K., Fuchs, M., Pearson, M., 2021. What constitutes a compassionate response. The important role of culture. Emotion 21, 1610–1624.
Kroupin, I., Davis, H.E., Henrich, J., 2024. Beyond Newton: why assumptions of universality are critical to cognitive science, and how to finally move past them. Psychological Review.
Krys, K., Haas, B.W., Igou, E.R., Kosiarczyk, A., Kocimska-Bortnowska, A., et al., 2023. Introduction to a culturally sensitive measure of well-being: combining life satisfaction and interdependent happiness across 49 different cultures. Journal of Happiness Studies 24, 607–627.
Krys, K., Vignoles, V.L., Almeida, I., Uchida, Y., 2022. Outside the "cultural binary": understanding why Latin American collectivist societies foster independent selves. Perspectives on Psychological Science 17, 1166–1187.

Kuhn, M.H., McPartland, T., 1954. An empirical investigation of self-attitudes. American Sociological Review 19, 68–76.

Kung, F.Y.H., Kim, Y.-H., Yang, D.Y.-J., Cheng, S.Y.Y., 2016. The role of regulatory fit in framing effective negative feedback across cultures. Journal of Cross-Cultural Psychology 47, 696–712.

Lachlan, R.F., Crooks, L., Laland, K.N., 1998. Who follows whom? Shoaling preferences and social learning of foraging information in guppies. Animal Behaviour 56, 181–190.

LaFromboise, T., Coleman, H.L.K., Gerton, J., 1993. Psychological impact of biculturalism: evidence and theory. Psychological Bulletin 114, 395–412.

Lawless, N.M., Lucas, R.E., 2011. Predictors of regional well-being: a county level analysis. Social Indicators Research 101, 341–357.

Layous, K., Lee, H., Choi, I., Lyubomirsky, S., 2013. Culture matters when designing a successful happiness-increasing activity: a comparison of the United States and South Korea. Journal of Cross-Cultural Psychology 44, 1294–1303.

Lee, C.S., Talhelm, T., Dong, X.W., 2023. People in historically rice-farming areas are less happy and socially compare more than people in wheat-farming areas. Journal of Personality and Social Psychology 124, 935–957.

Lee, J., Adams, G., 2021. Cultural–ecological moderation of physical attractiveness bias: attractiveness-based discrimination or discrimination of attractiveness? Social Psychological and Personality Science 12, 1165–1174.

Lee, S.W.S., Oyserman, D., Bond, M.H., 2010. Am I doing better than you? That depends on whether you ask me in English or Chinese: self-enhancement effects of language as a cultural mindset prime. Journal of Experimental Social Psychology 46, 785–791.

Leu, J., Wang, J., Koo, K., 2011. Are positive emotions just as positive across cultures? Emotion 11, 994–999.

Levine, C.S., Miyamoto, Y., Markus, H.R., Rigotti, A., Boylan, J.M., Park, J., et al., 2016. Culture and healthy eating: the role of independence and interdependence in the United States and Japan. Personality & Social Psychology Bulletin 42, 1335–1348.

l'Haridon, O., Vieider, F.M., 2019. All over the map: a worldwide comparison of risk preferences. Quantitative Economics 10, 185–215.

Li, L.M.W., Adams, G., Kurtis, T., Hamamura, T., 2015. Beware of friends: the cultural psychology of relational mobility and cautious intimacy. Asian Journal of Social Psychology 18, 124–133.

Li, L.M.W., Masuda, T., Lee, H., 2018. Low relational mobility leads to greater motivation to understand enemies but not friends and acquaintances. British Journal of Social Psychology 57, 43–60.

Li, M., Li, W.-Q., Li, L.M.W., 2019. Sensitive periods of moving on mental health and academic performance among university students. Frontiers in Psychology 10, 1289.

Li, X., Han, M., Cohen, G.L., Markus, H.R., 2021. Passion matters but not equally everywhere: predicting achievement from interest, enjoyment, and efficacy in 59 societies. Proceedings of the National Academy of Sciences 118, e2016964118.

Lieberman, P., McCarthy, R.C., 2013. The evolution of speech and language. In: Henke, W., Tattersall, I. (Eds.), Handbook of Paleoanthropology. Springer, Berlin.

Liu, C.-H., Chiu, Y.-H.C., Chang, J.-H., 2017. Why do Easterners have lower well-being than Westerners? The role of others' approval contingencies of self-worth in the cross-cultural differences in subjective well-being. Journal of Cross-Cultural Psychology 48, 217–224.

Liu, S.S., Morris, M.W., Talhelm, T., Yang, Q., 2019. Ingroup vigilance in collectivistic cultures. Proceedings of the National Academy of Sciences 116, 14538–14546.

Lockhart, K.L., Nakashima, N., Inagaki, K., Keil, F.C., 2009. From ugly duckling to swan? Japanese and American beliefs about the stability and origins of traits. Cognitive Development 23, 155–179.

Lockwood, P., Marshall, T.C., Sadler, P., 2005. Promoting success or preventing failure: cultural differences in motivation by positive and negative role models. Personality and Social Psychology Bulletin 31, 379–392.

Lomas, T., 2024. Exploring associations between income and wellbeing: new global insights from the Gallup World Poll. The Journal of Positive Psychology 19 (4), 629–646.
Lu, J.G., Jin, P., English, A.S., 2021. Collectivism predicts mask use during COVID-19. Proceedings of the National Academy of Sciences 118, e2021793118.
Lu, L., Gilmour, R., 2004. Culture and conceptions of happiness: individual oriented and social oriented SWB. Journal of Happiness Studies 5, 269–291.
Luria, A.R., 1976. Cognitive Development: Its Cultural and Social Foundations. Harvard University Press, Cambridge, MA.
Ma, V., Schoeneman, T.J., 1997. Individualism versus collectivism: a comparison of Kenyan and American self-concepts. Basic and Applied Social Psychology 19, 261–273.
Ma, X., Tamir, M., Miyamoto, Y., 2018. A socio-cultural instrumental approach to emotion regulation: culture and the regulation of positive emotions. Emotion 18, 138–152.
Ma-Kellams, C., Blascovich, J., McCall, C., 2012. Culture and the body: East-West differences in visceral perception. Journal of Personality and Social Psychology 102, 718–728.
Maass, A., Karasawa, M., Politi, F., Suga, S., 2006. Do verbs and adjectives play different roles in different cultures? A cross-linguistic analysis of person representation. Journal of Personality and Social Psychology 90, 734–750.
Maddux, W.W., Yang, H., Falk, C., Adam, H., Adair, W., et al., 2010. For whom is parting with possessions more painful? Cultural differences in the endowment effect. Psychological Science 21, 1910–1917.
Maguire, E.A., Gadian, D.G., Johnsrude, I.S., Good, C.D., Ashburner, J., Frackowiak, R.S.J., Frith, C.D., 2000. Navigation-related structural changes in the hippocampi of taxi drivers. Proceedings of the National Academy of Sciences 97, 4398–4403.
Maitner, A.T., Mackie, D.M., Pauketat, J.V.T., Smith, E.R., 2017. The impact of culture and identity on emotional reactions to insults. Journal of Cross-Cultural Psychology 48, 892–913.
Markus, H.R., Kitayama, S., 1991. Culture and the self: implications for cognition, emotion, and motivation. Psychological Review 98, 224–253.
Markus, H.R., Kitayama, S., 2010. Cultures and selves: a cycle of mutual constitution. Perspectives on Psychological Science 5, 420–430.
Martin, C.F., Bhui, R., Bossaerts, P., Matsuzawa, T., Camerer, C.F., 2014. Experienced chimpanzees are more strategic than humans in competitive games. Scientific Reports 4, 5182.
Masuda, T., Ellsworth, P.C., Mesquita, B., Leu, J., Tanida, S., van de Veerdonk, E., 2008a. Placing the face in context: cultural differences in the perception of facial emotion. Journal of Personality and Social Psychology 94, 365–381.
Masuda, T., Gonzalez, R., Kwan, L., Nisbett, R.E., 2008b. Culture and aesthetic preference: comparing the attention to context of East Asians and Americans. Personality and Social Psychology Bulletin 34, 1260–1275.
Masuda, T., Nisbett, R.E., 2001. Attending holistically vs. analytically: comparing the context sensitivity of Japanese and Americans. Journal of Personality and Social Psychology 81, 922–934.
Masuda, T., Shi, S., Varma, P., Fisher, D., Shirazi, S., 2022. Do surrounding people's emotions affect judgment of the central person's emotion? Comparing within cultural variation in holistic patterns of emotion perception in the multicultural Canadian society. Frontiers in Human Neuroscience 16.
Mathews, G., 2012. Happiness, culture, and context. International Journal of Wellbeing 2 (4), 299–312.
May, R.M., 1997. The scientific wealth of nations. Science 275, 793–796.
Mesquita, B., 2001. Emotions in collectivist and individualist contexts. Journal of Personality and Social Psychology 80, 68–74.
Mesquita, B., 2022. Between Us: How Cultures Create Emotions. Norton, New York, NY.
Mesquita, B., Karasawa, M., 2002. Different emotional lives. Cognition and Emotion 16, 127–141.
Mezulis, A.H., Abramson, L.Y., Hyde, J.S., Hankin, B.L., 2004. Is there a universal positive bias in attributions?: A meta-analytic review of individual, developmental, and cultural differences in the self-serving attributional bias. Psychological Bulletin 130, 711–747.

Miller, G.A., 2003. The cognitive revolution: a historical perspective. Trends in Cognitive Sciences 7 (3), 141–144.
Miller, J.G., 1984. Culture and the development of everyday social explanation. Journal of Personality and Social Psychology 46, 961–978.
Miller, J.G., Bersoff, D.M., 1992. Culture and moral judgment: how are conflicts between justice and interpersonal obligations resolved? Journal of Personality and Social Psychology 62, 541–554.
Miller, J.G., Goyal, N., Wice, M., 2017. A cultural psychology of agency: morality, motivation, and reciprocity. Perspectives on Psychological Science 12, 867–875.
Miyamoto, Y., Kitayama, S., 2002. Cultural variation in correspondence bias: the critical role of attitude diagnosticity of socially constrained behavior. Journal of Personality and Social Psychology 83, 1239–1248.
Miyamoto, Y., Nisbett, R.E., Masuda, T., 2006. Culture and the physical environment: holistic versus analytic perceptual affordances. Psychological Science 17, 113–119.
Miyamoto, Y., Uchida, Y., Ellsworth, P.C., 2010. Culture and mixed emotions: co-occurrence of positive and negative emotions in Japan and the United States. Emotion 10, 404–415.
Morris, M., Peng, K., 1994. Culture and cause: American and Chinese attributions for social and physical events. Journal of Personality and Social Psychology 67, 949–971.
Moshontz, H., Campbell, L., Ebersole, C.R., et al., 2018. The psychological science accelerator: advancing psychology through a distributed collaborative network. Advances in Methods and Practices in Psychological Science 1, 501–515.
Mosquera, P.M.R., Manstead, A.S.R., Fischer, A.H., 2002. The role of honour concerns in emotional reactions to offences. Cognition and Emotion 16, 143–163.
Muthukrishna, M., Bell, A.V., Henrich, J., Curtin, C.M., Gedranovich, A., et al., 2020. Beyond Western, Educated, Industrial, Rich, and Democratic (WEIRD) psychology: measuring and mapping scales of cultural and psychological distance. Psychological Science 31, 678–701.
Muthukrishna, M., Henrich, J., Slingerland, E., 2021. Psychology as a historical science. Annual Review of Psychology 72, 717–749.
Muthukrishna, M., Schaller, M., 2020. Are collectivistic cultures more prone to rapid transformation? Computational models of cross-cultural differences, social network structure, dynamic social influence, and cultural change. Personality and Social Psychology Review 24, 103–120.
Muthukrishna, M., Shulman, B.W., Vasilescu, V., Henrich, J., 2014. Sociality influences cultural complexity. Proceedings of the Royal Society B 281, 1774.
Na, J., Kitayama, S., 2011. Spontaneous trait inference is culture-specific: behavioral and neural evidence. Psychological Science 22, 1025–1032.
Na, J., McDonough, I.M., Chan, M.Y., Park, D.C., 2016. Social-class differences in consumer choices: working-class individuals are more sensitive to choices of others than middle-class individuals. Personality & Social Psychology Bulletin 42, 430–443.
Naaman, M., Boase, J., Lai, C.H., 2010. Is it really about me?: Message content in social awareness streams. In: Proceedings of the 2010 ACM Conference on Computer Supported Cooperative Work. Association for Computing Machinery, Savannah, GA, pp. 189–192.
Newcomb, T.M., 1961. The prediction of interpersonal attraction. The American Psychologist 11, 575–586.
Newell, A., Shaw, J.C., Simon, H.A., 1959. Report on a general problem-solving program [Conference session]. International Conference on Information Processing. Paris, France.
Ng, T.K., Cheng, C.H.K., 2010. The effects of intimacy, passion, and commitment on satisfaction in romantic relationships among Hong Kong Chinese people. Journal of Psychology in Chinese Societies 11, 123–146.
Nielsen, M., Haun, D., Kartner, J., Legare, C.H., 2017. The persistent sampling bias in developmental psychology: a call to action. Journal of Experimental Child Psychology 162, 31–38.
Nisbett, R.E., 2003. The Geography of Thought. Free Press, New York.
Nisbett, R.E., Cohen, D., 1996. Culture of Honor: The Psychology of Violence in the South. Westview Press, Boulder, CO.

Nisbett, R.E., Peng, K., Choi, I., Norenzayan, A., 2001. Culture and systems of thought: holistic vs. analytic cognition. Psychological Review 108, 291–310.
Norenzayan, A., Choi, I., Nisbett, R.E., 2002a. Cultural similarities and differences in social inference: evidence from behavioral predictions and lay theories of behavior. Personality & Social Psychology Bulletin 28, 109–120.
Norenzayan, A., Choi, I., Peng, K., 2007. Cognition and perception. In: Kitayama, S., Cohen, D. (Eds.), Handbook of Cultural Psychology. Guilford Press, New York, pp. 569–594.
Norenzayan, A., Smith, E.E., Kim, B.J., Nisbett, R.E., 2002b. Cultural preferences for formal versus intuitive reasoning. Cognitive Science 26, 653–684.
Nowak, A., Gelfand, M., Borkowski, W., Cohen, D., Hernandez, I., 2016. The evolutionary basis of honor cultures. Psychological Science 27, 12–24.
Nunn, N., 2008. The long-term effects of Africa's slave trades. The Quarterly Journal of Economics 123, 139–176.
Nunn, N., Wantchekon, L., 2011. The slave trade and the origins of mistrust in Africa. American Economic Review 101, 3221–3252.
Oishi, S., Cha, Y., Komiya, A., Ono, H., 2022. Money and happiness: the income-happiness correlation is higher when income inequality is higher. PNAS Nexus 1 (5), pgac224.
Oishi, S., Diener, E., 2003. Culture and well-being: the cycle of action, evaluation, and decision. Personality & Social Psychology Bulletin 29, 939–949.
Oishi, S., Graham, J., Kesebir, S., Galinha, I.C., 2013. Concepts of happiness across time and cultures. Personality & Social Psychology Bulletin 39, 559–577.
Oishi, S., Ishii, K., Lun, J., 2009. Residential mobility and conditionality of group identification. Journal of Experimental Social Psychology 45, 913–919.
Oishi, S., Lun, J., Sherman, G.D., 2007. Residential mobility, self-concept, and positive affect in social interactions. Journal of Personality and Social Psychology 93, 131–141.
Oishi, S., Miao, F.F., Koo, M., Kisling, J., Ratliff, K., 2012. Residential mobility breeds familiarity-seeking. Journal of Personality and Social Psychology 102, 149–162.
Oishi, S., Tsang, S., 2022. The socio-ecological psychology of residential mobility. Journal of Consumer Psychology 32, 519–536.
Ou, C., Lou, N.M., Maheshka, C., Shi, M., Takemura, K., Cheung, B., Heine, S.J., 2025. Healthy sleep durations appear to vary across cultures. Proceedings of the National Academy of Sciences 122 (19), e2419269122.
Oyserman, D., Lee, S.W.S., 2008. Does culture influence what and how we think? Effects of priming individualism and collectivism. Psychological Bulletin 134, 311–342.
Pelham, B., Hardin, C., Murray, D., Shimizu, M., Vandello, J., 2022. A truly global, non-WEIRD examination of collectivism: the global collectivism index (GCI). Current Research in Ecological and Social Psychology 3, 100030.
Peng, K., Nisbett, R.E., 1999. Culture, dialectics, and reasoning about contradiction. American Psychologist 54, 741–754.
Peristiany, J.G., 1965. Honor and Shame: The Values of Mediterranean Society. Weidenfeld and Nicolson, London.
Phillips, L.T., Stephens, N.M., Townsend, S.S.M., Goudeau, S., 2020. Access is not enough: cultural mismatch persists to limit first-generation students' opportunities for achievement throughout college. Journal of Personality and Social Psychology 119, 1112–1131.
Plaut, V.C., Adams, G., Anderson, S.L., 2009. Does attractiveness buy happiness? "It depends on where you're from". Personal Relationships 16, 619–630.
Prentice, D., Miller, D., 1996. Pluralistic ignorance and the perpetuation of social norms by unwitting actors. In: Zanna, M. (Ed.), Advances in Experimental Social Psychology. Academic Press, San Diego, CA, pp. 161–209.
Prinz, F., Schlange, T., Asadullah, K., 2011. How much can we rely on published data on potential drug targets? Nature Reviews Drug Discoveries 10, 712–713.
Putnam, R.D., 2000. Bowling Alone: The Collapse and Revival of American Community. Simon & Schuster, New York.

Putnam, R.D., Leonardi, R., Nanetti, R.Y., 1993. Making Democracy Work. Princeton University Press, Princeton, NJ.
Rad, M.S., Martingano, A.J., Ginges, J., 2018. Toward a psychology of homo sapiens: making psychological science more representative of the human population. Proceedings of the National Academy of Sciences 115, 11401–11405.
Rattan, A., Savani, K., Naidu, N.V.R., Dweck, C.S., 2012. Can everyone become highly intelligent? Cultural differences in societal consequences of beliefs about universal potential for intelligence. Journal of Personality and Social Psychology 103, 787–803.
Ricart-Huguet, J., 2022. Why do different cultures form and persist? Learning from the case of Makerere University. Journal of Modern African Studies 60, 429–456.
Ricart-Huguet, J., Paluck, E.L., 2023. When the sorting hat sorts randomly: a natural experiment on culture. Quarterly Journal of Political Science 18, 39–73.
Richerson, P.J., Boyd, R., 2005. Not by Genes Alone. University of Chicago Press, Chicago, Il.
Roets, A., Schwartz, B., Guan, Y., 2012. The tyranny of choice: a cross-cultural investigation of maximizing-satisficing effects on well-being. Judgment and Decision Making 7, 689–704.
Roos, P., Gelfand, M.J., Nau, D., Lun, J., 2015. Societal threat and cultural variation in the strength of social norms: an evolutionary basis. Organizational Behavior and Human Decision Processes 129, 14–23.
Rosenberg, M., 1965. Society and the Adolescent Self-Image. Princeton University Press, Princeton.
Ross, L.D., Amabile, T.M., Steinmetz, J.L., 1977. Social roles, social control, and biases in social-perception processes. Journal of Personality and Social Psychology 35, 485–494.
Ross, M., Xun, W.Q.E., Wilson, A.E., 2002. Language and the bicultural self. Personality & Social Psychology Bulletin 28, 1040–1050.
Rozin, P., 2001. Social psychology and science: some lessons from Solomon Asch. Personality and Social Psychology Review 5, 2–14.
Rozin, P., Fischler, C., Shields, C., Masson, E., 2006. Attitudes towards large numbers of choices in the food domain: a cross-cultural study of five countries in Europe and the USA. Appetite 46, 304–308.
Ruby, M.B., Falk, C.F., Heine, S.J., Villa, C., Silverstein, O., 2012. Not all collectivisms are equal: Opposing preferences for ideal affect between East Asians and Mexicans. Emotion 12, 1206–1209.
Rudy, D., Sheldon, K.M., Li, Y., Kamble, S., Bi, X., Palermo, F., 2015. Who chooses best? Explaining the interactive effect of culture and decision maker on children's intrinsic motivation. Journal of Cross-Cultural Psychology 46, 471–488.
Ryder, A.G., Yang, J., Zhu, X., Yao, S., Yi, J., Heine, S.J., Bagby, R.M., 2008. The cultural shaping of depression: somatic symptoms in China, psychological symptoms in North America? Journal of Abnormal Psychology 117, 300–313.
Sampson, R.J., Raudenbush, S.W., Earls, F., 1997. Neighborhoods and violent crime: a multilevel study of collective efficacy. Science 277, 918–924.
San Martin, A., Schug, J., Maddux, W.W., 2019. Relational mobility and cultural differences in analytic and holistic thinking. Journal of Personality and Social Psychology 116, 495–518.
San Martin, A., Sinaceur, M., Madi, A., Tompson, S., Maddux, W.W., Kitayama, S., 2018. Self-assertive interdependence in Arab culture. Nature Human Behaviour 2, 830.
Savani, K., Alvarez, A., Mesquita, B., Markus, H.R., 2013. Feeling close and doing well: the prevalence and motivational effects of interpersonally engaging emotions in Mexican and European American cultural contexts. International Journal of Psychology 48, 682–694.
Savani, K., Markus, H.R., 2012. A processing advantage associated with analytic perceptual tendencies: European Americans outperform Asians on multiple object tracking. Journal of Experimental Social Psychology 48, 766–769.
Savani, K., Markus, H.R., Conner, A.L., 2008. Let your preference be your guide? Preferences and choices are more tightly linked for North Americans than for Indians. Journal of Personality and Social Psychology 95, 861–876.

Savani, K., Markus, H.R., Naidu, N.V.R., Kumar, S., Berlia, N., 2010. What counts as a choice? U.S. Americans are more likely than Indians to construe actions as choices. Psychological Science 21, 391–398.

Savani, K., Morris, M.W., Naidu, N.V.R., 2012. Deference in Indians' decision making: introjected goals or injunctive norms? Journal of Personality and Social Psychology 102, 685–699.

Savani, K., Morris, M.W., Naidu, N.V.R., Kumar, S., Berlia, N.V., 2011. Cultural conditioning: understanding interpersonal accommodation in India and the United States in terms of the modal characteristics of interpersonal influence situations. Journal of Personality and Social Psychology 100, 84–102.

Schaller, M., Muthukrishna, M., 2021. Modeling cultural change: computational models of interpersonal influence dynamics can yield new insights about how cultures change, which cultures change more rapidly than others, and why. The American Psychologist 76, 1027–1038.

Schein, E.H., 2004. Organizational Culture and Leadership. John Wiley & Sons, San Francisco, CA.

Schug, J., Yuki, M., Horikawa, H., Takemura, K., 2009. Similarity attraction and actually selecting similar others: how cross-societal differences in relational mobility affect interpersonal similarity in Japan and the USA. Asian Journal of Social Psychology 12, 95–103.

Schug, J., Yuki, M., Maddux, W., 2010. Relational mobility explains between- and within-culture differences in self-disclosure to close friends. Psychological Science 21, 1471–1478.

Schulz, J.F., Bahrami-Rad, D., Beauchamp, J.P., Henrich, J., 2019. The church, intensive kinship, and global psychological variation. Science 366, 6466. eaau5141.

Schunk, F., Trommsdorff, G., König-Teshnizi, D., 2022. Regulation of positive and negative emotions across cultures: does culture moderate associations between emotion regulation and mental health? Cognition and Emotion 36, 352–363.

Schwartz, B., 2004. The Paradox of Choice: Why More Is Less. HarperCollins, New York.

Seder, J.P., Oishi, S., 2008. Friendculture: Predictors of diversity in the social networks of college students. Poster session presented at the annual meeting. Society for Personality and Social Psychology, Albuquerque, NM.

Segall, M.H., Campbell, D.T., Herskovits, M.J., 1963. Cultural differences in the perception of geometric illusions. Science 139, 769–771.

Senft, N., Campos, B., Shiota, M.N., Chentsova-Dutton, Y.E., 2021. Who emphasizes positivity? An exploration of emotion values in people of latino, Asian, and European heritage living in the United States. Emotion 21, 707–719.

Seo, M., Kim, Y.-H., Tam, K.-P., Rozin, P., 2016. I am dumber when I look dumb in front of many (vs. few) others: a cross-cultural difference in how audience size affects perceived social reputation and self-judgments. Journal of Cross-Cultural Psychology 47, 1019–1032.

Seth, A., Cao, J., Shi, X., Dotsch, R., Liu, Y., Bos, M.W., 2023. Cultural differences in friendship network behaviors: a snapchat case study. In: Proceedings of the 2023 CHI Conference on Human Factors in Computing Systems, pp. 1–14.

Shachar, R., 1991. His and her marital satisfaction: the double standard. Sex Roles 25, 451–467.

Shepard, R.N., 2004. How a cognitive psychologist came to seek universal laws. Psychonomic Bulletin & Review 11, 1–23.

Shimizu, Y., Uleman, J.S., 2021. Attention allocation is a possible mediator of cultural variations in spontaneous trait and situation inferences: eye-tracking evidence. Journal of Experimental Social Psychology 94, 104115.

Shu, T.-M., Lam, S.-F., 2016. Is it always good to provide positive feedback to students? The moderating effects of culture and regulatory focus. Learning and Individual Differences 49, 171–177.

Shweder, R.A., 1990. Cultural psychology: what is it? In: Stigler, J.W., Shweder, R.A., Herdt, G. (Eds.), Cultural Psychology: Essays on Comparative Human Development. Cambridge University Press, Cambridge, pp. 1–43.

Shweder, R.A., Bourne, E.J., 1982. Does the concept of the person vary cross-culturally? In: Marsella, A.J., White, G.M. (Eds.), Cultural Conceptions of Mental Health and Therapy. Kluwer, New York, NY.

Silk, J.B., Brosnan, S.F., Vonk, J., Henrich, J., Povinelli, D.J., et al., 2005. Chimpanzees are indifferent to the welfare of unrelated group members. Nature 437, 1357–1359.

Simmons, J.P., Nelson, L.D., Simonsohn, U., 2011. False-positive psychology: undisclosed flexibility in data collection and analysis allows presenting anything as significant. Psychological Science 22 (11), 1359–1366.

Simons, D.J., Shoda, Y., Lindsay, D.S., 2017. Constraints on generality (COG): a proposed addition to all empirical papers. Perspectives on Psychological Science 12, 1123–1128.

Sims, T., Tsai, J.L., Jiang, D., Wang, Y., Fung, H.H., Zhang, X., 2015. Wanting to maximize the positive and minimize the negative: implications for mixed affective experience in American and Chinese contexts. Journal of Personality and Social Psychology 109, 292–315.

Singelis, T.M., 1994. The measurement of independent and interdependent self-construals. Personality & Social Psychology Bulletin 20, 580–591.

Skolnick, A.S., 1987. The Intimate Environment: Exploring Marriage and Family. Little, Brown, Boston.

Snibbe, A.C., Markus, H.R., 2005. You can't always get what you want: social class, agency, and choice. Journal of Personality and Social Psychology 88, 703–720.

Sprecher, S., Chandak, R., 1992. Attitudes about arranged marriages and dating among men and women from India. Free Inquiry in Creative Sociology 20, 1–11.

Stamkou, E., van Kleef, G.A., Homan, A.C., Gelfand, M.J., van de Vijver, F.J., et al., 2019. Cultural collectivism and tightness moderate responses to norm violators: effects on power perception, moral emotions, and leader support. Personality & Social Psychology Bulletin 45, 947–964.

Steele, C.M., 1988. The psychology of self-affirmation: sustaining the integrity of the self. In: Berkowitz, L. (Ed.), Advances in Experimental Social Psychology, vol. 21. Academic Press, San Diego, CA, pp. 261–302.

Stewart, E.A., Simons, R.L., 2006. Structure and culture in African American adolescent violence: a partial test of the "code of the street" thesis. Justice Quarterly 23, 1–33.

Stockemer, D., Praino, R., 2015. Blinded by beauty? Physical attractiveness and candidate selection in the US house of representatives. Social Science Quarterly 96, 430–443.

Suddendorf, T., 2013. The Gap. Basic Books, New York, NY.

Suh, E.M., 2002. Culture, identity consistency, and subjective well-being. Journal of Personality and Social Psychology 83, 1378–1391.

Swallow, K.M., Wang, Q., 2020. Cultural influences on how people divide continuous sensory experience into events. Cognition 205, 104450.

Tajfel, H., Turner, J.C., 1986. The social identity theory of inter-group behavior. In: Worchel, S., Austin, W. (Eds.), Psychology of Intergroup Relations, 2nd ed. Nelson-Hall, Chicago, pp. 7–24.

Talhelm, T., 2018. Hong Kong liberals are WEIRD: analytic thought increases support for liberal policies. Personality & Social Psychology Bulletin 44, 717–728.

Talhelm, T., Dong, X., 2024. People quasi-randomly assigned to farm rice are more collectivistic than people assigned to farm wheat. Nature Communications 15, 1782.

Talhelm, T., English, A.S., 2020. Historically rice-farming societies have tighter social norms in China and worldwide. Proceedings of the National Academy of Sciences 117, 19816–19824.

Talhelm, T., Haidt, J., Oishi, S., Zhang, X., Miao, F.F., Chen, S., 2015. Liberals think more analytically (more "WEIRD") than conservatives. Personality & Social Psychology Bulletin 41, 250–267.

Talhelm, T., Lee, C.-S., English, A.S., Wang, S., 2023. How rice fights pandemics: nature-crop-human interactions shaped COVID-19 outcomes. Personality & Social Psychology Bulletin 49, 1567–1586.

Talhelm, T., Oishi, S., Zhang, X., 2019. Who smiles while alone? Rates of smiling lower in China than U.S. Emotion 19, 741–745.

Talhelm, T., Zhang, X., Oishi, S., Shimin, C., Duan, D., Lan, X., Kitayama, S., 2014. Large-scale psychological differences within China explained by rice versus wheat agriculture. Science 344, 603–608.

Tamir, D.I., Mitchell, J.P., 2012. Disclosing information about the self is intrinsically rewarding. PNAS 109, 8038–8043.

Tamir, M., Ito, A., Miyamoto, Y., Chentsova-Dutton, Y., Choi, H.J.H., et al., 2024. Emotion regulation strategies and psychological health across cultures. American Psychologist 79 (5), 748–764.

Tay, L., Morrison, M., Diener, E., 2014. Living among the affluent: boon or bane? Psychological Science 25, 1235–1241.

Taylor, S.E., Brown, J.D., 1988. Illusion and well-being: a social psychological perspective on mental health. Psychological Bulletin 103, 193–210.

Tesser, A., Crepaz, N., Beach, S.R.H., Cornell, D., Collins, J.C., 2000. Confluence of self-esteem regulation mechanisms: on integrating the self-zoo. Personality & Social Psychology Bulletin 26, 1476–1489.

Thalmayer, A.G., Toscanelli, C., Arnett, J.J., 2021. The neglected 95% revisited: is American psychology becoming less American? The American Psychologist 76, 116–129.

Thomson, R., Yuki, M., Talhelm, T., Schug, J., Kito, M., et al., 2018. Relational mobility predicts social behaviors in 39 countries and is tied to historical farming and threat. Proceedings of the National Academy of Sciences 115, 7521–7526.

Thrasher, J., Handfield, T., 2018. Honor and violence. Human Nature 29, 371–389.

Tian, Y., Bian, L., 2023. Should leaders conform? Developmental evidence from the United States and China. Journal of Experimental Psychology. General 152, 3153–3166.

Tomasello, M., 2014. A Natural History of Human Thinking. Harvard University Press, Cambridge, MA.

Tomasello, M., Carpenter, M., Call, J., Behne, T., Moll, H., 2005. Understanding and sharing intentions: the origins of cultural cognition. Behavioral and Brain Sciences 28, 675–735.

Trafimow, D., Triandis, H.C., Goto, S.G., 1991. Some tests of the distinction between the private self and the collective self. Journal of Personality and Social Psychology 60, 649–655.

Travaglino, G.A., Abrams, D., de Moura, G.R., 2014. Men of honor don't talk: the relationship between masculine honor and social activism against criminal organizations in Italy. Political Psychology 37, 183–199.

Triandis, H.C., 1972. The Analysis of Subjective Culture. Wiley, New York.

Triandis, H.C., 1994. Culture and Social Behavior. McGraw-Hill, New York.

Triandis, H.C., 1995. Individualism and Collectivism. Westview Press, Boulder, CO.

Triandis, H.C., 1996. The psychological measurement of cultural syndromes. The American Psychologist 51, 407–415.

Triandis, H.C., McCusker, C., Hui, C.H., 1990. Multimethod probes of individualism and collectivism. Journal of Personality and Social Psychology 59, 1006–1020.

Tsai, J.L., 2007. Ideal affect: cultural causes and behavioral consequences. Perspectives on Psychological Science 2, 242–259.

Tsai, J.L., Knutson, B.K., Fung, H.H., 2006a. Cultural variation in affect valuation. Journal of Personality and Social Psychology 90, 288–307.

Tsai, J.L., Louie, J., Chen, E., Uchida, Y., 2006b. Learning what feelings to desire: socialization of ideal affect through children's storybooks. Personality & Social Psychology Bulletin 32, 1–14.

Tsai, J.L., Simeonova, D.I., Watanabe, J.T., 2004. Somatic and social: Chinese Americans talk about emotion. Personality & Social Psychology Bulletin 30, 1226–1238.

Twenge, J.M., Campbell, W.K., 2001. Age and birth cohort differences in self-esteem: a cross-temporal meta-analysis. Personality and Social Psychology Review 5, 321–344.

Uchida, Y., Nakayama, M., Bowen, K.S., 2022. Interdependence of emotion: conceptualization, evidence, and social implications from cultural psychology. Current Directions in Psychological Science 31, 451–456.

Uskul, A.K., Cross, S.E., 2019. The social and cultural psychology of honour: what have we learned from researching honour in Turkey? European Review of Social Psychology 30, 39–73.

Uskul, A.K., Cross, S.E., Sunbay, Z., Gercek-Swing, B., Ataca, B., 2012. Honor bound: The cultural construction of honor in Turkey and the Northern United States. Journal of Cross-Cultural Psychology 43, 1131–1151.

Uskul, A.K., Kirchner-Hausler, A., Vignoles, V.L., Rodriguez-Bailon, R., Castillo, V.A., et al., 2023. Neither Eastern nor Western: Patterns of independence and interdependence in Mediterranean societies. Journal of Personality and Social Psychology 125, 471–495.

Uskul, A.K., Kitayama, S., Nisbett, R.E., 2008. Ecocultural basis of cognition: farmers and fishermen are more holistic than herders. Proceedings of the National Academy of Sciences of the United States of America 105, 8552–8556.

Uz, I., 2015. The index of cultural tightness and looseness among 68 countries. Journal of Cross-Cultural Psychology 46, 319–335.

Vaesen, K., MacDonald, K., Scherjon, F., van Veen, E., Roebroeks, W., 2021. Chimpanzees do not exhibit widespread cultural diffusion. Proceedings of the National Academy of Sciences 118, e2116917118.

Van Boven, L., 2000. Pluralistic ignorance and political correctness: the case of affirmative action. Political Psychology 21, 267–276.

Vandello, J.A., Cohen, D., 1999. Patterns of individualism and collectivism across the United States. Journal of Personality and Social Psychology 77, 279–292.

Vandello, J.A., Cohen, D., 2003. Male honor and female fidelity: implicit cultural scripts that perpetuate domestic violence. Journal of Personality and Social Psychology 84, 997–1010.

Varnum, M.E.W., Grossmann, I., Kitayama, S., Nisbett, R.E., 2010. The origin of cultural differences in cognition: the social orientation hypothesis. Current Directions in Psychological Science 19, 9–13.

Vauclair, C.-M., Wilson, M., Fischer, R., 2014. Cultural conceptions of morality: examining laypeople's associations of moral character. Journal of Moral Education 43, 54–74.

Veenhoven, R., 2014. World Database of Happiness. Erasmus University, Rotterdam, Netherlands. Retrieved from http://worlddatabaseofhappiness.eur.nl.

Vignoles, V.L., Owe, E., Becker, M., Smith, P.B., Easterbrook, M.J., Brown, R., et al., 2016. Beyond the 'East-West' dichotomy: global variation in cultural models of selfhood. Journal of Experimental Psychology: General 145, 966–1000.

Vohs, K.D., Baumeister, R.F., Schmeichel, B.J., Twenge, J.M., Nelson, N.M., Tice, D.M., 2008. Making choices impairs subsequent self-control: a limited-resource account of decision making, self-regulation, and active initiative. Journal of Personality and Social Psychology 94, 883–889.

Voigtländer, N., Voth, H.-J., 2012. Persecution perpetuated: the medieval origins of anti-semitic violence in Nazi Germany. The Quarterly Journal of Economics 127, 1339–1392.

Vygotsky, L.S., 1929. The problem of the cultural development of the child II. Journal of Genetic Psychology 36, 414–434.

Wang, H., Masuda, T., Ito, K., Rashid, M., 2012. How much information? East Asian and North American cultural products and information search performance. Personality & Social Psychology Bulletin 38, 1539–1551.

Wei, L., English, A.S., Talhelm, T., Li, X., Zhang, X., Wang, S., 2023. People in tight cultures and tight situations wear masks more: evidence from three large-scale studies in China. Personality & Social Psychology Bulletin 51 (7), 1121–1138.

White, C.J.M., Muthukrishna, M., Norenzayan, A., 2021. Cultural similarity among coreligionists within and between countries. Proceedings of the National Academy of Sciences 118, e2109650118.

Whiten, A., 2021. The psychological reach of culture in animals' lives. Current Directions in Psychological Science 30, 211–217.

Whiten, A., Goodall, J., McGrew, W.C., Nishida, T., Reynolds, V., et al., 1999. Cultures in chimpanzees. Nature 399, 682–685.

Williamson, H.C., Bornstein, J.X., Cantu, V., Oyku, C., Farnish, K.A., Schouweiler, M.T., 2022. How diverse are the samples used to study intimate relationships? A systematic review. Journal of Social and Personal Relationships 39 (4), 1087–1109.

Wills, T.A., 1981. Downward comparison principles in social psychology. Psychological Bulletin 90, 245–271.

Witkin, H.A., 1969. Social Influences in the Development of Cognitive Style. Rand McNally, New York.

Wormley, A.S., Kwon, J.Y., Barlev, M., Varnum, M.E.W., 2023. How much cultural variation across the globe is explained by ecology? Proceedings of the Royal Society, B 290, 20230485.

Wrangham, R., 2009. Catching Fire: How Cooking Made Us Human. Basic Books, New York.

Wundt, W., 1921. Elements of Folk Psychology. Allen & Unwin, London.

Xu, X., Whyte, M.K., 1990. Love matches and arranged marriages: a Chinese replication. Journal of Marriage and the Family 52, 709–722.

Yamada, J., Kito, M., Yuki, M., 2017. Passion, relational mobility, and proof of commitment: a comparative socio-ecological analysis of an adaptive emotion in a sexual market. Evolutionary Psychology 15.

Yamagishi, T., 1988. Exit from the group as an individualistic solution to the free rider problem in the United States and Japan. Journal of Experimental Social Psychology 24, 530–542.

Yamagishi, T., Yamagishi, M., 1994. Trust and commitment in the United States and Japan. Motivation and Emotion 18, 129–166.

Yoo, J., Martin, J., Niedenthal, P., Miyamoto, Y., 2022. Valuation of emotion underlies cultural variation in cardiovascular stress responses. Emotion 22, 1801–1814.

Youyou, W., Yang, Y., Uzzi, B., 2023. A discipline-wide investigation of the replicability of psychology papers over the past two decades. Proceedings of the National Academy of Sciences 120 (6), e2208863120.

Yuki, M., Schug, J., Horikawa, H., Takemura, K., Sato, K., Yokota, K., et al., 2007. Development of a scale to measure perceptions of relational mobility in society. CERSS Working Paper 75. Hokkaido University, Center for Experimental Research in Social Sciences, Sapporo, Japan.

Zheng, X., Ghoul, S.E., Guedhami, O., Kwok, C.C.Y., 2013. Collectivism and corruption in bank lending. Journal of International Business Studies 44, 363–390.

Zhu, Y., Zhang, L., Fan, J., Han, S., 2007. Neural basis of cultural influence on self-representation. NeuroImage 34, 1310–1316.

Chapter 2

Ethnographic records, folklore, and AI☆

Stelios Michalopoulos
Brown University, CEPR, and NBER, Providence, RI, United States

1 Introduction

In his Marshall Lectures, delivered at the University of Cambridge in 1985 on the mechanics of economic development, the late Nobel laureate Robert E. Lucas wrote: "*once one starts to think about them (the drivers of economic development), it is hard to think about anything else*." And for the next decades, growth and development economists did just this. Broadly speaking, research in the field coalesced around two distinct approaches: the historical and the experimental. The recent Sveriges Riksbank Prizes in Economic Sciences in Memory of Alfred Nobel aptly recognize these two research strands.

On the one hand, the 2024 Prize highlights the historical foundations of present-day institutions in the colonized world. According to the press release, "Daron Acemoglu, Simon Johnson, and James Robinson have demonstrated the importance of societal institutions introduced during colonization in shaping differences in countries' path to prosperity". On the other hand, the 2019 Nobel was bestowed on Abhijit Banerjee, Esther Duflo, and Michael Kremer for "introducing a new approach (field experiments) to obtaining reliable answers about the best ways to combat global poverty by dividing this issue into smaller, more manageable questions."[1]

But how did the research on the drivers of economic development evolve to this point? In the 1990s, a testing ground for competing growth theories emerged, fueled by new theoretical insights and the growing availability of internationally comparable output data, primarily via the Penn World Table (PWT) Project. This enabled comparisons across a large number of countries (for an overview, see Barro (1999)). Empirical works on cross-country growth

☆ The extensive discussions with Elias Papaioannou over the years have helped shape the contours of this chapter. I would also like to thank Paola Giuliano (the Editor) for her concise and detailed feedback and acknowledge the valuable comments provided by participants at the Economics of Culture conference at Northwestern University. Daniele Goffi provided superlative assistance.

[1] For a thorough review of the 2019 and 2024 laureates contributions, see Olken (2020) and Papaioannou (2025), respectively.

Handbook of Culture and Economic Behavior, Volume 1, ISSN 3051-1682
https://doi.org/10.1016/bs.hceb.2026.01.002

regressions and development accounting blossomed, leading to a vibrant body of work on the conditional correlates of economic growth since World War II. The focus areas included traditional candidates, such as the accumulation of physical and human capital and financial development, but also touched on aspects that were rarely discussed up to that point, including the role of geographic and social attributes and institutional arrangements. These empirical findings, in turn, spurred further theoretical work and fed back into empirical research.

This turn in the literature of slowly incorporating historical and social features of a country's legacy was in contrast to the dominant neoclassical approach. The latter would leave little room for a deeper understanding of important historical events in the growth process, such as colonization, institutional changes, and geographic and cultural characteristics. Elements that social scientists would instinctively see as deeply intertwined with economic behavior. Not explicitly accounting for the role of history, geography-ecology, and culture (religion, beliefs, family ties, norms) had relegated these fundamental aspects to being viewed empirically as the *residual* of the growth process.[2]

However, as the cross-country growth literature matured, it faced increasing empirical challenges, ranging from coefficient instability due to multicollinearity, small sample sizes, and limited degrees of freedom to measurement error, outliers, and variable data quality across countries. Even running millions of regressions (e.g., Sala-i-Martin et al. (2004)), identifying robust correlates became difficult (Ciccone and Jarociński, 2010; Johnson et al., 2013). Furthermore, identification issues persisted, despite innovative approaches leveraging aspects of the colonial history as a source of variation (see, e.g., Acemoglu et al. (2001); Hall and Jones (1999); La Porta et al. (1998); Mauro (1995)).

In the early 2000s, the field of micro-development started adopting randomization techniques, raising the standard for empirical identification (Duflo et al., 2007). This shift highlighted a growing divide between the rigorously identified but (initially) narrowly focused micro-development studies and the broader but less credible lessons from cross-country analyses. This gap provided a fertile ground for research exploring large-scale within-country variation. This approach, coined by Michalopoulos and Papaioannou (2018) as "meso", aimed to balance the strengths and weaknesses of both macro- and micro studies by applying microeconomic empirical tools to answer broader questions, often using large, global datasets.

The rise of geographic information systems (GIS) and the increasing availability of large spatial data, such as satellite images of nighttime light density, opened new avenues for research. These unconventional data sources, along with historical natural experiments, expanded the range of questions

2 The disregard of history by economists was not limited to the literature on economic growth or macroeconomics. The total number of economic history papers published in general interest journals had declined as economists moved from transparent, intuitive theories and applied methods to more complex, often esoteric, mathematical structures and elaborate quantitative approaches.

economists began to tackle. As a result, a tectonic shift has taken place in the research of the historical roots of comparative development. To appreciate the scope of this change see the contributions in the recent Handbooks of Historical Political Economy and Historical Economics edited by Jenkins and Rubin (2024) and Bisin and Federico (2021), respectively, and the literature reviews by Margo (2018), Michalopoulos and Papaioannou (2020), Nunn (2020) and Voth (2021).

By shifting the focus to within-country analyses, economists studying the causes of underdevelopment had to engage productively with neighboring disciplines to leverage valuable insights. Working with conjectures and lifetime works of anthropologists, ethnographers, political scientists, social psychologists, historians, and even folklorists became increasingly common. This willingness to cross disciplinary boundaries was driven by the realization that understanding the local context and the historical process that shaped it is a sine qua non to recognize the constraints and catalysts of (economic) change.

This interdisciplinary approach has been facilitated to a great extent by building on meticulously curated databases crafted by eminent scholars. Examples include the Ethnographic Atlas and the Standard Cross-Cultural Sample compiled by George Peter Murdock, the Folklore Motif Index constructed by Yuri Berezkin, and the myriads of databases available from earth scientists. The resulting cross-pollination of disciplines has proved fertile ground for expanding the scope of economic questions.

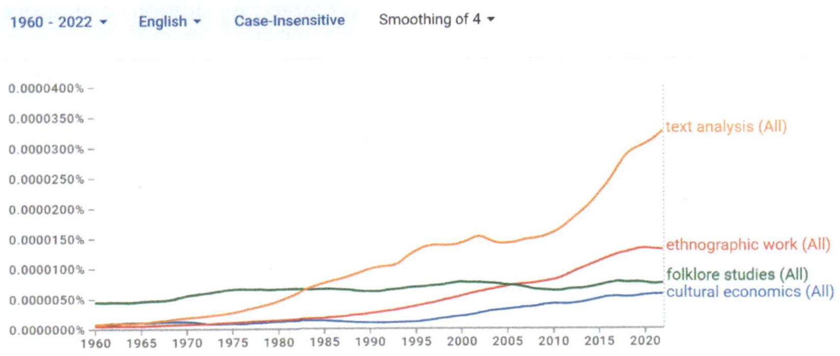

FIGURE 1 Evolution of concepts in book production over the last 60 years.

Thematic evolution

To better understand the context in which the literature evolved, it is useful to analyze the frequency of four key concepts in the corpus of English books over time. In Fig. 1, we prompt Google Ngram Viewer to plot the usage frequency of the main concepts that form the basis of the present study. Namely, mentions of "ethnographic work," "text analysis," "folklore studies", and "cultural economics".[3] Interest in folklore studies has been stable for the last sixty years, reflecting the mature state of the discipline. During the same period, mentions of ethnographic work have steadily risen, particularly after the 1990s. Just a few years later, "cultural economics" appears to have gained some currency in the world of book writing, whereas text analysis skyrockets, particularly after 2010.

This Handbook chapter weaves these seemingly disparate themes through the lenses of cultural economics. I critically review the literature on the drivers of comparative economic development, paying particular attention to how ethnographic and folklore records have been used to deepen our understanding of the interaction between culture and economic behavior. I will also highlight how folklore records can complement the ethnographic material. Additionally, I will explore how advances in text analysis have revolutionized the field and revisit the work of Michalopoulos and Xue (2021), henceforth MX, by offering concrete guidelines on how to leverage Large Language Models (LLMs) to extract values and norms from folkloric motifs. In conclusion, I will offer some thoughts on open questions and future research.

2 Murdock's ethnographic work and his critics

In this section, I examine the contributions of George Peter Murdock, a pioneering cross-cultural anthropologist whose work has been widely employed by economists seeking to uncover the historical foundations of comparative development. This discussion draws on White and Brudner-White (1988).

Murdock was the leading advocate of the empirical tradition in anthropology, emphasizing direct comparison of societies. His major contribution was to develop a scientific framework that would enable anthropology to evolve into a comparative and formal science capable of testing and (dis)proving theories using a global data set. George Peter Murdock is renowned for compiling and organizing the following corpora. First, along with colleagues, he initiated the Cross-Cultural Survey (1937) project at Yale's Institute of Human Relations, which aimed at systematically categorizing and organizing data from various societies worldwide, providing a foundation for cross-cultural comparisons. This was a precursor to the more comprehensive work in his later years. Arguably, it laid the groundwork for what is considered perhaps as Murdock's most influential creation, the Human Relations Area Files (HRAF), designed as a vast repository of ethnographic material from cultures worldwide. He aimed to make this data accessible for comparative research, with detailed descriptions of the social, cultural, and economic practices of different societies. The HRAF uses a standardized coding system called the Outline of Cultural Materials (OCM). This system assigns specific numerical codes to topics and themes (e.g., kinship,

[3] The data comes from the Google Ngram Viewer, a tool that allows one to explore language usage trends over time by searching through a vast collection of books, documents, and other textual sources.

economy, religion) to help organize and classify the textual information for easier retrieval and comparative research. It remains one of the largest collections of ethnographic information ever assembled. Its extant digital platforms, the eHRAF World Cultures and eHRAF Archaeology, are continuously expanded and updated with new ethnographic records, societies, and archaeological traditions. They are currently maintained by the Human Relations Area Files, Inc., a non-profit research organization at Yale University.

However, the main reason that HRAF has not been productively employed by economists interested in culture and historical comparative development is because of its primarily textual nature, providing rich qualitative descriptions of societies. Converting nuanced ethnographic descriptions to quantifiable bits had long been viewed as an academic task best left to the specialists. This is precisely why the subsequent comparative works by Murdock, the Ethnographic Atlas (EA), and the Standard Cross-Cultural Sample (SCCS) became the go-to databases for comparative work among empirically-minded social scientists and economists in particular.

The EA and the SCCS

The EA is a systematic compilation of attributes for over 1200 societies with global coverage. A monumental output that came to life thanks to Murdock's prodigious memory for ethnographic detail and vast erudition, having read and digested over 10,000 ethnographic books and articles. Although many of his students worked on coding projects, he relied on their coding over his own only when they had done the primary ethnography, and even then, he was meticulous about catching coding errors. The EA includes information on more than 60 group attributes, including subsistence pattern, family structure, and social organization. This Atlas has been widely used for cross-cultural studies and has been revised and expanded several times after its initial publication in 1967 (Murdock, 1967). One of the key revisions was undertaken by anthropologist Douglas R. White and others in the 1980s (White and Brudner-White, 1988), with updated data and additional societies included.

Various scholars have also contributed to revisions and extensions of the Atlas with the latest attempt to integrate more ethnographic data by Giuliano and Nunn (2018). The latter update is particularly valuable as it incorporates groups from Eastern Europe and Siberia that have been underrepresented in the EA. Moreover, the authors have matched the ancestral characteristics of groups in the extended EA to more than 7000 language groups in the Ethnologue producing an unprecedented coverage of ancestral traits of contemporary languages across the globe.

Murdock's complementary output was the 186-society Standard Cross-Cultural Sample (Murdock and White, 1969). He created this sample to address the need for a more systematic and scientifically rigorous comparison of cultures. It is a subset of the HRAF, providing a selected set of societies to facilitate hypothesis testing. For Murdock, the culture area classifications were not an end in themselves, but a means to sampling design. Murdock's cultural provinces were a central part of the Murdock and White (1969) sample.

Through these works, Murdock provided a structured, empirical basis for anthropological research, allowing for scientific testing and cross-cultural analysis across a wide range of human societies. The last product of his scholarship was the geographic and ethnographic mapping of 563 societies in the Atlas of World Cultures (1981). He also founded and edited the journal *Ethnology* to provide an outlet for ethnographic and cross-cultural data.

Murdock's contributions in perspective

To better understand the intellectual environment in anthropology and appreciate Murdock's contributions and reactions to his work, it is important to keep in mind that for decades, anthropologists had been fiercely divided over the very idea of subscribing to a method and framework for the comparison of societies. On the one hand, scholars following the tradition of prominent anthropologists, including Tylor (1871), Morgan (1877), and Spencer and Gillen (1899), remained cultural evolutionists, broadly embracing the view that human societies develop over time and follow three stages of evolution: savagery, barbarism, and civilization. However, most adopted antievolutionism and were starkly opposed to wide-ranging comparisons. For them, the mandate was to study societies holistically and in their own context. Under Franz Boas, for example, the dominant paradigm was historical particularism, i.e., the importance of understanding each culture and society on its own terms (Boas, 1896, 1901).[4]

Therefore, the fundamental premise of making direct statistical comparisons between groups was heavily debated. In many respects, Murdock's work laid bare the complex theoretical and methodological task of the comparativist. How do we come up with a consistent definition of what constitutes a group, the unit of observation, and how to operationalize it empirically? Once one has answered the first question, she needs to decide how many dimensions of the group's social, economic, and institutional environment to code. For each dimension, how many distinct categories to admit? Are these categories fixed and stable or time-varying and ephemeral? Should we develop codes that are region-specific or strive for universal classifications? In other words, can different aspects of different societies even be compared? If so, how wide-ranging can the comparison be? Is there enough evidence to support a given categorization? What is the threshold for admitting evidence in favor or against the presence of a given trait?[5]

4 Murdock did share the view with Boas that cultural variation could also be explained by mechanisms of diffusion, trade, and a shared (historical and geographic) environment. These considerations were paramount in shaping his efforts to design the SCCS to minimize such influences.

5 These questions, seen from today's perspective, are similar to the debate and advances surrounding the core problem of dimensionality reduction in fields that deal with large numbers

Given this background, it is not surprising that Murdock's work was met with skepticism and sometimes outright hostility. Joseph Tobin, for example, in 1990 starts his critique of the HRAF with the following passage: "*What if I were to tell you of a bold experiment in anthropological writing in which ethnographies are being chopped up and then jumbled together... a French physical anthropologist's 1899 study of cranial dimensions of natives of the Toba tribal group, follows a 1968 study of Toban religious beliefs by a Mennonite missionary/anthropologist, which follows an American culture and personality theorist's 1974 paper on children's doll play among the Toba. A series of numbers and dots running down the margins gives you the option of sequencing your reading in a variety of ways, including the usual beginning to end. Would it matter if I were to tell you that the idea for this radical text was not developed in 1987 by a Nobel-prize-winning Argentinian novelist, but instead in 1937 by an American behavioral scientist searching for a unified theory of human behavior?*" As evident in this polemic, Murdock's efforts brought the profession's attention to the incomplete nature of the ethnographic record, which, if anything, became itself a subject of contention.

Needless to say, Murdock's classification was not perfect. For example, some of Murdock's codes obscure regional variations that he thought were inimical to finding universal regularities.[6] Nevertheless, Murdock's judgment about cultural classifications has been verified by various studies, including Driver et al. (1972), Driver and Coffin (1974), and Driver et al. (1974).

Moreover, Murdock (1949) was well aware, for example, that patterns of kinship behavior form a continuum (following Eggan (1937)), even while he tried to break that continuum into defensible but useful segments. His coding tried to do justice to the descriptive content of ethnographies, within the limitations of a comparative framework, and to identify these limitations rather than ignore them, analyzing where anthropologists stood as a discipline in the process of data collection. The debate over residence categories is a case in point, Goodenough (1956). Murdock's classification of the types of residence grew ever more complex as the debate intensified. The initially simple six-part code of Murdock (1949) had, by the EA in 1967, been augmented with life-cycle variability and additional types to accommodate the countervailing view that these residence patterns are not norms or rules of society, but individual choices under constraints.

Finally, in an effort to circumscribe the geographic and temporal relevance of the coding, all of Murdock's codes, from the Atlas forward, are pinpointed to a specific local entity at a particular period. In addition, SCCS aimed to address many of these concerns by including societies from a wide range of geographic

of observations and/or variables, such as signal processing, speech recognition, neuroinformatics, text analysis, and bioinformatics.

6 For example, White and Burton (1988) found that Murdock's tripartite classification of polygyny obscures the major regional differences in marriage forms that emerge when the grounds for limited and general polygyny are identified.

regions to represent the global diversity of human cultures, prioritizing those that were not historically or geographically dependent on each other to reduce the risk of overlap or bias. This resulted in a sample that included a variety of social, political, and economic systems, from small-scale hunter-gatherer groups to large, complex states. To minimize measurement error, groups were selected based on the availability of reliable and in-depth ethnographic data, ensuring that the comparisons were grounded in strong empirical evidence.

Africa and its people

In addition to his global compilations, Murdock also developed an interest in the African continent (Murdock, 1959). This book remains one of the key texts for understanding African ethnography from a comparative perspective and laid the foundation for subsequent anthropological studies on African societies.

This work has also been criticized for the limitations of its typological and static approach. For example, Kopytoff (1988) critically engaged with Murdock's work on Africa, particularly regarding Murdock's cultural and social categorization systems and his structural-functional approach to African societies. Kopytoff launched several critiques of Murdock's approach. First, he criticized Murdock for treating African societies as static entities, failing to account for historical changes and fluidity. Second, Kopytoff claimed that Murdock's framework was implicitly ethnocentric, rooted in Western understandings of social structure, universalizing Western concepts of family, kinship, and political organization, which could not align with African social realities. He believed that Murdock imposed external categories on African cultures rather than understanding them on their own terms. He stressed that to understand African societies one needed to earnestly embrace the role of individual agency, local innovations, adaptability, and the dynamic and negotiable nature of African societies exemplified in their complex kinship systems, elements that Murdock's rigid comparative scheme by construction could not accommodate.

3 Ethnographic material in economics research

Ethnographic and linguistic records have two main manifestations. The first involves mapping ethnic, linguistic, and cultural groups, and the second concerns the characteristics that ethnographers have compiled for the underlying societies.

3.1 Ethnographic maps

Researchers investigating the drivers of economic development faced a new spatial reality as they moved from country-level to within-country analysis. Beyond country boundaries, a plethora of alternative mappings of the social landscape awaited. While economists were focused on countries as the primary unit of analysis, linguists, ethnographers, and social historians had been busy cataloging the diversity in the social fabric within developing countries and beyond.

These sometimes global representations include (i) the classical Soviet Atlas Narodov Mira constructed by the Miklukho-Maklai Institute of Ethnology and Anthropology (1964), which researchers have digitized and georeferenced, producing the "Georeferencing of Ethnic Groups" (GREG) (Weidmann et al., 2010). (ii) The World Language Mapping System (WLMS), a GIS database that depicts the spatial boundaries of linguistic groups catalogued by the Ethnologue (Gordon and Grimes, 2005).[7] A third source that has often been used is Murdock's mapping of ethnic groups in Africa. Murdock's (1959) book on the cultural history of the African continent contained a map from the author's own drawing, showing the approximate territorial boundaries of the various tribes and nations distinguished in the text. Fig. 2 below reproduces this map. Starting with Nunn (2008), who digitized and georeferenced Murdock's work and made it publicly available, scholars interested in precolonial Africa have used it productively. Below, I review some of these works.

3.2 Combining ethnographic maps and records

Aggregating the ethnographic evidence

At the turn of the 21st century, economists constrained by the availability of measures of local economic development aggregated the underlying ethnographic and linguistic characteristics at the country level using ethnolinguistic maps to explore how these country aggregates influenced national economic performance. Early examples of this work include Mauro (1995) and Easterly and Levine (1997), who used information from the Atlas Narodov Mira project to construct measures of ethnolinguistic fragmentation at the country level and link its variation to corruption levels and economic growth, respectively. Focusing on Africa, Gennaioli and Rainer (2007) combine the information from the EA with the ethnic composition of the countries listed by the Atlas Narodov Mira to calculate the share of the population in each African country that traces its ancestry to historically centralized groups, finding that countries with a stronger state apparatus among their indigenous population performed better than others.[8] Similarly, Nunn (2008) combines information on the location of groups within a country from Murdock's Tribal Map with the number of en-

[7] The latter provides information on all known living languages, as well as languages that have become extinct since 1951. This includes information on names, dialects, population estimates, location, vitality level, usage, and second language information. The Ethnologue draws information from a variety of sources, including books, reference sources, serials, and government publications, and is updated with a new edition approximately every four years.

[8] A similar pattern was established in a global sample by Bockstette et al. (2002), who, going through the historical literature, constructed measures of state antiquity, i.e., a variable capturing the depth of experience with state during the last 2 millennia. See Borcan et al. (2018) for an extension of the state antiquity index.

slaved individuals from various sources to arrive at country-level estimates of slavery across Africa, establishing a strong negative relationship between the legacy of slavery and country-level economic performance.

These early contributions showed that historical legacies as coded in ethnographies may hold significant promise in explaining differences in comparative development, but at the same time highlighted the limits of cross-country works as the degrees of freedom, particularly for studies focusing on countries in a single continent, were severely curtailed. This realization paved the way for moving the analysis across groups within countries, allowing researchers to empirically estimate models including country-fixed effects and ensure that the established associations were not driven by the myriad country-wide differences in the correlates that the cross-country growth literature had been busy identifying up to that point. The pivot from cross-country to cross-group analysis gave a much-needed boost to the literature on the roots of culture and economic performance.

Moving the analysis within countries

The EA is often complemented by Murdock's tribal map, particularly for studies focusing on the African continent.[9] Among the first works to move beyond country borders and explore ethnic-level variation is the work by Nunn and Wantchekon (2011), who combine contemporary individual-level survey data with historical data on slave shipments by ethnic group and find that individuals whose ancestors were heavily raided during the slave trade are less trusting today. Other early papers in this genre have focused on the origins and consequences of political centralization across African societies. For example, in Michalopoulos and Papaioannou (2013) we provide evidence of the importance of historical ethnic institutions in shaping Africa's economic landscape. In particular, we establish that regions historically inhabited by ethnic groups characterized by centralized institutions, i.e., those with more hierarchical political systems, exhibit higher economic development today.

Fenske (2014) and Alsan (2015) explore the trade and epidemiological origins of statehood in the continent, respectively. Specifically, Fenske tests Bates' explanation of precolonial African states, linking trade across ecological boundaries to state formation. The author establishes empirically that African societies in ecologically diverse environments had more centralized states. Exploring the potential mechanisms connecting trade to states, he found that trade supported class stratification between rulers and ruled. Alsan highlights the importance of the TseTse fly, which is unique to Africa and transmits a parasite that is harmful to humans and lethal to livestock. She shows that ethnic groups

9 In her chapter in the Handbook of Historical Economics, Lowes (2021) discusses how economists have leveraged the Ethnographic Atlas, revealing its extensive use among those interested in understanding the variation in institutions, culture, and comparative development across groups within modern countries. I refer the interested reader to Table 6.1 in the published version for a comprehensive coverage of these works.

inhabiting TseTse-suitable areas were less likely to use domesticated animals and the plow, less likely to be politically centralized, and had lower population density. The evidence suggests that current economic performance is affected by TseTse through the channel of precolonial political centralization.

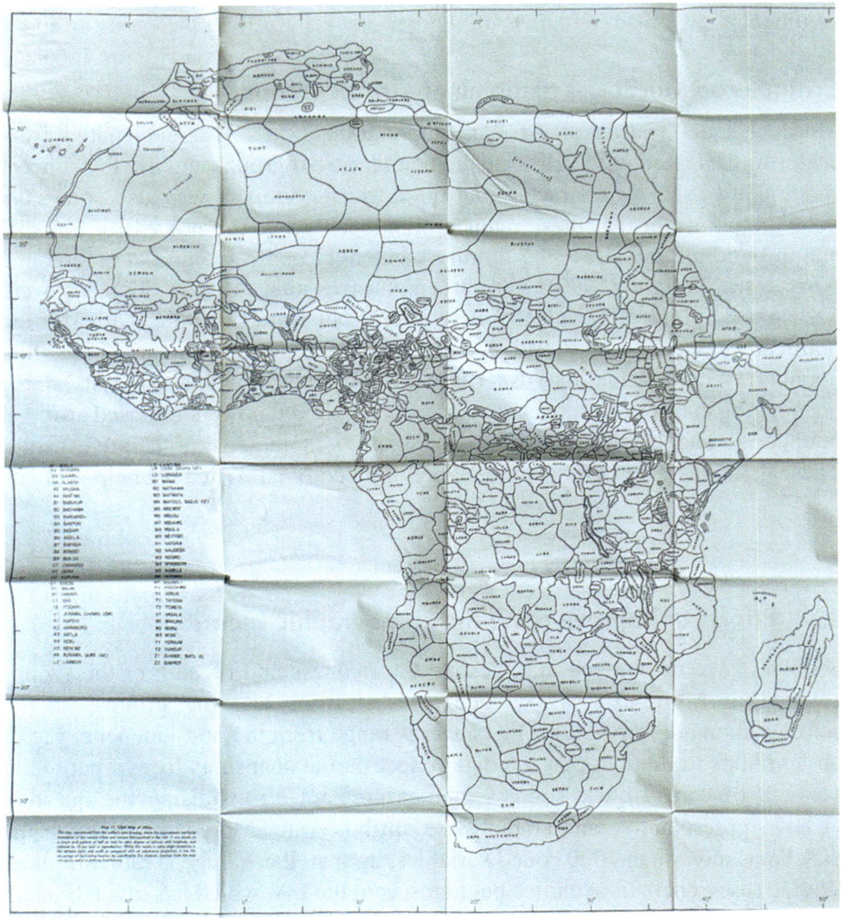

FIGURE 2 Tribal map of Africa – pocket inside back cover of the 1959 book by George Peter Murdock, Africa: Its Peoples and their Culture History.

Moving beyond the role of political centralization, Enke (2019) stresses the paramount importance of kinship structure in shaping moral systems, showing how societies with a historically tightly knit kinship structure regulate behavior through communal moral values, revenge taking, emotions of external shame, and notions of purity and disgust. In loose kinship societies, on the other hand, cooperation appears to be enforced through universal moral values, internalized guilt, altruistic punishment, and an apparent rise and fall of moralizing religions.

In Michalopoulos et al. (2019), we test Diamond's hypothesis that prolonged exposure to agriculture sets societies on a favorable developmental path. By examining how ancestral economic lifeways influence contemporary economic status in Africa, we find that individuals tracing their lineage to farming groups outperform those from pastoral backgrounds, even within the major cities of the continent.

Critiques on Murdock's mapping of African groups

Murdock's delineation of African ethnic groups was also not spared from criticism. His attempt to delineate the boundaries of groups and use the concept of ethnicity itself for characterizing the African continent was also contested. Scholars point out that these maps are endogenous to the process of colonial nation-building and stress the fluidity of identity and residence in precolonial Africa, see Wright (1999). Wright emphasizes that African societies were not rigidly bounded, homogeneous "tribes", but were dynamic, with shifting political alliances, migrations, and interactions between groups. These fluid boundaries complicate the use of the term "tribe", which suggests fixed, unchanging entities. Moreover, he argues that colonial powers imposed artificial boundaries and labels on African societies to fit their administrative needs. These divisions did not reflect the reality of precolonial Africa but helped create it.

3.3 Efforts to improve upon the ethnographic record

Scholars have recognized that, despite the richness and breadth of the groups covered in Murdock's work, the recorded traits and the groups' spatial configuration are imperfect. The concerns range from the non-independence of observations to the fact that the data reflect partial snapshots from a particular point in time, and other sources of measurement error, raising the question of how representative and stable these attributes are. Moreover, although the SCCS has more than 1000 coded variables, its spatial coverage is rather limited, leaving researchers little choice but to resort to the EA, which has much broader group coverage at the expense of having access to only a handful of indicators that are directly useful. Economists have pursued multiple strategies to navigate these constraints.

How much can we trust existing maps?

A stream of research has sought to better understand the drivers of these groups' spatial distribution. Establishing, for example, that the underlying geographical and ecological landscape shapes the territorial extent of groups as delineated by ethnographers and linguists would suggest constraints on how malleable ethnicity is.

In Michalopoulos (2012), I explore the determinants of ethnolinguistic diversity within as well as across countries, shedding light on its geographic origins. The empirical analysis conducted across countries, virtual countries, and pairs of contiguous pixels establishes that geographic heterogeneity, captured by variation in regional land quality and elevation, is a fundamental determinant of contemporary linguistic diversity. The findings are consistent with the proposed hypothesis that differences in land endowments gave rise to location-specific human capital, leading to the formation of localized ethnicities.

In the same spirit, in a subsequent study focusing on Africa and its exceptional levels of diversity, Cervellati et al. (2019) uncover the role of the ecological environment in shaping tribal diversity in the continent. Specifically, they theorize how malaria exposure may cause multiple geographically clustered groups with high endogamy rates because voluntary isolation would limit the extent of malaria outbreaks. They proceed to document its role in shaping tribal diversity in Murdock's map as well as contemporaneous ethnic diversity in Africa. Interestingly, they show that malaria is a main driver of precolonial ethnic diversity in Africa but not in the Americas, where the pathogen was absent before the European colonization.[10] Ashraf and Galor (2013) show that distance from pre-historical migration routes inversely predicts ethnic diversity, whereas Ahlerup and Olsson (2012) find that the duration of human settlements since prehistoric times has a strong positive association with current levels of ethnolinguistic diversity.

The findings of these studies bridge the two opposing strands of thought regarding the formation and spatial extent of ethnic groups. On the one hand, establishing that deep geographic and ecological determinants explain a significant fraction of the observed linguistic diversity is consistent with the primordial view qualifying ethnic groups as deeply rooted, clearly drawn entities (Geertz, 1963). On the other hand, showing that geography alone cannot account for all the variation in contemporary ethnic diversity, and in particular establishing that there is no link between geographic and ethnic diversity in those places where the historically indigenous populations today constitute a minority, see Michalopoulos (2012), provides evidence in favor of the constructivist or instrumentalist school of thought. This view highlights the contingent and situational character of ethnicity, with modern states' policies being a significant determinant of the observed diversity; see Barth (1969). See also Blouin and Mukand (2019), who show that the salience of ethnic identity can be manipulated by governments exploiting variation in the exposure to government propaganda in post-genocide Rwanda.

[10] Outside economics, studies in the fields of linguistics, anthropology, and sociology have also examined the relationship between the environment and cultural diversity. For example, Mace and Pagel (1995) use historical maps of native populations in North America at the time of contact by Europeans and show that more diverse habitats sustained more native groups. Also, Nettle (1998, 1999) looks at the global distribution of languages and finds that countries characterized by low rainfall and short growing seasons sustain fewer languages.

Another way to address concerns that specific configurations of group mappings are not driving a study's main argument is to use alternative delineations of the same phenomenon. For example, in Alesina et al. (2016), we investigate the consequences and origins of between-group inequality across countries. Combining satellite images of nighttime luminosity with the homelands of ethnolinguistic groups, we construct measures of ethnic inequality. We use both the GREG and the Ethnologue databases reviewed above to ensure that our findings do not hinge on a particular set of ethnic borders. Although this robustness alleviates concerns that the patterns are map-dependent, it also raises the possibility that any mapping would deliver the same pattern. If so, this would negate the argument. To better understand how informative ethnic boundaries are above and beyond arbitrary map partitions, we created ethnic Gini coefficients using perturbed ethnic regions.[11] We then proceed to show that the ethnic inequality derived by these locally perturbed ethnic boundaries has less explanatory power than the one based on the original mappings.

Finally, digitizing hitherto unexplored maps to obtain a sharper view of the ethnic landscape during the time period of interest has been a fruitful avenue in supplementing existing maps. Lowes (2022), for example, explores how matrilineal versus patrilineal kinship structures shape incentives for cooperation within the household. After establishing her findings in the context of Africa overall using Murdock's map, she zooms in on the DRC, digitizing a map of Vansina (1966) reflecting multiple groups in one area and finer cultural distinctions. The resulting dataset includes information on more than 380 groups in the DRC, a decisive improvement over what the Murdock Map and Atlas cover in this area.

Account for measurement error

Much of the criticism of Murdock's work reviewed above was centered on the limited availability of the ethnographic sources, which were often deemed scattered and lacking historical depth. This debate from the economists' perspective has often been interpreted as meaning *there is substantial measurement error in how ethnographies have been translated into numbers*. In the presence of classical measurement error, that is, when the right-hand side variable in a regression analysis is measured with error, this leads to attenuation bias, that is, the estimated coefficient between the independent and dependent variables is

---

[11] Using as inputs the centroids of ethnic-linguistic homelands, we generate Thiessen polygons that have the unique property that each polygon contains only one input point and that any location within a polygon is closer to its associated point than to a point within any other polygon. Hence, the resulting Thiessen polygons have exactly the same centroids as the original linguistic and ethnic homelands in the Ethnologue and GREG databases, respectively, the key difference being that the actual homelands have idiosyncratic shapes.

systematically biased toward zero.[12] In this context, the use of geographic attributes as an instrument for the ethnographic trait serves a dual purpose: first, to correct for measurement error, and second, to address omitted variables that could bias the results. This also explains why the instrumented ethnographic trait often yields a much larger coefficient estimate than its OLS counterpart.

A direct way to tackle the issue of historical depth is to reconstruct existing attributes from the Atlas, tracing their evolution over time whenever possible. A nice illustration is the work by Depetris-Chauvin (2016). Motivated by the observation that Murdock's map offers a snapshot of political centralization around the 19th and early 20th century (the period the typical society in the EA is pinpointed), the author combines a wide variety of historical sources to construct an original measure of long-term exposure to statehood at the subnational level. Armed with this measure, he shows that historical political centralization decreases the likelihood of contemporary civil conflict. This study shows how to add a time dimension to the ethnographic record. In Michalopoulos et al. (2018) we adopt a similar procedure. Specifically, we digitize the location of trade routes from several historical maps at different points in time, and construct a time series of trade routes' proximity at the pixel level in the Old World, from the pre-Islamic period until the 19th century. Given that the EA does not include group-level trade measures, our coding fills this gap.

Deal with phylogenetic and spatial dependence across groups

In a recent methodological paper, Gershman and Mumladze (2025) attempt to address the well-known problem of cultural non-independence due to common ancestry in the context of the EA. It is worthwhile to note that this concern was the chief reason for Murdock to construct the SCCS (from the EA). The authors start their analysis by showing that many characteristics in the Atlas exhibit phylogenetic signal, i.e., they are more similar among societies with closer ancestral ties. This observed phylogenetic correlation leads to severe inefficiency of the standard OLS estimator compared to phylogenetic generalized least squares (PGLS), which they propose. The appropriate clustering of standard errors partially, but not entirely, mitigates the problem.

A related issue concerns spatial autocorrelation as variables are geographically clustered, meaning nearby observations are more likely to be similar, inflating statistical significance. Voth (2021) reviews how the addition of geographic controls, region fixed effects, and applying the Conley correction of standard errors further mitigate spatial autocorrelation. Moreover, recent advances in spatial econometrics, see Müller and Watson (2024), offer strategies

[12] When measurement error is non-classical, things become more complex as one needs to specify the direction of the bias with respect to both the outcome variable and the possibly omitted variables in the residual.

for valid inference in regressions with persistent spatial data. See Becker et al. (2025) for a practitioner's guide for applied researchers on this topic.

Reconstruct missing traits one at a time

The uneven coverage of groups and their social attributes prompted scholars to dig into the ethnographic record independently and reconstruct, through their own reading, a new trait at a time. This was a necessary step to test a hypothesis whose empirical validity could not be ascertained with what the EA offered. Notable examples of this approach include the work of Moscona et al. (2020) who construct information on the presence of segmentary lineage systems in Africa. They use published ethnographies, the primary source being the Ethnographic Survey of Africa, a series of studies edited by Daryll Forde and published between the 1940s and 1970s. Lowes et al. (2025) are in the process of digitizing this wealth of text.[13]

In another study, Moscona and Seck (2024) ask how social organization shapes patterns of economic interaction and the effects of national policy, focusing on the distinction between age-based and kin-based groups in sub-Saharan Africa. Since the latter classification is not readily available in the EA, after consulting an extensive set of secondary sources, the authors made that determination for groups in Kenya and Uganda.

A final illustration of works that complement the material in the EA is the recent study by Espín-Sánchez et al. (2024). The authors of this exciting work put together new data on the practice of rain rituals around the world and explore how the rainfall profile in the region may explain the emergence of such rituals.

These efforts are crucial in filling knowledge gaps in specific aspects of society, while highlighting the need for a more systematic and comprehensive Atlas update. This is where folklore records can make a significant difference.

Validate the EA with contemporary surveys

The ideal way to validate the Atlas and address the expressed skepticism among cultural anthropologists reviewed above, would be through representative data collected from recorded societies when the ethnographers made their observations. As I will show below, this is one of the several advantages of integrating folklore in our analysis. Bahrami-Rad et al. (2021) rely on the next best alternative: data from the descendants of the populations documented in the Atlas. The authors first link the societies in the EA to the ethnic groups that 790,000 individuals from the Demographic and Health Surveys identify with across 43 countries. They then show that ethnographers' accounts about life in preindustrial societies, as captured in the EA, are informative across a wide range of contemporary attributes. In most cases, these accounts show strong and significant correlations with the self-reports of descendants from the same

[13] Combining this underutilized corpus with the tools of machine learning and LLM, as explained below, offers a promising avenue to expand our empirical understanding of African societies.

societies. These associations likely represent a lower bound, suggesting that the Atlas offers a meaningful and reliable source of information on human cultures.

3.4 Searching for causality in unexpected places: borderlands

A growing literature has relied on natural experiments to establish causal relationships in macroeconomics. See Diamond and Robinson (2010) and Fuchs-Schündeln and Hassan (2016) for a thorough review. In this context, the use of maps and the spatial delineation of cultural entities has greatly aided the rise of plausibly identified research designs, bringing the credibility revolution in empirical research of works at the intersection of macroeconomics, economic history, and economic development (Angrist and Pischke, 2010). Moving the inquiry for the roots of comparative development within countries, one may now exploit a wide range of identification strategies to overcome the limited degrees of freedom inherent to cross-country works.

Comparing political, social, and economic outcomes at the border of national, subnational, ethnic, linguistic, and historical entities has emerged as a leading empirical strategy. Efforts to link a region's heritage with its current performance have particularly benefited from spatial regression discontinuity designs, mainly because demarcating boundaries (of groups, empires, historical events, and zones of influence) on modern territories is relatively easier than tracing the history of the lineage of a given individual. Looking at places, for example, on both sides of a historical boundary, one may juxtapose contemporary indicators and trace the legacy of whatever it was that historically differed between the two regions. This strategy has been fruitfully applied to examining the role of institutions that tend to have a territorial base.

What enabled economists to look at border regions?

Borders have long fascinated social scientists, producing a rich narrative of the historical, social, and institutional context of these areas. This has given rise to the independent field of border studies. Contributors include political scientists, sociologists, ethnologists, psychologists, anthropologists, linguists, economists, art historians, physical geographers, and even specialists in more technical sciences.

Understanding the economic activity in these areas and the factors that influence it was mostly inaccessible to development and growth economists, hindering the exchange of ideas between economics and related fields. Quite simply, before incorporating GIS into their empirical tools, development economists could largely overlook the complexities of spatial development, and urban economists would focus on cities with available data (Henderson and Thisse, 2004). The lack of reliable indicators for local economic performance made large-scale empirical studies difficult. However, over the past two decades, this has changed dramatically with the advent of satellite imagery capturing nighttime light density, popularized among economists by Henderson et al.

(2012), the availability of high-resolution spatial data, and georeferenced mappings of conflict. See Duranton et al. (2015) for its impact on urban economics.

Comparing outcomes across ethnic borders within countries

By implementing spatial regression discontinuity designs, essentially comparing adjacent entities along a given boundary, one may successfully account for factors that vary smoothly in space and hence mitigate concerns related to bias arising from variation in geographic elements. Michalopoulos and Papaioannou (2013) conduct such an analysis across dozens of pairs of adjacent ethnic groups using the ethnic boundaries delineated in Murdock's Tribal Map of Africa. In this study, we compare within the same country how average luminosity changes as one crosses from the historical homeland of a politically centralized ethnic group into the territory of a stateless (during the precolonial era) society, finding that economic performance declines discontinuously at the boundary. This is consistent with the idea that the ethnic-specific institutional heritage matters for a group's economic performance today. This empirical strategy has been adopted in the literature on the ethnic-specific origins of African development and conflict, see, for example, Moscona et al. (2020).

Comparing outcomes across country borders within ethnicities

The colonial boundaries in Africa were drawn by the colonizers in European capitals before the arrival of the colonists and were largely preserved after decolonization. The arbitrariness in the border creation led to the partitioning of more than a quarter of preexisting ethnic groups across the nascent African nations.[14] From an econometric perspective, this creates a natural experiment, i.e., a framework where one can hold ethnicity constant and explore how differences in countrywide characteristics influence within-group outcomes.

A representative example of this type is the work of Michalopoulos and Papaioannou (2014), where we investigate whether regional disparities in development across national borders in Africa today are shaped by differences in national institutions. To control for ethnic-specific factors, we conduct our analysis within groups whose ancestral lands were split by colonial borders. The within-ethnic homeland analysis reveals that variation in national institutions does not shape local development as reflected in luminosity. While the lack of any association contradicts research stressing the causal impact of institutions on development, it is in line with the African historiography that stresses the role of ethnic rather than national features and emphasizes the inability of the central

14 In Michalopoulos and Papaioannou (2016), after showing that split groups were similar in many respects to nonpartitioned ones, we empirically establish, using high-precision georeferenced data on local events of political violence, that partitioned ethnic homelands have suffered disproportionately from state-sponsored violence and discrimination, uncovering the violent consequences of the colonial border design.

government to broadcast power far from the capital (Herbst, 2000). Consistent with this interpretation, we show that (i) various proxies of state capacity decline as one moves away from the capital cities and (ii) national-level institutions translate into within-ethnicity differences in economic activity for groups whose partitions are close to the capital cities on both sides of the country border.

Several studies have adopted the same empirical design to explore differences in national characteristics within African partitioned ethnicities to neutralize the role of ethnic-specific characteristics. These include Dickens (2018), who explores the extent of ethnic politics in African groups over time. Anderson (2018) studies how differences in legal origins determine current-day female HIV rates within partitioned ethnic groups. Poyker (2023) explores how regime stability shapes the persistence of traditional practices. Laitin and Ramachandran (2022) show that the reliance on colonial languages as mediums of instruction reduces the formation of human capital, suggesting that retaining colonial languages is an important factor in explaining economic failures in post-colonial Africa. Ali et al. (2019) use individual-level data to compare observations across anglophone–francophone borders in sub-Saharan Africa and find that anglophone citizens are less likely to identify themselves in national terms (relative to ethnic terms), highlighting the colonial legacy on ethnic salience.

4 Folklore studies to the rescue

The literature that has flourished linking past historical events and ethnographic traits to contemporary cultural and economic outcomes has been missing a crucial input: the cultural fabric of societies, not today but in the past. Thanks to large representative surveys, including the Global Preferences Surveys by Falk et al. (2018), the World Values Surveys and their corresponding regional ones, along with the many Barometers launched in different (sub)continents, we now possess an unusually detailed global mapping of contemporary economic preferences, beliefs, norms, and attitudes.

However, while it has been possible to argue orally that these cultural attributes arose *historically* directly from the phenomenon under study, these claims have lacked empirical backing. In this context, economists have often leveraged famous conjectures put forward by eminent anthropologists to increase the plausibility of the hypothesis tested. See, for example, Alesina et al. (2013) for a careful test of Boserup's hypothesis on the role of the plow in shaping gender norms. This absence of historical cultural traits also had broader implications. It has rendered academic efforts to document cultural change over long periods of time intractable. This situation has also led to criticism of the comparative development literature, as articulated by Austin (2008), who argued that the field often makes sweeping claims about historical outcomes based on excessively large regional units and an insufficient number of cases. This overgeneralization *compresses* history, resulting in oversimplified and frequently inaccurate explanations for economic development.

Amidst this debate and stalemate, an unexpected breakthrough came from an unlikely source: the myths, legends, and tales of our ancestors. Although these narratives have traditionally fallen far outside the scope of conventional economic analysis, humanists have long been captivated by their ability to reveal our societies' historical and cultural heritage.

Bringing folklore to the table

In 2021, MX introduced a global compilation of oral traditions into the field of economics. The Folklore and Mythology Catalog includes 2564 motifs drawn from 958 oral traditions. This database represents the lifetime work of renowned anthropologist and folklorist Yuri Berezkin. See, for example, Berezkin (2015), Berezkin (2016), and d'Huy et al. (2023). This extraordinary corpus was made possible by Berezkin's prodigious ability to absorb and synthesize information from more than 6000 books, articles, and monographs on folklore from different oral traditions and time periods written in different languages. Berezkin defines a motif as an episode or image found within a collection of narratives recorded in an ethnolinguistic community. A title and a brief description accompany each motif in the Berezkin catalog, and what we know is whether that particular motif is present or not in the specific oral tradition. Thus, the underlying data is text.

MX employ two approaches to quantify aspects of folklore. The first is a dictionary-based method, which analyzes text by breaking it into individual words and linking their counts to the attributes one aims to measure. This straightforward and commonly used technique is enhanced by incorporating the top-50 *related terms* for any keywords of interest. These related terms are derived from word embeddings according to ConceptNet.[15] The second approach involves human classification, where individuals evaluate the content of each motif to identify and categorize its attributes.

MX do three things to show the value of integrating traditional narratives into the analytical toolkit of economists and political scientists studying the origins of comparative development, gender norms, morality, psychology, and culture. First, they validate the catalog by showing that the motifs in a group's oral tradition correspond to key aspects of their physical environment. For instance, lore in earthquake-prone areas is rich in earthquake-related motifs. Groups residing on fertile lands emphasize crops in their stories, and groups near rivers or in colder climates feature themes with analogous landscapes. Second, they show how information may be extracted from a group's oral tradition to complement its ethnographic record. Third, MX propose a method to recover a group's cultural heritage by having multiple individuals read and classify motifs.

15 Similar to how humans understand the world, ConceptNet is a semantic network that uses nodes and edges to represent concepts and their relationships. It originated from the Open Mind Common Sense crowdsourcing project at the MIT Media Lab. Its knowledge is derived from various sources, including expert-created resources, crowd-sourcing, and games with a purpose, see Speer and Lowry-Duda (2017).

They then apply this method to create proxies for trust, risk-taking attitudes, and gender norms.

The main output of this research has been made publicly available and is a catalog containing over 12,000 variables that quantify the intensity of concepts across 958 oral traditions from Berezkin's database, 1245 out of the 1265 groups in the Ethnographic Atlas, and 199 contemporary countries. Additionally, it includes three human-coded measures of (i) risk representation, measured by the proportion of motifs where challenges are overcome versus those where they are not, (ii) trust, measured by the share of motifs where tricksters' antisocial behavior is punished versus not, and (iii) gender representation, based on the stereotypical roles assigned to genders in the motifs.[16]

Armed with measures of narrative differences between groups and countries, scholars have used folklore to derive bilateral measures of cultural proximity in the spirit of Spolaore and Wacziarg (2009); see D'Amato and Russo (2025) for an application.

Moreover, in Michalopoulos and Rauh (2024) we ask why certain movies are more successful in some markets than others and whether the entertainment products we consume reflect our core beliefs. To answer these questions, we use machine learning to measure a movie's plot similarity to the motifs in the Catalogue. Globally, films mirroring local lore get wider screenings and generate more revenue. Across US markets, movies matching ancestral stories attract more interest. Finally, films promoting risk taking, revenge seeking, and traditional gender roles perform better across markets with similar historical and contemporary norms. Choosing to watch modern adaptations of stories passed down from our ancestors on the big screen reinforces cultural identity.

In what follows, I do two things. First, I illustrate with concrete examples the catalog's potential for complementing the ethnographic record while discussing how other scholars have fruitfully employed this corpus, see Table 1. Second, I outline a procedure for utilizing large language models (LLMs) alongside human ratings to fully unlock the catalog's potential.

4.1 Decrease measurement error and complete existing ethnographic variables

MX connected oral traditions in the Berezkin database with 1245 of the 1265 groups in the EA, systematically integrating for the first time societal narratives with their coded ethnographic characteristics, see Figs. 3 and 4. Of the 20 groups in the EA that were not matched to an oral tradition, 10 come from Africa and 7 from the Americas.

16 https://dataverse.harvard.edu/dataset.xhtml?persistentId=doi:10.7910/DVN/IXOHKB.

TABLE 1 Examples of works using the folklore catalogue.

Authors	Outlet	Explanatory Variable	Outcome Variable
Becker (2024)	Review of Economic Studies	reliance on pastoralism	women depicted as sexual in folklore
Brulé (2023)	Annual Review of Political Science	trade opportunities	gender bias in folklore
Dincecco et al. (2024)	CEPR	conflict	gender bias in folklore
Malein and Beltrán Tapia (2024)	CEPR	famine	gender bias in folklore
Horvath and Lahtinen (2025)	Finance Research Letters	gender bias in folklore	firms' corporate cash holdings
Bertocchi et al. (2024)	IZA	abstinence and chastity in folklore	postpartum abstinence
Delis et al. (2023a)	Journal of Banking & Finance	overcoming challenges in folklore	stock market participation
Delis et al. (2023b)	Journal of Corporate Finance	overcoming challenges in folklore	firm financing costs
Han et al. (2024)	SSRN	overcoming challenges in folklore	corporate innovation
Marigo and Weill (2024)	LaRGE	overcoming challenges in folklore	access to credit
Lagakos et al. (2025)	NBER	overcoming challenges in folklore	resilience in life
Cao et al. (2021)	NBER	revenge in folklore	violence and conflict in folklore
Schläpfer (2024)	Journal of Economic Behavior & Organization	revenge in folklore	foul play in soccer leagues
Le Rossignol and Lowes (2022)	NBER	transhumant pastoralism	milk, cattle, tent, travel in folklore
Le Rossignol et al. (2022)	NBER	magic in folklore	is magic stigmatized?
Enke (2023)	Nature Human Behaviour	trade and money in folklore	shame and guilt in folklore
Link (2024)	IDEAS	transport animals	trade and numbers in folklore
Saenger (2022)	mimeo, Harvard University	elder respect in folklore	environmental stability
Dessi et al. (2023)	CEPR	shame and guilt in folklore	self-confidence
Lopez-Manuel (2023)	SSRN	despotic institutions	individualism/collectivism in folklore
Eruchimovitch et al. (2023)	Journal of Economic Growth	cereal-rice suitability difference	individualism/collectivism in folklore
Litina and Roca Fernández (2024)	The Economic Journal	eclipses in folklore	thinking-related motifs
Kikuta (2024)	IDE	# of solar eclipses	eclipses in folklore
Fan et al. (2024)	Economica	rice-farming areas	family in folklore
D'Amato and Russo (2025)	Journal of Economic Growth	bilateral differences in folklore	bilateral differences in income
Michalopoulos and Rauh (2024)	NBER	movie-country's folklore similarity	movie success

FIGURE 3 Integrating contributions from social scientists into economics.

Notes: This figure plots the Ethnographic Atlas groups matched with an oral tradition in Berezkin's Catalogue.

FIGURE 4 Groups with ethnographic and folklore data.

Lowering measurement error in the historical record is far from a trivial undertaking. As already discussed, many of the critiques of the EA have focused on the scarcity and incompleteness of the record on which Murdock relied to quantify the corresponding attributes. Hence, bringing along a wealth of readily coded aspects from the group's folklore can help mitigate these concerns.[17] For example, having two noisy proxies of the same underlying attribute may allow researchers to quantify the role of error-in-variables. This is usually done in

---

17 Measurement error considerations have also been recognized in cross-country studies linking a nation's colonial past to its present, see, for example, Albouy (2012).

the context of estimating two-stage-least-squares specifications "instrumenting" one proxy for the other. Under error orthogonality of Murdock's classification and Berezkin's compilation of folklore stories, this 2SLS approach allows the researcher to account for error-in-variables (see Wooldridge (2002) and Krueger and Lindahl (2001) for an application).

The number of motifs in a given society reflects both the extent of the underlying material (both original and sampled by Berezkin himself) and the variation in the plurality of images across traditions. Distinguishing between the two is difficult, but recognizing that the uneven coverage across societies is of first-order importance, I always normalize the number of concept-related motifs by the total number of motifs in the corresponding oral tradition to capture the intensity of the phenomenon studied. In addition, I include controls for the ln(# of publications) per oral tradition and the ln(year of the earliest publication). Accounting for these dimensions is important as it absorbs variation in the diversity of the underlying sources, as well as the timing of the earliest (usually most comprehensive) publication detailing the tales and legends of the group.[18]

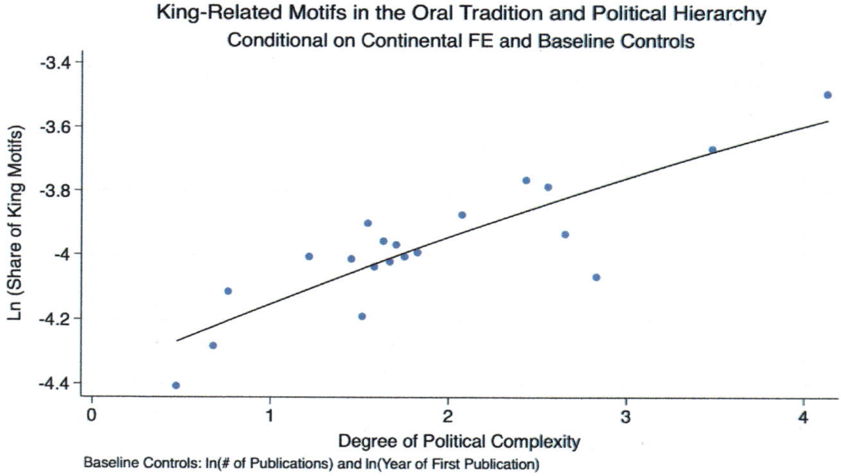

FIGURE 5 King-related concepts and politically centralized groups.

In Fig. 5, I illustrate the strong relationship between the degree of political complexity recorded by Murdock in the EA and the intensity of the king-related motifs as quantified by MX, while in Fig. 6, I show how the share of subsistence from pastoralism in the EA moves in tandem with a more frequent mention of pastoralism-related terms in the motifs. Concepts from ConceptNet related to pastoralism and mentioned in the motifs are: cattle, graze, herdsman, pasture,

18 Early folklorists, for example, were often missionaries or curious intellectuals, whereas later generations were frequently scholars, including anthropologists conducting fieldwork in small-scale societies.

herd, livestock, and agriculture. Establishing that folklore-based measures align with analogous traits in the EA increases confidence in the EA-coded traits.

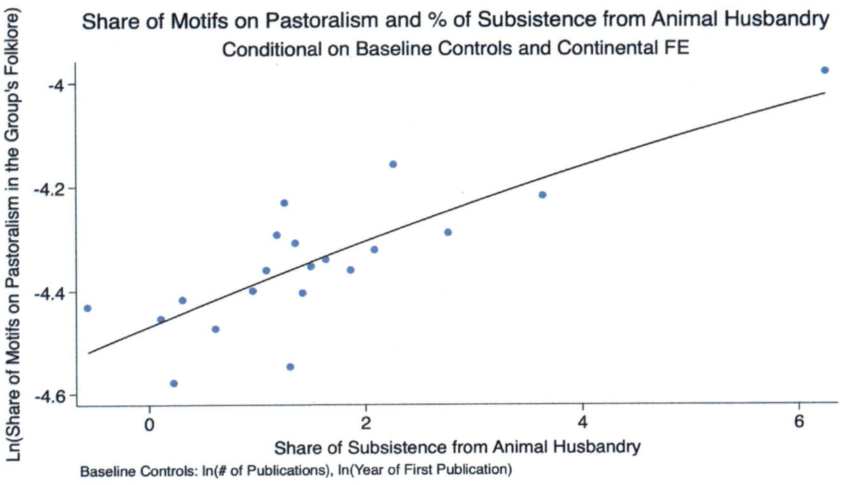

FIGURE 6 Pastoral motifs in herding groups.

In the EA, data on the typical society was collected primarily in the late 19th and early 20th centuries. Interestingly, this is also the modal period of the earliest publication for an oral tradition. Hence, both the ethnographic characteristics and the stories recorded reflect the conditions observed by the ethnographers and folklorists around the same point in time. Nevertheless, it is useful to keep in mind that what appears in folklore images is potentially from a period long before the one captured by the EA. Hence, the comparisons between an EA trait and the analogously derived one from its folklore can shed some light on the continuity of traits over longer horizons.

Finally, MX demonstrate how to fill in missing values in the ethnographic record using folklore. For example, they show that researchers can estimate a group's level of political complexity when it is not recorded in the EA by analyzing the prevalence of king-related motifs in that group's folklore.[19] Similarly, they illustrate how an important EA variable that measures the presence of high gods, which has missing values for about 40% of the EA entries, can be completed using folklore-coded attributes on awards, supernatural elements, and punishment. Anthropologists have argued that these three are prominent themes in the lore of societies with high gods. Using machine learning to predict the ethnographic attributes from a group's folklore and vice versa strikes me as a fruitful avenue to create a robust cross walk between the EA, the SCCS, and the Folklore Catalogue.

19 Concepts from ConceptNet related to kings and mentioned in the motifs are: king, queen, official, ruler, prince and princess.

4.2 Add new groups, missing from the ethnographic record

Societies traditionally considered the domain of historians have received less attention from ethnographers. This has partly contributed to the reluctance of ethnographers to include groups from Europe and Asia, resulting in an imbalanced representation in the EA, with a disproportionate focus on the Americas and Africa and limited coverage of other regions.

Berezkin's coverage of oral traditions does not suffer from this imbalance. As a result, it covers the oral tradition of 33 European groups *not included* in the EA. These include the Galicians, the Aragonese, and the Catalans in Spain, the Bretons in France, the Romansh in Switzerland, and the Scottish and the Welsh in the UK.[20] Moreover, there are 190 additional groups located in Asia. Integrating these groups into the EA would almost double the coverage of groups in both continents, currently standing at 219 in Asia and 30 in Europe. However, Berezkin's coverage is not only strong in these two continents. In South (North) America, there are 86 (51) groups with oral traditions beyond the 90 (306) societies in the EA. See Fig. 7 for the societies with oral traditions but no ethnographic coverage.

Notes: This figure plots the groups with an oral tradition *missing* from the EA.

FIGURE 7 Groups with folklore data not represented in the EA.

4.3 Quantify not-yet-recorded attributes

A dimension along which the transformation of the Folklore Catalogue into quantifiable bits has resonated with the literature is by providing proxies for aspects of a group missing altogether from the EA. A notable example is the presence of trade, a topic of instinctive interest to economists. Fig. 8 illustrates the spatial distribution of groups in the Folklore Catalogue, featuring at least one trade-related motif. This map offers a visualization of the extent of preindustrial market economies—an essential economic dimension not covered by the EA.

[20] Giuliano and Nunn (2018) have added 42 societies mainly from Siberia and Eastern Europe.

This metric has been used by Enke (2023) to explore how market forces shape the intensity of guilt, shame, and anger, as well as male dominance, respectively. Link (2024) explores how the presence of domesticable transport animals gave rise to trade.

Notes: This figure highlights in orange the Berezkin groups that have at least one motif related to trade. I use the top-50 trade-related words according to ConceptNet.

FIGURE 8 Presence of trade-related motifs in a group's oral tradition.

As mentioned above, economists and economic historians have attempted to complement the EA by adding new dimensions based on their particular interests. Espín-Sánchez et al. (2024), for example, measure rainmaking for the groups in the Atlas by extensively consulting the anthropological literature, drawing on 370 sources covering 1208 ethnic groups. The literature overview is fascinating, as for many groups they document rich narrative accounts of rainmaking practice.[21]

The themes highlighted by the authors are at the heart of folklore studies. Hence, the Folklore Catalogue can be readily utilized for research attempts that aim at systematically extracting quantifiable dimensions from groups' narratives. As an example, in Fig. 9, I illustrate the groups that have motif k38d in their folklore. The latter reads: "A monster blocks sources of water and asks in exchange for human victims or valuables. Hero kills the monster." A total of 130 groups have this particular episode in their tradition; 26 in Asia, 12 in Europe, 91 in Africa, and 1 in North America. There are roughly 20 motifs in the Folklore Catalogue that describe episodes related to rainmaking. This example is meant to illustrate the Catalogue's versatility in filling in the ethnographic record.

[21] The Cherokee dance for rain and sing a song for the Great Spirit; the Herero sprinkle a calf with water, allow it to wander around, and then sacrifice the animal; Iranian women wage a mock battle and capture the animals of their neighbors to release them only when it rains; the people of Shandong, China, beseech the rain dragon for rain, and if it refuses, abuse the dragon and desecrate its temple.

Several studies have used the Catalogue to extract the intensity of specific practices and traits. These include (i) abstinence and chastity-related motifs used by Bertocchi et al. (2024) to explore how the former shape fertility patterns in Africa today, (ii) the incidence of revenge-related motifs and foul play in soccer by Schläpfer (2024), and the incidence of conflicts in Cao et al. (2021), (iii) the link between motifs on eclipses and thinking-related images by Litina and Roca Fernández (2024), (iv) magic-related motifs and their stigmatization by Le Rossignol and Lowes (2022), and (v) individualistic and collectivistic motifs by Eruchimovitch et al. (2023) and Lopez-Manuel (2023).

Notes: This figure highlights in orange the groups that have motif *k38d* in their folklore. Motif *k38d* reads "A monster blocks sources of water (or sends floods) and usually gives some (promises not to send floods) in exchange for human victims or valuables. Hero kills the monster".

FIGURE 9 Spatial distribution of motif k38d.

Extracting norms and values from motifs

One crucial aspect of Berezkin's work is that his goal was to compile a catalog of images and episodes from oral traditions *refraining from* interpreting their moral lessons or uncovering hidden meanings. Hence, the motifs are based on symbols, metaphors, analogies, and indirect representations of abstract ideas and morals. As a result, abstract terms like honesty, patience, and courage are rarely explicitly mentioned in the Catalogue. This approach minimizes subjective interpretation in folklore analysis, but it also makes it challenging to infer values, norms, and beliefs based only on counting concepts and related words.

This realization is what prompted MX to have human subjects evaluate motifs along specific dimensions, namely the portrayal of risk taking, trust, and gender norms. The uniqueness of these proxies explains why these have been used in a variety of settings. For example, in terms of gender norms, Becker (2024) shows that groups historically reliant on pastoralism have a higher prevalence of motifs depicting women as sexual in their oral tradition. Similarly, Dincecco et al. (2024) link the historical occurrence of conflict in

India to the prevalence of male-biased folklore, while Malein and Beltrán Tapia (2024) examine cohorts before, during and after the 1891–1892 Russian famine, demonstrating differential gender mortality in regions with gender-biased folklore. Finally, Brulé (2023) finds a link between trade opportunities and gender representation.

Images and episodes depicting characters facing challenges are common in oral traditions. However, while some groups portray these encounters as ending in tragedy, others emphasize the protagonist's ability to emerge victorious against the odds. MX found that traditions where challenges are more often successfully resolved are more entrepreneurial. Similar patterns are observed among CEOs (Han et al., 2024) and across regions in firms' investment behavior (Delis et al., 2023a). Finally, in Lagakos et al. (2025) we show that U.S. respondents in the 1930s tracing their lineage to countries with oral traditions rich in narratives overcoming adversities often narrate life histories emphasizing perseverance and resilience in the face of hardship.

5 Using LLMs to read folklore: opportunities and pitfalls

MX coded 3 values and attitudes that are important to economists. Nevertheless, the World Values Surveys have dozens of variables of potential interest, including patience, aspirations, reciprocity, role models, attitudes toward violence, strangers, the elderly (Saenger, 2022), the community, the importance of imagination, obedience, independence, hard work, and honesty, to name just a few. How should one go about quantifying these aspects? In 2021 when MX was published, the authors encouraged more human readings to get at these values. In MX, we employed, for example, Amazon Mechanical Turks (MTurk). The latter is a marketplace for work that requires human intelligence. The Mechanical Turk service offers access to a diverse, on-demand, scalable workforce and gives workers a selection of thousands of tasks to complete whenever it is convenient. Chan and Holosko (2016) and Buhrmester et al. (2018) offer an overview of its extensive use in the social sciences.

Over the past two years, advancements in LLMs have reshaped the field of text analysis, fundamentally altering established best practices.

How to handle LLM's output?

The ease of obtaining answers from an ever-increasing number of LLMs posits a series of questions. The central one is whether a researcher should unconditionally trust the LLM output. For example, it is widely known that LLMs hallucinate, i.e., the model generates information that is false, misleading, or not based on real data. This, of course, is not unique to LLMs as humans may also produce erroneous output. In fact, MTurk requesters have realized that attention among (online) workers should not be taken for granted. As a result, a set of evolving guidelines on how to recognize and minimize inattention have been proposed. This is usually done in the context of randomly inserted attention checks throughout the survey batches and ensuring that the output used is only from MTurks that have not failed the attention checks. In case the attention check gets answered incorrectly, all classifications specific to that MTurk are reassigned to other workers.

Below, I propose a methodology inspired by Lagakos et al. (2025) (LMV) for deploying LLM capabilities within the context of the Folklore Catalogue, Fig. 10. The process begins with the creation of a ground-truth dataset curated by humans, which serves as a benchmark for evaluating the LLM's output. If the results successfully pass a specialized version of the Turing (1950) test developed by LMV and applied in this study, the approach can be scaled across the entire Catalogue. Otherwise, further refinement through prompt engineering is recommended.

FIGURE 10 Algorithmic transformation of stories into data.

5.1 Introduction to the setting

In this section, I illustrate the workflow. To obtain the GPT data, we used the supported chat completion API. Fig. 11 shows an example of an API request.

```
{'custom_id': 'a19b',
 'method': 'POST',
 'url': '/v1/chat/completions',
 'body': {'model': 'gpt-4o-2024-08-06',
  'messages': [{'role': 'system',
    'content': 'You are a helpful assistant. You will be provided with a short text. Based s
olely on the information provided, determine whether the text suggests the presence of a mal
e character. Respond {Yes} or {No} and provide a confidence score for your answer (0-10) onl
y. Please do not be lazy. Every male character matters.'},
   {'role': 'user',
    'content': 'By snail in summer, by bird in winter: For its sky voyage, the Sun chooses d
raught animals according to the season, riding a slow one in the summer time and a quick one
in the winter time. Or a young man carries the Sun in the winter time and the old man in the
summer time'}],
  'max_tokens': 60,
  'seed': 1746192,
  'temperature': 0}}
```

FIGURE 11 Prompt for the presence of gendered character(s).

This API is used to *chat* with the chosen LLM and requires the researcher to create a completion object with specified roles. In our application, we used the *system* role and the *user* role.[22] The *system* role provides the specified model with instructions on what to do and how to structure its output, while the *user* represents the end user. Fig. 11 also shows that the API allows the researcher to specify the model, a maximum length for the GPT-generated answer measured in tokens, and two additional parameters, which are the temperature and the seed. The temperature, ranging from 0 to 1, regulates how creative/stochastic the GPT output is.

Towards reproducible output

One natural question concerns the reproducibility of GPT-generated output. Due to the inherent non-determinism of AI models, perfect replication is not guaranteed. Nevertheless, as explained by OpenAI,[23] in the newest models, including GPT-4o that we use in this paper, by setting a fixed integer seed and matching all other parameters, such as temperature and the maximum number of tokens, one can generate largely reproducible output. We set the temperature to 0 and specify a seed and maximum number of tokens for our requests.

There is one additional setting that is beyond the control of the researcher and affects output's reproducibility. This is the system fingerprint. The latter is an identifier for the current combination of model weights, infrastructure, and other configuration options used by OpenAI servers to generate the output. It changes whenever one edits any of the request parameters or when OpenAI updates the infrastructure behind their models, which can happen often.

We used the previously shown layout to get motif evaluations by GPT on topics such as gender representation, antisocial behavior, and challenges. The first prompt we used to obtain gender attributes assessments follows closely what MX asked the MTurks. This is shown in Fig. 12.

5.2 A Turing test

As ratings from LLMs become increasingly easy to generate, the next question is how much should one trust this output and whether there is a way to evaluate it.

To examine the extent to which LLM responses differ from those among MTurks, I follow the intuitive approach of LMV. Specifically, I apply a variant of the Turing (1950) test that asks whether the LLM's answers stand out from the human answers. The basic idea is to compute the fraction of instances where GPT-4 matches the modal human score. The key thing to note is that we don't

---

22 OpenAI also provides for the *assistant* role used to interact with different models or complex tasks. Assistants can also be tuned in terms of their personality and capabilities. For a complete explanation of the various roles, refer to the original OpenAI documentation, available at https://platform.openai.com/docs/guides/text-generation/building-prompts.

23 https://platform.openai.com/docs/advanced-usage/reproducible-outputs.

```
{'custom_id': 'a19b',
 'method': 'POST',
 'url': '/v1/chat/completions',
 'body': {'model': 'gpt-4o-2024-08-06',
  'messages': [{'role': 'system',
    'content': 'You will be provided with a short text featuring male characters. Based onl
y on the information provided, classify the portrayal of the male characters choosing from
the following categories: \'Violent/Dominant/Independent\', \'Submissive/Dependent/Lacking
Agency\', \'Physically Active\', \'Engaged in Domestic Affairs\', \'Sexual\', \'Intelligent
\', \'Naive/Stupid\'. Multiple categories may be chosen. Provide a confidence score from 0
to 10 and your reasoning. Output only a JSON table with the following structure: {"Confiden
ce": YOUR SCORE, "Categories": [CHOSEN CATEGORY1, CHOSEN CATEGORY2,...], "Reasoning": YOUR
REASONING}'},
   {'role': 'user',
    'content': 'By snail in summer, by bird in winter: For its sky voyage, the Sun chooses
draught animals according to the season, riding a slow one in the summer time and a quick o
ne in the winter time. Or a young man carries the Sun in the winter time and the old man in
the summer time'}],
  'max_tokens': 120,
  'seed': 1746192,
  'temperature': 0}}
```


FIGURE 12 Prompt for gender attributes.

have a ‘ground truth’ of representation in our motifs; hence, the modal human score serves this role. Establishing that the LLM finds the modal human score with a frequency within the range of the human readers, we will conclude that it has passed the indistinguishability test. This approach captures the spirit of Turing’s original test, which asked whether one could identify which answers came from a human and which came from a computer. Passing our test for a particular question means that GPT’s answers do not stand out relative to the other human readers for that question.[24]

Given that classifying a motif is inherently subjective and humans may disagree on the actual meaning of a given text, we started by constructing the ground truth of the between-raters heterogeneity. We implemented this procedure as follows: for a given question, we quantified how often a set of human raters agrees with the modal choice among the other raters (i.e., with the leave-one-out modal choice). This metric allows us to gauge how much humans vary in their assessment regarding the presence of a specific attribute across motifs. For example, if all raters agree with the modal answer over a set of motifs and GPT disagrees, this will be indicative of GPT failing the Turing test as it will be easy to single out GPT’s output from the rest. Conversely, if individuals are more often torn between options, then it will be harder to pinpoint which set of those answers is AI-generated.

We now describe the ingredients necessary for its implementation. First, we need to define the sets of human ratings against which we will compare

24 Dell (2025) recommends fine-tuning the algorithm on a test sample before evaluating it on a separate validation sample to avoid overfitting. However, in our case, we already have the full set of human ratings for the relevant traits, so splitting the data into training and validation sets is less applicable. Our goal is more modest. We aim to evaluate whether GPT, when asked questions similar to those posed to human raters, can produce comparable responses. When this is not the case, we seek to understand how to adjust the initial prompts to improve alignment.

GPT's ratings. Second, since the goal is to measure whether GPT's ratings deviate from human ones, we need to establish a human ratings-based agreement benchmark against which to assess the performance of AI-generated output. Last, it is important to define the testing procedure, including clear criteria for what qualifies as passing or failing the test.

Concerning the creation of multiple sets of ratings over the same set of motifs, a natural choice would be to compare the ratings of a *single* MTurk worker to those among the rest. While this approach is certainly sensible and followed by LMV, the MTurk data MX collected in 2020 led to an unbalanced panel of workers and motifs, where many workers rated a handful of motifs. This could be problematic in our case, since it is possible that a particular worker consistently agrees or disagrees with the majority opinion simply due to their limited number of ratings.[25]

The following procedure allows us to generate sets of ratings per motif with a consistent number of ratings, avoiding the (dis)agreement circumstances generated by the imbalance in the number of motifs rated by individual MTurks. The procedure works as follows. We group MTurk workers and their ratings into waves. We assign to each MTurk-motif pair a random number using a seed.[26] Then, we sort these workers per motif by that random number. Finally, for each motif separately, we assign workers to waves based on their random sort order: workers sorted in the first position are assigned to wave 1, workers sorted in the second position are assigned to wave 2, and so on. This approach is sketched in Fig. 13.

In the toy example presented in Fig. 13, we started with an unbalanced data set of 8 MTurk workers, rating on average 3.5 motifs, and ended up with 3 MTurk waves rating on average 9.3 motifs. Additionally, by using 100 different seeds, we allow for different wave realizations.

Moving to the second ingredient of the test, it is crucial to understand the dimension of agreement against which we want to evaluate GPT responses. Imagine a motif rated by two workers answering the male characters' portrayal question in Fig. 12. Suppose the first worker chose only "Physically Active" whereas the second one chose only "Violent/Dominant/Independent." Since there are only two workers, the previous description of the test would be equivalent to checking whether the first worker agrees with the second. If one compares workers only based on their choice, then one would infer complete disagreement between the two workers. However, doing so would miss several pieces of information, i.e., that both workers agreed that the portrayal is not

---

[25] MX assigned only a few motifs per worker on average to prevent the classification from being overly influenced by a small number of MTurk contributors. To ensure a broadly representative input, MX divided the set of motifs into smaller subsets, distributing them among different workers for independent evaluation.

[26] We generated 100 consecutive integers, starting with an initial seed of 12345 to ensure replicability. Each of these integers was then used as the primary seed for the procedure described in the text.

Worker ID	Motif ID	A	Random Number	Motif Row Order	Wave ID
Worker 2	Motif 1	0	0.12	1	Wave 1
Worker 4	Motif 1	0	0.35	2	Wave 2
Worker 3	Motif 1	1	0.45	3	Wave 3
Worker 1	Motif 1	1	0.54	4	Wave 4
Worker 3	Motif 2	1	0.32	1	Wave 1
Worker 1	Motif 2	1	0.65	2	Wave 2
Worker 6	Motif 2	0	0.72	3	Wave 3
Worker 2	Motif 3	1	0.15	1	Wave 1
Worker 4	Motif 3	0	0.20	2	Wave 2
Worker 4	Motif 4	1	0.30	1	Wave 1
Worker 1	Motif 4	0	0.65	2	Wave 2
Worker 6	Motif 4	1	0.55	3	Wave 3
Worker 3	Motif 5	1	0.10	1	Wave 1
Worker 5	Motif 5	1	0.25	2	Wave 2
Worker 2	Motif 5	0	0.55	3	Wave 3
Worker 2	Motif 6	1	0.85	1	Wave 1
Worker 6	Motif 6	0	0.40	2	Wave 2
Worker 7	Motif 6	1	0.75	3	Wave 3
Worker 6	Motif 7	1	0.22	1	Wave 1
Worker 4	Motif 7	1	0.30	2	Wave 2
Worker 7	Motif 7	0	0.50	3	Wave 3
Worker 4	Motif 8	1	0.15	1	Wave 1
Worker 6	Motif 8	0	0.70	2	Wave 2
Worker 7	Motif 9	0	0.40	1	Wave 1
Worker 5	Motif 9	1	0.60	2	Wave 2
Worker 5	Motif 10	1	0.10	1	Wave 1
Worker 7	Motif 10	1	0.25	2	Wave 2
Worker 8	Motif 10	0	0.75	3	Wave 3

FIGURE 13 Example dataset.

"Naive" nor "Intelligent," etc. For this reason, we will have a measure of agreement between GPT and the mode of the MTurk waves and one MTurk wave and the mode among the remaining ones for every motif and for every possible attribute.

Given the definition of waves and the dimension of agreement, the next step is to establish the agreement benchmark that will be used to evaluate GPT. For each iteration and each possible answer, we first define binary variables to determine whether or not a particular answer was chosen for each motif. Then, for each motif, we compared the answer of each wave to its corresponding leave-one-out mode. In case the mode was not unique, i.e., when the remaining waves were exactly split between the presence and absence of a trait, agreement was set by default. Then, we computed the share of times each wave agreed with the mode among the remaining waves for each possible attribute. As mentioned above, there are usually at least 9 waves for which we have ratings for all motifs.

We usually have other waves with fewer observations. To further reduce the sensitivity of the test, we dropped waves with less than 15 motifs rated.

In the end, we compared the GPT responses with the MTurk wave mode for every iteration and computed the share of motifs for which GPT agreed with the mode across waves.[27] Then, we checked whether this statistic falls below, within, or above the leave-one-out range of agreement coming from comparing the corresponding MTurk wave with the leave-one-out mode. Finally, we collapsed our agreement measures across iterations to obtain two different outputs. First, we derived how often GPT falls below, within, or above such an agreement range. Second, we computed the average share of agreement between GPT and MTurk waves and the minimum and maximum of the wave-specific agreement ranges averaged across 100 iterations. The former share informed us on how well GPT did compared to MTurk waves. Indeed, we considered the Turing test to pass if GPT responses exceed the minimum of the agreement range among MTurks' waves (with the minimum averaged across 100 iterations).

The next section will go behind the scenes of our analysis of gender norms and present how we approached the issue of prompt engineering, hoping this would be useful to researchers interested in applying similar methodologies.

5.3 Using LLMs to study gender norms in the folklore catalogue

The first step in any analysis involving generating LLM output is getting the *right* prompt. While prompt engineering is currently more of an art than science, pre-setting the temperature, the seed, and the maximum number of tokens and using a statistical test along the lines of what I just discussed against which to judge whether the prompt delivers what the researcher is asking seem reasonable starting points.

To replicate the MX gender classification exercise, we first asked GPT about the presence of male/female characters in a motif and to provide a confidence score for the answer, as shown in Fig. 11. Then, conditional on a positive response, we asked GPT to classify the portrayal across 8 categories: "Violent/Dominant/Independent", "Submissive/Dependent/Lacking Agency", "Physically Active", "Engaged in Domestic Affairs", "Sexual", "Intelligent", and "Naive/Stupid." The full prompt is shown in Fig. 12. Since GPT itself may assess how confident it is about the answers it provides, we added this to the prompt.[28]

[27] We first compare MTurk and GPT on whether they perceive the presence of the same theme/character and conduct further analysis on the subset of motifs where both GPT and the mode across MTurk waves agree whether a topic is present, that is, the specific motif describes antisocial behavior or challenges, or has male/female characters present. For what concerns gender traits, we further excluded motifs where GPT identified a gendered character but refused to classify their traits.

[28] Additionally, we use this score to explore whether our Turing test results were sensitive to focusing on GPT ratings with higher confidence scores. We found this not to be the case in our setting.

Furthermore, we asked GPT to explain its classification to gauge the rationale for its choice. Reading through these explanations helps the researcher understand how GPT interprets the current prompt and guides him in refining the prompt to align more closely with what the researcher is attempting to extract. This proved useful in our case. Specifically, it became clear that one classification that was particularly distinct between GPT and MTurks was the "Submissive/Dependent" aspect for both genders. Upon reviewing the GPT-provided explanation, we discovered several instances where MTurk workers interpreted the motif as portraying female characters in that manner, but GPT did not. Examining the motifs with such disagreements made us realize that, unlike humans, GPT was not recognizing the concept of 'Lacking Agency' as part of that category. As a result, we explicitly included that qualification in the prompt.

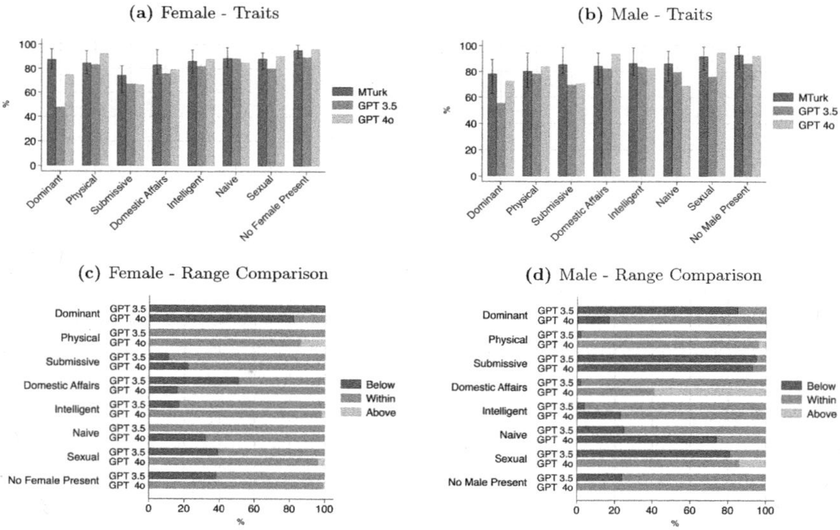

Notes: Panels 14a and 14b illustrate how often GPT 3.5 and GPT 4o agree with the MTurk mode. The within-MTurk range of agreement is also depicted. For the latter, we estimate the agreement of each wave of MTurks with the corresponding leave-one-out mode. Panels 14c and 14d show how often GPT 3.5 and GPT 4o fall within the trait-specific range of agreement derived from MTurks.

FIGURE 14 Turing test for gender traits.

In Figs. 14a and 14b, we report how often GPT models 3.5 and 4o agree with the MTurks' modal answer. Importantly, for each classification, we also display the within-MTurk range of agreement. When the GPT bar is below the MTurk range, this indicates that the LLM-generated output fails the Turing test. In Figs. 14c and 14d, we detail how often GPT falls below, within, and above the MTurk range across the 100 iterations of reshuffling MTurk ratings across waves.[29]

Figs. 14a and 14b reveal two clear patterns. First, comparing the output of GPT 3.5 Turbo with that of the most updated model as of October 2024 (GPT 4o), one can see a clear improvement in how often GPT performs at least as well as MTurk waves across most traits. For instance, the attributes 'Sexual' and 'Engaged in Domestic Affairs,' along with accurately identifying the presence of a gendered entity, demonstrated significant improvement for both genders. This is an encouraging finding, suggesting that ongoing AI model improvements, reflected in future model versions, will further increase overall accuracy. Second, we note the robust performance of GPT 4o in classifying the traits "Sexual" and "Physically active" for both genders. In total, in 13 (9) out of the 16 classifications, GPT 4o (3 Turbo) passes the Turing test.

However, looking at Figs. 14a and 14b, we can see that the submissive attribute for male characters and the dominant and naive traits for female characters fail the Turing test. Furthermore, Panels 14c and 14d reinforce this impression by reporting the share of times GPT disagrees with MTurk waves.


```
{'custom_id': 'a19b',
 'method': 'POST',
 'url': '/v1/chat/completions',
 'body': {'model': 'gpt-4o-2024-08-06',
  'messages': [{'role': 'system',
    'content': 'You are a helpful assistant. Please indicate whether male and female charact
ers are portrayed stereotypically. This means that males appear more dominant, violent, inde
pendent and physically active, while women appear more submissive, engaged in domestic affai
rs and lacking agency. Choose only one category for each gender among (1) defy stereotypes (
2) are portrayed stereotypically (3) no gender representation (4) not enough information to
make a judgment. Also, provide an explanation (Max 180 tokens). Please, do not be lazy, ever
y gender matters. Structure your answer in JSON format as { FEMALE CATEGORY: your category f
or females, MALE CATEGORY: your category for males, EXPLANATION: your explanation }}'},
   {'role': 'user',
    'content': 'By snail in summer, by bird in winter: For its sky voyage, the Sun chooses d
raught animals according to the season, riding a slow one in the summer time and a quick one
in the winter time. Or a young man carries the Sun in the winter time and the old man in the
summer time'}],
  'max_tokens': 180,
  'seed': 1746192,
  'temperature': 0}}
```


FIGURE 15 Revised prompt for gender bias.

An alternative prompt

The results for gender traits match parallel research on how well GPT responses can mimic human perceptions regarding the portrayal of gender traits, (Cappelen, 2024). Hence, I decided to take a step back, conceptually speaking, and approach the problem differently. In fact, if the goal is to assess overall gender bias in motifs/text, inquiring about each specific dimension of gender portrayal may be counterproductive. Providing overly detailed prompt

[29] In the few instances that the GPT-agreement rate exceeds the range of agreement among humans, this implies that GPT gets the modal answer among humans more consistently than any of the individual sets of ratings.

details may even result in the model focusing disproportionately on the detailed instructions, effectively *forgetting* broader knowledge on that subject. Hence, it may display what is known as "catastrophic forgetting" (Luo et al., 2023; Tian et al., 2024).[30] See the discussion and examples in Salinas and Morstatter (2024) and Leidinger et al. (2023).

So, instead of trying to assess every single dimension of a stereotype separately in a motif, we used a prompt that asks GPT whether known stereotypes are present and whether the gendered character defies or confirms such stereotypes (in that specific motif). Fig. 15 reports the prompt.

Therefore, according to our prompt, the representation of a motif reinforces male stereotypes if male characters are more dominant, violent, independent, physically active, and less engaged in domestic affairs than female characters. In contrast, male stereotypes are defied if the opposite is true. Fig. 16 presents the results of the Turing test applied to the output of this new prompt. Each bar in Panels 16a and 16b shows the average agreement of GPT 3.5 Turbo, GPT 4o, and MTurk waves for a given aspect. Furthermore, the MTurk agreement range obtained from across waves is shown on the leftmost bar for every trait. One can see that this prompt performs reasonably well compared to the MTurk waves using the most up-to-date model. Furthermore, Panels 16c and 16d reveal how often the GPT falls below, within, and above our agreement range. In particular, we see that GPT 4o falls more often than not within such a range. Given that these results look reasonable, we use a definition of gender bias coming from this prompt in our replication exercise.

Consider motif *k27z2c*, which reads, "Prince marries a girl to lock her up: A prince marries a poor girl only to lock her up in her room. She outwits him". GPT 4o finds female characters to defy their stereotypes, while male characters are portrayed stereotypically. The following explanation is provided: "The female character defies stereotypes as she outwits the prince, showing intelligence and agency despite being initially placed in a submissive position. The male character is portrayed stereotypically as he is dominant and controlling, using his power to imprison the girl, which aligns with traditional stereotypes of male dominance and aggression". Similarly, consider motif f60, which reads: "Trickster cures maiden: A girl gets sick. A man comes to cure her but only copulates with her or makes an attempt to do so." All MTurks agree that the man acts stereotypically, and GPT agrees with this judgment.

MX define male dominance bias as the share of motifs in which men are portrayed as more dominant, less submissive, less engaged in domestic affairs, and more physically active than women in a given oral tradition. In the current application, I define male dominance bias as the difference between the share of motifs in which male characters reinforce their stereotypes and the share of motifs in which male characters defy them, plus the corresponding

30 This is a well-documented phenomenon in machine learning, particularly in neural networks. It occurs when a model fine-tuned or trained on new data overwrites existing knowledge, *forgetting* previously learned patterns.

difference for females. Notice that these definitions are qualitatively equivalent since we defined stereotypical gender representation as "males appear more dominant, violent, independent, and physically active, while women appear more submissive, engaged in domestic affairs, and lacking agency".

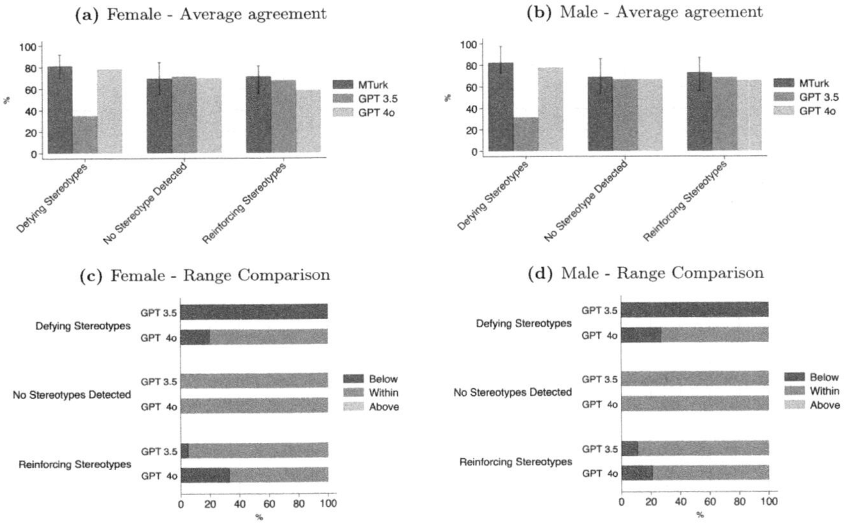

Notes: Panels 16a and 16b illustrate how often GPT 3.5 and GPT 4o agree with the MTurk mode. The within-MTurk range of agreement is also depicted. For the latter, we estimate the agreement of each wave of MTurks with the corresponding leave-one-out mode. Panels 16c and 16d show how often GPT 3.5 and GPT 4o fall within the trait-specific range of agreement derived from MTurks.

FIGURE 16 Turing test for gender bias.

Table 2 shows the result of the replication exercise where controls for the log earliest year of publication and the log number of publications are taken into account. Panel A presents the original MTurk classification of the motifs used in MX, whereas Panel B uses the GPT classification. Normalized beta coefficients are presented for ease of interpretation. By comparing the coefficients in each column (specification) vertically across panels, one can assess the stability of the estimated relationships based on who performed the motif classification. The cross-country correlation of the GPT and MTurk-based male dominance bias is 0.63.

Fig. 17 plots the cross-country association between female labor force participation in 2019 and male bias as derived by GPT. Columns 1 and 2 of Table 2 reveal a country-level negative association between male dominance bias and female labor force participation. In Column 1, an increase of one standard deviation in male dominance bias is associated with an approximate 0.33-0.38 st. dev. decrease in female labor force participation in 2019. When

TABLE 2 Gender roles in folklore and females in the labor force: historically and today.

Dependent Variable	Female labor force participation in 2019		Male Dominance Bias in the Oral Tradition					
	(1)	(2)	(3)	(4)	(5)	(6)	(7)	(8)
Panel A: Original Sample and MTurk Classification								
Male Dominance bias in the oral tradition	−0.3826***	−0.3723***						
	(0.0759)	(0.0862)						
Men contribute more than women in agriculture; EA			0.4023***	0.3408***	0.1885**			
			(0.1057)	(0.1094)	(0.0827)			
Plow is indigenous to the society; EA						0.5572***	0.6058***	0.3592**
						(0.1298)	(0.0812)	(0.1774)
Adj. R^2	0.136	0.145	0.056	0.083	0.201	0.049	0.064	0.179
N	174	174	702	702	702	1131	1131	1131
Controls	✓	✓	✓	✓	✓	✓	✓	✓
Continent FE		✓		✓			✓	
Country FE					✓			✓
Panel B: Original Sample and GPT Classification								
Male Dominance bias in the oral tradition	−0.3284***	−0.2887***						
	(0.0699)	(0.0745)						
Men contribute more than women in agriculture; EA			0.2101*	0.2016*	0.2085**			
			(0.1147)	(0.1013)	(0.0939)			
Plow is indigenous to the society; EA						0.4852***	0.3441***	0.3219*
						(0.1098)	(0.0784)	(0.1654)
Adj. R^2	0.100	0.115	0.018	0.044	0.148	0.042	0.067	0.181
N	174	174	702	702	702	1131	1131	1131
Controls	✓	✓	✓	✓	✓	✓	✓	✓
Continent FE		✓		✓			✓	
Country FE					✓			✓

Notes: Controls include ln(# of publications) and ln(year of first publication) for the oral tradition. Female labor force participation and male dominance bias are standardized. Heteroskedasticity-robust standard errors are used in columns (1) and (2) in the cross-country sample, while in the EA sample in columns (3) to (8), standard errors are clustered at the language-family level. ***, **, * denote significance at 1%, 5%, and 10% levels, respectively.

we account for the broad continental differences in Column 2, the magnitude of the association between male bias and female labor force participation in the GPT-generated output declines slightly but remains precisely estimated.

Columns (3)–(8) focus on ethnic groups in the EA. In particular, we follow MX in looking at the sex differences in agriculture, defined as an indicator for men contributing more than women to agriculture (Columns 3-5) and an indicator for possessing the plow before the Europeans' arrival. Using the GPT classification for male bias, we continue to find evidence of male bias in the folklore of societies that used the plow historically and where men contribute more to agricultural labor. Although the magnitudes are larger for the MTurk-based male bias, once we compare oral traditions of groups within the same country, the estimated coefficients from GPT and MTurk are very similar.

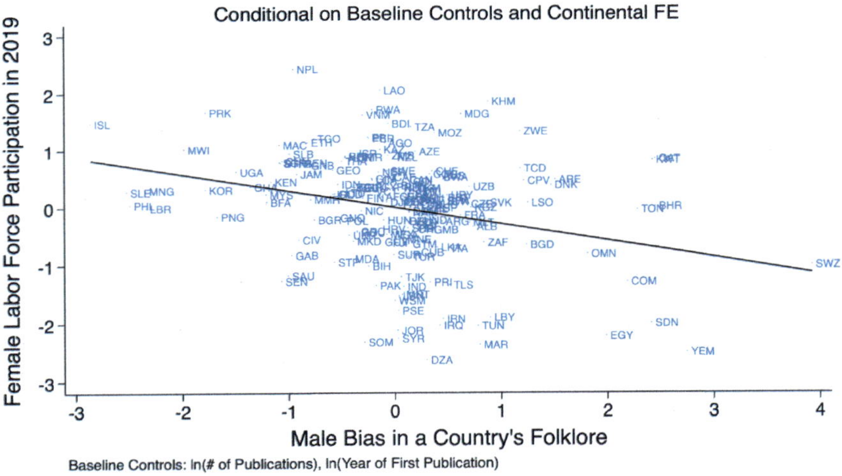

FIGURE 17 GPT-rated male bias and female labor force participation in 2019.

5.4 Using LLMs to code challenges and antisocial behavior from the folklore catalogue

Coding antisocial behavior

In this section, I follow the steps established above to code, using an LLM, how challenges and antisocial behavior are portrayed in folklore motifs. I focus on these two aspects because MX provide MTurk ratings for these attributes. There are 87 motifs related to challenges and 281 motifs related to tricksters and deceitful behavior.

For each trait, I present four exhibits. The first exhibit corresponds to two prompts: one inquiring about the trait's presence and the other about its classification. In the second, we report the results from the Turing test assessing whether GPT's rate of agreement with the modal MTurk answer falls within

(a) Presence


```
{'custom_id': 'a13a', 'method': 'POST', 'url': '/v1/chat/completions', 'body': {'model': 'gpt-4o-202
4-08-06', 'messages': [{'role': 'system', 'content': 'You will be provided with a short text. Based
solely on the information provided, determine whether the text describes a character deliberately en
gaging in any sort of antisocial behavior, be it absurd, obscene or deceiving. Respond {Yes} or {No}
and provide a confidence score for your answer (1-10) only.'}, {'role': 'user', 'content': 'Raven hi
des the Sun: A raven steals (hides) the Sun or tries to do it'}], 'max_tokens': 60, 'seed': 1746192,
'temperature': 0}}
```


(b) Classification


```
{'custom_id': 'a13a',
 'method': 'POST',
 'url': '/v1/chat/completions',
 'body': {'model': 'gpt-4o-2024-08-06',
  'messages': [{'role': 'system',
    'content': "You will be provided with a short text featuring a character engaging in anti-social
behavior. Based solely on the information provided, determine the outcome of the character's action
s. Respond with {Unclear} if there is not enough information to determine the outcome, if the outcom
e is not explicitly stated, or if there are mixed outcomes. Respond with {Unsuccessful} if the anti-
social behavior clearly fails or leads to punishment. Provide evidence from the text that explains y
our choice.Respond with {Successful} if the anti-social behavior is clearly successful and no punish
ment is mentioned. Provide evidence from the text that explains your choice. Use only the informatio
n provided to choose. Choose only one answer and your reasoning (max 60 tokens). Provide a confidenc
e score from 0 to 10."},
   {'role': 'user',
    'content': 'Raven hides the Sun: A raven steals (hides) the Sun or tries to do it'}],
  'max_tokens': 60,
  'seed': 1746192,
  'temperature': 0}}
```


FIGURE 18 Prompts for antisocial behavior.

the range of agreement among MTurks. In the third exhibit, we plot the cross-country association between the corresponding GPT-generated value and the variable of interest. Finally, in the last exhibit, we replicate the cross-country associations, comparing the coefficient estimates from the proxies based on MTurk ratings and GPT, respectively.

Let's start with the coding of antisocial behavior. The prompt we use follows what MX asked the MTurks, i.e., to classify the outcome of the character engaging in antisocial behavior. We allow for unclear, successful, and unsuccessful categorizations. See Figs. 18a and 18b. Here is an example of how GPT rates motif h17, which reads: "Ring of defenders around chief: Ancestors surround their (dead) chief trying to defend him or his corpse. A trickster gets to go through the ring, kills the chief or steals and devours his heart". GPT-provided explanation: "Successful, the text states that a trickster successfully gets through the ring of defenders and either kills the chief or steals and devours his heart, indicating the antisocial behavior was successful. Confidence score: 9."

In Figs. 19a and 19b, I show that along these 3 dimensions, i.e., whether a trickster is successful (following MX we lump together instances where the trickster is clearly successful and those where he is not clearly punished), unsuccessful, or no deceiving behavior is detected, the GPT agrees with the modal MTurk more often than most individual MTurks do. In Fig. 20 and Table 3, I demonstrate that societies where antisocial behavior is frequently punished tend to report higher levels of trust, as measured by both the World Values Survey and the Global Preferences Dataset. In addition, countries with oral traditions where tricksters are not allowed to escape the consequences of their antisocial behavior also show higher levels of GDP per capita. The magnitudes are comparable to the MTurk-derived trust measures. One cannot reject the null hypothesis that the estimated coefficients between the GPT and MTurk-based measures are the same. This is not surprising, since the cross-country association between MTurk and GPT assessment of relative punishment for antisocial behavior is 0.78.

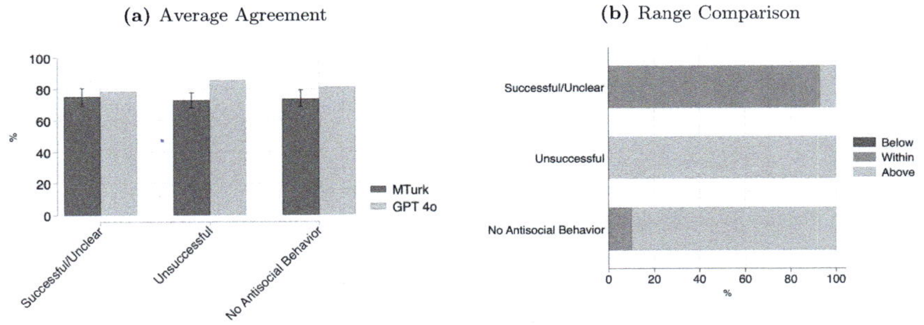

Notes: Panel 19a shows how often GPT 4o agrees with the MTurk mode. The within-MTurk range of agreement is also depicted. For the latter, we estimate the agreement of each wave of MTurks with the corresponding leave-one-out mode. Further, Panel 19b shows how often GPT 4o falls within the trait-specific range of agreement derived from MTurks.

FIGURE 19 Turing test for antisocial behavior.

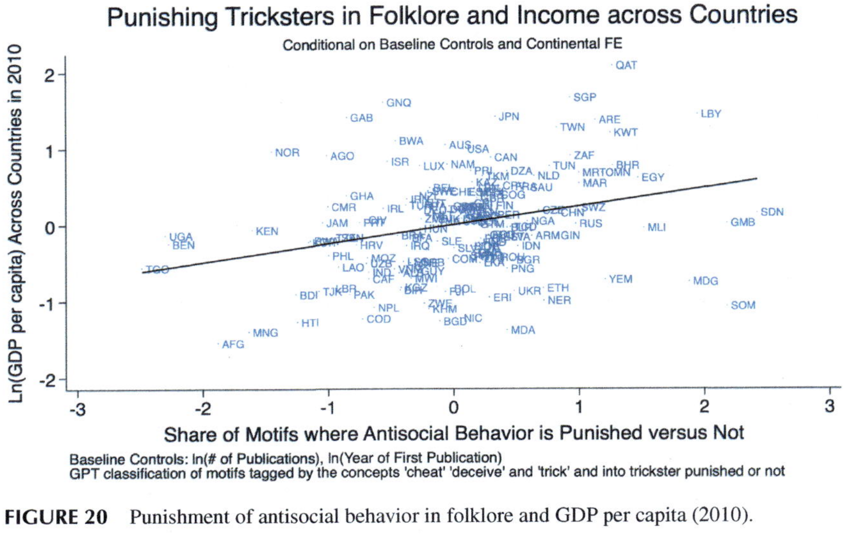

FIGURE 20 Punishment of antisocial behavior in folklore and GDP per capita (2010).

TABLE 3 Portrayal of antisocial behavior in folklore and contemporary trust and income.

	Trust (WVS/EVS)		Trust (GPS)		ln(GDP pc in 2010)	
	(1)	(2)	(3)	(4)	(5)	(6)
Panel A: Original Sample and MTurk Classification						
Relative punishment of antisocial behavior	0.4659***	0.3861***	0.5245***	0.3828*	0.4178***	0.2201***
	(0.1203)	(0.1349)	(0.1111)	(0.2097)	(0.0686)	(0.0734)
Adj. R^2	0.205	0.317	0.188	0.194	0.382	0.550
N	104	104	76	76	160	160
Controls	✓	✓	✓	✓	✓	✓
Continent FE		✓		✓		✓
Panel B: Original Sample and GPT Classification						
Relative punishment of antisocial behavior	0.2877***	0.1955*	0.5035***	0.3945**	0.3961***	0.2435***
	(0.1030)	(0.1159)	(0.1127)	(0.1959)	(0.0656)	(0.0783)
Adj. R^2	0.157	0.274	0.213	0.199	0.376	0.560
N	104	104	76	76	160	160
Controls	✓	✓	✓	✓	✓	✓
Continent FE		✓		✓		✓

Notes: Controls include ln(# of publications) and ln(year of first publication) for the oral tradition. Dependent variables and relative punishment measures are standardized. Heteroskedasticity-robust standard errors are used. ***, **, * denote significance at 1%, 5%, and 10% levels, respectively.

Coding how challenges are portrayed

Regarding the coding of how challenges are depicted, I implement a prompt that asks GPT to infer whether characters manage to overcome a challenging situation or not. I allow for unclear, successful, and unsuccessful categorizations. See Figs. 21a and 21b. Following MX, I group together instances where GPT (MTurk) classifies the outcome of a challenge as either successful or unclear, creating a clear contrast with motifs where the challenging situation results in an unambiguous loss. Take, for example, motif m35, which reads: "Cold enduring competition: Two animal persons compete to see who could withstand cold all the night. At dawn one is dead". The GPT-explanation reads: "Unsuccessful – One of the competitors did not survive the night, indicating they did not overcome the challenge. Confidence score: 9."

The cross-country correlation between the MTurk and GPT ratings on the relative incidence of unsuccessful challenges is 0.93. In Figs. 22a and 22b, we show that along all these 3 dimensions, i.e., whether someone weakly overcomes a challenging situation, or fails, or there is actually no challenge involved, the GPT agrees with the modal MTurk more often than the average wave of MTurks. In Fig. 23 and Table 4, we show that societies where challenges are more likely to lead to disasters are less risk seeking. Furthermore, countries with oral traditions stressing the downside of engaging in difficult and challenging situations engage less in entrepreneurship and are less innovative, as reflected in the patent rate. These patterns are similar to the MTurk-derived measures of challenges.

(a) Presence


```
{'custom_id': 'a23a', 'method': 'POST', 'url': '/v1/chat/completions', 'body': {'model': 'gpt-4o-202
4-08-06', 'messages': [{'role': 'system', 'content': 'You will be provided with a short text. Based
solely on the information provided, determine whether the text contains any contests, challenges, or
difficult situations. Respond {Yes} or {No} and provide a confidence score for your answer (1-10) on
ly.'}, {'role': 'user', 'content': 'Who will see the Sun first?: Two persons or animals argue about
who of them will be the first to see the rising sun. One who seemed to have less chances wins'}], 'm
ax_tokens': 60, 'seed': 1746192, 'temperature': 0}}
```


(b) Classification


```
{'custom_id': 'a23a',
 'method': 'POST',
 'url': '/v1/chat/completions',
 'body': {'model': 'gpt-4o-2024-08-06',
  'messages': [{'role': 'system',
    'content': 'You will be provided with a short text featuring a difficult or challenging situation.
Based solely on the information provided, determine whether or not the character(s) in the text overco
me the challenge or difficulty. Respond with {Unclear} if there is not enough information to determine
the outcome, if the outcome is not explicitly stated, or if there are mixed outcomes. Respond with {Su
ccessful} if they clearly overcome the challenge and {Unsuccessful} if they clearly do not. Choose onl
y one answer and your reasoning (max 60 tokens). Provide a confidence score from 0 to 10.'},
   {'role': 'user',
    'content': 'Who will see the Sun first?: Two persons or animals argue about who of them will be th
e first to see the rising sun. One who seemed to have less chances wins'}],
  'max_tokens': 60,
  'seed': 1746192,
  'temperature': 0}}
```


FIGURE 21 Prompts for challenge.

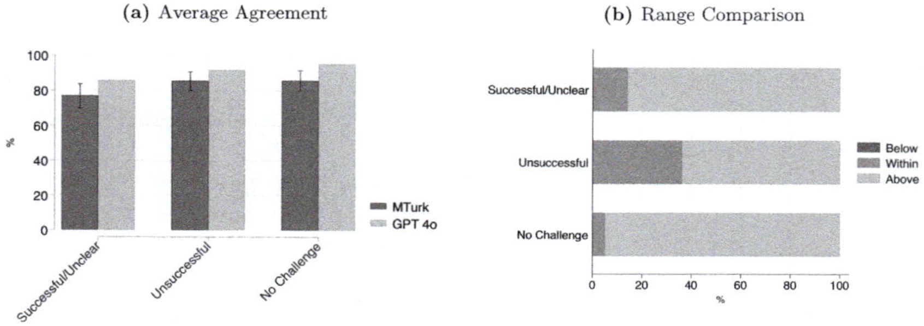

Notes: Panel 22a compares how often GPT 4o agrees with the MTurk mode. The within-MTurk range of agreement is also depicted. For the latter, we estimate the agreement of each wave of MTurks with the corresponding leave-one-out mode. Panel 22b shows how often GPT 4o ratings fall within the trait-specific range of agreement derived from MTurks.

FIGURE 22 Turing test for challenge.

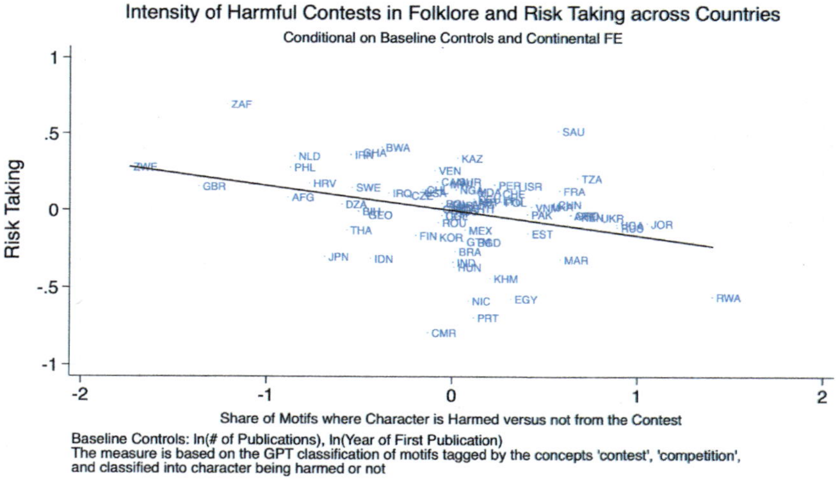

FIGURE 23 Harmful competition in folklore and risk-taking attitudes.

Open questions and a personal reflection

In the Folklore project, the motif-coding by MTurks took about a month to complete, costing roughly 2800 USD. Finding multiple, highly rated MTurks to avoid having all motifs classified by a few became an increasingly binding constraint. This meant constantly monitoring the completion of a given batch and intervening when it got stuck for days. Maintaining a diverse, high-quality pool of MTurks eventually slowed the process to a halt.

TABLE 4 Portrayal of challenges in folklore and risk taking and entrepreneurship today.

	Risk Taking (GPS)				ln(# of patents from country's residents per 100,000 in 2006–2018)		ln(New business registrations per 1000 people ages 15–64 in 2006–2018)	
	(1)	(2)	(3)	(4)	(5)	(6)	(7)	(8)
Panel A: Original Sample and MTurk Classification								
All Challenge Motifs	0.3815***	0.3985**						
	(0.1238)	(0.1619)						
Character is Successful			0.5103**					
			(0.1929)					
Character is not Successful			−0.0995					
			(0.0987)					
Character is neither Successful nor Unsuccessful			0.2948*					
			(0.1511)					
Character is relatively Unsuccessful				−0.5851***	−0.2487***	−0.1848**	−0.3504***	−0.1940**
				(0.1662)	(0.0920)	(0.0802)	(0.0822)	(0.0830)
Adj. R^2	0.130	0.235	0.266	0.274	0.409	0.535	0.263	0.343
N	76	76	76	76	140	140	147	147
Controls	✓	✓	✓	✓	✓	✓	✓	✓
Continent FE		✓	✓	✓		✓		✓
Panel B: Original Sample and GPT Classification								
All Challenge Motifs	0.3380***	0.3971**						
	(0.1230)	(0.1717)						
Character is Successful			0.3657*					
			(0.1995)					
Character is not Successful			−0.0484					
			(0.1061)					
Character is neither Successful nor Unsuccessful			0.3927**					
			(0.1726)					
Character is relatively Unsuccessful				−0.5424***	−0.2886***	−0.2016***	−0.3347***	−0.1965**
				(0.1691)	(0.0849)	(0.0748)	(0.0771)	(0.0795)
Adj. R^2	0.118	0.236	0.251	0.253	0.416	0.536	0.260	0.346
N	76	76	76	76	140	140	147	147
Controls	✓	✓	✓	✓	✓	✓	✓	✓
Continent FE		✓	✓	✓		✓		✓

Notes: Controls include ln(# of publications) and ln(year of first publication) for the oral tradition. Dependent variables and challenge-related variables are standardized. Heteroskedasticity-robust standard errors are used. ***, **, * denote significance at 1%, 5%, and 10% levels, respectively.

In September 2024, the LLM cost about 1.35 USD for the same amount of work and took roughly 30 minutes to complete. As the analysis shows, the LLM output requires human ground truth to be trusted, but the returns are substantial. My hope is that this exploration serves as a proof of concept, demonstrating that, under the right conditions, GPT can extract values from folkloric motifs as effectively as a group of human subjects.

It is important to note that best practices in this area are evolving with many open questions. For example, what is the appropriate number of human readings/ratings per input? Should the subjects rating the text be familiar with the culture whose text they are rating? How many inputs (in our case, motifs) should be classified before implementing the Turing approach? In addition, one may debate whether passing the Turing test by getting above the minimum of the agreement range is sufficient or should instead be taken as an intermediate step towards an end product. Lastly, since these variables are generated from a prompt designed by the researcher, what are the appropriate statistical adjustments? A growing set of scholars engaging with these fundamental questions increases our optimism that best practices will soon emerge. See, for example, Battaglia et al. (2024); Compiani et al. (2023); Wei and Malik (2022); Zhang et al. (2023), and Ludwig et al. (2025).

6 Outlook and future research

Strengthening the link to humanities

The current Handbook Chapter has (hopefully) highlighted the connections that economists interested in understanding the roots and consequences of cultural, institutional, and economic variation across societies have forged with neighboring disciplines, particularly anthropologists, ethnographers, and folklorists. However, establishing a strong connection with the humanities has been less successful.

The humanities include the academic study of philosophy, religion, history, language arts (literature, writing, oratory, rhetoric, poetry, etc.), the performing arts (theater, music, dance, etc.), and the visual arts (painting, sculpture, photography, filmmaking, etc.). Despite efforts in the digital humanities to systematically use digital resources, effectively harnessing unstructured text remains a challenge. This weak link has become more apparent with the rapid growth of digitized books and online content, emphasizing the importance of extracting meaningful insights from them. Not surprisingly, a growing literature on text-to-data methods has emerged to close this gap; see Ash and Hansen (2023); Beach and Hanlon (2023); Gentzkow et al. (2019); Lagakos et al. (2025).

In Michalopoulos and Papaioannou (2025), we combine insights from musicology with a century-long comprehensive compilation of song production in Greece to explore how artists tracing their lineage to native populations and the 1920s refugees differ in their lyrical themes, emotional tone, and worldviews expressed in the lyrics. The study reveals how historical critical junctures can influence artistic expression across generations, shaping how music reflects and transmits cultural memory and identity.

A complementary strand of recent work attempts to extract information from images. Examples include the work by Gorin et al. (2025) who rely on a large, open-access repository of art collections, and develop an algorithm to classify the emotions conveyed through paintings covering most of Europe from the 15th century onward. In a related study, Voth and Yanagizawa-Drott (2023) present new methods for using images as a high-frequency, detailed source to study cultural change. Their approach measures visual similarity across time and geography, allowing us to track when and where influential style trends emerge. To demonstrate these methods, they analyze over 14 million US high school yearbook photos of graduating seniors, offering a large-scale view of how styles persist and evolve. Finally, Adukia et al. (2023) develop AI methods to convert images from children's books into data in the US. Their analysis shows lighter average skin tones, underrepresentation of Black and Latinx characters, and greater symbolic inclusion of females in images than in text, highlighting visual patterns of inequality and change over time.

Looking ahead

The arrival of LLMs is revolutionizing research on comparative development. I have already reviewed its transformative power in the context of using it to "read" and quantify aspects of folkloric motifs.

Folkloric motifs are just one application of how LLMs can be fruitfully applied in extracting quantifiable bits from text. However, the possibilities are tremendous. What do we learn by integrating rich unstructured text, including narratives, books, life histories, interviews, and diaries, into our toolkit? They are likely to have important insights on questions that are at the heart of decision theory, behavioral economics, happiness studies, and culture, including how memory is formed, what gives meaning to one's personal life, how one reasons about her actions, how life events shape one's attitudes and vice versa, and what is the taxonomy of preferences in the general population not as assumed by economists, but as narrated by individuals themselves.[31]

Economists embrace new tools only after painstaking reflection and detailed examination, often resulting in a considerable lag in adoption compared to other disciplines. However, over the last few months, while working on this chapter, the profession has witnessed a rapid increase in the number of studies by economists using LLM-generated output and investigating the usage of this technology (see the weekly working paper series of the National Bureau of

31 In LMV, for example, we explore an iconic product of the New Deal's Federal Writers' Project, the American Life Histories manuscripts produced by a team of writers traveling the United States to record the lives of thousands of older Americans for posterity, to quantify the narrators' experiences, economic fortunes, and perspectives on what brought happiness, satisfaction, and meaning into their lives.

Economic Research, NBER, and the Centre for Economic Policy Research, CEPR, respectively).

It is evident that the integration of LLMs in the arsenal of economists interested in understanding culture, human behavior, and beyond is developing at a dizzying pace. As with any new general-purpose technology, it will take some time to appreciate the contours of what LLMs can and cannot do for us. The excitement and ambivalence among academics are palpable as best practices are only now being chartered, and novel studies, hitherto infeasible, become a possibility. I find myself wondering what the next edition of the Handbook of Culture and Economic Behavior may look like.

References

Acemoglu, D., Johnson, S., Robinson, J.A., 2001. The colonial origins of comparative development: an empirical investigation. American Economic Review 91 (5), 1369–1401.

Adukia, A., Eble, A., Harrison, E., Runesha, H.B., Szasz, T., 2023. What we teach about race and gender: representation in images and text of children's books. The Quarterly Journal of Economics 138 (4), 2225–2285.

Ahlerup, P., Olsson, O., 2012. The roots of ethnic diversity. Journal of Economic Growth 17, 71–102.

Albouy, D.Y., 2012. The colonial origins of comparative development: an empirical investigation: comment. American Economic Review 102 (6), 3059–3076.

Alesina, A., Giuliano, P., Nunn, N., 2013. On the origins of gender roles: women and the plough. The Quarterly Journal of Economics 128 (2), 469–530.

Alesina, A., Michalopoulos, S., Papaioannou, E., 2016. Ethnic inequality. Journal of Political Economy 124 (2), 428–488.

Ali, M., Fjeldstad, O.-H., Jiang, B., Shifa, A.B., 2019. Colonial legacy, state-building and the salience of ethnicity in sub-Saharan Africa. The Economic Journal 129 (619), 1048–1081.

Alsan, M., 2015. The effect of the TseTse fly on African development. American Economic Review 105 (1), 382–410.

Anderson, S., 2018. Legal origins and female HIV. American Economic Review 108 (6), 1407–1439.

Angrist, J.D., Pischke, J.-S., 2010. The credibility revolution in empirical economics: how better research design is taking the con out of econometrics. The Journal of Economic Perspectives 24 (2), 3–30.

Ash, E., Hansen, S., 2023. Text algorithms in economics. Annual Review of Economics 15 (1), 659–688.

Ashraf, Q., Galor, O., 2013. Genetic diversity and the origins of cultural fragmentation. American Economic Review 103 (3), 528–533.

Austin, G., 2008. The 'reversal of fortune' thesis and the compression of history: perspectives from African and comparative economic history. Journal of International Development 20 (8), 996–1027.

Bahrami-Rad, D., Becker, A., Henrich, J., 2021. Tabulated nonsense? Testing the validity of the Ethnographic Atlas. Economics Letters 204, 109880.

Barro, R., 1999. Human capital and growth in cross-country regressions. Swedish Economic Policy Review 6, 237–277.

Barth, F., 1969. Ethnic Groups and Boundaries: The Social Organization of Culture Difference. Waveland Press.

Battaglia, L., Christensen, T., Hansen, S., Sacher, S., 2024. Inference for regression with variables generated from unstructured data. arXiv preprint. arXiv:2402.15585.

Beach, B., Hanlon, W.W., 2023. Historical newspaper data: a researcher's guide. Explorations in Economic History 90, 101541.
Becker, A., 2024. On the economic origins of concerns over women's chastity. The Review of Economic Studies. rdae084.
Becker, S., Boll, D., Voth, H.-J., 2025. Spatial Unit Roots in Regressions: a Practitioner's Guide and a Stata Package. Discussion paper, Warwick Economics Research Papers.
Berezkin, Y., 2015. Folklore and mythology catalogue: its lay-out and potential for research. In: Frog, Leslie-Jacobsen, H.F., Hopkins, J.S. (Eds.), The Retrospective Methods Network Newsletter. In: Between Text and Practice: Mythology, Religion and Research, vol. 10. Folklore Studies/Dept. of Philosophy, History, Culture and Art Studies University of Helsinki, Helsinki, pp. 58–70.
Berezkin, Y., 2016. Peopling of the new world in light of the data on distribution of folklore motifs. In: Kenna, R., MacCarron, M., MacCarron, P. (Eds.), Maths Meets Myths: Quantitative Approaches to Ancient Narratives (Understanding Complex Systems), vol. 10. Springer Verlag, pp. 71–89.
Bertocchi, G., Dimico, A., Falco, C., 2024. Family Planning and Ethnic Heritage: Evidence from Sub-Saharan Africa. Discussion paper, IZA Discussion Papers.
Bisin, A., Federico, G., 2021. Merger or acquisition? An introduction to the handbook of historical economics. In: Bisin, A., Federico, G. (Eds.), The Handbook of Historical Economics. Academic Press. pp. xv–xxxviii.
Blouin, A., Mukand, S.W., 2019. Erasing ethnicity? Propaganda, nation building, and identity in Rwanda. Journal of Political Economy 127 (3), 1008–1062.
Boas, F., 1896. The limitations of the comparative method of anthropology. Science 4 (103), 901–908.
Boas, F., 1901. The mind of primitive man. Science 13 (321), 281–289.
Bockstette, V., Chanda, A., Putterman, L., 2002. States and markets: the advantage of an early start. Journal of Economic Growth 7 (4), 347–369.
Borcan, O., Olsson, O., Putterman, L., 2018. State history and economic development: evidence from six millennia. Journal of Economic Growth 23 (1).
Brulé, R.E., 2023. Women and power in the developing world. Annual Review of Political Science 26 (1), 33–54.
Buhrmester, M.D., Talaifar, S., Gosling, S.D., 2018. An evaluation of Amazon's Mechanical Turk, its rapid rise, and its effective use. Perspectives on Psychological Science 13 (2), 149–154.
Cao, Y., Enke, B., Falk, A., Giuliano, P., Nunn, N., 2021. Herding, warfare, and a culture of honor: Global evidence. Working Paper 29250. National Bureau of Economic Research.
Cappelen, C., 2024. Using Large Language Models to Classify Cultural Heritage. Working Paper.
Cervellati, M., Chiovelli, G., Esposito, E., 2019. Bite and divide: Malaria and ethnolinguistic diversity. CEPR Discussion Paper No. DP13437.
Chan, C., Holosko, M.J., 2016. An overview of the use of Mechanical Turk in behavioral sciences: Implications for social work. Research on Social Work Practice 26 (4), 441–448.
Ciccone, A., Jarociński, M., 2010. Determinants of economic growth: will data tell? American Economic Journal. Macroeconomics 2 (4), 222–246.
Compiani, G., Morozov, I., Seiler, S., 2023. Demand estimation with text and image data. CESifo Working Paper.
D'Amato, M., Russo, F., 2025. Cultural doorways in the barriers to development. Journal of Economic Growth. https://doi.org/10.1007/s10887-025-09253-7.
Delis, M.D., Dioikitopoulos, E.V., Ongena, S., 2023a. Population diversity and financial risk-taking. Journal of Banking & Finance 151, 106852.
Delis, M.D., Hasan, I., Iosifidi, M., Tsoumas, C., 2023b. Economic preferences for risk-taking and financing costs. Journal of Corporate Finance 80, 102423.
Dell, M., 2025. Deep learning for economists. Journal of Economic Literature 63 (1), 5–58.
Depetris-Chauvin, E., 2016. State History and Contemporary Conflict: Evidence from Sub-Saharan Africa. Documentos de Trabajo 475. Instituto de Economia. Pontificia Universidad Católica de Chile.

Dessi, R., Ren, J., Zhao, X., 2023. Shame, Guilt, and Motivated Self-Confidence. Centre for Economic Policy Research.

Diamond, J., Robinson, J.A., 2010. Natural Experiments of History. Harvard University Press.

Dickens, A., 2018. Ethnolinguistic favoritism in African politics. American Economic Journal: Applied Economics 10 (3), 370–402.

Dincecco, M., Fenske, J., Gupta, B., Menon, A., 2024. Conflict and Gender Norms. CEPR Discussion Paper No. DP18920.

Driver, H.E., Coffin, J.L., 1974. Statistical classification of North American Indian ethnic units from the driver-Massey sample. In: Comparative Studies by Harold E. Driver and Essays in His Honor, pp. 205–224.

Driver, H.E., Jorgensen, J.G., Aberle, D.F., 1974. Comparative Studies by Harold E. Driver and Essays in His Honor. HRAF Press, New Haven.

Driver, H.E., Kenny, J.A., Hudson, H.C., Engle, O.M., 1972. Statistical classification of North American Indian ethnic units. Ethnology 11 (3), 311–339.

Duflo, E., Glennerster, R., Kremer, M., 2007. Using randomization in development economics research: a toolkit. In: Handbook of Development Economics, vol. 4, pp. 3895–3962.

Duranton, G., Henderson, V., Strange, W., 2015. Foreword. In: Duranton, G., Henderson, J.V., Strange, W.C. (Eds.), Handbook of Regional and Urban Economics. In: Handbook of Regional and Urban Economics, vol. 5. Elsevier. pp. xv–xvi.

d'Huy, J., Le Quellec, J.-L., Thuillard, M., Berezkin, Y.E., Lajoye, P., Oda, J., 2023. Little statisticians in the forest of tales: towards a new comparative mythology. Fabula 64 (1–2), 44–63.

Easterly, W., Levine, R., 1997. Africa's growth tragedy: policies and ethnic divisions. The Quarterly Journal of Economics 112 (4), 1203–1250.

Eggan, F., 1937. Historical changes in the Choctaw kinship system. American Anthropologist 39 (1), 34–52.

Enke, B., 2019. Kinship, cooperation, and the evolution of moral systems. The Quarterly Journal of Economics 134 (2), 953–1019.

Enke, B., 2023. Market exposure and human morality. Nature Human Behaviour 7 (1), 134–141.

Eruchimovitch, I., Michaeli, M., Sarid, A., 2023. On the coevolution of individualism and institutions. Journal of Economic Growth, 1–42.

Espín-Sánchez, J.-A., Gil-Guirado, S., Ryan, N., 2024. Praying for rain. Working Paper 31411. National Bureau of Economic Research.

Falk, A., Becker, A., Dohmen, T., Enke, B., Huffman, D., Sunde, U., 2018. Global evidence on economic preferences. The Quarterly Journal of Economics 133 (4), 1645–1692.

Fan, C., Jiang, M., Zhang, B., 2024. Beyond cultural norms: how does historical rice farming affect modern firms' family control? Economica 91 (363), 770–808.

Fenske, J., 2014. Ecology, trade, and states in pre-colonial Africa. Journal of the European Economic Association 12 (3), 612–640.

Fuchs-Schündeln, N., Hassan, T.A., 2016. Natural Experiments in Macroeconomics. Handbook of Macroeconomics, vol. 2. Elsevier, pp. 923–1012.

Geertz, C., 1963. Old Societies and New States: the Quest for Modernity in Asia and Africa. The Free Press of Glencoe, New York.

Gennaioli, N., Rainer, I., 2007. The modern impact of pre-colonial centralization in Africa. Journal of Economic Growth 12 (3), 185–234.

Gentzkow, M., Kelly, B.T., Taddy, M., 2019. Text as data. Journal of Economic Literature 57, 535–574.

Gershman, B., Mumladze, T., 2025. Common Ancestry, Uncommon Findings: Revisiting Cross-Cultural Research in Economics. American University. Mimeo.

Giuliano, P., Nunn, N., 2018. Ancestral characteristics of modern populations. Economic History of Developing Regions 33 (1), 1–17.

Goodenough, W.H., 1956. Residence rules. Southwestern Journal of Anthropology 12 (1).

Gordon, R.G., Grimes, B.F., 2005. Ethnologue: Languages of the World, 15th edition. SIL International.
Gorin, C., Heblich, S., Zylberberg, Y., 2025. State of the Art: Economic Development Through the Lens of Paintings. University of Toronto. Mimeo.
Hall, R.E., Jones, C.I., 1999. Why do some countries produce so much more output per worker than others? The Quarterly Journal of Economics 114 (1), 83–116.
Han, J., Ji, X., Pan, Z., 2024. Inherited Culture and Corporate Innovation. Available at SSRN 4979871.
Henderson, J.V., Storeygard, A., Weil, D.N., 2012. Measuring economic growth from outer space. American Economic Review 102 (2), 994–1028.
Henderson, J.V., Thisse, J.-F., 2004. Foreword. In: Henderson, J.V., Thisse, J.-F. (Eds.), Cities and Geography. In: Handbook of Regional and Urban Economics, vol. 4. Elsevier. pp. xxvii–xxviii.
Herbst, J., 2000. States and Power in Africa: Comparative Lessons in Authority and Control. Princeton University Press.
Horvath, J., Lahtinen, K.D., 2025. Cross-country gender bias and corporate cash holdings. Finance Research Letters, 106820.
Jenkins, J.A., Rubin, J., 2024. The Oxford Handbook of Historical Political Economy. Oxford University Press.
Johnson, S., Larson, W., Papageorgiou, C., Subramanian, A., 2013. Is newer better? Penn World Table revisions and their impact on growth estimates. Journal of Monetary Economics 60 (2), 255–274.
Kikuta, K., 2024. Eclipse: How Darkness Shapes Violence in Africa. Institute of Developing Economies, Japan External Trade Organization (JETRO).
Kopytoff, I., 1988. George Peter Murdock's contributions to African studies. Behavior Science Research 22 (1–4), 41–49.
Krueger, A.B., Lindahl, M., 2001. Education for growth: why and for whom? Journal of Economic Literature 39 (4), 1101–1136.
La Porta, R., Lopez-de-Silanes, F., Shleifer, A., Vishny, R.W., 1998. Law and finance. Journal of Political Economy 106 (6), 1113–1155.
Lagakos, D., Michalopoulos, S., Voth, H.-J., 2025. American Life Histories. Mimeo Brown University, Working Paper 33373. National Bureau of Economic Research.
Laitin, D.D., Ramachandran, R., 2022. Linguistic diversity, official language choice and human capital. Journal of Development Economics 156, 102811.
Le Rossignol, E., Lowes, S., 2022. Ancestral livelihoods and moral universalism: Evidence from transhumant pastoralist societies. Working Paper 30259. National Bureau of Economic Research.
Le Rossignol, E., Lowes, S., Nunn, N., 2022. The Social Consequences of Traditional Religion in Contemporary Africa. Working Paper 29695. National Bureau of Economic Research.
Leidinger, A., van Rooij, R., Shutova, E., 2023. The language of prompting: what linguistic properties make a prompt successful? In: Bouamor, H., Pino, J., Bali, K. (Eds.), Findings of the Association for Computational Linguistics: EMNLP 2023. Association for Computational Linguistics, Singapore, pp. 9210–9232.
Link, A., 2024. Beasts of Burden, Trade, and Hierarchy: The Long Shadow of Domestication. ZBW-Leibniz Information Centre for Economics, Kiel, Hamburg.
Litina, A., Roca Fernández, È., 2024. Solar eclipses and the origins of critical thinking and complexity. The Economic Journal 134 (660), 1545–1577.
Lopez-Manuel, L., 2023. Despotic Political Systems and the Historical Evolution of Social Preferences. Available at SSRN 4610526.
Lowes, S., 2021. Ethnographic and field data in historical economics. In: The Handbook of Historical Economics. Elsevier, pp. 147–177.
Lowes, S., 2022. Kinship Structure and the Family: Evidence from the Matrilineal Belt. Working Paper 30509. National Bureau of Economic Research.

Lowes, S., Moscona, J., Nunn, N., Seck, A.-A., 2025. Digitizing the Ethnographic Survey of Africa: New Data on Pre-Colonial sub-Saharan African Culture and Politics. Mimeo UCSD.

Ludwig, J., Mullainathan, S., Rambachan, A., 2025. Large Language Models: an Applied Econometric Framework. Working Paper 33344. National Bureau of Economic Research.

Luo, Y., Yang, Z., Meng, F., Li, Y., Zhou, J., Zhang, Y., 2023. An empirical study of catastrophic forgetting in large language models during continual fine-tuning. arXiv preprint. arXiv:2308.08747.

Mace, R., Pagel, M., 1995. A latitudinal gradient in the density of human languages in North America. Proceedings of the Royal Society of London. Series B, Biological Sciences 261 (1360), 117–121.

Malein, V., Beltrán Tapia, F.J., 2024. Culture, Economic Stress, and Missing Girls. CEPR.

Margo, R.A., 2018. The integration of economic history into economics. Cliometrica 12 (3), 377–406.

Marigo, J.-B., Weill, L., 2024. Once upon a Loan: How Folk Tales Shape Access to Credit. Discussion paper. Laboratoire de Recherche en Gestion et Economie (LaRGE), Université de Strasbourg.

Mauro, P., 1995. Corruption and growth. The Quarterly Journal of Economics 110 (3), 681–712.

Michalopoulos, S., 2012. The origins of ethnolinguistic diversity. American Economic Review 102 (4), 1508–1539.

Michalopoulos, S., Naghavi, A., Prarolo, G., 2018. Trade and geography in the spread of Islam. The Economic Journal 128 (616), 3210–3241.

Michalopoulos, S., Papaioannou, E., 2013. Pre-colonial ethnic institutions and contemporary African development. Econometrica 81 (1), 113–152.

Michalopoulos, S., Papaioannou, E., 2014. National institutions and subnational development in Africa. The Quarterly Journal of Economics 129 (1), 151–213.

Michalopoulos, S., Papaioannou, E., 2016. The long-run effects of the scramble for Africa. American Economic Review 106 (7), 1802–1848.

Michalopoulos, S., Papaioannou, E., 2018. Spatial patterns of development: a meso approach. Annual Review of Economics 10 (1), 383–410.

Michalopoulos, S., Papaioannou, E., 2020. Historical legacies and African development. Journal of Economic Literature 58 (1), 53–128.

Michalopoulos, S., Papaioannou, E., 2025. Songs of Refugees. Discussion paper. Mimeo. Brown University.

Michalopoulos, S., Putterman, L., Weil, D.N., 2019. The influence of ancestral lifeways on individual economic outcomes in sub-Saharan Africa. Journal of the European Economic Association 17 (4), 1186–1231.

Michalopoulos, S., Rauh, C., 2024. Movies. Working Paper 32220. National Bureau of Economic Research.

Michalopoulos, S., Xue, M.M., 2021. Folklore. The Quarterly Journal of Economics 136 (4), 1993–2046.

Miklukho-Maklai Institute of Ethnology and Anthropology, 1964. Atlas Narodov Mira. Department of Geodesy and Cartography of the State Geological Committee of the Soviet Union.

Morgan, L.H., 1877. Ancient Society. Belknap Press, Cambridge, MA.

Moscona, J., Nunn, N., Robinson, J.A., 2020. Segmentary lineage organization and conflict in sub-Saharan Africa. Econometrica 88 (5), 1999–2036.

Moscona, J., Seck, A.A., 2024. Age set versus kin: culture and financial ties in East Africa. American Economic Review 114 (9), 2748–2791.

Murdock, G.P., 1949. Social Structure. Macmillan, New York.

Murdock, G.P., 1959. Africa: Its Peoples and Their Culture History. McGraw-Hill.

Murdock, G.P., 1967. Ethnographic atlas: a summary. Ethnology 6 (2), 109–236.

Murdock, G.P., White, D.R., 1969. Standard cross-cultural sample. Ethnology 8 (4), 329–369.

Müller, U.K., Watson, M.W., 2024. Spatial unit roots and spurious regression. Econometrica 92 (5), 1661–1695.

Nettle, D., 1998. Explaining global patterns of language diversity. Journal of Anthropological Archaeology 17 (4), 354–374.
Nettle, D., 1999. Linguistic Diversity. Oxford Univ Press, Oxford, UK.
Nunn, N., 2008. The long-term effects of Africa's slave trades. The Quarterly Journal of Economics 123 (1), 139–176.
Nunn, N., 2020. The historical roots of economic development. Science (New York, N.Y.) 367 (6485), eaaz9986.
Nunn, N., Wantchekon, L., 2011. The slave trade and the origins of mistrust in Africa. American Economic Review 101 (7), 3221–3252.
Olken, B.A., 2020. Banerjee, duflo, kremer, and the rise of modern development economics. Scandinavian Journal of Economics 122 (3), 853–878.
Papaioannou, E., 2025. Institutions, history, antagonisms, and development. Scandinavian Journal of Economics 127 (3), 511–575.
Poyker, M., 2023. Regime stability and the persistence of traditional practices. Review of Economics and Statistics 105 (5), 1175–1190.
Saenger, L.Y., 2022. Respect Your Elders? The Economic Origins and Political Consequences of Attitudes Toward the Aged. Bachelor's thesis. Harvard University Engineering and Applied Sciences.
Sala-i-Martin, X., Doppelhofer, G., Miller, R.I., 2004. Determinants of long-term growth: a Bayesian averaging of classical estimates (BACE) approach. American Economic Review 94 (4), 813–835.
Salinas, A., Morstatter, F., 2024. The butterfly effect of altering prompts: how small changes and jailbreaks affect large language model performance. In: Ku, L.-W., Martins, A., Srikumar, V. (Eds.), Findings of the Association for Computational Linguistics: ACL 2024. Association for Computational Linguistics, Bangkok, Thailand, pp. 4629–4651.
Schläpfer, A., 2024. Cross-cultural differences in retaliation: evidence from the soccer field. Journal of Economic Behavior & Organization 223, 216–233.
Speer, R., Lowry-Duda, J., 2017. Conceptnet at semeval-2017 task 2: extending word embeddings with multilingual relational knowledge. arXiv preprint. arXiv:1704.03560.
Spencer, B., Gillen, F.J., 1899. The Native Tribes of Central Australia. Macmillan and Company, Limited.
Spolaore, E., Wacziarg, R., 2009. The diffusion of development. The Quarterly Journal of Economics 124 (2), 469–529.
Tian, S., Li, L., Li, W., Ran, H., Ning, X., Tiwari, P., 2024. A survey on few-shot class-incremental learning. Neural Networks 169, 307–324.
Tobin, J., 1990. The HRAF as radical text? Cultural Anthropology 5 (4), 473–487.
Turing, A.M., 1950. Computing machinery and intelligence. Mind 59 (236), 433–460.
Tylor, E.B., 1871. Primitive Culture: Researches into the Development of Mythology, Philosophy, Religion, Art, and Custom, vol. 2. J. Murray.
Vansina, J., 1966. Introduction à l'ethnographie du Congo, vol. 1. Centre de Recherche et d'Information SocioPolitiques, Université Lovanium.
Voth, H.-J., 2021. Chapter 9 – Persistence – myth and mystery. In: Bisin, A., Federico, G. (Eds.), The Handbook of Historical Economics. Academic Press, pp. 243–267.
Voth, H.-J., Yanagizawa-Drott, D., 2023. Image(s). CEPR Discussion Paper 16624.
Wei, Y., Malik, N., 2022. Unstructured Data, Econometric Models, and Estimation Bias. USC Marshall School of Business Research Paper Sponsored by iORB.
Weidmann, N.B., Rød, J.K., Cederman, L.-E., 2010. Representing ethnic groups in space: a new dataset. Journal of Peace Research 47 (4), 491–499.
White, D.R., Brudner-White, L.A., 1988. The Murdock legacy: the ethnographic atlas and the search for a method. Behavior Science Research 22 (1–4), 59–81.
White, D.R., Burton, M.L., 1988. Causes of polygyny: ecology, economy, kinship, and warfare. American Anthropologist 90 (4), 871–887.
Wooldridge, J.M., 2002. Econometric Analysis of Cross Section and Panel Data. The MIT Press.

Wright, D.R., 1999. "What do you mean there were no tribes in Africa?": thoughts on boundaries—and related matters—in precolonial Africa. History in Africa 26, 409–426.
Zhang, J., Xue, W., Yu, Y., Tan, Y., 2023. Debiasing Machine-Learning-or AI-Generated Regressors in Partial Linear Models. Available at SSRN 4636026.

Chapter 3

On the measurement of social heterogeneity☆

Klaus Desmet[a], Ignacio Ortuño-Ortín[b], and Romain Wacziarg[c]

[a]*SMU, NBER, and CEPR, Department of Economics and Cox School of Business, Southern Methodist University, Dallas, TX, United States,* [b]*UC3M, Department of Economics, Universidad Carlos III de Madrid, Getafe, Madrid, Spain,* [c]*UCLA and NBER, UCLA Anderson School of Management, Los Angeles CA, United States*

1 Introduction

Heterogeneity between individuals forms the basis of political economy: without differences, there is no disagreement, no need to reach social choices by aggregating disparate preferences and interests, and no conflict. In recent times, issues surrounding diversity and identity have been central to social debates. In advanced industrialized democracies, identity politics, political polarization, culture wars, and the effects of immigration on culture and policy occupy commentators and scholars alike. In emerging economies, the persistence of ethnic and religious conflict continues to represent a central obstacle to modernization and growth. The growing interest in what separates us is no coincidence: in many societies, evolving social rifts, stemming from disagreements between individuals and between groups, have the potential to undermine social trust, the functioning of democracies, the provision of public goods, the efficiency of transactions between economic agents, and civil peace. Diversity, on the other hand, can also strengthen societies and organizations, by fostering creativity and innovation. However, our understanding of the relevant dimensions of social heterogeneity and of the proper way to measure diversity remains incomplete. Measuring social heterogeneity, in short, is central to our understanding of the forces that shape diversity, and of its effects on political economy outcomes.

Arguably, social scientists have long been cavalier about the measurement of social heterogeneity. They have relied on arbitrary choices of dimensions along which to measure social heterogeneity, and equally arbitrary functional forms

☆ This paper was written for the *Handbook of Culture and Economic Behavior*. We thank Paola Giuliano, Nathan Nunn as well as participants at the Economics of Culture Conference at Northwestern University in October 2024 for useful comments.

Handbook of Culture and Economic Behavior, Volume 1, ISSN 3051-1682
https://doi.org/10.1016/bs.hceb.2026.02.001

to create measures of diversity. In this chapter, we discuss the measurement of social heterogeneity, addressing two major issues.

The first issue is: heterogeneity of what? Humans differ along a wide range of traits – gender, race, income, cultural beliefs and values, religious affiliations, among many others. Yet social scientists often pick an arbitrary subset of these as the focus of their analysis. It is only by understanding the broad range of dimensions of social heterogeneity that we can hope to focus on the ones most likely to be relevant for a given topic of inquiry. Moreover, scholars have traditionally relied on predefined traits such as language or ethnicity, to capture the relevant dimensions of social heterogeneity. However, such measures correlate weakly – or even not at all – with observed measures of disagreement on social and moral issues (Desmet et al., 2017). When one defines groups through exogenous markers like gender, race, ethnicity, location, etc., one sees a tremendous amount of within-group variation in the fundamental building blocks of social disagreement: values, norms, and attitudes. Thus, a recent approach has sought to go directly to the core elements along which people might disagree – the very subjects of those disagreements.

The second issue is: how does one measure heterogeneity? Even if we can agree on what separates us – i.e., the relevant dimensions of heterogeneity – there remain many degrees of freedom in the choice of functional forms to capture heterogeneity in the most relevant way. Social scientists often choose their preferred measures *ex ante*, without paying attention to possible alternatives that may yield distinct insights. Yet distinctions between various measures can have first-order implications for our understanding of the causes and effects of social heterogeneity. Fractionalization has effects distinct from polarization. For example, polarization may be more predictive of civil conflict than fractionalization, as societies are more prone to war and conflict when a few large groups dominate than when there are many small groups (Montalvo and Reynal-Querol, 2005b). The level of aggregation at which groups are defined also matters. For instance, one might treat different dialects of Italian as distinct groups, or alternatively, as part of a single group. For some outcomes, such as economic growth, heterogeneity may be detrimental, even if groups are finely defined, whereas for other outcomes, such as redistribution, heterogeneity only becomes relevant if groups are more coarsely defined (Desmet et al., 2012). The possible interaction between different dimensions of heterogeneity–whether they are cross-cutting or mutually reinforcing–is also relevant. For example, the risk of conflict may be especially heightened when ethnic differences coincide with cultural differences (Desmet et al., 2017).

In this chapter, we seek to provide clarity on these issues, by covering much of the work that social scientists have done in the past decades, in their efforts to quantify social heterogeneity. We proceed in three steps. The first step is theoretical. We provide a theoretically-founded and comprehensive typology of heterogeneity measures (Section 2). Our unified framework delivers a wide range of measures of social heterogeneity. The assumptions that deliver each of them are transparent, allowing a clear understanding of the circumstances under which a given measure is appropriate for the question at hand.

The second step is descriptive. We calculate a wide class of measures using a range of data sources, and characterize the global landscape of social heterogeneity (Section 3). Across the world, there is wide variation in all measures – whether considering identity traits like language or religion, or whether considering cultural beliefs and values. Moreover, these measures are imperfectly correlated with each other, suggesting that which one is used in empirical applications matters. We document, for instance, that cultural heterogeneity and ethnic heterogeneity are uncorrelated. We highlight the main measurement issues that the recent literature has confronted, and conclude the section with an explicit consideration of the endogenous determination of heterogeneity.

In the third step, we turn to inferences on the effects of heterogeneity. That is, we survey how different indices of diversity correlate with socioeconomic outcomes such as growth, government effectiveness, redistribution, or conflict. We show that the dimensions of heterogeneity under consideration – and the specific functional forms used to calculate the indices – have first-order effects on the inferences that can be drawn from the use of social heterogeneity measures (Section 4). Here we learn that simple narratives on the effects of diversity are elusive, but that nonetheless, much has been learned – and remains to be discovered – on the political economy effects of social heterogeneity.

2 A theoretical approach to measuring social heterogeneity

In this section, we present a common framework that rationalizes many of the most widely used indices of heterogeneity. Our aim is to provide microfoundations for these different indices. The framework that we propose draws on the concept of antagonism introduced by Esteban and Ray (1994). This is a natural foundation for modeling social tension as arising from antagonism between individuals of different groups. Depending on what causes this antagonism at the individual level, the average degree of tension in society maps into different indices of heterogeneity. In this way, our model is able to encompass many of the standard measures of heterogeneity used in the literature.

In our approach, individuals belong to identity groups. We use the term identity in the sense of some demographic trait that defines group members. It may refer to ethnicity, race, language, religion, gender, income, political party, etc. An individual's identity might also be at the intersection of some of these groups. In that case, the relevant identity groups might be Muslim female, Christian male, etc. For now, we take identity groups as exogenous, and each individual belongs to just one group, without having the possibility of changing groups. Later, we discuss the possibility of endogenizing identity, in line with the recent literature on identity choices (e.g., Akerlof and Kranton, 2000; Shayo, 2009).

In addition to belonging to an identity group, individuals are also characterized by their positions on cultural issues. We use the term culture in a broad sense – it encompasses values, norms, and attitudes on a wide range of moral, political, and socioeconomic questions. Examples of cultural issues include abortion, redistribution, gender equality, and immigration policies. As with identity, for now we assume that each individual has a fixed position in cultural space. Later, we explore the possibility that these positions could endogenously change.

Our framework takes the view that the utility individuals derive from their interactions with others may be influenced by their identity and their cultural values. Suppose that interactions with individuals who share similar cultural values are likely to be more beneficial *(cultural homophily)*, or that interactions with the same identity group might be more rewarding *(identity homophily)*. We refer to the (negative) utility that an individual experiences from interacting with others that differ as antagonism, following the conceptual framework by Esteban and Ray (1994). Antagonism depends on the alienation felt towards others. It may also depend on the degree of identification with one's own group. Overall antagonism in society is then the expected antagonism experienced by a random individual. Depending on the form alienation and identification take, overall antagonism can be measured by different indices of heterogeneity. In that sense, we adopt a broader view compared to Esteban and Ray (1994), whose focus was limited to obtaining a measure of polarization.

Before providing further details about the framework, a few remarks are in order. First, while homophily in identity or culture is our main assumption, heterophily would deliver the same measures of heterogeneity (the negative utility we refer to as antagonism would now be positive utility). A more neutral term than antagonism might be preferable, but our work builds on Esteban and Ray (1994), so we retain the term "antagonism" despite its negative connotation. This has no bearing on whether the measures are negatively or positively related to political economy outcomes of interest, which remains an empirical issue. Second, while heterogeneity affects utility in our setup, it could also affect productivity: heterogeneity could hinder coordination, lowering productivity, or it could promote collective creativity, raising productivity. Thus, our framework should be understood as one among potentially multiple microfoundations that can give rise to some of the standard indices of heterogeneity. In Section 2.5, we further elaborate on these points.

2.1 Basic framework

Consider a society with a population of N individuals, partitioned into J identity groups, indexed by $j = 1, \cdots, J$. Groups differ by some identity marker, such as ethnicity, language, gender, or religion. For example, if the society is Canada, and the identity marker is language, there would be two main groups: French speakers and English speakers. Denote by N_j the population of group j, and by $s_j = N_j/N$ the share of the population belonging to group j. Each individual belongs to one group, so that $\sum_{j=1}^{J} N_j = N$. There are Q cultural dimensions, indexed by $q = 1, \ldots, Q$. For each cultural dimension q, there are $R(q)$ possible positions, indexed by $r(q)$. To simplify notation, we assume that $R(q) = R$, but this restriction can easily be dropped.

An individual's type is then characterized by an identity group j and a vector v of her positions on the different cultural dimensions:

$$v = \{r(1), r(2), ..., r(Q)\}$$

Individuals of the same cultural type have the same vector v. Suppose there are K cultural types of individuals. Denote by N_k the number of individuals of cultural type k, where $\sum_{k=1}^{K} N_k = N$, and by $s_k = N_k/N$ the share of individuals of cultural type k. We also use the notation $s_{r(q)}$ to refer to the share of the population that holds position $r(q)$ on cultural dimension q. At the level of identity group j, the share of the population that holds position $r(q)$ is denoted by $s^j_{r(q)}$. We further use the notation $r(k, q)$ as the position in cultural dimension q held by individuals of cultural type k. We can then write $v(k)$ as the vector of individuals of cultural type k:

$$v(k) = \{r(k, 1), r(k, 2), ..., r(k, Q)\}.$$

We suppose that an agent interacts with all other agents in society and that the antagonism she experiences depends on those interactions. In our discussion, the term antagonism is equivalent to disutility.

2.2 Cultural heterogeneity

In this subsection we assume that antagonism only depends on cultural issues, and not on identity. That is, we assume homophily in culture, but not in identity. As an example, individuals feel antagonism towards others with different views on abortion, but not towards people of a different ethnic group. Under this assumption, social antagonism arises from disagreement on substantive issues, as opposed to identity markers – a common assumption in political science, for instance, where heterogeneity in political preferences drives differences in voter behavior.

Cultural fractionalization index (CF)

Consider an individual who randomly encounters another individual, and compares their positions on a random cultural dimension. Define the antagonism experienced by that individual as the expected disagreement with the other individual. Formally, an individual of cultural type k experiences an expected level of antagonism or disutility equal to:

$$a_k = \frac{1}{Q} \sum_{k'=1}^{K} d\left(v_k, v_{k'}\right) s_{k'} \tag{1}$$

where $d\left(v_k, v_{k'}\right)$ is the *Hamming distance* between cultural vectors v_k and $v_{k'}$ – the number of cultural dimensions along which cultural types k and k' hold different positions. In the case of one cultural dimension, the Hamming distance is a simple binary measure: an individual experiences an antagonism of one towards another individual if their positions differ, without regard for how much their positions differ. For instance, an individual who is "in favor" of abortion would feel the same antagonism towards someone who is "strongly in favor" as towards someone who is "strongly against".

The probability that an individual of cultural type k disagrees with a random individual on a random issue can also be expressed as one minus the probability that they agree on that issue. Hence, we can rewrite (1) as

$$a_k = 1 - \frac{1}{Q} \sum_{q=1}^{Q} s_{r(k,q)} \tag{2}$$

The average antagonism agents experience in society can then be obtained by taking the population-weighted average of antagonism (2) across all types:

$$a = \sum_{k=1}^{K} s_k \left(1 - \frac{1}{Q} \sum_{q=1}^{Q} s_{r(k,q)}\right) \tag{3}$$

Expression (3) can be rewritten as an average across individuals instead of across types:

$$CF = \frac{1}{Q} \sum_{q=1}^{Q} \left(1 - \sum_{r(q)=1}^{R} s_{r(q)}^2\right) = \frac{1}{Q} \sum_{q=1}^{Q} \left(\sum_{r(q)=1}^{R} s_{r(q)} \left(1 - s_{r(q)}\right)\right) \tag{4}$$

This is the *cultural fractionalization* index (CF) of Desmet et al. (2017). It is equal to the expected antagonism experienced by a random individual who encounters another random individual and discusses a random cultural issue. Equivalently, it measures the probability that two randomly chosen individuals disagree on a randomly chosen cultural dimension.

Greenberg cultural fractionalization index (CFD)

Rather than measuring whether cultural types k and k' disagree on a cultural dimension, we now take into account how much they disagree. Going back to a previous example, an individual who is "in favor" of abortion would have less disagreement with someone who is "strongly in favor" than with someone who is "strongly against". Instead of using the Hamming distance between cultural vectors, we use the sum of the L1 (Manhattan) distances between the positions on the different cultural dimensions:

$$d\left(v_k, v_{k'}\right) = \sum_{q=1}^{Q} \left| r(k,q) - r(k',q) \right| \tag{5}$$

In that case, the expected antagonism experienced by an individual of type k becomes:

$$a_k = \frac{1}{Q} \sum_{k'=1}^{K} \sum_{q=1}^{Q} \left| r(k,q) - r(k',q) \right| s_{k'} \tag{6}$$

As before, the average antagonism in society is the population-weighted average of antagonism across cultural types:

$$a = \frac{1}{Q} \sum_{k=1}^{K} \sum_{k'=1}^{K} \sum_{q=1}^{Q} \left| r(k,q) - r(k',q) \right| s_{k'} s_k \tag{7}$$

Instead of averaging across cultural types, we can also average across individuals. In that case, (7) becomes

$$CFD = \frac{1}{Q} \sum_{q=1}^{Q} \sum_{r(q)=1}^{R} \sum_{r'(q)=1}^{R} \left| r(q) - r'(q) \right| s_{r(q)} s_{r'(q)} \tag{8}$$

The expression (8) measures the expected cultural distance between two randomly chosen individuals on a randomly chosen cultural dimension. This is similar to Greenberg's B index with the groups defined by the different cultural positions. We therefore refer to it as the *Greenberg cultural fractionalization* index (CFD). Of course, instead of using the distance measure (5), we could also use other distance measures, such as the Euclidean distance.

Cultural polarization index (CP)

So far, we have assumed that antagonism originates exclusively from the alienation individuals feel towards others who have different cultural views. In the general alienation-identification framework of Esteban and Ray (1994), an individual experiences not just alienation towards others with a different view, she also feels identified with people who think like her. Alienation and identification interact, in the sense that the stronger an individual feels identified with her own group of like-minded people, the more alienation towards those with different views translates into antagonism.

Because the cultural vector is multi-dimensional, we need to decide whether we view being like-minded as being of the same cultural type, or whether we define it dimension by dimension. In what follows, we take the latter view. As in Esteban and Ray (1994), identification with the group of like-minded people increases with the size of the group. The degree of identification that an individual with position $r(q)$ feels is given by $s_{r(q)}^{\alpha}$, with $\alpha > 0$. This same individual also experiences alienation towards others with a different view. For now, we assume that the intensity of disagreement does not matter, so the degree of alienation is simply the share of people with whom she disagrees, $(1 - s_{r(q)})$.

As described before, antagonism is then the result of the interaction between alienation and identification. Specifically, for a given cultural dimension q, the antagonism felt by an individual with position $r(q)$ is given by $s_{r(q)}^{\alpha} \times (1 - s_{r(q)})$. Taking the average across all individuals and all cultural dimensions gives the overall antagonism in society:

$$CP = \frac{1}{Q} \sum_{q=1}^{Q} \sum_{r(q)=1}^{R} s_{r(q)}^{1+\alpha} \left(1 - s_{r(q)}\right) \tag{9}$$

This is the *cultural polarization* index in Desmet et al. (2017), which is based on the polarization index in Reynal-Querol (2002).

Cultural polarization with distances index (CPD)

It is straightforward to incorporate the intensity of disagreement into this index of cultural polarization. To do so, suppose the distance between two individuals with positions $r(q)$ and $r'(q)$ along dimension q is given by $|r(q) - r'(q)|$, as in the Greenberg cultural fractionalization index. The degree of identification experienced by an individual with position $r(q)$ on dimension q is still given by $s_{r(q)}^{\alpha}$. In that case, overall antagonism in society can be written as:

$$CPD = \frac{1}{Q} \sum_{q=1}^{Q} \sum_{r(q)=1}^{R} \sum_{r'(q)=1}^{R} s_{r(q)}^{1+\alpha} \left|r(q) - r'(q)\right| s_{r'(q)} \tag{10}$$

We refer to this index as *cultural polarization with distances* (CPD), which is equivalent to index (14) in Duclos et al. (2004). It is to the cultural polarization index (CP) what Greenberg's cultural fractionalization (CFD) is to the standard cultural fractionalization (CF) index.

2.3 Identity heterogeneity

In this subsection we assume the opposite of the previous subsection – cultural views are irrelevant, antagonism depends only on an individual's identity group j. As an example, individuals feel antagonism or disutility towards people of a different ethnic group, but not towards others with different views on abortion. Following the same logic as before, we can derive the equivalent versions of the four indices above.

Ethnolinguistic fractionalization index (ELF)

When an individual interacts with someone of a different identity group, she experiences one unit of alienation. For now, the only thing that matters is whether the other individual belongs to a different identity group, not how different the other identity group is. Identification with the own group plays no role. In that case, the average antagonism experienced by an individual of group j is $a^j = 1 - s^j$. Averaging across all individuals and all groups yields the level of antagonism in society:

$$ELF = \sum_{j=1}^{J} s_j(1 - s_j) = 1 - \sum_{j=1}^{J} (s_j)^2 \tag{11}$$

This is the well-known *ethnolinguistic fractionalization* index (ELF), first proposed by Bruk et al. (1964), and extensively used in the economics literature since Easterly and Levine (1997), Alesina et al. (1999), and Alesina et al. (2003).[1] The ELF index measures the probability that two randomly drawn individuals belong to different identity groups. It is similar to the CF index in (4), with the difference that ELF is measured in one (identity) dimension rather than multiple (cultural) dimensions. In spite of its name, the identity marker that defines groups need not be ethnicity or language, it could also be religious affiliation or any other identity marker.

Greenberg ethnolinguistic fractionalization index ($ELFD$)

Suppose individuals care not just about whether others are of a different identity group, but also how distant the other group is from their own. Denote the distance between identity groups j and j' by $d(j, j')$. For instance, if language is the identity marker, this distance could refer to how far apart languages are in a linguistic tree. If an individual of group j experiences antagonism of $d(j, j')$ when meeting someone from group j', average antagonism in society is:

$$ELFD = \sum_{j=1}^{J} \sum_{j'=1}^{J} d(j, j') s^j s^{j'} \tag{12}$$

We refer to this as the *Greenberg ethnolinguistic fractionalization* index; it measures the expected distance between the identity groups of two randomly drawn individuals.

Ethnolinguistic polarization index (ELP)

Assume that antagonism originates not just from the alienation felt towards other groups, but also from the strength of identification with the own group. The degree of identification experienced by an individual of group j with her

[1] One minus this index is the well-known Herfindahl-Hirschman concentration index.

own group is s_j^{α}, with $\alpha > 0$. The average alienation felt by that same individual towards other groups, $(1 - s_j)$, then interacts with how strongly she identifies with her own group to yield the individual's average antagonism, $s_j^{\alpha} \times (1 - s_j)$. Averaging across all individuals of all groups gives average antagonism in society:

$$ELP = \sum_{j=1}^{J} s_j^{1+\alpha}(1 - s_j) \tag{13}$$

This is the *ethnolinguistic polarization* index (ELP) as defined by Reynal-Querol (2002).

Ethnolinguistic polarization with distances index ($ELPD$)

Consider the same identification-alienation approach as in ELP, but now assume that alienation does not simply depend on the share of people who are from a different group, but on how distant the other groups are. Specifically, the alienation experienced by an individual of group j towards someone from group j' is given by $d(j, j')$. When interacting with the degree of identification with the own group, an individual of group j experiences a degree of antagonism towards someone of group j' of $s_j^{\alpha} \times d(j, j')$. Averaging over all individuals and groups yields a measure of antagonism in society:

$$ELPD = \sum_{j=1}^{J} \sum_{j'=1}^{J} s_j^{1+\alpha} d(j, j') s_{j'} \tag{14}$$

This is the *ethnolinguistic polarization with distances* ($ELPD$), equivalent to index (14) in Duclos et al. (2004).

2.4 The degree of overlap between different dimensions of heterogeneity

Rather than assuming that antagonism originates from alienation towards other cultural types or other identity groups, here we consider that antagonism has to do with how culturally different identity groups are. In other words, an individual does not experience antagonism from interacting with other identity groups if they hold the same cultural values, and neither does she experience antagonism from interacting with other cultural types if they are from the same identity group. Antagonism only arises when there is overlap between identity groups and cultural positions. For instance, individuals feel antagonism towards people of another ethnic group only if they also hold different views on abortion.

In this subsection we focus on the overlap between identity heterogeneity and cultural heterogeneity. Of course, we could in the same way consider the overlap between different dimensions of identity heterogeneity, or between different dimensions of cultural heterogeneity. For instance, we could consider the extent to which ethnicity and religion overlap, or the extent to which people's views on abortion and redistribution coincide. This would lead to the same functional forms for metrics of heterogeneity based on overlap between different individual attributes.

As we will see, there are different approaches to measuring the overlap between different dimensions of heterogeneity. These overlap measures have often been used in the segregation literature (for an overview, see, e.g., Reardon and Firebaugh, 2002). In that context, consider geographic areas or institutions (e.g., neighborhoods, schools, etc.) instead of identity groups, and consider individual characteristics (e.g., race, income, etc.) instead of cultural values. If then the neighborhoods coincide with income levels, or if the schools overlap with race, we would say there is segregation in income or race. In our discussion, we talk about overlap, rather than segregation, but the two terms refer to the same conceptual phenomenon.

2.4.1 *Chi-square and related measures*

χ^2 index

Our first measure of overlap between identity and culture relies on the χ^2 statistic. To understand the intuition behind this statistic, consider different identity groups, and a single cultural issue with different possible positions. Then create a contingency table, with the rows representing the different identity groups and the columns representing the different cultural positions. If culture and identity are unrelated, all the rows of the contingency table should have the same relative frequencies. At the opposite extreme, if each identity group has a different position on the cultural issue, then knowing the identity of an individual gives us perfect information about his cultural position. The χ^2 statistic is a measure of the disproportion in these frequencies, and it can be used as a test of independence in contingency tables. In our context, we do not use the χ^2 measure for the purpose of hypothesis testing, but rather as a measure of the overlap between identity and culture.

Suppose that, for a given cultural dimension q, the alienation experienced by an agent of identity group j and cultural position $r(q)$ depends on comparing the share of individuals in his own group that holds the same position, $s^j_{r(q)}$, and the share of individuals in all of society that holds that position, $s_{r(q)}$. Taking his group as reference point, he experiences alienation if the rest of society has a smaller share of people with his position. Specifically, the antagonism an individual of identity group j and cultural position $r(q)$ experiences is given by:

$$a^j_{r(q)} = \frac{s^j_{r(q)}}{s_{r(q)}} - 1 \tag{15}$$

If the ratio $s^j_{r(q)}/s_{r(q)}$ is smaller than one, (15) is negative, so agents experience negative antagonism. In this case, the proportion that holds his cultural position is higher in society overall than in his own group, so he experiences higher utility from interacting with all individuals than with only individuals of his group.

Averaging across all cultural dimensions, we can write the antagonism experienced by someone of identity group j and cultural type k as:

$$a^j_k = \frac{1}{Q}\sum_{q=1}^{Q}\frac{s^j_{r(k,q)} - s_{r(k,q)}}{s_{r(k,q)}} \tag{16}$$

Averaging across groups j and cultural types k yields average antagonism in society:

$$a = \frac{1}{Q}\sum_{j=1}^{J}\sum_{k=1}^{K}\sum_{q=1}^{Q}\left(\frac{s^j_{r(k,q)} - s_{r(k,q)}}{s_{r(k,q)}}\right)s^j_k s^j \tag{17}$$

Instead of averaging across groups and types, we can equivalently average over individuals. Desmet et al. (2017) show that average antagonism can then be written as the χ^2 statistic:

$$a = \chi^2 = \frac{1}{Q}\sum_{j=1}^{J}\sum_{r(q)=1}^{R}\sum_{q=1}^{Q}\frac{s^j\left(s_{r(q)} - s^j_{r(q)}\right)^2}{s_{r(q)}} \tag{18}$$

where, for each cultural dimension q, the term $\sum_{j=1}^{J}\sum_{r(q)=1}^{R}\frac{s^j\left(s_{r(q)}-s^j_{r(q)}\right)^2}{s_{r(q)}}$ is equal to the well-known $\bar{\chi}^2_q$ statistic divided by total population. This normalization makes it easier to compare societies with different populations. We denote this normalized statistic by χ^2_q. Thus, the χ^2 statistic in (18) is the average χ^2_q over the different cultural dimensions. The stronger the overlap between identity groups and cultural positions, the higher the index.

Indices related to χ^2

Closely related to the χ^2 index is Cramér's V, which, for a given dimension q is defined as $\sqrt{\frac{\chi^2_q}{t}}$, where t is the smaller of $J-1$ and $R-1$ (Cramér, 1946). This normalization ensures that V is between zero and one. This is the index used by Selway (2011b) to study the overlap between ethnicity and religious identity. Also closely related is the index of geographic segregation used by Alesina and Zhuravskaya (2011). It corresponds to our χ^2 measure multiplied by $1/(J-1)$.

Reardon and Firebaugh (2002) discuss the χ^2 index within the family of "measures of association" and justify it by the fact that the ratio $s^j_{r(q)}/s_{r(q)}$ reflects the extent to which group j is overrepresented in cultural position q.

Starting from this ratio, one can consider other variants. For instance, suppose we took a log transformation of this ratio as a measure of the antagonism felt by someone of group j and cultural position $r(q)$. In this case, $a^j_{r(q)} = \log(s^j_{r(q)}/s_{r(q)})$. Aggregating over individuals yields an average antagonism measure equal to the G^2 statistic:

$$a = G^2 = \frac{1}{Q}\sum_{j=1}^{J}\sum_{r(q)=1}^{R}\sum_{q=1}^{Q}\log\left(\frac{s^j_{r(q)}}{s_{r(q)}}\right)s^j_{r(q)}s^j \tag{19}$$

Within the family of measures of association, Reardon and Firebaugh (2002) argue that the index that satisfies certain axioms and properties that best capture the concept of segregation is related to the mutual information index. In our case, the mutual information index measures the reduction in uncertainty about an individual's cultural positions that results from knowing her identity. It can be shown that the χ^2 index is up to an order of approximation equal to the mutual information index (Cover and Thomas, 2006, p. 400).

Identification and χ^2

The antagonism underlying the χ^2 index is due to alienation towards other identity groups with different cultural positions, without the degree of identification playing a role. As with the polarization indices discussed before, we could incorporate identification with the own group as an additional driver of antagonism. When doing so, there are different ways of defining an individual's group. A person could feel identified with her identity group, with the group that shares her cultural positions, or with the group that shares both her identity and her cultural positions. Here, we focus on the first option, so that the degree of identification of an individual from identity group j is $(s^j)^\alpha$. Hence, the antagonism experienced by an individual of identity group j and cultural position $r(q)$ on cultural dimension q is $(s^j)^\alpha(s^j_{r(k,q)} - s_{r(k,q)})/s_{r(k,q)}$. In that case, average antagonism in society is:

$$\chi^2_I = \frac{1}{Q}\sum_{q=1}^{Q}\sum_{j=1}^{J}\sum_{r(q)=1}^{R}\frac{\left(s^j\right)^{1+\alpha}\left(s_{r(q)} - s^j_{r(q)}\right)^2}{s_{r(q)}} \tag{20}$$

Obviously, this variant of the index loses its connection to the χ^2 statistic.

2.4.2 *Diversity decomposition*

An alternative way to measure the overlap between identity and culture is to decompose total cultural heterogeneity into between- and within-group heterogeneity. The share of total cultural heterogeneity that is due to between-group differences can then be interpreted as the degree of overlap between identity and culture. For instance, if each identity group is culturally as heterogeneous as the overall population, then there are no between-group differences and there is no overlap between identity and culture. In contrast, if identity groups are culturally homogeneous but different from each other, then there is complete overlap between identity and culture.

F_{ST} index

This diversity decomposition approach is similar to the one used in the analysis of variance. Here, we discuss the F_{ST} index, which is widely used in population genetics. Within the family of relative diversity indices, Reardon and Firebaugh (2002) refer to a similar index as R, which is also equivalent to the τ_b index in Goodman and Kruskal (1954). We define the F_{ST} index separately for each cultural dimension, and then take the average. For a given cultural dimension q, the overall cultural fractionalization in society is

$$CF_q = \left(1 - \sum_{r(q)=1}^{R} s_{r(q)}^2\right) \tag{21}$$

For each identity group j, we can also define within-group cultural fractionalization on cultural dimension q as

$$CF_q^j = \left(1 - \sum_{r(q)=1}^{R} (s_{r(q)}^j)^2\right) \tag{22}$$

Average within-group cultural fractionalization on cultural dimension q is then

$$CF_q^W = \sum_{j=1}^{J} s^j CF_q^j = \sum_{j=1}^{J} s^j \left(1 - \sum_{r(q)=1}^{R} (s_{r(q)}^j)^2\right) \tag{23}$$

The share of overall cultural fractionalization that is not due to within-group fractionalization on dimension q is:

$$F_{ST_q} = \frac{CF_q - CF_q^W}{CF_q} \tag{24}$$

This corresponds to the share of overall cultural heterogeneity that is due to between-group fractionalization, i.e., Wright's fixation index F_{ST} (Wright, 1949; Nei, 1973). To illustrate the meaning of this index, suppose identity is defined by race (Black, White) and suppose the cultural dimension refers to abortion (in favor, against). If the shares of Blacks and Whites who are in favor are identical, there is no overlap between identity and culture. Knowing someone's identity does not reveal anything about their views on abortion, and

F_{ST_q} would be zero. If, instead, all Blacks are in favor of abortion and all Whites against, or vice versa, then there is complete overlap between identity and culture. Knowing someone's identity is enough to also know their view on abortion, and F_{ST_q} would be one.

Averaging (24) across the different cultural dimensions then gives us the average cultural fixation in society:

$$F_{ST} = \frac{1}{Q} \sum_{q=1}^{Q} \frac{CF_q - CF_q^W}{CF_q} \tag{25}$$

An alternative to averaging the ratios across cultural dimensions would be to separately average the numerators and the denominators in (24), as done in Cavalli-Sforza et al. (1994).

Relative advantages of F_{ST} and χ^2

What are the relative advantages of the F_{ST} and the χ^2 indices as measures of the overlap between culture and identity? As we will see in Section 3, both indices are highly correlated, so from a practical point of view there is little difference between using one or the other. In fact, if for a given cultural dimension there are only two possible positions, both indices coincide. One advantage of the F_{ST} index is its popularity. Another is its ease of interpretation. However, justifying this index within the antagonism framework of Esteban and Ray (1994) is less obvious. One possibility is to assume that the antagonism that an individual of identity group j experiences is decreasing in the ratio of the probability that two random people of her group disagree to the probability that two random people in society as a whole disagree. In other words, assume that the antagonism experienced by someone of group j on cultural dimension q is given by $1 - CF_q^j/CF_q$. If the ratio CF_q^j/CF_q is high, the individual is used to seeing people disagreeing in her own group, and so experiences less antagonism from the disagreement she observes in society overall. Averaging this measure of antagonism $1 - CF_q^j/CF_q$ across individuals gives the F_{ST} index in Eq. (25). What makes this micro-foundation different (and maybe less obvious) compared to other indices is that an individual's antagonism does not come from the tension of interacting with people that hold a different view from her, but rather from observing disagreement in society. More specifically, two individuals from the same group j, with different cultural positions $r(q)$, experience the same alienation.

Another disadvantage is that the F_{ST} index can sometimes produce paradoxical results, as noted in Jost (2008) and Desmet et al. (2017). To illustrate this, suppose there are two identity groups of equal size and one cultural dimension with four possible positions, a, b, c, and d. Consider two societies. In the first society, in one group the frequency vector of the different positions is $\{0.1, 0.9, 0, 0\}$, i.e., 10% of the group has position a and 90% has position b, whereas in the other group the frequency vector is $\{0.9, 0.1, 0, 0\}$. As a result, F_{ST} in the first society is 0.64. In the second society, the two frequency vectors of the two groups are $\{0.5, 0.5, 0, 0\}$ and $\{0, 0, 0.5, 0.5\}$. It seems obvious that in the second society culture and identity overlap more strongly than in the first society, yet in the second society $F_{ST} = 0.33$. The reason for the lower F_{ST} in the second society is the higher degree of within-group heterogeneity. This drives down the share of overall heterogeneity that is due to between-group heterogeneity.

Diversity decomposition with distances

It is straightforward to do a similar diversity decomposition, starting from the Greenberg cultural fractionalization index (CFD), rather than from the standard cultural fractionalization index (CF). For a particular cultural dimension q, we can write CFD_q as:

$$CFD_q = \sum_{r(q)=1}^{R} \sum_{r'(q)=1}^{R} \left| r(q) - r'(q) \right| s_{r(q)} s_{r'(q)} \tag{26}$$

Average within-group Greenberg cultural fractionalization on cultural dimension q is then

$$CFD_q^W = \sum_{j=1}^{J} s^j CFD_q^j \tag{27}$$

The index of between-group differentiation that takes into account distances between cultural positions is referred to as the Φ_{ST_q} index and it is given by:

$$\Phi_{ST_q} = \frac{CFD_q - CFD_q^W}{CFD_q} \tag{28}$$

In population genetics this index is often referred to as the index of genetic differentiation. Averaging across cultural dimensions yields:

$$\Phi_{ST} = \frac{1}{Q} \sum_{q=1}^{Q} \Phi_{ST_q} \tag{29}$$

2.4.3 Cross-cuttingness

Another alternative to measure the overlap between identity and culture is the index of cross-cuttingness used in the political science literature (Rae and Taylor, 1970; Selway, 2011b). Intuitively, when identity and culture cross-cut, belonging to different identity groups is unrelated to holding different cultural views. In that sense, a high degree of cross-cuttingness implies a low level of overlap. Hence, the index of cross-cuttingness should be interpreted as a negative overlap index.

Formally, the cross-cuttingness of a cultural dimension q, denoted by XC_q, is defined as the expected share of a random pair of individuals with both members either being in the same identity group with different cultural positions or being in different identity groups with the same cultural positions. Thus,

$$XC_q = \sum_{r(q)=1}^{R} s_{r(q)}^2 + \sum_{j=1}^{J} \left(s^j\right)^2 - 2 \sum_{r(q)=1}^{R} \sum_{j=1}^{J} \left(s^j s_{r(q)}^j\right)^2 = 2F_q^c - CF_q - ELF \tag{30}$$

where

$$F_q^c = 1 - \sum_{r(q)=1}^{R} \sum_{j=1}^{J} \left(s^j s_{r(q)}^j\right)^2 \tag{31}$$

so F_q^c is fractionalization defined over groups that are defined by both identity and culture. As usual, XC_q can be averaged over cultural dimensions q to yield the overall degree of overlap, XC.

Although this index captures one aspect of the overlap between identity and culture, it is conceptually very different from the χ^2 and F_{ST} indices (see Desmet et al., 2017, for further discussion). The XC index is sensitive to changes in group sizes that are not associated with changes in the degree to which identity is informative about a person's cultural positions. In the empirical work in Desmet et al. (2017) the (negative) correlations between XC and χ^2 and F_{ST} are relatively low, -0.43 and -0.45 respectively, given that these three indices are meant to capture the same underlying phenomenon.

One issue is that the XC index is not so easy to justify using our conceptual framework. A higher degree of cross-cuttingness implies less antagonism because it increases the probability that two random people are either of the same identity group or hold the same cultural beliefs. While this is intuitive, we would also expect less antagonism if two random people are more likely to be both of the same identity group *and* have the same cultural positions. However, the cross-cutting index (30) does not take this second effect into account.

To address this, we now propose a variant of the XC index which emphasizes interactions between individuals rather than the information that knowing someone's identity carries about cultural positions. Start by focusing on a single cultural dimension. Suppose that an individual, when interacting with others, experiences alienation only if the other person is from a different identity group and also holds a different cultural view. Equivalently, an individual does not experience alienation towards others if at least he shares an identity or a cultural position. Thus, the antagonism experienced by someone of identity group j and cultural position $r(q)$ is the share of people who do not belong to group j and do not have cultural position $r(q)$:

$$a^j_{r(q)} = 1 - (s^j + \sum_{j' \neq j} s^{j'} s^{j'}_{r(q)}) \tag{32}$$

Average antagonism in society on cultural dimension q is then:

$$\begin{aligned} CC_q = a_q &= \sum_{j=1}^{J} \sum_{r(q)=1}^{R} s^j s^j_{r(q)} \left(1 - (s^j + \sum_{j' \neq j} s^{j'} s^{j'}_{r(q)})\right) \\ &= 1 - \sum_{j=1}^{J} \sum_{r(q)=1}^{R} \left(s^j\right)^2 s^j_{r(q)} - \sum_{j=1}^{J} \sum_{r(q)=1}^{R} s^j s^j_{r(q)} \left(\sum_{j' \neq j} s^{j'} s^{j'}_{r(q)}\right) \\ &= 1 - \sum_{j=1}^{J} \left(s^j\right)^2 - \sum_{r(q)=1}^{R} \left(s_{r(q)}\right)^2 + \sum_{j=1}^{J} \sum_{r(q)=1}^{R} \left(s^j s^j_{r(q)}\right)^2 \\ &= CF_q + ELF - F^c_q \end{aligned} \tag{33}$$

Note that the antagonism experienced by someone of identity group j with cultural position $r(q)$ can also be written as:

$$a^j_{r(q)} = \sum_{j \neq j'} \sum_{r'(q) \neq r(q)} s^{j'} s^{j'}_{r'(q)} \tag{34}$$

and therefore CC_q can be written as:

$$CC_q = \sum_{j=1}^{J} \sum_{r(q)=1}^{R} \sum_{j \neq j'} \sum_{r'(q) \neq r(q)} s^j s^j_{r(q)} s^{j'} s^{j'}_{r'(q)} \tag{35}$$

Averaging over all cultural dimensions yields the alternative index of cross-cuttingness:

$$CC = \frac{1}{Q} \sum_{q=1}^{Q} CC_q \tag{36}$$

Duclos et al. (2004) propose a similar index, where identity is given by ethnicity and individuals differ in income, rather than in cultural positions.

Identification and cross-cuttingness

So far, we have assumed that antagonism only arises from alienation towards others. As with the other indices, one could add a role for identification with the own group. Here the own group could be defined as either the identity group, the group with the same cultural position, or the group with both the same identity and the same cultural position. Here, we adopt the first alternative: the level of identification of an individual of identity group j is given by $(s^j)^\alpha$. In this case, the level of antagonism experienced by someone of identity group j with cultural position $r(q)$ is given by $\sum_{j \neq j'} \sum_{r'(q) \neq r(q)} (s^j)^\alpha s^{j'} s^{j'}_{r'(q)}$, so that average antagonism on cultural dimension q becomes:

$$CC_q = \sum_{j=1}^{J} \sum_{r(q)=1}^{R} \sum_{j \neq j'} \sum_{r'(q) \neq r(q)} (s^j)^{1+\alpha} s^j_{r(q)} s^{j'} s^{j'}_{r'(q)} \tag{37}$$

If, instead, we assume that identification depends on the size of the group formed by individuals who share both their identity group and their cultural position, we get a slightly different index:

$$\overline{CC}_q = \sum_{j=1}^{J} \sum_{r(q)=1}^{R} \sum_{j \neq j'} \sum_{r'(q) \neq r(q)} (s^j s^j_{r(q)})^{1+\alpha} s^{j'} s^{j'}_{r'(q)} \tag{38}$$

This index (38) is related to the polarization index in equation (17) of Duclos et al. (2004) or the P^2 index in Desmet et al. (2017).

Cross-cuttingness with distances

It is easy to incorporate distances between cultural positions within the cross-cuttingness framework. For a given cultural dimension q, the antagonism experienced by an individual of group j and position $r(q)$ is:

$$a^j_{r(q)} = \sum_{j \neq j'} \sum_{r'(q) \neq r(q)} s^{j'} s^{j'}_{r'(q)} \left| r(q) - r'(q) \right| \tag{39}$$

The equivalent of (35) then becomes:

$$CCD_q = \sum_{j=1}^{J} \sum_{r(q)=1}^{R} \sum_{j \neq j'} \sum_{r'(q) \neq r(q)} s^j s^j_{r(q)} s^{j'} s^{j'}_{r'(q)} \left| r(q) - r'(q) \right| \tag{40}$$

2.5 Further discussion of heterogeneity measures

Antagonism and disutility

The micro-foundations we have presented to justify the different heterogeneity indices are based on the antagonism concept of Esteban and Ray (1994). In our framework, greater heterogeneity leads to more antagonism, and hence to higher disutility. The negative relationship between heterogeneity and utility is a consequence of assuming homophily – people have a preference for associating either with other like-minded people or with their own identity group. However, the concept of heterogeneity need not have a negative connotation. In certain contexts, people might derive positive utility from associating with others who are different from them. In this alternative case of heterophily, we could use the same framework and we could generate the same heterogeneity indices, with the only difference that negative utility (or antagonism) would now be interpreted as positive utility.

The same discussion applies to our overlap measures. In our framework, we have justified indices of overlap by assuming that antagonism between different identity groups only arises if these groups also have different cultural values. Greater overlap between identity and culture leads to more antagonism, and hence to higher disutility. However, having a high degree of overlap need not always be a source of tension. For example, Jha (2013) and Becker and Pascali (2019) focus on the overlap between identity and professional activity, finding that inter-ethnic relations are better if groups specialize in *different* activities. As specialization makes groups interdependent, there is a mutual benefit from interacting. More generally, depending on the context, interacting with individuals and groups that are different may affect utility negatively or positively. This does not change the functional forms of the indices. The issue of whether such indices bear positive or negative relationships with observable political economy outcomes remains an empirical issue.

Alternative micro-foundations of heterogeneity measures

The micro-foundations that we have presented so far assume that interacting with people from different groups affects an individual's utility. One could imagine an alternative setup, where cooperating with people from other groups has costs and benefits in terms of productivity. For example, Lazear (1999) explores this trade-off in the context of global firms. He argues that although workers from different cultures and languages impose coordination and integration costs, there must also be strong enough complementarities between them for global firms to exist. The model in Lazear (1999) is not meant to generate diversity indices, but his insights might be used as an alternative micro-foundation for some of these indices – based on the effect of heterogeneity on productivity rather than utility.

2.6 Cultural evolution

So far, we have taken an individual's positions on different cultural issues as exogenously given. Of course, individuals may sometimes change their views. At a societal level, these changes translate into culture evolving and changing over time. In this subsection we outline a simple model of cultural change, allowing us to illustrate some of its main drivers and implications. In doing so, we follow the model of Desmet and Wacziarg (2021), which builds on previous work by, among others, Boyd and Richerson (1988), Bisin and Verdier (2000), Kuran and Sandholm (2008) and Richerson and Boyd (2008).

Consider a society with two equally-sized identity groups, j and $-j$ (e.g., Blacks and Whites), and one cultural issue with two possible positions, r and

$-r$ (e.g., believe in God and don't believe in God). For now, we continue to assume that individuals cannot choose their identity group. Time is discrete, $t = 1, 2, \ldots$, and each agent has one child. Cultural evolution depends on the vertical transmission of values, the pressure to conform, and the diffusion of cultural innovations. In what follows, we describe these different forces within the context of the framework of Desmet and Wacziarg (2021).

Vertical transmission and innate values

There is imperfect vertical transmission of cultural values between a parent and a child. In particular, only a share of children inherits the value of their parent. The higher the share, the stronger the vertical transmission of values.[2] Although Desmet and Wacziarg (2021) take this share as given, one could endogenize it to capture the purposeful decision by a parent to transmit a particular value to his child as in Bisin and Verdier (2000). The value an agent is born with is her innate value, and it provides a baseline utility to her.

Pressure to conform

One reason people may change their values is the pressure to conform. When an individual socializes within their identity group, they may perceive a benefit from conforming to the group's majority value. One driver of this conformism is that people who frequently interact may have an incentive to coordinate on the same value. Another driver is the cost of standing out. Assume the utility benefit from conforming increases in the share of the own group that holds the majority value, but it is heterogeneous across individuals. That is, some individuals are more conformist than others, and are therefore more prone to adopt their group's majority value. As an example, a Black individual born as a non-believer in God may find it more beneficial to become a believer the larger the share of Black individuals who are believers in God and the stronger his propensity to conform.

The diffusion of cultural innovations

Another reason people may change their values is the tendency to follow cultural innovations or fads. A cultural innovation can be thought of as an existing value that becomes socially more acceptable or fashionable. Some individuals may find it appealing to adopt this value, switching from the non-innovating to the innovating position. Suppose the utility benefit of adopting the innovating value is increasing in the share of the own group that holds this value. As with conformism, the tendency to adopt the innovating value varies across agents (and possibly across groups), as some are more sensitive to fads, fashions and

2 Vertical transmission can be also affected by the degree of cultural similarity between parents. In societies with a lot of assortative mating, the values of the parents can be passed on more strongly to the children. Although important, we do not consider here how heterogeneity within the family may affect the transmission of values, and the resulting social heterogeneity and antagonism experienced by individuals.

social trends than others. In some cases, the diffusion of cultural innovations may turn the minority view into the majority view.

Patterns of cultural evolution

Each period, each individual compares the utility of holding different positions. Based on this utility comparison, he decides whether to keep his current value or to switch to the alternative value. Different types of individuals take different decisions, depending on their innate values, their group's majority value, the innovative value in society, their tendency to conform, and their tendency to imitate cultural innovations. Aggregating these decisions yields laws of motion for the share of the population across different groups holding different values. This simple model generates insights that illuminate some of the patterns that characterize cultural evolution.

A first result relates to how cultural fractionalization and divisions between groups depend on the pressure to conform and on the strength of intergenerational values transmission. With stronger pressure to conform, individuals have a greater incentive to switch to their group's majority value. As a result, the steady-state majority share becomes larger. With stronger intergenerational values transmission, the constraint on how high the majority share can become is weakened. Taken together, higher degrees of conformism and intergenerational transmission reduce within-group cultural fractionalization, CF^W. Whether this also lowers overall fractionalization depends on whether both groups conform to the same majority value. If they do, CF also drops, and there is no increase in between-group differentiation, F_{ST}. If, in contrast, the two groups conform to different majority values, overall fractionalization CF does not go down, and there is growing between-group differentiation F_{ST}.

As an illustration, consider Democrats and Republicans in the US, two groups that hold different majority values. As argued by Desmet and Wacziarg (2021), the emergence of new interaction technologies, such as social media, has made it easier for everyone to seek out people of their own group. Being less exposed to members of the other group would then translate into a higher pressure to conform to their own group's majority view. This would result in an increase in F_{ST}, and could help explain growing partisan polarization in the U.S.

A second result relates to the impact of cultural innovations on cultural fractionalization. Suppose both groups start off holding the same majority value, with innovation affecting the minority value. If people have a strong propensity to adopt innovations, fads diffuse easily and eventually take over, becoming the new majority norm. As the original consensus breaks down, there is initially growing disagreement. However, as the old majority norm gets increasingly replaced by a new majority norm, agreement between individuals once again increases. This translates into a hump-shaped transition path for cultural fractionalization.

As an illustration, consider people's views on the legality of marijuana use. As shown by Desmet and Wacziarg (2021), in the early 1990s, there was a strong consensus that it should be illegal, with 83% of the U.S. population subscribing to this view according to the General Social Survey (GSS). Since then, the consensus has shifted, and by 2018 only 35% was still in favor of keeping marijuana use illegal. During this transition path, CF followed a hump-shaped path.

2.7 Endogenous identity

In the same way that people have a choice about the cultural values they hold, they may sometimes also be able to choose their identity. In fact, the model of Desmet and Wacziarg (2021) presented above contemplates this possibility. Consider an individual born with the minority value of her identity group. In addition to holding on to her group's minority value or adopting her group's majority value, Desmet and Wacziarg (2021) introduce a third option: she can switch identity groups. For example, a liberal Republican might prefer to become a Democrat, rather than either suffering the cost of being in the minority or succumbing to the pressure of becoming conservative. Of course, if identity were defined by less malleable traits, such as race, then the option of changing identity groups may not be available, or could be more costly.

The choice of identity builds on work by Akerlof and Kranton (2000) who introduced identity into the utility function. In their setup, the utility an individual derives from their identity depends on the status of the group they belong to (e.g., "man" or "woman") and on how well their behavior matches their group's prescriptions (e.g., how well a man's behavior subscribes to that of an "ideal man"). To endogenize identity choice, Shayo (2009, 2020) considers a situation where each individual belongs to different social groups, but they each identify with only one of them. The utility of identifying with a particular group depends on its social status and on the individual's perceived distance from the group. For example, compare two residents of Catalonia: a Catalan speaker and a Spanish speaker. They can choose to identify with either their region (Catalonia) or their nation (Spain). If Catalonia were poor and had low status, both may prefer to identify with Spain. If, instead, Catalonia had similar income levels to Spain, then the Catalan speaker may identify with Catalonia and the Spanish speaker with Spain, because of the lower perceived distances to, respectively, the region and the country.

3 The global landscape of diversity

In this section, we draw on the indices derived in Section 2 to describe the global landscape of social heterogeneity. Most of our focus is on cross-country comparisons, but we also provide some examples of within-country variation, and of the evolution of diversity through time. Beyond the descriptive goal of characterizing the extent of diversity across the globe along a range of dimensions – ethnicity, language, cultural values, etc. – we also make some general points. First, we show that the major indices of diversity are only imperfectly correlated with each other. Hence, in empirical applications it matters which dimensions of heterogeneity are considered, and which functional forms are employed. Second, across countries, measures of ethnic or linguistic diversity are essentially uncorrelated with measures of diversity in attitudes, norms and values. It can therefore be expected that these various measures bear different relationships with different socio-economic outcomes of interest to social scientists, such as public goods provision, civil conflict, redistribution, and economic performance: ethnolinguistic diversity cannot simply be taken as a proxy for heterogeneity in cultural values. Third, the reason that identity-based diversity is uncorrelated with values-based diversity is that an overwhelming share of the variation in cultural values occurs within groups: there is very little overlap between ethnicity and culture. The surprising and widespread extent of within-group cultural heterogeneity serves as a cautionary tale for those who would too readily, through stereotypes or prejudice, systematically ascribe certain views and attitudes to specific identity groups.

3.1 The landscape of identity heterogeneity

In this subsection, we calculate and discuss some of the main indices of heterogeneity that are based on specific identity markers. These include the standard ethnolinguistic fractionalization index (ELF), Greenberg's ethnolinguistic fractionalization index ($ELFD$), and the ethnolinguistic polarization index (ELP).

Ethnolinguistic fractionalization (ELF)

The ethnolinguistic fractionalization index (ELF), given by Eq. (11), measures the probability that two randomly drawn individuals belong to different identity groups. Recall the microfoundations of this index: the antagonism an individual feels towards another individual is one if they belong to different identity groups, and zero if they belong to the same group. The ELF index can then be interpreted as the expected antagonism between two randomly drawn individuals. Since what matters is whether the two individuals belong to the same identity group or not, the ELF index ignores the distance between groups (this is equivalent to assuming that the distance between any two groups is one).

Two key characteristics of the ELF index are worth noting. First, for a given number of identity groups, the index reaches its maximum when all groups are of the same size. Second, if all identity groups are of equal size, then a society with a larger number of groups has a higher ELF index. Together, this implies that fractionalization tends to be high in a society composed of many small identity groups (ELF is maximized when each individual belongs to a different group).

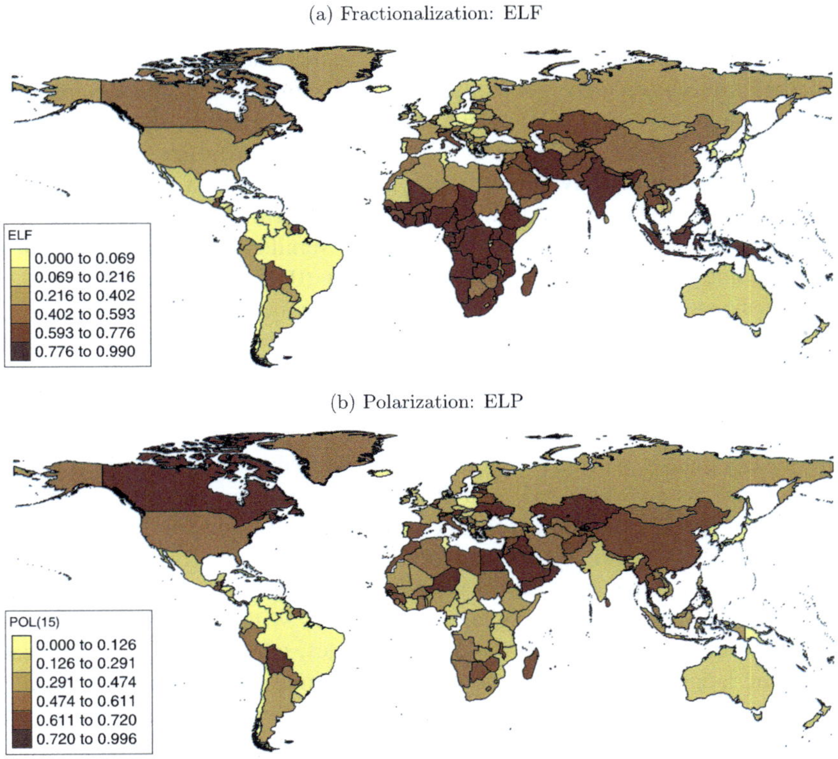

FIGURE 1 Different heterogeneity measures.
Note: Panel (a) depicts the ethnolinguistic fractionalization index (ELF) and (b) the ethnolinguistic polarization index (ELP). Source of underlying data: Desmet et al. (2009).

Fig. 1 (a) depicts the ELF index across the world for the case where identity is defined by language. The data on languages come from the 15th edition of the Ethnologue project (Ethnologue, 2005), which provides information on the number of speakers and the geographic distribution of almost 7000 languages around the world. The country with the highest ELF is Papua New Guinea, with more than 800 language groups, all of them small. The region in the world with the highest average level of ELF is Sub-Saharan Africa. In fact, almost all of the top-20 countries are in that region, with India being a notable exception. These countries tend to have many languages, with none of them dominating. The region with the lowest level of ELF is South America and the Caribbean.[3]

[3] Common sources for the linguistic composition of countries in Latin America and the Caribbean, such as Ethnologue (2005) or the Geo-Referencing of Ethnic Groups dataset (Weidmann et al., 2010) often fail to identify separate ethnic groups if those groups do not speak a separate language, and the wide prevalence of Spanish and Portuguese in these countries results in low levels of measured linguistic diversity in this region irrespective of the source for the data.

The examples above focus on linguistic fractionalization. Of course, the ELF index can also be used to measure ethnic fractionalization, religious fractionalization, or more generally, fractionalization of any identity marker. One relevant question is how ethnic, linguistic, and religious fractionalization relate to each other. Alesina et al. (2003) construct measures of these three indices, using country-level information from the Britannica (2000) and other sources. They find a relatively high correlation between linguistic and ethnic fractionalization (0.70, p-value 0.00), and a significantly lower correlation between linguistic and religious fractionalization (0.25, p-value 0.00).

Consistent with this, Desmet et al. (2025) document that in many parts of the world ethnicity coincides with language. They come to this conclusion by comparing the Geo-Referencing of Ethnic Groups (GREG) dataset (Weidmann et al., 2010), to the Ethnologue dataset.[4] For Africa, there is a one-to-one mapping between ethnic groups and languages. For the rest of the world, the GREG dataset typically identifies each nationality with one ethnic group (e.g., Germans in Germany), and it only distinguishes between subgroups when they speak a different language, such as the Basques in Spain. Desmet et al. (2025) also compare data on language and religion, by relying on the Joshua Project (https://joshuaproject.net/) which identifies, for all peoples in all countries, their primary language and religion. Within countries, people of the same religion often speak multiple languages, whereas people who speak the same language almost always practice the same religion. In other words, religious groups are linguistically heterogeneous, whereas language groups are religiously homogeneous. This is consistent with linguistic fractionalization and religious fractionalization having a relatively low correlation. It also implies that language groups are more cohesive than religious groups, making it more likely for language to define group identity. To reinforce this point, Desmet et al. (2025) show that of the hundreds of subnational regions around the globe that have active secessionist movements, very few have a distinct religion without also having a distinct language: Zanzibar (Tanzania), Northern Ireland (United Kingdom) and Bangsamoro (Philippines). Many other examples, where religion may be a driver of secessionism, also have linguistic differences. Examples include Chechnya (Russia), Tibet (China), and Punjab (India).

Ethnolinguistic polarization (ELP)

The standard ethnolinguistic polarization index is given by Eq. (13). Here we follow Reynal-Querol (2002) and set $\alpha = 1$, so

$$ELP = \sum_{j=1}^{J} s_j^2 (1 - s_j). \tag{41}$$

[4] The GREG dataset is based on the *Atlas Narodov Mira* (Bruk et al., 1964).

As explained in the theory section, alienation towards other groups interacts with identification with the own group to give rise to antagonism. Specifically, an individual of group j feels an alienation of 1 towards someone from another group, and an alienation of 0 towards people of his own group. At the same time, he experiences a level of identification s_j^α with his own group. The two forces interact, so that the antagonism an individual of group j feels towards someone of another group is $s_j^\alpha \times 1$. The idea is that an individual's antagonism gets amplified if he identifies more strongly with his own group, which happens when the size of his group is larger. Taking the average antagonism between all individuals then yields Eq. (41). Similar to the ELF index, the ethnolinguistic polarization index (ELP) does not take into account distances between groups. This is equivalent to saying that it considers the distance between any two groups to be equal to one.

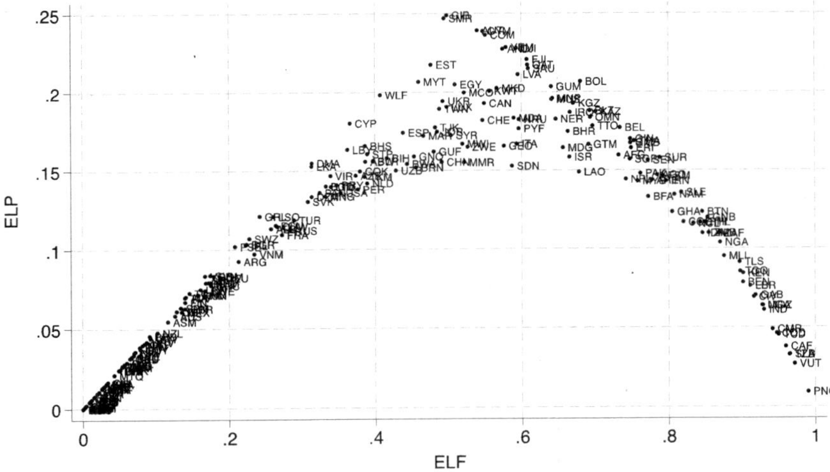

FIGURE 2 Ethnolinguistic fractionalization (ELF) and polarization (ELP).
Figure depicts the ethnolinguistic fractionalization index (ELF) and the ethnolinguistic polarization index (ELP), based on 224 countries. Source of data: Desmet et al. (2009).

In contrast to the ELF index, which reaches its maximum when each individual belongs to a different group, the ELP index reaches its peak when there are two groups of equal size. When focusing on languages as identity marker, Fig. 2 shows that there is a clear hump-shaped relationship between fractionalization and polarization. Countries with low levels of linguistic fractionalization tend to have low levels of linguistic polarization, but the same is true for countries with high levels of linguistic fractionalization. As mentioned before, Papua New Guinea is linguistically the most fractionalized country in the world, because it is made up of hundreds of groups. However, this large number of small groups also results in a low level of polarization. In contrast, Estonia, dominated by two major language groups – Estonian-speaking and Russian-speaking – exhibits one of the highest levels of polarization despite its moderate level of fractionalization. Using data on 225 countries, the correlation between ELP and ELF is 0.56.

Aggregation of groups

An important question when measuring heterogeneity is how to define identity groups. Consider the example of linguistic groups in Mexico. Using information from the *Encyclopedia Britannica*, Alesina et al. (2003) identify 37 language groups in Mexico. In contrast, using information from the Ethnologue project, Desmet et al. (2009) identify 291 language groups in the same country. At first sight, having more detailed data would seem to be preferable to less detailed data. However, of the 291 languages in Mexico according to the Ethnologue, more than 50 are different variants of Mixtec. Hence, to avoid overestimating the degree of heterogeneity, it might be sensible to aggregate these variants into one common Mixtec group.

The approach of aggregating related language variants into a single group raises another critical question: when should two languages be combined into the same group? For instance, should Ligurian and Lombard, two variants of Italian, be grouped together? And what about Italian and French, both Romance languages, or Italian and German, both Indo-European languages? Before answering these questions, we need a formal methodology for aggregating languages. Desmet et al. (2012) propose using a linguistic tree to define groups at varying levels of aggregation. To illustrate their methodology, Fig. 3 displays the linguistic tree of the main languages spoken in Pakistan. At the most disaggregated level, there are seven main languages: Panjabi, Pashto, Sindhi, Seraiki, Urdu, Balochi, and Brahui. Going up the tree, the number of groups declines, as the level of aggregation rises. For instance, at level 3, three linguistic groups are left: Iranian, Indo-Aryan, and Northern Dravidian, whereas at level one, we are left with the two main language families: Dravidian (Brahui) and Indo-European (all others).

This way of aggregating languages is referred to as a phylogenetic approach, because a linguistic tree describes the family structure of world languages. Coarse linguistic divisions, at high levels of aggregation, describe divisions that go back thousands of years. For example, the division between Indo-European and all others is estimated to have occurred almost 9000 years ago. In contrast, finer linguistic divisions, obtained at low levels of aggregation, originated more recently. For example, the division between different variants of Modern Greek is estimated to have happened less than 1000 years ago.

We now illustrate how to compute the ethnolinguistic fractionalization (ELF) measure at different levels of aggregation. Fig. 4 depicts a hypothetical language tree. Each of the seven leaves at level 2 represents a living language. The three nodes at level 1 represent the (extinguished) mother languages of the existing languages. The node at level 0 represents the common ancestor

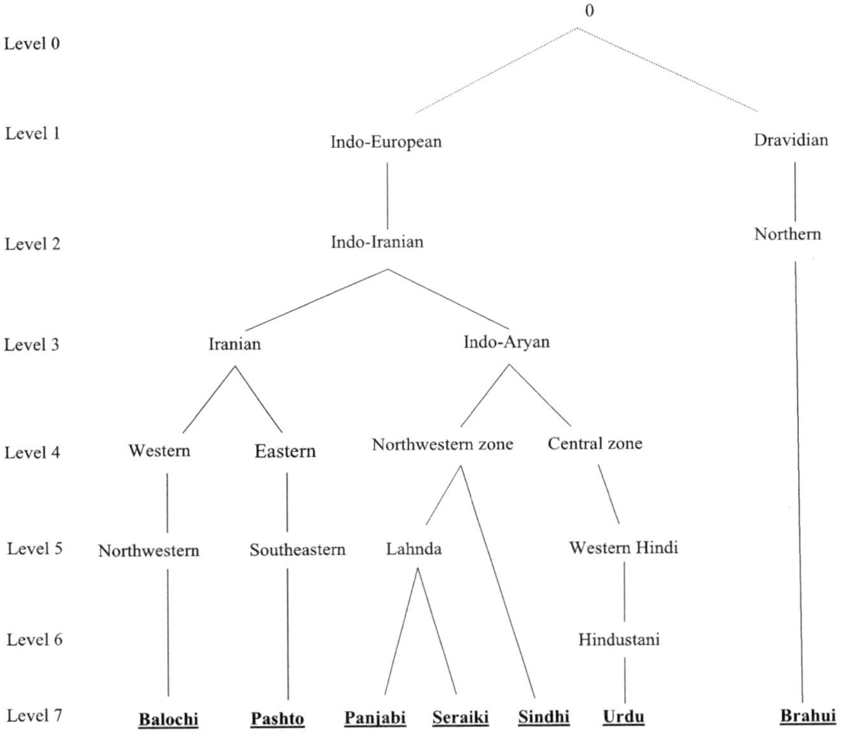

FIGURE 3 Linguistic tree of the main languages spoken in Pakistan.
Source: Desmet et al. (2012).

language of the three mother languages. The number below each living language at level 2 indicates the population shares of the corresponding languages. At level 2, the ELF index, taking the seven living languages as different groups, yields $ELF(2) = 1 - 3 \times (0.2^2) - 4 \times (0.1^2) = 0.84$. At level 1, the seven living languages are aggregated into 3 distinct groups A, B, and C, resulting in $ELF(1) = 1 - 0.4^2 - 2 \times (0.3^2) = 0.66$. In our empirical applications we use the linguistic tree of the Ethnologue which has 15 levels. Hence, for each society, we can define the ELF index at 15 different levels of aggregation, where level 15 refers to the most disaggregated level (e.g., all the variants of Mixtec would be considered separate groups) and level 1 refers to the most aggregated level (e.g., Indo-European versus other major language families). By analogy we can compute the ethnolinguistic polarization (ELP) index at different levels of aggregation too. Of course, this approach is not limited to languages. Gomes (2013) uses a relatedness tree of religions to measure religious fractionalization at different levels of aggregation.

Fig. 5 shows a world map of ethnolinguistic fractionalization, where language groups are measured at the highest level of aggregation. At this

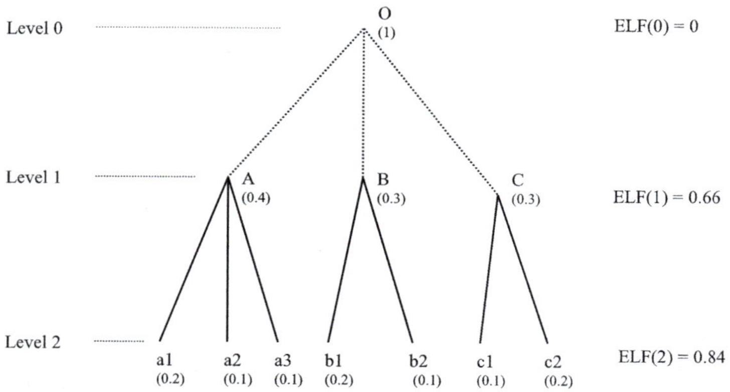

FIGURE 4 Hypothetical linguistic tree.
Source: Desmet et al. (2012).

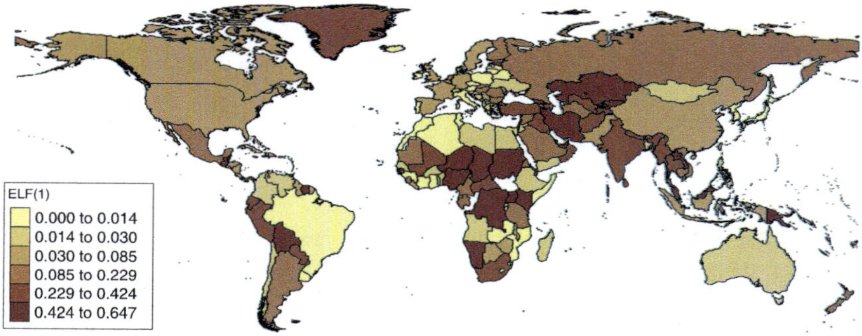

FIGURE 5 ELF at highest level of aggregation.
Note: Figure depicts the ethnolinguistic fractionalization index (ELF) at the highest level of linguistic aggregation, i.e., at the level where groups are defined at the level of language families (Indo-European, Afro-Asiatic, Niger-Congo,..). Source of underlying data: Desmet et al. (2012).

level groups are defined by broad language families (Indo-European, Afro-Asiatic, Niger-Congo,...). As can be seen by comparing with Panel (a) of Fig. 1, aggregating languages into broad families changes the ranking of some countries dramatically. For instance, when considering the almost 50 languages in Zambia as separate groups, the country ranks in the top 10% of most diverse countries. However, almost 80% of these languages are of the Niger-Congo family, and 99.5% of the population speaks a language belonging to that family. As a result, when aggregating languages at the level of these broad families, Zambia drops from the top decile to the bottom quartile in terms of ethnolinguistic fractionalization. The case of Zambia is not an exception in Sub-Saharan Africa, where many countries appear relatively more homogeneous when only differentiating between the large language families. In the Sahel, the situation is different: aggregating has little effect on the ranking. For example, in

Chad, there are around 135 languages, making the country very heterogeneous when measuring ELF without aggregating languages. However, in contrast to Zambia, one-third of the population speaks an Afro-Asiatic language, one-third a Nilo-Saharan language, and one-third a Niger-Congo language. As a result, Chad continues to be one of the linguistically most heterogeneous countries, even when grouping languages into broad families. Using data on 225 countries, the correlation between ethnolinguistic fractionalization based on the most disaggregated definition of languages, $ELF(15)$, and the one based on the most aggregated definition of languages, $ELF(1)$, is 0.53. This is slightly lower than the correlation between ELF and ELP which stands at 0.56.

So far, we have not addressed the maybe most important question: at what level of aggregation should we measure ELF or ELP? If we are interested in deep cleavages that go back many millennia, then focusing on $ELF(1)$ or $ELF(2)$ would be reasonable. If, instead, we are interested in all cleavages, including shallow ones that are more recent, then focusing on $ELF(15)$ would be more preferable. Naturally, the appropriate level of coarseness depends on the political economy outcome we are attempting to explain. As we argue in Section 4 of this chapter, heterogeneity measures based on coarse divisions are more predictive of civil conflict, whereas heterogeneity measures based on fine divisions are more predictive of economic growth.

Distance between groups

Going back to our example of Mexico, another way of dealing with the 50 different variants of Mixtec is to take into account the distances between languages when measuring heterogeneity. Before discussing how this changes the standard indices of diversity, we describe the different ways of defining distances between languages.

One method for defining distances between languages is to rely on lexicostatistical studies. As an example, Dyen et al. (1992) compute the share of cognates – words that have an unbroken descent from a common ancestor – for each pair of 95 Indo-European languages, using a list of 200 words. Based on these data, Ginsburgh et al. (2005) define the distance between languages j and k, denoted by τ_{jk}, as one minus the share of cognates between j and k. One drawback is that Dyen et al. (1992) only cover Indo-European languages.[5] Another method for defining distances between languages is to rely on a linguistic tree diagram, similar to the one depicted in Fig. 3. For example,

5 A more recent method uses the Levenshtein distance to measure the proximity in the phonetic pronunciation of words in different languages (see, for instance, Petroni and Serva, 2010). This method allows for a more continuous measure of linguistic distance for all languages, not just those of the Indo-European group. The different methodologies for assessing distances between languages are discussed in Ginsburgh and Weber (2016).

Fearon (2003) defines the distance between languages j and k as:

$$\tau_{jk} = 1 - (\frac{\ell_{jk}}{\ell^{max}})^{\delta} \tag{42}$$

where ℓ_{jk} is the number of shared branches between j and k, ℓ^{max} is the maximum number of branches between any two languages, and δ is a parameter that determines how fast the distance declines as the number of shared branches increases. This same approach is also used by Desmet et al. (2009), who use data from the Ethnologue project, which provides a tree for the almost 7000 languages in its database.

When measuring linguistic distances in (42), an important question relates to the value of δ, which determines how rapidly the distance between two languages increases as the number of shared branches decreases. For instance, compare Japanese and English, which share zero branches, to German and French, which share one branch, as both are Indo-European languages. If we use $\delta = 0.5$, as in Fearon (2003), the distance between German and French would be 0.74, while the distance between Japanese and English would be 1. In contrast, if we use $\delta = 0.05$, as in Desmet et al. (2009), the distance between German and French would be only 0.13, whereas the distance between Japanese and English would still be 1. Essentially, a low value of δ implies relatively small distances as long as languages share at least one branch.

Similarly to the question about the appropriate level of linguistic aggregation, one can ask what a good value of δ might be. As we discuss in Section 4.3, Desmet et al. (2009) let the data determine the optimal value. Specifically, they investigate how linguistic diversity affects redistribution. When incorporating linguistic distances in their measure of diversity, they find that a value of $\delta = 0.05$ best explains this relationship. This suggests that redistribution is negatively affected by linguistic diversity, especially when languages belong to completely different families – a point we explore in more detail in Section 4.3.

Greenberg's ethnolinguistic fractionalization index (ELFD)

The Greenberg ethnolinguistic fractionalization index ($ELFD$), given by (12), generalizes the ELF index by incorporating linguistic distances between languages. It measures the expected distance between two randomly chosen individuals. If the antagonism an individual feels towards another individual is equal to the distance between them, then this index measures the average antagonism between two random individuals. In what way might we view this index as a generalization of the ELF index? If we were to take a binary distance metric, i.e., if $\tau_{jj} = 0$ and $\tau_{jk} = 1$ for $j \neq k$, then the $ELFD$ index simplifies to the ELF index. In other words, the ELF index can be interpreted as the expected distance between two random individuals when the distance metric is binary.

Naturally, Greenberg's ethnolinguistic fractionalization index no longer has the characteristic that diversity is maximized when all groups are of equal size. For instance, starting from an equal distribution of population across groups, moving some people from a group that is relatively close to the rest of society to a group that is relatively distant may increase heterogeneity as measured by the $ELFD$ index.

When measuring diversity, we discussed two ways of accounting for the fact that some languages are more closely related than others. We either aggregate related languages into the same group, or we incorporate distances into our measure of heterogeneity, as in Greenberg's ethnolinguistic fractionalization index. With the former approach, we need to decide the level of aggregation. Do we group only close variants of the same language, or do we aggregate at a higher level? With the latter approach, we get around this decision by assigning distances between languages. Although an advantage, it also blurs the concept of what constitutes a group. Indeed, because the $ELFD$ index captures the expected distance between two individuals, there is a less clear notion of group identification. In some contexts, the notion of a group may not be crucial, but in other situations, it is essential. For example, conflict often occurs between well-defined groups. Hence, if we aim to understand the relationship between heterogeneity and conflict, it may be desirable to base our diversity measure on a clear group structure.

That said, depending on the value of δ when measuring the $ELFD$ index, and depending on the value of aggregation when measuring the ELF index, the two approaches may be comparable. As an example, consider the case of $\delta = 0.05$. As already mentioned, with such a low value of δ, distances between different languages will be relatively small as long as they share at least one branch. In other words, distances only become large when two languages belong to entirely different families, say, the Indo-European and the Afro-Asiatic families. This is not unlike aggregating languages up to the level of language families, in which case the distances between a pair of languages are one if they belong to different families and zero otherwise. Hence, we would expect the $ELFD$ index with $\delta = 0.05$ to be similar to the $ELF(1)$ index. This is indeed the case: the correlation between the two indices is 0.99.[6]

3.2 The landscape of cultural heterogeneity

3.2.1 Data on values, norms, and attitudes

While the first approach used by social scientists relied on metrics based on predefined identity traits, as discussed in Section 3.1, more recently scholars have tried to capture social heterogeneity by directly considering traits representing individuals' norms, values, and attitudes. The first approach

6 It is straightforward, using the same data, to also compute ethnolinguistic polarization with distances ($ELPD$), as defined in 2.3.

relied on demographic or economic data on race, ethnicity, religious affiliation, urbanicity, gender, etc., but the more recent approach starts from survey data on stated values and cultural traits. The latter data had previously been used to study specific cultural traits such as religiosity, trust, life satisfaction, or attitudes toward immigrants, among many others. More recently, social scientists have started using them to capture cultural heterogeneity, by looking at within-society variation in stated preferences. Examples of such approaches include Desmet et al. (2017) and Desmet and Wacziarg (2021), which we discuss in greater detail below.

An advantage of relying on measures of heterogeneity based on surveys of values, norms, and attitudes is that they capture dimensions of beliefs that are directly relevant for some specific types of socio-economic outcomes of interest. For instance, when it comes to politics, it stands to reason that differences in beliefs about public policies would be directly connected to voting behavior. The importance of heterogeneity in values relative to other measures of social heterogeneity, as determinants of political, social, and economic outcomes, is ultimately an empirical issue. We explore this issue in Section 4. But the *prima facie* case for such measures mattering is straightforward based on the fact that they are designed to capture disagreement on the big social and economic issues of the day. Such is the case for the main surveys used in this context, such as the World Values Survey (WVS), the Global Preference Survey (GPS) or the Gallup World Poll – for cross-national purposes – or the General Social Survey (GSS) and the American National Election Studies (ANES) – in the U.S. context. Measures of heterogeneity based on identity traits, in contrast, have often been developed and used as mere *proxies* for heterogeneity in values and beliefs. As we document below, however, the two concepts are rather different, and the correlation between heterogeneity based on values and heterogeneity based on identity is weak at best.

Despite their advantage, values-based measures of heterogeneity are not without drawbacks. A particular drawback concerns measurement error: respondents may not report their "true" values to surveyors. Such misreporting of underlying beliefs could stem from inattention, low stakes in answering truthfully, or a more deliberate process of obfuscation, such as preference falsification (Kuran, 1987). Such biases could be systematically related to characteristics of societies where the surveys are conducted. For instance, respondents may be reluctant to criticize governmental authorities in autocracies, or may not be willing to deviate from majority religious beliefs in deeply religious societies. Other drawbacks of survey-based measures of values heterogeneity are more commonly discussed drawbacks of survey data: the choice of questions to ask is arbitrary and dependent on the goals of those designing the survey, the precise wording of questions can have a large influence on responses, the context of the survey may introduce bias in answers, etc. Some, but not all of these drawbacks can be addressed using careful research designs.

Some of these concerns have spurred efforts to validate stated preferences with either revealed preferences or actual behavior elicited in experimental settings. On the one hand, Obradovich et al. (2022) query Facebook's Marketing API to collect for 225 countries and territories the share of users interested in 60,000 different topics. They use these data to compute cross-country differences in preferences. Cuevas et al. (2021) use a similar approach to measure the gender gap in preferences. In contrast to surveys, Facebook interests yield a bottom-up revealed measure of preferences, covering whatever users find interesting, rather than what social scientists deem important. On the other hand, the Global Preference Survey (Falk et al., 2018) uses experimental validation of questions on "time preference, risk preference, positive and negative reciprocity, altruism, and trust from 80,000 people in 76 countries." (p. 1645). Experimental validation, however, is costly and experimentally validated survey answers are typically available only for a small set of questions, rather than for the expansive question sets available in more commonly used surveys, such as the WVS and the GSS.

3.2.2 *Cultural fractionalization across countries*

Based on our work in Desmet et al. (2017), we now discuss measures of cultural fractionalization. The underlying data are from the Integrated World Values Survey – European Values Survey, for five survey waves between 1981 and 2008, covering 76 countries. We focus on survey questions that the WVS itself categorizes as questions on norms, values, and attitudes, and that are given a category label (family, politics and society, religion and morals, etc.). These exclude questions on the socio-demographic characteristics of the respondents (race, gender, age, etc.). The questions on cultural values are either binary, ordered on a scale, or multinomial but unordered. We consider a set of 808 questions asked in all countries, with an average number of questions per country of 294, and an average number of respondents per country-question of 1,497. To ensure a relatively comparable set of questions across countries, we further restrict attention to questions that are asked in at least 50 countries. For the resulting set of questions, we compute CF_q for each question and then average these across all questions to obtain the overall index of cultural fractionalization, CF. We also compute cultural fractionalization with distances (CFD) and cultural polarization (CP), as in Section 2.2.

Table 1 displays correlations between measures of cultural heterogeneity and measures of ethnolinguistic diversity discussed in Section 3.1, while Fig. 6 displays CF on a world map. Several lessons emerge. First, there is only a weak correlation between cultural fractionalization and ethnolinguistic fractionalization. For instance, the correlation between ELF (computed using self-reported ethnicity and language data in the WVS) and CF is −0.03. In other words, the two measures are not correlated at all. This is surprising in light of the fact that ethnolinguistic fractionalization had often been used, in the past literature, as a proxy for the level of disagreement on social and

TABLE 1 Correlations of cultural measures with ethnolinguistic measures.

	$ELF^{(a)}$	$ELF^{(b)}$	$ELF^{(c)}$	$ELFD$	$ELFP$	CF	CFD
$ELF^{(b)}$	0.6513	1					
	(75)	(76)					
$ELF^{(c)}$	0.8239	0.6765	1				
	(195)	(74)	(224)				
$ELFD$	0.4463	0.4130	0.6054	1			
	(195)	(74)	(224)	(224)			
$ELFP$	0.3337	0.3256	0.5570	0.4382	1		
	(195)	(74)	(224)	(224)	(224)		
CF	0.0119	−0.0303	−0.1759	−0.0164	−0.2293	1	
	(75)	(76)	(74)	(74)	(74)	(76)	
CFD	0.0352	0.0488	−0.1508	0.0125	−0.2180	0.8098	1
	(75)	(76)	(74)	(74)	(74)	(76)	(76)
CP	0.0263	0.0042	−0.1572	0.0335	−0.2493	0.8224	0.8028
	(75)	(76)	(74)	(74)	(74)	(76)	(76)

Note: This table displays pairwise correlations between the main measures of ethnolinguistic heterogeneity discussed in Section 3.1 and the main measures of cultural heterogeneity discussed in the present section. We include three measures of ethnolinguistic diversity: (a) refers to the measure of linguistic fractionalization from Alesina et al. (2003); (b) is the measure of ethnolinguistic fractionalization among WVS respondents, from Desmet et al. (2017); (c) is the measure of linguistic fractionalization from Desmet et al. (2009). In the rest of the table, $ELFD$ is the Greenberg index and $ELFP$ refers to ethnolinguistic polarization, both from Desmet et al. (2009). The last three rows display correlations with cultural fractionalization (CF), cultural fractionalization with distances (CFD) and cultural polarization (CP), from Desmet et al. (2017). The number of countries is in parentheses.

political issues. It is not. The pattern is the same when ELF is measured using the ethnolinguistic classification in Alesina et al. (2003) or the linguistic classification in Desmet et al. (2009). Second, similarly low correlations are found between ethnolinguistic diversity and other measures of cultural diversity, CFD and CP. Third, different measures of cultural diversity (CF, CFD or CP) are correlated at about 80% with each other – so they capture related but not identical concepts of diversity, and it matters potentially which one is used as a determinant of political economy outcomes.

Interesting lessons also emerge from Fig. 6. There is substantial variation in CF around the world. Regions with high levels of cultural heterogeneity include most industrial democracies, as well as India (Desmet et al., 2017). Those with low levels of heterogeneity include countries in North Africa and the Middle East, as well as China. Muslim-majority countries and autocracies tend to have lower levels of CF. China, for instance, stands in stark contrast with India.

There are several interpretations for these patterns. There could be bias in respondents answering the surveys truthfully in societies with strict religious, moral or political codes, where deviating from such codes can be personally costly. Autocracy might be more sustainable in societies with more homogeneous cultural values, whereas democracy as a system of government might be more necessary to resolve disagreements peacefully in contexts with high levels of social disagreement. Finally, some of these correlations may reflect causality running from democracy or per capita income to the level of cultural fractionalization. Modernization theories, for instance, imply that pluralism should increase as societies develop and become more tolerant of alternative viewpoints, norms, and lifestyles. These observations suggest interesting directions for future research, but it is not our goal here to address them in greater detail.

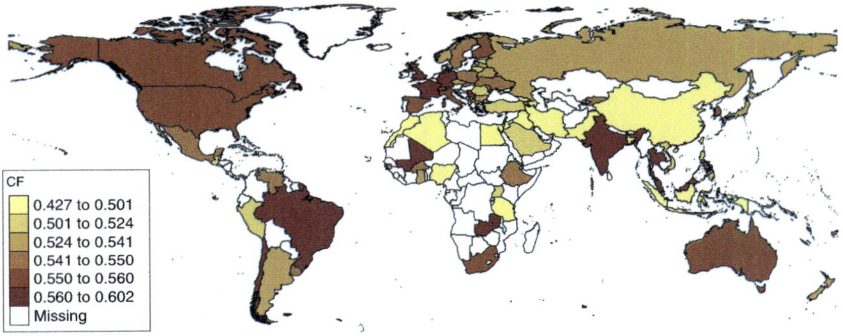

FIGURE 6 Map of CF around the world.
Note: This Figure is a map of CF around the world, using data for 76 countries. Source of underlying data: Desmet et al. (2017).

3.2.3 *Cultural fractionalization over time in the United States*

While the above discussion focused on the cross-country context, measures of cultural heterogeneity based on survey data can also be used to study the evolution of cultural diversity within countries, by using surveys that ask the same questions at different points in time. Desmet and Wacziarg (2021) follow such an approach for the United States. This paper uses data from the General Social Survey (GSS), from 1972 to 2018, to characterize the evolution of CF through time. The data consist of 32 waves of the GSS, but the data are aggregated into 2-wave sets in order to increase the number of available questions. The survey questions that are retained are those that pertain to norms, attitudes, and values, and that are asked at least once in each 2-wave set. This results in 76 questions on cultural norms that are used to compute CF. Fig. 7 displays this variable over time. It reveals a U-shaped pattern whereby CF was high in the early 1970s, at the time of the Vietnam War and Watergate, and then gradually declined to reach a minimum in the early 1990s. It then started to rise again to roughly match its value at the beginning of the sample period.

Averaging CF over 76 questions masks interesting variation across questions. Only about 12% of the questions display significantly U-shaped dynamics, while 25% show a monotonically increasing CF and 29% display a monotonically decreasing CF. Different question types display different patterns. For

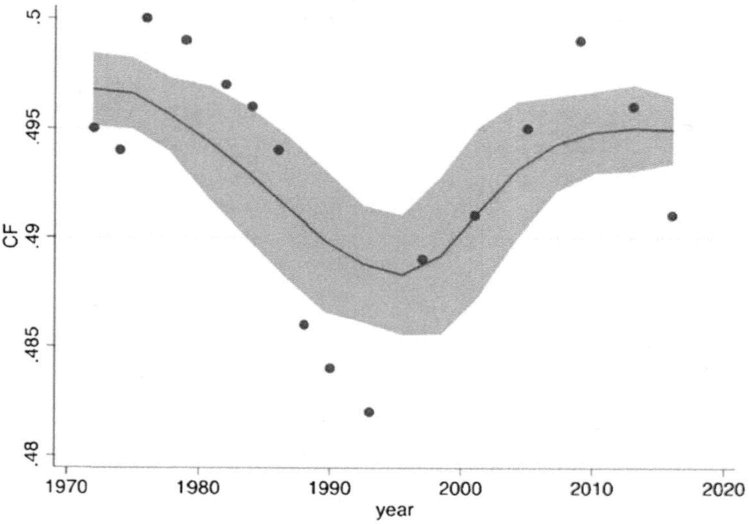

FIGURE 7 CF in the United States, 1972–2018.
Note: Cultural fractionalization (CF), 1972–2018. Source: Desmet and Wacziarg (2021). This graph represents overall cultural fractionalization in the U.S., as measured by the probability that two random respondents answer a random question of the GSS differently. The dots denote the actual numbers, the curve represents a nonlinear approximation, and the shaded area the 95 percent confidence interval.

instance, questions on free speech and personal freedoms, including gun ownership, are the subject of declining disagreements, whereas questions on abortion and church attendance display increasing diversity. The latter changes may reflect the rising – but still minority – share of respondents who profess to have no religion. Questions on confidence in government or government spending priorities have CF values that have barely changed over time.

3.3 The landscape of overlap between multiple dimensions of heterogeneity

A recent literature explores measures of overlap (or cross-cuttingness) between different dimensions of heterogeneity. Examples of such measures include segregation metrics, capturing the overlap between spatial location and ethnic identity (Alesina and Zhuravskaya, 2011); metrics of ethnic inequality, capturing the overlap between income levels and ethnic identity (Alesina et al., 2016b); measures of the overlap between religion and ethnicity (Selway, 2011a); and measures of the overlap between cultural values and ethnic identity (Desmet et al., 2017). The general idea behind these measures is that while a single dimension of heterogeneity may have uncertain effects on political economy outcomes, when the degree of overlap between two dimensions is high (that is, when their degree of cross-cuttingness is low, so that the cleavages reinforce each other, in the terminology of Rae and Taylor, 1970), social effects might be more significant. For instance, while religious cleavages and ethnic cleavages alone may not be conducive to civil conflict, when they overlap with each other, so that members of a given religious group also tend to be members of a given ethnic group, social heterogeneity may lead to conflict. The measures themselves have varying functional forms depending on the specific topic under investigation, but usually take forms similar to the main measures of overlap that we microfounded in Section 2.4.

3.3.1 Overlap measures across countries

A salient example of overlap measures are the χ^2 and F_{ST} indices developed in Desmet et al. (2017) and discussed here, from a conceptual perspective, in Section 2.4. When applied to culture and ethnicity, these measures capture the extent of between-ethnic-group variation in cultural values: if χ^2 or F_{ST} take on high values, there is a lot of cultural variation between groups relative to variation within groups. In this case, knowing one's ethnic group is informative for knowing one's cultural values. An equivalent way to describe these characteristics is that cultural and ethnic cleavages are overlapping, or reinforcing.

Following Desmet et al. (2017), the data we use here to calculate these measures are the same as those used to measure CF in Section 3.2, with the same sample and selection of cultural values questions. Additionally, we used self-reported language and ethnicity to capture ethnic cleavages, i.e. we use the classification that served as the basis for computing $ELF^{(a)}$ in Table 1. Indeed, to calculate χ^2 and F_{ST}, one needs to have information on both a person's ethnicity and on their cultural values – a feature that is sometimes available in survey data on cultural attitudes, norms, and values, such as the GSS and the WVS. Using these data, we compute χ^2 and F_{ST} at the country level for a cross-section of 76 countries.

In what follows, we focus on F_{ST}. In practice, χ^2 and F_{ST} are very highly correlated (98%), so it matters little which one we use empirically, despite the differences in these indices' theoretical properties discussed in Section 2.4. Here we choose to focus on F_{ST} because it is more intuitive to interpret: it ranges from 0 to 1 and represents the share of the total variation in culture that occurs between ethnic groups. A high value indicates that culture overlaps more strongly with ethnic identity, while a low value indicates that there is a high degree of within-group variation in culture, relative to the total variation.

The mean of F_{ST} across countries is 0.012. That is, on average, only a little more than 1% of the variation in culture occurs between groups. This is a surprisingly small number. Most variation in culture occurs within ethnic groups. This contrasts with the results that would be obtained if all the WVS data were stacked across all countries, and the groups were defined by the respondent's country of residence rather than ethnicity. In that case, we find a value for F_{ST} equal to 7.4%. Thus, ethnicity is less informative of the within-country variance in culture than country of residence is informative of the global variance in culture. The fact that most cultural variation occurs within ethnic groups explains the surprising lack of correlation, documented in 3.2, between cultural fractionalization (CF) and ethnic fractionalization (ELF). This correlation would be much higher if ethnicity were more predictive of culture or, equivalently, if a higher degree of cultural heterogeneity occurred between ethnic groups.

This discussion of average values, however, masks interesting variation across countries. Fig. 8 shows a map of F_{ST}. Regions with higher degrees of overlap between ethnicity and culture include many parts of Asia as well as Sub-Saharan Africa, while countries in Western Europe as well as the U.S. and Australia display smaller values. In general, countries farther away from the Equator have smaller values of F_{ST}. There is also a clear negative relationship between per capita income and F_{ST}: culture and ethnicity are more divorced from each other in richer, modern societies, while F_{ST} is higher in poorer societies, more "primordial" societies. Strikingly, the country with the highest value of F_{ST} is India (5.88%) and the country with the lowest value is Japan (0.1%).[7]

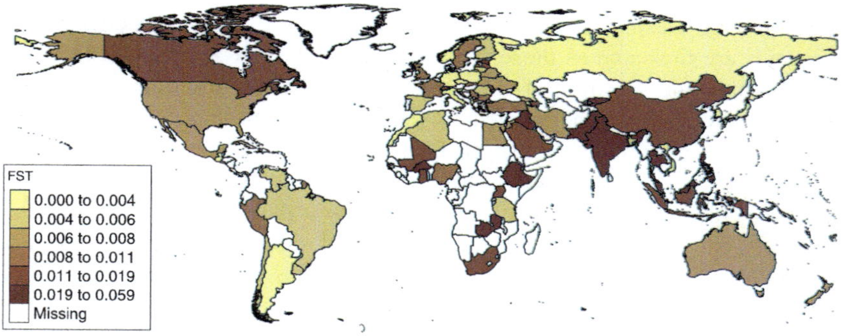

FIGURE 8 Map of F_{ST} around the world.
Note: This Figure is a map of F_{ST} around the world, using data for 76 countries. Source of underlying data: Desmet et al. (2017).

Table 2 displays correlations between various measures of heterogeneity, including overlap measures. A few observations are in order. First, there is a positive correlation between F_{ST} and ELF. Indeed, without ethnic heterogeneity, there can be no between-group cultural variation. For instance, in our sample, South Korea and Italy display no ethnic diversity, so their F_{ST} is zero. Conversely, India is very ethnically diverse, so there is a lot of scope for overlap between ethnicity and culture. However, this is not a tight relationship: some countries are ethnically very diverse yet have low levels of F_{ST}, as illustrated by the fact that the correlation between F_{ST} and $ELF^{(b)}$

7 We exclude from this comparison Italy and South Korea, because in the WVS these have a level of ethnic heterogeneity equal to zero.

TABLE 2 Correlations between ELF, CF, F_{ST} and Φ_{ST}.

	$ELF^{(b)}$	CF	F_{ST}
CF	−0.0303	1	
F_{ST}	0.6198	0.1787	1
Φ_{ST}	0.6278	0.1852	0.9976

Note: This table displays correlations between various measures of ethnic heterogeneity, cultural heterogeneity, and overlap between ethnicity and culture. $ELF^{(b)}$ is the measure of ethnolinguistic fractionalization among WVS respondents. All the variables are from Desmet et al. (2017), and the sample consists of 76 countries.

stands at 0.62. Second, the association between F_{ST} and CF, while positive, is quite weak. Third, it matters little whether we consider an index that takes into consideration distances between answers (Φ_{ST}) or not (F_{ST}), as the two are extremely highly correlated. This is perhaps a result of the fact that many WVS questions on culture are binary, and that a relatively small share involve answers arrayed on a scale, where there is a natural metric of distance between answers.

The broad variation in the degree of overlap between culture and ethnicity is not specific to these particular traits. Indeed, Alesina and Zhuravskaya (2011) report a high degree of heterogeneity across countries in the extent of ethnic spatial segregation (a measure of the overlap between ethnic identity and location), Alesina et al. (2016b) report a high degree of heterogeneity in ethnic inequality (a measure of the overlap between income levels and ethnic identity), and Selway (2011b) shows that the degree of overlap between religion and ethnicity varies significantly across countries. These authors further show that these various measures of overlap are predictive of political economy outcomes across countries, as we discuss in Section 4.

While the application here used data from the WVS, it is possible to conduct the same exercise with other surveys. For instance, Desmet et al. (2017) report some results using the Afrobarometer and Latinobarómetro. The results are consistent with those obtained from the WVS: in both datasets, the ability of ethnic identity to predict cultural values is very small, as only about 1% of the variation in culture occurs between ethnic groups. As in the WVS, the degree of overlap between ethnicity and culture was relatively high in Sub-Saharan African countries, and rather small in Latin American countries.

3.3.2 Cultural divides over time in the United States

The existence of surveys of cultural values that ask the same questions across survey waves opens up the possibility of looking at the evolution of overlap measures through time. Moreover, there is no reason to limit the analysis to the overlap between culture and ethnicity: it is possible to look at other dimensions of identity, to study whether they are predictive of culture. These two goals are pursued in Desmet and Wacziarg (2021), in the context of the United States. This paper uses data from the already mentioned 32 waves of the GSS (see Section 3.2), and calculates F_{ST} over time to measure cultural divides along a wide range of identity traits. Indeed, the share of between-group variation in culture is a measure of how culturally differentiated these groups are, so it can be used as a measure of cultural divides between groups defined by specific cleavages. Desmet and Wacziarg (2021) consider six such cleavages, namely family income (by quintile), gender, political party identification, religion, race and urbanicity.[8]

The first lesson to emerge from this exercise is a confirmation that between-group variation usually takes on very small values, so that, once again, an overwhelming share of the variation in cultural values occurs within groups, regardless of the type of cleavage. Stereotypes that attribute certain cultural values to certain groups are sometimes directionally correct, but almost always incorrect in terms of magnitudes, because cultural traits are always very weakly predicted by identity traits. To illustrate this statement, Table 3 displays the value of F_{ST} across the six cleavages under consideration. For readability, we show the data for a selected number of two-wave groupings at a seven- or eight-year interval.[9] Across all waves, the average value of F_{ST} varies between 0.6% for gender and 2.1% for religion. These numbers are quite small, but they vary across cleavage: by far the smallest cultural divide is between genders, and the biggest one is between religious groups. Party identification and family income also display relatively high divides, while race and urbanicity take on values of 1.1% – quite in line with what prevails between ethnic groups on average across countries.

In addition to variation across cleavages, cultural divides also vary through time in interesting ways. Such time variation can be gleaned from Table 3, but is more easily seen in Fig. 9. There we can see that some cleavages display stable cultural divides: race and family income. Others display falling divides: urbanicity and gender (although, for the latter, from a very low base). Finally, party identification and religion display sharply increasing divides, in line with the frequently heard observation about a culture war between the main political parties in the United States. Desmet and Wacziarg (2021) also show that the evolution of these divides through time depends, not only on the cleavages under consideration, but also on the specific cultural trait under consideration. For instance, views on free speech have been the subject of falling divides across

8 For each cleavage, there is a varying number of groups. For instance, gender admits two groups (male / female) while party identification admits seven categories (strong Democrat, Democrat, Democratic-leaning independent, independent, Republican-leaning independent, Republican, and strong Republican). Across all six cleavages, the median number of groups is five.

9 The entire data appears as Table 1 in Desmet and Wacziarg (2021).

various groups, however defined, while views on homosexual relationships are more divisive between groups now that a substantial proportion of the population has become more accepting of gay lifestyle and gay marriage.

TABLE 3 Cultural divides by time period and cleavage (selected two-wave groupings, 1972–2018 waves).

Time period	Family income	Gender	Party ID	Race	Religion	Urbanicity
1972	0.020	0.006	0.016	0.012	0.024	0.015
1979	0.018	0.006	0.011	0.010	0.022	0.013
1986	0.020	0.007	0.012	0.015	0.018	0.011
1993	0.015	0.006	0.011	0.009	0.018	0.009
2001	0.017	0.007	0.013	0.011	0.021	0.008
2009	0.019	0.006	0.018	0.012	0.024	0.009
2016	0.016	0.005	0.023	0.013	0.026	0.008
Average	0.018	0.006	0.014	0.011	0.021	0.011

Note: Time period refers to two-wave groupings. For instance, 1972 refers to pooled data over the 1972 and 1973 waves of the GSS. Cultural divides are measured by F_{ST}. The average value shown on the last line is computed across all available two-wave groupings, not only those displayed.

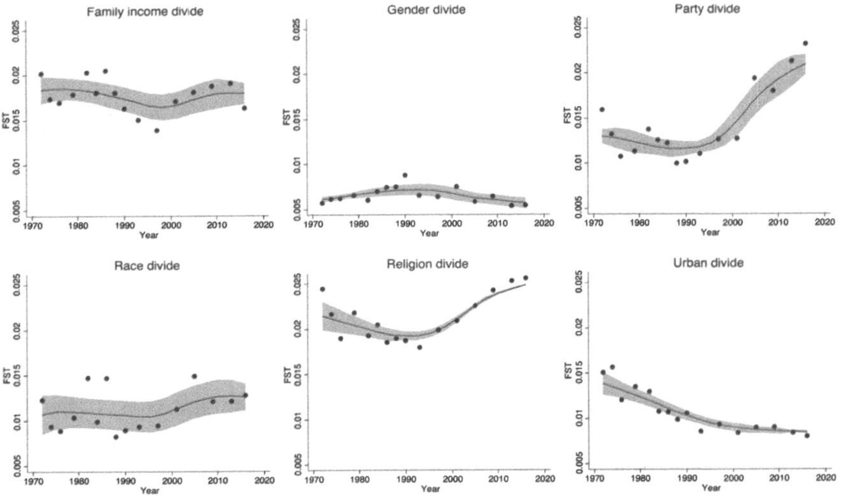

FIGURE 9 F_{ST} in the United States, 1972–2018, for Six Identity Traits.
Note: This figure displays the time path of F_{ST} in the United States for six identity traits, between 1972 and 2018. Source: Desmet and Wacziarg (2021). The dots denote the actual numbers, the curve represents a nonlinear approximation, and the shaded area the 95 percent confidence interval.

It is interesting to ponder the reasons for these contrasting dynamics. Desmet and Wacziarg (2021) propose a model of cultural change, that we already outlined in Section 2.6. In this model, an individual's cultural traits result from three forces: intergenerational transmission from their parents; conformism to the views of the majority of their group; and susceptibility to minority innovations that may gradually diffuse through society despite being initially espoused by a small minority. The model also allows individuals to switch groups (sorting) rather than to change their cultural values. Desmet and Wacziarg (2021) then derive the dynamic paths of cultural traits as a function of various model parameters, in particular parameters that describe the strength of intergenerational transmission, the degree of susceptibility to influence from the majority, the degree of susceptibility to cultural innovations, and the ease of sorting across groups.

The model offers a lens through which observed cultural dynamics can be interpreted: conformism is stronger when within-group interactions are made easier. Hence, the introduction of a technology that facilitates intra-group contact could lead to deeper divides if the dominant cultural traits of each group are different. For instance, the internet allowed persons of particular political proclivities to more easily seek out and interact with people with similar views. Sorting across political parties is also easier than sorting across, say, races, which can serve to enhance the dynamics of growing divides across political lines. Such divides can also arise from the diffusion of cultural innovations, such as the acceptance of gay lifestyles, that spreads unevenly between different groups. For instance, acceptance of gay lifestyles spreads more rapidly among more secular individuals than among the more religious, contributing to the increase in the cultural divide between religious groups, as the number of those professing having "no religion" has increased. Desmet and Wacziarg (2021) elaborate on these and other examples of cultural evolution having implications for changes in cultural divides across specific identity cleavages and cultural traits.

3.4 The origins of diversity

We conclude this section by briefly discussing a recent literature that examines the determinants of diversity. As discussed above, there is wide variation in social heterogeneity – however measured – across the globe. This variation is not the result of randomness. In recent years, a growing literature has studied the origins of such diversity. Below we contrast deeply-rooted origins with factors that operate at shorter horizons.

In a seminal paper, Ashraf and Galor (2013b) start from the fact that the degree of genetic diversity in human populations, as measured by expected heterozygosity, declines as one moves away in space from the location of the origin of Homo Sapiens in East Africa. Indeed, the country with the highest degree of genetic diversity in the world is Ethiopia, and the country with the smallest level is Bolivia. This is because of the serial founder effect: as populations migrated away from the origin of humanity, each successive wave of migrants carried less and less of the genetic diversity of previous migrants. Populations that descend from those who migrated a long time ago (such as the Ethiopians, who are located at the origin) are therefore more diverse than those who arrived much more recently (such as the indigenous populations of the Americas, who are thought to be descended from a relatively small number of founding individuals).

In turn, genetic diversity is positively associated with other forms of diversity, such as ethnic and linguistic diversity (Ashraf and Galor, 2013a). It is indeed the case, for instance, that Sub-Saharan Africa, as noted earlier, is one of the most ethnically diverse regions in the world – and this anecdote has broader validity across countries. Genetic diversity is not only correlated positively with ethnic diversity, but also with cultural traits. For instance, in recent work, Galor et al. (2023) show that proximity to East Africa, in other words genetic diversity, is strongly correlated with the diversity of cultural motifs observed in Berezkin's *Folklore and Mythology Catalogue* (Berezkin, 2023): places with more genetic diversity have more diversity in cultural traits, as measured by folklore motifs.

While the serial founder effect and the pattern of prehistoric human migration have explanatory power for current diversity, it is obviously not the only factor. Geography also matters. A series of recent papers has documented the lasting effects of geographic features on diversity and on cultural traits. These would be too numerous to comprehensively survey here. A salient example is Michalopoulos (2012), a paper that documents the fact that locations with more geographic variability (heterogeneous land quality and elevations) tend to have a higher degree of linguistic diversity. The argument is that differences in geographic endowments led to cultural differentiation as different populations adapted to and took advantage of distinct ecological "niches". Another example looking at variability through time rather than through space is Giuliano and Nunn (2021), a paper documenting that greater climatic variability is associated with lower cultural persistence through time. This has implications for cultural diversity as locations with more climatic variability can be expected to have more diversity, since cultural traits can change more rapidly in such locations.

While prehistoric migratory patterns and persistent geographic characteristics are a deeply rooted and increasingly well-established determinant of premodern levels of cultural diversity, they are by no means the only determinant. To begin with, the discovery of the New World, and the colonial era that followed, scrambled the distribution of world populations through mass migrations – either forced (as in the case of the slave trade) or more voluntary (as in the case of the migration of 60 million Europeans to the New World during the Age of Mass Migrations between 1850 and 1920). This made some regions of the world, such as the Americas, or Oceania, vastly more diverse than they previously were (Nunn and Qian, 2010). Beyond the complex process of cultural change brought about by migration, long-run cultural evolution also led to changes in the distribution of cultural traits in all human societies, with consequent implications for diversity. Evolutionary forces such as selection of certain cultural traits based on the degree of fitness that they confer also led to cultural change. This is the subject of a vast literature that was pioneered by evolutionary anthropologists Robert Boyd and Peter J. Richerson (see for instance Boyd and Richerson, 1988), and carried forward by Joseph Henrich (see for instance Henrich, 2016). In the more recent past, higher frequency changes have occurred through more rapid horizontal transmission across populations, brought about by the ease of communication and travel over great distances. Some of the forces of cultural change that we discussed in Section 2, when reviewing Desmet and Wacziarg (2021), are of this nature: they operate on a rapid timescale, and often lead to widespread cultural change across vast swaths of the world, with consequent implications for cultural heterogeneity.

The various factors that give rise to social diversity operate to different degrees and at different time scales on different traits. Phenotypic traits like skin color are likely the most closely linked to deeply rooted factors, as they are biologically transmitted across generations. Language, while culturally transmitted, is nonetheless mostly transmitted vertically between generations, and therefore also evolves slowly, so linguistic diversity is likely to still display the effects of deeply-rooted traits, as illustrated by the aforementioned paper by Michalopoulos (2012). Religious values, and more generally cultural values, attitudes, and norms, are more susceptible to large changes at short horizons, because they are not only vertically transmitted, but also comparatively more susceptible to horizontal or oblique transmission.

While the discussion above is by nature incapable of doing justice to the now-vast literature on the endogenous determination of culture, ethnicity, and language, it hopefully serves to give a sense of the broad scope of the recent scholarship on the distribution of identity and culture across the globe.

4 The political economy of social heterogeneity

So far, we have discussed some theoretical foundations for the measurement of social heterogeneity, and, based on the resulting indices applied to data on a wide range of traits, we have provided some descriptive information on the global landscape of diversity. Ultimately, of course, social scientists care about the measurement of social heterogeneity because of its potential to account for political, social, and economic outcomes. This is the subject of this section. We survey the literature on the effects of social heterogeneity on outcomes such as growth, redistribution, conflict, and secessionism. This literature is vast, so our goal is not to be comprehensive, but to provide a general sense of the main strands of the literature, and to cover salient themes that have emerged from the study of the effects of diversity. Since this chapter is on measurement, we pay particular attention to measurement issues, providing multiple examples where measurement choices condition the inferences that can be drawn from data concerning the effects of social heterogeneity.

We begin with the cross-national literature. Country-level assessments of diversity are the context in which most of the measures described earlier in this chapter were developed. However, the now enormous literature on the effects of social heterogeneity greatly transcends the cross-national context. In recent years, scholars have devoted considerable efforts to understanding the effects of diversity at a subnational or regional level.[10] At the end of this section, we turn to this more granular approach. There, we provide a sense of the main categories of studies on the effects of diversity within regions or countries, and highlight the relevance of careful measurement in such contexts.

4.1 Ethnolinguistic cleavages and political economy outcomes

One of the earliest studies in economics using a measure of ethnolinguistic fractionalization is Paolo Mauro's study of the effects of corruption on investment and growth (Mauro, 1995), where ELF (calculated with data on ethnic group shares from the *Atlas Narodov Mira*) is used as an instrument for subjective measures of corruption. While the exclusion restriction employed in this paper would nowadays be the subject of many questions, the paper can be credited for spurring a big literature focused on the direct effects of ELF on a variety of political economy outcomes.

One of the first major references in this tradition is Easterly and Levine (1997), where the same measure of diversity is argued to account for a significant portion of Africa's growth shortfall over the 1960–1990 period.[11] In this study, a high value of ELF is also associated with a wide range of negative outcomes in terms of the quality of government policies, partly explaining its deleterious effect on economic growth. Alesina et al. (2003) expand this approach in three ways: first, they consider a broader set of political economy outcomes, including redistribution and civil conflict; second, they examine the effect of linguistic, ethnic, and religious diversity separately; third, they consider both measures of fractionalization and of polarization. The paper reaches broadly similar conclusions as those of Easterly and Levine (1997): there is a generally negative, though not always statistically significant, correlation between various measures of diversity and the quality of government, economic growth, and redistribution; and a generally positive correlation with civil conflict. Finally, a pair of important papers by Marta Reynal-Querol and

[10] There is also a large literature at an even more micro level, studying the effects of diversity within groups, teams, and organizations. This can take the form of observational studies or experimental studies. Salient references include Lazear (1999), Hong and Page (2001), Habyarimana et al. (2009), and more recently Corno et al. (2022), among numerous others. The literature on the effects of diversity at the team, firm, or organizational levels is assessed and surveyed in, for instance, Page (2017) and Bertrand and Duflo (2017). However, this literature, while important and highly relevant to our understanding of the effects of diversity, does not rely on measures of social heterogeneity, the focus of this chapter, so we do not dwell on it here.

[11] Earlier references on the relationship between linguistic diversity and development include Fishman (1966) and Pool (1972). For an overview see Nettle (2000).

José Montalvo (Reynal-Querol, 2002; Montalvo and Reynal-Querol, 2005b) focus more closely on ethnic polarization, which is maximized when two equally-sized groups are at loggerheads, finding that polarization measures are stronger predictors of civil conflict than fractionalization measures. This finding highlights the importance of choosing the correct functional form to capture the relevant dimension of ethnic heterogeneity.[12]

These early contributions and the large literature that accompanied them are the subject of a widely-cited literature review by Alesina and La Ferrara (2005). In a broad survey of the cross-national and within-country literature on ethnic diversity and economic performance, this paper concludes that diversity entails both costs and benefits, and that the net effect may depend on third variables, such as income levels or the quality of institutions. A fair read of the literature on ethnolinguistic fractionalization, up to this point, is indeed that the average effect of ethnolinguistic fractionalization on economic performance is negative, but that countries with higher incomes and better institutions, like the United States, can escape this broad pattern and turn diversity into a strength. Another lesson is that measurement matters – both in the sense of functional forms, and in the sense of the dimension of heterogeneity being captured (whether ethnic, linguistic or religious). In the subsections that follow, we offer detailed examples of the importance of careful measurement in the scholarship on the political economy effects of social heterogeneity.

While the bulk of the literature on ethnic divisions is now over twenty years old, work on this topic has continued apace more recently. This is not surprising, given the continued salience of issues surrounding diversity and identity in recent years. Among the more recent contributions, we would be remiss if we did not mention closely related work examining the effects of genetic diversity. As mentioned earlier, genetic diversity is strongly correlated with ethnic diversity (Ashraf and Galor, 2013a). However, unlike ethnic fractionalization or polarization, genetic diversity is measured, not from group-level frequencies, but from individual-level data.

A salient reference in this tradition is Ashraf and Galor (2013b). In this paper, the authors find that genetic diversity (i.e. migratory distance from Addis Ababa) bears a non-monotonic relationship with the level of pre-modern economic development, measured by population density in 1500. The same non-monotonic relationship holds for contemporary economic development (measured by per capita income), when adjusting for ancestry (i.e. correcting for post-Columbian population movements). The authors extensively document

---

[12] This insight is further refined and enriched in Esteban et al. (2012), who show theoretically that polarization should be a more appropriate predictor of conflict when such conflict is over public goods (and group cohesion is high), while fractionalization should be more predictive of conflict when such conflict is over private goods (and group cohesion is low). Empirically they find that both ethnic polarization and fractionalization are predictive of conflict, suggesting that a mix of disagreements over public and private goods prevails in many cases of conflict observed across countries, and that in such cases group cohesion is likely to be high.

the fact that genetically very diverse and very homogeneous populations were historically poorer and remain so, while societies at intermediate levels of genetic diversity (heterozygosity) tend to be the most developed. They interpret these facts, much like in the survey by Alesina and La Ferrara (2005), as resulting from a trade-off: diversity brings benefits in terms of problem solving, innovation and creativity, lifting economic performance; but it also introduces antagonism between individuals, resulting in lack of coordination and possibly conflict, with deleterious effects on development.[13]

4.2 Linguistic classifications, conflict, and growth

The early literature used an arbitrary definition of linguistic and ethnic groups. However, the level of ethnolinguistic diversity depends on how finely or coarsely groups are defined. In Section 3, we discussed Zambia, a country with almost 50 languages. If each of these languages is treated as a distinct group, Zambia ranks in the top decile of the world's most diverse countries. However, since almost all these languages belong to the Niger-Congo family, Zambia appears ethnolinguistically much more homogeneous when diversity is measured at the level of broad linguistic families. This raises the question of the appropriate level of aggregation for measuring diversity. Desmet et al. (2012, 2016) suggest that the optimal level may vary, depending on the political economy outcome being examined. To investigate this issue, they compare the predictive power of different diversity indices at different levels of aggregation for civil conflict, redistribution, economic growth, and public goods provision. Below we briefly describe their findings for conflict and growth.

Civil conflict: deep cleavages

To determine how finely or coarsely ethnolinguistic groups should be defined when analyzing the impact of diversity on civil conflict, Desmet et al. (2012) adopt the same specification as the seminal study by Fearon and Laitin (2003) on the determinants of conflict. The only modification is the substitution of ELF and ELP indices at different levels of aggregation for the diversity measure used in Fearon and Laitin (2003). Table 4 reports the results for three levels of aggregation (1, 6, and 15).

The key finding is that the effect of ethnolinguistic diversity on conflict onset falls monotonically as the level of aggregation decreases. This pattern holds for both ethnolinguistic fractionalization (ELF) and ethnolinguistic polarization (ELP). In fact, it is only at the highest level of aggregation, where groups are defined at the level of broad linguistic families, that the coefficients on linguistic ELF and ELP are positive and statistically significant. The magnitude of the

13 A very recent contribution by Cesur and Yıldırım (2024) uses the data from Ashraf and Galor (2013b) to look at the effects of genetic diversity on subjective well-being. They find strong negative effects of genetic diversity on various measures of subjective well-being, with no evidence of a hump-shaped profile.

effect is considerable: a one standard deviation increase in $ELF(1)$ is associated with a rise in the probability of conflict of 13% of the variable's mean (the mean probability of civil war onset is 1.67%).

This finding suggests that the "us" versus "them" divide in civil conflicts is especially relevant when the warring parties are separated by deep historical cleavages. Only then does ethnolinguistic diversity seem to have a direct impact on the probability of civil war. In other words, the willingness to go to war, rather than to settle disputes peacefully, is greater when cleavages go back thousands of years.

Economic growth: shallow cleavages

As mentioned earlier, Easterly and Levine (1997) argued that ethnolinguistic diversity contributed to Africa's growth tragedy. These cross-country results were later confirmed and extended by Alesina et al. (2003). To examine the impact of linguistic cleavages at various levels of aggregation on economic growth, Desmet et al. (2012) use a specification derived from an augmented Solow model. Table 5 reports the results. In contrast to civil conflict, the effect of ELF on economic growth becomes greater in magnitude and more significant when the level of aggregation falls: the standardized beta is equal to 2.46% for $ELF(1)$ and rises to around 22% for levels $ELF(11)$ and higher. Consistent with Alesina et al. (2003), polarization measures seem to be unrelated to growth.

To further interpret these findings, compare China and India. According to the Penn World Tables 6.2 (Heston et al., 2006), over the period 1970–2004 China averaged an annual growth rate in real GDP per capita of 6.9%, compared to 2.7% in India. Using the coefficient on $ELF(15)$ in column (3) of Table 5, a predicted 14.7% of the growth difference between India and China over 1970–2004 is accounted for by the higher level of $ELF(15)$ in India. In contrast, the share of the growth differential accounted for by differences in $ELF(1)$ is only 2.11%, and that difference is not statistically significant.

In contrast to conflict, which seems to be driven by deep cleavages going back thousands of years, economic growth is negatively impacted even when distinctions across linguistic groups are small. One reason might be that economic growth requires groups to coordinate, interact and cooperate in production and trade networks. Such coordination and interaction may already suffer for relatively minor linguistic differences between groups.

Fractionalization versus polarization

Some of the earlier literature on diversity and conflict found no statistically significant effect of ethnic or religious fractionalization on the probability of civil wars (Fearon and Laitin, 2003). In a seminal paper that we already cited, Montalvo and Reynal-Querol (2005b) argue that fractionalization is not the appropriate measure to capture the impact of diversity on conflict. Instead, they propose that conflict is more likely to arise in polarized societies. The

TABLE 4 Civil conflict and linguistic diversity (1945–1999).

Dependent variable: Onset of civil war	(1) ELF(1)	(2) ELF(6)	(3) ELF(15)	(4) ELP(1)	(5) ELP(6)	(6) ELP(15)
ELF	1.157	0.04	−0.165			
	(0.545)**	(0.417)	(0.466)			
ELP				0.72	−0.324	−0.669
				(0.318)**	(0.427)	(0.483)
Lagged civil war	−0.901	−0.852	−0.845	−0.913	−0.87	−0.874
	(0.255)***	(0.257)***	(0.259)***	(0.257)***	(0.265)***	(0.259)***
Log lagged GDP/cap	−0.616	−0.613	−0.627	−0.615	−0.619	−0.61
	(0.140)***	(0.152)***	(0.153)***	(0.140)***	(0.146)***	(0.143)***
Log lagged population	0.311	0.293	0.3	0.31	0.3	0.298
	(0.068)***	(0.071)***	(0.071)***	(0.067)***	(0.071)***	(0.069)***
Mountainous	0.009	0.009	0.009	0.009	0.008	0.009
	(0.005)*	(0.005)*	(0.005)*	(0.005)*	(0.005)*	(0.004)**
Noncontiguous state	0.616	0.518	0.511	0.639	0.445	0.432
	(0.357)*	(0.355)	(0.349)	(0.360)*	(0.365)	(0.361)
Oil exporter	0.621	0.724	0.746	0.601	0.742	0.783
	(0.246)**	(0.243)***	(0.245)***	(0.248)**	(0.241)***	(0.244)***
New state	1.766	1.775	1.78	1.763	1.783	1.793
	(0.367)***	(0.369)***	(0.368)***	(0.367)***	(0.370)***	(0.373)***
Instability	0.643	0.646	0.645	0.645	0.649	0.661
	(0.214)***	(0.218)***	(0.217)***	(0.213)***	(0.217)***	(0.217)***
Democracy lagged	0.016	0.019	0.02	0.016	0.02	0.02
	(0.020)	(0.021)	(0.021)	(0.020)	(0.021)	(0.021)

Source: Desmet et al. (2012), Table 3. Robust standard errors, clustered at the level of countries, in parentheses; * significant at 10%; ** significant at 5%; *** significant at 1%. All columns involve 5733 observations from 142 countries from 1945 to 1999. The table reports logit coefficients, not marginal effects. All columns include the following additional controls (estimates not shown): Dummies for French legal origin, UK legal origin, Socialist legal origin, regional dummies for Latin America & Caribbean, Sub-Saharan Africa, East and Southeast Asia. All specifications include an intercept term. Results are robust to controlling for the growth of GDP per capita, the growth of GDP per capita lagged, a lagged dichotomous indicator of democracy (instead of the Polity2 index), a squared term for ELF (or POL), a dummy for the new world (and interaction between the new world dummy and diversity), and an anocracy dummy. Results are also robust to introducing ELF(1), ELF(6) and ELF(15) simultaneously (or, similarly, POL(1), POL(6) and POL(15)). The data are from Fearon and Laitin (2003), except for ELF (authors' own calculations) and legal origin from La Porta et al. (1999).

intuition is straightforward and aligns with the view of Horowitz (2000): conflict is more likely when society is composed of two large groups than when it is fragmented into many smaller groups. Empirically, they show that while ethnic fractionalization does not have a statistically significant effect on the likelihood

TABLE 5 Growth and linguistic diversity (1970–2004).

Dependent variable: Economic growth	(1) ELF(1)	(2) ELF(6)	(3) ELF(15)	(4) ELP(1)	(5) ELP(6)	(6) ELP(15)
ELF	−0.279	−1.056	−1.412			
	(0.933)	(0.576)*	(0.473)***			
ELP				−0.205	−0.667	0.25
				(0.537)	(0.531)	(0.573)
Log initial real per capita GDP	−1.209	−1.153	−1.143	−1.214	−1.208	−1.203
	(0.234)***	(0.219)***	(0.230)***	(0.234)***	(0.234)***	(0.231)***
Investment share of GDP	0.043	0.032	0.032	0.044	0.038	0.043
	(0.034)	(0.031)	(0.031)	(0.034)	(0.032)	(0.034)
Avg. schooling years in total population aged 25+	0.211	0.193	0.186	0.212	0.233	0.208
	(0.098)**	(0.092)**	(0.095)*	(0.097)**	(0.095)**	(0.096)**
Growth of population	−0.599	−0.524	−0.508	−0.595	−0.526	−0.634
	(0.196)***	(0.204)**	(0.184)***	(0.198)***	(0.214)**	(0.194)***
Log population	0.197	0.22	0.225	0.197	0.194	0.198
	(0.151)	(0.147)	(0.145)	(0.150)	(0.150)	(0.151)
Interaction between openness and log population	−0.005	−0.005	−0.004	−0.005	−0.005	−0.005
	(0.002)**	(0.002)**	(0.002)**	(0.002)**	(0.002)**	(0.002)**
Openness (imports + exports over GDP)	0.046	0.045	0.041	0.046	0.044	0.046
	(0.017)***	(0.017)**	(0.017)**	(0.017)***	(0.018)**	(0.017)***
R-squared	0.54	0.56	0.57	0.54	0.55	0.54

Source: Desmet et al. (2012), Table 6. Robust standard errors in parentheses. * significant at 10%; ** significant at 5%; *** significant at 1%. All columns involve 100 countries. All columns include the following additional controls (estimates not shown): Regional dummies for Latin America and Caribbean, Sub-Saharan Africa, East and Southeast Asia, legal origins dummies for British legal origin, French legal origin, Socialist legal origin and German legal origin. All specifications include an intercept term. Investment, schooling, population growth, log population and openness are entered as period averages; log initial per capita income is for 1970. The data on income per capita, income growth, population, population growth, openness and investment are from the Penn World Tables, version 6.2 (Heston et al., 2006). The data on human capital are from Barro and Lee (2001). The diversity measures are based on the authors' calculations using the Ethnologue database.

of conflict, ethnic polarization does. In contrast, in related work they establish that when it comes to economic development, ethnic fractionalization has a direct negative impact on growth (Montalvo and Reynal-Querol, 2005a).

How do these findings relate to the discussion above? When examining the determinants of civil wars, Desmet et al. (2012) show that both linguistic fractionalization (ELF) and linguistic polarization (ELP) have a positive and statistically significant effect on conflict, but only when measured at high levels of aggregation. The reason both measures yield similar effects is that, at high levels of aggregation, $ELF(1)$ and $ELP(1)$ are very highly correlated ($r = 0.988$). This is not surprising: when languages are aggregated into broad linguistic families, such as Indo-European or Afro-Asiatic, there are often only one or two groups per country, making the two measures perfectly correlated. At the same time, it is worth noting that neither $ELF(15)$ nor $ELP(15)$ has a statistically significant effect on conflict. This suggests that choosing the appropriate level of aggregation may sometimes be more important than distinguishing between fractionalization and polarization. As for the effect of diversity on economic growth, Montalvo and Reynal-Querol (2005a) and Desmet et al. (2012) reach a similar conclusion: fractionalization plays a more significant role as a direct driver of economic growth than polarization.

4.3 Inter-group distances and redistribution

Altruistic attitudes tend to be more prevalent within groups than across groups. This may explain why the U.S., where the income distribution has a strong racial component, does not have a European-style welfare state (Alesina et al., 2001). However, cross-country studies have often failed to find a statistically significant effect of ethnolinguistic diversity on the degree of redistribution (Alesina et al., 2003).

Because earlier studies had not taken into account the distinctiveness of groups, Desmet et al. (2009) examine whether inter-group solidarity is stronger between groups that are more similar. In a cross-country setting, they compare the impact of the Greenberg ethnolinguistic fractionalization index ($ELFD$) and the standard ethnolinguistic fractionalization index (ELF) on the degree of redistribution, measured as transfers and subsidies as a share of GDP. Table 6 reports the results. To make results comparable to previous work, they use specifications similar to the ones used by La Porta et al. (1999) and Alesina et al. (2003). As can be seen in columns (1)–(3), a higher degree of $ELFD$ is associated with a lower degree of redistribution, and the effect is statistically significant at either the 1% or the 5% level. Hence, when taking into account the distance between groups, they found a statistically robust effect of diversity on redistribution.

The magnitude of the effect is substantial: focusing on column (2), an increase in $ELFD$ by one standard deviation is predicted to lower redistribution as a share of GDP by 0.97 percentage points. Given that the average level of redistribution is 9.5% of GDP, this is a relatively large effect. As an example, compare Paraguay, with a level of redistribution of 2.3%, and Uruguay, with a level of redistribution of 13.1%. The greater linguistic diversity of Paraguay is predicted to lower redistribution by 5.6 percentage points compared to Uruguay.

Whether including linguistic distances is relevant for our understanding of redistribution is ultimately an empirical question. Columns (4)–(6) report results for the same regressions as columns (1)–(3), with the difference that we substitute the standard ethnolinguistic fractionalization index (ELF) for the version that incorporates linguistic distances ($ELFD$). As can be seen, ELF

TABLE 6 Redistribution and linguistic diversity (1985–1995).

Dependent variable: Redistribution	(1) ELFD	(2) ELFD	(3) ELFD	(4) ELF	(5) ELF	(6) ELF
ELFD	−6.313	−5.071	−4.042			
	[2.60]**	[2.79]***	[2.32]**			
ELF				−4.763	−2.207	−1.666
				[2.41]**	[1.44]	[1.19]
GDP per capita 1985–1995		1.792	1.037		1.676	0.968
		[3.95]***	[2.05]**		[3.65]***	[1.88]*
UK legal origin		3.554	4.59		3.168	4.367
		[1.58]	[2.39]**		[1.38]	[2.19]**
French legal origin		3.853	4.011		3.715	3.965
		[1.52]	[1.72]*		[1.42]	[1.66]
Socialist legal origin		8.441	8.666		7.626	8.22
		[2.72]***	[2.93]***		[2.43]**	[2.77]***
Scandinavian legal origin		6.104	6.626		5.716	6.412
		[1.44]	[1.73]*		[1.32]	[1.66]
Catholic 1980		0.02	0.034		0.022	0.036
		[1.00]	[1.64]		[1.08]	[1.73]*
Muslim 1980		−0.079	−0.024		−0.081	−0.024
		[3.93]***	[1.04]		[3.82]***	[1.02]
Protestant 1980		−0.041	−0.02		−0.045	−0.022
		[1.11]	[0.51]		[1.19]	[0.54]
Population 1985–1995			0.054			0.125
			[0.20]			[0.46]
Population above 65			0.685			0.7
			[4.11]***			[4.05]***
Observations	105	102	102	105	102	102
R-squared	0.6569	0.8203	0.8436	0.6581	0.8147	0.8401

Source: Desmet et al. (2009), Tables 1 and 2. Robust t-statistics in square brackets. * significant at 10%; ** significant at 5%; *** significant at 1%. Additional controls in all columns (estimates not shown) include a small island dummy, latitude, and regional dummies for Latin America, Sub-Saharan Africa, East Asia & Pacific. All specifications include an intercept term. Data sources are described in Desmet et al. (2009).

loses statistical significance. This suggests that the willingness to redistribute depends on how different groups are – solidarity travels easier across groups when they are more closely related to each other.

4.4 Local segregation and interactions

Cross-country studies often ignore the geography of diversity. Consider two countries with the same level of diversity, but in one country the different groups live geographically separated, while in the other the different groups are evenly spread across the country's geography. In Belgium, for example, many Dutch speakers rarely interact with French speakers in their daily lives, because both groups reside in geographically distinct regions. In contrast, in Mauritius there is more local diversity, so that an individual may easily use English, Kreol Morisien, French, and Bhojpuri in daily life. Does the spatial distribution of ethnolinguistic groups matter for different political economy outcomes, such as people's willingness to contribute to public goods?

The microfoundations for the different measures of diversity that we provided in Section 2 emphasized the animosity arising from the interaction between people of different groups. In that framework, we used the term interaction in a broad sense. It referred to the abstract type of interaction that occurs at the level of the society at large, but also to the more personal interaction that people encounter in their daily lives. Both types of interaction need not have the same effect on animosity. In fact, contact theory, first developed by the psychologist Allport (1954), posits that repeated interpersonal contact between people tends to reduce prejudice and conflict between individuals of different groups. Important in this theory is that the change in prejudice extends to the entire out-group: if a Dutch-speaking Belgian has more contact with French-speaking Belgians, it affects his prejudice towards all French-speaking Belgians. Because of this, local mixing may mitigate the overall negative impact of diversity in society.

A seminal study on the geography of diversity is Alesina and Zhuravskaya (2011) who examine the effect of spatial segregation of ethnic and linguistic groups on different measures of the quality of government, such as political stability, government effectiveness, control of corruption, and the rule of law. Using a cross-country regression approach, they find that greater segregation leads to lower quality of government. One potential mechanism underlying this negative effect is the lower inter-group trust observed in many segregated societies.

When examining the geography of diversity and its impact on political economy outcomes, it is important to consider the most appropriate way of measuring the spatial distribution of ethnolinguistic groups. Hodler et al. (2021) axiomatize an index of ethnic segregation that takes into account both ethnic and spatial distances. This index allows for a decomposition into three components: generalized fractionalization, spatial dispersion, and the alignment of spatial and ethnic distances. It clarifies that a society may be more segregated for three distinct reasons: higher spatial distance, greater ethnic distance, and stronger overlap between geography and ethnicity. This aligns with our discussion in Sections 2 and 3, where we described segregation as the overlap between geography and identity. What sets this index apart from some other segregation indices, such as the one used by Alesina and Zhuravskaya (2011), is its explicit consideration of distance. This incorporation of distance has the advantage of making the index independent of how exactly the government draws subnational borders. In terms of substantive results, they find the opposite of Alesina and Zhuravskaya (2011): the quality of government tends to be higher if ethnic groups live further apart.

Rather than focusing on indices of segregation, Desmet et al. (2020) start with the contact hypothesis which argues that the intensity of local interactions with the out-group affects the antagonism an individual feels towards the out-group in the society at large. Formally, they assume that the intensity of an individual's local interaction with another group is increasing in the local share of that group; and how much this affects his antagonism towards that other group in the rest of society depends on the aggregate share of that group. To illustrate this with a simple example, the local interaction of a Dutch-speaking Belgian with French-speaking Belgians depends on the local share of French speakers, but how much that interaction affects the overall antagonism she experiences towards that group depends on the aggregate share of French speakers. This yields a complementarity between the local group share and the aggregate group share in their effects on an individual's antagonism. The intuition for this complementarity is straightforward: the change in an individual's opinion about another group can only have an important impact on her overall antagonism if that other group is sizable in the society at large. When averaging across individuals, this yields an index that is a linear combination of the society's overall fractionalization and a term that captures the complementarity between local and overall diversity. They refer to this latter term as the degree of local-global ethnolinguistic complementarity.

When examining the effect of this index on a variety of public goods outcomes related to health, education, and infrastructure, Desmet et al. (2020) find that the negative effect of overall ethnolinguistic fractionalization is mitigated by the degree of complementarity between local and overall diversity. The magnitudes of the effects are large: a one standard deviation increase in local-global ethnolinguistic complementarity is associated with an increase in child survival by 0.75 per hundred live births. To put this figure into perspective, in its relation to child mortality, it is equivalent to a 48 percent increase in GDP per capita. This result supports the contact hypothesis: more local contact with the out-group diffuses antagonism towards that out-group not just locally, but in the society at large.

4.5 Heterogeneity and secessionism

There are currently active secessionist movements in 52% of countries and 14.7% of subnational regions (Desmet et al., 2025). When evaluating the drivers of secessionism, a commonly held view is that having a separate identity in terms of language, ethnicity, religion, or culture is important, but so is being relatively rich, with neither condition being sufficient (Sorens, 2005). This could explain why we see support for secession in Catalonia and Flanders, relatively wealthy regions with a distinct language, but not in Galicia and Wallonia, regions with different languages but economically lagging. However, it is not always obvious that both conditions need to be satisfied for secessionism to take hold. Regions such as Aceh and Tibet have significant pro-independence movements, in spite of their relatively low income per capita (Horowitz, 1981). There, having a separate identity may be a sufficient condition for regions wanting to secede.

To analyze the relative importance of income per capita and ethnolinguistic diversity, Desmet et al. (2025) propose and quantify a political economy model where people are less willing to contribute to a public good if they are richer or if they have an identity that is different from the rest of the country. Specifically, consider a country C partitioned into different geographic regions, indexed by ℓ, and into different identity groups, indexed by j. Denote by $y(\ell, C)$ the income per capita of a resident of region ℓ and by $Y(C)$ the total income of country C. Public goods are financed by a proportional income tax $\tau(C)$. An individual of group j residing in region ℓ in country C has quasi-linear preferences across private consumption and public consumption, yielding the following indirect utility function:

$$v(y(\ell, C), s(j, C), \tau(C), Y(C)) = (1-\tau(C))y(\ell, C) + \alpha s(j, C)^{\delta}(\tau(C)Y(C))^{\beta} \tag{43}$$

where $\alpha > 0$, $\beta, \delta \in [0, 1]$, and $s(j, C)$ is the share of the population in country C that belongs to identity group j. As a result, the utility an individual derives from consuming the public good is increasing in the share of the population that belongs to his group. Eq. (43) implies that an individual prefers lower taxes if either her income per capita is higher or the size of her identity group is smaller. Her actual utility of living in region ℓ in country C depends on $\tau(C)$ which is decided by majority vote.

To determine whether an individual of identity group j residing in region ℓ favors secession, she considers the utility she would get if her region became an independent country:

$$v(y(\ell), s(j, \ell), \tau(\ell), Y(\ell)) = y(\ell)(1 - \tau(\ell)) + \alpha s(j, \ell)^{\delta}(\tau(\ell)Y(\ell))^{\beta} \tag{44}$$

where $s(j, \ell)$, $Y(\ell)$, and $\tau(\ell)$ are all different from their values if ℓ were to remain as part of country C. Taking into account the endogenous tax rates $\tau(C)$ and $\tau(\ell)$, individual j from region ℓ would support independence if (44) is greater than (43). It is easy to show that the benefits from seceding are (i) decreasing in the identity group's national share, $s(j, C)$, (ii) increasing in the identity group's regional share, $s(j, \ell)$, and (iii) increasing in the income per capita of the region, $y(\ell)$.

In a calibrated version of the model, Desmet et al. (2025) analyze the propensity to secede across 3153 subnational regions in 177 countries. Fig. 10 shows the model-generated support for secessionism across the globe. The top-10% of regions with strongest support for secessionism include Flanders (Belgium), Quebec (Canada), Tibet (China), Tigray (Ethiopia), Saarland (Germany), Punjab (India), Aceh (Indonesia), Sardinia (Italy), Okinawa (Japan), Limburg (Netherlands), Chechnya (Russia), West Darfur (Sudan), and Galicia (Spain).

FIGURE 10 Model-based share of regional population in favor of secession.
Source: Desmet et al. (2025) Figure 4. It depicts the model-generated share of the population in favor of secession for each of the 3153 subnational regions. Darker colors indicate stronger support for secession.

Counterfactual analysis can help us understand the relative importance of income per capita and ethnolinguistic identity as drivers of secessionism. Removing linguistic identity differences between subnational regions lowers the support for secession from an average of 10.1% of the regional population to 0.2%, whereas removing differences in income per capita has almost no impact on the demand for secession. This suggests that identity trumps income in determining a region's propensity to secede. Another relevant counterfactual consists of removing within-region linguistic heterogeneity. Doing so increases the support for secessionism from 10.1% to 21.1%. Fig. 11 shows the increase in support for secession if subnational regions were linguistically homogeneous. Overall, these different counterfactual analyses show that separatism is stronger not just when a region is ethnolinguistically heterogeneous with respect to the rest of the country, but also when it is ethnolinguistically homogeneous within.

4.6 Conflict and the overlap between ethnicity and culture

An extensive literature has related ethnolinguistic diversity to civil war. In Section 4.2 we discussed the evidence showing that civil war is more likely when there are deep cleavages between ethnolinguistic groups (Desmet et al., 2012) and when society is more polarized (Montalvo and Reynal-Querol,

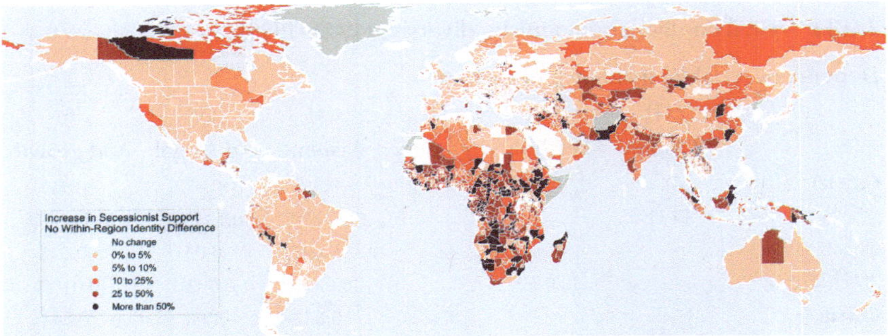

FIGURE 11 Increase in secessionism when eliminating within-region differences.
Source: Desmet et al. (2025) Figure 8. For each subnational region, the figure depicts the increase in support for secession if people were to ignore within-region identity differences in the case of independence. Darker colors indicate a larger increase in the support for secession.

2005b). In this subsection we ask whether civil war and conflict are more likely in societies where ethnicity overlaps with other dimensions of heterogeneity.

Using data from over 100 countries, Gubler and Selway (2012) find that civil war onset is almost twelve times less probable in societies where ethnicity is cross-cut by socio-economic class, geographic region, and religion. That is, in countries where there is less overlap between ethnicity and these other dimensions of heterogeneity, there is less civil war. This result is intuitive. Suppose religion cross-cuts ethnicity, so that the religious composition of the different ethnic groups is the same. This makes it more likely that people of different ethnic groups share the same religion. This would tend to mitigate the antagonism between ethnic groups, reducing the chance of conflict.

Desmet et al. (2017) consider the overlap between ethnicity and another important dimension of heterogeneity: culture. From our discussion in Section 3, we already know that the correlation between ethnic diversity and cultural diversity is close to zero. The degree of overlap between ethnicity and culture is small: in a sample of 76 countries, the share of cultural heterogeneity that is due to differences between ethnic groups is on average 1.2%. However, the degree of between-group variation in culture does vary significantly across countries, as we discussed in Section 3.3. Thus, one can ask whether the degree of overlap between culture and ethnicity affects the probability of war and conflict.

To answer this question, Desmet et al. (2017) regress the incidence of civil war on a set of standard determinants, distinguishing between cultural fractionalization, ethnic fractionalization, and the overlap between ethnicity and culture. Table 7 reports the results. Focusing on column (4), where the three measures of diversity are introduced jointly, we see that higher ethnic fractionalization is only weakly associated with lower incidence of conflict. In contrast, cultural fractionalization reduces conflict. While maybe surprising, one interpretation is that high levels of cultural diversity reflect societies that are more tolerant of different views. As for the overlap between ethnicity and

TABLE 7 Civil conflict and linguistic diversity (1945–1999).

Dependent variable: Incidence of civil war						
	(1) CF only	(2) ELF only	(3) χ^2 only	(4) Baseline	(5) Add legal	(6) Add growth
Cultural fractionalization	−0.187			−0.391	−0.472	−0.417
	[0.117]			[0.117]***	[0.135]***	[0.114]***
Ethnolinguistic fractionalization		0.019		−0.037	−0.041	−0.035
		[0.017]		[0.021]*	[0.022]*	[0.019]*
Chi-square			0.472	0.87	0.992	0.84
			[0.172]***	[0.227]***	[0.248]***	[0.212]***
Lagged war	0.86	0.868	0.864	0.84	0.84	0.833
	[0.028]***	[0.026]***	[0.026]***	[0.030]***	[0.032]***	[0.032]***
Log lagged GDP per capita	−0.005	−0.008	−0.007	0.003	0.005	0.003
	[0.006]	[0.005]	[0.004]*	[0.005]	[0.006]	[0.004]
Log lagged population	0.011	0.012	0.013	0.012	0.015	0.011
	[0.003]***	[0.003]***	[0.003]***	[0.003]***	[0.003]***	[0.003]***
Observations	2921	2921	2921	2921	2705	2850
Pseudo R-squared	0.752	0.752	0.754	0.758	0.754	0.771

Notes: Robust standard errors clustered at the country level in brackets. * $p < 0.1$, ** $p < 0.05$, *** $p < 0.01$. Columns report marginal effects. All columns include dummies for Latin America and Caribbean; Sub-Saharan Africa; East and Southeast Asia. Additional controls in all columns (not shown) include: Fraction mountainous territory, dummy for country with non-connected territory, oil dummy, new state dummy, political instability, lagged democracy score, legal origins dummies (UK, French, Socialist – columns 5 and 6 only), GDP growth and its lag (column 6 only). All specifications include an intercept term. This table reports estimates from a logit regression of a binary indicator of civil conflict on 3 diversity measures as well as a series of control variables. The data are a panel of at most 69 countries from 1945 to 1999, sourced from Fearon and Laitin (2003).

culture, χ^2 is a significant predictor of conflict incidence (at the 1% level). The magnitude of the effect is large: the logit marginal effect of χ^2 is equal to 0.87, implying that a one standard deviation change in χ^2 raises the probability of conflict by 2.35 percentage points. Overall, these results seem to indicate that ethnic diversity may matter for civil conflict, but only to the extent that it overlaps with cultural cleavages.

Together with the aforementioned findings on ethnic segregation as a determinant of the quality of government, the relevance of the overlap between culture and ethnicity as a predictor of civil wars suggests that a consideration of multiple dimensions of heterogeneity – and their interactions – is central to our understanding of the complex relationship between social heterogeneity and political economy outcomes. Such complex effects involving multiple dimensions of heterogeneity have been documented in a wide range of contexts. The overlapping dimensions of heterogeneity are not necessarily between geography and ethnicity (as in studies of segregation), or between culture and ethnicity (as in Desmet et al., 2017). The dimensions can be quite specific to given cases and circumstances, and the effects of overlap can be positive. For instance, in a now-classic paper, Saumitra Jha shows that medieval trading ports of the West Coast of India were much less prone to Hindu-Muslim riots in the 1850–1995 period than towns that were not medieval trading cities – despite being more ethnically mixed (Jha, 2013). He interprets these findings through the lens of interethnic complementarities between Hindus and Muslims, that were specific to trading towns due to medieval trade between India and Arabia, and led to the development of persistent institutions that still, to this day, support greater trust between communities in these locations. In this case, the overlap is between occupational complementarity and religious identity, and the effects of overlap are to *reduce* conflict: equally diverse towns where the complementarities were not present experienced *more* violence between Hindus and Muslims.

4.7 Within-country evidence on the effects of heterogeneity

While most of the studies surveyed above focus on the cross-national context, economists have long been interested in understanding the effects of diversity within countries. Some of the same measurement issues encountered in the cross-national context – such as the choice of relevant dimensions of heterogeneity and of functional forms for the diversity measures – apply to this more granular literature. And some of the substantive findings offer useful qualifiers to the inferences drawn from cross-national data.

This is a voluminous literature, so we focus on some salient references. Early work on diversity at the subnational level examined variation across cities. Alesina et al. (1999) show that more racially fractionalized cities in the U.S. tend to spend less on public goods. They interpret this finding as indicating that those affiliated with a given group are unwilling to pay for benefits that accrue to members of the other group – either because preferences over what kind of public goods to provide differ between groups, or directly because of animosity between groups.[14]

Results of a similar flavor were found in a variety of contexts. For instance, Beach and Jones (2017) find that the degree of diversity of city councils in California is negatively associated with spending on public goods. Dahlberg et al. (2012) exploit a natural experiment: the exogenous relocation of immigrants across Swedish municipalities between 1985 and 1994. They find that in municipalities that received more immigrants, individual preferences turned toward favoring less redistribution. Algan et al. (2016) study the effect of diversity on housing conditions at the very local level: apartment blocks in France. For identification, they exploit the fact that the allocation of social

14 This logic applies, not only to racial or ethnic groups, but also to other forms of heterogeneity, such as age. For instance, Poterba (1997) writes that "an increase in the fraction of elderly residents in a jurisdiction is associated with a significant reduction in per-child educational spending" in the United States.

housing in France is done without reference to ethnic identity or ethnic preference, generating exogenous variation in ethnic composition. Their results suggest that apartment blocks with higher ethnic fractionalization have worse housing conditions and more blight. They conclude that "diversity leads to social anomie, preventing the emergence of social norms and collective action".

Deleterious effects of ethnic diversity on public goods and redistribution have also been documented in the context of developing countries. Miguel and Gugerty (2005) found that more ethnically diverse locations had a lower provision of public goods in rural western Kenya. In a pair of papers, Kaivan Munshi and Mark Rosenzweig study the effect of ethnic divisions at the level of wards in India, concluding that "ethnic diversity (...) significantly reduces the supply of local public goods in India" (Munshi and Rosenzweig, 2015, 2018).

While the contributions discussed above tend to find negative effects of diversity on political economy outcomes, such negative effects are by no means a universal feature of research looking at local effects, suggesting that the specific institutional context, the specific dimension of heterogeneity, and the specific interactions between various dimensions of diversity are all important considerations when assessing the effects of diversity. Papers by Ottaviano and Peri (2006) and Bellini et al. (2013) are notable examples finding positive effects of diversity when looking at immigrant populations. Ottaviano and Peri (2006) study birthplace diversity (measured by the fractionalization index applied to residents' origin countries) at the level of 160 U.S. metropolitan areas between 1970 and 1990. They find that cities that became more diverse as a result of immigration experienced higher wage growth and higher rents, for *U.S.-born citizens*. This suggests that greater birth country diversity positively affects the productivity of natives. Admittedly, the paper does not fully address the issue of selection of immigrants to cities with preexisting characteristics that may account for both higher productivity and higher diversity. Nonetheless, the paper identifies an important potential channel whereby the diversity of a city may have positive effects. These findings were largely confirmed by Bellini et al. (2013) in the context of the regions of Europe, where greater birthplace country diversity is associated with higher productivity.[15]

Also noteworthy is the paper by Montalvo and Reynal-Querol (2021). These authors use very granular worldwide data, at a spatial resolution of one degree by one degree, to study how local diversity affects economic performance. At this level of spatial resolution, direct data on income is not available, so they use the growth in nighttime light density, measured by satellites, to capture economic performance. To measure local ethnic fractionalization, they use detailed maps depicting the location of ethnic groups, from GREG (Weidmann

[15] Alesina et al. (2016a) reach similar conclusions in a cross-country context, finding that immigrant birthplace diversity, while uncorrelated with ethnolinguistic diversity, is positively correlated with economic performance and prosperity. The authors find that this is driven particularly by skilled immigrants in richer countries, and argue that the findings are "suggestive of skill-complementarities between immigrants and native workers".

et al., 2010). They find a consistently positive effect of ethnolinguistic fractionalization on growth of nighttime lights, after controlling for country fixed effects and a wide range of observable cell characteristics. This effect holds strongly in Africa, where additionally, the authors are able to show that the presence of interethnic markets – i.e., markets located close to ethnic borders – helps explain the finding. In other words, ethnic specialization in production can help account for why ethnically diverse grid cells have higher levels of growth.

Positive effects of diversity have also been detected in specific countries. A salient paper in this area is Bazzi et al. (2019), which contains compelling causal identification. It also demonstrates the importance of measurement. The context is that of Indonesia, where in the 1980s two million individuals from diverse Indonesian ethnic groups were (voluntarily) resettled from Java and Bali to newly-created villages in the outlying islands. The destinations of the migrants, and the resulting ethnic composition of the villages, were as good as random. This so-called Transmigration Program was an attempt at nation-building, to dissociate ethnic identity from geography and prevent groups from seceding. It also offers exogenous variation in ethnic group size at the local level. The paper shows that a measure of ethnic fractionalization is positively associated with the use of Indonesian as a language at home, as opposed to the ethnic language of the resettled individuals. Fractionalization is also positively associated with interethnic marriage. However, the opposite pattern holds with respect to ethnic polarization – in villages where ethnic polarization was high, the integration of ethnic minorities was weaker. For social scientists, this paper illustrates both the potential of resettlement programs to offer exogenous variation in ethnic composition, and the substantive importance of considering alternative measures of social heterogeneity. More broadly, it reaches important lessons on the design of communities to maximize integration and nation-building, by showing that it is better to mix many small groups than to create relatively equally-sized large groups. In reaching this conclusion, the paper confirms many of the lessons on the effects of fractionalization and polarization found in the cross-national literature on conflict.

5 Conclusion

In this chapter, we have attempted a general overview of the large and still growing literature on the measurement of social heterogeneity. We began with theory. Building on the alienation-identification framework of Esteban and Ray (1994), we showed that a wide range of measures of heterogeneity – fractionalization, polarization, and others – can be derived from simple microfoundations, by making alternative assumptions on the manner in which social divisions affect antagonism between individuals. All these measures can be applied to data on underlying group shares, where the groups are based either on identity (language, ethnicity, religious affiliation, etc.) or on cultural values (belief in God, values on free speech, etc.). The framework can also accommodate a growing class of heterogeneity measures that depend on the degree of overlap between various dimensions of heterogeneity, such as class and religion, ethnicity and cultural values, geographic location and language, etc. We concluded this section with a brief discussion of the growing theoretical literature that seeks to endogenize culture and identity. Future research on the theory of diversity measurement should incorporate more refined microfoundations to the framework we have presented. While scholars have begun to better understand the forces that explain the emergence and diffusion of certain identities and cultural traits, they have not fully drawn out the theoretical implications of the endogenous determination of culture and identity for social heterogeneity. This is a promising avenue for future research.

In the second part of this chapter, we brought the theory to the data and calculated a range of measures of social heterogeneity using different data sources. Several salient themes emerged. First, all the measures of heterogeneity we considered display considerable variation across the world. Diversity in cultural values is higher in richer, more democratic societies, while diversity in language and ethnicity tends to be higher in poorer countries. Second, we documented the fact that ethnolinguistic and cultural diversity are not correlated at all across countries. To the extent that scholars study social disagreements on substantive issues, then, it is not appropriate to take ethnic divisions as a proxy for preference heterogeneity. Third, new survey data on people's actual beliefs, values, and norms is a growing and promising approach to study social heterogeneity in a range of contexts – for example in the study of political polarization. Fourth, we explored several patterns of overlap between various dimensions of heterogeneity. Our main example was that of the overlap between ethnicity and culture. This overlap is very small everywhere: ethnicity is not very predictive of cultural values and – equivalently – most cultural variation occurs within rather than between groups. This explains why ethnic diversity is uncorrelated with cultural diversity. We concluded this section with a discussion of the origins of diversity – both deeply-rooted and more immediate. Descriptive work on the characteristics of human societies in terms of cultural diversity is in its infancy. New techniques to tease out cultural traits from written texts, artifacts, ancient folklore, and other sources, provide the prospects of measuring historical cultural traits in a time varying manner. New techniques of text analysis, machine learning and artificial intelligence more broadly open exciting new avenues on the data-gathering front.

Finally, in the third part of this chapter, we surveyed the vast literature on the effects of social heterogeneity on political economy outcomes. We focused mostly on cross-national studies, since the measures of diversity that we discussed previously were primarily developed in this context. We described some of the main findings of the literature on the effects of ethnic, linguistic, and cultural diversity. The literature teaches us that the specific functional form, the specific dimension of heterogeneity, and the specific geographic and historical context, condition the inferences that can be drawn from data. In other words, measurement issues are central to our understanding of the effects of diversity. We concluded this section with a discussion of a very promising area of research, which is to look at the effects of diversity at a granular, local level – or even at the level of a single country or subnational jurisdiction. The findings there are contrasting and subtle, obviating sweeping statements that diversity is "good" or "bad". While local studies sometimes lack the generality of worldwide approaches, they offer advantages in terms of causal identification and mechanisms. We hope and expect to see a generalization of such granular, within-country approaches.

The scholarship devoted to the measurement of social heterogeneity is well-established, yet it remains an exciting area of study given the salience of issues surrounding cultural diversity broadly defined. There exist promising avenues for progress on the theory, data and identification fronts.

References

Akerlof, G., Kranton, R., 2000. Economics and identity. The Quarterly Journal of Economics 115 (3), 715–753.

Alesina, A., Baqir, R., Easterly, W., 1999. Public goods and ethnic divisions. The Quarterly Journal of Economics 114 (4), 1243–1284.

Alesina, A., Devleeschauwer, A., Easterly, W., Kurlat, S., Wacziarg, R., 2003. Fractionalization. Journal of Economic Growth 8 (2), 155–194.

Alesina, A., Harnoss, J., Rapoport, H., 2016a. Birthplace diversity and economic prosperity. Journal of Economic Growth 21 (2), 101–138.

Alesina, A., La Ferrara, E., 2005. Ethnic diversity and economic performance. Journal of Economic Literature 43 (3), 762–800.

Alesina, A., Michalopoulos, S., Papaioannou, E., 2016b. Ethnic inequality. Journal of Political Economy 124 (2), 428–488.

Alesina, A., Zhuravskaya, E., 2011. Segregation and the quality of government in a cross section of countries. American Economic Review 101 (5), 1872–1911.

Alesina, A., Glaeser, E.L., Sacerdote, B., 2001. Why doesn't the US have a European-style welfare system? Brookings Papers on Economic Activity 2001 (2), 187–277.

Algan, Y., Hémet, C., Laitin, D.D., 2016. The social effects of ethnic diversity at the local level: a natural experiment with exogenous residential allocation. Journal of Political Economy 124 (3), 696–733.

Allport, G., 1954. The Nature of Prejudice. Addison-Wesley, Reading, MA.

Ashraf, Q., Galor, O., 2013a. Genetic diversity and the origins of cultural fragmentation. The American Economic Review 103 (3), 528–533.

Ashraf, Q., Galor, O., 2013b. The "Out of Africa" hypothesis, human genetic diversity and comparative economic development. American Economic Review 103 (1), 1–46.

Barro, R.J., Lee, J.-W., 2001. International data on educational attainment: updates and implications. Oxford Economic Papers 53 (3), 541–563.

Bazzi, S., Gaduh, A., Rothenberg, A.D., Wong, M., 2019. Unity in diversity? How intergroup contact can foster nation building. American Economic Review 109 (11), 3978–4025.

Beach, B., Jones, D.B., 2017. Gridlock: ethnic diversity in government and the provision of public goods. American Economic Journal: Economic Policy 9 (1), 112–136.

Becker, S.O., Pascali, L., 2019. Religion, division of labor, and conflict: anti-semitism in Germany over 600 years. American Economic Review 109 (5), 1764–1804.

Bellini, E., Ottaviano, G.I.P., Pinelli, D., Prarolo, G., 2013. Cultural diversity and economic performance: evidence from European regions. In: Crescenzi, R., Percoco, M. (Eds.),

Geography, Institutions and Regional Economic Performance. Springer Berlin Heidelberg, Berlin, Heidelberg, pp. 121–141.

Berezkin, Y.E., 2023. Folklore and Mythology Catalogue: Its Lay-Out and Potential for Research. Museum of Anthropology & Ethnography (Kunstkamera). European University at Saint Petersburg.

Bertrand, M., Duflo, E., 2017. Field experiments on discrimination. In: Banerjee, A., Duflo, E. (Eds.), Handbook of Field Experiments, Volume 1. North-Holland, pp. 309–393.

Bisin, A., Verdier, T., 2000. "Beyond the melting pot": cultural transmission, marriage, and the evolution of ethnic and religious traits. The Quarterly Journal of Economics 115 (3), 955–988.

Boyd, R., Richerson, P.J., 1988. Culture and the Evolutionary Process. University of Chicago Press, Chicago.

Bruk, S.I., Apenchenko, V.S., Telberg, V.G., 1964. Atlas Narodov Mira. Miklukho-Maklai Ethnological Institute at the Department of Geodesy and Cartography of the State Geological Committee of the Soviet Union, Moscow.

Cavalli-Sforza, L.L., Menozzi, P., Piazza, A., 1994. The History and Geography of Human Genes. Princeton University Press, Princeton, NJ.

Cesur, R., Yıldırım, S., 2024. The Misery of Diversity. NBER Working Paper 33163.

Corno, L., La Ferrara, E., Burns, J., 2022. Interaction, stereotypes, and performance: evidence from South Africa. American Economic Review 112 (12), 3848–3875.

Cover, T.M., Thomas, J.A., 2006. Elements of Information Theory. John Wiley & Sons, Hoboken, NJ.

Cramér, H., 1946. Mathematical Methods of Statistics. Princeton University Press, Princeton, NJ.

Cuevas, Á., Cuevas, R., Desmet, K., Ortuño-Ortín, I., 2021. The Gender Gap in Preferences: Evidence from 45,397 Facebook Interests. NBER Working Paper 29451.

Dahlberg, M., Edmark, K., Lundqvist, H., 2012. Ethnic diversity and preferences for redistribution. Journal of Political Economy 120 (1), 41–76.

Desmet, K., Gomes, J.F., Ortuño-Ortín, I., 2020. The geography of linguistic diversity and the provision of public goods. Journal of Development Economics 143, 102384.

Desmet, K., Ortuño-Ortín, I., Wacziarg, R., 2012. The political economy of linguistic cleavages. Journal of Development Economics 97 (2), 322–338.

Desmet, K., Ortuño-Ortín, I., Wacziarg, R., 2016. Linguistic cleavages and economic development. In: Ginsburgh, V., Weber, S. (Eds.), The Palgrave Handbook of Economics and Language. London: Palgrave Macmillan UK, pp. 425–446.

Desmet, K., Ortuño-Ortín, I., Wacziarg, R., 2017. Culture, ethnicity and diversity. American Economic Review 107 (9), 2479–2513.

Desmet, K., Ortuño-Ortín, I., Weber, S., 2009. Linguistic diversity and redistribution. Journal of the European Economic Association 7 (6), 1291–1318.

Desmet, K., Ortuño-Ortín, I., Özak, Ö., 2025. Is secessionism mostly about income or identity? A global analysis of 3,153 subnational regions. Economic Journal 135 (668), 1261–1299.

Desmet, K., Wacziarg, R., 2021. The cultural divide. Economic Journal 131 (637), 2058–2088.

Duclos, J.-Y., Esteban, J., Ray, D., 2004. Polarization: concepts, measurement, estimation. Econometrica 72 (6), 1737–1772.

Dyen, I., Kruskal, J.B., Black, P., 1992. An Indo-European classification: a lexicostatistical experiment. Transactions of the American Philosophical Society 82 (5). iii–132.

Easterly, W., Levine, R., 1997. Africa's growth tragedy: policies and ethnic divisions. The Quarterly Journal of Economics 112 (4), 1203–1250.

Encyclopedia Britannica, 2000. Chicago.

Esteban, J., Mayoral, L., Ray, D., 2012. Ethnicity and conflict: an empirical study. American Economic Review 102 (4), 1310–1342.

Esteban, J., Ray, D., 1994. On the measurement of polarization. Econometrica 62 (4), 819–851.

Ethnologue, 2005. Ethnologue: Languages of the World (15 ed.). SIL International, Dallas TX.

Falk, A., Becker, A., Dohmen, T., Enke, B., Huffman, D., Sunde, U., 2018. Global evidence on economic preferences. The Quarterly Journal of Economics 133 (4), 1645–1692.

Fearon, J., 2003. Ethnic and cultural diversity by country. Journal of Economic Growth 8 (2), 195–222.
Fearon, J.D., Laitin, D.D., 2003. Ethnicity, insurgency, and civil war. American Political Science Review 97 (1), 75–90.
Fishman, J.A., 1966. Some contrasts between linguistically homogeneous and linguistically heterogeneous polities. Sociological Inquiry 36 (2), 146–158.
Galor, O., Klemp, M., Wainstock, D., 2023. The Impact of the Prehistoric Out of Africa Migration on Cultural Diversity. NBER Working Paper 31274.
Ginsburgh, V., Ortuño-Ortín, I., Weber, S., 2005. Disenfranchisement in linguistically diverse societies: the case of the European Union. Journal of the European Economic Association 3 (4), 946–965.
Ginsburgh, V., Weber, S., 2016. Linguistic distances and ethnolinguistic fractionalization and disenfranchisement indices. In: Ginsburgh, V., Weber, S. (Eds.), The Palgrave Handbook of Economics and Language. Palgrave Macmillan UK, London, pp. 137–173.
Giuliano, P., Nunn, N., 2021. Understanding cultural persistence and change. The Review of Economic Studies 88 (4), 1541–1581.
Gomes, J.F., 2013. Religious Diversity, Intolerance and Civil Conflict. Economic Series Working Paper 13-11. Universidad Carlos III de Madrid.
Goodman, L.A., Kruskal, W.H., 1954. Measures of association for cross classifications. Journal of the American Statistical Association 49 (268), 732–764.
Gubler, J.R., Selway, J., 2012. Horizontal inequality, cross-cutting cleavages, and civil war. The Journal of Conflict Resolution 56 (2), 206–232.
Habyarimana, J., Humphreys, M., Posner, D.N., Weinstein, J.M., 2009. Coethnicity: Diversity and the Dilemmas of Collective Action. Russell Sage Foundation, New York, NY.
Henrich, J., 2016. The Secret of Our Success: How Culture Is Driving Human Evolution, Domesticating Our Species, and Making Us Smarter. Princeton University Press, Princeton.
Heston, A., Summers, R., Aten, B., 2006. Penn World Table Version 6.2. Center for International Comparisons of Production, Income and Prices, University of Pennsylvania, Philadelphia.
Hodler, R., Valsecchi, M., Vesperoni, A., 2021. Ethnic geography: measurement and evidence. Journal of Public Economics 200, 104446.
Hong, L., Page, S.E., 2001. Problem solving by heterogeneous agents. Journal of Economic Theory 97 (1), 123–163.
Horowitz, D.L., 1981. Patterns of ethnic separatism. Comparative Studies in Society and History 23 (2), 165–195.
Horowitz, D.L., 2000. Ethnic Groups in Conflict. University of California Press, Berkeley.
Jha, S., 2013. Trade, institutions, and ethnic tolerance: evidence from South Asia. American Political Science Review 107 (4), 806—-832.
Jost, L., 2008. G_{ST} and its relatives do not measure differentiation. Molecular Ecology 17 (18), 4015–4026.
Kuran, T., 1987. Chameleon voters and public choice. Public Choice 53 (1), 53–78.
Kuran, T., Sandholm, W.H., 2008. Cultural integration and its discontents. The Review of Economic Studies 75 (1), 201–228.
La Porta, R., Lopez-de-Silanes, F., Shleifer, A., Vishny, R., 1999. The quality of government. Journal of Law, Economics, & Organization 15 (1), 222–279.
Lazear, E.P., 1999. Globalisation and the market for team-mates. Economic Journal 109 (454), C15–C40.
Mauro, P., 1995. Corruption and growth. The Quarterly Journal of Economics 110 (3), 681–712.
Michalopoulos, S., 2012. The origins of ethnolinguistic diversity. American Economic Review 102 (4), 1508–1539.
Miguel, E., Gugerty, M.K., 2005. Ethnic diversity, social sanctions, and public goods in Kenya. Journal of Public Economics 89 (11), 2325–2368.
Montalvo, J.G., Reynal-Querol, M., 2005a. Ethnic diversity and economic development. Journal of Development Economics 76 (2), 293–323.

Montalvo, J.G., Reynal-Querol, M., 2005b. Ethnic polarization, potential conflict, and civil wars. American Economic Review 95 (3), 796–816.

Montalvo, J.G., Reynal-Querol, M., 2021. Ethnic diversity and growth: revisiting the evidence. Review of Economics and Statistics 103 (3), 521–532.

Munshi, K., Rosenzweig, M., 2015. Insiders and Outsiders: Local Ethnic Politics and Public Goods Provision. NBER Working Paper 21720.

Munshi, K., Rosenzweig, M., 2018. Ethnic Diversity and the Under-Supply of Local Public Goods. Working Paper. Yale University.

Nei, M., 1973. Analysis of gene diversity in subdivided populations. Proceedings of the National Academy of Sciences 70 (12), 3321–3323.

Nettle, D., 2000. Linguistic fragmentation and the wealth of nations: the Fishman-Pool hypothesis reexamined. Economic Development and Cultural Change 48 (2), 335–348.

Nunn, N., Qian, N., 2010. The Columbian exchange: a history of disease, food, and ideas. The Journal of Economic Perspectives 24 (2), 163–188.

Obradovich, N., Özak, Ö., Martín, I., Ortuño-Ortín, I., Awad, E., Cebrián, M., Cuevas, R., Desmet, K., Rahwan, I., Cuevas, Á., 2022. Expanding the measurement of culture with a sample of two billion humans. Journal of the Royal Society Interface 19 (190), 20220085.

Ottaviano, G.I., Peri, G., 2006. The economic value of cultural diversity: evidence from US cities. Journal of Economic Geography 6 (1), 9–44.

Page, S.E., 2017. The Diversity Bonus: How Great Teams Pay Off in the Knowledge Economy. Princeton University Press, Princeton, NJ.

Petroni, F., Serva, M., 2010. Measures of lexical distance between languages. Physica A: Statistical Mechanics and its Applications 389 (11), 2280–2283.

Pool, J., 1972. National development and language diversity. In: Fishman, J.A. (Ed.), Advances in the Sociology of Language, Volume 2 Selected Studies and Applications. De Gruyter Mouton, Berlin, Boston, pp. 213–230.

Poterba, J.M., 1997. Demographic structure and the political economy of public education. Journal of Policy Analysis and Management 16 (1), 48–66.

Rae, D.W., Taylor, M.J., 1970. Analysis of Political Cleavages. Yale University Press, New Haven, CT.

Reardon, S.F., Firebaugh, G., 2002. Measures of multigroup segregation. Sociological Methodology 32 (1), 33–67.

Reynal-Querol, M., 2002. Ethnicity, political systems, and civil wars. The Journal of Conflict Resolution 46 (1), 29–54.

Richerson, P.J., Boyd, R., 2008. Not by Genes Alone: How Culture Transformed Human Evolution. University of Chicago Press, Chicago.

Selway, J.S., 2011a. Cross-cuttingness, cleavage structures and civil war onset. British Journal of Political Science 41 (1), 111–138.

Selway, J.S., 2011b. The measurement of cross-cutting cleavages and other multidimensional cleavage structures. Political Analysis 19 (1), 48–65.

Shayo, M., 2009. A model of social identity with an application to political economy: nation, class, and redistribution. American Political Science Review 103 (2), 147–174.

Shayo, M., 2020. Social identity and economic policy. Annual Review of Economics 12 (1), 355–389.

Sorens, J., 2005. The cross-sectional determinants of secessionism in advanced democracies. Comparative Political Studies 38 (3), 304–326.

Weidmann, N.B., Rød, J., Cederman, L.E., 2010. Representing ethnic groups in space: a new dataset. Journal of Peace Research 47 (4), 491–499.

Wright, S., 1949. The genetical structure of populations. Annals of Human Genetics 15 (1), 323–354.

Chapter 4

The global variation in risk and time preferences ☆

Anke Becker[a], Christina Borner[b], Thomas Dohmen[c,d], Armin Falk[c], David Huffman[e], and Uwe Sunde[b]
[a]*Harvard Business School, Boston, MA, United States,* [b]*LMU Munich, Munich, Germany,* [c]*University of Bonn, Bonn, Germany,* [d]*Maastricht University, Maastricht, Netherlands,* [e]*Cornell University, Ithaca, NY, United States*

1 Introduction

Risk and time preferences are central components of economic decision making. Conceptually, preference parameters for risk taking and time discounting directly emerge from economists' standard utility framework. Empirically, preferences have been shown to be heterogeneous with respect to, e.g., gender (Croson and Gneezy, 2009; Falk and Hermle, 2018; Charness and Gneezy, 2012), age (Dohmen et al., 2017; Josef et al., 2016), cognitive ability (Dohmen et al., 2010; Benjamin et al., 2013; Dohmen et al., 2018), and personality traits (Becker et al., 2012; Jagelka, 2024), and they are relevant for understanding choices related to, e.g., education, the labor market (Dohmen et al., 2011; Bonin et al., 2007; Golsteyn et al., 2014), investments and savings (Dohmen et al., 2011), or health behavior (Bergeot and Jusot, 2023; Anderson and Mellor, 2008).

A fairly recent and growing literature has measured people's preferences for time and risk on an international scale. The aim is to study worldwide variation in preferences and to assess the generalizability of results and patterns documented previously only in more limited, regionally focused samples. While these 'global' data sets differ in terms of the employed preference measures, population samples and survey methodology, research findings based on their

☆ The authors are grateful to Benjamin Enke, Nathan Nunn, and participants of the 2024 Kabiller Science of Empathy Conference: The Economics of Culture for helpful comments, and Elisa Winter and Fedor Shafranov for outstanding research assistance. Thomas Dohmen gratefully acknowledges funding by the German Science Foundation (Deutsche Forschungsgemeinschaft, DFG) through CRC TRR 224 (Project A05) and Germany's Excellence Strategy – EXC 2126/1-390838866 as well as through NSF Award 2201888. Uwe Sunde gratefully acknowledges funding by the German Science Foundation (Deutsche Forschungsgemeinschaft, DFG) through CRC TRR 190 (project number 280092119) and Project 491578970.

Handbook of Culture and Economic Behavior, Volume 1, ISSN 3051-1682
https://doi.org/10.1016/bs.hceb.2026.02.012

data suggest that the variation in risk and time preferences across the globe is, at least partly, 'cultural' in nature. For example, differences in economic preferences between populations are larger for population pairs with greater ancestral distance, a measure for the time that has passed since two populations shared a common ancestor (Becker et al., 2020). Average levels of patience are higher in countries that had higher crop yields, rendering agricultural investments more attractive in pre-industrial times, consistent with cultural adaptation (Galor and Özak, 2016). There is also evidence that preferences are transmitted 'socially', e.g., through parents (Dohmen et al., 2012; Kosse and Pfeiffer, 2012; Falk et al., 2021b; Zumbuehl et al., 2021) or peers (Lahno and Serra-Garcia, 2015; Kosse et al., 2020; Schwerter, 2024), a key part of many definitions of culture.

This chapter intends to take stock of the research on the global variation in risk and time preferences, to highlight the differences and similarities across the different datasets, to summarize their key findings, and to identify empirical regularities that emerge robustly from the different studies. In doing so, we direct attention to studies that collect data on preferences for a sufficiently large number of countries around the world and that have representative population samples. In particular, we focus on the Global Preferences Survey (Falk et al., 2018, henceforth GPS), the World Values Survey (Inglehart et al., 2020, henceforth WVS), and the preference data collected by Ruggeri et al. (2022, henceforth Ruggeri). In addition, we discuss data sets with global coverage that are based on convenience and student samples: the INTRA data (Rieger et al., 2015), the Maps data (Vieider et al., 2015; L'Haridon and Vieider, 2019), and the GLOBE data (House et al., 2004), all of which are discussed in more detail below. To broaden the country-level coverage and reduce measurement error, we also create a new, synthetic dataset that can be used to study how country-level preference measures relate to country characteristics. We construct this dataset using a methodology that combines the existing datasets with global coverage to achieve comparable country-level measures of risk preference and patience for an extended range of countries. We denote this the Synthetic World Aggregate Preferences (SWAP) data.

The aforementioned datasets measure risk and time preferences in various ways, and also differ in some respects in terms of how data were collected. The Maps data contain measures from incentivized choice experiments. Although these are widely considered the gold standard in preference measurement, it is typically infeasible to collect them for large representative samples on a global scale. Most similar to these incentivized experiments, the GPS contains measures from hypothetical choice experiments. The GPS measures are constructed as the linear combination of measures—typically a combination of behavior in a hypothetical choice experiment and a qualitative self-assessment—that jointly best predict choices in incentivized preference elicitation tasks (Falk et al., 2023). The most commonly used type of measure across the other datasets is qualitative questions that ask the individual respondents to subjectively self-report their own willingness to take risks or to trade off future against present-day rewards. Regarding data collection methodology, some datasets were constructed mostly with telephone interviews, while others used in-person interviews or online survey platforms.

Given the differences in population samples, measures, survey methodology, countries covered, as well as the inherent challenges in comparing survey measures across different cultures, our objective is to shed light on the following questions: Do the different data sets reveal a similar global variation in preferences? Do countries that are classified as more risk averse or more patient in one dataset also exhibit higher average risk aversion and patience in another? Are the country-level correlates of preferences, such as GDP, consistent across data sets? Do the data sets reveal similar individual-level correlates across countries—for example, is the average gender gap in willingness to take risks present and comparable in all data sets? Comparing across datasets is valuable because it addresses a fundamental challenge in cross-country preference research: do differences in survey responses reflect genuine preference differences, or merely cultural variation in how respondents interpret or understand particular question wordings or formats? If the latter, we would expect country rankings and the relationships between preferences and outcomes to diverge across datasets. If, however, similar patterns emerge robustly despite variation in survey design, this suggests that cross-country differences in measured preferences capture, at least in part, actual underlying differences.

We document six empirical regularities that emerge robustly from the different data sets that share comparable (but far from identical) survey measures of risk and time preferences. First, these different data sets reveal similar patterns of heterogeneity in preferences across the globe, especially when considering direct measures of respondents' preferences and representative samples of the population. We conclude that differences in preference variation that do emerge across datasets can likely be attributed to differences in sample composition and measurement. Second, the stability of country-by-country rankings in economic preferences depends on the specific measures. We find higher stability for measures that ask individual respondents directly about their own preference, rather than asking about, e.g., their assessment of certain attributes in the general population of a country. Moreover, we find higher stability for measures based on representative population samples. Third, at the country level, economic preferences exhibit consistent correlations with aggregate characteristics such as income, education, and institutions. These are even stronger in the synthetic dataset that measures country-level risk preference and patience across an extended range of countries. Fourth, at the individual level, economic preferences show consistent patterns of differences between women and men. Women tend to be more risk averse and less patient. These gender differences emerge for the majority of countries in all datasets. Fifth, preferences show systematic heterogeneity across age groups. In particular, people's willingness to take risks declines with age, a pattern that emerges from various datasets for the majority of countries. Sixth, at the individual level, preferences show consistent correlations with socioeconomic status, as proxied by income. In many countries, individuals in higher income deciles are less risk averse and exhibit higher levels of patience.

In sum, our analyses reveal important consistencies regarding the nature of economic preferences across cultures. This is remarkable, given the variation in methodology and sampling procedures used in the different data sets. The observed consistencies within and between countries, and the relationships of economic preferences to important outcomes, underline the usefulness of running large-scale international assessments of preference measures, and suggest that differences in preferences are an important component of cultural variation.

The remainder of this chapter is structured as follows. Section 2 presents the conceptual background related to preference elicitation in large representative samples. Section 3 contains information about available data sets with global coverage that will be used for the empirical analysis. Section 4 presents evidence for the global distribution of preferences across the different data sets. Sections 5 and 6 discuss correlation patterns with country-level and individual-level variables. Section 7 provides a brief discussion of global variation in social and other preferences, and Section 8 concludes with an outlook regarding avenues for future work.

2 Measures of risk and time preferences

2.1 Conceptual background

Economic thinking about risk and time preferences has been shaped profoundly by utility theory, particularly expected utility theory (EUT) in the domain of risk preference (Von Neumann and Morgenstern, 1944) and the discounted utility (DU) model in modeling time preference (Samuelson, 1937; Frederick et al., 2002). Within the EUT framework, individuals are assumed to evaluate utility derived from lotteries over consumption by calculating their expected utility. This theoretical structure has strongly influenced economists' attempts to infer risk preferences from choices between lotteries. Likewise, the DU framework has led economists to use intertemporal trade-offs in consumption as a means of measuring time preference, typically by observing how individuals discount future outcomes relative to present ones.

As a result, elicitation protocols have been developed to measure risk preferences from lottery choices and time preferences from intertemporal trade-offs in controlled laboratory environments. The preferred methodology of economists has been to use real incentives for these measurements, with the aim of reducing noise due to factors like inattention. However, measuring risk and time preferences in controlled laboratory settings, and with real incentives, is time consuming and financially expensive to implement in large-scale studies, limiting the scope of analysis to small and often selective samples.

One potential solution to this challenge is to reduce the costs for elicitation by using non-incentivized versions of the traditional lottery and intertemporal-tradeoff protocols. There is evidence that hypothetical lottery measures, and hypothetical time preference measures, are correlated with, and sometimes extremely similar to, their incentivized counterparts (for an early survey and more recent work, see Camerer and Hogarth, 1999; Falk et al., 2023; Brañas-Garza et al., 2023), consistent with measuring the same underlying trait albeit potentially with noise.

However, important measurement problems remain even when attempting to measure the preference parameters specified in the EUT or DU frameworks under controlled laboratory conditions with or without incentives, as the experimental environment may not be fully congruent with the theoretical framework. For instance, conceptually, EUT is defined over lifetime wealth, whereas laboratory lotteries typically involve small-stake monetary outcomes (Rabin, 2000). Similarly, DU concerns consumption streams, yet experiments often use monetary rewards, which themselves can be re-allocated over time. Further complications arise because the utility function assumed in theory is not directly observable, making it difficult to infer deep preference parameters from observed choices.

In addition, economic theories such as the EUT and DU frameworks may be too narrow to capture the full range of factors shaping people's risk preferences and time preferences (see, e.g., Kahneman and Tversky, 1979; Frederick et al., 2002).[1] If the theoretical framework itself captures only a limited aspect of how individuals evaluate risk or time, then lottery-choice and inter-temporal choice measures derived from it are likewise narrow. Consequently, such measures may miss important dimensions of how people perceive and respond to risk or time in everyday life, such as emotional, contextual, or motivational factors or broader notions of risk and delay that fall outside the expected utility or discounted utility model.[2] This raises a further measurement problem: if the underlying theory is incomplete or overly restrictive, measures based strictly on it may not capture the construct of interest, i.e., the broader disposition to take or avoid risk or the willingness to delay gratification across contexts. Moreover, experimental

1 Empirical evidence shows that EUT often fails to predict actual behavior in real-world contexts (see, e.g., Charness et al., 2020) and that individuals' decisions frequently violate the axioms of expected utility (for surveys see, e.g., Starmer, 2000; Barberis, 2013). Likewise, intertemporal choices often violate the DU model (for a survey see, e.g., Cohen et al., 2020).

2 Everyday decision-making is shaped largely by uncertainty rather than reflecting choices between lotteries with known outcome probabilities. As a consequence, individuals may draw on how they typically decide under uncertainty even when confronted with lottery choices. When asked to assess their own willingness to take risks, they may therefore likewise refer to their inclination to make decisions under uncertainty, which may in fact describe their real-world behavior in risky situations more accurately.

elicitation protocols are fairly abstract and might lead to confusion, and the use of heuristics as a consequence of a lack of familiarity.

In practice, economists therefore face a trade-off between maintaining theoretical closeness to EUT (or DU) and achieving empirical relevance. Measures closely aligned with EUT and DU are conceptually clear, which often makes them the preferred choice of behavioral and experimental economists, who are interested in measuring theoretically-rooted parameters. At the same time, these measures may be empirically narrow, especially in settings that require broader conceptualizations of risk and time preferences. This might be achieved by broader, more intuitive and naturalistic measures that can be obtained in survey settings and that are often used in studies in cultural economics, despite the cost of less direct interpretability within a specific theoretical framework.

One alternative for obtaining such broader measures is the use of qualitative questions that ask individuals to assess their own willingness to take risks or to forgo current consumption for future consumption. Although such measures lack a direct interpretation as parameters of EUT or DU models and may be affected by limited self-knowledge, reporting biases, or differences in scale use, they can capture broader, dispositional aspects of preference that manifest across multiple domains.[3] These measures also offer an alternative elicitation approach that may sidestep certain types of complexity specific to quantitative measures, such as complexities of evaluating probabilities and implied interest rates (e.g., Enke and Shubatt, 2023), again with the caveat that retrieving an assessment of one's preference from introspection and scale use in reporting this answer has its own complexities. A further advantage is that they can be implemented at relatively low cost in large surveys. The following section briefly introduces standard incentivized elicitation protocols and then presents survey-based measures that are easier to implement and therefore especially suitable for large-scale studies.

Measuring risk and time preferences across diverse cultures also presents several challenges. First, survey wording may be interpreted differently across cultural contexts. The standard mitigation is back-translation: one individual translates questions into the local language, another translates back to the original, and if the meaning is preserved, this provides some reassurance of equivalence. This procedure is imperfect, however. Hypothetical quantitative measures may be less susceptible to cultural interpretation differences than qualitative measures, providing one reason to favor these for cross-country

[3] Evidence, in particular in psychology, has shown that risk preferences are highly context dependent, a feature missing in the standard EUT framework (see, e.g. Weber et al., 2002). Supporting this view, Dohmen et al. (2011) show that the best predictor of risky behavior in a given domain, e.g., holding stocks, is a qualitative question framed narrowly in that context, e.g., willingness to take risks in financial matters. They also find, however, that a broader question about willingness to take risks in general is the best all-around predictor across a range of risky domains, for example also predicting self-employment, smoking, and participating in risky leisure activities.

comparisons. On the other hand, they introduce other difficulties. Stake sizes must be adjusted for local income levels, typically using country-level average or median income, which is inherently imprecise. Cross-country variation in inflation can also be problematic, although questions can instruct respondents to assume a particular inflation rate. A second challenge in comparing measures of preferences across countries is that decision heuristics or responses to question complexity and framing may vary across countries due to factors such as education levels. Whether quantitative or qualitative measures better elicit true preference differences in view of these factors remains unclear.

These challenges motivate the approach taken in this chapter: comparing results across multiple cross-country datasets that differ substantially in wording, structure, and the use of quantitative elements. To the extent that similar country rankings emerge across datasets—despite these methodological differences—the rankings are unlikely to be driven entirely by cultural variation in question interpretation, and may instead reflect genuine preference differences.

2.2 Risk preferences

A commonly used tool to elicit risk preferences in behavioral economics literature is the multiple price list, in which respondents make choices between alternatives that involve different levels of risk.[4] This approach was introduced by Binswanger (1980, 1981) and has since been widely used in various variants (see, e.g., Holt and Laury, 2002; Harrison et al., 2007; Dohmen et al., 2010).[5] Typically, these multiple price lists involve relatively small stakes. A prominent example is the laboratory design of Holt and Laury (2002), in which subjects face ten decisions between two lotteries with fixed outcomes but varying probabilities, with the probability of the first outcome increasing from 1/10 to 10/10. As most subjects switch from the safer to the riskier option as probabilities change, individual risk aversion can be inferred from the switching point.[6]

An alternative lottery-choice measure with large but hypothetical stakes was introduced in the Health and Retirement Study and analyzed by Barsky et al. (1997).[7] Respondents choose between a safe lifetime job and otherwise equivalent jobs offering different probabilities of income gains or losses.

---

4 Other elicitation methods involving choices between risky prospects have been proposed in the economics and psychology literature (see, e.g., Gneezy and Potters, 1997; Sharpe et al., 2000; Eckel and Grossman, 2002; Andreoni and Sprenger, 2012; Crosetto and Filippin, 2013).

5 Andersen et al. (2006) provide a discussion on the advantages and limitations of this approach.

6 Simpler formats, such as choices between a lottery and a safe payment, have been used in subsequent work (Dohmen et al., 2010), and more refined designs have been implemented in large representative samples (see, e.g., Donkers et al., 2001; von Gaudecker et al., 2011). Surveys of methods are provided by Charness et al. (2013), and payoff-varying price lists have been proposed to account for probability weighting (Drichoutis and Lusk, 2016).

7 See also Kimball et al. (2008, 2009).

Instead of a multiple price list, this approach uses an adaptive staircase procedure (see Cornsweet, 1962) in which each question is tailored to previous responses, successively narrowing the bounds around the respondent's indifference point. By focusing on the indifference region, this method achieves similar informational content with fewer questions.[8] Another advantage of the survey measure used by Barsky et al. (1997) is its domain-specific framing, which may enhance predictive power for employment-related risk choices; a disadvantage is that the narrow context may confound preferences with individual or environmental characteristics (e.g., age, labor market environment, etc.), requiring additional assumptions about unobserved heterogeneity. Its hypothetical nature also allows for high stakes that meaningfully vary lifetime wealth.

An alternative to incentivized or hypothetical lottery-choice experiments is the use of qualitative self-assessments of willingness to take risks. Dohmen et al. (2011) showed that answers to a qualitative self-report question are robustly correlated with choices in an incentivized price list lottery experiment. Respondents assess their general willingness to take risks on an 11-point Likert scale ranging from 0 ('not at all willing to take risks') to 10 ('very willing to take risks'). Although the correlation is imperfect, reflecting both noise and the possibility that self-assessments capture broader aspects of risk preferences relevant for behavior under risk or uncertainty, these findings validate that the qualitative measure has an overlap with what is captured by incentivized lottery experiments.

A key advantage of qualitative self-assessments is that they require minimal survey time and do not involve incentivization, making them particularly well suited for inclusion in large-scale population surveys. This has led to their widespread use in surveys worldwide (see, e.g., Ding et al., 2010; Hardeweg et al., 2013) and their inclusion in major representative household panels, including the BHPS, HILDA, HRS, PSID, SOEP, and SHARE.

A recent development combines hypothetical lottery measures with qualitative self-assessments of willingness to take risks. Falk et al. (2023) compare the out-of-sample predictive power of linear combinations of roughly thirty different survey measures about willingness to take risks. They find that the strongest performance is achieved by combining a non-incentivized lottery experiment and the general risk question of Dohmen et al. (2011), with the qualitative measure adding explanatory power beyond the lottery task alone. A closely performing alternative combines a staircase lottery design with the general risk question. While predictive power is imperfect, consistent with noise and broader notions of risk preferences, this combined measure has been adopted for large-scale global fielding (Falk et al., 2018), where it predicts risky behaviors at the individual level and risk-related institutions at the country level.

8 Variants of this adaptive procedure have since been adopted in modern elicitation methods, including Falk et al. (2023) and Wang et al. (2024).

Replications of the validation exercises in Falk et al. (2023) across countries yield similar mappings, but also suggest that quantitative elicitation formats, such as multiple price lists, are more reliable predictors and less sensitive to environmental heterogeneity than qualitative self-reports (see, e.g., Bauer et al., 2020; Kosfeld and Sharafi, 2024; Kosfeld et al., 2025). The advantages of using multiple items for eliciting risk preferences are well-documented (see, e.g. Vieider et al., 2015; Menkhoff and Sakha, 2017), partly reflecting measurement error in both quantitative and qualitative measures. Quantitative tasks require comprehension of probabilistic information and cognitive effort, which likely contributes to their correlation with cognitive ability (see, e.g., Dohmen et al., 2010; Andersson et al., 2016; Dohmen et al., 2018). Qualitative measures reduce some complexity but still rely on introspection and are subject to noise due to differences in scale use or risk perception, and are likewise related to cognitive ability (Dohmen et al., 2010).[9] As a result, measurement error is more pronounced in representative population samples than in student or otherwise selected samples (see, e.g., Dohmen et al., 2011).

2.3 Patience

The standard tools to elicit time preferences or, more generally, patience, are very similar. The goal is to isolate how much compensation an individual respondent would require to wait for the realization of a later payoff instead of an earlier payoff. In studies eliciting patience using multiple price lists, participants typically face a series of choices that reveal their preferences for receiving rewards at different times (e.g., Coller and Williams, 1999). Specifically, respondents choose between smaller, sooner rewards (e.g., \$100 now) and larger, later rewards across multiple scenarios (\$101, \$102, ..., \$150 12 months later). The switching point from sooner to later rewards provides a measure of their impatience, as reflected in their discount rate, because later rewards typically involve larger amounts (e.g., \$108 in 12 months instead of \$100 today, i.e., a discount rate of 8%). As for risk preferences, the elicitation of time preferences can involve incentivized choices or hypothetical versions of the same or similar choice scenarios, including staircase measures that use titration to identify an individual's discount rate under the assumption of the DU framework (for surveys, see, e.g., Frederick et al., 2002; Cohen et al., 2020).[10]

Again, an alternative approach to elicit measures of patience involves qualitative self-assessments. Here, respondents state their agreement with statements about individual patience. One example is the question about the respondent's willingness to give up something that is beneficial for them today in order to benefit more from that in the future, on a scale from 0 (unwilling) to

9 For a formal treatment of survey responses and measurement error, see Falk et al. (2021a).

10 An additional complication for the elicitation of time preferences arises in the presence of risk aversion, i.e., concave utility in the EUT framework (see Andersen et al., 2008, for details).

10 (very willing, see Falk et al., 2023). Responses to subjective self-assessments provide an ordinal measure of patience.

Various versions of non-incentivized quantitative measures, including price lists and staircases, as well as qualitative measures of patience have been validated as predictors of choices in incentivized multiple price list elicitations (see, e.g., Vischer et al., 2013; Falk et al., 2023). Falk et al. (2023) find that a combined measure including both quantitative and qualitative items has the best out-of-sample predictive power. The GPS data include such a combined measure, comprising a staircase measure and a qualitative self-assessment of patience (Falk et al., 2018). Fewer studies have implemented patience measures in large population-wide surveys than for risk preferences. Moreover, validation studies have found greater heterogeneity in the validity of subjective self-assessments for time preferences than for risk preferences (see, e.g., Bauer et al., 2020; Kosfeld and Sharafi, 2024; Kosfeld et al., 2025).

3 Data sets with global coverage

This section introduces several data sets that contain preference measures elicited at a global scale or in a large sample of countries. We conduct a brief discussion of the data sets, focusing on those with roughly comparable measures of preferences and coverage. The discussion does not aim for an exhaustive list of global preference data, but rather focuses on the most extensive and easily accessible data sets.[11]

3.1 Representative samples

3.1.1 Global Preferences Survey/Gallup

The Global Preferences Survey (GPS) measures risk, time, and social preferences (including altruism, positive reciprocity, negative reciprocity, and trust) for a sample of approximately 80,000 individual respondents drawn as representative samples from 76 countries around the world, covering 90 percent of both the world's population and global income (Falk et al., 2018).[12] The GPS was conducted as part of the Gallup World Poll in 2012. The survey items used in the GPS are based on an experimentally validated survey module (Falk et al., 2023). The survey items have been translated into local languages applying a back-translation procedure in addition to pre-testing for cultural appropriateness, and involve monetary stakes of comparable sizes across countries.

The measure of risk preferences combines a qualitative item assessing a respondent's subjective willingness to take risks and a quantitative item based on a series of hypothetical lottery choices. The qualitative item asks individuals to rate their willingness to take risks on a scale from 0 (unwilling) to 10

---

[11] Other work includes, e.g., Meissner et al. (2023) who use representative samples for eight European countries.

[12] See also gps.econ.uni-bonn.de/home.

(very willing), following Dohmen et al. (2011). The quantitative item presents respondents with a sequence of five interdependent choices between a varying safe payment and a binary lottery offering either a positive payment or no payment, each with 50% probability. To ensure comparability across countries, payments were adjusted based on purchasing power parity and relative to median household income for each country. The responses are combined using weights derived from the validation of these survey items (see Falk et al., 2018, 2023, for details).

Time preferences were elicited in a similar way, combining survey responses to a quantitative and a qualitative survey item. The quantitative item confronted respondents with five interdependent choices between an immediate payment and varying future payments with a 12-month delay, assuming no inflation. The qualitative survey question asked individuals to rate their willingness to forgo something that is beneficial for them today in order to benefit more from that in the future, on a scale from 0 (unwilling) to 10 (very willing). As with risk preferences, the two measures were combined using weights established through the validation of the questions (see Falk et al., 2018, 2023, for details). More recently, Burro et al. (2022) elicited time preferences using a simpler (binary) question about preferences for an earlier or later income (PELI) in a sample of 65 countries and documented a high correlation with the GPS measures in the 44 countries for which both measures are available.

3.1.2 World Values Survey

The World Values Survey (WVS) is one of the most widely used cross-national surveys in the social sciences, containing a large number of survey items on human values, beliefs and attitudes (Inglehart et al., 2020).[13] Conducted globally almost every five years since 1981, the WVS provides representative comparative data, with seven waves available to date. Our analysis utilizes data from wave 6 (2010–2014), which was conducted around the same time as the other representative data sets. This wave includes responses from almost 90,000 individuals across 60 countries.[14]

While the WVS does not contain experimentally validated measures for economic preferences, it offers proxies frequently used in the literature.[15] Risk preferences are assessed through a qualitative self-evaluation question, asking respondents to what extent they think they are similar to a person for whom having an exciting life, taking risk and adventure are important. Responses are given on a six-point scale, ranging from "not at all like me" to "very much like me". Time preferences are not measured by asking respondents how they solve an intertemporal trade-off. Instead the WVS asks respondents whether

13 See also www.worldvaluessurvey.org.

14 Robustness checks with wave 5 (2005–2009) deliver similar results.

15 The items in the WVS are constructed through rigorous protocols that ensure cross-national comparability, including independent back-translations, expert review, and comparisons against the master questionnaire.

they consider thrift, saving money and things to be particularly important qualities for children. This question is part of a list of 11 qualities, from which respondents can select up to five that they find most relevant. Since this measure does not elicit respondents' time preferences directly by confronting them with intertemporal trade-offs, we consider this measure to be fairly indirect, and potentially affected by other factors (such as education styles or altruism).

3.1.3 Ruggeri et al. (2022)

The data from Ruggeri et al. (2022) were collected using online tools via the Qualtrics survey platform and include responses from over 13,500 respondents from 61 countries. The sampling process involved multiple stages, starting from an initial convenience sample of 5–10 participants to ensure comprehension of survey questions. This was followed by the recruitment of approximately 30 participants in each country by local country teams to verify functionality. Finally, full-scale recruitment in the general population and data collection were conducted, but without ensuring representativeness.

The data collection aimed to investigate various "anomalies" in intertemporal choice behavior, including present bias and subadditivity. The empirical analysis below leverages the fact that the dataset includes measures of risk preferences and time preferences that are comparable to those included in the GPS and WVS data sets. Risk preferences were assessed using a survey question that asked respondents to choose their preferred option from a set of five alternatives: (i) a sure payment of \$50, (ii) a binary lottery with 75% probability of obtaining \$67 (25% probability of obtaining \$0), (iii) a binary lottery with 67% probability of obtaining \$75 (33% probability of obtaining \$0), (iv) a binary lottery with 50% probability of obtaining \$100 (50% probability of obtaining \$0), (v) and a binary lottery with 25% probability of obtaining \$200 (75% probability of obtaining \$0).

Time preferences were elicited using several survey items. In the baseline scenario, respondents chose between an immediate payment (which corresponded to approximately 10% of the average national household income) or delayed payment of 110% of the immediate amount after 12 months. If they opted for the immediate payment, they were subsequently offered a delayed payment of 120% of the immediate amount. If they still preferred the immediate payment, they were presented with a final option of 150% of the immediate amount as the delayed payment. Conversely, participants who initially chose the delayed payment were given follow-up choices of 102% and 101%, respectively. Additional scenarios featured alternative stakes, including negative payments (losses) or varying time frames to extract subadditivity. A broader discounting score based on all scenarios, ranging from 0 (always preferring delayed gains or earlier losses) to 19 (always preferring immediate gains or delayed losses) was computed. For our analysis, we differentiate between two measures: the broader discounting score (referred to as the combined measure) and the initial survey item of the baseline scenario (single measure), which excludes loss aversion and other dimensions of intertemporal choice.

3.2 Convenience samples and student samples

Not all data sets with preference measures at a global scale involve representative country samples or samples of the general population; some are elicited in more specific samples, such as university students. On the one hand, the fact that student samples are not representative of the broader population in each country might raise concerns about selection bias and external validity in a general population context. On the other hand, student samples offer the advantage of comparability with typical subject pools used in laboratory experiments for preference elicitation. In view of several existing studies that have used student samples or convenience samples to reveal global variation in economic preferences, we incorporate the largest respective data sets in our analysis.

3.2.1 INTRA data (Rieger et al., 2015)

The International Test on Risk Attitudes (INTRA) is a data set that has been constructed by Rieger, Wang, and Hens in collaboration with researchers and labs at various universities around the world (see Rieger et al., 2015, for details). The preference data were collected from a sample of approximately 7,000 undergraduate students (primarily first- and second-year) across 53 countries. The average age was 21.5 years, and the gender distribution was roughly balanced.

The dataset includes survey measures for risk preferences, time preferences and other preferences (see Rieger et al., 2015; Wang et al., 2016; Rieger et al., 2021). Specifically, participants responded to 14 decision-making questions, including ten lottery-based questions to elicit risk preferences, three questions related to time preferences, and one question measuring ambiguity aversion. Additionally, the survey included questions on other attitudes and values, such as the Hofstede Values Survey Module (Hofstede and McCrae, 2004), as well as questions on happiness and socio-demographic background. The monetary values used in the multiple price list tasks were denominated in local currency and adjusted based on the monthly average incomes and expenses of local students, while also accounting for purchasing power parity.

Risk preferences were elicited by measuring participants' willingness to pay for various hypothetical lotteries involving gains with different probabilities (for details, see Rieger et al., 2015).[16] The analysis below relies on survey responses in which participants stated the maximum amount they would be willing to pay for different lotteries, e.g., a lottery offering a 40% chance of winning $0, and a 60% chance of winning the equivalent of $100.[17]

16 Additional lotteries involving losses or mixed outcomes were used to elicit loss aversion.

17 Alternative lotteries featured payoffs of $0 and $400 or $0 and $10,000, with probabilities of 10% and 90%. Our analysis includes respondents with complete answers to lotteries 1–6 in the

Time preferences were measured using a quantitative survey item eliciting respondents' preferences in decisions between an immediate payment and a delayed payment. Concretely, respondents were asked about whether or not they preferred varying payments $X delayed by one year to an immediate payment of $100.[18]

3.2.2 *Maps data (Vieider et al., 2015; L'Haridon and Vieider, 2019)*

Another dataset with global coverage includes measures of risk preferences from a sample of approximately 3,000 students in 30 different countries (see Vieider et al., 2015; L'Haridon and Vieider, 2019). Preferences were measured by eliciting certainty equivalents for 44 binary prospects that varied in terms of payment amounts, probabilities, domains (gains or losses), and source of uncertainty (known or ambiguous probabilities). In addition, the dataset contains responses to a qualitative question assessing the general subjective willingness to take risks, identical to the validated measure used by Dohmen et al. (2011). As documented by Vieider et al. (2015), responses to this general risk question correlate with incentivized lottery choices both within and across countries. For our empirical analysis, we use the mean of the standardized responses to the general risk question and the certainty equivalent of the first lottery as our measure of risk preferences.

3.2.3 *GLOBE data (House et al., 2004)*

The Global Leadership and Organizational Behavior Effectiveness Project (GLOBE) developed measures of societal culture, as reflected in shared motives, values, beliefs, and identities transmitted across generations. These measures span nine dimensions of societal culture, based on data collected from over 17,000 middle managers in 951 organizations in 62 countries (House et al., 2004).[19]

One of these dimensions, uncertainty avoidance, reflects the extent to which societies seek to mitigate uncertainty through social norms, rules, and procedures. The measure of uncertainty avoidance is based on responses to four questions assessing the extent to which a society relies on social norms, rules, and procedures to alleviate unpredictability of future events, and the tendency to seek orderliness, consistency, structure, formal procedures, and laws to cover situations in their daily lives. Each of these questions measures agreement on a Likert scale from 1 (strongly agree) to 7 (strongly disagree).

---

study. The final measure is derived by winsorizing responses at the 99th percentile, standardizing them and averaging across the six items.

[18] Alternative choices involved a binary decision between an immediate payment of $3,400 and a payment of $3,800 after one month. For the analysis, we use responses to items 1–3, including only respondents who provided answers to all three items. The final measure was derived by winsorizing responses at the 95th percentile, standardizing them, and averaging across the three items.

[19] See also the GLOBE Project website https://globeproject.com/study_2004_2007.

Time preferences are captured by a dimension on future orientation. This dimension consists of four questions about practices regarding planning for the future instead of taking life events as they occur. Responses are given on a Likert scale from 1 to 7. Individual responses for both dimensions were aggregated at the country level by averaging and then standardized.

Notably, these responses do not measure the uncertainty avoidance or future orientation of individual respondents but instead reflect country-level measures of risk attitudes and future orientation that are based on the assessment of managers and capture the broader cultural context in which they are embedded. As a result, the GLOBE data provide insights into aggregate (country-level) variation, but differ conceptually from the other data sets. Our interest in including the GLOBE is mainly for comparability with literature that has used this data set as a source of variation in culture related to risk and time preferences, and for comparison of the respective data patterns.

4 Economic preferences: a global view

4.1 The global distribution of preferences

We begin by documenting the global distribution of risk-taking and patience using maps, which show the geographic coverage and distribution of the respective measures across different datasets. To aid comparability despite variation in measurement approaches, we aggregate standardized individual-level measures to the country level. For the GLOBE data, which contains country-level observations only, the standardization is implemented at the country level and variation is therefore higher by construction than in country-level measures derived from data sets with individual-level observations. We then normalize these values relative to the corresponding average for the USA, which allows us to compare, across datasets, whether the measures for the willingness to take risk or patience for a particular country all deliver a similar value relative to the USA.

☐ Stylized Fact 1: Preferences exhibit considerable heterogeneity around the world.

4.1.1 The global distribution of risk preferences

Fig. 1 presents the global distributions of risk preferences. Both the GPS and WVS reveal broadly similar global patterns. Relative to the USA, the average willingness to take risks in most countries, especially in Europe, Asia, and Oceania, is smaller (risk aversion is larger), but some countries, especially in Africa, exhibit a greater willingness to take risks (risk aversion is smaller). The color pattern, which is comparable in terms of scale (measured in standard deviations), is, perhaps surprisingly, similar, with Europe exhibiting populations that are about a fourth of a standard deviation less willing to take risks. Similar findings apply to Latin America, Asia, and Australia/Oceania. A notable difference is visible for India and Russia. The data collected by Ruggeri et al. (2022), on the contrary, which has a smaller worldwide coverage than the GPS or WVS, exhibits quite different patterns, with most countries more willing to take risks than the USA (except for Japan and Uruguay). The INTRA and Maps studies also cover a smaller number of countries, but use student samples. Similar to the GPS and WVS, the data sets indicate higher risk aversion in Europe compared to the USA. They also align in the ranking of some Latin American and Asian countries, though some inconsistencies exist. The INTRA data show a greater willingness to take risks in China—contrasting with the GPS, WVS, and Maps data, but aligning with the Ruggeri data. Meanwhile, the risk preference patterns in the GLOBE data partly resemble those in the representative samples, especially so for Western Europe, Asia and Oceania.[20]

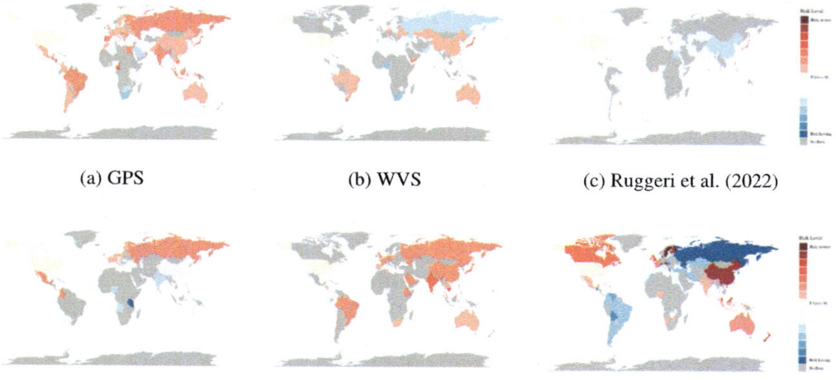

(a) GPS (b) WVS (c) Ruggeri et al. (2022)

(d) INTRA (e) Maps Data (f) GLOBE

Note: Country averages of standardized preference measures, ranging from dark red (very risk-averse) to dark blue (very risk-loving); values are normalized to the respective average for the USA (yellow).

FIGURE 1 Average Willingness to Take Risk (Relative to USA).

4.1.2 The global distribution of patience

The analogous pattern for the global distribution of patience is depicted in Fig. 2. According to the GPS, virtually all countries have populations that are, on average, less patient than the U.S. population. The pattern emerging from the other data sets is very similar. Specifically, the data from Ruggeri et al. (2022) closely align with the GPS data, showing that the populations of most countries are less patient than the U.S. population. This finding holds regardless of whether using a comparable measure based on a trade-off between an immediate payment versus delayed payment or a combined measure incorporating different

[20] As mentioned above, the comparison for the GLOBE data needs to be restricted to qualitative interpretations as the standard deviations are by construction higher than for the other data sets.

time delays in both the gain and loss domains. Also, the two data sets with global coverage of convenience samples—the INTRA data, which includes students and their mentors, and the GLOBE data, which surveys middle managers' assessments—exhibit patterns that closely resemble those found in the GPS data. The only exception is the pattern observed in the WVS, which indicates that many countries—particularly in Europe and Asia—have more patient populations than the USA. One potential explanation for this discrepancy lies in the survey items used to elicit time preferences. The measure of patience in the WVS asks about qualities encouraged in children at home. In contrast, the measures used in GPS, Ruggeri et al. (2022), and the INTRA data set, which ask individuals about their own patience, are more closely aligned.

In sum, the findings document pronounced heterogeneity in economic preferences across the world. Moreover, the observed patterns are similar for comparable preference measures and samples. In this context, it is interesting to note that the results for the GPS and WVS align closely for risk preferences, a domain for which both data sets use at least one rather similar survey item. In contrast, results diverge for time preferences, where the elicitation methods differ significantly. A reversed pattern appears in the comparison between the GPS data and the data from Ruggeri et al. (2022): time preference measures are closely aligned, and so are the cross-country patterns, while risk preference measures and cross-country patterns differ. This suggests that the variations in empirical patterns are primarily driven by differences in the measurement methods, whereas differences in respondent samples have a more moderate impact.

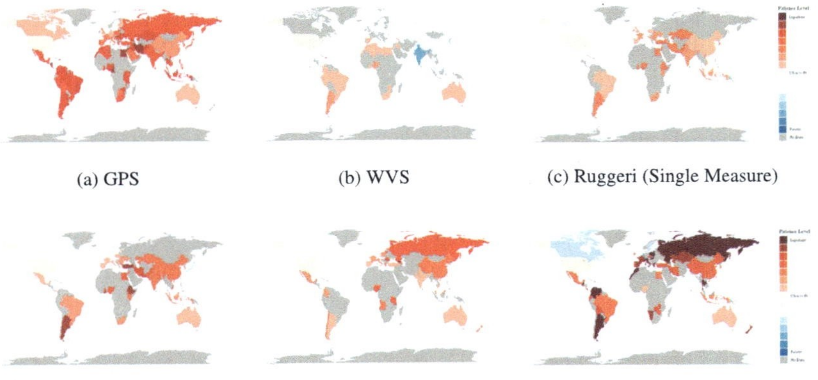

(a) GPS (b) WVS (c) Ruggeri (Single Measure)

(d) Ruggeri (Combined Measure) (e) INTRA (f) GLOBE

Note: Country averages of standardized preference measures, ranging from dark red (very impatient) to dark blue (very patient); values are normalized to the respective average for the USA (yellow).

FIGURE 2 Average Patience (Relative to USA).

4.2 Cultural heterogeneity

The significant heterogeneity in preferences across the world raises questions about systematic patterns. The variation could reflect stable differences arising from cultural heterogeneity, but an alternative possibility is that the rankings could be largely driven by noise. In this section we address the possibility of noise in two ways. We explore the robustness of preference rankings within any given dataset to noise arising from sampling variation. We then explore more rigorously whether different datasets yield similar rankings of countries, consistent with a systematic underlying cultural variation emerging from these multiple attempts at global measurement. From this analysis, we establish our second stylized fact:

☐ Stylized Fact 2: Within data sets, rank correlations across countries are stable with respect to sampling. Between data sets, rank correlations across countries are positively correlated.

4.2.1 Cultural heterogeneity: risk

Although data sets such as the GPS and the WVS—and to a lesser extent the data from Ruggeri et al. (2022)—are designed to be representative of the general population, variation in sampling may influence a country's position in the global preference distribution. To investigate the stability of the global patterns of heterogeneity in risk preferences, we rank countries by their average willingness to take risks. We then replicate this ranking based on sub-samples of 30% of respondents for 100 iterations of sub-sampling. For each country, we calculate the rank correlation across iterations. The resulting correlations indicate a high consistency of rankings.[21] This is especially true for the data sets that rely on representative samples, the GPS and the WVS, which exhibit rank correlations between the 30%-sub-samples larger than 0.95 with very low dispersion (standard deviations of ranks are 3.61 and 2.34, respectively). The other data sets still exhibit average rank correlations around 0.7–0.8, but these are much less tightly clustered around the mean, so that re-sampling results in greater rank variability.[22] These results indicate that, at least for the WVS and GPS, sampling variation among respondents of a country contributes rather little to the measured global variation of risk preferences, making it plausible that country differences in risk preferences reflect cultural variation.

Fig. 3 provides a complementary analysis by plotting the average ordinal ranking of countries based on the average willingness to take risks of their populations, along with the standard deviations of these ranks.[23] In the data sets with representative population samples, such as the GPS and WVS, country

[21] The respective results are displayed in Fig. A1.

[22] The corresponding standard deviations are 9.62 for the data by Ruggeri et al. (2022), 6.21 for the INTRA data, and 4.11 for the Maps data.

[23] Fig. A2 in the Appendix presents the corresponding results for re-sampling with fixed absolute sample sizes (200 individuals).

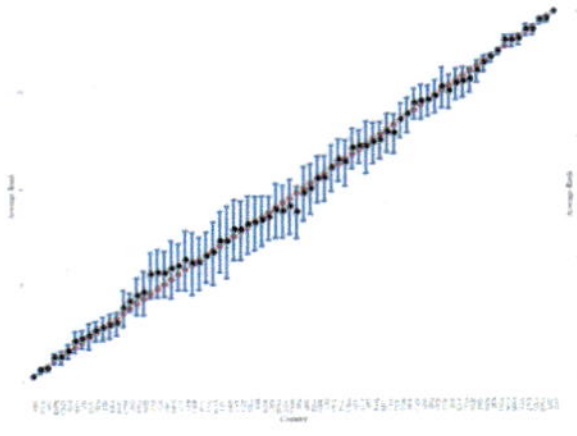

(a) GPS

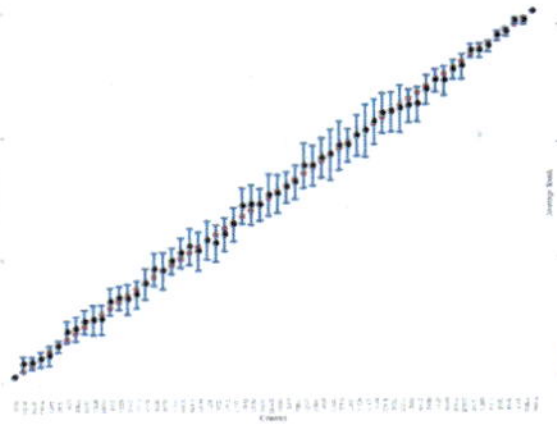

(b) WVS

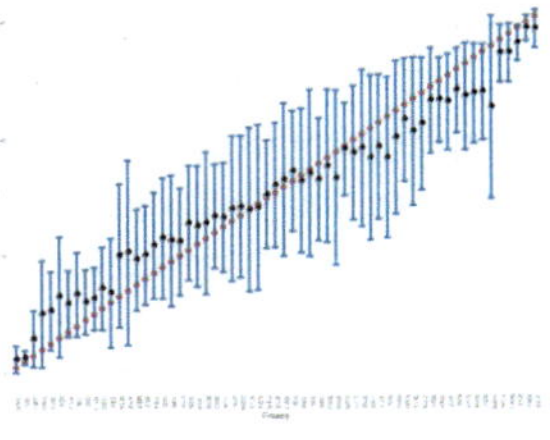

(c) Ruggeri et al. (2022)

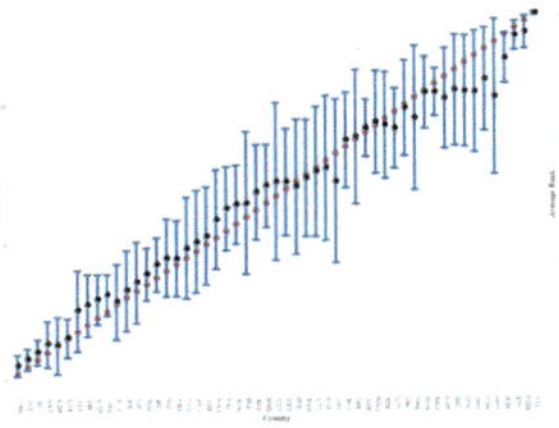

(d) INTRA

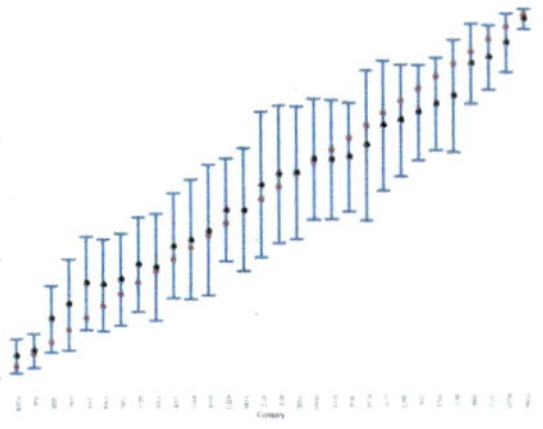

(e) Maps Data

Note: The figures plot average ranks and standard deviations for 100 iterations of taking a sub-sample of 30% of the observations of a country. The red dots represent the actual ranking based on the entire samples, and the countries are arranged in ascending order of these actual ranks. Blue whiskers represent standard deviations.

FIGURE 3 Rank Consistency: Risk.

rankings show little sensitivity to re-sampling. Greater variability appears in the middle of the rank distribution compared to the extremes: If countries in the center of the distribution are closer in terms of the absolute average preference, the same degree of sampling variation (i.e., the same variation around the estimated mean) leads to higher variation in ranks. Data sets with less representative samples—Ruggeri et al. (2022), INTRA, and Maps—also exhibit some degree of rank stability, though with greater variation in the ordinal ranking of countries as indicated by the larger standard deviations.[24] This increased variability may stem from smaller sample sizes or more heterogeneous samples across countries.[25]

Since the data sets cover different sets of countries, the rank order plots are not directly comparable. To address this, we constructed plots using normalized ordinal ranks, ranging from 0 to 1. Instead of average risk-taking by country, these plots show average risk-taking by country rank. A similar result emerges, comparing across datasets: There is an (inverted) S-shaped pattern.

[24] Due to the lack of information at the individual level, the GLOBE data is excluded from this analysis.

[25] For instance, student samples might be more selective in some countries than in others with respect to access to a tertiary education path and selection into particular programs, such as economics.

Rankings at the extremes are stable and largely invariant, while the flat middle section indicates little heterogeneity, making rankings there susceptible to small sampling changes.[26] This is in line with the higher variability observed in the center of the distribution for the re-sampling exercise (Fig. 3).[27]

We also examine how comparable country rankings are across different data sources. To do so, we compute cross-country correlations of the risk measures. We use the set of countries that overlap in each pairwise comparison. Table 1 shows that risk preference measures are positively correlated across most data sets, indicating broadly similar country rankings, although with substantial heterogeneity. The Ruggeri et al. (2022) ranking shows only a weak positive association with the GPS data, and the GLOBE project stands out as the only case with negative correlations relative to two other data sets. Clearly, these correlations are attenuated due to the previously discussed imperfect within-dataset rank correlation that is due to sampling error.[28]

TABLE 1 Correlation matrix between data sets: Risk.

	GPS	WVS	Ruggeri	INTRA	Maps Data	GLOBE
GPS	-	0.31	0.05	0.30	0.33	−0.19
WVS	38	-	0.22	0.12	0.27	0.31
Ruggeri	43	32	-	0.22	0.38	0.10
INTRA	40	29	39	-	0.07	−0.13
Maps Data	25	19	18	19	-	0.25
GLOBE	42	33	35	37	18	-
Relative overall	1.00	1.45	1.08	0.81	0.99	0.23
Relative overall (excluding GLOBE)	1.00	0.81	0.72	0.76	0.63	

Note: Rank correlations are taken of all common countries between two data sets (risk). Top right are Spearman correlation coefficients, bottom left are number of overlapping countries between the data sets. The relative overall correlation is constructed as the weighted sum of correlation coefficients, with the number of overlapping countries between two data sets as weights, and normalized to the respective sum for the GPS for comparability.

Note also that the raw correlations are not directly comparable as each pairwise estimate is based on a different number of overlapping countries. The GPS shows the largest overlap overall (with a total of 188 country-pairs across all other data sets). To assess which data set aligns most closely with the others, the bottom rows of Table 1 report a weighted overall correlation measure, where correlations are weighted by the number of overlapping countries and normalized relative to the GPS. The WVS exhibits the largest overall correlation

26 See also Appendix Fig. A3.

27 See also Appendix Fig. A4.

28 Correlations here and in the following are obtained without correcting for measurement error, i.e., coefficients might be underestimated. Appendix Table A1 shows the corresponding results for sub-samples restricted to a similar age of respondents in the range 18–30.

of the risk preference measures with the other data sets, followed by the data by Ruggeri et al. (2022). However, GLOBE's negative correlation with two data sets casts doubt on the consistency of its measure of risk preferences, which is not surprising given that, in contrast to all other data sets, the GLOBE data is not based on respondents' measures of their own preferences, but captures managers' assessments of the country's population's tendency to avoid risks. Therefore, we also report the weighted score when excluding the GLOBE's correlation coefficient. This paints a more consistent picture with all data sets exhibiting relatively high scores, with the GPS revealing the highest score.

4.2.2 *Cultural heterogeneity: patience*

The analysis of cultural heterogeneity for patience yields similar patterns. We find that re-sampling does not greatly affect the country ranking in patience, with rank correlations exceeding 0.95 for the two representative data sets, the GPS and the WVS, and little variation (standard deviations of 2.86 and 2.54, respectively).[29] The corresponding rank correlations for the data sets based on convenience samples and students are only moderately lower.[30]

Fig. 4 documents the rank consistency for each of the data sets.[31] The rank correlation obtained with each data set is largely insensitive to re-sampling. Again, the stability is slightly weaker for countries in the center of the respective rank distribution.[32]

Table 2 shows the respective correlation results for patience obtained with different data sets. Again, the results show substantial heterogeneity. Interestingly, however, the results reveal an even more coherent picture than for risk preferences: All correlations of patience measures across data sets are positive, indicating the consistency of measures across data sets, but the correlations vary in size. The largest correlations are found between the measures contained in the GPS and in the data by Ruggeri et al. (2022) and in the INTRA data. Naturally, the two scores provided by Ruggeri et al. (2022) are highly correlated with each other and therefore only one of them is included in the respective weighted sums. Unsurprisingly, the highest relative overall correlation is obtained for the GPS data, closely followed by the other data sets except the WVS. Given that the WVS exhibits the lowest correlation coefficients across all data sets, this suggests that the measure might capture different dimensions of time preferences or other traits.[33]

29 See Appendix Fig. A5 for the resulting distributions of rank correlations based on 100 replications with sub-samples of 30% of respondents.

30 The respective standard deviations are 5.26 and 3.69 for the baseline measure and the combined measure, respectively, in the data by Ruggeri et al. (2022), and 4.44 for the INTRA data.

31 The corresponding figure for re-sampling based on an absolute number of draws is shown in the Appendix, see Fig. A6.

32 Likewise, Appendix Fig. A7 shows the corresponding figure for the normalized ranks.

33 Appendix Table A2 contains the corresponding results for the sub-sample of respondents aged 18–30.

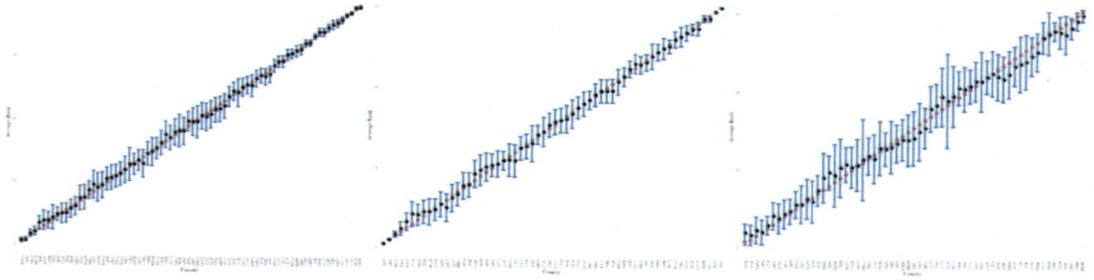

(a) GPS (b) WVS (c) Ruggeri (Single Measure)

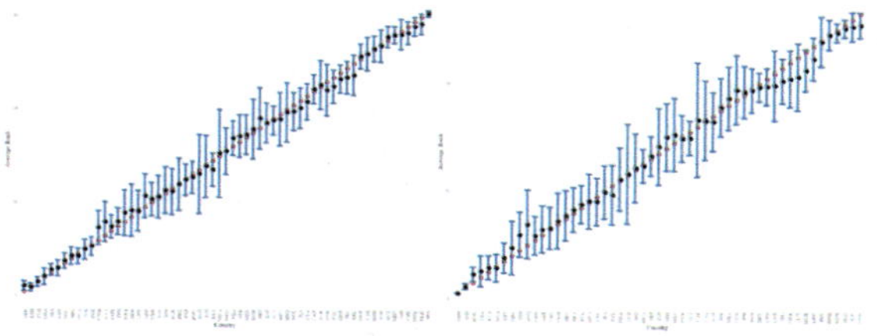

(d) Ruggeri (Combined Measure) (e) INTRA

Note: The figures plot average ranks and standard deviations for 100 iterations of taking a sub-sample of 30% of the observations of a country. The red dots represent the actual ranking based on the entire samples, and the countries are arranged in ascending order of these actual ranks. Blue whiskers represent standard deviations.

FIGURE 4 Rank Consistency: Time.

TABLE 2 Correlation matrix between data sets: Patience.

	GPS	WVS	Ruggeri (Single)	Ruggeri (Combined)	INTRA	GLOBE
GPS	-	0.39	0.66	0.69	0.66	0.62
WVS	38	-	0.41	0.44	0.03	0.23
Ruggeri (Single)	43	32	-	0.92	0.56	0.55
Ruggeri (Combined)	43	32	61	-	0.66	0.52
INTRA	40	29	39	39	-	0.60
GLOBE	42	33	35	35	37	-
Relative overall (S)	1.00	0.38	0.86		0.74	0.78
Relative overall (C)	1.00	0.39		0.90	0.77	0.76

Note: Rank correlations are taken of all common countries between two data sets (patience). Top right are Spearman correlation coefficients, bottom left are number of overlapping countries between the data sets. The relative overall correlation is constructed as the weighted sum of correlation coefficients, with the number of overlapping countries between two data sets as weights, and normalized to the respective sum for the GPS for comparability. The relative overall correlations are constructed by excluding one of the Ruggeri measures: (S) considers only the single measure, while in (C) only the value of the combined measure is used.

Summing up, we find considerable stability with respect to sampling within data sets. The stability between data sets is primarily driven by the respective preference measures contained in the data sets.

4.3 Extending the scope: global variation in risk and time preferences

One shortcoming of the analysis of economic preferences using different data sets with numerous countries is the limited overlap of countries across data sets. This, together with the heterogeneity in measures of risk and time preferences, implies that the information on global variation in preferences is limited by the comparability of measures across different samples of countries. For instance, the overlap of countries in the GPS with any other of the data sets comprises at most 43 countries, and the subset of countries for which all data sets of global coverage are available is down to 8 for measures of risk preferences and 15 for measures of time preferences. While the limited overlap in the sets of countries used in different datasets makes comparison more difficult, a silver lining is that combining the different datasets could expand the total number of countries for which there is at least one type of measure for each preference. Combining the information from different data sets is also a potential way to reduce measurement error because for many countries a synthesized data set contains multiple observations.

The main challenge to aggregating the different datasets is isolating common factors from the various measures of these preferences that involve different survey items, response scales, and country samples. Here, we follow an approach proposed by Rieger et al. (2021) for the case of time preferences. This approach combines the standardized preference measures from different data sets by using a principal component analysis (PCA) and extracting a common preference factor. The corresponding PCA weight for a particular measure that is missing in a country (since the respective measure has not been elicited in this country) is set to zero, and the PCA weights are renormalized to sum to one for each country. The synthetic measure of global preference variation is then obtained by predicting the weighted average of standardized measures for each country.

We apply this methodology separately to measures of risk preferences and of time preferences using all available data sets, except for restricting to one of the two versions of the Ruggeri data (single measure) for time preferences. The corresponding synthetic measures will be denoted as Synthetic World Aggregate Preferences for Risk (SWAP-Risk) or Time (SWAP-Time), respectively. We note that one might construct measures of global variation in preference that overcome the challenge of small overlap and different measures in different ways. Nevertheless, we illustrate this procedure as a useful tool of how to combine different data sets with individual responses to particular preference measures to obtain a data set with larger scope and broader global coverage.

Moreover, it is straightforward to extend the procedure to incorporate other data sets or newly available studies with the same or different measures.

Table 3 presents summary statistics of the resulting synthetic global preference measures in terms of the number of countries for which the synthetic measures are constructed and the correlations of the synthetic measures with the various individual-level measures of risk and time preferences from the different data sets.

TABLE 3 Construction of Synthetic Global Preference Measures.

	Risk (SWAP-Risk)		Time (SWAP-Time)	
	Number of Countries Overlap	Correlation Coefficient	Number of Countries Overlap	Correlation Coefficient
GPS	76	0.66	76	0.86
WVS	60	0.76	60	0.72
Ruggeri	61	0.67	61	0.87
INTRA	53	0.53	53	0.77
Maps Data	30	0.61		
GLOBE	57	0.60	57	0.80
Total	116		116	

Note: The table lists the contributions of the different data sources to the Synthetic World Aggregate Preferences (SWAP) measures, in terms of the number of countries and the correlation coefficient.

Fig. 5 shows the emerging world maps for global variation in risk preferences and patience. The respective values for the individual countries are listed in Appendix Table A3.

(a) Risk (b) Time

Note: Standardized values per country, ranging from dark red (very risk-averse / very impatient) to dark blue (very risk-loving / very patient) in comparison to USA.

FIGURE 5 Synthetic Global Preference Measures: Average Risk and Patience (Relative to USA).

4.4 Potential deep determinants of cultural heterogeneity in risk and time preferences

Evidence of cultural heterogeneity in risk and time preferences raises many fascinating questions about where such differences might come from. In this section we briefly survey a recently emerging literature that has sought to understand deep determinants of preference differences across countries, restricting our attention to studies that span multiple countries. We also extend previous work on how differences in risk and time preferences around the globe are related to ancient migration patterns, exploring robustness to a broader range of datasets and countries.

From a theoretical perspective, heterogeneity in preferences is likely to be the result of heterogeneous environmental conditions and evolutionary dynamics that lead to a selection of specific preference types, partly in combination with other traits such as cognitive intelligence (see, e.g., Robson, 2001; Robson and Samuelson, 2011). Primary candidates for such environmental conditions are mortality risk (Robson and Samuelson, 2010) or the frequency of decisions and the severity of decision errors (Netzer, 2009). In addition, social interactions, population composition, and societal interactions have been shown to determine the emergence of stable preference patterns (Alger et al., 2020; Alger and Weibull, 2019).

One strand of empirical research examines the relationship of preferences, especially risk preferences, to geography, environment, and lifestyle of ancestors. Howden and Levin (2023) use GPS data and country-level panels to show that lifetime exposure to greater climatic variation reduces individuals' willingness to take risks. They interpret this as operating through an informational channel about higher background risk. Geography has also been implicated in shaping risk preferences through its influence on occupations and lifestyles. Cai et al. (2022) combine historical ethnographic data on sea-fishing with the GPS measure of risk preference to demonstrate that having sea-fishing ancestors is associated with greater willingness to take risks. They argue that this can reflect the ancient sorting of individuals into sea-fishing according to willingness to venture onto the risky environment of local seas, and subsequent transmission of their risk preferences to later generations. Chan and Luo (2025) show, using GPS data, that having ancestors who had a pastoral occupation (herding) is associated with increased willingness to take risks. They argue that this occupation exposed ancestors to idiosyncratic risks, and that the development of tactical responses to risk, like herd diversification, may have instilled a greater tolerance for risk that was transmitted to subsequent generations. Similarly, Nazarova (2024) finds in WVS data (and other data sources) that ancestral nomadic lifestyles — shaped by environmental factors like availability of animals suitable for long-distance travel — predict greater willingness to take risks. Geographic factors have also been linked to cross-country differences in patience. Galor and Özak (2016) demonstrate that pre-industrial suitability of local land for agricultural investment is associated with the development of patience, as measured by WVS data. The proposed channel is that returns to investment fostered a future-oriented mindset that was passed on in the form of patience.

Various within-country studies have also documented relationships of risk preferences and patience to environmental factors, especially extreme weather events and disasters, with adverse events generally decreasing willingness to take risks and decreasing patience (Cameron and Shah, 2015; Cassar et al., 2017; Hanaoka et al., 2018; Di Falco and Vieider, 2022; Jaramillo et al., 2025).

A second strand of research has investigated the relationship of preferences to cultural factors of religion and language. Although ancient, such factors are socially constructed, raising the possibility that they are not determinants, but rather could have co-evolved with certain preferences. Chen (2013) studies the relationship of linguistic structure to patience as proxied by savings behavior across a large set of countries, finding that languages that force a stark separation between present and future are associated with a lesser propensity to save, and Falk et al. (2018) show similar findings of reduced patience using the GPS patience measure and a broader set of countries.[34] Studies on religion and preferences have mainly used subject pools from individual countries, and have found that Catholics are relatively more willing to take risks than, e.g., Protestants (Noussair et al., 2013; Benjamin et al., 2016), while finding little evidence of a relationship between religion and patience (Benjamin et al., 2016).

A third approach has been taken by Becker et al. (2020), who seek to explain absolute differences across countries rather than preference levels. They show that ancient migration patterns out of Africa help explain the global distribution of risk and time preferences. Using GPS data, they find that populations separated longer by earlier migrations exhibit significantly greater differences in risk preferences. There is a positive, but smaller and not statistically significant impact of time of separation on differences in patience. The authors hypothesize that one mechanism through which ancestral temporal difference may magnify preference differences is through distinct historical experiences.

We extend the analysis of Becker et al. (2020) across multiple datasets, using various preference measures and a larger set of countries. The variable of interest is a composite measure of ancestral genetic distance.[35] Table 4 replicates their findings, confirming that greater ancestral distance predicts larger absolute differences in average risk preferences between countries. In contrast to Becker et al. (2020), we find that the relationship is even stronger for patience. Notably, the synthetic datasets also show significant, quantitatively large associations with ancestral distance, suggesting preferences are deeply

---

[34] Roberts et al. (2015) replicate the analysis in Chen (2013) accounting for relatedness among languages, and find robust although weaker relationships.

[35] In contrast to Becker et al. (2020), we only construct the index as the unweighted average of the standardized values of two measures of genetic distance (based on Spolaore and Wacziarg, 2018), but not linguistic distance.

TABLE 4 Absolute Preference Difference and Ancestral Distance.

	Dependent variable: Absolute difference in preference level						
	GPS	**WVS**	**Ruggeri**	**INTRA**	**Maps Data**	**GLOBE**	**SWAP-Risk**
Panel A: Risk							
Ancestral distance	0.24***	0.10	0.00	0.13*	0.05*	0.06***	0.13**
	(0.09)	(0.07)	(0.05)	(0.07)	(0.03)	(0.01)	(0.05)
Country FE	Yes	Yes	Yes	Yes	Yes	Yes	Yes
Observations	2,701	1,653	1,653	1,326	435	1,596	6,105
R^2	0.63	0.48	0.52	0.66	0.58	0.46	0.60
	GPS	**WVS**	**Ruggeri (S)**	**Ruggeri (C)**	**INTRA**	**GLOBE**	**SWAP-Time**
Panel B: Patience							
Ancestral distance	0.06	0.27***	0.24**	0.23**	0.09*	0.04	0.12***
	(0.04)	(0.07)	(0.10)	(0.10)	(0.05)	(0.04)	(0.04)
Country FE	Yes	Yes	Yes	Yes	Yes	Yes	Yes
Observations	2,701	1,653	1,653	1,653	1,326	1,596	6,105
R^2	0.53	0.59	0.32	0.45	0.72	0.46	0.45

Note: Ancestral distance is measured in terms of a composite index of ancestral genetic distance following Becker et al. (2020). The index is computed as unweighted average of the standardized values of two measures of genetic distance, see text. The index is standardized. Country fixed effects are included and standard errors are clustered for both countries separately.

rooted in cultural differences and demonstrating the value of combining datasets for cross-validation.

5 Economic preferences: country-level correlates

In this section, we explore whether the preference measures obtained from different data sets as well as the synthetic global preference data set exhibit comparable correlations with country-level characteristics. This analysis provides several insights. First, it offers an additional way to validate whether the preference measures across different data sets capture comparable information. Second, it assesses whether the associations between different economic preferences and aggregate correlates found in the literature remain robust across different data sets, which are based on different measures and population samples. Strictly speaking, this analysis should be restricted to data sets with representative population samples. However, for completeness and comparability with previous studies that have used these preference measures as proxies for cultural variation across countries or populations, we also include data sets based on more selected samples, such as student samples.

We conduct the analysis for different dimensions of characteristics: income per capita and democracy as two measures that are frequently used in the literature to capture variation in socio-economic development and institutional quality, respectively. In addition, we present results for correlates that have been used in previous work on single data sets (see, e.g., Falk et al., 2018) so that the following analysis complements existing studies by providing a sense of the comparability of the results across preference measures from different data and of the systematic variation in preferences as a part of culture.

☐ Stylized Fact 3: Preferences exhibit consistent cross-country correlations with socio-economic development.

5.1 Aggregate correlates: risk

Table 5 presents the results for the correlation between countries of various aggregate variables with measures of risk preferences from the different data sets. Each coefficient corresponds to a separate regression with the corresponding number of observations.

Estimates in the first column capture the relationship between risk preferences and GDP per capita as a measure of overall economic development. The results reveal a negative correlation of willingness to take risks and the level of development for all data sets. Moreover, the relation is not statistically significant for the GPS, Ruggeri and Maps data. At first sight, this finding appears surprising, as higher incomes are typically associated with a higher willingness to take risks at the level of individuals or households (see, e.g., Dohmen et al., 2011). However, this finding aligns with earlier results that have reported a similar unconditional association across countries (see, e.g., Falk et al., 2018). The literature also suggests a discrepancy in the association between risk preferences and income at the aggregate and household level: the relationship of risk tolerance with GDP is typically found to be negative, whereas the relationship with income within countries is positive (see Falk et al., 2018; Bouchouicha and Vieider, 2019).

The results in the second column refer to the correlation of risk preferences with self-employment, measured in terms of the self-employment share in the working-age population. The decision to become self-employed is associated with more risky earnings than employed work, and thus constitutes a deliberately risky choice that has been shown to correlate with risk preferences in previous literature (see, e.g., Barsky et al., 1997; Dohmen et al., 2011). In fact, the results indicate that the cross-country correlation between the average willingness to take risks and self-employment across countries is positive. As with GDP per capita, the correlation is not statistically significant for the GPS, Ruggeri and Maps data.

The third set of results refers to the relation between country-level variation in risk preferences and country-level variation in expenditures for research and development (R&D), measured as share of GDP. The estimates reveal a

TABLE 5 Regression Coefficients for Aggregate Correlates: Risk.

	Dependent variable:				
Risk measured in:	**GDP per capita (in logs)**	**Self-employment share**	**R&D**	**Education (in years)**	**Institutions: Democracy**
GPS	−0.581	12.175	−0.610	−0.570	−3.246
	(0.391)	(8.570)	(0.458)	(0.924)	(2.040)
Observations	75	76	51	72	74
R^2	0.029	0.027	0.035	0.005	0.034
WVS	−0.890**	19.656**	−1.058**	−2.154**	−1.912
	(0.387)	(9.303)	(0.482)	(1.050)	(2.735)
Observations	59	59	43	53	58
R^2	0.085	0.073	0.105	0.076	0.009
Ruggeri	−1.040	21.635	−0.944	−1.737	−14.030***
	(0.673)	(16.718)	(0.863)	(1.831)	(3.290)
Observations	61	61	49	54	60
R^2	0.039	0.028	0.025	0.017	0.239
INTRA	−1.118***	37.345***	−0.500	−2.395***	−5.128***
	(0.245)	(6.320)	(0.385)	(0.615)	(1.535)
Observations	53	52	43	47	51
R^2	0.289	0.411	0.040	0.252	0.186
Maps Data	−0.613	24.973	−1.984**	−1.003	1.822
	(0.679)	(16.904)	(0.733)	(1.826)	(4.120)
Observations	30	30	24	28	30
R^2	0.028	0.072	0.250	0.011	0.007
GLOBE	−0.403***	5.045*	−0.549***	−0.677**	−0.688
	(0.123)	(2.801)	(0.136)	(0.281)	(0.755)
Observations	57	56	44	55	56
R^2	0.164	0.057	0.279	0.099	0.015
SWAP-Risk	−0.305***	6.824***	−0.461***	−0.543**	−1.221**
	(0.097)	(2.151)	(0.115)	(0.244)	(0.560)
Observations	114	115	80	103	112
R^2	0.081	0.082	0.171	0.047	0.041

Note: Sources: Penn World Tables (GDP per capita), World Bank (self-employment, R&D), Barro-Lee Educational Attainment Data Set (average years of schooling), Polity V (democratic quality, polity2-index). All data is for the year 2010.

negative correlation for preference measures from all data sets. While surprising at first sight, this correlation largely reflects the negative correlation with overall development as proxied by GDP per capita. The fourth column includes results for education.

The last set of results pertains to institutional quality, measured by an index of the quality of democratic institutions. Democracy has been used extensively as a proxy for inclusive institutions that are viewed as a determinant of economic development that is potentially even more fundamental than human capital (see, e.g., Acemoglu et al., 2014). Across all data sets except for the Maps data, a negative correlation with the democratic quality index is observed, but it is only significant for the Ruggeri and INTRA data.

Overall, the synthetic global measure of risk preferences (SWAP-Risk) captures these overall patterns and exhibits significant associations with all country-level covariates: negative with GDP per capita, R&D, the education level and democracy, and positive with the self-employment share. This illustrates its potential usefulness in providing a global measure of risk preferences with a broad coverage of countries. Moreover, this measure accounts for approximately 4–17% of the cross-country variation in aggregate correlates, which is comparable to the variation accounted for by other measures of cultural heterogeneity used in previous work.[36]

5.2 Aggregate correlates: patience

Table 6 contains the corresponding results for patience. As before, the first column contains the results for GDP per capita as an overall measure of economic development. All data sets reveal a strong positive and (with the exception of the WVS) significant association between patience and GDP per capita. It should be noted, however, that a positive association might be the result of mechanisms that run both ways. On the one hand, patience induces greater incentives for investment, knowledge accumulation and other activities that are beneficial for economic development in the long-run (see, e.g., Sunde et al., 2022). On the other hand, a higher level of economic development and better living conditions might foster greater patience (see, e.g., Sunde et al., 2026). Again, the discrepancy in the pattern obtained with the WVS might be related to the measurement of patience, which might capture traditional education styles focusing on instilling conservative values to children, rather than individual patience.

The second column contains the results for the savings rate as a proxy for capital accumulation. The association is positive but weak for most data sets, with the GPS exhibiting the strongest association among all data sets. The third set of results refers to total factor productivity (TFP) whose association with patience is positive for measures from all data sets, with the exception of the WVS. The fourth column contains results for the correlation of time preferences with education, measured in terms of average years of schooling. Education can

36 For instance, in analysis comparable to that in Table 5, the cross-country variation in GDP per capita explained by trust is 13–17% (using GPS or WVS measures of trust and the respective samples), 5% by individualism, 8.9% by religiosity, and 1.2% by a composite measure of civic values (all based on WVS measures).

TABLE 6 Regression Coefficients for Aggregate Correlates: Time.

	Dependent variable:				
Time measured in:	GDP per capita (in logs)	Savings Rate	TFP	Education (in years)	Institutions: Democracy
GPS	1.607***	0.053**	0.238***	3.599***	5.359***
	(0.271)	(0.021)	(0.058)	(0.633)	(1.608)
Observations	75	75	62	72	74
R^2	0.325	0.077	0.222	0.316	0.134
WVS	0.639	0.040	−0.144	2.405**	2.324
	(0.410)	(0.034)	(0.103)	(1.041)	(2.802)
Observations	59	59	48	53	58
R^2	0.041	0.023	0.041	0.095	0.012
Ruggeri (Single)	2.037***	0.041	0.230**	4.429***	6.431***
	(0.259)	(0.027)	(0.098)	(0.768)	(1.835)
Observations	61	61	51	54	60
R^2	0.512	0.038	0.102	0.390	0.175
Ruggeri (Combined)	1.414***	0.011	0.124*	3.292***	5.095***
	(0.169)	(0.019)	(0.068)	(0.487)	(1.182)
Observations	61	61	51	54	60
R^2	0.542	0.006	0.063	0.467	0.243
INTRA	0.840***	0.041**	0.320***	1.761***	3.004**
	(0.167)	(0.016)	(0.064)	(0.646)	(1.144)
Observations	53	53	48	47	51
R^2	0.332	0.122	0.353	0.142	0.123
GLOBE	0.321**	0.020**	0.046	0.754***	0.966
	(0.127)	(0.009)	(0.029)	(0.277)	(0.750)
Observations	57	57	54	55	56
R^2	0.104	0.089	0.045	0.123	0.030
SWAP-Time	0.606***	0.019***	0.086***	1.441***	1.803***
	(0.083)	(0.007)	(0.021)	(0.200)	(0.545)
Observations	114	114	89	103	112
R^2	0.322	0.068	0.156	0.341	0.091

Note: Sources: Penn World Tables (GDP per capita, savings, TFP), Barro-Lee Educational Attainment Data Set (average years of schooling), Polity V (democratic quality, polity2-index). All data is for the year 2010.

be seen as an alternative measure of overall economic development in light of the relevance of human capital for productivity and development (Diebolt and Hippe, 2019; Sunde et al., 2022). The estimates reveal a positive and significant correlation between patience and education for all data sets. The last set of results for aggregate correlates refers to institutional quality, measured by an index of the quality of democratic institutions. The resulting pattern shows positive and significant associations, except for the WVS and the GLOBE data, for which the correlations are insignificant.

Taken together, these findings are largely consistent with earlier results of consistent patterns for data sets that have comparable measures of risk and time preferences, and diverging patterns for data sets with measures that are less closely linked to the underlying preference and thus less reliable. Specifically, it is notable how the patterns for time preferences obtained with the WVS deviate. This could reflect the fact that the measure of time preference in the WVS refers to respondents' assessment that "patient" behavior in specific domains is an important trait to be instilled in children, rather than eliciting respondents' own patience. Similarly, the GLOBE data exhibit differing patterns while the responses reflect an assessment of middle managers about the cultural predispositions in the overall population, rather than the respondents' own traits.

Also here, the synthetic global measure of time preference (SWAP-Time) exhibits significant associations with all aggregate correlates, and thereby offers a useful complement to the individual data sets. Moreover, the explanatory power of this measure for variation in aggregate correlates is considerable, especially for GDP and education.[37]

Taken together, the aggregate results show that risk and time preferences constitute an important and behaviorally relevant part of a society's culture. Above and beyond other cultural markers, such as religion, values or social norms, economic preferences are systematically associated with central country-level outcomes and account for a similar or even larger fraction of the respective cross-country variation than other measures of cultural heterogeneity.

6 Economic preferences: individual-level correlates

6.1 General patterns

In this section, we turn to the relationships of economic preferences to individual-level traits. Specifically, we focus on three dimensions of heterogeneity that have been found to correlate with individual preferences: gender, age, and socio-economic status (in terms of household income). Whereas gender and age are plausible drivers of preference heterogeneity at the individual level, the mechanisms behind the correlation between preferences and socio-economic status could potentially go both ways. In fact, existing evidence supports the notion of stable preferences and systematic heterogeneity along these dimensions (Sahm, 2012; Schildberg-Hörisch, 2018; Frey et al., 2017; Falk et al., 2021b). Moreover, while our analysis does not aim for causal statements, it builds on

[37] In view of a recent literature on religious norms and modernization in sociology, additional results for an index of secular values show similar patterns. Specifically, the secularization index exhibits a mostly negative association with the willingness to take risks (except for a positive association in the data by Ruggeri et al. (2022)), and a positive association with patience.

earlier research that has shown systematic heterogeneity in preferences along these dimensions (Dohmen et al., 2011; Falk et al., 2018; Frey et al., 2021).

Table 7 contains the results of regressions of measures of risk preferences in different data sets on a core set of individual characteristics—gender, age, and socio-economic status. The age profile is captured by a quadratic specification in light of previous evidence for non-linear age profiles (e.g., Dohmen et al., 2017). For each data set, we present the results for two specifications, without and with controls for socio-economic status (income). All specifications account for country-specific differences in risk preferences in terms of country fixed effects.

A first insight from the results concerns the relative importance of within-country variation in risk preferences as compared to between-country variation. Estimates from specifications without controls other than country fixed effects reveal that systematic between-country variation only accounts for 10–15% of the total variation in risk preferences.[38] This finding, which is in line with earlier reports, suggests that a major part of variation in preferences is not accounted for by systematic variation between populations of countries.

The estimation results for the individual characteristics show a consistent gender difference in risk preferences: Women are significantly less willing to take risks than men across all data sets. In terms of age profile, the estimates suggest a lower willingness to take risks at higher ages, although the age profiles are concave for some data sets, convex for others, and insignificant in the INTRA and Maps data. Finally, a higher income is associated with a greater willingness to take risks.

Table 8 contains the corresponding results for patience. Also in this preference domain, systematic variation between countries only accounts for a small fraction of the total variation.[39]

The estimation results for the individual characteristics reveal more heterogeneous patterns than for risk preferences. Specifically, women tend to be more impatient in the GPS data and in the data by Ruggeri et al. (2022), at least when the contrast in the baseline scenario is used to measure patience. The results for the combined measure reveal no significant gender difference, as do the results for the INTRA data. In contrast, the results obtained with the WVS data reveal a positive effect, suggesting greater patience among female respondents. The age patterns are similar across data sets and suggest a hump-shaped (concave) age profile, except for the WVS. Also, the effect for socio-economic status is different across data sets. These results provide further evidence for the sensitivity of the findings with respect to the specific preference measures contained in the

38 Specifically, the R^2 from the respective regressions of a specification with country fixed effects are 0.1 for the GPS, 0.11 for the WVS, 0.03 for the data by Ruggeri et al. (2022), 0.12 for the INTRA data, and 0.08 for the Maps data. The GLOBE data only contains observations at the country level.

39 Specifically, between-country variation only accounts for 0.14 of the variation in the GPS data (in terms of an R^2), 0.11 in the WVS, 0.09 in the raw measure and 0.23 in the combined measure of the data by Ruggeri et al. (2022), and 0.21 in the INTRA data.

TABLE 7 Individual-Level Correlates: Risk.

	GPS		WVS		Ruggeri		INTRA	Maps Data	
	(1)	(2)	(3)	(4)	(5)	(6)	(7)	(8)	(9)
1 if female	−0.205***	−0.199***	−0.216***	−0.212***	−0.161***	−0.160***	−0.249***	−0.138***	−0.140***
	(0.014)	(0.014)	(0.015)	(0.015)	(0.016)	(0.016)	(0.040)	(0.039)	(0.041)
Age	−0.001	−0.002	−0.025***	−0.024***	−0.017***	−0.018***	0.003	−0.020	−0.022
	(0.002)	(0.002)	(0.003)	(0.003)	(0.005)	(0.005)	(0.032)	(0.026)	(0.026)
$(Age)^2/100$	−0.012***	−0.011***	0.014***	0.014***	0.012**	0.013**	−0.001	0.047	0.047
	(0.002)	(0.002)	(0.003)	(0.003)	(0.006)	(0.005)	(0.055)	(0.042)	(0.041)
Income (in logs)		0.067***		0.312***		0.024			0.177***
		(0.008)		(0.043)		(0.015)			(0.054)
Country FE	Yes	Yes	Yes	Yes	Yes	Yes	Yes	Yes	Yes
Observations	79,439	79,439	86,220	83,504	13,269	13,267	6,367	2,939	2,675
R^2	0.15	0.16	0.16	0.16	0.05	0.05	0.13	0.09	0.09

Note: Standard errors are clustered at the country level.

TABLE 8 Individual-Level Correlates: Patience.

	GPS		WVS		Ruggeri (Single)		Ruggeri (Combined)		INTRA
	(1)	(2)	(3)	(4)	(5)	(6)	(7)	(8)	(9)
1 if female	−0.074***	−0.070***	0.039***	0.036***	−0.139***	−0.140***	0.013	0.012	0.013
	(0.013)	(0.013)	(0.012)	(0.011)	(0.028)	(0.028)	(0.019)	(0.019)	(0.023)
Age	0.007***	0.006***	0.004**	0.004**	0.019***	0.020***	0.002	0.003	0.009
	(0.002)	(0.002)	(0.002)	(0.002)	(0.006)	(0.006)	(0.005)	(0.005)	(0.019)
$(Age)^2/100$	−0.015***	−0.014***	0.001	0.000	−0.022***	−0.022***	−0.006	−0.006	−0.001
	(0.002)	(0.002)	(0.002)	(0.002)	(0.007)	(0.007)	(0.006)	(0.006)	(0.026)
Income (in logs)		0.046***		−0.095**		−0.015		−0.015	
		(0.009)		(0.037)		(0.013)		(0.013)	
Country FE	Yes	Yes	Yes	Yes	Yes	Yes	Yes	Yes	Yes
Observations	79,472	79,472	89,319	86,149	13,269	13,267	13,237	13,235	6,364
R^2	0.16	0.16	0.12	0.12	0.10	0.10	0.23	0.23	0.22

Note: Standard errors are clustered at the country level.

surveys. The patience measure in the WVS consistently delivers different results from the patience measures in the other data sets.

6.2 Gender differences across countries

To investigate the universality of these findings, we consider whether and to what extent these patterns hold in the different countries contained in the respective data sets. As a first dimension, we consider differences in preferences between women and men.

☐ Stylized Fact 4: Preferences exhibit consistent patterns of differences between women and men.

The literature has documented consistent differences in the willingness to take risks between women and men, with women typically being found to be less willing to take risks than men. This perception is based on survey evidence for gender differences in risk (Charness and Gneezy, 2012) and evidence in psychology (see, e.g., Byrnes et al., 1999, for a meta study that reports evidence for women being more risk averse). These gender differences are present in many countries, comprising both patriarchal and matriarchal societies (Gneezy et al., 2009; Falk et al., 2018) and seem to become visible around puberty (Khachatryan et al., 2015). More recent evidence suggests that above and beyond mean differences in preferences between women and men, men exhibit greater variability (Thoeni and Volk, 2021). In addition, gender differences in risk (and other) preferences have been shown to decline with the level of economic development and gender equality (Falk and Hermle, 2018). Recent work suggests that this association, sometimes referred to as gender equality paradox, is accounted for by systematic cultural variation across countries (Berggren and Bergh, 2025).

Fig. 6(a) plots the results for gender differences in terms of the coefficients for gender from regressions of individual responses to the question about the willingness to take risks on gender, age, and household income. The regressions allow for country-specific gender coefficients, but hold the age and income coefficients constant across countries and include country-specific intercepts. The results reveal almost exclusively positive coefficient estimates, indicating that in almost all countries and across all data sets, men are more willing to take risks than women, thus generalizing the results from Table 7. Specifically, the coefficient estimates are negative (i.e., women are more willing to take risks than men) in 4 out of 76 countries in the GPS data, in only one country (out of 60) in the WVS, in 12 out of 61 countries in the data by Ruggeri et al. (2022), and eight out of 27 countries in the Maps data.

Existing evidence is less conclusive when it comes to gender differences in time preferences. According to earlier meta-studies on the relation between time preference (delay of gratification) and gender, women are more patient (Silverman, 2003), whereas more recent evidence appears to find the opposite (Falk et al., 2018; Falk and Hermle, 2018).

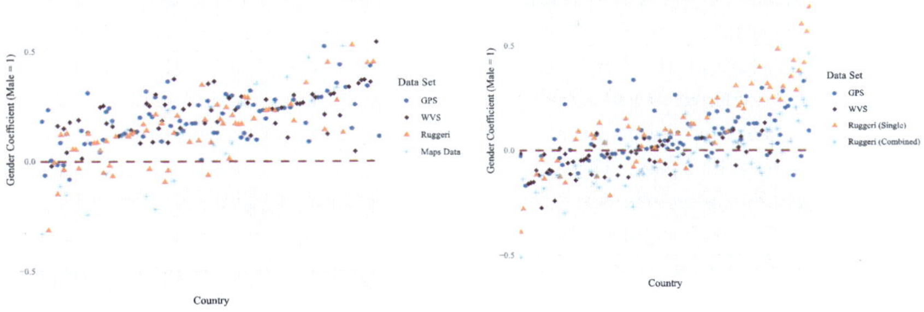

(a) Risk (b) Time

Note: This figure plots gender differences in preferences across countries for each data set. Positive values indicate that men are more risk-loving/patient than women.

FIGURE 6 Gender Differences.

The results depicted in Fig. 6(b) are consistent with this (mixed) evidence. In a majority of countries and data sets, men appear to be more patient than women, although the opposite is found for a considerable set of countries and data sets, complementing the estimates shown in Table 8. Importantly, these patterns do not appear to be driven by specific data sets or questions.

Another pattern that has gained attention in the recent literature is the extent to which gender differences in preferences vary by the level of economic development. Evidence suggests that gender differences in preferences are greater in economically more developed and more gender equal countries (Falk and Hermle, 2018; Cuevas et al., 2021). Replicating this analysis by relating the country-specific gender coefficients for risk and time preferences for the different data sets (as in Fig. 6) to GDP per capita delivers a similar pattern: on average, gender differences are more pronounced in richer countries (see Appendix Fig. A8). In fact, the estimated slope coefficients for the large and representative data sets (GPS and WVS) are quantitatively very similar, while the relation is less pronounced in the samples with convenience and student samples.

6.3 Differences by age

The second dimension of individual heterogeneity in economic preferences we study is age. Here, we investigate the universality of heterogeneity in preferences across age groups.

☐ Stylized Fact 5: Preferences show systematic heterogeneity across age groups.

Conceptually, one might think of different reasons for expecting risk preferences and time preferences to be correlated with age. These include lifetime experiences (Kettlewell, 2019), cohort differences (Dohmen et al., 2017), as well as variation in the prospective length of life (Sunde et al., 2026). Existing evidence has found a declining propensity to take risks at higher ages (Dohmen et al., 2011; Mata et al., 2011; Josef et al., 2016; Mata et al., 2016; Dohmen et al., 2017; Fitzenberger et al., 2022).

In line with existing evidence, Table 7 shows a negative age gradient in the willingness to take risks. This gradient is close to linear and universal across all data sets. The regression results are robust to more flexible specifications of the age profile. Specifically, the results are similar in terms of the coefficients for age bins in regressions that also control for gender, household income, and country-specific intercepts.[40] The only exceptions are outliers for some age bins in data sets with non-representative samples (INTRA and Maps).

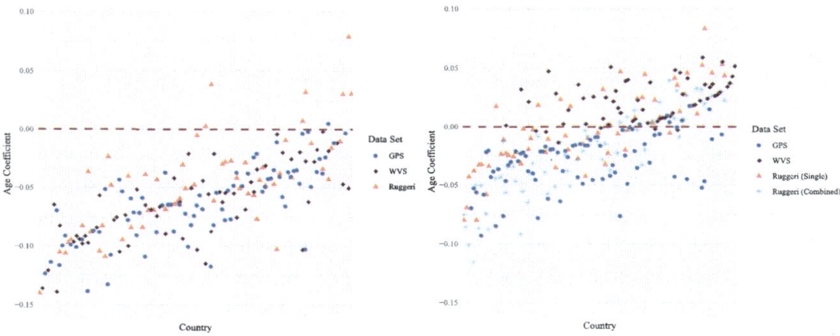

(a) Risk (b) Time

Note: This figure plots the age coefficients for the different countries for the different preferences and datasets. To obtain the age group coefficients, gender, income and country fixed effects are included in the model.

FIGURE 7 Age Coefficients.

Fig. 7 reports the corresponding results for country-specific age patterns (based on five-year age groups) in regressions of risk preferences and time preferences on gender, income, and country fixed effects. As for the gender differences, this analysis sheds light on the universality of age patterns across countries. Overall, the majority of age coefficients on risk preferences is negative (189 out of 197 coefficient estimates), indicating that the willingness to take risks declines with age in almost all countries and data sets.[41] While the estimates in Table 8 suggest a hump-shaped age pattern in patience on average, the picture for country-specific linear age patterns for patience is less uniform,

[40] See Appendix Fig. A9.

[41] The Ruggeri data exhibit positive age coefficients for 7 countries and negative coefficients for 54 countries. The corresponding numbers are 1 vs. 75 in the GPS, and exclusively negative coefficients in the WVS data.

with 157 out of 258 coefficients being negative and a greater discrepancy in the estimates across data sets.[42] Moreover, there is greater variability at higher ages across data sets.[43] Patience declines monotonically with age in the GPS, stays almost constant across age groups in the data by Ruggeri et al. (2022), and increases with age in the WVS. Again, this might be related to the measure for patience elicitation in the WVS, which might reflect parenting style and altruistic values, rather than individual time preferences. The other data exhibit less coherent patterns and more variability across age groups.

Moreover, these overall age patterns exhibit moderate heterogeneity. For instance, the gender differences are fairly comparable across age groups.[44] At the same time, the differences across age groups exhibit some visible differences between women and men. In particular, the age profiles for women are less pronounced than those for men.[45]

6.4 Differences by socioeconomic status

The third dimension of preference heterogeneity is socio-economic status, as reflected by individual income.

- ☐ Stylized Fact 6: Preferences exhibit consistent correlations with socioeconomic status at the individual level.

To explore preference heterogeneity in this dimension, we present the coefficient estimates for income bins (in terms of country-specific income deciles) from regressions of individual responses to the question about the willingness to take risks (or patience), with additional controls for gender, age bins, and country-specific intercepts.

Fig. 8(a) presents the corresponding results for the willingness to take risks. Consistent with the estimates in Table 7, the results when allowing for country-specific associations reveal an almost uniformly positive income gradient: individuals in higher income groups are more willing to take risks. This pattern is consistent with, and generalizes, earlier findings in the literature (see, e.g. Dohmen et al., 2011; Falk et al., 2018; Bouchouicha and Vieider, 2019).

A similar pattern is found for patience, as indicated by the results of a positive income gradient shown in Fig. 8(b) for the GPS data and the data by Ruggeri et al. (2022). Again, the WVS data on patience reveal the opposite pattern, which is presumably due to the measure for patience, complementing the findings of Table 8.

To explore the universality of these patterns across countries, Fig. 9 plots the country-specific slope coefficients for income in regressions that account for

42 In particular, while only 6 out of 76 countries exhibit a positive age coefficient in the GPS data, the corresponding number for the WVS data is 53 out of 60.

43 See Appendix Fig. A9.

44 See Appendix Fig. A10.

45 See Appendix Figs. A11 and A12.

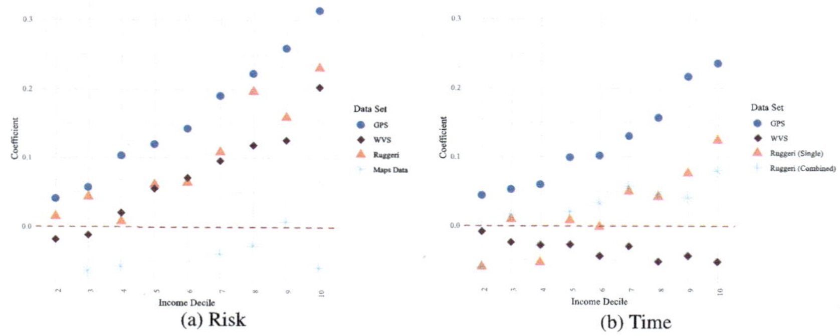

Note: This figure plots the coefficients of income deciles for the different preferences and datasets. To obtain the income coefficients, gender, age group, and country fixed effects are included in the model. Coefficients are measured relative to income decile 1.

FIGURE 8 Differences by Socioeconomic Status: Income Deciles.

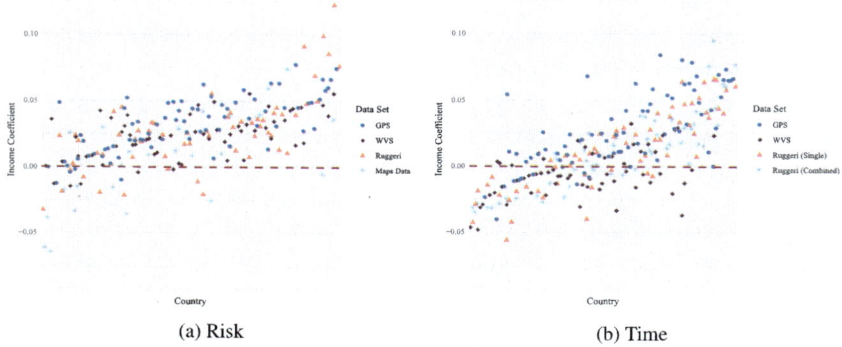

Note: This figure plots the income decile coefficients for the different countries for the different preferences and datasets. To obtain the income decile coefficients, gender, age group, and country fixed effects are included in the model.

FIGURE 9 Income Decile Coefficients.

gender and age, as in the previous estimates. The results reveal that individual income and willingness to take risks exhibit a positive association in a large majority of country observations (195 out of 225 coefficient estimates are positive). These patterns are even more pronounced for the data sets based on representative samples.[46]

[46] The income coefficients are positive in 71 of 76 countries in the GPS data, in 55 of 60 countries in the WVS, and in 52 of 61 countries in the Ruggeri data. In contrast, in the Maps data, which is mostly based on a sample of students, only 17 of 28 coefficients are positive.

A similar pattern emerges for the association between income and patience, although the pattern is slightly more mixed (163 out of 258 coefficient estimates are positive). A closer look reveals, however, that this discrepancy can be mostly explained by different findings in the WVS data with the patience measure that refers to patience as a desirable trait for children rather than individual patience.[47]

Also correlations of economic preferences with individual income exhibit only moderate heterogeneity. Specifically, the patterns are very similar regardless of whether considering the entire sample of countries, or when restricting attention to high-income and low-income countries, respectively.[48]

7 Extending the scope: global variation in other preferences

The main focus of this chapter is on risk and time preferences. There are, however, also large, international data sets that cover other types of preferences, in particular social preferences. In the following, we discuss a few examples. We note that, unlike time and risk preferences, there is little overlap in the specific notion of the respective preference measures, rendering a comparison between data sets difficult.

The GPS contains three measures of social preferences, together with a measure of trust (see Falk et al., 2018). The preference measures assess three important facets of social preferences, altruism, positive reciprocity and negative reciprocity, respectively. Altruism is measured with the help of two items. The first is the self-reported willingness to donate to a charity, in terms of the amount individuals would donate in case they won the equivalent of 1,000 Euros in a lottery. The second measures the self-assessed willingness to share with others without expecting anything in return (measured on a Likert scale from 0 to 10). Positive reciprocity is based on responses to two items as well. A qualitative item asks whether a respondent is willing to return a favor on an 11-point Likert scale. A quantitative item elicits willingness to reciprocate a favor, where the reward varies according to six levels of values. Negative reciprocity is measured with the help of three survey items, the individual willingness to take revenge when treated unjustly, even at a cost, willingness to punish unfair behavior toward themselves or toward a third party (all measured on a Likert scale). As shown in Falk et al. (2018), altruism, positive reciprocity and trust are significantly positively correlated. All preference measures also show significant variation between countries and vary systematically with important economic and social outcomes, both at the individual and the country-level. At the individual level, for example, altruism correlates well with individual

47 The GPS data exhibits positive coefficients in 64 out of 76 countries, and the Ruggeri data exhibit positive coefficients in 40 (39) of 61 countries for the basic (combined) measure of time preference, whereas the WVS only delivers positive income coefficients in 20 out of 60 countries.

48 For details, see Appendix Figs. A13 and A14.

willingness to donate money, volunteer time or help a stranger, while positive reciprocity is positively associated with having friends one can count on or being in a relationship. At the country-level, negative reciprocity is, for example, correlated with conflict and a "culture of honor" as shown in detail in Cao et al. (2021).

The World Values Survey (WVS) also contains a measure related to notions of altruism. It refers to the agreement as to whether or not it is important to teach children that being selfish (or unselfish) is important. The WVS and the GPS measures have an overlap of 36 countries and display a weak positive rank order correlation of 0.09. In terms of rank stability within data sets, the pattern for altruism is similar to that for risk and time preferences. Specifically, for both WVS and GPS re-sampling appears to have a minor impact on the ranking of countries in the different data sets. In addition, for both WVS and GPS, women tend to be more altruistic than men in most countries, and age as well as income have a positive effect on observed altruism.

Another international data set on prosocial preferences is Cohn et al. (2019) who use a "wallet experiment" design. Specifically, research assistants deposited more than 17,000 wallets at different places (such as museums or post offices) in 355 cities across 40 countries. Each wallet contained a business card of the presumed "owner" and varying amounts of money. The rate at which the "owner" of a wallet was contacted serves as a measure of "civic honesty". The authors report relatively high levels of civic honesty across countries. Moreover, the likelihood to return a wallet typically increases in the amount of money contained in the wallet, a finding they interpret as an expression of altruism in combination with image concerns. On measures of civic capital, see also Guiso et al. (2011).

A different approach is taken by Rhoads et al. (2021). They provide a country-level measure of altruism building on responses to seven different dimensions of altruistic behaviors. These involve, e.g., charitable donations, volunteering time, helping strangers, or willingness to donate blood or a kidney. Depending on data availability, responses for the different questions are available for different sets of countries (from 48 to 152 countries). The country-level altruism measure is computed as the average response to these items, which come from various data sets. The measure is positively associated with population-level subjective well-being and individualist values.

Recent work by Cappelen et al. (2025) provides global evidence regarding the relationship-specific nature of altruism. The degree of universalist preferences reflects whether altruism depends on the identity or group membership of other persons. They survey 64,000 individuals in 60 countries around the world and find that universalism is associated with a broader radius of trust. Based on a similar sample, Almås et al. (2025) investigate the global distribution of fairness preferences that relate to the acceptance of inequality depending on the source of this inequality. Their findings report evidence on the global distribution of fairness preferences, efficiency preferences, beliefs about the source of inequality and the cost of redistribution, as well as preferences for redistribution.

Another publicly available data set that measures an important prosocial preference is Andre et al. (2024) who study the willingness to fight climate change, in a globally representative sample. Their data is based on 125 representative country samples with almost 130,000 respondents, representing 96 percent of the world's gross domestic product and 92 percent of the global population. They find widespread support for climate action with 69 percent of the global population expressing a willingness to contribute 1 percent of their monthly household income, 86 percent endorsing pro-climate social norms and 89 percent demanding intensified political action. A related research question has been addressed by Dechezleprêtre et al. (2025) in a sample of 40,000 respondents in 20 countries.

More systematic research on global prosocial preferences with comparable measures constitutes an interesting avenue for future research.

8 Concluding remarks and outlook

This chapter has reviewed the existing evidence on global variation in economic preferences. After a brief and selective overview of available data sets and measures of risk and time preferences across the globe, we documented six empirical regularities that emerge robustly across different data sources.

First, economic preferences exhibit substantial variation across the globe. While some of this variation stems from differences in measurement and, to a lesser extent, sample composition, the overall distribution of global preferences is fairly comparable across representative population studies using reliable measures.

Second, the stability of country rankings in economic preferences depends on measurement. Our analysis of rank stability across data sets shows that preference rankings are more consistent for measures that ask individuals about their own preference, and in data sets with representative respondent samples.

Third, economic preferences exhibit consistent systematic correlations with country-level factors. Specifically, the average willingness to take risks is lower in richer countries, while the average level of patience tends to be higher. The same pattern emerges for average levels of education and institutional quality, as proxied by democracy. These patterns are replicated with synthetic global preference measures that combine the various measures from all available data sets. Moreover, greater ancestral distance is associated with larger differences in preferences across countries.

The remaining stylized facts refer to individual-level correlates. Our fourth fact states that economic preferences differ systematically between women and men. On average, women are less willing to take risks and show lower levels of patience. This gender difference is found in the majority of countries. Fifth, economic preferences vary with age. Willingness to take risks declines with age, while patience follows a less clear pattern. Sixth, preferences correlate with socioeconomic status at the individual level. Specifically, individuals in higher country-specific income deciles are more willing to take risks and more patient.

The goal of this chapter was to take stock of how data on the global variation in risk and time preferences has advanced our understanding of patterns of global variation and heterogeneity in the domains of risk and time preferences, rather than delivering results on a specific issue. In fact, many aspects of the risk and time preference variation are not well understood and give rise to a wide range of future research questions.

For example, we are just beginning to understand better the ultimate and proximate forces shaping the global variation in risk and time preferences. Exceptions include, e.g., the work by Galor and Özak (2016) and Galor and Savitskiy (2018) that illustrates the role of ancestral climatic and environmental conditions in shaping risk and time preferences, the work by Chen (2013) that provides evidence for coevolutionary processes between language and preferences, and work by Becker et al. (2020) that shows that differences in preferences across populations are rooted in temporally distant migration movements.

Similarly, important knowledge gaps remain about population level changes in risk and time preferences over time. A natural next step to the efforts in collecting global data on these preferences is to continue the systematic data collection repeatedly. This would provide the basis for knowing the instances of population level changes in preferences, the time scale at which they take place, and promises to shed light on the sources and drivers of such population level changes. Previous research on drivers of changes in preferences over time has shown, e.g., that exposure to natural disasters or macroeconomic shocks affects people's willingness to take risks (Hanaoka et al., 2018; Bernile et al., 2017; Malmendier and Nagel, 2011; Giuliano and Spilimbergo, 2024; Schildberg-Hörisch, 2018) and people's willingness to trade off present day against future rewards (Akesaka, 2019; Callen, 2015). Open questions pertain to, e.g., the persistence of such effects, their universality and their heterogeneity with regards to population specific characteristics, particular environments, or institutions.

Finally, extending to global survey data more generally, we have yet to study and understand the relationship between 'culture' and survey methods. For example, we do not know whether people's willingness to select into surveys depends on their culture. Likewise, we have little knowledge about whether responses are biased 'culturally' or how the survey methodology, e.g., phone interviews versus in person interviews, interacts with cultural norms and values. And, if so, what does this mean for interpreting data on the global variation in preferences, beliefs and attitudes?

Appendix A Supplementary material

Supplementary material related to this chapter can be found online at https://doi.org/10.1016/bs.hceb.2026.02.012.

References

Acemoglu, D., Gallego, F.A., Robinson, J.A., 2014. Institutions, human capital, and development. Annual Review of Economics 6, 875–912.

Akesaka, M., 2019. Change in time preferences: evidence from the great East Japan earthquake. Journal of Economic Behavior & Organization 166, 239–245.

Alger, I., Weibull, J.W., 2019. Evolutionary models of preference formation. Annual Review of Economics 11, 329–354.

Alger, I., Weibull, J.W., Lehmann, L., 2020. Evolution of preferences in structured populations: genes, guns, and culture. Journal of Economic Theory 185, 104951.

Almås, I., Cappelen, A.W., Sørensen, E.Ø., Tungodden, B., 2025. Fairness Across the World. NHH Dept. of Economics Discussion Paper, 06/2025.

Andersen, S., Harrison, G.W., Lau, M.I., Rutström, E.E., 2006. Elicitation using multiple price list formats. Experimental Economics 9, 383–405.

Andersen, S., Harrison, G.W., Lau, M.I., Rutström, E.E., 2008. Eliciting risk and time preferences. Econometrica 76, 583–618.

Anderson, L.R., Mellor, J.M., 2008. Predicting health behaviors with an experimental measure of risk preference. Journal of Health Economics 27, 1260–1274.

Andersson, O., Holm, H.J., Tyran, J.-R., Wengström, E., 2016. Risk aversion relates to cognitive ability: preferences or noise? Journal of the European Economic Association 14, 1129–1154.

Andre, P., Boneva, T., Chopra, F., Falk, A., 2024. Globally representative evidence on the actual and perceived support for climate action. Nature Climate Change 14, 253–259.

Andreoni, J., Sprenger, C., 2012. Risk preferences are not time preferences. American Economic Review 102, 3357–3376.

Barberis, N.C., 2013. Thirty years of prospect theory in economics: a review and assessment. The Journal of Economic Perspectives 27, 173–196.

Barsky, R.B., Juster, F.T., Kimball, M.S., Shapiro, M.D., 1997. Preference parameters and behavioral heterogeneity: an experimental approach in the health and retirement study. The Quarterly Journal of Economics 112, 537–579.

Bauer, M., Chytilová, J., Miguel, E., 2020. Using survey questions to measure preferences: lessons from an experimental validation in Kenya. European Economic Review 127, 103493.

Becker, A., Deckers, T., Dohmen, T., Falk, A., Kosse, F., 2012. The relationship between economic preferences and psychological personality measures. Annual Review of Economics 4, 453–478.

Becker, A., Enke, B., Falk, A., 2020. Ancient origins of the global variation in economic preferences. The American Economic Review: Papers and Proceedings 110, 319–323.

Benjamin, D., Choi, J., Fisher, G., 2016. Religious identity and economic behavior. Review of Economics and Statistics 98, 617–637.

Benjamin, D.J., Brown, S.A., Shapiro, J.M., 2013. Who is 'behavioral'? Cognitive ability and anomalous preferences. Journal of the European Economic Association 11, 1231–1255.

Bergeot, J., Jusot, F., 2023. Risk, time preferences, trustworthiness and COVID-19 preventive behavior: evidence from France. The European Journal of Health Economics 19, 1–11.

Berggren, M., Bergh, R., 2025. Simpson's gender-equality paradox. Proceedings of the National Academy of Sciences 122, e2422247122.

Bernile, G., Bhagwat, V., Rau, P.R., 2017. What doesn't kill you will only make you more risk-loving: early-life disasters and CEO behavior. The Journal of Finance 72, 167–206.

Binswanger, H.P., 1980. Attitudes toward risk: experimental measurement in rural India. American Journal of Agricultural Economics 62, 395–407.

Binswanger, H.P., 1981. Attitudes toward risk: theoretical implications of an experiment in rural India. The Economic Journal 91, 867–890.

Bonin, H., Dohmen, T., Falk, A., Huffman, D., Sunde, U., 2007. Cross-sectional earnings risk and occupational sorting: the role of risk attitudes. Labour Economics 14, 926–937.

Bouchouicha, R., Vieider, F.M., 2019. Growth, entrepreneurship, and risk-tolerance: a risk-income paradox. Journal of Economic Growth 24, 257–282.

Brañas-Garza, P., Jorrat, D., Espín, A.M., Sánchez, A., 2023. Paid and hypothetical time preferences are the same: lab, field and online evidence. Experimental Economics 26, 412–434.

Burro, G., McDonald, R., Read, D., Taj, U., 2022. Patience decreases with age for the poor but not for the rich: an international comparison. Journal of Economic Behavior & Organization 193, 596–621.

Byrnes, J.P., Miller, D.C., Schafer, W.D., 1999. Gender differences in risk taking: a meta-analysis. Psychological Bulletin 125, 367.

Cai, X., Gangadharan, L., Lu, Y., Zhao, X., 2022. Does a Sea Fishing Legacy Explain Differences in Risk Attitudes and Entrepreneurship? Working Paper.

Callen, M., 2015. Catastrophes and time preference: evidence from the Indian Ocean earthquake. Journal of Economic Behavior & Organization 118, 199–214.

Camerer, C.F., Hogarth, R.M., 1999. The effects of financial incentives in experiments: a review and capital-labor production framework. Journal of Risk and Uncertainty 19, 7–42.

Cameron, L., Shah, M., 2015. Risk-taking behavior in the wake of natural disasters. The Journal of Human Resources 50 (2), 484–515.

Cao, Y., Enke, B., Falk, A., Giuliano, P., Nunn, N., 2021. Herding, Warfare, and a Culture of Honor: Global Evidence. NBER Working Paper, 29250.

Cappelen, A.W., Enke, B., Tungodden, B., 2025. Universalism: global evidence. American Economic Review 115, 43–76.

Cassar, A., Healy, A., von Kessler, C., 2017. Trust, risk, and time preferences after a natural disaster: experimental evidence from Thailand. World Development 94, 90–105.

Chan, M., Luo, L., 2025. The Economic Origins of Risk Preferences. Working Paper.

Charness, G., Gneezy, U., 2012. Strong evidence for gender differences in risk taking. Journal of Economic Behavior & Organization 83, 50–58.

Charness, G., Gneezy, U., Imas, A., 2013. Experimental methods: eliciting risk preferences. Journal of Economic Behavior & Organization 87, 43–51.

Charness, G., Garcia, T., Offerman, T., Villeval, M.C., 2020. Do measures of risk attitude in the laboratory predict behavior under risk in and outside of the laboratory? Journal of Risk and Uncertainty 60, 99–123.

Chen, M.K., 2013. The effect of language on economic behavior: evidence from savings rates, health behaviors, and retirement assets. American Economic Review 103, 690–731.

Cohen, J., Ericson, K.M., Laibson, D., White, J.M., 2020. Measuring time preferences. Journal of Economic Literature 58, 299–347.

Cohn, A., Maréchal, M.A., Tannenbaum, D., Zünd, C.L., 2019. Civic honesty around the globe. Science 365, 70–73.

Coller, M., Williams, M.B., 1999. Eliciting individual discount rates. Experimental Economics 2, 107–127.

Cornsweet, T.N., 1962. The staircase-method in psychophysics. The American Journal of Psychology 75, 485–491.

Crosetto, P., Filippin, A., 2013. The 'bomb' risk elicitation task. Journal of Risk and Uncertainty 47, 31–65.

Croson, R., Gneezy, U., 2009. Gender differences in preferences. Journal of Economic Literature 47, 448–474.

Cuevas, A., Cuevas, R., Desmet, K., Ortuño-Ortín, I., 2021. The Gender Gap in Preferences: Evidence from 45,397 Facebook Interests. NBER Working Paper 29451. National Bureau of Economic Research, Cambridge, MA.

Dechezleprêtre, A., Fabre, A., Kruse, T., Planterose, B., Chico, A.S., Stantcheva, S., 2025. Fighting climate change: international attitudes toward climate policies. American Economic Review 115, 1258–1300.

Diebolt, C., Hippe, R., 2019. The long-run impact of human capital on innovation and economic development in the regions of Europe. Applied Economics 51, 542–563.

Di Falco, S., Vieider, F.M., 2022. Environmental adaptation of risk preferences. The Economic Journal 132.

Ding, X., Hartog, J., Sun, Y., 2010. Can We Measure Individual Risk Attitudes in a Survey? IZA Discussion Paper, 4807.

Dohmen, T., Falk, A., Huffman, D., Sunde, U., 2010. Are risk aversion and impatience related to cognitive ability? American Economic Review 100, 1238–1260.

Dohmen, T., Falk, A., Huffman, D., Sunde, U., Schupp, J., Wagner, G.G., 2011. Individual risk attitudes: measurement, determinants, and behavioral consequences. Journal of the European Economic Association 9, 522–550.

Dohmen, T., Falk, A., Huffman, D., Sunde, U., 2012. The intergenerational transmission of risk and trust attitudes. The Review of Economic Studies 79, 645–677.

Dohmen, T., Falk, A., Golsteyn, B.H.H., Huffman, D., Sunde, U., 2017. Risk attitudes across the life course. The Economic Journal 127, F95–F116.

Dohmen, T., Falk, A., Huffman, D., Sunde, U., 2018. On the relationship between cognitive ability and risk preference. The Journal of Economic Perspectives 32, 115–134.

Donkers, B., Melenberg, B., van Soest, A., 2001. Estimating risk attitudes using lotteries – a large sample approach. Journal of Risk and Uncertainty 22, 165–195.

Drichoutis, A.C., Lusk, J.L., 2016. What can multiple price lists really tell us about risk preferences? Journal of Risk and Uncertainty 53, 89–106.

Eckel, C.C., Grossman, P.J., 2002. Sex differences and statistical stereotyping in attitudes toward financial risk. Evolution and Human Behavior 23, 281–295.

Enke, B., Shubatt, C., 2023. Quantifying lottery choice complexity. Tech. Rep. National Bureau of Economic Research.

Falk, A., Hermle, J., 2018. Relationship of gender differences in preferences to economic development and gender equality. Science 362, eaas9899.

Falk, A., Becker, A., Dohmen, T., Enke, B., Huffman, D., Sunde, U., 2018. Global evidence on economic preferences. The Quarterly Journal of Economics 133, 1645–1692.

Falk, A., Henkel, L., Neuber, T., Strack, P., 2021a. Limited Self-Knowledge and Survey Response Behavior. CESifo Working Paper, 9179.

Falk, A., Kosse, F., Pinger, P., Schildberg-Hörisch, H., Deckers, T., 2021b. Socio-economic status and inequalities in children's IQ and economic preferences. Journal of Political Economy 129, 2504–2545.

Falk, A., Becker, A., Dohmen, T., Huffman, D., Sunde, U., 2023. The preference survey module: a validated instrument for measuring risk, time, and social preferences. Management Science 69, 1935–1950.

Fitzenberger, B., Mena, G., Nimczik, J., Sunde, U., 2022. Personality traits across the life cycle: disentangling age, period, and cohort effects. The Economic Journal 132, 2141–2172.

Frederick, S., Loewenstein, G., O'Donoghue, T., 2002. Time discounting and time preference: a critical review. Journal of Economic Literature 40, 351–401.

Frey, R., Pedroni, A., Mata, R., Rieskamp, J., Hertwig, R., 2017. Risk preference shares the psychometric structure of major psychological traits. Science Advances 3, 1–13.

Frey, R., Richter, D., Hertwig, R., Mata, R., 2021. Identifying robust correlates of risk preference: a systematic approach using specification curve analysis. Journal of Personality and Social Psychology 120, 538–557.

Galor, O., Özak, Ö., 2016. The agricultural origins of time preference. American Economic Review 106, 3064–3103.

Galor, O., Savitskiy, V., 2018. Climatic Roots of Loss Aversion. Working Paper.

Giuliano, P., Spilimbergo, A., 2024. Aggregate Shocks and the Formation of Preferences and Beliefs. Working Paper.

Gneezy, U., Potters, J., 1997. An experiment on risk taking and evaluation periods. The Quarterly Journal of Economics 112, 631–645.

Gneezy, U., Leonard, K.L., List, J.A., 2009. Gender differences in competition: evidence from a matrilineal and a patriarchal society. Econometrica 77, 1637–1664.

Golsteyn, B.H., Grönqvist, H., Lindahl, L., 2014. Adolescent time preferences predict lifetime outcomes. The Economic Journal 124, F739–F761.

Guiso, L., Sapienza, P., Zingales, L., 2011. Civic capital as the missing link. In: Benhabib, J., Bisin, A., Jackson, M.O. (Eds.), Handbook of Social Economics. Elsevier, Amsterdam, pp. 417–480. Chap. 10.

Hanaoka, C., Shigeoka, H., Watanabe, Y., 2018. Do risk preferences change? Evidence from the great East Japan earthquake. American Economic Journal: Applied Economics 10, 298–330.

Hardeweg, B., Menkhoff, L., Waibel, H., 2013. Experimentally validated survey evidence on individual risk attitudes in rural Thailand. Economic Development and Cultural Change 61, 859–888.

Harrison, G.W., Lau, M.I., Rutström, E.E., 2007. Estimating risk attitudes in Denmark: a field experiment. Scandinavian Journal of Economics 109, 341–368.

Hofstede, G., McCrae, R.R., 2004. Personality and culture revisited: linking traits and dimensions of culture. Cross-Cultural Research 38, 52–88.

Holt, C.A., Laury, S.K., 2002. Risk aversion and incentive effects. American Economic Review 92, 1644–1655.

House, R.J., Hanges, P.J., Javidan, M., Dorfman, P.W., Gupta, V. (Eds.), 2004. Culture, Leadership, and Organizations: The GLOBE Study of 62 Societies. Sage Publications.

Howden, W., Levin, R., 2023. The Global Impacts of Climate Change on Risk Preferences. Working Paper.

Inglehart, R., Haerpfer, C., Moreno, A., Welzel, C., Kizilova, K., Diez-Medrano, J., Lagos, M., Norris, P., Ponarin, E., Puranen, B. (Eds.), 2020. World Values Survey: All Rounds – Country-Pooled Datafile. JD Systems Institute, Madrid.

Jagelka, T., 2024. Are economists' preferences psychologists' personality traits? A structural approach. Journal of Political Economy 132, 910–970.

Jaramillo, P., LaFave, D., Novak, L.K., 2025. Extreme Weather Events Impact Risk Tolerance and Time Preferences. The World Bank Economic Review, lhaf018.

Josef, A.K., Richter, D., Wagner, G.G., Hertwig, R., Mata, R., 2016. Stability and change in risk-taking propensity across the adult life span. Journal of Personality and Social Psychology 111, 430–450.

Kahneman, D., Tversky, A., 1979. Prospect theory: an analysis of decision under risk. Econometrica 47, 263–291.

Kettlewell, N., 2019. Risk preference dynamics around life events. Journal of Economic Behavior & Organization 162, 66–84.

Khachatryan, K., Dreber, A., von Essen, E., Ranehill, E., 2015. Gender and preferences at a young age: evidence from Armenia. Journal of Economic Behavior & Organization 118, 318–332.

Kimball, M.S., Sahm, C., Shapiro, M.D., 2008. Imputing risk tolerance from survey responses. Journal of the American Statistical Association 103, 1028–1038.

Kimball, M.S., Sahm, C., Shapiro, M.D., 2009. Risk preferences in the PSID: individual imputations and family covariation. American Economic Review 99, 363–368.

Kosfeld, M., Sharafi, Z., 2024. The preference survey module: evidence on social preferences from Tehran. Journal of the Economic Science Association 10, 152–164.

Kosfeld, M., Sharafi, Z., Sontag-Gonzalez, M., Zou, N., 2025. Measuring Economic Preferences with Surveys and Behavioral Experiments. CEPR Discussion Paper, 19845.

Kosse, F., Pfeiffer, F., 2012. Impatience among preschool children and their mothers. Economics Letters 115, 493–495.

Kosse, F., Deckers, T., Pinger, P., Schildberg-Hörisch, H., Falk, A., 2020. The formation of prosociality: causal evidence on the role of social environment. Journal of Political Economy 128, 434–467.

Lahno, A.M., Serra-Garcia, M., 2015. Peer effects in risk taking: envy or conformity? Journal of Risk and Uncertainty 50, 73–95.

L'Haridon, O., Vieider, F., 2019. All over the map: a worldwide comparison of risk preferences. Quantitative Economics 10, 185–215.

Malmendier, U., Nagel, S., 2011. Depression babies: do macroeconomic experiences affect risk taking? The Quarterly Journal of Economics 126, 373–416.

Mata, R., Josef, A.K., Samanez-Larkin, G.R., Hertwig, R., 2011. Age differences in risky choice: a meta-analysis. Annals of the New York Academy of Sciences 1235, 18–29.

Mata, R., Josef, A.K., Hertwig, R., 2016. Propensity for risk taking across the life span and around the globe. Psychological Science 27, 231–243.

Meissner, T., Gassmann, X., Faure, C., Schleich, J., 2023. Individual characteristics associated with risk and time preferences: a multi country representative survey. Journal of Risk and Uncertainty 66, 77–107.

Menkhoff, L., Sakha, S., 2017. Estimating risky behavior with multiple-item risk measures. Journal of Economic Psychology 59, 59–86.

Nazarova, A., 2024. Ethnic Roots of Risk Attitudes: the Impact of Ancestral Lifestyle on Risk Taking Behaviour. Working Paper.

Netzer, N., 2009. Evolution of time preferences and attitudes toward risk. American Economic Review 99, 937–955.

Noussair, C.N., Trautmann, S.T., van de Kuilen, G., Vellekoop, N., 2013. Risk aversion and religion. Journal of Risk and Uncertainty 47, 165–183.

Rabin, M., 2000. Risk aversion and expected-utility theory: a calibration theorem. Econometrica 68, 1281–1292.

Rhoads, S.A., Gunter, D., Ryan, R.M., Marsh, A.A., 2021. Global variation in subjective well-being predicts seven forms of altruism. Psychological Science 32, 1247–1261. pMID: 34237223.

Rieger, M.-O., Wang, M., Hens, T., 2015. Risk preferences around the world. Management Science 61, 637–648.

Rieger, M.-O., Wang, M., Hens, T., 2021. Universal time preferences. PLoS ONE 16, e0245692.

Roberts, S.G., Winters, J., Chen, K., 2015. Future tense and economic decisions: controlling for cultural evolution. PLoS ONE 10, e0132145.

Robson, A.J., 2001. The biological basis of economic behavior. Journal of Economic Literature 39, 11–33.

Robson, A.J., Samuelson, L., 2010. The evolution of intertemporal preferences. American Economic Review 100, 1919–1935.

Robson, A.J., Samuelson, L., 2011. The evolutionary foundations of preferences. In: Benhabib, J., Bisin, A., Jackson, M.O. (Eds.), Handbook of Social Economics, vol. 1A. Elsevier, Amsterdam, pp. 221–310.

Ruggeri, K., et al., 2022. The globalizability of temporal discounting. Nature Human Behaviour 6, 1386–1397.

Sahm, C.R., 2012. How much does risk tolerance change? Quarterly Journal of Finance 2, 1250020.

Samuelson, P.A., 1937. A note on measurement of utility. The Review of Economic Studies 4, 155–161.

Schildberg-Hörisch, H., 2018. Are risk preferences stable? The Journal of Economic Perspectives 32, 135–154.

Schwerter, F., 2024. Social reference points and risk taking. Management Science 70, 616–632.

Sharpe, W.F., Goldstein, D.G., Blythe, P.W., 2000. The Distribution Builder: a Tool for Inferring Investor Preferences. Preprint.

Silverman, I.W., 2003. Gender differences in delay of gratification: a meta-analysis. Sex Roles 49, 451–463.

Spolaore, E., Wacziarg, R., 2018. Ancestry and development: new evidence. Journal of Applied Econometrics 33, 748–762.

Starmer, C., 2000. Developments in non-expected utility theory: the hunt for a descriptive theory of choice under risk. Journal of Economic Literature 38, 332–382.

Sunde, U., Dohmen, T., Enke, B., Falk, A., Huffman, D., Meyerheim, G., 2022. Patience and comparative development. The Review of Economic Studies 89, 2806–2840.

Sunde, U., Falk, A., Hermle, J., 2026. Life expectancy, age, and patience. The Economic Journal. Forthcoming.

Thoeni, C., Volk, S., 2021. Converging evidence for greater male variability in time, risk, and social preferences. Proceedings of the National Academy of Sciences 118, e2026112118.

Vieider, F.M., Lefebvre, M., Bouchouicha, R., Chmura, T., Hakimov, R., Krawczyk, M., Martinsson, P., 2015. Common components of risk and uncertainty attitudes across contexts and domains: evidence from 30 countries. Journal of the European Economic Association 13, 421–452.

Vischer, T., Dohmen, T., Falk, A., Huffman, D., Sunde, U., Schupp, J., Wagner, G.G., 2013. Validating an ultra-short survey measure of patience. Economics Letters 120, 142–145.

von Gaudecker, H.-M., van Soest, A., Wengström, E., 2011. Heterogeneity in risky choice behavior in a broad population. American Economic Review 101, 664–694.

Von Neumann, J., Morgenstern, O. (Eds.), 1944. Theory of Games and Economic Behavior. Princeton University Press, Princeton.

Wang, M., Rieger, M.-O., Hens, T., 2016. How time preferences differ: evidence from 53 countries. Journal of Economic Psychology 52, 115–135.

Wang, Z., Snowberg, E., Camerer, C., 2024. Dynamically Optimized Sequential Experimentation. NBER Working Paper 33013. National Bureau of Economic Research.

Weber, E.U., Blais, A.-R., Betz, N.E., 2002. A domain-specific risk-attitude scale: measuring risk perceptions and risk behaviors. Journal of Behavioral Decision Making 15, 263–290.

Zumbuehl, M., Dohmen, T., Pfann, G., 2021. Parental involvement and the intergenerational transmission of economic preferences, attitudes and personality traits. The Economic Journal 131, 2642–2670.

Part II

Theories of culture

Chapter 5

The nature of culture

Robert Boyd[a] **and Peter J. Richerson**[b]
[a]*School of Human Evolution and Social Change, Institute of Human Origins, Arizona State University, Tempe, AZ, United States,* [b]*Department of Environmental Science and Policy, University of California, Davis, CA, United States*

In recent decades economists have taken an interest in how culture affects behavior (Guiso et al., 2024; Bisin and Verdier, 2023). Guiso et al. (2006) define culture as "those customary beliefs and values that ethnic, religious, and social groups transmit fairly unchanged from generation to generation". Other economists interested in culture tend to define culture similarly (Fernández, 2011; Alesina and Giuliano, 2015; Bisin and Verdier, 2011), but see (Acemoglu and Robinson, 2021). Much of this work is empirical and seeks to determine whether variation in important, economically interesting behavior is affected by cultural differences. Some of this work focuses on aggregate behavior, for example differences in savings rate or trust between nations or firms (Alesina and Giuliano, 2015; Guiso et al., 2006; Gorton et al., 2022; Cao et al., 2021). Other research asks how individual cultural differences affect individual behaviors (Fernández, 2011). An important research tradition uses cultural continuity to explain long-term persistence of the effects of past environments (e.g. Nunn, 2014; Guiso et al., 2016; Grosjean, 2014).

There is also a theoretical literature in economics in which culture is modeled using population dynamic models (Bisin and Verdier, 2001b; Tabellini, 2008; Guiso et al., 2008; Bisin and Verdier, 2011; Besley and Persson, 2019). Most economists cite works in evolutionary anthropology from the 1980's as inspiration for the population dynamic approach to culture (Cavalli-Sforza and Feldman, 1981; Boyd and Richerson, 1985). Such models take culture to be socially acquired beliefs and values held by individuals in a population. The goal is to understand how the distribution of cultural traits in the population changes through time as individuals acquire and modify their beliefs and values in response to social and economic conditions. Most of this work assumes that children are socialized by their parents, and that parents prefer that their children have the same beliefs and values that they do (Bisin and Verdier, 2023). Evolution occurs when people modify their beliefs and transmit the changed beliefs to their children. Thus parents' preferences determine the direction of cultural change.

Handbook of Culture and Economic Behavior, Volume 1, ISSN 3051-1682
https://doi.org/10.1016/bs.hceb.2026.02.009

There is an older, and larger literature in evolutionary anthropology in which culture is defined as information acquired by individuals by imitation or teaching (Cavalli-Sforza and Feldman, 1981; Boyd and Richerson, 1985; Henrich, 2016; Mesoudi, 2016; Boyd, 2017; Brown and Lala, 2024; Hewlett et al., 2024; Henrich and Boyd, 1998; Henrich and Gil-White, 2001; Richerson et al., 2016; Richerson and Boyd, 1978; Boyd et al., 2011). Information flows modify individuals' ideas in the short run and in the long run create a common history for large groups, and culture is understood as a population dynamic phenomenon. Mathematical tools from population biology are used to model cultural change.

There are two important differences between this tradition and the research on culture in economics.

First, economic research tends to focus on norms and basic attitudes. Most behavior can be explained by individual rational choice, but culture is necessary to explain some behavior, particularly differences between groups. In contrast, work in evolutionary anthropology supposes that a wide variety of traits are culturally transmitted (Sturtevant, 1978–2022). People acquire their language, norms, and institutions governing family structure, social stratification, internal security, clubs, relations with other societies, belief systems involving religion, cosmology, secular ideology, ritual practices including both religious and civil celebrations, technological knowledge and a vast range of other beliefs about the world. Culture is not a tightly structured holistic system, but a collection of messy systems of variously related parts (Boyd et al., 1997). A variety of processes act to shape cultural content. Some cultural variants may be more attractive, easier to learn, or easier to remember. People may tend to imitate the successful, or the more common trait, or traits exhibited by particular kinds of models. The processes that shape content in different domains can be quite different. For example, variant tools often have conspicuously different functional results. Superior innovations tend to spread rapidly. Artistic and linguistic evolution is often driven by neophilia, not function (Martindale, 1990; Deutscher, 2005). Norms are often subject to frequency dependent selection.

Second, much of the work in evolutionary anthropology seeks to understand human culture as an evolved adaptation. Humans are an outlier in the natural world. We have the largest geographic range of any terrestrial species, surviving in virtually every habitat. We are clever creatures, but this alone cannot explain our spectacular ecological success. Rather it is the fact that our ability to learn from each other allows human populations to gradually accumulate knowledge, institutions, and technology that no individual could create on their own (Boyd et al., 2011; Henrich, 2016; Boyd, 2017). The theory of cultural evolution developed in evolutionary anthropology is a handy modeling framework. But it is more than that. It extends the self-interested choice framework by explaining the origins of preferences and priors in a way that is consistent with the facts of human evolution, and so explains the essential nature of culture in human life and society, an explanation that has important implications for how economists should think about culture.

We believe that thinking about culture in this way is likely to have important benefits for economics. In the last section of this paper we give a number of examples of such benefits:

- Culture is not just norms, values, and shared understandings; it includes a wide range of beliefs.
- People are predisposed to adopt the beliefs of those around them. Most culture is not acquired from parents.
- Culture is shaped by individual preferences and transmission biases, including evolved biases that cause people to learn behaviors that were beneficial over human evolution.
- Gene-culture coevolution provides an explanation for prestige.
- Evolutionary reasoning suggests an explanation for costly displays that is different than signaling models.
- Cultural group selection can help explain the evolution of norms and institutions supporting cooperation.
- Political institutions structure collective decision-making that also helps explain the evolution of norms and other institutions.
- Population dynamic processes are consistent with a wide range of rates of cultural change.

Population dynamic models are not widely used by researchers in cultural anthropology, the academic discipline that has done the most to study culture over the last century and a half. Instead, cultural anthropologists have long used a wide range of distinct, and often incompatible definitions of culture (Kroeber and Kluckhohn, 1952). Most conceptualize culture as inherently a property of groups, but there are some approaches that are consistent with population dynamic models in which individuals and groups play key, but different, roles.

Here, we begin by locating the population dynamic models of culture used in evolutionary anthropology within the diverse range of culture concepts used by other anthropologists. We then explain how population dynamic models fit within accounts of human evolution, with a particular focus on how the coevolution of genes and culture has led to dramatic increases in the technical and social sophistication of human socio-economic systems, thus providing an explanation for the singular aspects of *Homo sapiens*. Finally, we argue that thinking about culture as an evolved adaptation makes predictions about how cultural learning works that should be of interest to economists even if they are not interested in human evolution in the long term. The decisions people make today are driven by genes and culture that evolved as adaptations over the last 2.8 million years of the genus *Homo*.

1 Population thinking in cultural anthropology

Culture is a central concept in cultural anthropology, but anthropologists do not agree about what culture is, or why it changes. For much of its history, anthropology defined culture as *shared* beliefs and therefore, a property of groups, not individuals. This concept of culture was central to cultural anthropology through much of the 20th century, mainly due to the writings of Franz Boas and his many influential students (e.g. Lowie, 1917; Kroeber, 1917). It holds that:

- Culture is a property of groups.
- Culture is socially acquired.
- A group's culture includes a wide range of traits including technology, institutions, and religion.
- These traits form an organized, coherent whole.

This way of thinking is also consistent with ordinary English usage. A common dictionary definition of culture is "the customs, arts, social institutions, and achievements of a particular nation, people, or other social group" (Oxford Languages Dictionary).

Boas and his followers knew that sometimes people within a culture had different beliefs and values, that individual traits frequently diffused from one group to another, and that such processes were important for understanding culture change, but they never developed a systematic theory describing how intracultural variation shaped the dynamics of culture. The Boasian culture concept held sway in American cultural anthropology through the first half of the 20th century. The concept of culture was not as central in British social anthropology which emphasized social structure and its function, an approach associated with Bronislaw Malinowski and A.R. Radcliffe-Brown (Barnard, 2021; Eriksen and Nielsen, 2013).

Within cultural anthropology, the Boasian culture concept has been elaborated and criticized in many different ways. (See Keesing, 1974; Risjord, 2012; Barnard, 2021; Engelke, 2018 for histories of the culture concept). Many anthropologists believed that culture evolved progressively so that the scale and complexity of societies tended to increase over time (e.g. White, 1943; Sahlins and Service, 1960; Steward, 1972), and this view still has some currency, especially in archeology (Johnson and Earle, 2000). Some anthropologists viewed culture through a functionalist lens. For example, cultural ecology, an important school in the 1960's and 70's, held that culture served to adapt cultural groups to their ecological and economic circumstances, often solving problems arising from externalities such as preventing over exploitation of game resources or regulating population growth (Harris, 2001; Steward, 2004; Rappaport, 1970). Some contemporary anthropologists, who typically call themselves human behavioral ecologists, follow this tradition but use concepts and models from evolutionary biology to undergird their functionalism (Winterhalder and Smith, 2017).

Many other anthropologists came to reject the idea that culture included behaviors and artifacts, and instead thought of it as a system of shared beliefs and understandings. Structuralists drew on concepts from linguistics and focused on social patterns, particularly kinship and kinship terminology as cognitive systems of relationships (e.g. Lévi-Strauss, 1971). Symbolic anthropologists viewed culture as a system of shared meanings expressed in the ongoing social behavior of members of a culture (Geertz, 2008). Much of this work is written in an interpretive frame, rather than the scientific approach of earlier cultural anthropologists. The goal was to provide a rich description of how members of a culture understood the world. For example, in Clifford Geertz's famous "Notes on a Balinese Cockfight" we get an evocative ethnographic account of a cockfight in Bali and the betting that surrounds it, and we sense that we have learned something significant about the nature of status in Bali. But there are no hypotheses, and no actual data. Or as Geertz put it, anthropology is "not an experimental science in search of law but an interpretive one in search of meaning" (Geertz, 2008).

Towards the end of the 20th century, many cultural anthropologists came to feel that the prevailing idea that culture was a set of shared meanings portrayed culture as a unified system of norms and beliefs, and so was unable to represent the perspectives of different people within a society (Clifford and Marcus, 1986). Of particular importance, the holistic culture concept did not allow agency for those who were marginalized. These views were very influential with the Clifford and Marcus book having been cited almost 20,000 times. Moreover, many felt that the culture concept in particular and anthropology in general were complicit in colonialism. To take a particularly distasteful example, during Apartheid an important plank in the platform of the National Party in South Africa was that black Africans needed to be kept separate in order to keep their cultures intact (Engelke, 2018). Such considerations have led many anthropologists to be skeptical about the usefulness of the culture concept.

A number of anthropologists have developed "distributed" models of culture (Rodseth, 1998; Shore, 1998; Barth, 2002; Sperber, 1985; Boyd and Richerson, 1985) that reject the notion that cultures are unified wholes. Instead, culture is conceptualized as knowledge or practice that is distributed across the minds of a population. Different minds may hold different beliefs, knowledge, and other kinds of information and the key is to explain how social life shapes the spread of different variants. For example, Fredrik Barth (1990, 1987) describes how cosmological knowledge is transmitted in secret nighttime initiation rituals among the Ok of highland New Guinea, and compares this process to how local Muslim and Hindu beliefs are learned in quiet classrooms in Bali. The first setting favors the spread of beliefs leading to high arousal and rapid evolution, the second to a cooler, but more elaborate, more codified, and slowly evolving theology. Barth also emphasized the importance of individual decision-making in shaping institutions (Barth, 2011, 2020). One of the most influential contemporary proponents of a distributed model of culture is the cognitive anthropologist Dan Sperber (Sperber, 1985, 1996) who conceptualizes culture as mental representations distributed throughout a population. Most mental representations are private, but some spread through a population analogous to the way viruses spread. Sperber and his school (Atran, 1998; Boyer, 2023;

Morin, 2016; Miton and DeDeo, 2022) believe that interpersonal transmission is usually noisy and biased, and as a consequence representations that fit with people's cognitive architecture will tend to be most common. Sperber has a strongly modularist view of cognition and this leads him and others in this school to a nativist view, and they have done ambitious empirical work motivated by this view of culture (see Miton, 2024 for a review). We are skeptical of this approach. There is active debate about the psychology of social learning (Gelpi and Buchsbaum, 2023; Gweon, 2021; Vélez and Gweon, 2021; Olsson et al., 2020) and reliable replication of observed behavior is widespread. Compared to other primates, humans acquire novel traits rapidly and accurately, and they are also more likely to imitate behaviors that have no obvious function (Whiten et al., 2017; Tomasello, 1996; Dean et al., 2014). This makes sense because humans must acquire a very large repertoire of cultural traits in many different environments, and the function of many elements in complex traits is not obvious to learners. Many non-human animal social learning systems rely lightly on social learning and heavily on innate cognitive mechanisms, but repertoire sizes are much smaller than in the human case.

Another distributed model is rooted in evolutionary anthropology, and it is to this model we now turn.

2 Evolutionary models of culture

Human populations are the repositories of immense amounts of information that persists over time. Language provides a clear example. Native speakers of a language in small-scale illiterate societies typical of our ancestors typically know the meanings of 5–10 thousand words, phonological rules that specify how these are pronounced, and complex grammatical rules that specify how words are combined to convey meaning. The communicative function of language means that the many speakers of a language must use very similar meanings for words structured by similar grammatical rules. These are transmitted within communities with sufficient fidelity that linguistic descent can be tracked over thousands of years, even though the descendant languages become mutually unintelligible in a millennium or so (e.g. Haak et al., 2015; Mollica and Piantadosi, 2019). Much of the work on culture in economics focuses on traits like norms and social identity, but in fact a variety of beliefs are culturally acquired—including a vast range of beliefs ranging from the everyday to the esoteric. Many beliefs are directly related to economic activity. Foragers learn how to make tools, which plants are toxic and which are edible, the habits of prey species, how to construct shelters, how to navigate, and much, much more. The same goes for culture in modern urban societies. By the time American children reach puberty most know a lot about the world. Of course, kids learn lots of stuff on their own—where their house is and whether they like to eat tomatoes. But LOTS of other stuff is culturally acquired. They know that the earth spins on its axis and orbits the sun, that disease is caused by tiny, invisible organisms, that cars produce air pollution, that police can use DNA to identify criminals, and that electricity somehow flows through wires. The list is very long. But very little of this vast store of information results from individual experience. We believe that the earth orbits the sun and diseases are caused by invisible germs because the people around us teach us these things. This knowledge is acquired culturally. Scientists acquire the tools and techniques to directly experience phenomena in their field but outside of it, we rely on culture for our beliefs like everyone.

Another way to grasp the importance of culture in shaping everyday beliefs is to compare what all of us know with what culturally related people believed in the past. David Wootton (2015) describes some of the beliefs of an educated Englishman in 1600.

> *He believes in witchcraft... He believes witches can summon up storms that sink ships at sea... He believes in werewolves... He believes mice are spontaneously generated in piles of straw... He believes that a murdered body will bleed in the presence of the murderer. He believes that there is an ointment which, if rubbed on a dagger that has caused a wound, will cure the wound. He believes that the shape, color and texture of a plant can be a clue to how it will work as a medicine... He believes that it is possible to turn base metal into gold, although he doubts that anyone knows how to do it. He believes that nature abhors a vacuum. He believes the rainbow is a sign from God and that comets portend evil. He believes that dreams predict the future, if we know how to interpret them. He believes, of course, that the earth stands still.*

None of the readers of this article shares any of these beliefs. Of course, 16th century London is different than London today. But nothing in individual experience explains why the Londoner of that day believed in spontaneous generation while the modern Londoner rejects this idea as nonsense. Both acquired their beliefs from the people around them. The difference is that since the 16th century many scientific ideas have seeped into the pool of common knowledge. Lay people "know" these things even though most of them are as unfamiliar with their evidentiary basis as their 16th century forebears were of their common knowledge.

There is also ample evidence that different traits often have different histories, particularly because some kinds of information readily diffuse from one population to its neighbors, while other kinds of information are less likely to move between populations. Again language provides a good example. Words for unfamiliar concepts like "mesa" and "weekend" readily diffuse from one speech community to others, while words which every language has like "one" and "mother" and structural aspects of morpho-syntax are borrowed less frequently than, for example, phonological features (Thomason, 2001). Phylogenetic studies of technology (Jordan, 2014; Risjord, 2012) and norms (Cowlishaw and Mace, 1996; Jordan et al., 2009) suggest that many other kinds of traits diffuse among populations along paths dependent on social structure.

Defining culture as transmitted information is crucial because information can replicate. People transmit lots of things besides information: wealth, artifacts, and modified environments (Odling-Smee et al., 2003), but the dynamics of material inheritances are quite different than inherited cultural information. Think about farming. Information, like farming skills, can be replicated relatively cheaply, but farms cannot. A typical pioneering farm family can produce several farmers, but only one farm. Thus we focus on the information that is stored in human heads, and recently in off-line media, how to make artifacts rather than the artifacts themselves.

In cultures without widespread literacy (which is to say all cultures until the last couple of thousand years), this information was mainly stored in human brains (Cantlon and Piantadosi, 2024). Genes store a great deal of information, but there is not much genetic variation between human groups. Modest amounts of technological information can be stored in physical objects. Existing bows may provide models for the dimensions and materials of future bows, but there are many aspects of the manufacture of bows that are hard to reverse engineer, and many complex, causally opaque technologies like food processing can only be reverse engineered by solving a high dimensional optimization problem, something usually impossible until the development of modern R&D technology and finance. Before writing, recipes for brewing beer were stored in the minds of brewers, not in the beer itself. The culture of non-literate societies persists over time and exhibits phylogenetic patterns so writing is not essential for the properties of culture, although once writing, and especially printing, became common, they had important effects (Goody, 1975; Wootton, 2015).

The fact that cultural information is stored in brains and transmitted by teaching, imitation, and other forms of social learning means that a causal theory of cultural content must explain why some cultural items spread throughout populations and persist through time while others do not. So, we need a theory that accounts for the processes that cause people to acquire the knowledge and beliefs that they have, and how this depends on the distribution of cultural knowledge in the population, and how different variants affect the lives of the people who hold those variants. Some processes may be psychological—a propensity to disproportionately adopt commonly observed variants will cause common variants to become even more common, and other processes may be practical decisions—some variants may lead to high payoffs that lead to widespread, rapid adoption, like the cell phone. The population dynamic models used in population genetics and epidemiology provide a useful set of conceptual and mathematical tools to create such a theory. And so, beginning in the 1970's biologists and evolutionary anthropologists began to develop population dynamic models of culture (Cavalli-Sforza and Feldman, 1981; Boyd and Richerson, 1985).

One of their principal aims was to develop a theory of cultural change that could be incorporated into the Darwinian theory of organic evolution and explain the striking differences between humans and other species. These are:

- We are much better at adapting to a large range of habitats than any other creature. We have a larger geographical and ecological range than any other terrestrial animal species. Most primate species are limited to part of a continent and a limited range of habitats. By 10,000 years ago humans occupied the entire planet except for Antarctica and a few remote islands, and were adapted to habitats ranging from desert to rain forest to tundra, using a wide range of technologies.
- There is much greater variation in behavior among human groups than among groups of other animals. In other species, different groups have very similar subsistence strategies and social organization, and the differences that do exist are mainly due to exogenous environmental variation. Unusually successful organic innovations, like flight in birds, give rise to swarms of species deploying the innovation in a host of specialized forms. Evolutionary biologists call this an adaptive radiation. Different human groups have different forms of social organization and subsistence. Much of this variation has important effects on fitness, persists for generations, and exhibits phylogenetic history, but much is not due to underlying environmental or genetic variation. We constitute a massive adaptive radiation mostly based on cultural variation.
- Humans have complex behaviors that show adaptive design, but are not evolved, genetically transmitted traits shaped by natural selection. For example, reading has many of the attributes said to identify the output of an evolved module, but until a few hundred years ago, very few people could read.
- Despite our success, many human behaviors are more or less highly maladaptive. For example, some of us climb mountains, grow flowers, and have devoted more time and energy to writing scientific papers than raising a fitness optimizing number of children.

The striking differences between humans and other species are not just the result of farming and industrial production. Ten thousand years ago, when every person was a forager, we were already qualitatively different than other animals. These differences evolved over the last two million years or so. Our ancestors were ape-like creatures much like other mammals. By the beginning of the Holocene, 12,000 years ago, human hunter-gatherers occupied every corner of the globe, cooperated in large numbers, made intricate, locally appropriate tools and other artifacts, and had diverse norms and institutions.

This leads to the obvious question: How could such an unusual species evolve? Evolution has been creating vertebrate species for more than 500 million years, and we are outliers in comparison with every single one of them. Something very unusual happened during the Pleistocene evolution of our species, and it is of great interest to know what it was. Our behavior today largely reflects a long history of exploiting cultural adaptations and suffering from the maladaptive tradeoffs and other costs of our hyper-cultural adaptation.

A common answer is that we became smarter than other animals. Beginning about 2.5 million years ago brain sizes in the hominin lineage began to increase, and by 500,000 years ago, we had larger brains scaled for body size than any other animal (Kimbel and Villmoare, 2016). There is evidence that humans are better at causal reasoning than other species and this enables us to adjust our behavior in response to new environments (Bender and Beller, 2019; Vaesen, 2012). This leads to better tools and more productive subsistence techniques allowing us to survive in a wider range of environments. We also seem to be better at theory of mind than other species and it is plausible that this enables us to negotiate more complex, mutually beneficial social arrangements (Vaesen, 2012).

However, greater cognitive ability alone cannot explain how humans are able to adapt to such a wide range of environments. Other animals solve most of the problems they need to solve on their own. In many social species social learning from others plays an important but relatively modest role compared to humans (Whitehead et al., 2019). It can help individuals learn adaptive traits, but in virtually every case, they can, and do, learn the same traits without social input. In stark contrast, people do not solve most of the problems they need to solve on their own. Even in small-scale foraging societies, people depend on tools, foraging techniques, and ecological knowledge that no individual could invent by themselves (Boyd et al., 2011; Henrich, 2016; Boyd, 2017). Instead, human populations gradually accumulate solutions over time, and our exceptional social learning abilities allow these solutions to spread from one individual to another and so be preserved over time. Nor does greater cognitive ability obviously explain the extensive variation among human groups, or the tree-like patterning of this variation through time. Nor is it obvious why increased intelligence will lead to obviously maladaptive behavior. We also need to explain how humans, but apparently not other species, can pay the very high overhead costs of the huge brains that support our intelligence and culture (Heldstab et al., 2022).

On the other hand, the unusual features of the human species follow naturally if culture acts like a system of inheritance. Suppose that people are strongly motivated to adopt the beliefs and behavior of those around them, often without much modification. Such a system yields a psychology consistent with our desiderata. First, the repeated action of a little bit of adaptive innovation coupled with accurate social learning can lead to the accumulation of complex adaptations that no individual is likely to invent on their own. Second, an inheritance system of descent with modification naturally leads to a phylogenetic pattern, particularly if norms or network externalities create barriers to the flow of ideas among groups. Third, cultural transmission greatly amplifies the possibility that cooperative norms will evolve via some combination of group selection on cultural variation and prosocially motivated political and social actions. Fourth, the learning rule encourages people to ignore their own experience and motivations when they are uncertain, and this sometimes allows maladaptive behaviors to spread, sometimes by "madness of crowds" runaway processes (Richerson and Boyd, 2022). Importantly, tools and cooperation allow humans to operate very productive economies that not only pay the high overhead costs of our big brains but also provide the where-with-all to expand demographically at very high rates under favorable circumstances.

In the next section we present a very simple model that shows that under the right conditions, natural selection *can* favor a psychology that supports culture as an inheritance system.

3 The evolution of unbiased social learning

A number of models suggest that selection *can* favor a psychology that causes most people to adopt beliefs just because others hold those beliefs when it is difficult to evaluate which beliefs are correct (Boyd and Richerson, 1985; Rogers, 1988; Boyd and Richerson, 1988b; Aoki and Feldman, 2014; Hoppitt and Laland, 2008; Laland, 2004; Aoki et al., 2005; Wakano et al., 2004). Here we describe a recent simple model that illustrates the logic of this claim, and shows how different kinds of biased transmission can evolve (Perreault et al., 2012; Perreault and Boyd, 2022). Of course, any tractably simple model fails to capture many important processes shaping cultural evolution, and we will discuss some fundamental extensions below.

Here is the intuition behind the model: Suppose that a population lives in a variable environment. The environment changes slowly so that individuals live all of their lives in one environmental state. Individuals have two kinds of information about what is the genetic fitness maximizing behavior in the current environment and use this information to choose how to behave. First, they observe environmental cues that allow them to make inferences about the current environmental state. People use a variety of creative processes to generate new adaptive variants, but for simplicity we will refer to these inferential processes as individual learning. Moreover, they can estimate how likely this process is to produce a correct answer. Sometimes individual learning is a sure thing, but sometimes it is unlikely to yield the right answer. Second, learners observe the behavior of several individuals from the previous generation and can copy the behavior of those individuals. The central question is: Suppose that most of the individuals that they observe are doing one thing, but their own inference from environmental cues is telling them to do something different. When should individuals rely on individual learning, and when should they copy the behavior of others? The answer depends on their estimate of how good their individual learning is and how slowly environments are changing. If you are confident that individual learning is accurate, you should ignore the behavior of others, and rely on your own experience. Perhaps you have, by rare chance, observed a normally cryptic bit of animal behavior or the tell-tale trace of a hidden edible plant that reveals a new hunting or gathering strategy. However, if your own experience is more ambiguous and your confidence is low, it is better to imitate the behavior of others in your group (Boyd and Richerson, 1988b; Perreault et al., 2012). If individuals innovate only when they are likely to be right, almost all of the information flowing into the population will be accurate. Most people imitate because accurate individual learning is rare, and as long as the environment changes slowly, accurate information accumulates in the population and can be accessed by imitating others. It seems plausible that a strategy that uses environmental cues when they happen to be reliable, but depends on imitation when they are not, could be favored by selection because the occasional use of unusually reliable cues plus blind copying would cause the most commonly observed behavior to be the best behavior. To test this intuition, we need to model the cultural evolution of how people behave, given a learning psychology, and then allow the learning psychology to evolve genetically.

3.1 Optimal learning in a variable environment

Consider a large population living in an environment which can exist in two states, imaginatively labeled *state 1* and *state 2*. Each generation, the environment switches with probability γ and stays the same with probability $1 - \gamma$. This means that over the long run the environment is equally likely to be in each state. Individuals acquire one of two behaviors, *behavior 1* and *behavior 2* by either individual or social learning. Behavior 1 is favored by selection when the environment is in state 1 and behavior 2 is favored when the environment is in state 2. The relative fitness advantage of the favored behavior in each environment is the same.

Individuals observe a non-social cue, x, that provides probabilistic information about the state of the environment. Values of the environmental cue are normally distributed with mean μ and variance equal to one when the environment is in state 1 and with mean $-\mu$ and variance one when the environment is in state 2. Thus positive values of x support the inference that the environment is in state 1 and negative values support the inference that it is in state 2. The parameter μ is a measure of how accurately the environmental cue allows individuals to predict the state of the environment. The larger the absolute value of x, the better predictor the environmental cue is, but also the rarer it is.

Each individual also observes n models sampled from the previous generation. Here, we assume that models are identical except for their behavior. We relax this assumption below. Then the value of the social cue, y, is the number of observed models exhibiting behavior 1. Let p be the expected frequency of the behavior favored by selection in the population. Thus p is the frequency of behavior 1 when the environment is in state 1, and, from the symmetry of the model, p is the frequency of behavior 2 when the environment is in state 2. Then the conditional probability of y given that the environment is in state 1 is binomial with parameters p and n.

With these assumptions, the probability that the environment is in state 1 conditioned on the observed values of x and y is greater than one half if

$$y - \frac{1}{2}n > -gx$$

where

$$g = \frac{\mu}{\ln\left(\frac{p}{1-p}\right)}$$

(see Perreault et al., 2012 for a complete derivation). Because the expected frequency of the trait favored in the current environment, p, is greater than one half, g is positive. Thus, if x is positive and $y > n/2$, both environmental and social cues indicate that the environment is in state 1 and the expected fitness maximizing choice is behavior 1. Similarly, if x is negative and $y < n/2$, the rule indicates that behavior 2 is best. The magnitude of g becomes important when the cues point in opposite directions. Suppose, for example, that an individual observes more than half of her models using behavior 1 but observes a negative environmental cue that indicates she is in environment 2. Now, both sides of the inequality are positive. If g is small, in absolute value, the environmental cue is weighted less heavily; if it is large, the environmental cue is weighted more heavily.

3.2 The evolutionarily stable learning psychology

However, individuals cannot calculate the value of g because it depends on the expected frequency p and the mean of the cue distribution, μ. These are features of the environment over the long term that individuals cannot observe. Instead, the value of g is a representation of how an individual's learning psychology weights the importance of social and environmental information. Very small values of g correspond to placing a greater reliance on doing what others do, and less on individual inference. To determine whether natural selection can lead to the evolution of "blind imitation," which is just doing what others do, we need to let g evolve and see whether there are any conditions that favor the evolution of small values of g.

To model this process we assume that the value of g is controlled by one of m alleles at a haploid genetic locus. The ith allele has a learning rule characterized by the parameter g_i and has frequency q_i. Individuals first acquire their genotype through genetic transmission. Then, they observe members of the previous generation and the environmental cue, and determine whether they should adopt behavior 1 or behavior 2. Finally, viability selection adjusts the genotypic frequencies.

The fitnesses of the alleles depend on the average frequency of the two behaviors in the population over time. When the adaptive behavior is common, selection will favor small values of g that place a heavy emphasis on the social cue; when it is not, selection will favor larger values of g. This means that we must also derive an expression for how these frequencies change in the population as a result of learning given the distribution of different values of g in the population and the rate of switching of the environment between the two states. The distributions of learning rules and behaviors coevolve, each affecting the dynamics of the other. We iterate this system of $2m$ recursions in a given varying environment numerically until a joint stationary distribution of genotypic and behavioral frequencies is reached. The mathematical and simulation details are given in Perreault et al. (2012).

These evolutionary simulations lead to two interesting results:

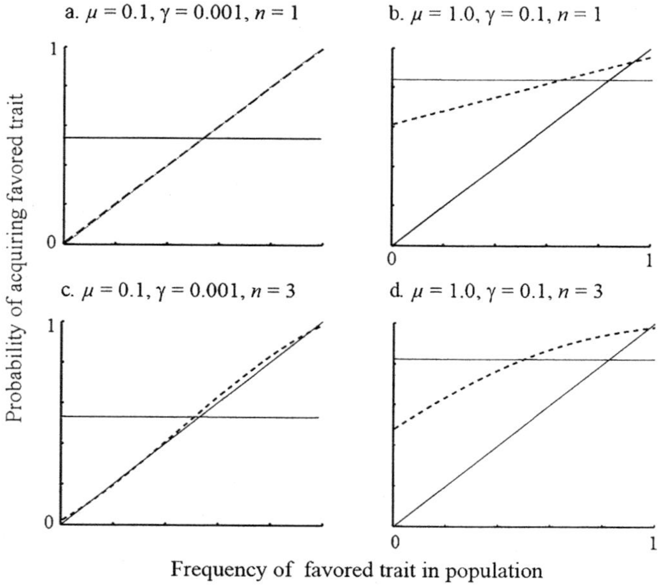

FIGURE 1 Dashed lines give the probability of acquiring the favored trait as a function of the frequency of that trait in the population at the evolutionary steady state for two levels of environmental cue quality ($\mu = 0.1, 1$). The horizontal line is the probability of acquiring the favored variant based on individual learning alone. The 45° line is the probability of acquiring the favored variant by imitating a randomly chosen individual. Panels a and b assume that learners are only able to observe the behavior of one model ($n = 1$) while panels c and d assume that there are three models ($n = 3$). In panels a and c the environment changes every 1000 time periods on average ($\gamma = 0.001$), while in b and d it changes every 10 time periods. We compare the evolutionary equilibrium outcome to two benchmarks: (1) the horizontal line gives probability of acquiring the favored trait if the learner ignores the social information and relies only on the environmental cue, and (2) the 45° line gives the probability of acquiring the favored trait if the learner ignores the environmental cue, and imitates a random individual.

Slowly changing environments and inaccurate individual learning favor more social learning. The results plotted in Fig. 1 indicate that natural selection can favor a strong reliance on social cues. When the environmental information is accurate and environments change rapidly (panels b and d) selection favors a little imitation and individual learning predominates. In contrast, when learning is noisy and environments change slowly (panels a and c) selection favors a learning rule in which almost everybody relies on the social cue and imitates the behavior of an individual from the previous generation. As a result, for any value of y, the equilibrium learning rule recursion lies closer to individual learning when μ is large. Conversely, as the quality of the environmental information decreases, selection favors putting less weight on it and relying instead on social information. When more than one individual is available to imitate, selection favors a stronger reliance on the social cue and the probability of acquiring the favored behavior is higher, and this increases the equilibrium frequency of the behavior (Fig. 1 panels c and d).

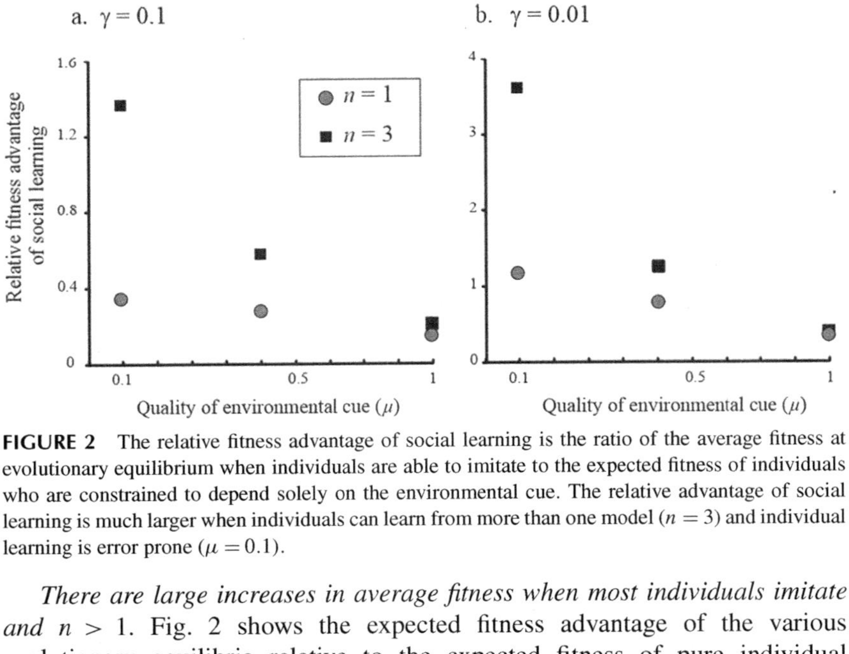

FIGURE 2 The relative fitness advantage of social learning is the ratio of the average fitness at evolutionary equilibrium when individuals are able to imitate to the expected fitness of individuals who are constrained to depend solely on the environmental cue. The relative advantage of social learning is much larger when individuals can learn from more than one model ($n = 3$) and individual learning is error prone ($\mu = 0.1$).

There are large increases in average fitness when most individuals imitate and $n > 1$. Fig. 2 shows the expected fitness advantage of the various evolutionary equilibria relative to the expected fitness of pure individual learners. When $n = 1$, there may be a substantial reliance on imitation at evolutionary equilibrium, but the average fitness of the population decreases. However, when $n = 3$ and selection favors reliance on the social cue, there is a large increase in average fitness. This effect persists for larger values of n.

In this simple model social learning is favored in the information acquisition economy because it allows populations to tap information from many individual attempts to learn the state of the environment. Note that individuals cannot calculate that this is the best strategy—they do not have access to the necessary information. Rather natural selection on genes shapes their learning psychology so that when environments change relatively slowly, they are innately predisposed to imitate the common behavior in the population.

4 Biased social learning can enhance cultural adaptation

So far we have assumed that when individuals imitate, they weight different individuals equally. Social learning is biased when learners place more weight on the behavior of some individuals compared to other individuals. Several types of bias are possible. Here we consider two.

4.1 Content bias

Content bias occurs when some content is more attractive or easier to learn than other content. Sometimes content bias may be adaptive. For example, Wertz (2019) has shown that small children are much more cautious about touching or eating unfamiliar plants than other novel objects. Hunter-gatherer children frequently forage on their own, and because wild plants often contain toxins, this bias is plausibly the result of genetic adaptation. Barrett and Broesch (2012) have shown that both children living in Santa Barbara and in rain forest villages in eastern Ecuador more readily learn and better remember which animals are dangerous than which animals are plant eaters. Other times, content bias may arise from acquired cognitive factors. For example, the use of bloodletting to cure disease occurs in many unrelated cultures (Miton et al., 2015) and persists because it is more memorable than other treatments. Miton (2024) provides many examples of content bias in social learning. Bloodletting is potentially an example of a case in which general content biases that are useful on average may sometimes go astray. Content bias can also be maladaptive if the success of a cultural practice is normally poor but only rare successes attract the attention of social learners. High risk criminal behaviors may result in failure and obscurity for most poor people who attempt them, but a few lucky gangsters become conspicuous successes (Velilla et al., 2025).

There was no content bias in the model analyzed above because both environments were equally likely, and the relative fitness effects of having the favored behavior in each environment were the same. If these assumptions are relaxed, the optimal behavioral rule becomes biased. For example, suppose that the fitness of the favored behavior in environment 1 is d_1 and in environment 2 it is d_2, π is the expected fraction of the time the environment is in state 1, and p_1 and p_2 are the frequency of the expected frequencies of the favored trait in environments 1 and 2. Then the fitness maximizing behavior rule becomes (Perreault and Boyd, 2022):

$$y - \frac{n}{2} > -gx + b$$

Where g gives the relative weight of the environmental and social cues. The parameter b is given by

$$b = \frac{\ln\left(\frac{1-\pi}{\pi}\right) + \ln\left(\frac{d_1}{d_2}\right)}{\ln\left(\frac{p_1 p_2}{(1-p_1)(1-p_2)}\right)}.$$

In the symmetric case, $b = 0$. When the payoff of the favored behavior in environment 1 is greater than in environment 2 ($d_1 > d_2$) then $b < 0$. This means that other things being equal, learners are more likely to adopt behavior 1. Notice that if b is large enough in absolute value, the learner will ignore both cues and adopt behavior 1. Behavior has become innate.

4.2 Payoff bias

Payoff bias occurs when social learners can estimate the fitness associated with different cultural variants, and preferentially imitate relatively higher payoff behaviors. This creates a selection-like process that tends to increase the representation of variants that covary with genetic fitness. If fitness is difficult to estimate and correlations between particular variants and fitness are weak, most people will imitate, approximately at random. Nonetheless, over time the weak payoff bias will cause the population to evolve toward traits that increase fitness. In many environments, it may be difficult to determine which traits are correlated with fitness and so proxies are used. One useful proxy could be who other people are imitating. This can lead to adaptation but may also lead to the spread of maladaptive traits (Henrich and Gil-White, 2001). Imitating the majority may also enhance local adaptation, but increase the variation among local populations. Biased teaching occurs when social models selectively teach one variant in preference to others they know.

We add payoff bias to the model above by allowing learners to observe the behaviors and the fitness of the n models that they potentially may imitate. The observed payoff of an individual with the favored behavior is a normally distributed random variable with mean $\mu + d$ and variance v and the payoff of an individual with the disfavored behavior is a normally distributed variable with mean μ and variance v. The common mean, μ, is itself a normally distributed random variable with mean zero and a very large variance. This means that the absolute magnitudes of payoffs provide no information about the state of the environment, but that the difference between the payoffs is informative.

With these assumptions the optimal decision rule becomes

$$y - \frac{n}{2} > G\left(\frac{y(n-y)}{n}\right)(\bar{w}_2 - \bar{w}_1) - gx$$

where as before y is the number of models with behavior 1, $\bar{w}_i$ is the observed average payoff of individuals with behavior i, and x is the value of the environmental cue. The parameter g has the same meaning as in the model above. The parameter G gives the relative weight of the difference in mean payoffs as a cue

$$G = \frac{d}{v \ln\left(\frac{p}{1-p}\right)}.$$

Notice that the importance of payoff bias depends on the variance of behavior within the sample of social learning models. As the variance of behavior in the sample declines, so too does the relative importance of the payoff cue. As a result payoff bias is less effective when either most people in a population have the favorable trait or very few do, or if individual's sample of the population to learn from is small.

As in the previous model, learners do not have access to the information necessary to compute G and so we assume it is a component of innate individual psychology that gives the weight that learners put on the observed difference in payoffs information compared to the commonness of two behaviors, and the environmental cue. To determine the effect of payoff bias we simulated the coevolution of genes affecting G and g and the frequency of the two behaviors over time until a stationary distribution was reached. Payoff bias becomes more important as the environmental cue decreases in quality, and as the rate of environmental change decreases. When payoff bias is significant, it leads to a substantial increase in average fitness compared to a population using only unbiased imitation (see Perreault and Boyd, 2022 for the details).

5 What's in it for economists

Distributed models of cultural evolution borrow heavily from economics and game theory. At the core of the theory are boundedly rational actors consuming and using genetic and cultural information to make a living. Individuals are modeled as smart innovators, vendors, and shoppers in the marketplace of ideas as they can realistically be. Collectively, they more or less successfully create institutions and normative constraints on individual behavior to solve problems of coordination and the dilemma of cooperation. The contribution of the evolutionary models is to keep track of the market-wide and long-term dynamics of the information economy. In turn, we argue that the distributed models and the concepts behind them offer tools that economists find useful when their questions touch on the population dynamic properties of the information economy.

There is no doubt that we are descended from an ape-like creature that lived several million years ago, and in the interim, our species has been radically transformed. It might seem obvious that our evolutionary history and the processes that shaped it would be relevant to understanding why people are the way that they are, and, consequently, the social sciences would incorporate ideas from evolutionary anthropology. But this is not the case. Scholars in most of the social sciences have paid little attention to our evolutionary origins.

Economics is a partial exception to this generalization. Although evolutionary thinking does not play a central role in economics, economists have made more use of evolutionary ideas than other social sciences. Evolutionary reasoning has been used to explain the features of preferences already assumed in economic models, things like time preference, risk preference, the role of trust and why people behave altruistically toward kin (Robson, 2001, 2002; Netzer, 2009; Seabright, 2010). There has also been some work using evolutionary reasoning to explain the "irrationalities" observed by behavioral economists (Netzer, 2009; Polanía et al., 2024), and some economists have used evolutionary ideas to support the more controversial idea that people have prosocial preferences (Fehr and Fischbacher, 2003; Bowles, 2006).

We believe that the models of culture developed in evolutionary anthropology will be useful to economists for three reasons: First, most economists who have thought about culture have adopted a distributed model in which beliefs and social attitudes are distributed across individuals in a population. Theories of cultural evolution developed in evolutionary anthropology have used existing ideas and mathematical techniques from population biology, and provide a handy framework for distributed models of culture. Given the nature of economic theory, it is unsurprising that this framework has already been adopted and modified by economists (Bisin and Verdier, 2023). Second, linking the nature of preferences and priors to an understanding of human evolution is an important link to the rest of science. Consilience, the idea that all of science is linked in a single causal web, is important in the physical and biological sciences. Think about the origin of life. We really want to know how chemistry produced living things. Consilience is not given much importance in social sciences, but it should be. Third, and most important, thinking about culture as an evolved adaptation provides useful insights about the role of culture and how to model it. Economic theory depends on the nature of preferences and priors, the explanation for which economists usually outsource to other sciences like psychology. Evolution is the ultimate source of preferences and priors. A theory which assumed that people were completely unselfish or had no time preference is inconsistent with our origins as evolved organisms. In the same way, the adaptive theory of cultural evolution makes predictions about the nature of culture and cultural change. We sketch some of these below.

5.1 Culture includes more than norms, values, and shared understandings

There is much evidence that enhanced cognitive processes alone cannot explain our ability to adapt to a wide range of environments using techniques and social organization that vary widely (Boyd et al., 2011; Henrich, 2016; Richerson and Boyd, 2022). The cumulative cultural evolution of knowledge, tools and institutions has played a crucial role in the evolution of our species. This means that culture must allow the transmission of complex traits with sufficient accuracy that cumulative improvement can occur. Our very large, energy hungry brain that makes possible both complex cognition and cultural learning is extremely costly, as is a prolonged pre-reproductive childhood that provides time to learn most of the information provided by cultural evolution. These costs had to be balanced by adaptive advantages, and this strongly suggests that culture is more than the set of shared understandings that are the focus of attention of many contemporary anthropologists. Practical knowledge, tools and institution-sustaining norms are all culturally transmitted as well and are fundamental to the economies that produce the where-with-all to pay the high overhead costs of our cultural system. This does not mean that shared meaning and other aspects of "imaginative" culture are without economic interest. Professional sports, for example, are selling meaningful participation in ersatz tribal conflicts and they are big business.

5.2 People are predisposed to adopt the beliefs of those around them

In the period between birth and maturity, people have to acquire large amounts of information about the local environment, and much of it is very difficult for individuals to vet on their own. The evolutionary model of culture strongly predicts that human psychology is structured so that people acquire this information by learning from the people around them. It is as if people are born with priors that hold that what they see people around them doing is adaptive in the current environment. This does not mean that behavior remains unchanged. Individual learning and more complex forms of creativity introduce new cultural variants into populations. If observed behavior varies, various kinds of biased social learning may cause some variants to increase in frequency. Of course, sometimes people acquire information that causes them to modify the socially acquired behaviors and this will lead to cultural change as well.

This picture is at variance with the longstanding idea that culture is transmitted mainly through the efforts of parents to socialize their children (Harris, 2009; Collins et al., 2002). This assumption is incorporated in a number of influential models of cultural evolution developed in economics (Bisin and Verdier, 2001a,b). In contrast, the evolutionary approach predicts that culture is acquired by members of the younger generation because their evolved psychology motivates them to hoover up useful, but hard to verify, information by absorbing the knowledge and imitating behavior of peers and older non-parental individuals. They will often learn from parents, because parents are more likely to be care givers, and simple propinquity means that they will be the most readily available source of cultural information. As children get older they will more easily observe the behavior of other people, both adults and peers. To the extent that cultural learning is biased, acquiring information from this larger sample will increase the chance of getting the most adaptive cultural variants. Children may also learn from parents when teaching helps acquire a skill because parents are more likely to pay the costs of teaching.

There is much data supporting this view of social learning. Broad cross-cultural surveys of how children learn subsistence skills (Lew-Levy et al., 2017, 2023) and social norms (Lew-Levy et al., 2018) and in-depth ethnographic studies (Lew-Levy et al., 2021; Kline et al., 2013) support this picture. Kids initially learn from their parents, but as they get older, peers, older kids, and a variety of adults play a crucial role. Cross-cultural experiments suggest that sharing norms converge to locally common beliefs in late childhood (House et al., 2013). In the US, parent-offspring correlations for political attitudes are substantial (Jennings et al., 2009), but twin studies indicate that little of the correlation is due to common family environment (Alford et al., 2005). In the short term social learning experiments performed by psychologists, participants faithfully imitate actions that are not causally relevant to the reward as long as they cannot infer why the causally irrelevant action was performed (Hoehl et al., 2019). Consistent with the model, experimental work shows that reliance on imitation increases as the difficulty of individual learning increases (Baron et al., 1996).

5.3 Culture is shaped by individual preferences and transmission biases

Humans have relied on cumulative cultural adaptation for at least a few hundred thousand years, and perhaps longer (Paige and Perreault, 2024). The evidence comes from archaeological sites with complex tools and production processes that are too sophisticated for individuals to repeatedly invent on their own. To cite just a few examples: birch tar adhesive has been found at a number of sites that date to more than 100,000 years ago. Manufacturing birch tar in quantity requires cooking birch bark in anaerobic conditions, requiring complex heating techniques (Schmidt et al., 2023). Twisted, multi-ply cordage has been found at a Neanderthal site that dates to more than 40,000 years ago (Hardy et al., 2013). More than 150,000 years ago, humans in southern Africa heat-annealed stone to improve its knapping qualities (Schmidt, 2016).

The antiquity of cultural adaptation means that natural selection has been working on human psychology of social learning for a long time, and we should expect that social learning should be biased in ways that increase chances that learners acquire adaptive information. We have already seen that selection can favor content and payoff biases. Other research suggests that social learning should be biased in favor of more commonly observed behaviors, in favor of models who are similar to the learner, older models, and models who are prestigious, and a wide range of experimental and observational data supports these predictions (Boyd and Richerson, 1985; Henrich, 2016; Morgan et al., 2012; Kendal et al., 2018).

There is debate about the relative importance of biased transmission and individual learning. Many psychologists believe that reliable replication of observed behavior occurs frequently enough to serve as a basis for modeling the population dynamics of cultural change (Gelpi and Buchsbaum, 2023; Gweon, 2021; Vélez and Gweon, 2021; Olsson et al., 2020). On this view, biased transmission plays a crucial role in cumulative cultural evolution (Henrich, 2016; Boyd, 2017). However, Dan Sperber (Sperber, 1985) and his school (Atran, 1998; Boyer, 2023; Morin, 2016; Miton and DeDeo, 2022) believe that accurate cultural learning is very difficult, and occurs only infrequently. Rather, humans must depend upon genetically transmitted cognitive structures to largely reconstruct "cultural" behaviors using only scanty social cues. A highly gene-based view very much like this was pioneered by E.O. Wilson (1978). This belief is based on one strand of the cognitive science literature that holds that it is very difficult to infer the mental representations by observing the behavior. It is certainly true that many non-human social learning systems, such as the classic Norway rat diet learning system conform to this intuition (Galef, 1982). It seems likely that some domains of human behavior are similar. For example, high-level athletic performance requires very extensive individual practice. On the other hand, experiments comparing the social learning capabilities of humans and other primates show that humans are much more efficient social learners (Dean et al., 2012). Language is a particularly efficient way of transmitting cognitively complex concepts to learners (Carey, 2009). It is hard to understand how children can accurately learn the large, unique vocabulary of their languages without sophisticated social learning strategies (Bloom, 2002). The largest share of the information content of languages is in their idiosyncratic vocabularies, not the possibly more innate syntax (Mollica and Piantadosi, 2019).

5.4 Gene-culture coevolution provides an explanation for prestige

Many authors who have written about the role of culture in human evolution see genetic evolution as being in the driver's seat because genetic evolution shapes the psychology that determines which cultural traits spread and which do not (e.g. Lumsden and Wilson, 1981; Alexander, 1974; Tooby and Cosmides, 1992). There is no doubt that our evolved psychology does play an important role in shaping cultural evolution. But it is also true that cultural evolution gives rise to novel environments that change how natural selection shapes our brains and bodies. This process, called gene-culture coevolution, can lead to completely novel outcomes.

The evolution of prestige provides a good example. In other social animals status is associated with strength and power. Dominant individuals acquire social influence by coercion. In humans status has two dimensions (Henrich and Gil-White, 2001; Jiménez and Mesoudi, 2019). Like other animals we have dominance. But we also have prestige in which social status is voluntarily conferred on successful or skillful individuals. Stalin was dominant; Einstein was prestigious.

Thinking about the evolution of social learning provides an explanation for why humans have two forms of social status. We have seen that natural selection will favor a social learning psychology that weights models according to their relative fitnesses. This requires observable cues of fitness. It is useful to divide these into two broad categories—skill-based cues that indicate fitness relevant traits in specific domains like hunting or sewing, and broad-based success cues of relative fitness that aggregate skill in many domains (Henrich, 2016). For many kinds of traits, learning from somebody requires being around them for substantial amounts of time, and so people will compete for access to especially skillful or successful individuals. Thus, we should expect learners to "pay" for access to especially successful people with social deference. This is the first order reason for prestige. Fitness is notoriously difficult to measure, and differences of a few percent really matter, especially when aggregated over many traits. Moreover, environments vary a lot and so cues of skills and success will also vary from one environment to another. This means that selection will favor cues that are useful in a wide range of environments. Henrich and Gil-White (2001) argue that such bias is a propensity to imitate people who other people imitate. People who other people admire and want to imitate are prestigious.

This is a good general rule, but it also can lead to a positive feedback process that swamps the effect of first-order cues of skill and success so that people become prestigious because lots of people attend to them. Henrich (2016) calls this the "Paris Hilton" effect. A similar dynamic may explain why advertisers pay celebrities who are prestigious due to skill in one domain (e.g. football) to endorse products completely unrelated to that domain (e.g. bundled home and car insurance).

5.5 Evolutionary reasoning suggests a novel explanation for costly displays

The fact that learners are motivated to acquire beliefs and behavior by learning from others creates the potential for manipulation (Henrich, 2009; Seabright, 2017). In many circumstances, people who serve as "models" will be aware that they can manipulate what others learn from them by modifying their behavior so learners acquire behavior that serves the model's interests, not those of the learner.

This is not likely to be a problem when learners observe on-going behavior especially in small-scale societies in which individuals' behavior is observed repeatedly and intimately by many people who in turn gossip about it (Henrich, 2009). Children can learn what is good to eat by watching what others eat. Young men learn how to make their bows by watching older men make their bows (Harris et al., 2021). Learners acquire many traits by imitating things that their models are already doing. Deception is difficult because models are doing what they think best. An older man might know how to make a superior bow, and would prefer others not learn how to make this bow in order to preserve his advantage. But if learners can readily observe the bow that he uses when hunting, concealment won't be possible.

The scope for manipulation is much greater when beliefs are transmitted verbally and behavior isn't easily observed. A man who knows how to make a particularly potent arrow poison might provide an inferior recipe to others and manufacture his own poison in private. A naughty parent we know, who really likes to eat artichoke hearts, encouraged his young kids' initial suspicion of them in order to eat theirs as well as his. Such deception is likely to be especially important for hard to verify beliefs. An experienced hunter tells a young man that the failure to share a kill will lead to bad luck in future hunts, or a priest preaches that god rewards those who live a life of poverty and devotion to the church. In both cases, the teacher may benefit from the learner adopting the belief.

Joe Henrich (2009, 2016) has argued that social learning psychology predisposes us to copy behavior that has costly, observable entailments. Or, in other words, by only imitating people who put their money where their mouth is. An older man is a proficient hunter who shares his kills so you adopt his belief that stinginess leads to bad luck, but if he doesn't hunt any more but advocates sharing, you do not. If the priest is willing to go to the stake in defense of his beliefs, observers are more likely to think he sincerely believes. But this creates a transmission bias that favors costly proofs of honesty—what Henrich calls credibility enhancing displays (or CREDs). This bias will lead to the spread of exaggerated costly displays (Jordan et al., 2017; Kraft-Todd et al., 2018).

Notice that this mechanism for explaining exaggerated displays is quite distinct from the usual signaling models in which individuals signal that they are of a valuable, but unobservable, type by engaging in behavior that is less costly for them than for individuals who are of a different type. Such costly signals can pay because they benefit by honestly revealing their type. CREDs are different in two important ways. First, the costly signal spreads because social learning psychology predisposes learners to adopt beliefs that underlie the display. There is no requirement that the signaler receives a private benefit; indeed she will tend to pay private costs. The fervent believer accepts martyrdom because she is committed to her religious belief. Second, unlike costly signaling, the CRED mechanism explains why behaviors like martyrdom cause others to adopt the underlying beliefs, something that does not follow from the signaling explanation for costly displays.

5.6 Cultural group selection can explain the evolution of norms supporting cooperation

Humans are much more cooperative than other vertebrates. People in human societies cooperate in large groups of distantly related or unrelated individuals to produce collective goods. They construct shared capital facilities like drivelines, fish traps, fortifications, and irrigation works, they risk their lives in large-scale warfare, and they maintain public order (Boyd and Richerson, 2022). People who cooperate in large groups to produce collective goods incur a personal cost, but the effect of their contribution on their own fitness is very small. This kind of behavior is unknown among other vertebrate species. Some, like communally nesting birds and chimpanzees, cooperate with distantly related individuals in small groups to produce collective goods, but very few vertebrate species do this in larger groups, and the few that do, like African mole rats, live in groups of close kin.

The non-human pattern fits with accounts of the evolution of social behavior. Hamilton's (Hamilton, 1964) theory of kin selection says that when relatives interact, selection acts as if individuals place a positive value on the fitness of others. Because ants and termites can have many siblings, selection can favor collective action in truly immense societies. But the reproductive biology of most vertebrates limits the number of close relatives, and kin selection does not favor large-scale cooperation. Reciprocity can motivate cooperation between individuals and small groups but its effects decline rapidly with numbers of participants (Boyd and Richerson, 1988a). People cooperate in large groups, something that is unique among vertebrates. So, the evolution of large-scale human cooperation is a puzzle—something must be added to the usual account, as Hamilton (1975) recognized.

The cultural evolution of social norms and institutions provides an alternative route to the evolution of large-scale cooperation. Institutions (systems of rules that operate at the level of social systems) and norms (subordinate rules that regulate human behavior according to the institutionalized division of labor) structure social interactions in every human society (Elsenbroich and Gilbert, 2014; Brennan et al., 2013; Bicchieri, 2005, 2016; Mackie et al., 2015; Roughley and Bayertz, 2019; Edgerton, 1985; Currie et al., 2016). They specify which kinds of behaviors are desirable and which are forbidden, and reach into every corner of life—who you can marry, how you should dress, how you raise your children, what kinds of contracts are allowed, which god you may worship—the list is long. These requirements are socially enforced. Norm violators may lose status, access to mutual aid, and face monetary or corporal punishment. There is great variation in the content of norms and institutions among societies, and there is evidence that this variation is culturally transmitted (Handley and Mathew, 2020). For example, linguistically related societies have more similar norms than less closely related societies (Mackie et al., 2015). Moreover, on average, norms and institutions support collective action and other forms of cooperative behavior (Currie et al., 2021).

Norms and institutions create incentives that stabilize a vast range of behaviors, and these incentives can maintain differences in norms between neighboring groups even though people and ideas move between groups. This means that differences will be stable through time, and when groups split, daughter groups will resemble their parent. When a vast range of outcomes is evolutionarily stable, knowing that a norm is evolutionarily stable isn't very informative. A satisfying account of human large-scale cooperation must specify the processes that give rise to the particular kinds of norms that are observed—an "equilibrium selection mechanism" in the jargon of evolutionary game theory. We have argued that intergroup competition is one such mechanism (Boyd and Richerson, 1982). Neighboring groups often compete—militarily, economically, and for prestige. The norms and institutions that predominate in a group can affect whether a group survives, whether it expands, whether it is imitated by its neighbors, and whether it attracts immigrants. Norms and institutions causing a group to survive will become more common than those that lead to extinction (Boyd and Richerson, 1990). Similarly, norms and institutions that lead to group expansion, are more likely to be imitated (Boyd and Richerson, 2002), or attract more immigrants (Boyd and Richerson, 2009) will also increase compared to those that don't. There is much empirical evidence that these processes, which we collectively term "cultural group selection," have played a role in shaping the kinds of culturally transmitted norms and institutions we observe in human societies (Richerson et al., 2016; Handley and Mathew, 2020).

5.7 Population dynamic processes are consistent with a wide range of rates of cultural change

Acemoglu and Robinson (2021) argue that population dynamic models of cultural evolution only can explain gradual change on the generational time scale, not more rapid or discontinuous change. Cultures often change slowly and this can explain the long-term persistence of economic and social phenomena. However, culture can also evolve very quickly. There are several reasons for this. First, much cultural information is transmitted horizontally among peers or from prestigious individuals to many learners (Cavalli-Sforza and Feldman, 1981) and so culture can evolve much more rapidly than genes. Second, the rate at which new traits can spread due to selective forces depends on how often individuals update their beliefs and how dense cultural learning networks are. People may update their ideas about fashion on weekly time scales and when this is coupled with tipping point dynamics, for example, the frequency of Hush Puppy wearing can change rapidly in a population of hipsters (Gladwell, 2006). Laboratory studies of cultural evolution also exhibit substantial change in a few cultural "generations," which are often far shorter than the human biological generation (Derex and Boyd, 2015; Thompson et al., 2022). Third, learning processes often depend on external cues that are correlated across individuals in a population, and so abrupt environmental changes can lead to extremely rapid cultural change. The rapid spread of millenarian beliefs in Melanesia provides an illustrative example. According to Burridge (1969), these societies were based on status competition over property. Colonial powers introduced new prestige goods which were not available to colonized people. This triggered a crisis in which existing prestige norms could not be satisfied, leading in turn to the innovation of "cargo cults" which promised access to European goods by magical means.

6 Conclusion

There is little consensus within anthropology about what culture is, how it changes, or even whether it is a useful concept. The population dynamic models described in this paper are one of several approaches in which culture is conceptualized as information distributed across the minds of individuals in a population. What makes it different from other population dynamic models is a commitment to understanding culture in terms of organic evolution. The capacities that make *Homo sapiens* hyper-cultural organisms evolved because culture allows adaptation to a wide range of habitats in the chaotic environments of the Pleistocene. Human populations adapt, accumulating useful information over time—sometimes rapidly, sometimes over many generations. This means that much culturally transmitted information is acquired by imitation and teaching. Of course, children learn a great deal about the world through individual learning, but this is not nearly enough. The complex, hard to learn information must be acquired through cultural transmission. The world is diverse and complex, and individuals cannot learn all that they need to know on their own in the time available to learn it. At least initially, we do what the people we grow up around do. Some traits are easier to vet than others and these may change relatively rapidly as adults modify what they have imitated. But many traits, especially in simpler societies without writing, may persist little changed for generations. The commitment to an evolutionary approach also implies that it doesn't make sense to limit culture to symbols or deep systems of meaning. Culture is adaptive because it allows the cumulative evolution of all kinds of traits—knowledge about the environment, technology, symbolic styles, norms, and systems of meaning. Finally, the evolutionary approach implies that culture is not solely transmitted as parents socialize children, shaping them in accordance with social norms and institutions. Children are designed to avidly seek information from their social world because that is much better than trying to figure out stuff on their own. Human children have to learn so much to be competent adults that even if they could in principle learn a given trait on their own, learning it more quickly by teaching or imitation saves precious time. Of course, some traits may benefit from effortful teaching by adults, and parents may often be more willing to expend such effort, and be less likely to mislead their own offspring. But much social information is demonstrated in the observable, everyday behavior of adults. How they get food, how they make shelters, how they dress, and of course the norms that they obey and enforce. Human economies for the last few hundred thousand years rest on cultural foundations and their often rapid changes are driven by cultural evolutionary processes.

References

Acemoglu, D., Robinson, J.A., 2021. Culture, institutions and social equilibria: a framework. Technical report. National Bureau of Economic Research.

Alesina, A., Giuliano, P., 2015. Culture and institutions. Journal of Economic Literature 53 (4), 898–944.

Alexander, R.D., 1974. The evolution of social behavior. Annual Review of Ecology and Systematics 5 (1), 325–383.

Alford, J.R., Funk, C.L., Hibbing, J.R., 2005. Are political orientations genetically transmitted? American Political Science Review 99 (2), 153–167.

Aoki, K., Feldman, M.W., 2014. Evolution of learning strategies in temporally and spatially variable environments: a review of theory. Theoretical Population Biology 91, 3–19.

Aoki, K., Wakano, J., Feldman, M., 2005. The emergence of social learning in a temporally changing environment: a theoretical model. Current Anthropology 46 (2), 334–340.

Atran, S., 1998. Folk biology and the anthropology of science: cognitive universals and cultural particulars. Behavioral and Brain Sciences 21 (4), 547–569.

Barnard, A., 2021. History and Theory in Anthropology. Cambridge University Press.

Baron, R.S., Vandello, J.A., Brunsman, B., 1996. The forgotten variable in conformity research: impact of task importance on social influence. Journal of Personality and Social Psychology 71 (5), 915.

Barrett, H.C., Broesch, J., 2012. Prepared social learning about dangerous animals in children. Evolution and Human Behavior 33 (5), 499–508.

Barth, F., 1987. Cosmologies in the Making: a Generative Approach to Cultural Variation in Inner New Guinea. Number 64 in Cambridge Studies in Social Anthropology. Cambridge University Press.

Barth, F., 1990. The guru and the conjurer: transactions in knowledge and the shaping of culture in Southeast Asia and Melanesia. Man, 640–653.

Barth, F., 2002. An anthropology of knowledge. Current Anthropology 43 (1), 1–18.

Barth, F., 2011. Nomads of south Persia-the Basseri tribe of the Khamseh Confederacy. Read Books Ltd.

Barth, F., 2020. Political Leadership Among Swat Pathans. London School of Economics Monographs on Social Anthropology, vol. 19. Routledge.

Bender, A., Beller, S., 2019. The cultural fabric of human causal cognition. Perspectives on Psychological Science 14 (6), 922–940.

Besley, T., Persson, T., 2019. Democratic values and institutions. American Economic Review: Insights 1 (1), 59–76.

Bicchieri, C., 2005. The Grammar of Society: The Nature and Dynamics of Social Norms. Cambridge University Press.

Bicchieri, C., 2016. Norms in the Wild: How to Diagnose, Measure, and Change Social Norms. Oxford University Press.

Bisin, A., Verdier, T., 2001a. Agents with imperfect empathy may survive natural selection. Economics Letters 71 (2), 277–285.

Bisin, A., Verdier, T., 2001b. The economics of cultural transmission and the dynamics of preferences. Journal of Economic Theory 97 (2), 298–319.

Bisin, A., Verdier, T., 2011. The Economics of Cultural Transmission and Socialization. Handbook of Social Economics, vol. 1. Elsevier, pp. 339–416.

Bisin, A., Verdier, T., 2023. Advances in the economic theory of cultural transmission. Annual Review of Economics 15 (1), 63–89.

Bloom, P., 2002. How Children Learn the Meanings of Words. MIT Press.

Bowles, S., 2006. Group competition, reproductive leveling, and the evolution of human altruism. Science 314 (5805), 1569–1572.
Boyd, R., 2017. A Different Kind of Animal: How Culture Transformed Our Species. Princeton University Press.
Boyd, R., Durham, W.H., Borgerhoff Mulder, M., Richerson, P.J., 1997. Are cultural phylogenies possible? In: Weingart, P., Mitchell, S.D., Richerson, P.J., Maasen, S. (Eds.), Human by Nature: Between Biology and the Social Sciences. Lawrence Erlbaum, pp. 355–386.
Boyd, R., Richerson, P.J., 1982. Cultural transmission and the evolution of cooperative behavior. Human Ecology 10, 325–351.
Boyd, R., Richerson, P.J., 1985. Culture and the Evolutionary Process. University of Chicago Press.
Boyd, R., Richerson, P.J., 1988a. The evolution of reciprocity in sizable groups. Journal of Theoretical Biology 132 (3), 337–356.
Boyd, R., Richerson, P.J., 1988b. An evolutionary model of social learning: the effects of spatial and temporal variation. In: Zentall, T.R., Galef, B.G. (Eds.), Social Learning. Psychology Press, pp. 41–60.
Boyd, R., Richerson, P.J., 1990. Group selection among alternative evolutionarily stable strategies. Journal of Theoretical Biology 145 (3), 331–342.
Boyd, R., Richerson, P.J., 2002. Group beneficial norms can spread rapidly in a structured population. Journal of Theoretical Biology 215 (3), 287–296.
Boyd, R., Richerson, P.J., 2009. Voting with your feet: payoff biased migration and the evolution of group beneficial behavior. Journal of Theoretical Biology 257 (2), 331–339.
Boyd, R., Richerson, P.J., 2022. Large-scale cooperation in small-scale foraging societies. Evolutionary Anthropology: Issues, News, and Reviews 31 (4), 175–198.
Boyd, R., Richerson, P.J., Henrich, J., 2011. The cultural niche: why social learning is essential for human adaptation. Proceedings of the National Academy of Sciences 108 (supplement_2), 10918–10925.
Boyer, P., 2023. The Naturalness of Religious Ideas: A Cognitive Theory of Religion. Univ. of California Press.
Brennan, G., Eriksson, L., Goodin, R.E., Southwood, N., 2013. Explaining Norms. Oxford University Press, USA.
Brown, G.R., Lala, K.N., 2024. Sense and Nonsense: Evolutionary Perspectives on Human Behaviour. Oxford University Press.
Burridge, K., 1969. New Heaven, New Earth: a Study of Millenarian Activities. Schocken Books.
Cantlon, J.F., Piantadosi, S.T., 2024. Uniquely human intelligence arose from expanded information capacity. Nature Reviews Psychology 3 (4), 275–293.
Cao, Y., Enke, B., Falk, A., Giuliano, P., Nunn, N., 2021. Herding, warfare, and a culture of honor: Global evidence. Technical report. National Bureau of Economic Research.
Carey, S., 2009. The Origin of Concepts. Oxford University Press.
Cavalli-Sforza, L.L., Feldman, M.W., 1981. Cultural Transmission and Evolution: A Quantitative Approach. Princeton University Press.
Clifford, J., Marcus, G.E., 1986. Writing Culture: The Poetics and Politics of Ethnography. Univ. of California Press.
Collins, W.A., Maccoby, E.E., Steinberg, L., Hetherington, E.M., Bornstein, M.H., 2002. Contemporary research on parenting: the case for nature and nurture. In: Annual Progress in Child Psychiatry and Child Development 2000–2001, pp. 125–154.
Cowlishaw, G., Mace, R., 1996. Cross-cultural patterns of marriage and inheritance: a phylogenetic approach. Ethology and Sociobiology 17 (2), 87–97.
Currie, T., Turchin, P., Bednar, J., Richerson, P.J., Schwesinger, G., Steinmo, S., Wacziarg, R., Wallis, J., 2016. Evolution of institutions and organizations. In: Wilson, D.S., Kirman, A. (Eds.), Complexity and Evolution: Toward a New Synthesis for Economics. In: Strüngmann Forum Reports, vol. 19. MIT Press, pp. 201–236.
Currie, T.E., Campenni, M., Flitton, A., Njagi, T., Ontiri, E., Perret, C., Walker, L., 2021. The cultural evolution and ecology of institutions. Philosophical Transactions of the Royal Society B 376 (1828), 20200047.

Dean, L.G., Kendal, R.L., Schapiro, S.J., Thierry, B., Laland, K.N., 2012. Identification of the social and cognitive processes underlying human cumulative culture. Science 335 (6072), 1114–1118.

Dean, L.G., Vale, G.L., Laland, K.N., Flynn, E., Kendal, R.L., 2014. Human cumulative culture: a comparative perspective. Biological Reviews 89 (2), 284–301.

Derex, M., Boyd, R., 2015. The foundations of the human cultural niche. Nature Communications 6 (1), 8398.

Deutscher, G., 2005. The Unfolding of Language: An Evolutionary Tour of Mankind's Greatest Invention. Macmillan.

Edgerton, R.B., 1985. Rules, Exceptions, and Social Order. Univ. of California Press.

Elsenbroich, C., Gilbert, N., 2014. Modelling Norms. Springer.

Engelke, M., 2018. How to Think Like an Anthropologist. Princeton University Press.

Eriksen, T.H., Nielsen, F.S., 2013. A History of Anthropology. Pluto Press.

Fehr, E., Fischbacher, U., 2003. The nature of human altruism. Nature 425 (6960), 785–791.

Fernández, R., 2011. Does culture matter? Handbook of Social Economics 1, 481–510.

Galef Jr, B.G., 1982. Studies of social learning in Norway rats: a brief review. Developmental psychobiology. The Journal of the International Society for Developmental Psychobiology 15 (4), 279–295.

Geertz, C., 2008. Thick description: toward an interpretive theory of culture. In: Oakes, T.S., Price, P.L. (Eds.), The Cultural Geography Reader. Routledge, pp. 41–51.

Gelpi, R., Buchsbaum, D., 2023. Children as cultural explorers: how imitation, pedagogy, and selective trust prepare children for learning in the cultural niche. PsyArXiv.

Gladwell, M., 2006. The Tipping Point: How Little Things Can Make a Big Difference. Little, Brown.

Goody, J., 1975. Literacy in Traditional Societies. Cambridge University Press.

Gorton, G.B., Grennan, J., Zentefis, A.K., 2022. Corporate culture. Annual Review of Financial Economics 14 (1), 535–561.

Grosjean, P., 2014. A history of violence: the culture of honor and homicide in the US south. Journal of the European Economic Association 12 (5), 1285–1316.

Guiso, L., Sapienza, P., Zingales, L., 2006. Does culture affect economic outcomes? The Journal of Economic Perspectives 20 (2), 23–48.

Guiso, L., Sapienza, P., Zingales, L., 2008. Social capital as good culture. Journal of the European Economic Association 6 (2–3), 295–320.

Guiso, L., Sapienza, P., Zingales, L., 2016. Long-term persistence. Journal of the European Economic Association 14 (6), 1401–1436.

Guiso, L., Sapienza, P., Zingales, L., 2024. Embedded culture as a source of comparative advantage. Technical report. National Bureau of Economic Research.

Gweon, H., 2021. Inferential social learning: cognitive foundations of human social learning and teaching. Trends in Cognitive Sciences 25 (10), 896–910.

Haak, W., Lazaridis, I., Patterson, N., Rohland, N., Mallick, S., Llamas, B., Brandt, G., Nordenfelt, S., Harney, E., Stewardson, K., et al., 2015. Massive migration from the steppe was a source for Indo-European languages in Europe. Nature 522 (7555), 207–211.

Hamilton, W.D., 1964. The genetical evolution of social behaviour. Journal of Theoretical Biology 7 (1), 1–52.

Hamilton, W.D., 1975. Innate social aptitudes of man: an approach from evolutionary genetics. In: Narrow Roads of Gene Land. Vol. 1: Evolution of Social Behaviour. Oxford University Press, pp. 315–352.

Handley, C., Mathew, S., 2020. Human large-scale cooperation as a product of competition between cultural groups. Nature Communications 11 (1), 702.

Hardy, B.L., Moncel, M.-H., Daujeard, C., Fernandes, P., Béarez, P., Desclaux, E., Navarro, M.G.C., Puaud, S., Gallotti, R., 2013. Impossible Neanderthals? Making string, throwing projectiles and catching small game during marine isotope stage 4, (Abri du Maras, France). Quaternary Science Reviews 82, 23–40.

Harris, J.A., Boyd, R., Wood, B.M., 2021. The role of causal knowledge in the evolution of traditional technology. Current Biology 31 (8), 1798–1803.
Harris, J.R., 2009. The Nurture Assumption: Why Children Turn Out the Way They Do. Revised and updated. Simon and Schuster.
Harris, M., 2001. The Rise of Anthropological Theory: A History of Theories of Culture. AltaMira Press.
Heldstab, S.A., Isler, K., Graber, S.M., Schuppli, C., van Schaik, C.P., 2022. The economics of brain size evolution in vertebrates. Current Biology 32 (12), R697–R708.
Henrich, J., 2009. The evolution of costly displays, cooperation and religion: credibility enhancing displays and their implications for cultural evolution. Evolution and Human Behavior 30 (4), 244–260.
Henrich, J., 2016. The Secret of Our Success: How Culture Is Driving Human Evolution, Domesticating Our Species, and Making Us Smarter. Princeton University Press.
Henrich, J., Boyd, R., 1998. The evolution of conformist transmission and the emergence of between-group differences. Evolution and Human Behavior 19 (4), 215–241.
Henrich, J., Gil-White, F.J., 2001. The evolution of prestige: freely conferred deference as a mechanism for enhancing the benefits of cultural transmission. Evolution and Human Behavior 22 (3), 165–196.
Hewlett, B.S., Boyette, A.H., Lew-Levy, S., Gallois, S., Dira, S.J., 2024. Cultural transmission among hunter-gatherers. Proceedings of the National Academy of Sciences 121 (48), e2322883121.
Hoehl, S., Keupp, S., Schleihauf, H., McGuigan, N., Buttelmann, D., Whiten, A., 2019. 'Over-imitation': a review and appraisal of a decade of research. Developmental Review 51, 90–108.
Hoppitt, W., Laland, K.N., 2008. Social processes influencing learning in animals: a review of the evidence. Advances in the Study of Behavior 38, 105–165.
House, B.R., Silk, J.B., Henrich, J., Barrett, H.C., Scelza, B.A., Boyette, A.H., Hewlett, B.S., McElreath, R., Laurence, S., 2013. Ontogeny of prosocial behavior across diverse societies. Proceedings of the National Academy of Sciences 110 (36), 14586–14591.
Jennings, M.K., Stoker, L., Bowers, J., 2009. Politics across generations: family transmission reexamined. The Journal of Politics 71 (3), 782–799.
Jiménez, Á.V., Mesoudi, A., 2019. Prestige-biased social learning: current evidence and outstanding questions. Palgrave Communications 5 (1).
Johnson, A.W., Earle, T.K., 2000. The Evolution of Human Societies: From Foraging Group to Agrarian State. Stanford University Press.
Jordan, F.M., Gray, R.D., Greenhill, S.J., Mace, R., 2009. Matrilocal residence is ancestral in Austronesian societies. Proceedings of the Royal Society B: Biological Sciences 276 (1664), 1957–1964.
Jordan, J.J., Sommers, R., Bloom, P., Rand, D.G., 2017. Why do we hate hypocrites? Evidence for a theory of false signaling. Psychological Science 28 (3), 356–368.
Jordan, P., 2014. Technology as Human Social Tradition: Cultural Transmission Among Hunter-Gatherers, vol. 7. Univ. of California Press.
Keesing, R.M., 1974. Theories of culture. Annual Review of Anthropology 3 (1), 73–97.
Kendal, R.L., Boogert, N.J., Rendell, L., Laland, K.N., Webster, M., Jones, P.L., 2018. Social learning strategies: bridge-building between fields. Trends in Cognitive Sciences 22 (7), 651–665.
Kimbel, W.H., Villmoare, B., 2016. From Australopithecus to Homo: the transition that wasn't. Philosophical Transactions of the Royal Society B: Biological Sciences 371 (1698), 20150248.
Kline, M.A., Boyd, R., Henrich, J., 2013. Teaching and the life history of cultural transmission in Fijian villages. Human Nature 24, 351–374.
Kraft-Todd, G.T., Bollinger, B., Gillingham, K., Lamp, S., Rand, D.G., 2018. Credibility-enhancing displays promote the provision of non-normative public goods. Nature 563 (7730), 245–248.
Kroeber, A.L., 1917. The superorganic. American Anthropologist 19 (2), 163–213.

Kroeber, A.L., Kluckhohn, C., 1952. Culture: A critical review of concepts and definitions. Papers of the Peabody Museum of American Archaeology and Ethnology, Harvard University.

Laland, K.N., 2004. Social learning strategies. Learning & Behavior 32 (1), 4–14.

Lévi-Strauss, C., 1971. The Elementary Structures of Kinship. Beacon Press.

Lew-Levy, S., Lavi, N., Reckin, R., Cristóbal-Azkarate, J., Ellis-Davies, K., 2018. How do hunter-gatherer children learn social and gender norms? A meta-ethnographic review. Cross-Cultural Research 52 (2), 213–255.

Lew-Levy, S., Reckin, R., Lavi, N., Cristóbal-Azkarate, J., Ellis-Davies, K., 2017. How do hunter-gatherer children learn subsistence skills? A meta-ethnographic review. Human Nature 28, 367–394.

Lew-Levy, S., Ringen, E.J., Crittenden, A.N., Mabulla, I.A., Broesch, T., Kline, M.A., 2021. The life history of learning subsistence skills among Hadza and BaYaka foragers from Tanzania and the republic of Congo. Human Nature 32, 16–47.

Lew-Levy, S., van den Bos, W., Corriveau, K., Dutra, N., Flynn, E., O'Sullivan, E., Pope-Caldwell, S., Rawlings, B., Smolla, M., Xu, J., et al., 2023. Peer learning and cultural evolution. Child Development Perspectives 17 (2), 97–105.

Lowie, R.H., 1917. Culture & Ethnology. DC McMurtrie.

Lumsden, C.J., Wilson, E.O., 1981. Genes, Mind, and Culture: The Coevolutionary Process. Harvard University Press, Cambridge, MA.

Mackie, G., Moneti, F., Shakya, H., Denny, E., 2015. What Are Social Norms? How Are They Measured. UNICEF Working Paper. University of California at San Diego, San Diego.

Martindale, C., 1990. The Clockwork Muse: The Predictability of Artistic Change. Basic Books.

Mesoudi, A., 2016. Cultural evolution: a review of theory, findings and controversies. Evolutionary Biology 43, 481–497.

Miton, H., 2024. Cultural attraction. In: Tehrani, J.J., Kendal, J., Kendal, R. (Eds.), Oxford Handbook of Cultural Evolution. Oxford, pp. 1–24.

Miton, H., Claidière, N., Mercier, H., 2015. Universal cognitive mechanisms explain the cultural success of bloodletting. Evolution and Human Behavior 36 (4), 303–312.

Miton, H., DeDeo, S., 2022. The cultural transmission of tacit knowledge. Journal of the Royal Society Interface 19 (195), 20220238.

Mollica, F., Piantadosi, S.T., 2019. Humans store about 1.5 megabytes of information during language acquisition. Royal Society Open Science 6 (3), 181393.

Morgan, T.J., Rendell, L.E., Ehn, M., Hoppitt, W., Laland, K.N., 2012. The evolutionary basis of human social learning. Proceedings of the Royal Society B: Biological Sciences 279 (1729), 653–662.

Morin, O., 2016. How Traditions Live and Die. Oxford University Press.

Netzer, N., 2009. Evolution of time preferences and attitudes toward risk. American Economic Review 99 (3), 937–955.

Nunn, N., 2014. Historical development. Handbook of Economic Growth 2, 347–402.

Odling-Smee, F.J., Laland, K.N., Feldman, M.W., 2003. Niche Construction: The Neglected Process in Evolution. Monographs in Population Biology, vol. 37. Princeton University Press, Princeton.

Olsson, A., Knapska, E., Lindström, B., 2020. The neural and computational systems of social learning. Nature Reviews. Neuroscience 21 (4), 197–212.

Paige, J., Perreault, C., 2024. 3.3 million years of stone tool complexity suggests that cumulative culture began during the middle Pleistocene. Proceedings of the National Academy of Sciences 121 (26), e2319175121.

Perreault, C., Boyd, R., 2022. Evolution of social learning with payoff and content bias. Games 13 (1), 7.

Perreault, C., Moya, C., Boyd, R., 2012. A Bayesian approach to the evolution of social learning. Evolution and Human Behavior 33 (5), 449–459.

Polanía, R., Burdakov, D., Hare, T.A., 2024. Rationality, preferences, and emotions with biological constraints: it all starts from our senses. Trends in Cognitive Sciences 28 (3), 264–277.

Rappaport, R.A., 1970. Pigs for the Ancestors: Ritual in the Ecology of a New Guinea People. Yale University Press.
Richerson, P., Baldini, R., Bell, A.V., Demps, K., Frost, K., Hillis, V., Mathew, S., Newton, E.K., Naar, N., Newson, L., et al., 2016. Cultural group selection plays an essential role in explaining human cooperation: a sketch of the evidence. Behavioral and Brain Sciences 39, e30.
Richerson, P.J., Boyd, R., 1978. A dual inheritance model of the human evolutionary process I: basic postulates and a simple model. Journal of Social and Biological Structures 1 (2), 127–154.
Richerson, P.J., Boyd, R., 2022. What sort of mind/brain is compatible with cultural adaptation? Journal of Cognition and Culture 22 (5), 390–405.
Risjord, M., 2012. Models of culture. In: The Oxford Handbook of Philosophy of Social Science. Oxford University Press, Oxford, pp. 387–408.
Robson, A.J., 2001. The biological basis of economic behavior. Journal of Economic Literature 39 (1), 11–33.
Robson, A.J., 2002. Evolution and human nature. The Journal of Economic Perspectives 16 (2), 89–106.
Rodseth, L., 1998. Distributive models of culture: a sapirian alternative to essentialism. American Anthropologist 100 (1), 55–69.
Rogers, A.R., 1988. Does biology constrain culture? American Anthropologist 90 (4), 819–831.
Roughley, N., Bayertz, K., 2019. The Normative Animal? On the Anthropological Significance of Social, Moral, and Linguistic Norms. Oxford University Press.
Sahlins, M., Service, E., 1960. Evolution and Culture. University of Michigan Press, Ann Arbor.
Schmidt, P., 2016. The 'sand-bath' and lithic heat treatment in the South African Middle Stone Age: Myth or reality? African Archaeological Review 33 (2), 99–105.
Schmidt, P., Koch, T.J., Blessing, M.A., Karakostis, F.A., Harvati, K., Dresely, V., Charrié-Duhaut, A., 2023. Production method of the Königsaue birch tar documents cumulative culture in Neanderthals. Archaeological and Anthropological Sciences 15 (6), 84.
Seabright, P., 2010. The Company of Strangers: A Natural History of Economic Life. Princeton University Press.
Seabright, P., 2017. Adaptable, cooperative, manipulative, and rivalrous. In: A Different Kind of Animal: How Culture Transformed Our Species. Princeton University Press.
Shore, B., 1998. Culture in Mind: Cognition, Culture, and the Problem of Meaning. Oxford University Press.
Sperber, D., 1985. Anthropology and psychology: towards an epidemiology of representations. Man, 73–89.
Sperber, D., 1996. Explaining Culture: A Naturalistic Approach. Oxford Blackwell.
Steward, J., 2004. Cultural ecology and multilinear evolution. Visions of Culture: An Introduction to Anthropological Theories and Theorists, 193.
Steward, J.H., 1972. Theory of Culture Change: The Methodology of Multilinear Evolution. University of Illinois Press.
Sturtevant, W., 1978–2022. Handbook of North American Indians, vol. 1–15. Smithsonian Institution Press.
Tabellini, G., 2008. The scope of cooperation: values and incentives. The Quarterly Journal of Economics 123 (3), 905–950.
Thomason, S., 2001. Language Contact, an Introduction. Georgetown University Press.
Thompson, B., Van Opheusden, B., Sumers, T., Griffiths, T., 2022. Complex cognitive algorithms preserved by selective social learning in experimental populations. Science 376 (6588), 95–98.
Tomasello, M., 1996. Do apes ape? In: Heyes, C.M., Galef, B.G. (Eds.), Social Learning in Animals: The Roots of Culture. Academic Press, pp. 319–346.
Tooby, J., Cosmides, L., 1992. The psychological foundations of culture. The Adapted Mind: Evolutionary Psychology and the Generation of Culture 19 (1), 1–136.
Vaesen, K., 2012. The cognitive bases of human tool use. Behavioral and Brain Sciences 35 (4), 203–218.

Vélez, N., Gweon, H., 2021. Learning from other minds: an optimistic critique of reinforcement learning models of social learning. Current Opinion in Behavioral Sciences 38, 110–115.
Velilla, A.P., Beheim, B., Smaldino, P.E., 2025. The development of risk attitudes and their cultural transmission. SocArXiv Papers.
Wakano, J.Y., Aoki, K., Feldman, M.W., 2004. Evolution of social learning: a mathematical analysis. Theoretical Population Biology 66 (3), 249–258.
Wertz, A.E., 2019. How plants shape the mind. Trends in Cognitive Sciences 23 (7), 528–531.
White, L.A., 1943. Energy and the evolution of culture. American Anthropologist 45 (3), 335–356.
Whitehead, H., Laland, K.N., Rendell, L., Thorogood, R., Whiten, A., 2019. The reach of gene–culture coevolution in animals. Nature Communications 10 (1), 2405.
Whiten, A., Ayala, F.J., Feldman, M.W., Laland, K.N., 2017. The extension of biology through culture. Proceedings of the National Academy of Sciences 114 (30), 7775–7781.
Wilson, E.O., 1978. On Human Nature. Harvard University Press, Cambridge, MA.
Winterhalder, B., Smith, E.A., 2017. Evolutionary ecology and the social sciences. In: Evolutionary Ecology and Human Behavior. Routledge, pp. 3–24.
Wootton, D., 2015. The Invention of Science: A New History of the Scientific Revolution. Penguin, UK.

Chapter 6

Do liberal-democratic institutions sustain the values they require? Endogenous social preferences and why they matter☆

Samuel Bowles[a,b] and Katrin Schmelz[a,c]
[a]*Santa Fe Institute, Santa Fe, NM, United States,* [b]*CORE Econ, University College London, London, United Kingdom,* [c]*Technical University of Denmark, Kongens Lyngby, Denmark*

1 Introduction

Do liberal-democratic institutions cultivate "the spirit of liberty", as John Stuart Mill suggested (1998 [1859], p. 78)? Or instead, might liberal democracy fail the test proposed by John Rawls half a century ago, namely, that in order to be viable in the long run, a social order must "generate its own supportive moral attitudes" (Rawls, 1971, p. 399)?

Cases that appear to have fallen short of Rawls' requirement are not hard to come by: the collapse of the Weimar Republic's fledgling liberal democracy with the election of Adolf Hitler, and more recently the electoral successes of Recep Erdoğan, Narendra Modi, Donald Trump and other authoritarian leaders. But we can also today look back on well over a century of liberal democracy, for example in the Nordic countries and New Zealand, where liberal-democratic institutions seem to have reproduced the values upon which their sustainability depends. Yet, we do not have a good understanding of the conditions under which the coevolution of liberal democracies and the corresponding societal preferences and values succeeds or fails.

We read Rawls' dictum to mean that a well-governed society requires preferences that support the particular forms of cooperation and pro-social behaviors essential to the functioning of its basic institutions. It is based on three

☆ We thank Sascha Becker, Laura Araújo De Freitas, Benjamin Enke, Hetty Marx, Nathan Nunn, Elizabeth Paluck and Sherry Wu for helpful comments. Raphael Strerath provided research assistance. We are grateful for financial support from the Emergent Political Economies (EPE) Program at the Santa Fe Institute, and to Caroline Seigel of the SFI library.

Handbook of Culture and Economic Behavior, Volume 1, ISSN 3051-1682
https://doi.org/10.1016/bs.hceb.2026.06.002

propositions regarding the relationship between institutions and preferences, that we take up in the pages that follow. First, social preferences like reciprocity, generosity, or fairness, as well as social norms, are endogenous, meaning that their evolution is shaped by institutions. Second, these other-regarding elements of a society's culture matter: liberal governance – or indeed any set of societal governing institutions – could not be sustained on the basis of entirely amoral and self-regarding preferences. Third, the preferences that are essential to the workability of a social system differ depending on the nature of its institutions (e.g., other-regarding and ethical preferences may be less essential to the functioning of markets than to the functioning of a liberal democracy). A consequence is that a viable society's institutions and its population's distribution of preferences must serve as complements, each contributing to the conditions required for the successful functioning and perpetuation of the other.

A possible failure of this institution-preference complementarity is what prompted Joseph Schumpeter to think that "the capitalist order tends to destroy itself" (1950, p. 448). Like Schumpeter, responding to the rise of Fascism and Communism, Gabriel Almond and Sidney Verba outlined what the complementarity of liberal democratic institutions and preferences required. They wrote that "a democratic form of participatory political system requires ... a political culture consistent with it," reasoning that "particular psychological tendencies ... are important for the functioning of political systems." Almond and Verba stressed the importance of "civic virtue and its consequences for the effectiveness and stability of the democratic polity; and ... the kind of community life, social organization, and upbringing of children that fosters civic virtue" (1963, pp. 12, 33, 3, 5, vii).

A troubling response to Rawls and to Almond and Verba was suggested by Daniel Bell in his *The Cultural Contradictions of Capitalism* (Bell, 1976). Bell's central hypothesis was that the functioning of a system of markets, elections, the rule of law, and other liberal institutions depends on values and social norms that are endogenous and are endangered by these very institutions. In similar vein, the philosopher Peter Berkowitz wrote that "liberalism depends on virtues that it does not readily summon and which it may even stunt or stifle" (Berkowitz, 1999, p. xiii).[1]

It follows from this set of ideas that to sustain a liberal-democratic society, institutions may best be designed not only to embody liberty, democracy and associated structural ideals, but also to cultivate and sustain the set of other-regarding preferences that provide the cultural complement for liberal-democratic institutions. This idea is not new. Political philosophers from Aristotle to Thomas Aquinas, Jean-Jacques Rousseau, Edmund Burke and John Stuart Mill recognized some form of civic virtue as an essential foundation of good government.

[1] See also: Alexis de Tocqueville (1945 [1830]), Joseph Schumpeter (1950), Jürgen Habermas (1975) and Edmund Burke (1890 [1790]). For a review, see Bowles (2011).

"Legislators make the citizens good by inculcating habits in them," Aristotle wrote in the *Ethics*. "It is in this that a good constitution differs from a bad one" (1962 [335–322 BCE], p. 103). A century and a half earlier, Confucius had provided advice about how Aristotle's legislators do this, and about the pitfalls to be avoided: "Guide them with government orders, regulate them with penalties, and the people will seek to evade the law and be without shame. Guide them with virtue, regulate them with ritual, and they will have a sense of shame and become upright" (2007 [475–221 BCE], p. 20).

But through a 21st century lens, reference to virtue and shame as the basis of a well-ordered society appears quaint, and to some misguided. Economics has for the most part followed not Aristotle, but instead David Hume, who in his *Essays: Moral, Political, and Literary* (1742) wrote: "Political writers have established it as a maxim, that in contriving any system of government . . . every man ought to be supposed to be a knave and to have no other end, in all his actions, than his private interest. By this interest we must govern him, and, by means of it, make him, notwithstanding his insatiable avarice and ambition, cooperate to public good" (1898 [1742], pp. 117–18).

This approach – knave-proof institutional and policy design – came to define how economists think when it comes to public policy or institutional design (e.g. in fields such as welfare economics, optimal taxation and contracts, mechanism design, or optimal deterrence). It might be thought that Kenneth Arrow and Gerard Debreu's "invisible hand theorem" had vindicated this approach, as it had provided conditions under which an entirely self-interested population could implement an efficient allocation of resources through a process of competition. (Debreu thought as much, telling the French daily *Le Figaro* that "The superiority of the liberal economy . . . has been demonstrated mathematically," 1984, p. 80 referring to his theorem with Arrow.)

In the pages that follow we explain why we believe that the constitution-for-knaves approach is mistaken. Our view is based in part on developments within microeconomic theory itself. It has long been understood (including by Arrow himself, 1971) that the main axiom under which Arrow and Debreu's efficiency result would obtain – the absence of uncompensated external effects, or complete contracts for short – does not apply to any real economy. Modern mechanism design has demonstrated that in a world of entirely amoral and self-interested actors, even cleverly designed public policies (mechanisms) are limited in the extent to which they can mitigate the resulting market failures.

In practice, too, fines, rewards, and other material inducements along with legal constraints often do not work very well in the absence of a supportive culture: no matter how well designed to harness the avarice of knaves (as Hume put it), incentives and constraints cannot alone provide the foundations of good governance. Moreover, a constitution designed for knaves not only would fail in a hypothetical population of entirely amoral and self-regarding citizens. In an empirically plausible population of both knaves and civic-minded citizens, it could make the citizens more knave-like by crowding out their social preferences that are essential to effective governance.

The above reasoning suggests a different representation of the relationship between institutions and culture, one that supports a framework for policy and institutional design less in line with Hume than with Aristotle and Confucius. In this alternative conception, the endogenous nature of other-regarding and ethical preferences plays a central role. The reason is that the functioning and sustainability of institutions depends on other-regarding and ethical preferences that may themselves either be sustained, making the institution-culture configuration dynamically stable, or be undermined, possibly leading to an institutional turnover.

We turn first (in Section 2) to the origin of *Homo economicus* – characterized by an exogenous set of amoral and self-regarding preferences – as the behavioral axiom for economic reasoning and institutional design. We demonstrate its inadequacy, particularly in light of the unavoidable shortcomings of contracts and laws as forms of governance in the absence of other-regarding social preferences including altruism, reciprocity and fairness.

Given that these social preferences are essential to good governance, we need to understand the evolution of preferences, which we take up in the next three sections. In Section 3, we review empirical evidence that institutions affect preferences. Section 4 introduces biological and cultural models of the evolution of other-regarding preferences, along with examples of their application. The parameters defining the stationary and stable distribution of preferences in these models provide insights on how alternative institutions might support the evolution of distinct cultures.

Having illustrated the ways in which institutions affect the distribution of preferences, in Section 5 we turn to the effect of culture on the evolution of institutions, modeling the co-evolution of institutions and culture. We illustrate a culture-institutions co-evolutionary process by two applications. The first is the emergence of the nation state as the dominant political form in Europe over the last half-millennium, along with complementary cultural changes. The second is the coevolutionary dynamics of the extent of hierarchy entailed by the labor contract offered by employers (institutions) and workers' value of autonomy (preferences).

In Section 6 we begin with a case of policy design – ancient mechanism design in Athens at the time of Aristotle – illustrating the value of exploring a possible alternative to the conventional exogenous-preferences approach. We then ask what we have learned and point to some gaps and important lines for new research, and we identify two required revisions of economic theory suggested by these models and evidence. First, we propose what we term an *Augmented Nash Equilibrium*, which extends the conventional concept so as to account not only for endogenous beliefs (as in a Bayesian Nash Equilibrium), but also the endogenous nature of preferences. Second, we point to the normative challenges posed by the endogenous nature of preferences and the fact that the perpetuation of liberal and democratic institutions may require public policies or institutional design favoring the evolution of some preferences over others.

Before developing this set of ideas, we will clarify our use of terms, beginning with the elements of the preferences, beliefs and constraints approach that constitutes the workhorse model in economics and decision theory for understanding human behavior.

By *preferences* we mean an individual's pro or con assessment of the states that their own actions may bring about including tastes (as is conventional in economics) but also ethical commitments, habits, and psychological dispositions. Beliefs are an individual's understanding of how the actions they take map onto the resulting states that their actions may bring about (and are not the focus of this chapter). In the preferences, beliefs and constraints approach, these three terms are sufficient to explain people's actions. We term *social preferences* such as altruism or spite as *other-regarding* if they take account of the effects of one's actions on the states experienced by others.

We define *institutions* broadly here as the population-level laws, informal rules, and conventions that give a durable structure to social interactions. *Liberal-democratic institutions* are the rules of the game initially laid down in such founding documents of political liberalism as the American *Bill of Rights* (1791) or the French *Declaration of the Rights of Man and the Citizen* (1789), today including not only formal equality of political rights and the rule of law, but also virtually universal suffrage in fair elections that select political leadership, bodily autonomy, and the absence of substantial barriers to occupational and geographical mobility based on race, gender, religion, or other accidents of birth.

Finally, by *liberal-democratic values* we mean preferences that contribute to the appropriate workings of liberal-democratic institutions and their sustainability over time. Note that some liberal-democratic values are closely aligned with specifically liberal-democratic institutions, for example the value one places on individual autonomy, agency and interpersonal tolerance. Other elements – willingness to comply with legitimate authority, for example – are essential to the functioning of virtually any system of governance at the societal level, as Schumpeter recognized when he wrote that "no social system can work ... in which everyone is ... guided by nothing except his own ... utilitarian ends" (1950, p. 448).

2 A constitution for knaves: origins and second thoughts

Our analysis of the relationship among these terms – preferences, liberal-democratic values, and liberal-democratic institutions – begins with two traditions in economics and philosophy that hold contrasting views on the nature of preferences. The first, stemming from Aristotle and epitomized in classical economics by Adam Smith, Jeremy Bentham and John Stuart Mill, recognizes that social preferences are essential for a well-governed society. Moreover, because preferences are endogenous, our evaluations of alternative institutions should include an assessment of the preferences they are likely to cultivate.

The second tradition embraces the assumptions that preferences are not only self-regarding, but exogenously given – not as an empirical description of real people but as a thought experiment. An early exponent was Thomas Hobbes, who invited his readers to "consider men as if ... sprung out of the earth, and suddenly, like mushrooms, come to full maturity without any kind of engagement to each other" (Hobbes, 1949 [1642], p. 100). George Stigler and Gary Becker expressed a similar view in their essay *De Gustibus Non Est Disputandum*: "One does not argue about tastes for the same reason that one does not argue about the Rocky Mountains – both are there, and will be there next year, too, and are the same to all men." They added, in case the reader had missed the point, that: "The establishment of the proposition that one may usefully treat tastes as stable over time and similar among people is the central task of this essay" (Stigler and Becker, 1977, p. 76).

In this section, we explain how in the late 19th century the second tradition – from Hobbes to Becker and Stigler – displaced the first to become dominant among economists, and how their thought experiment came to be taken by many economists as more than that, namely as a fact about human behavior that should guide the design of institutions and public policy. We then explain how developments since the late 20th century – in behavioral economics, mechanism design, and the economics of asymmetric information and incomplete contracts – provide both reasons to favor the Aristotelian tradition, and the means to update it in light of modern economics, a task that we take up in later sections.

2.1 Origins: Hume's constitution for knaves

The long road from Aristotle's legislators inculcating good habits in citizens to Hume's constitution that would harness the avarice of knaves to promote the public good took a decisive turn in the sixteenth century with Niccolò Machiavelli. In a passage anticipating Hume's dictum on knaves (and even his wording), Machiavelli wrote: "Anyone who would found a republic and order its laws must assume that all men are wicked [and] ... never act well except through necessity ... it is said that hunger and poverty make them industrious, laws make them good" (1984, pp. 69–70). Machiavelli's "laws make them good" might sound a bit like Aristotle's legislators "inculcating good habits" in the public. But here, Machiavelli uses "good" (*buoni*) to describe actions induced by constraints, not internalized values.

However, like Aristotle but unlike many modern economists, Machiavelli did not imagine that good governance was possible in a self-interested ("corrupt") citizenry: "neither laws nor orders can be found that are enough to check a universal corruption. For as good customs have need of laws to maintain themselves, so have laws need of good customs so as to be observed" (Machiavelli, 1984, p. 109). Here Machiavelli is recognizing the complementarity of preferences and institutions.

Two centuries later and a generation before Hume advocated his constitution for knaves, Bernard Mandeville offered a precursor of Hume's dictum in his *The Fable of the Bees*. The book scandalized readers, who, like Aristotle, believed that good citizens were the *sine qua non* of good governance. The *Fable* announced in its subtitle that the work contained "several discourses to demonstrate that human frailties ... may be turn'd to the advantage of civil society, and made to supply the place of moral virtues," with the result, he wrote, that "the worst of all the multitude did something for the common good."

Just as Machiavelli saw the foundation of good government not in human nature but in the human capacity to design institutions, for Mandeville it was "the dextrous Management of a skillful Politician" that allowed the "Private Vices" to be "turned into Publick Benefits" (Mandeville, 1988, p. 369). The *Fable* is thus a precursor to modern mechanism design, a body of thought that devises institutional settings (mechanisms) that will implement socially valued outcomes as Nash equilibria among citizens with "unrestricted preferences".

This latter expression means that "private vices" such as Hume's "avarice" are included as possible motivations among the citizenry of a well-governed society. In other words, an acceptable mechanism has to work for knaves. In contrast to the Aristotelian view that good laws make good citizens, Mandeville's *Fable* suggested that the right institutions might harness shabby motives to elevated ends. It was left to Adam Smith's invisible hand to provide a mechanism – competitive markets and well-defined property rights – that might accomplish this improbable alchemy in the private economy.

The same logic – harnessing avarice for the public good – was applied to the structure of government. Jeremy Bentham, whose *Introduction to the Principles of Morals and Legislation* (1970 [1789]) is considered to be the first text in public economics, offered guidance on how Hume's dictum could guide the design of public policy. For the design of compensation systems for public officials, for example, he offered his "Duty and Interest junction principle: Make it each man's interest to observe ... that conduct which it is his duty to observe" (Bentham and Bowring, 1962, p. 380).

In short, let prices do the work of morals.

While harnessing self-interest was their leitmotif, none of these writers believed that citizens are actually knaves, least of all Hume himself, who pioneered the study of the evolution of social norms. In the sentence immediately following the passage laying down his dictum about knaves, Hume mused that it is "strange that a maxim should be true in politics which is false in fact." And Hobbes, after inviting his reader to consider how people would behave in his hypothetical state of nature, cautioned: "I believe it was never generally so" (2005 [1651], p. 101). The knave-proof constitution was advocated on grounds of prudence, not realism about human motivations.

In practice, the policies advocated by the classical economists did not overlook appeals to ethical and other-regarding motives. For example, Bentham, who as we saw above, pioneered the idea of aligning self-interested incentives with a social planner's societal objectives, also advocated well-designed public policy as a way of inculcating what Aristotle called "good habits":

> *"A punishment may be said to be ... a moral lesson, when by reason of the ignominy it stamps upon the offence, it is calculated to inspire the public with sentiments of aversion towards those pernicious habits and dispositions with which the offence appears to be connected; and thereby to inculcate the opposite beneficial habits and dispositions." (Bentham, 1970 [1789], p. 26)*

Among the classical economists, Bentham was not exceptional in treating preferences as endogenous. John Stuart Mill, embracing the *doux commerce* logic of Voltaire and Montesquieu, in his *Principles of Political Economy* (1848) held that:

> *"[The] economic advantages of commerce are surpassed in importance by those of its effects which are intellectual and moral. It is hardly possible to overrate the value ... of placing human beings in contact with persons dissimilar to themselves and with modes of thought and action unlike those with which they are familiar." (Mill, 1965 [1848], p. 594)*

The classical economists were thus quite aware that what later came to be called *Homo economicus* was a simplification, one that differed from what they knew about human behavior, but one that would clarify, among other things, how policies that altered economic incentives would affect behavior. Here is John Stuart Mill in 1844, among the last of the classical economists, laying down boundaries and key assumptions of economics that would remain with us until very recently:

> *[Political economy] "does not treat of the whole of man's nature ... it is concerned with him solely as a being who desires to possess wealth, ... it predicts only such ... phenomena ... as take place in consequence of the pursuit of wealth. It makes entire abstraction of every other human passion or motive." (Mill, 1994 [1844], p. 52)*

He pointedly observed that this is "an arbitrary view of man" (Mill, 1994 [1844], p. 56).

What economists since the turn of the 20th century have set aside is the possibility that moral and other pro-social behavior would be affected – perhaps adversely – by incentives and constraints based policies designed to harness self-interest. Since the advent of the neoclassical school, most economists have routinely made the assumption that other-regarding motives are absent. If they recognized motives other than self-interest, they took for granted that the two sets of motives – the moral sentiments and material interests (in the language of the classical economists) – are additively separable (using contemporary mathematical terminology).

Separability here means that the effects of variations in the one do not depend on the level of the other, so that, for example, greater use of monetary incentives appealing to the material interests to promote a societal objective such as the provision of public goods will not diminish the force of other-regarding ethical motives (the moral sentiments) towards the same end. The implicit assumption of separability has led economists, even while recognizing people's other-regarding and ethical preferences, to ignore the conditions under which ethical and other-regarding concerns would flourish and favorably affect societal outcomes, including the sustainability of its institutional structure.

2.2 Doubts: why not a constitution for knaves?

Three developments in economics since 1970 suggest shortcomings of the knave-proof constitution as an ideal: evidence from behavioral economics suggesting that *Homo economicus* is in the minority in most populations (Section 2.2.1), results from mechanism design and the microeconomics of exchanges with incomplete contracts suggesting that social preferences are an indispensable component of good governance (Section 2.2.2), and evidence from social psychology, anthropology as well as economics that these and other preferences are endogenously affected by institutions, raising the possibility that a constitution for knaves may tend to produce knaves (Section 3).

2.2.1 Social preferences are common

Experimental evidence suggests that many people prefer to treat others fairly, punish unfair actions, reciprocate kind behaviors, and cooperate with like-minded people. A key experiment in these findings is the Ultimatum Game (first implemented by Güth et al. 1982) in which a first mover can offer any share of an asset to the second mover (including all or none of it), who may accept (receiving the offer) or reject, in which case both players receive nothing. The players' identities are not known to each other, and the stakes are substantial in some experiments.

When played in 15 small-scale societies in Africa, Asia and Latin America, as well as among student populations around the world, second movers routinely rejected what they regarded as unfair offers resulting in zero payoffs. Thus, participants effectively paid substantial sums (foregoing the "unfair" offer they could have accepted) to punish the first mover's unfairness and to avoid participating in an unjust interaction (Henrich et al., 2001). More recent studies (for the most part with students in higher income countries) provide evidence of similar fairness norms (as reviewed in Fehr and Charness, 2024).

Miettinen et al. (2020) found that the standard *Homo economicus* model of behavior explained just 28 percent of their experimental observations, much less than models based on unconditional altruism (44 percent) or inequality aversion (60 percent). Using data from a wide range of experiments, Ernst Fehr and Simon Gächter (2000b) estimated that those exhibiting reciprocal choices were twice as common as those exhibiting conventional self-regarding outcome-oriented preferences. Loewenstein et al. (1989) found in their experiments that just 29 percent of subjects were "ruthless competitors [who] consistently prefer to come out ahead of the other party regardless of the type of relationship" [p. 433]. Similarly, in a one-shot Public Goods Game, Urs Fischbacher, Simon Gächter and Ernst Fehr (2001) classified a third of their subjects as free riders, whereas 50% were conditional cooperators who, when paired with another cooperator, forgo payoff gains that would be available by defecting (with the remaining share being other types).

Social preferences can also take the form of people's willingness to criticize, chastise and otherwise discourage anti-social behavior even at a cost to oneself, which is an essential complement to the activities of the state in upholding the rule of law. This has been observed in many populations playing experimental Public Goods Games in which players have the option to punish their peers, i.e., reduce the payoffs of other players after seeing how much each member has contributed to the public good. Peer punishment of free riders sustains very high levels of cooperation in a game for which the dominant strategy for an entirely self-regarding player is to neither contribute nor engage in costly punishment (Fehr and Gächter, 2000a; Herrmann et al., 2008; Gächter et al., 2010).

People are not only willing to incur costs to punish free-riders who have adversely affected their own payoffs, but also in cases where the punisher's own payoffs are not reduced by the free riding (Fehr and Fischbacher, 2003, 2004). This is consistent with the hypothesis that peer punishment is motivated by moral reasoning rather than personal anger or retribution motives.

Taking account of these preferences does not require overturning the conventional preferences, constraints and beliefs approach to understanding human behavior. Strong experimental evidence indicates that when individuals give to others (e.g., in a Dictator Game), they respond to the price of giving much as they respond to any other price, for example, giving more when it costs them less to benefit another person, such that their behavior conforms to the transitivity assumptions and other requirements of rational choice (Andreoni and Miller, 2002).

2.2.2 *The liberal trilemma: the impossibility of a liberal constitution for knaves*

This evidence that generous and fair-minded preferences are common comes as good news, as few would question Schumpeter's affirmation that other-regarding and ethical preferences are essential to any process of governance. Bentham advised aligning the "interests" of public servants to match their "duties". But no one, including Bentham, thought this to be sufficient to secure good government. Economists since Marshall and Pigou have recognized that market failures are unavoidable, even ubiquitous, and have had no reason to object to Kenneth

Arrow's observation that "ethical and moral codes ... are reactions of society to compensate for market failures" (1971, p. 22).

The modern microeconomics of incomplete contracts in labor, credit, and other markets has underscored the ubiquity of market failures, for which Arrow pointed out the mitigating effects of social norms – for example, a work ethic in the labor market, or truth telling by borrowers about their intended use of a loan. But could not well-designed policies address market failures irrespective of citizens' preferences? The idea would be that government policy could give "the invisible hand a helping hand" as *The Economist* (2007) put it, explaining the mission of mechanism design when three of its leading scholars were awarded the Nobel Prize in 2007.

The holy grail of this field has been to design a set of incentives and constraints (i.e., a mechanism) to address the problem of market failure that both works and is liberal, summarized by three minimal requirements. First, there can be no restrictions on the kinds of preferences people may have. Thus, the mechanism must work even if individuals are entirely self-interested and amoral.

The first requirement has come to be termed liberal neutrality in philosophy, expressed by Ronald Dworkin's dictum that "political decisions must be ... independent of any particular conception of the good life, or of what gives value to life" (Dworkin, 1985, p. 191). Peter Jones likewise writes: "It is not the function of the state to impose the pursuit of any particular set of ends upon its citizens" (Jones, 1989, p. 9).

Second, whatever the citizens' preferences are, the mechanism must rely on individuals' voluntary participation in their economic activities. They must be free to choose their own courses of action, guided by their own preferences, including opting out of any possible exchange or other interaction. In economic language, the outcome must satisfy the individual's participation constraint, i.e., each must regard participating in the mechanism as better than not doing so. The outcome must also be incentive compatible, meaning that whatever the individual does while participating must be motivated by the individual's own preferences.

The second requirement rules out mandatory participation in an exchange. Along with the first requirement, voluntary participation expresses the standard liberal commitments to individual liberty and the state's neutrality on matters concerning individuals' conceptions of the good.

And third, the mechanism must eliminate the market failure, meaning that the Nash equilibria of interactions governed by the mechanism must be Pareto-efficient. Call these three conditions preference neutrality, voluntary participation, and efficiency.

The Nobel Prize Committee of the Royal Swedish Academy of Sciences that honored Eric Maskin, Leonid Hurwicz and Roger Myerson for their contributions to mechanism design explained what they had discovered as follows. A paper by Hurwicz, the committee pointed out, had proved a "negative result" concerning voluntary participation: in the presence of private information, "no incentive-compatible mechanism which satisfies the participation constraint can produce Pareto-optimal outcomes." Referring to Maskin's joint work with Jean-Jacques Laffont, and Myerson's joint work with Mark Satterthwaite, the committee members wrote: "In a large class of models Pareto efficiency is incompatible with voluntary participation, even if there are no public goods" (Royal Swedish Academy of Sciences, 2007, p. 9). Mechanism design, it appeared, had failed in its quest for mechanisms to address market failures that would have Pareto-efficient outcomes while respecting preference neutrality and voluntary participation.

The extent of the problem is illustrated by a one-shot buyer-seller interaction called a "double auction" because both buyers and sellers are looking for the counterpart who will give them the best price. In a double auction, prospective buyers and sellers are paired, each knows how much they value the good held by the prospective seller, and they simultaneously announce prices: for the seller, the least price at which she will part with the good, and for the buyer, the maximum price he is willing to pay. If the seller's announced least price is less than the buyer's announced maximum price, then a trade will occur, the actual price being somewhere between the two announced prices. If the seller's announced least price exceeds the buyer's maximum price, then no transaction takes place.

The double-auction setting is important because Pareto efficiency should not be difficult to sustain in this type of interaction, even without the help of a mechanism designer. The reason is that it features none of the familiar impediments to efficient bargaining and market exchange, such as ill-defined property rights, incomplete contracts, or, as in the case of public goods, the impossibility of excluding those who have not contributed to its provision from enjoying the public good. Barring these impediments, buyers or sellers knowing only their own preferences and the prices offered or asked by their trading counterparts should be able to bargain their way to an efficient allocation, eventually exhausting all potential gains from trade and hence, by definition, implementing a Pareto-efficient outcome.

But surprisingly, this is not the case. The problem is that when traders meet, they have no incentive to reveal their true valuations of the goods that may be exchanged, since, as is plausible, these stated valuations will influence the eventual price at which they transact if they make a deal. Knowing this, the prospective seller of a good will overstate the lowest price at which she will sell, and the would-be buyer will understate the highest price at which he is willing to buy.

The key result of investigations of the double auction is that if traders care only about maximizing their expected gains, it is never in either party's interest to truthfully reveal their evaluation. This is the case even if the other party is reporting truthfully (Gibbard, 1973; Laffont and Maskin, 1979). As a result, the buyer's announced maximum price will sometimes fall short of the seller's

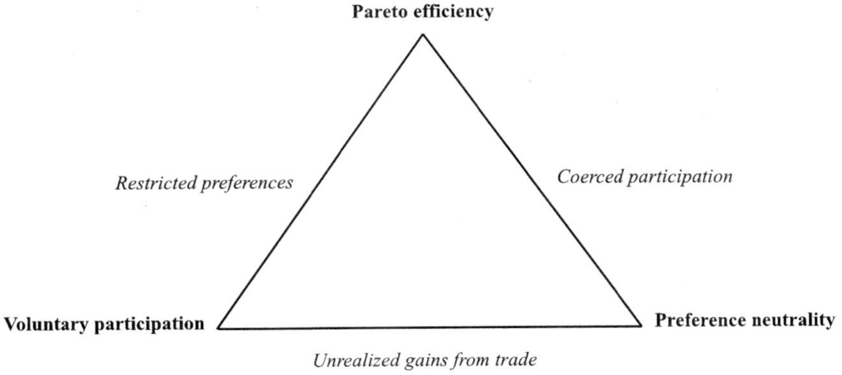

FIGURE 1 The liberal trilemma: The impossibility of satisfying all three liberal desiderata: Pareto efficiency, preference neutrality, and voluntary participation. The terms at the vertices are the three liberal desiderata, only two of which can obtain simultaneously; the terms in italics on the edges between the vertices are the consequences of realizing the two desiderata connected by the edge, but not the third desideratum opposite to the edge. Source: Bowles (2016).

announced minimum price, so no trade will take place, even when the buyer's true valuation of the good is greater than the seller's. This means that some mutually beneficial exchanges will not be consummated, resulting in a Pareto inefficient outcome.

Fig. 1 summarizes what we call the liberal trilemma (Bowles, 2016). What mechanism design has discovered is that the three conditions of liberal constitutional design and public policy – neutrality with respect to preferences, voluntary participation, and Pareto efficiency – are not generally compatible. Consider each pair of vertices of the triangle in the figure, and why the excluded vertex is not feasible. Between each pair of liberal desiderata, the phrase in italics is the consequence of realizing the two desiderata connected by this edge but excluding the third.

If voluntary participation is combined with preference neutrality – the base of the triangle – some would-be mutually beneficial exchanges will not occur (because both parties would misreport their selling and buying price), so there will be unrealized gains from trade, violating Pareto efficiency. This is what Myerson and Mark Satterthwaite (1983) showed for the example of the double auction. Pareto efficiency and preference neutrality are jointly feasible – the right-hand edge of the triangle – if people can be compelled to participate in a clever mechanism as designed by Kalyan Chatterjee (1982), even if some would prefer not to, violating the voluntary-participation condition. Finally, voluntary participation and Pareto efficiency are jointly feasible if the traders were predisposed to report honestly their true valuations out of a commitment to truth telling, an altruistic concern for the other trader, or some other reason. Individuals would then never walk away from a potential mutually beneficial trade. But demanding that traders place a sufficiently high value on honesty or altruism requires a violation of preference neutrality.

Abandoning preference neutrality offers a way out of the trilemma. If the traders were sufficiently altruistic, they would take account not only of the losses suffered by themselves because of forgone mutually beneficial trades, but also the losses suffered by their trading partners. As this would lead them to take account of the costs that their actions inflict on others, it would attenuate the resulting market failures (Hwang and Bowles, 2015; Lee et al., 2026).

The conclusion is that preference neutrality, voluntary participation, and Pareto efficiency are not jointly possible, even in a very simple exchange of goods. Thus, mechanism design fails to produce a constitution for knaves fit for a liberal-democratic society. Among the reasons is the liberal aversion to requiring people to participate in economic transactions against their will, and to allowing states to favor some kinds of preferences over others.

Another source of the trilemma is the limited extent to which intrinsically private information may be placed in a mechanism designer's hands or made legally verifiable so as to be the basis of complete and enforceable contracts. This is not only true as a practical matter but also, at least in a liberal society, a highly valued limit on the authority of states. Machiavelli stated the core message of the trilemma in his *Discourses* when he concluded that inducing the truly bad to act as if they were good "would be either a very cruel endeavor or altogether impossible," and would require "extraordinary means, including violence and a resort to arms" (Machiavelli, 1984). A state with the privacy-invading capacities and powers sufficient to acquire the information that would render contracts complete and ensure that all mutually beneficial trades were executed could not be called liberal.

In light of the dystopic aspects of what it would take to overcome the liberal trilemma, it is difficult to disagree with Tim Besley: "Perhaps then the solution can only lie in creating better people" (2013, p. 492). Recent empirical evidence on endogenous preferences suggests some ways that this might come about.

3 Institutions affect preferences: evidence

Institutions impose characteristic patterns of interaction on the people who make up a society, affecting who meets whom, on what terms, to perform which tasks, and with what expectation of rewards, including what one must do or be to acquire one's livelihood.

These rules of the game influence the way that aspects of personality, habits, tastes, identities, and values are differentially replicated in a population, endogenously shaping preferences. To recognize this fact, we posit a process by which new preferences are acquired and existing ones abandoned – natural selection on genes, for example, or a social learning process – and we show how differing institutions governing the social interactions that people have will support differing distributions of preferences in a population.

In recent decades, economists and other social scientists have accumulated substantial empirical evidence on the association of social norms and societal institutions (Bowles, 1998; Gächter et al., 2010; Gächter and Schulz, 2016; Tabellini, 2008a; Lane et al., 2023; Almond and Verba, 1963; Lonner et al., 1980; Inglehart and Welzel, 2005; Falk et al., 2018). Recent reviews are found in Nunn (2021) and Persson and Tabellini (2021). We here review some of the evidence particularly related to the endogenous nature of the social preferences that may contribute to the governance of liberal-democratic societies. We begin with the intrinsic challenges of measuring endogenous preferences.

3.1 Endogenous preferences and why it is difficult to identify them

We distinguish between two senses in which institutions may affect preferences: framing and learning. Framing effects arise because institutions – for example whether some action an individual may take is voluntary or required – provide information on the nature of the situation and the behavior appropriate to it. We characterize preferences subject to framing effects as situation-specific (borrowing from psychology), that is, reversible by a change in the situation. Such short-term framing effects do not help to answer the question raised at the outset of this chapter.

Institutions may also have durable learning effects that arise because institutions shape how people regularly interact (e.g., patterns of socialization, the feasible set of actions and associated rewards). The nature of these interactions may favor the long-term adoption of some preferences over others, such that learned preferences endure even after the conditions under which they were learned no longer exist. Due to these learning effects, preferences are endogenous with respect to institutions.

Experimental methods have demonstrated framing effects on preferences (e.g., Bowles and Polanía-Reyes, 2012; Fehr and Rockenbach, 2003; Gneezy and Rustichini, 2000; Falk and Kosfeld, 2006; Martinsson et al., 2019). In contrast, identifying the causal processes whereby the possible preference-learning effects of institutions might work has proven much more challenging. The reason is that the developmental processes by which we learn new preferences do not take place in the course of an hour-long experimental session, but over years or decades of upbringing and life experience.

Because preference change involves a long-term learning process and significant, plausibly exogenous changes in economic institutions are infrequent, compelling empirical studies of the impact of institutions on preferences are scarce (we review some exemplary studies below). Desiderata for an ideal research design are rarely jointly realized: Exogenous institutional changes or other natural experiments that could identify causal effects are few, and where these exist, the available evidence is typically from surveys and rarely includes data on economic behavior (experimental or other).

3.2 Empirical evidence on endogenous social preferences

Empirical studies of endogenous preferences have drawn on plausibly exogenous temporal or spatial discontinuities to identify causal effects of institutions on preferences. Important contributions to this literature include the following.

Nathan Nunn and Leonard Wantchekon (2011) exploited geographical differences in the extent to which enslaved people were taken from Africa along with contemporary survey responses to make a convincing case that slave trade had an enduring negative effect on interpersonal trust in the localities from which slaves were taken.

To estimate the effect of institutions on contemporary social norms, Sara Lowes and her co-authors (2017) studied populations on either side of what had been the boundaries of the Kuba Kingdom in early 17th century Central Africa, capturing differences in the degree of political centralization and state capacity. Their experimental data show that those now living where the centralized Kuba Kingdom once ruled were more likely to cheat for material gain and were less inclined to follow rules.

Similarly, Sascha Becker and his coauthors (2016) studied effects of historical exposure to the multi-ethnic Habsburg Empire, which was characterized by relatively well-functioning citizen-state interactions in a respected bureaucracy, as opposed to the Ottoman and Russian Empires, on citizens' preferences today. Their survey evidence shows that populations of modern day Ukraine, Poland, Montenegro, and Serbia living within the boundaries of what had been the Habsburg Empire at least a century earlier have substantially greater trust in the police and courts than did their fellow citizens living on the other side of the Habsburg border.

The staggered extension of the vote to women in Switzerland provided a treatment difference between age cohorts that Michaela Slotwinski and Alois Stutzer (2023) used to identify institutional changes as a cause of transformation of gender norms. Early exposure to female suffrage had a positive impact on female labor force participation and investment in human capital, as well as a negative impact on marital bonds.

Bruno Caprettini and Hans-Joachim Voth (2023) leveraged exogenous geographical variation in government spending along with individual data on bond purchases, volunteering for military service and bravery in battle to show that Americans who benefited from social spending during the New Deal were substantially more likely to exhibit patriotic behavior during World War II.

Benjamin Enke (2023) studied differences in the content of folklore among ethno-linguistic groups and found a strong positive association in the folklore between market-like themes and themes relating to social preferences and moral universalism. To motivate a causal interpretation of this evidence, he used local ecological diversity and proximity to trade routes as an exogenous influence on market exposure. The already mentioned cross-cultural experimental study by Joseph Henrich and his coauthors (2001) found that among 15 small-scale societies, subjects in populations with greater market exposure were more likely to make fair offers in the Ultimatum Game (closer to an even split) and were more likely to reject unequal offers.

To identify the effects of institutions of local self-governance, Devesh Rustagi (2024) used the end of noble rule in some Swiss municipalities in the 13th century that occurred due to the accidental deaths of the only legitimate heirs. Current residents of those localities were substantially more cooperative in a one-shot public goods experiment than those living in places where self-rule was not introduced until the 19th century. Inhabitants of municipalities with a long history of self-governance also engaged more in community associations and environmental protection activities, and were more likely to vote for the expansion of democratic rights in the 11 referendums held between 1960 and 2022 (expanding suffrage and citizenship, eliminating gender discrimination).

A suite of papers explores how the prevalent role of kinship relations in societal governance as opposed to more depersonalized relationships under the rule of law affects preferences concerning political participation and how order is sustained. Jonathan Schulz (2022) provides evidence that weak kin networks are associated with the formation of self-governing institutions and a preference for political participation. His evidence suggests that the medieval Catholic Church contributed to the advancement of democracy in Europe by dissolving strong kin networks (i.e., prohibiting cousin marriage). He shows that within European countries a proxy for civicness (national election voter turnouts) varies inversely with strong kin networks (proxied by cousin-marriages rates).

In an earlier paper, Schulz et al. (2019) provide evidence that greater exposure to kinship-based institutions is positively associated with obedience and conformity. Relatedly Enke (2019) found that in societies characterized by loose kinship ties both universal moral values that apply independently of group membership and internalized guilt are key in sustaining cooperation. In contrast, in kin-based societies behavioral regulation appears to be achieved via moral values specific to particular communities along with public shame.

Rather than identifying causal relationships by means of historical or spatial discontinuities, Fabian Kosse and his coauthors (2020) used a randomized controlled trial (RCT). They matched elementary school children with adult mentors who scored high on prosociality to interact over a period of a year. Children who interacted intensely with prosocial mentors scored higher on trust, altruism, and pro-sociality in everyday situations. This was true not only at the end of the treatment period, but also one year after the trial had ended.

The authors whose works we have reviewed here exploited convincing strategies to identify causal effects of institutions on preferences. They have also suggested plausible accounts about how institutions may have affected preferences in the cases studied. Lowes and her coauthors, for example, suggested that their result – weaker internalized morality among those whose ancestors lived under a more effective state – might reflect parents' lesser investment in inculcating norms of honesty in their children where in the past formal institutions had effectively enforced social norms. Henrich and his co-authors invoke John Stuart Mill's argument that by placing "human beings in contact with persons dissimilar to themselves," markets could cultivate attitudes of fairness towards strangers.

In related ongoing work, we examine whether exposure to a liberal-democratic institutional bundle – markets, private property, selection of leaders by elections, civil liberties and the rule of law – cultivates preferences for autonomy. Using survey and experimental evidence from post-Communist Europe, we study whether cohorts socialized under authoritarian institutions differ from younger cohorts whose formative years unfolded under more liberal-democratic conditions. We find patterns consistent with the view that liberal-democratic environments foster autonomy-valuing dispositions, while authoritarian environments foster tolerance of external control (Schmelz et al., 2026).

We conclude from this literature that institutions may shape not only incentives and opportunities, but also the preferences on which their own functioning depends.

3.3 Example: institutions affect attitudes towards independence and obedience

But none of these studies has provided direct empirical evidence on what Guido Tabellini (2008a) called the "missing link," namely the "precise mechanism of cultural transmission" (pp. 255 and 289). It seems likely that the mechanisms involved would include the way that institutions affect preferences both directly – in the way that they structure the interactions people engage in and the payoffs to adopting alternative behaviors – and indirectly by affecting socialization of the young both by parents and other adults. Important clues are provided by the anthropological and psychological literatures.

3.3.1 Causal mechanisms: the effects of work and economic institutions

Anthropologists have investigated how people come to have differing values about independence, compliance, and related dispositions. Studying the process of preference change in the transition from foraging to farming, Herbert Barry III, and his coauthors (1959) asked why "a particular society select[s] child training practices which will tend to produce a particular kind of typical personality?" They categorized 79 mostly illiterate small-scale societies according to the prevalent form of livelihood (animal husbandry, agriculture, hunting and fishing) and the related ease of food storage or other forms of wealth accumulation, the latter being a major correlate of dimensions of social structure such as wealth inequality and political hierarchy. Food storage is common in agricultural societies but not among foragers. They also collected evidence on forms of child-rearing, including obedience training, self-reliance, independence, and responsibility.

They found that in the populations that stored substantial amounts of food, child rearing practices emphasized obedience (controlling for other measures of social structure such as unilinearity of descent, extent of polygyny, levels of participation of women in the predominant subsistence activity, and size of population units). In the predominantly hunting-gathering populations doing little storage – "immediate returns economies" to anthropologists – parents stressed the development of independence in their children. These different approaches emerged, the authors write, "because this kind of typical personality is functional for the adult life of the society" (p. 51). They conclude that "knowledge of the economy alone would enable one to predict with considerable accuracy whether a society's socialization pressures were primarily toward compliance or assertion" (p. 59). The causal relationship is unlikely to run from child-rearing to economic structure, as the latter is dictated primarily by geography in the sample of societies under study.

The social psychologist Melvin Kohn and his coauthors (1990) explored a related topic: parents' value of self-determination as opposed to obedience in raising their children. In the U.S., Japan and Poland, they studied the relationship between self-direction in a person's work – autonomy in the selection and execution of tasks – and how important they as a parent thought self-direction and independence were for their children, as opposed to obedience. They found that parents who had substantial autonomy at work (directing the activities of others rather than being directed) valued self-direction substantially more than those with less autonomy at work.

Kohn et al. observe that people who exercise self-direction on the job also value self-direction more in other realms of their life like leisure activities and are less likely to exhibit fatalism, distrust, and self-depreciation. Their causal reasoning is that "social structure affects individual psychological functioning mainly by affecting the conditions of people's own lives" (p. 1006). The result is that "the experience of occupational self-direction [...] has a profound effect on people's values, orientation, and cognitive functioning" (p. 967).

Recent evidence consistent with Kohn's findings comes from an experiment by Sherry Wu and Elizabeth Paluck (2020) that was inspired by Kurt Lewin's early experiments on the effect of participatory (rather than hierarchical) workplace organization on workers' attitudes towards authority. They randomly selected groups of women textile workers in China to hold weekly meetings in which supervisors exercised no leadership role at all; the control work groups continued their conventional supervisor-directed meetings. After six weeks, the workers were asked to what extent they agree with the statement that "obedience and respect for authority are the most important virtues children should learn." They found that those who had been exposed to participatory meetings agreed with the statement less than the control group (the treatment effect was almost one standard deviation of the responses to the "obedience" question).

3.3.2 Causal mechanisms: the structure of schooling

If Wu and Paluck, Kohn and Barry III and their coauthors are right that preferences about autonomy versus obedience reflect the kinds of economic institutions governing one's activities, then it might follow that these same economic institutions would indirectly affect patterns of socialization beyond the family, for example in schools. Indeed, we find clues of exactly this in a small study of the similarity of reward systems in workplaces and schools, suggesting that the experience of schooling might produce adults with a psychological profile concerning autonomy and obedience that employers value in their workers.

The idea motivating the study was that for effective functioning, the structure of the firm as an institution defines a division of labor requiring not only different capabilities, but also different personalities for different roles as, for example, a manager and an employee. Schools, especially those serving families whose children are more likely to be employees than managers or owners, might then come to value the personality traits that employers also value in those who they hire.

At a series of workplaces in the Boston area – both private and public – Richard Edwards (1976; 1977) measured how supervisors valued the workers under their direction. He did this by eliciting their rankings of the workers' likelihood of being promoted or fired, and their relative job performance. He also used a peer-rating technique to elicit from each member of a work group the names of their co-workers that most closely corresponded to a list of 16 adjectives, including "creative," "consistent," "dependable," "independent" and "most likely to understand what is expected of them."

Using principal components analysis on these peer-rated personality measures of the workers, Edwards identified three largely orthogonal personality aspects that he termed "an awareness ... and commitment to follow the rules," "habits of predictability and dependability," and "internalization of the enterprise's goals and values" (1976, p. 58). Regressing the employees' supervisor rating on the value of these three components for the workers, he found large precisely estimated effects (normalized regression coefficients between a quarter and a third) even when conditioned on measures of the worker's IQ, level of education, age, parental socioeconomic status, and the socioeconomic status of their first job. Except for age, the estimated effect sizes of the conditioning variables were small and not even close to statistically significant.

Do schools reward the same traits as managers? Edwards (1977) performed the same peer ranking of students in their final year at a suburban high school in New York State (n=327) and obtained data on students' grades and cognitive scores. Fig. 2 shows the normalized regression coefficients estimated singly for each of the personality traits, controlling for measures of the students' IQ and scholastic achievement scores in both verbal and mathematical skills. The figure also shows the evidence on the personality traits of the "good worker" from the private firm and government data set reported above. The aspects of personality that are rewarded or penalized by teachers' grading practices (conditional on measures of cognitive performance) appear to be very similar to those that are favorably or adversely rated by work supervisors.

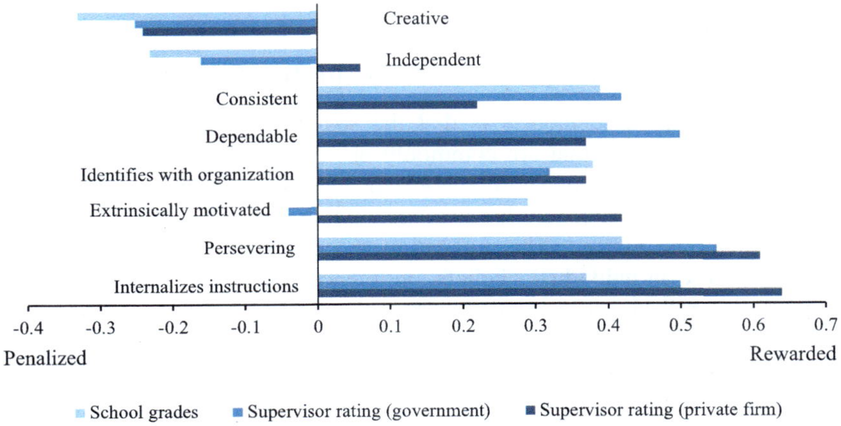

FIGURE 2 Peer-measured personality traits rewarded (+) and penalized (−) by work supervisors' ratings (Edwards, 1977) and teachers' grades (Bowles and Gintis, 1976). Own representation based on data from Meyer (1972).

The correspondence between the reward structures in an important institutional setting for adults (namely, work) and in schools provides a possible mechanism for the effect of institutions on preferences in this case. It may reflect parents', teachers' and employers' understanding of the psychological requisites for success in the labor market, which would then influence governmental educational policies. A schematic representation of this causal structure is presented in Fig. 3.

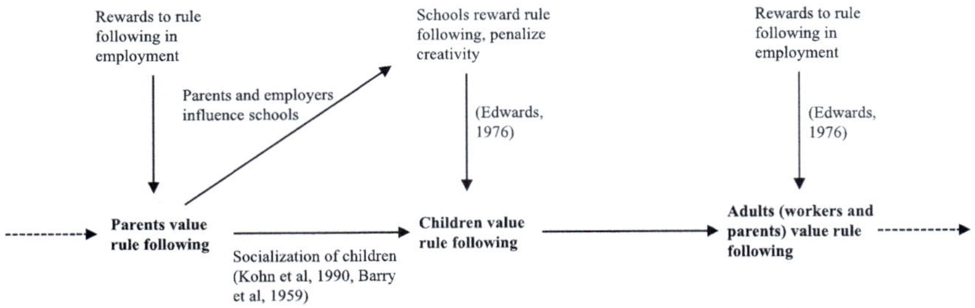

FIGURE 3 Mechanisms by which parents, schools, and workplaces may contribute to the influence of institutions on preferences. We illustrate possible mechanisms by which the value of following rules might be sustained through a combination of parental socialization and the experience of schooling and employment. Arrows indicate causal effects.

If this account is correct, we would expect the preference for personal autonomy and self-determination to be affected by the authority structures that regulate social interactions. Expanding similar reasoning beyond the workplace and schools, more hierarchical and less democratic societies would be expected to support a lesser value of autonomy and greater tolerance of being controlled by others. A series of evolutionary models provide insights on the causal processes that might be involved.

4 Institutions affect preferences: evolutionary models

The key idea in these models is that the societal institutions and patterns of individual behavior that are commonly observed are those that have been copied and diffused – in short, replicated – while competing rules of the game, beliefs, and preferences have suffered extinction (or have been replicated only in marginal niches). The replication process may be either cultural or genetic. Where an individual's beliefs, preferences, knowledge and other traits are socially learned from parents, others in the elder generation, and peers we refer to cultural evolution. Where replication is the result of genetic transmission from parents, the development of phenotypes from the inherited genotypes and their differential reproductive success, we refer to natural selection. (Robson and Samuelson (2026) model the ways in which natural selection could affect our utility functions, e.g. preferences towards risk and time.)

4.1 How natural selection could produce a cooperative species

Humans are unusual among animals in the extent to which we cooperate (except for the social insects). There are many self-interested reasons why people cooperate, e.g., exchanging goods for mutual benefit in a market, often in a context of repeated interactions where cooperative behavior can be subsequently rewarded. But as we have seen from the experimental evidence presented in Section 3, humans also bear costs to help others in situations with little or no expectation of material reward.

A strong case can be made that we became this way by the co-evolution of genes and culture, the two processes of replication affecting each other. A common instance of gene-culture co-evolution, called *cultural niche construction* by the biologists John Odling-Smee, Kevin Laland, and Marcus Feldman, is that "organisms ... construct aspects of their environment such as nests, holes, burrows, webs". Niche construction by humans can "modify the selective environment to which humans are exposed and may affect which genetic variants are transmitted" (2003, pp. 1, 247).

A well-documented example for gene-culture co-evolution by means of human niche construction is the spread of alleles (variants of genes) for adult lactose tolerance that occurred independently in at least three different populations following the domestication of goats, cows and other milk bearing animals eight millennia or so ago (Holden and Mace, 1997; Durham, 1991).

The environment favoring lactose tolerant alleles – farming – was culturally transmitted over generations.

More broadly, institutions are environments that humans construct and transmit culturally, regulating how we interact and how rewards are distributed among members of a population, which confers differential fitness advantages on people who behave in differing ways. Thus, institutions constitute part of the environment affecting gene selection and, of particular interest here, the selection of genes whose phenotypic expressions may take the form of preferences. Institutions, in biological terminology, are thus niches (Bowles, 2000).

It follows that the natural selection process itself could have favored the development of institution-building capacities among humans (a key idea in Machiavelli's thinking mentioned above). If the institutions constituting a particular niche confer fitness advantages on those occupying the niche, then we would expect that natural selection would favor "behavioral adaptations to enhance the efficiency of their niche construction" as noted by Odling-Smee and his co-authors (2003, p. 113). This means that the distribution of genotypes can affect the process of niche construction itself, thereby influencing the evolution of institutions.

We now provide an explanation of how this co-evolutionary process might have supported the construction of institutional niches contributing to the proliferation of alleles predisposing members of a population to altruistic and cooperative behaviors. The explanation in brief (based on Bowles and Gintis, 2011) is that preferences supporting altruistic cooperation became common in humans because in the environments we inhabited, cooperation was highly beneficial to the members of groups that practiced it. In addition, humans constructed institutions that minimized the costs borne by those with altruistic preferences competing for reproductive success with self-regarding fellow group members, while heightening the group-level advantages associated with the high levels of cooperation that these social preferences allowed. These institutions proliferated because the groups that adopted them secured high levels of within-group cooperation, which in turn favored the groups' survival, expansion and replication as a reproductive and cultural entity in the face of environmental challenges and conflicts with other groups.

4.1.1 Population structure and the evolution of a cooperative species

To model this process, we use the standard biological definition of altruism, which concerns its effects on fitness: the behaviors induced by an altruistic genotype increase the expected average fitness of members of this individual's group, while the altruistic individual would have higher fitness were they not the bearer of the altruistic genotype (Kerr et al., 2004).

Drawing on Bowles and Gintis (2011), we model a large population in which some are bearers of an allele that is expressed in altruistic behavior. (This

TABLE 1 The Altruism Game.

	A	N
A	*b*-*c*	-*c*
N	*b*	0

Shown are the row player's payoffs when paired with the column player. As A takes an altruistic action, conferring a benefit b on the other at a cost c to the actor with $b > c > 0$, this is a prisoners' dilemma game with N being the dominant strategy.

clonally transmitted single "allele for altruism" is a hypothetical simplifying device. Though altruism likely has a genetic component, there is no such allele.) When paired to interact in dyads, the altruists confer a fitness benefit of b on the other at a fitness cost of c to the altruist, while the non-altruists confer no benefits and bear no costs. Fitness payoffs for the row player being an altruist (A) or not (N) in this Altruism Game are shown in Table 1.

At the end of a period, each member of the population produces a number of exact replicas with a baseline fitness of $\beta_0 > c$ (to preclude negative fitness) plus the benefits and costs incurred in the interaction as given in Table 1. Letting $\pi^A(p)$ and $\pi^N(p)$ be the expected payoff to being an altruist or not in a population in which the fraction of altruists is p, and normalizing the total population to unity, the fraction of altruists in the next period p' is:

$$p' = \frac{p(\pi^A(p) + \beta_0)}{p\pi^A(p) + (1-p)\pi^N(p) + \beta_0} \tag{1}$$

which is just the number of altruists divided by the total population in the next period.

We are interested in Δp, the change in the fraction of the population that are altruists from one period to the next, which with a little rearranging, is

$$p' - p \equiv \Delta p = p(1-p)(\pi^A(p) - \pi^N(p)) \tag{2}$$

This is termed the replicator equation for trait x as it tracks its differential replication with respect to trait y. If matching to interact with others in the Altruism Game is random, then in a large population the probability that an altruist is matched with another altruist is approximately p, the fraction of the population that are altruists. Thus, given the payoffs in Table 1, $\pi^A(p) - \pi^N(p) = -c$, so we have

$$\Delta p = p(1-p)(-c) < 0 \tag{3}$$

Eq. (3) says that the direction and pace of the process of replication is given by the product of how frequently A's and N's are paired (which depends on p, namely, $p(1-p)$) and the net fitness costs of bearing the altruistic allele (which is independent of p, namely c). The fact that Eq. (3) must be negative shows why natural selection could not support the evolution of altruism (that would require $\Delta p > 0$) in a population that is randomly matched (termed "well-mixed" in population genetics).

But human populations are not well-mixed. We interact disproportionately with members of our own family, language group, neighborhood, workplace, and so on. These forms of assortative matching (that is, deviations from random matching) are what evolutionary biologists refer to as a structured population.

Fig. 4 illustrates this. The extent of assortation resulting from population structure is the difference in the probabilities of being paired with an A conditional on whether one is an A or not, that is $P(A|A) - P(A|N)$. If the extent of population structure is as shown in Fig. 4, the expected fitness of the two types $\pi^A = bP(A|A) - c$ and $\pi^N = bP(A|N)$ are equal, so from Eq. (2), $\Delta p = 0$, that is, p is stationary. If the extent of population structure were greater than shown in the figure, the fitness of A's would exceed that of N's, so the fraction of altruists in the population would increase.

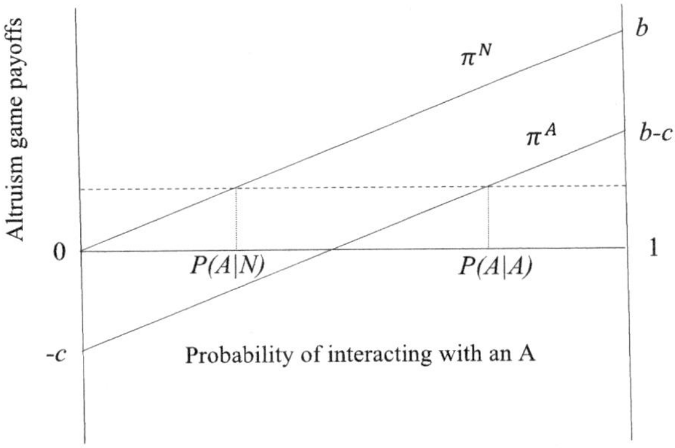

FIGURE 4 The evolution of an altruistic trait in a structured population. The horizontal axis shows the probability of interacting with an altruist for some given value of p, the fraction of the population that are altruists. The vertical axis is in units of expected fitness of the non-altruists and altruists based on the payoffs in Table 1 (π^N and π^A respectively, ignoring baseline fitness, a constant common to both types). In a structured (not well-mixed) population, $P(A|N)$ and $P(A|A)$, the probabilities of being matched with an A conditional on being respectively an N or an A differ, the latter exceeding the former by an amount that is increasing in the degree of population structure. The extent of population structure illustrated in the figure is just sufficient to offset the cost of altruism, that is, using Eq. (5), $(P(A|A) - P(A|N))b = c$, allowing the fraction of the population that are A's to be sustained.

An early statement of the importance of non-random matching is Hamilton's rule for the evolutionary success of altruism (Hamilton, 1964). The rule states that conferring a fitness benefit b on another individual at a direct fitness cost to oneself of c will be favored by natural selection if

$$rb > c \tag{4}$$

where r is the coefficient of genetic relatedness between the actor and the beneficiary (one half for siblings, a quarter for nieces and nephews, an eighth for cousins and so on), which is Hamilton's measure of population structure. It will vary from close to zero when most interactions are among total strangers to close to one half when most interactions are among siblings or parents and their offspring. Rowthorn (2006) offers a clear explanation of how Hamilton's rule works when applied to siblings. Hamilton's insight is far more general, however.

According to Hamilton's rule, helping another person increases the fitness of the altruistic allele by an amount $rb - c$, which if positive means that its population frequency will increase. His rule captures the key mechanism common to all models of the evolution of altruism, namely that an altruistic allele cannot proliferate if its bearers are no more likely to receive help from those with whom they interact than would occur by chance. We can rewrite Hamilton's rule in terms of the extent of population structure as

$$(P(A|A) - P(A|N))b > c \tag{5}$$

confirming that in a well-mixed population (e.g. with random matching, such that $P(A|A) = p = P(A|N)$), the evolution of an altruistic allele by natural selection is impossible.

All models of the evolution of altruistic behaviors share a positive assortment feature, meaning that a given type (A or N) is more likely to interact with their own type than would occur if matching were random. This includes not only models stressing preferential interaction among siblings or other close genetic family members, but also models of semi-isolated subpopulations in a larger population (which in this literature are termed demes). Ilan Eshel and Luigi Luca Cavalli-Sforza (1982, p. 1334) provide a glimpse of the variety of causes of assortment: "Kin, deme, niche, social group structure, ... and discrimination in the choice of companions are some of the possible sources of deviation from randomness."

A deme (subgroup of a population) may be a tribe, language community, or other ensemble of individuals in more frequent social interaction than with outsiders. In a structured population comprised of many partially isolated groups, the fraction of altruists in each group will differ. Thus, most altruists will be in groups with an above average number of other altruists. If groups are sufficiently different in their fraction of altruists, then most of the altruists will be in demes in which they are very likely to interact with altruists, benefiting mutually from their generosity, and altruists will experience few interactions with the non altruists (who exploit their altruism). This effect favoring the evolution of altruists in the population as a whole will be stronger the larger is the variance across groups in the fraction of their population that are altruists. This will be the case the less is the extent of migration among groups and the smaller are the groups (for reasons similar to sampling error).

Population structure will also exist within groups. Beyond the tendency of people to interact more with close genetic kin, people will have some information on the past behavior of group members. Thus, altruists, as Eshel and Cavalli-Sforza noted, may be able to discriminate against the non-altruists and as a result, more frequently interact with other altruists than would occur by chance.

To see how this would affect the evolution of an altruistic allele, suppose that groups are segmented, so that in the within-group pairing process, A's are more likely to interact with A's and N's with N's than would occur by random matching, and that the degree of this within-group segmentation differs across groups. We define $s_j \geq 0$ as the degree of segmentation in a group j, the difference in the conditional probability of an A being matched with an A and an N being matched with an A in the within-group pairing. Then the probability that an A-member of group j is matched with an A is not p_j but $P(A|A)_j = s_j + (1 - s_j)p_j \geq p_j$. The intuition for this expression is that with probability s_j, an altruist interacts with another altruist due to segmentation, and with probability $(1 - s_j)$, they interact with a random member of their group. Correspondingly, the probability that an N-member of group j is matched with an A is $P(A|N)_j = (1 - s_j)p_j \leq p_j$.

Using these probabilities, then we have $\pi_j^A - \pi_j^N = s_j b - c > -c$. In this model, segmentation is therefore part of the environment determining the reproductive success of altruists as opposed to non-altruists. If $s > c/b$, A's will on average do better than N's within groups and the A's will proliferate as a result of natural selection operating within the group.

For $s < c/b$, segmentation still reduces the expected payoff disadvantage of altruists because within a given group, they are disproportionately likely to meet other altruists, while N's are disproportionately likely to meet other N's in their group. Even though this does not reverse the payoff disadvantage of the altruists, segmentation can be complemented with other institutions that can support the genetic evolution of altruism, to which we now turn.

4.1.2 Reproductive leveling institutions and the evolution of altruism within groups

A second way that the selective pressures against an altruistic allele may be mitigated is termed reproductive leveling, meaning practices or institutions that reduce payoff differences between altruists and non-altruists by modifying the entries in Table 1. An example is the common practice among foragers and other human groups that some fraction of the resources an individual acquires – perhaps specific kinds of food as among the Ache (Kaplan and Hill, 1985) – is deposited in a common pot to be shared equally among all group members. In foraging societies the common pot may receive substantially more than half of the total food acquired (Fochesato and Bowles, 2015).

The effect of reproductive leveling is to reduce the minimal level of population structure, $(P(A|A) - P(A|N))$, that is sufficient to support the genetic evolution of an altruistic allele. Other forms of reproductive leveling reducing the expected fitness differences between altruists and non-altruists will have the same effect, e.g., a norm against polygynous marriage in a population among which richer individuals would have access to multiple wives.

We model the evolution of food sharing, monogamy and other forms of reproductive leveling as conventions, meaning practices to which adherence is in the (self-regarding) interest of each group member as long as most others follow the convention. Crucial to this process is the fact that food-sharing and other forms of reproductive leveling do not require the pre-existence of altruistic preferences: adherence to these conventions is a best response for self-interested individuals.

Reproductive leveling may be modeled as a linear tax at rate $t \in [0, 1)$, levied on the members' payoffs, with the proceeds distributed equally as transfers to all members of the population (as with food sharing practices, t here being the fraction of foods deposited in the common pot). This means that the difference between A's and N's payoffs $\pi^A - \pi^N$ is no longer $-c$ but instead $-(1-t)c$. Fig. 5 shows the effect of resource sharing on the payoff differences of the two types. The difference in the probability of being matched with an A (conditional on one's own type) that equalizes expected payoffs is no longer $P(A|A) - P(A|N)$ as shown in Fig. 4, but is now less, namely $P^T(A|A) - P^T(A|N)$. As a result, were the population structure as in Fig. 5, and the sharing institution in place ($t > 0$), then $\pi^A > \pi^N$, so p would increase. This shows how the egalitarian reproductive leveling practices common to foraging bands could have provided an environment in which natural selection would favor the evolution of a genetic predisposition to altruism.

Integrating both segmentation and reproductive leveling within groups into the model, the differences in the expected fitness of A's and N's within a group will now be $(1 - t_j)(s_j b - c)$, so we have a revised version of Eq. (3):

$$\Delta p_j = p_j(1 - p_j)(1 - t_j)(s_j b - c) \tag{6}$$

from which it is clear that both within group institutions – segmentation and reproductive leveling – retard within-group selection against the A's. As we have seen, for a sufficiently large level of segmentation, s_j, this may even reverse it.

4.1.3 Group competition: the coevolution of altruism, leveling, and segmentation

We turn now from modeling how segmentation and reproductive leveling institutions within groups may affect gene-culture co-evolution to consider institutions governing groups' survival or demise in between-group competition.

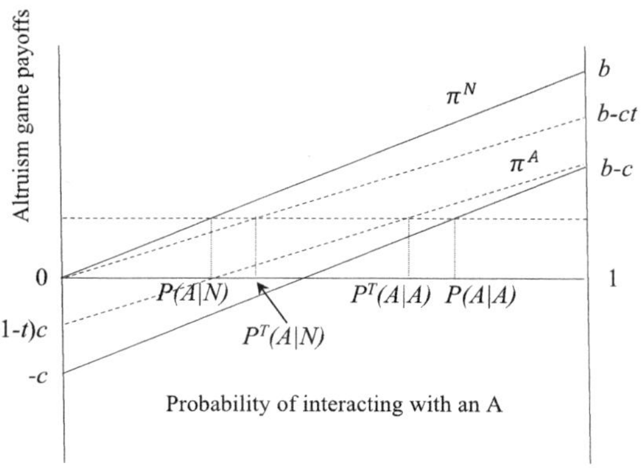

FIGURE 5 Reproductive leveling reduces the extent of population structure (positive assortment) necessary for the evolution of an altruistic trait. The fitness of the altruists and non-altruists (ignoring baseline fitness) are π^A and π^N, respectively. The horizontal axis measures the probability of being paired with an A for some given value of p. The dashed payoff lines indicate the effect of within-group resource sharing on the fitness cost of being an altruist and, as a result, on the degree of assortment required for natural selection to favor the evolution of altruism. For example if the entire population were A's, their before tax and transfer payoff, namely $b - c$, would be the population average payoff and their after tax and transfer payoff would not be affected because their taxes paid would be exactly offset by the tax-financed transfer they received. So they would both pay $t(b - c)$ in taxes and receive the same amount in transfer. For an N, however, the payoff under the tax and transfer institution would be $b(1 - t) + t(b - c) = b - ct$, as shown. For the values of c, b and t illustrated here, the altruistic trait will proliferate if the degree of assortment is greater than $P^T(A|A) - P^T(A|N)$, which is decreasing in the tax rate t.

The key idea is that groups with a larger fraction of altruists sustain higher levels of within-group cooperation and are therefore likely to prevail in conflicts with other groups, the (mostly non-altruistic) losers of these contests suffering elimination or reduced fitness. This provides an additional fitness benefit to being in a group with many altruists.

Bowles, with Jung-Kyoo Choi and Astrid Hopfensitz (2003) simulated a deme-structured population empirically calibrated to represent a population consisting of 20 hunter-gatherer groups during the Late Pleistocene. The question the simulation was designed to answer is: Would a population with empirically realistic migration rates, group sizes, payoffs to cooperative interactions, competition among groups and other attributes constitute an environment in which an altruistic allele could proliferate? The answer depends on the outcome of a race that pits within-group selection processes favoring non-altruists (assuming that Eq. (6) just above is negative) against the between-group competition process favoring altruists (most of whom will be in groups with more than the average number of altruists, which are as a result likely to prevail in contests).

In our simulated model, in addition to engaging in occasional conflicts, groups could adopt a reproductive leveling strategy in the form of a group-specific tax rate t_j, the coordination of which imposes costs on the group. Members could also exercise some (costly, imperfect) discrimination in who they interacted with within their group, resulting in a degree of segmentation in a group, $s_j < c/b$, thereby reducing (but not eliminating) the within-group fitness disadvantage of the altruists.

Our simulations thus modeled two selection processes operating simultaneously. Within-group individual selection tended to eliminate altruists. Between-group selection favored groups with substantial fractions of altruists. As a result it also favored institutions such as reproductive leveling and segmentation that mitigated the within-group selection processes operating against the altruists. We thus model the coevolution of individual preferences (altruist or not) and societal institutions (the extent of leveling and segmentation).

The initial state was a population without altruists and without leveling or segmentation. In the simulations, altruists introduced by rare mutation proliferated, as did the two group-level institutions: leveling and segmentation. The fraction of the population that were altruists after thousands of generations was higher the more frequent were inter-group conflicts, as expected given that between-group competition is the process favoring the evolution of altruism. Fig. 6 illustrates these results for four treatments.

The set of points labeled "No Institutions" were generated by simulations in which the possibility of segmentation within groups and reproductive leveling were turned off. Under these conditions, the frequency of group conflicts required to support even modest fractions of altruists in the population was substantial.

In the absence of these institutions, in simulations not shown in Fig. 6, the evolution of altruism occurred only if groups were much smaller than is likely to have been the case during the evolution of biologically modern humans, and migration rates were much lower than is empirically likely. But when groups were allowed to adopt reproductive leveling, within-group segmentation, or both, substantial fractions of altruistic alleles evolved for groups of realistic size and migration rates, and for quite modest levels of between-group conflict. Fig. 6 shows, for example, that when conflicts on average occur once every 4 generations (frequency 0.25 per generation) over half of the population are altruists.

These simulations suggest that altruistic behaviors, on the one hand, and reproductive leveling and within-group assortment institutions, on the other, all could have emerged and proliferated in an environment resembling the evolutionary environments of biologically modern humans. Bowles (2006) presents genetic, archaeological and ethnographic evidence that the conditions required for this scenario (that is, satisfying an expanded version of Hamilton's rule) may have obtained in the Late Pleistocene. Included are estimates of the genetic differentiation among hunter-gatherer groups, inter-group migration rates, and the frequency of and mortality rates in between-group warfare among hunter-gatherers. Similar results would follow if we had incorporated in our

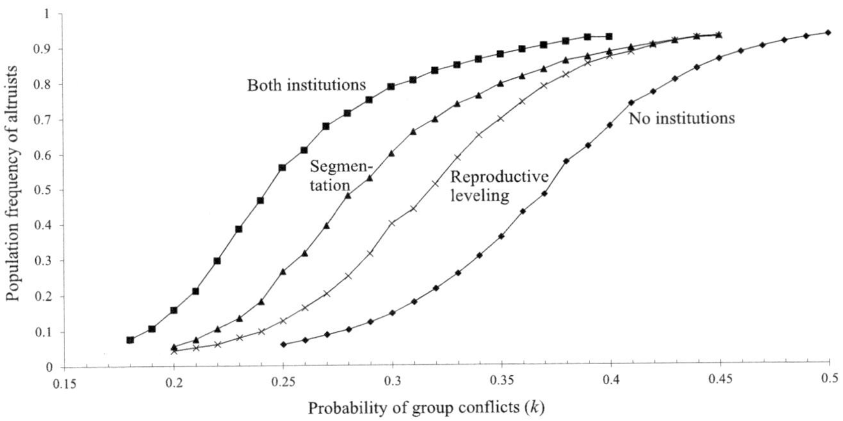

FIGURE 6 The coevolution of group-level institutions and individual altruism. Shown are the population frequencies of altruists for a given probability of group conflict in simulations in which no institutions are permitted to evolve, or reproductive leveling or segmentation alone are permitted, or both. Group-level institutions make it possible for altruistic behavior to evolve even when between-group conflicts are less frequent (Bowles et al., 2003). Each data point is the population share of altruists given the per generation frequency of between-group conflicts, averaged over 10 runs of 50,000 generations each. The horizontal distance between the "No institutions" curve and the other curves indicates the reduction in the frequency of group conflicts that is consistent with sustaining the given level of altruism in the population made possible by group-level institutions indicated by the other curves. The vertical distance between the curves shows the impact of institutions on the fraction of altruists in the population, for a given frequency of between-group conflict. Regarding these vertical comparisons, for infrequent conflict the two institutions – leveling and segmentation – are complements: at $k = 0.2$ for example, we see that the level of altruism sustained by both institutions together is greater than the sum of their separate effects. For greater frequency of conflicts the two institutions are substitutes.

model another empirical feature of our evolutionary past – environmental shocks (which were extraordinary during the Late Pleistocene) – and the advantages of cooperative groups in surviving them.

We have described a process whereby institutions such as within-group segmentation, reproductive leveling and inter-group conflicts provide an environment (niches, in biological terms) in which an individually costly genetically transmitted predisposition to group-beneficial altruistic cooperation may evolve. As we have seen in the simulations, these institutions proliferate across the population because of their contribution to the evolutionary success of altruistic cooperation, which in turn contributes to survival in conflicts with other groups.

The fact that frequent between-group warfare could have supported the evolution of altruistic alleles that contributed to sustaining the cooperation necessary to prevail in warfare is more than ironic; it suggests an unsettling possibility. Suppose that there were an allele that was expressed phenotypically in hostility towards "outsiders," meaning, members of different groups, and a willingness to inflict harm on them. Choi and Bowles (2007) modeled the co-evolution of "parochial altruism" represented by two hypothetical alleles, one for altruism and the other for out-group hostility. Their agent-based model (similar to that just described) shows that though the two alleles were not linked in any way, the simulated populations are overwhelmingly either parochial and altruistic, or neither. Though there is no genetic evidence to this effect, these results raise the possibility that a human genetic predisposition to altruism may have co-evolved with a less admirable predisposition: hostility towards "outsiders."

However, it would be a mistake to conclude that today the institutions that could accomplish the task assigned by Aristotle to his legislators – inculcating good habits in citizens – would replicate the environments that during the Pleistocene may have tipped natural selection in favor of a genetic predisposition for altruism. These included frequent warfare, hostility toward 'outsiders,' segmentation within groups, and limited migration. Our genetic legacy – possibly including parochialism as well as altruism – is not our destiny: *Homo sapiens* is a cultural animal.

We turn, therefore, to the ways that institutions affect the processes of cultural evolution, that is, the social learning by which we acquire and abandon preferences.

4.2 Institutions and the cultural evolution of preferences

A growing literature has explored the process by which institutions affect the cultural evolution of preferences, including important works by Bisin and Verdier (2000); Giuliano and Nunn (2021) and Akerlof and Kranton (2000). Recent reviews are found in Bowles et al. (2021); Nunn (2021), and Persson and Tabellini (2021). Seminal early theoretical works on endogenous preferences are Gintis (1972), Becker (1996), Sunstein (1996), Posner (2000), and Hirschman (1985); recent important additions are Mattauch et al. (2022), Kreps (2023) and Weizsäcker (2024).

In this section, after considering evidence suggesting a surprisingly limited role of parental transmission, we use a model of social learning to show how the process of cultural evolution may be affected by institutions. We present a hybrid model combining the intentional updating and socialization of the young as in Becker (1996) and Bisin and Verdier (2000) with social learning models inspired by population biology, socio-linguistics and anthropology (Boyd and Richerson, 1985; Cavalli-Sforza et al., 1982). In these models learning is an adaptation to one's social environment over the life course and is for the most part unwitting, more like acquiring one's home language or accent than acquiring knowledge or opinions.

The term "cultural inheritance," often understood as the storage and transmission of information, suggests a process similar to cultural artifacts like the family piano being passed on by parents to their offspring. But while parents are involved, cultures as we use the term here – including the distribution of preferences in a population – are not inherited in this sense, they are reproduced or modified daily by contemporary conditions by means of social learning.

4.2.1 *Parental transmission alone could not sustain between-group cultural differences*

Does learning from parents – termed vertical cultural transmission – provide an adequate basis for modeling the evolution of preferences? Food tastes provide a clue. These differ considerably between cultural groups, a major predictor of food likes and dislikes being one's nation or ethnic group of origin. Yet parental tastes are poor predictors of the tastes of adult offspring, even when the tastes of the two parents are themselves congruent. The mean correlation of parents' and adult offspring's tastes for particular foods (black coffee, lima beans, hot sauce, and so on) in the study by Paul Rozin (1991) is 0.17. He calls this the "family paradox" concerning "the sources of variance in preferences. Genetic factors and family influence account for a very small part" (Rozin, 1991, p. 101).

Measures of parent-offspring similarity for most of the traits relevant to the study of culture, too, seem to be quite limited. A meta-study of parent-child transmission of the so-called big five personality traits yields a mean correlation of 0.13 (Loehlin, 2005). Cavalli-Sforza et al. (1982) found parent-offspring correlations of 0.69 for religion and 0.48 for a measure of political values, but much lower correlations for other cultural traits (concerning beliefs, tastes in entertainment, etc.). Stefan Nowak's sample from Poland in the early 1970s (Nowak, 1981) yielded no significant correlation between parents' values and those of their (grown) children excepting religion. Melvin Kohn (1983, p. 3) concluded "that the relationships between parents and children's values are probably only modest in magnitude." Surveying a number of studies, he writes "studies of values have consistently found rather modest levels of agreement – correlations of roughly 0.15 to 0.25 – between parents and children."

In short, the available evidence does not support the inference of strong vertical transmission. We have shown elsewhere (Belloc and Bowles, 2013) that levels of intergenerational transmission implied by parent-offspring correlations of the magnitude cited in the previous paragraph would not sustain cultural differences between groups for more than a couple of generations (even if the groups initially differed sharply, say in food tastes, with one group relying mainly on bread and the other on noodles for carbohydrates).

Because cultural differences in tastes are maintained over long periods of time, much of social learning appears to occur at the societal rather than parental level. This motivates us to include what Boyd and Richerson (1985) term horizontal transmission (from age peers) and oblique transmission (from non-parental elders).

4.2.2 Social learning and the cultural evolution of preferences

To capture societal as well as parental aspects of social learning, we introduce *conformist learning* (Boyd and Richerson, 1985): the likelihood that an individual will adopt a particular behavior varies with the prevalence of that behavior in the population (independently of other influences on learning, such as relative payoffs). Conformist learning could arise if individuals simply sought to adopt what they consider to be the most common behavior. But conformism could also arise because social institutions privilege the most common behaviors in the process of social learning. This would be the case if the cultural models with the greatest exposure were those adhering to the most common behavioral norms, as occurs in most contemporary school systems, in which teachers tend to be drawn disproportionally from larger ethnic groups. (Note that in evolutionary models, conformism is a learning rule by which traits are learned or abandoned, distinct from conformism in psychology, that is, a feeling of discomfort or anxiety when one's beliefs or behaviors differ from those of other members of one's group, or strategic conformism as shown theoretically and experimentally by Dvorak et al. (2024) and Dvorak et al. (2026).)

To model these mechanisms, let there be one of two mutually exclusive traits (x and y) present in each member of a large population. The traits may be adherence to differing behavioral rules, food tastes, or any durable learned behavior that affects payoffs. These could include what economists conventionally term as preferences, including those of interest here, namely the presence or absence of a liberal-democratic value such as valuing personal agency or tolerance of others with different views or religions.

The model below represents behavioral updating as a process of switching from one trait to another. We ask how many copies of each trait are made at the end of each period. (An individual who leaves no copies in the next period has switched to the other trait; one who leaves two copies has retained his trait and been copied by another.) Thus, a constant number of individuals live forever and are simply bearers of the traits; it is the traits themselves that will be more or less successful in generating copies. The number of copies made is termed the cultural fitness of the trait, denoted $f_i, i \in (x, y)$, which is an increasing function of both the relative payoffs and (due to conformist learning) the population frequency of the two types.

The structure of the social learning process is as follows. Individuals implement the strategy dictated by their trait in a game that assigns payoffs to each depending on their own and others' behaviors. Suppose members of the population are randomly paired to interact in a symmetrical two-person game, the payoffs of which are denoted $\pi(i, j)$, i's payoff to playing trait i against a j-playing partner. For any population frequency of the x trait, $p \in [0, 1]$, the expected payoffs are thus

$$\begin{aligned} \pi^x(p) &= p\pi(x, x) + (1 - p)\pi(x, y) \\ \pi^y(p) &= p\pi(y, x) + (1 - p)\pi(y, y) \end{aligned} \tag{7}$$

We normalize the size of the population to unity.

In place of the payoff-monotonic genetic transmission process modeled in Section 4.1, here individuals will update in light of two pieces of information, their payoffs relative to others' and the frequency of the two traits in the population. The degree of conformity $\lambda \in [0, 1)$ measures the importance of the conformist aspect of the learning process relative to the payoff-based influences on updating, with $1 - \lambda$ being the relative importance of payoffs. Let the population frequency of the x-trait for which conformist learning exerts no effect be $\frac{1}{2}$, while for $p > \frac{1}{2}$ the prevalence of the x-trait in the population favors it relative to the y trait in the updating process, independently of the expected payoffs to the traits, which also depend on p. The expected cultural fitness of the two traits, f_x and f_y are then:

$$
\begin{aligned}
f_x &= \lambda(p - \frac{1}{2}) + (1 - \lambda)(\pi^x - \pi^y) \\
f_y &= \lambda(\frac{1}{2} - p) + (1 - \lambda)(\pi^y - \pi^x)
\end{aligned} \tag{8}
$$

Following the play of the game, some fraction of the population, $\omega \in (0, 1]$, may update their trait upon exposure to a "cultural model" (a competitor, a teacher, a coworker, or a neighbor, for example). If paired with a y-type cultural model and $f_x < f_y$, then an x-type will change to a y-type with probability $\beta(f_y - f_x)$; if $f_x \geq f_y$, the individual does not switch. (The adoption coefficient β is a positive constant scaled so that the probability of switching varies over the unit interval). This term in Eq. (9) captures the fact that the greater the cultural fitness difference between the two, the greater is the probability that the one with the lesser fitness will switch. Those who are paired with a cultural model of their own type do not switch. The analogous switching process holds for y-types.

For any distribution of the two traits, p, we know the expected payoffs, the magnitude and sign of the conformist learning effect, and the probabilities of an individual being matched with a cultural model with a different trait. From this information we have the following replicator equation

$$
p' - p \equiv \Delta p = \omega p(1 - p)\beta(f_x - f_y) = \omega p \beta(f_x - \underline{f}) \tag{9}
$$

where $\underline{f}$ is the group average cultural fitness. (Note that Eq. (9) has the same structure as the replicator Eq. (2) that modeled the genetic evolution of an altruistic trait, except that the frequency of unlike types meeting $p(1 - p)$ is here modified by the assumption that only a fraction of the population (ω) update in a given period.)

4.2.3 *Equilibrium preferences: the effects of payoff differences and conformism*

By equilibrium preferences we mean a value of p that is stationary in the replication process just modeled. From Eq. (9) it is clear that $\Delta p = 0$ either if p is 0 or 1 (so there is only one trait to replicate in the population) or if $f_x - f_y = 0$ (neither of the types is advantaged by cultural fitness, or, equivalently, $f_x - \underline{f} = 0$). To see what this latter equality entails, we use Eq. (8), finding that for $f_x - f_y = 0$ we must have that

$$\frac{\lambda(p-\frac{1}{2})}{1-\lambda} = \pi^y(p) - \pi^x(p) \tag{10}$$

When Eq. (10) is satisfied, p is stationary because the effect of conformist transmission (the left-hand side) just offsets the effects of differential payoffs (the right-hand side). Thus, in the presence of conformist transmission, and for $p \in (0, 1)$, the equilibrium payoffs to the trait favored by conformism will always be less than the payoffs of the less prevalent trait. The equilibrium distribution of traits, p^* is shown in Fig. 7.

For $p \in (0, 1)$, Δp takes the sign of $f_x - f_y$. An equilibrium is asymptotically stable if a small displacement away from the equilibrium is self-correcting. This requires that the conformist advantage for x conferred by a small increase in p is more than offset by the payoff advantage conferred on y by the same small increase in p. In Fig. 7, p^* represents the solution to Eq. (10) satisfying these conditions and hence, is an equilibrium distribution of traits that is stable (because the payoff effect line is steeper than the conformist learning effect line).

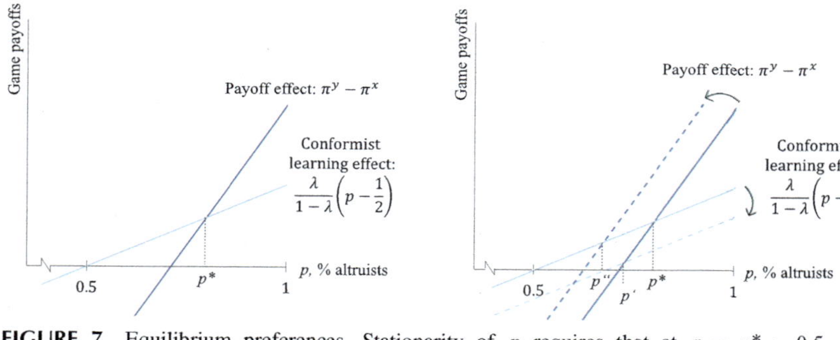

FIGURE 7 Equilibrium preferences. Stationarity of p requires that at $p = p^* > 0.5$, the conformist effect favoring the replication of x be offset by payoff advantages of y. On the left, the solid lines show an initial situation with the equilibrium distribution of preferences given by p^*. On the right, the dashed conformist learning effect (light blue) illustrates a reduction in the extent of conformist learning (relative to payoff based updating) shifting the equilibrium p to p'. The dashed payoff effect line (dark blue) illustrates an exogenous increase in the payoffs of trait y (shifting the equilibrium p to p'').

From Eq. (10) and Fig. 7 we see that conformism has two effects. First, Eq. (10) shows that prevalent strategies that yield low payoffs need not be eliminated: Preferences motivating behaviors that are not best responses defined over the game payoffs may persist in the population. For example, if the x trait were altruism and the game corresponded to the payoffs in Table 1, altruism (despite being a dominated strategy) could persist in the population as long as it was initially prevalent and conformist transmission was substantial.

Second, sufficiently high levels of conformism must violate the conditions for stability, converting p^* from a stable equilibrium to an unstable equilibrium that is the boundary of the two basins of attraction of the asymptotically stable equilibria at $p = 0$ and $p = 1$. Counterintuitively, conformism thus may help explain what is termed a punctuated equilibrium dynamic characterized by long periods of cultural stasis followed (punctuated by) a rapid cultural shift to a new equilibrium. Conformist learning may also account for the long-term survival of individually costly norms (such as smoking) whether group-beneficial or not (examples of the latter are documented by Robert Edgerton (1992) in his book *Sick Societies*).

We have taken the parameters of the cultural dynamic as given. But the social learning processes just described – the relative importance of conformism and payoffs in updating, for example – must have themselves evolved, presumably under the influence of natural selection, cultural group selection, chance and other evolutionary pressures. Taking account of the endogenous nature of the learning process, a plausible model must posit a learning process capable of reproducing itself.

Copying the successful could obviously be a learning rule that would proliferate. Conformist learning could also reproduce itself. There are compelling theoretical reasons to believe that if learning is costly and environmental conditions affecting payoffs sufficiently stable, conformist learning of traits will contribute to the material and reproductive success of individuals and hence might have evolved under the influence of either genetic or cultural transmission (Bowles, 2004; Boyd and Richerson, 1985; Henrich and Boyd, 1998; Miu et al., 2024).

In this section, motivated by the empirical evidence in Section 3, we have modeled the ways that the evolution of preferences may be affected by institutions. As we did for the social learning processes involved, we have for the most part taken the games structuring the interaction of players and its payoffs as given. (The modeling and simulation of within-group reproductive leveling and segmentation – both constituting changes in the game structure – in subsection 4.1.3 is an exception.)

But institutions – the rules of the game governing social interactions – too, evolve, sometimes in response to the actions taken by members of the population reflecting the distribution of preferences among them. The result is a process of coevolution of institutions and preferences. Examples include the emergence of nationalism as a common set of preferences contributing to changes in the structure of political systems, which in turn affected the further evolution of preferences. Another example: changing values concerning relations between men and women resulted in legal and other institutional changes regulating family structure and employment in ways that altered the social learning of preferences.

In the next section we take account of the fact that the distribution of preferences in a population will affect the dynamics of institutional change, the result being the coevolution of preferences and institutions (for a recent survey see Bowles et al. (2021)).

5 The co-evolution of preferences and institutions

Understanding the co-evolution of institutions and preferences is essential for an adequate response to our motivating question: Do liberal-democratic institutions sustain the values they require? Before taking up recent models of the culture-institutions co-evolutionary process, for concreteness we will begin with a historical case: the joint emergence of the modern national state along with a complementary state-friendly civic culture in Europe over the last half millennium.

5.1 The co-evolution of the national state and a civic culture

Eight centuries ago, in what is now Italy, there were more than two hundred distinct city-states. In South Germany, a half-millennium ago, there were sixty-nine free cities in addition to numerous bishoprics, principalities, duchies, and other state-like entities (Brady, 1985). The whole of Europe at that time was governed by about five hundred sovereign bodies.

But by World War I, fewer than thirty states remained. This culling of states not only thinned the number of sovereign bodies, it radically reduced the heterogeneity of forms of governance. A single political form – the national state – emerged, where once had ruled, according to Charles Tilly (1990, p. 5), "[e]mpires, city-states, federations of cities, networks of landlords, churches, religious orders, leagues of pirates, warrior bands, and many other forms of governance." Unlike the competing forms it eclipsed, the national state exhibited a centralized bureaucratic structure maintaining order over a defined territory, with the capacity to raise substantial revenues in the form of taxation and to deploy permanent armed forces. (Here we draw on Bowles (2004) and the works cited there.)

What explains the competitive success of this novel form of rule? The simple answer is that when national states warred with political entities ruled by different forms of governance, they tended to win. And Tilly writes, "No monarch could make war without securing the acquiescence of nearly all of his subject population, and the active cooperation of at least a crucial few" (1990, p. 75). Tilly further comments:

> *"Properly socialized citizens, furthermore, come to attach moral value to the payment of taxes; they monitor themselves and each other, blaming tax evaders as free riders." (p. 89)*

Successful national states assimilated the populations they absorbed, and they promoted and eventually required a common pattern of childhood socialization through schooling that Ernest Gellner describes as "exo-education," that is, childhood socialization by specialists who are not members of one's family or group of close associates (Weber, 1976; Gellner, 1983).

In part as a result of its success in Europe, replicas of the European national state were exported (often at gun point) and flourished throughout the world, displacing competing forms of governance. Under the auspices of the national state and the emerging capitalist economy, European populations grew rapidly – multiplying 15-fold in Britain in the four centuries after 1500, having grown hardly at all over the previous four centuries, and overshadowing population growth elsewhere in the world (except, perhaps, for eighteenth-century China). As a result, the global diffusion of the national state was promoted not only by competitive pressures on the states of the European periphery and beyond, but also by the substantial emigration of bearers of the European cultural traits and military capacities that had favored state-building in Europe.

In sum, the national state evolved because it won wars against populations governed by different institutions, and the ability to win wars depended on its peculiar ability to mobilize military resources including soldiers. This, in turn, was fostered by the diffusion of norms guiding individual behaviors that, while not (at least initially) individually advantageous, contributed to group success in war on the above reasoning. Among these are voluntary tax compliance, and willingness to risk danger in war for a ruler or nation.

Some scholars suggest that the formal prohibition of polygyny may have played a similar, if less obvious, role in securing popular cooperation with the projects of the elite, for example allowing the powerful to recruit others to their projects (including war). While reducing the advantages of the successful and powerful, enforced monogamy and its status as a social norm constraining elite privileges may have contributed to state building, as the evolutionary biologist Richard Alexander (1979) and others suggest. Herlihy and Klapisch-Zuber (1985, p. 157) write: "The great social achievement of the early Middle Ages was the imposition of the same rules of sexual and domestic conduct on both rich and poor."

Of course, national states eventually created legal and cultural environments in which those adhering to the norms that enhanced state war-making capacities suffered little or no material loss by comparison to those rejecting these norms. But the emergence and early diffusion of the national state may have relied critically on significant numbers of people complying with group-advantageous but individually costly norms, that is, acting altruistically.

Another well-documented empirical case of the co-evolution of cultures and institutions is the meteoric spread of Islam in the century following Mohammad's death – by 750 encompassing a broad swath from beyond the Indus River in the East to the Douro River in Spain in the West. This was possible because (according to Levy, 1957, p. 3) the faith in Allah provided "a bond far stronger though more subtle than that of kinship" that facilitated more inclusive systems of taxation and military recruitment and alliance.

Like the spread of Islam along with Islamic law and other institutions, the co-evolution of the European national state and a complementary civic culture required two components. First, the populations governed by the institutions in question survived in competition with other populations; and second, a distribution of preferences providing the behavioral foundations for those institutions was sustained in the population, in competition with alternative values.

With these two examples – Islamic law and the European national state and their associated preferences – we have illustrated how a particular preference-institution configuration won in competition with alternatives (the first condition above) while setting aside the question about within-group dynamics: how did that particular configuration persist in the populations in which it was initially established (the second condition)?

5.2 Modeling a preference-institution equilibrium

A number of recent works have explored the second of these conditions, under which a set of institutions and preferences for a particular population would be complementary, each providing conditions for the existence and sustainability of the other (Besley and Persson, 2019; Acemoglu and Robinson, 2021; Belloc and Bowles, 2017; Bisin and Verdier, 2023, 2024; Mokyr, 2016).

While it is common to model cultural dynamics as a decentralized evolutionary process, institutions are often taken to be imposed (by elites) and taken to be exogenously given until a change (also elite-imposed) occurs. Here we consider both preferences and institutions as evolving through the uncoordinated actions of individuals. In this setting, given some dynamical system representing the evolution of preferences and the rules of the game, we define a preference-institution equilibrium as *a distribution of preferences and a set of rules of the game such that the preferences are stationary given the rules of the game, which are themselves stationary given the distribution of preferences.*

For a case very similar to the historical evidence just described, Besley models the co-evolution of a civic culture in a large population of citizens, on the one hand, and state tax capacities and decisions about expenditures on common interest public goods determined by a political elite, on the other (Besley, 2020). The model provides insights on the "role of civic culture in building an effective fiscal state" and more generally its "historical emergence" and "how civic culture develops in the long run" (pp. 1307-08). Besley motivates this model by "one of the most striking features of twentieth century economic history ... the increase in the capacity of states to raise significant revenues as a share of national income." His model, Besley writes, represents a "complementarity between the strength of institutions and a quasi-voluntary tax compliance" or what we would term the coevolution of institutions and preferences.

For a related case, Tabellini (2008a and 2008b) studies how moral values that sustain cooperation and law enforcement institutions mutually reinforce each other. His model predicts that clan-based societies develop very different value systems than modern societies that rely on the abstract rule of law. While the former are characterized by moral values limited to one's close network, the latter exhibit internalized norms of general morality and cooperation over a large range of situations and interaction partners. He also shows that both limited and generalized morality reinforce the institutions under which they have emerged. An example is the different cultural and institutional trajectories of China and Europe (Greif and Tabellini, 2010).

Building on this work, Acemoglu and Robinson (2021) provide a framework for the interplay between institutions and culture where this is not only a gradually evolving process but can also include discontinuous spontaneous jumps. They also show how cultural configurations support different institutions, for example, how the emergence of democratic governance may depend on the linkages between the cultural attributes hierarchy, obedience and virtue.

These models provide insights on the co-evolution of political institutions and individual preferences, but their key idea – the possible complementarity of institutions and preferences – may be generalized to economic and other institutions. Jenna Bednar and Scott Page (2007), for example, study the kinds of behavioral rules that evolve when players with limited cognitive capacity play differing sets of overlapping games, resulting in cultural differences in the strategies adopted in any particular game. These games could represent interactions at work, within families, and in other non-state settings.

5.3 The co-evolution of contracts and preferences at work

The impact of our daily workplace experiences on how we develop as human beings has been recognized at least since Adam Smith wrote the following about working in the pin factory that he celebrated for the efficiency advantages of the division of labor:

> *"The man whose whole life is spent in performing a few simple operations, of which the effects are perhaps always the same, or very nearly the same, has no occasion to exert his understanding or to exercise his invention in finding out expedients for removing difficulties which never occur. He naturally loses, therefore, the habit of such exertion, and generally becomes as stupid and ignorant as it is possible for a human creature to become. ... Of the great extensive interests of his country he is altogether incapable of judging. ... His dexterity at his own particular trade seems, in this manner, to be acquired at the expense of his intellectual [and] social ... virtues."(Smith, 1937 [1776], p. 735)*

In Section 3.3 we reviewed work by anthropologists, social psychologists and economists, providing evidence that economic institutions, and the structure of work in particular, are social learning environments favoring the evolution of some personality traits, parenting styles and methods of educating the young over others. Here we explore how such effects of economic institutions on preferences may be modeled, along with the corresponding effects of preferences upon the evolution of institutions.

5.3.1 Complementary contracts and preferences

Drawing on Belloc and Bowles (2013), we study the evolutionary dynamics of preferences and institutions in an economy with two classes. These are large subpopulations, each of whose z members are paired randomly to interact with a member of the other class in a non-cooperative game governed by a set of institutions. The two classes may be workers and employers, sharecropping farmers and landlords, enslaved laborers and their owners, independent farmers and government officials, and so on.

As these examples suggest, these class relationships are asymmetric. The alternative economic institutions governing relations between the classes are one of two contracts. These regulate the work activities and income of the first class, the A's who are workers, or sharecroppers, for example. The two contracts are implemented by the members of the second class, the B's – the employers or landlords. The first class may adopt either of two alternative preferences (including social norms). The A's are agents and the B's are principals; agents perform some task (the amount or quality of work performed for example) that is essential to the objectives of the principal but that cannot be fully enforced by the principal due to the incomplete nature of the contract regulating their interactions.

To represent the complementarity between preferences and institutions, some contract-norms matches are more productive than others and can be Pareto-ranked. For concreteness, think of a somewhat idealized rendition of the institutional structure and preferences of workers in two firms, called: "Fiat" and "Volkswagen" (Jürgens, 2002; Nuti, 2011). In the former, a top-down management structure is matched with an oppositional workers' culture, the resulting frequent conflicts entailing reduced productivity. In the latter, an institutional structure based on rent-sharing and co-management matches with a work force that has adopted norms of cooperation with the management, resulting in high levels of productivity and, as a result, mutual gains.

What is important in this model is not only that the idealized Volkswagen match Pareto-dominates the Fiat match, but that the two matches are best responses for owners and workers alike. Given the oppositional preferences of Fiat's workers, the owners would do even worse if they implemented a co-management structure. Correspondingly, a militant oppositional culture would not benefit Volkswagen's workers given their employers' openness to cooperation and gain-sharing. These preference-institution complementarities are the basis of the sustainability of the contrasting suites of institutions and culture represented here by "Fiat" and "VW" and modeled in our Fiat-VW game.

Institutional differences in this model are captured by the two contracts, which reflect the core aspects of a firm's organizational structure and, hence, define the firm type. The two contracts differ in the degree of gain-sharing between employer and worker. In the fixed-wage contract denoted 0, the employer is the sole residual claimant, while the worker is paid a fixed wage and works under close supervision by the employer (as in some traditional manufacturing). In the partnership contract denoted 1, workers are motivated by gain-sharing with the employer, based on joint residual claimancy, as is the case in many legal practices, financial consulting, and in open-source software production and worker-owned cooperatives. (These two contracts are similar to what emerged endogenously in experiments reported in Bartling et al. (2012): a "control strategy" and a "trust strategy" with respectively "bad jobs with low discretion, low wages and little rent-sharing" and "good jobs with high discretion, high wages, and substantial rent-sharing" (p. 834).)

Preference differences matter for employers because a given set of preferences may have different effects on productivity depending on the nature of the incentives and constraints that are implemented by the contract. Thus, while some workers are self-regarding and extrinsically motivated (preferences 0), other workers care about the form of the contract under which they work *per se*, that is, in addition to the material payoffs they care about how they are treated by their employer (preferences 1). For these individuals, close supervision and threats of sanctions for non-compliance signal the employer's distrust or otherwise offend their reciprocal or other social preferences that are essential to mutually beneficial exchange, as has been found in a large number of observational and experimental studies (Bewley, 1999; Fehr et al., 2007; Falk and Kosfeld, 2006; Houser et al., 2008; Fehr and Rockenbach, 2003; Ziegelmeyer et al., 2012; Schmelz et al., 2026). Under the fixed wage contract, therefore, reciprocal workers will be worse off than selfish types who care only about their pay, and as a result they will work less than the selfish types.

Workers periodically quit or are terminated by their employer and seek an alternative employment match from the available pool of job vacancies, while employers likewise recruit a replacement worker from the pool of those available. This setup means that workers will be better off if they adopt reciprocity as a preference if most employers are offering cooperative contracts and, correspondingly, employers will profit by offering a cooperative contract if most workers are reciprocity minded. So the [1,1] contract-preference match in a population of mostly cooperative employers and mostly reciprocal workers could be a stationary state in the preference-institution co-evolutionary dynamic that we describe in the next section. For analogous reasons, a population of employers mostly offering the fixed wage contract to a population of workers most of whom are self-regarding could be a stationary state. Both of these stationary states constitute preference-institution equilibria as just defined in Section 5.2.

5.3.2 The coevolution of contracts and preferences

To explore the evolutionary dynamics in this two-class population, we need to know how their expected payoffs depend on the composition of the population and the type they adopt (that is, contracts implemented by employers and preferences adopted by workers). Their own type is indexed by j and the type with which they are paired by k, both $\in (0, 1)$ and classes by $i \in (A, B)$, with payoffs expressed as $\pi^i(j, k)$ so that, for example, $\pi^A(1, 0)$ is the payoff to a worker (A) of having adopted reciprocal preferences ($j = 1$) if paired with an employer offering a fixed wage contract ($k = 0$). The payoffs to the four possible preference-institutional matches are for both workers and employers $\pi^i(1, 1) > \pi^i(0, 0) > \pi^i(0, 1) = \pi^i(1, 0) = 0$ so that payoffs to the two "mismatches" are normalized to zero. We assume random pairing and a large population, so that the probability that a member of class i is matched with a type 1 of the other class is just ϕ_{-i}.

Expected payoffs for members of class i implementing contract j (or adopting preference j) are thus given by

$$v^i_j = (1 - \phi_{-i})\pi^i(j, 0) + \phi_{-i}\pi^i(j, 1) \tag{11}$$

so that, for example the expected payoff to a worker adopting reciprocal (that is type 1) preferences is

$$v^A_1 = (1 - \phi_{-i})\pi^i(1, 0) + \phi_{-i}\pi^i(1, 1) \tag{12}$$

Here, we capture the idea that actors update by switching to the type that would have been a best response in the recent past (termed myopic best response), where ϕ_{-i} denotes the fraction of individuals in the other class who implemented contract 1 (adopted preference 1) in the previous period. Expected payoffs for the members of the two classes when interacting with the other class are shown in Fig. 8.

The state space for this process (shown in Fig. 9) is all possible combinations of the number of individuals in the two classes, respectively, adopting preference 1 and implementing contract 1, $(z\phi^*_A, z\phi^*_B)$. The two matches with nonzero payoffs are Pareto-ranked Nash equilibria. In the Markov process that represents this model, the states in which all members of both classes adopt one or the other of these two profiles (denoted $\{0, 0\}$ and $\{z, z\}$) are evolutionarily stable preference-institution equilibria (technically, absorbing states) when all individuals best respond.

As in the models in Section 4.2, following matching, members of each class have the opportunity to update their contracts and preferences in such a way that contracts or preferences with higher average payoffs in the previous period tend to be adopted. This means that for any composition of the population (point in the state space) Eq. (11) gives us the expected payoffs of the two types and hence the expected change in the population composition in the next period.

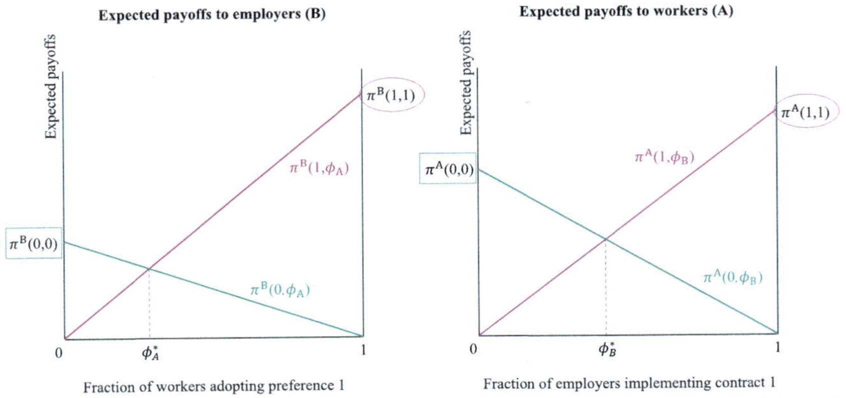

FIGURE 8 Expected payoffs to employers and workers in the Fiat-VW game. In the left panel, expected payoffs to employers who offer the gain sharing contract 1, $\pi^B(1, \phi_A)$, are increasing in the fraction of workers that have adopted reciprocity 1 as a preference. The right panel analogously shows that expected payoffs for workers from adopting reciprocity preferences are increasing in the fraction of employers implementing gain sharing contracts. The payoffs in the Pareto superior ("VW") and inferior ("Fiat") institution-preference matches are indicated by the circles and squares respectively.

Let the updating process be asynchronous (as in Binmore et al., 2003) with all members of one class updating first, followed by updating by the other class. When updating their contracts and preferences, best responding individuals maximize their expected payoffs based on the distribution of, respectively, preferences and contracts in the sub-population with which they were matched in the previous period.

But individuals are boundedly rational and even in the absence of cognitive failures they may deviate from a best response for reasons that are not in the model, for example hostility to the current institutions or culture and an attempt to disrupt the status quo. Thus in the updating process they occasionally adopt the preferences or contracts that are not a best response.

The probability of deviating from the best response (called idiosyncratic play) is strictly decreasing in both the expected cost of deviating from the best response and a parameter β that measures the degree to which employers and workers maximize their expected payoffs when updating. (If $\beta = 0$ individuals randomize when updating, if $\beta = \infty$ they always best respond.) For substantial values of β, once a population is close to either of the two preference-institution equilibria (0, 0 and z, z), the associated convention is likely to persist over very long periods.

The reason is that, for a large population and sufficiently best-responding individuals, and with a modest rate of idiosyncratic play, the expected waiting time for a realization of sufficient non-best responses to tip the process from the neighborhood of one convention to the basin of attraction of the other will be very prolonged. In this model, cultural-institutional equilibria are perpetuated in

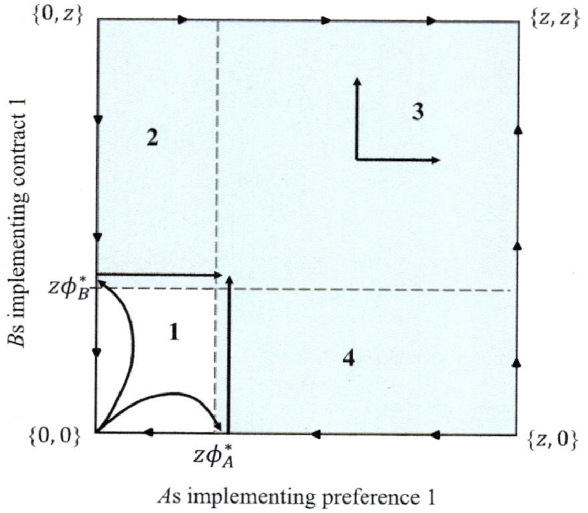

FIGURE 9 The preference-institutions state space and possible transitions. A point in the figure gives the numbers of employers (B's) and workers (A's) adopting the gain sharing contract and reciprocal preferences, respectively. The arrows in quadrant 3 illustrate the dynamics of this system. From the left panel of Fig. 8 we know that if $z\phi_A > z\phi_A^*$, B's expected payoffs would be maximized by implementing contract 1, so some employers would shift to the gain sharing contract. Correspondingly, if $z\phi_B > z\phi_B^*$, some workers would shift from self-interest to reciprocal preferences. The curved arrows in the lower left indicate two possible paths from the {0,0} preference-institution equilibrium ("Fiat") to the {z,z} equilibrium ("VW"), induced by the idiosyncratic play (i.e., deviating from the best response) of the workers (the curved arrow to the right) or the employers (the upwards curved arrow). Once outside of region 1, the dynamic will take the population to the "VW" institution-preference equilibrium $\{z, z\}$.

every period; inertia or "traditions" are not the reason, as individuals have just a single-period memory (when they update they consult only the distribution of play in the previous period).

The model formalizes what we mean by the sustainability of sets of preferences and institutions; and it also provides a framework for studying the decentralized dynamics by which transitions may occur. In the historical or contemporary settings which this model is designed to illuminate, idiosyncratic play is often coordinated and intentional. For example, families or entire lineages may update together reducing the effective number of independent actors and speeding up the expected waiting times to a transition. Strikes or other collective forms of resistance to the status quo have the same effect (see, for example, Wood, 2003; Bowles, 2004).

5.3.3 *The organization of work and the evolution of social preferences*

In this model, the convention with hierarchical work relationships and self-regarding workers could endure, even though the same populations of workers and employers (had their history been different) could sustain more cooperative and other-regarding interactions, also indefinitely. In other words, the difference between "Fiat" and "VW" may not be some intrinsic difference between "Italians" and "Germans" but instead the recent history of these populations of employers and workers.

Recalling the evidence presented in Sections 3.3.1 and 3.3.2, a more complete model of this process would take account of how alternative institutions governing the process of production may affect parents' and schools' socialization of children. This would suggest that hierarchical relationships at work might favor the evolution of what Schumpeter (1950, p. 448) termed "those habits of super- and subordination that are ... essential for the efficient working of the institutionalized leadership" of the conventional capitalist firm. In our terminology this would mean obedient rule followers rather than the autonomous and independent citizens posited as the ideal citizens of a liberal democracy.

Exactly this concern is raised by the assessment of one of the late 20th century's pre-eminent theorists of democratic politics, Robert Dahl. In a piece entitled "On removing certain impediments to democracy in the United States," he wrote:

> *"because the internal government of the corporation was not itself democratic but hierarchical and often despotic, the rapid expansion of this revolutionary form of economic enterprise meant that an increasing proportion of the demos would live out their working lives, and most of their daily existence, not within a democratic system but instead within a hierarchical structure of subordination." (Dahl, 1977, p. 8)*

With Kohn's and Wu and Paluck's accounts of the effect of hierarchical relationships at work cultivating values of independence and obedience in mind, Dahl's observation returns us to the question in the title of our essay "Do liberal-democratic institutions sustain the values they require?"

6 What have we learned and what do we need to learn?

We do not have a complete answer to the question. We have provided reasoning and evidence that institutions shape the evolution of preferences, including what we have called liberal-democratic values; and we have introduced models of this process.

We will close by raising some fundamental theoretical questions on the challenges of institutional design that were initially raised by the classical founders of economics. We suggest some revisions of the way we do economics that would better equip us for the task Aristotle set for his "legislators," namely designing institutions that would inculcate citizens' "good habits" or as Besley put it create "better people," to facilitate the workings and sustainability of "good" institutions. We will also point to gaps in the existing empirical and theoretical literature that suggest fruitful areas for new research.

But before doing this, we want to dispel the reader's suspicion that this task might be entirely our own utopian invention, one that no actual policy maker or constitution writer would ever take up. Our counter-example is one in which Aristotle himself may have participated, and it holds some lessons for economists today.

6.1 Mechanism design with endogenous preferences in Aristotle's Athens

When the Athenian citizens' assembly decided in 325 BCE to set up a colony and naval station in the Adriatic, far to the north and west of Greece, they took on an enormous project requiring thousands of people and 289 ships (Ober, 2008; Christ, 1990). And they had little time to spare: the window for safe navigation around the Peloponnesus would close in a matter of weeks. Neither the personnel nor the ships were at the moment under public orders; the settlers, oarsmen, navigators, and soldiers would have to be recruited from their private lives, and the ships outfitted for the mission (some would carry horses, since cavalry were involved). We know how they accomplished this because the assembly's decree was preserved. (Though Aristotle died three years after the Adriatic mission began, we have no evidence that he participated in the design of the campaign to mobilize resources for it.)

Trierarchs (ship commanders and equippers), appointed from among Athens's wealthy, were required to bring a fully outfitted ship to the docks at Piraeus by a given date. Those who felt unjustly burdened could appeal their assignment (called a liturgy). They would do this by challenging some other (also presumably wealthy) individual who had not been assigned a liturgy to either take on their liturgy, or else to exchange with the challenger all their real and personal property holdings. If the target of the challenge refused to do either, then a popular jury would determine which man's estate was the larger and should therefore bear the costs of the liturgy. By allowing citizens to use private information about their own and their neighbors' wealth to mitigate injustices in the assignment of the liturgy, this ingenious provision limited opposition to the provisioning of the mission.

The decree continues that the assembly would honor the "first [trierarch] to bring his ship [to Piraeus] with a crown of 500 drachmas and the second with a crown of 300 dr[achma]s and the third with a crown of 200 dr[achma]s," adding that "the herald of the Council [of 500] is to announce the crowns at the contest of the Thargelia [a festival] ... in order that the competitive zeal ... of the trierarchs towards the demos may be evident." The daily wage for a skilled worker at the time was about one drachma, so these were substantial rewards, even though they represented a tiny fraction of the total cost of executing a liturgy. Others contributing to the timely dispatch of the mission would be honored in similar style.

Lest there be any doubt about the elevated purpose served by these incentives, the decree spelled out the expected benefits of the Adriatic naval base: the Athenian people "may for all future time have its own commerce and transport in grain" as well as a "guard against the Tyrrhenians" (Etruscan pirates).

And for those unmoved by honors and rewards, there was a warning: "But if anyone to whom each of these things has been commanded does not do them in accordance with this decree, whether he be a magistrate or a private individual, the man that does not do so is to be fined 10,000 dr[achma]s," with the proceeds going to honor Athena. (The winners of prizes for the timely arrival of the ships at Piraeus most likely would have given their prizes as offerings to Athena, too.) The "crowns" such as those promised to the first trierarch who outfitted a ship were treated as prizes, not a fee for service. Their moral exhortations and monetary incentives were designed to be complements, not substitutes, the effect of each being enhanced by the presence of the other.

Collectively, the Athenian polis was an accomplished mechanism designer, recognizing that both the effectiveness of public policy and the sustainability of their concept of a good society would require taking account of the endogenous nature of social preferences. Their recruitment strategies for the Adriatic campaign seem designed to sustain what we would now call trust in government and to avoid the adverse effects of incentives and constraints that might otherwise have crowded out the citizens' willingness to contribute to the public good.

Are there possible insights that might arise from research into other deliberate attempts at the societal level to cultivate civic virtues, as in the religious and secular utopian communities of the 19th century (some of them continuing to the present)? Are there ways of empirically assessing Elinor Ostrom's (2000) caution that laws may "crowd out citizenship", as might be inferred from the work of Sara Lowes et al. (2017) on the Kuba Kingdom in Central Africa? How could we further explore Michael Taylor's conjecture that rather than seeing the autocratic Hobbesian state as a necessary response to the nature of Hobbesian man, we should consider Hobbes' Leviathan, instead, as the creator of Hobbesian man (Taylor, 1987)?

6.2 Possible implications for economics

Beyond the Athenians' evident skill in implementing a social learning environment that would "inculcate good habits," we think their design of the Adriatic campaign suggests two lessons which we mention in closing, recognizing that both raise difficult challenges that reach beyond the scope of this paper. The first is that we need to modify the Nash equilibrium as the workhorse concept of mechanism design. The second is that at least for public policy design and perhaps more broadly, we should reconsider the foundational liberal normative concept of preference neutrality.

6.2.1 Aristotelian mechanism design based on an augmented Nash equilibrium concept

The standard model of policy design in economics is that the designer implements a desired outcome by altering some aspects of the citizens' decision making environment – by means of altered incentives or constraints – so that the desired outcome is a Nash equilibrium. This, recall, is a strategy profile such that no individual acting alone could do better by implementing a different strategy, given the strategies adopted by others. Responding to John von Neumann's objection that people are not really all that uncooperative, Nash called it "the American way." (We learned this from the late Martin Shubik, Von Neumann's student.)

The Nash equilibrium is central to mechanism design because to succeed, the policy maker must displace the status quo in favor of an alternative outcome that will not only be implemented, but also persist given the preferences and resulting behaviors of the target citizens. In other words, to be implementable by the policy maker and to persist, the alternative outcome must be a Nash equilibrium. But to persist, the citizens' preferences motivating the behaviors that implement the designer's desired outcome must themselves be stationary.

The first lesson for economics that we draw from the evidence and models we have reviewed is that in thinking about the design of public policies and institutions, we need a revision of the Nash equilibrium concept to take account of how preferences are formed, and of the resulting impact of policy on preferences. We term this an *augmented Nash equilibrium*, and define it as a strategy profile and a set of beliefs and preferences all of which are stationary in the dynamical system describing the evolution of preferences and beliefs.

The key idea is not new. Bentham's plea that punishments should be designed as moral lessons as explained in Section 2 is an example. Many more recent works have taken up the idea that policy design could be enhanced by recognizing the endogenous nature of preferences (Kreps, 2023; Bowles, 2016; Ostrom, 2000; Besley, 2020; Nyborg et al., 2016; Posner, 2000).

A modern analogy to our augmented Nash equilibrium is suggested by the Lucas critique, concerning endogenous beliefs rather than preferences. Robert Lucas observed that taxes and other government interventions in the private economy affect not only the costs and benefits of actions citizens may take (as intended), but also their beliefs about the future actions of others (including the government), possibly in counter-productive ways. For example, announcing stiffer penalties for nonpayment of taxes provides an incentive to pay up, but it also may convey the information that non-compliance is common, leading otherwise honest citizens to cheat.

Lucas' point was that introducing a new economic policy is not simply re-calibrating a given model of how the economy works, but rather a structural change of the model itself (Lucas, 1976). Henry Aaron (1994) subsequently pointed to "the failure of economists to take the formation of preferences seriously," and went on to suggest that the Lucas critique be extended to cover preferences as well as beliefs.

By way of illustration, the two preference-institution equilibria in the Fiat and VW model in Section 5.3.2 are augmented Nash equilibria (the two stationary states [0,0] and $[z, z]$ in Fig. 9). This is because: *(i)* given the distribution of employer strategies in the population and given the preference updating model, the distribution of preferences in the population will not change, and correspondingly, *(ii)* given the distribution of preferences among workers and the model describing how employers update the contracts they offer, the distribution of contracts will not change. As a result, workers' and employers' beliefs about the distribution of contracts and workers' preferences respectively will not change.

The augmented Nash equilibrium provides an essential addition to the mechanism designer's or policy maker's toolkit. Notice that it accommodates not only endogenous preferences resulting from the learning processes modeled here, but also the effect that policies may have on preferences via the way that they frame a citizen's decision situation. The Athenians' framing the reward to the first trierarch to provide a fully equipped ship as a prize rather than a payment for service is an example.

A modern illustration of the challenge to policy design due to policy affecting preferences is evidence that policies seeking to modify individual behavior, if mandated rather than voluntary, may induce control averse responses. This is true even among those who fully agree with the behavioral change in the absence of a mandate, for example, adopting green lifestyle changes like reducing meat consumption or car use, and getting vaccination or other practices to address the covid pandemic (Schmelz, 2021; Schmelz and Bowles, 2021, 2022, 2026).

Taking account of the endogenous nature of preferences as well as beliefs is the key element in what we call *Aristotelian mechanism design*. This approach would be greatly enhanced by empirical studies identifying the extent and processes by which the incentives or constraints that a policy maker implements may affect preferences. Especially important would be to find ways of identifying elements of policy design such that incentives or constraints by which a policy is implemented would be complements to pre-existing ethical or other-regarding preferences – enhancing their contribution to addressing societal challenges – rather than substitutes, that is, crowding out social preferences.

Our models also show how a policy maker may engage in equilibrium selection in an environment with more than one preference-institution equilibrium. For example, returning again to the model of the co-evolution of contracts and preferences (Section 5.3), a one-time subsidy that induced employers to offer cooperative rent-sharing contracts in sufficient numbers to displace the population into the basin of attraction of the [1,1] cultural-institutional equilibrium would induce a shift to the Pareto superior convention, which would then be stationary in the absence of the subsidy. Important reference points for research in this area are the many works by economists, psychologists, and jurists addressing the challenge of climate policy design in cases where the extent of green preferences is endogenous (Truelove et al., 2014; Nyborg et al., 2016; Posner, 2000; Mattauch et al., 2022).

Critical advances in the underlying theory of cultural evolution would include going beyond learning from parents, which as we have shown may play a more modest role than is commonly thought. These advances should include modeling the influence of societal structures such as workplaces, markets, schools, and the state. Second, a priority would be to develop more empirically grounded models of the preference learning process itself to include some combination of forward-looking expected utility maximization common to classical game theory along with the backward looking and myopic best response approaches used here and in evolutionary game theory (Blume, 2003). Third, another bridge between classical and evolutionary game theory would be to develop models that incorporate both top-down aspects of leadership and imposition of learning environments in hierarchical settings, and the radically decentralized bottom-up approach of most evolutionary models (Acemoglu and Jackson, 2015). Finally, evolutionary dynamics depend critically on some people occasionally not best responding to the payoff structure of the game as modeled. Learning more about deviations from best response by treating them as intentional rather than mutation-like would be a valuable advance (Naidu et al., 2010; Bowles, 2004; Wood, 2003).

6.2.2 *Why it matters: liberal neutrality and the sustainability of liberal democracy*

We would be better able to exploit these opportunities for improved public policy and institutional design were we to do two things. On empirical grounds, the first would be to abandon the assumption that the actors in our models are invariably amoral and self-regarding. On normative grounds, the second would be to reconsider the principle of liberal neutrality on preferences, and instead, to recognize the value of cultivating the preferences required to sustain liberal-democratic institutions.

The idea that a constitution for knaves might actually work served as a device accommodating the liberal antipathy to public policies that promote any particular set of preferences. We do not dismiss this antipathy; nor are we unaware of the historical cases of authoritarian preference manipulation that motivate it (one of your authors was brought up under Communist Party rule). But we think the evidence and reasoning presented here raises the disturbing possibility that liberal neutrality on preferences could endanger the sustainability of liberal-democratic institutions.

Experimental evidence that other-regarding and ethical motives are common greatly expands the space of feasible policy interventions and institutional innovation. We clearly need an alternative to Hume's constitution for knaves.

But while modern economics provides a pretty well developed understanding of how an economy based entirely on amoral self-interest would function, we do not yet have a good idea of how an economy of knaves, saints, and zealots would work. Nor do we understand how a sustainable constitution for such a population would influence not only the quality of governance, but also the evolution over time of the proportion of these types making up the *dramatis personae* of our social life. Considered dynamically in this way and taking account of the dark side of other-regarding preferences – intolerance of "outsiders," for example – the challenge of good governance is far more difficult than heeding Hume's dictum. Some social preferences may be more difficult than self-interest to channel into socially valued or at least harmless ends.

For the liberal-democratic policy maker or mechanism designer the values of tolerance, generosity, fair-mindedness, autonomy, and a predisposition to cooperate with others are essential but fragile resources, which may be either empowered by legislation and public policy or diminished. This suggests an extension of Hume's dictum about knaves: good policies and constitutions are those that support socially valued ends not only by harnessing self-interest, but also by evoking, cultivating, and empowering the civic values and other social preferences essential to the effectiveness of public policy and the sustainability of societal institutions.

We do not yet know how to do this, but a sustainable liberal and democratic future may depend on figuring it out.

References

Aaron, Henry J., 1994. Distinguished lecture on economics in government: public policy, values, and consciousness. The Journal of Economic Perspectives 8 (2), 3–21.

Acemoglu, Daron, Jackson, Matthew O., 2015. History, expectations, and leadership in the evolution of social norms. The Review of Economic Studies 82 (2), 423–456.

Acemoglu, Daron, Robinson, James A., 2021. Culture, institutions and social equilibria: a framework. Discussion paper.

Akerlof, George A., Kranton, Rachel E., 2000. Economics and identity. The Quarterly Journal of Economics 115 (3), 715–753.

Alexander, R.D., 1979. Darwinism and Human Affairs. University of Washington Press, Seattle.

Almond, Gabriel Abraham, Verba, Sidney, 1963. The Civic Culture: Political Attitudes and Democracy in Five Nations. Princeton University Press, Princeton, New Jersey.

Andreoni, James, Miller, John, 2002. Giving according to GARP: an experimental test of the consistency of preferences for altruism. Econometrica 70 (2), 737–753.

Aristotle, 1962 [335–322 BCE]. Nicomachean Ethics. Bobbs-Merrill, Indianapolis.

Arrow, Kenneth J., 1971. Political and Economic Evaluation of Social Effects and Externalities. In: Frontiers of Quantitative Economics. North Holland, Amsterdam, pp. 3–23.

Barry, H. III, Child, I.L., Bacon, M.K., 1959. Relation of child training to subsistence economy. American Anthropologist 61 (1), 51–63.

Bartling, Björn, Fehr, Ernst, Schmidt, Klaus M., 2012. Screening, competition, and job design: economic origins of good jobs. American Economic Review 102 (2), 834–864.

Becker, Gary Stanley, 1996. Accounting for Tastes. Harvard University Press, Cambridge, MA.

Becker, S.O., Boeckh, K., Hainz, C., Woessmann, L., 2016. The empire is dead, long live the empire! Long-run persistence of trust and corruption in the bureaucracy. Economic Journal 126 (590), 40–74.

Bednar, J., Page, S., 2007. Can game(s) theory explain culture? The emergence of cultural behavior within multiple games. Rationality and Society 19 (1), 65–97.
Bell, Daniel, 1976. The Cultural Contradictions of Capitalism. Basic Books, New York.
Belloc, M., Bowles, S., 2013. The persistence of inferior cultural-institutional conventions. American Economic Review 103 (3), 93–98.
Belloc, M., Bowles, S., 2017. Persistence and change in culture and institutions under autarchy, trade, and factor mobility. American Economic Journal. Microeconomics 9 (4), 245–276.
Bentham, Jeremy, 1970 [1789]. An Introduction to the Principles of Morals and Legislation. Athlone Press.
Bentham, Jeremy, Bowring, John, 1962. The Works of Jeremy Bentham. Russell & Russell, New York.
Berkowitz, Peter, 1999. Virtue and the Making of Modern Liberalism. Princeton University Press, Princeton.
Besley, T., 2013. What's the good of the market: an essay on Michael Sandel's what money can't buy. Journal of Economic Literature 51 (2), 478–495.
Besley, Timothy, 2020. State capacity, reciprocity, and the social contract. Econometrica 88 (4), 1307–1335.
Besley, Timothy, Persson, Torsten, 2019. Democratic values and institutions. American Economic Review: Insights 1 (1), 59–76.
Bewley, Truman F., 1999. Why Wages Don't Fall During a Recession. Harvard University Press, Cambridge.
Binmore, Ken, Samuelson, Larry, Young, H. Peyton, 2003. Equilibrium selection in bargaining models. Games and Economic Behavior 45, 296–328.
Bisin, A., Verdier, T., 2000. "Beyond the melting pot": cultural transmission, marriage, and the evolution of ethnic and religious traits. The Quarterly Journal of Economics 115 (3), 955–988.
Bisin, Alberto, Verdier, Thierry, 2023. Advances in the economic theory of cultural transmission. Annual Review of Economics 15 (1), 63–89.
Bisin, A., Verdier, T., 2024. On the joint evolution of culture and political institutions: elites and civil society. Journal of Political Economy.
Blume, Lawrence E., 2003. How noise matters. Games and Economic Behavior 44, 251–271.
Bowles, Samuel, 1998. Endogenous preferences: the cultural consequences of markets and other economic institutions. Journal of Economic Literature 36 (1), 75–111.
Bowles, Samuel, 2000. Economic institutions as ecological niches. Behavioral and Brain Sciences 23 (1), 148–149.
Bowles, Samuel, 2004. Microeconomics: Behavior, Institutions, and Evolution. Princeton University Press, Princeton.
Bowles, Samuel, 2006. Group competition, reproductive leveling and the evolution of human altruism. Science 314, 1569–1572.
Bowles, Samuel, 2011. Is liberal society a parasite on tradition? Philosophy & Public Affairs 39 (1), 46–81.
Bowles, Samuel, 2016. The Moral Economy: Why Good Incentives Are No Substitute for Good Citizens. Yale University Press.
Bowles, Samuel, Choi, Jung-Kyoo, Hopfensitz, Astrid, 2003. The coevolution of individual behaviors and group level institutions. Journal of Theoretical Biology 223 (2), 135–147.
Bowles, Samuel, Choi, Jung-Kyoo, Hwang, Sung-Ha, Naidu, Suresh, 2021. How institutions and cultures change: an evolutionary perspective. In: Bisin, Alberto, Federico, Giovanni (Eds.), The Handbook of Historical Economics. Elsevier, pp. 391–433. Chap. 13.
Bowles, Samuel, Gintis, Herbert, 1976. Schooling in Capitalist America: Educational Reform and the Contradictions of Economic Life. Basic Books, New York.
Bowles, Samuel, Gintis, Herbert, 2011. A Cooperative Species: Human Reciprocity and Its Evolution. Princeton University Press, Princeton.
Bowles, Samuel, Polanía-Reyes, Sandra, 2012. Economic incentives and social preferences: substitutes or complements? Journal of Economic Literature 50 (2), 368–425.

Boyd, Robert, Richerson, Peter J., 1985. Culture and the Evolutionary Process. University of Chicago Press, Chicago, IL.

Brady, Thomas A., 1985. Turning Swiss: Cities and Empire, 1450-1550. Cambridge University Press, Cambridge.

Burke, Edmund, 1890 [1790]. Reflections on the Revolution in France. Macmillan, New York.

Caprettini, Bruno, Voth, Hans-Joachim, 2023. New deal, new patriots: how 1930s government spending boosted patriotism during World War II. The Quarterly Journal of Economics 138 (1), 465–513.

Cavalli-Sforza, Luigi Luca, Feldman, Marcus W., Chen, Kuang-Ho, Dornbusch, Sanford M., 1982. Theory and observation in cultural transmission. Science 218 (4567), 19–27.

Chatterjee, K., 1982. Incentive compatibility in bargaining under uncertainty. The Quarterly Journal of Economics 97 (4), 717–726.

Choi, Jung-Kyoo, Bowles, Samuel, 2007. The coevolution of parochial altruism and war. Science 318 (5850), 636–640.

Christ, Matthew, 1990. Liturgy avoidance and antidosis in classical Athens. Transactions of the American Philological Association 120, 147–169.

Confucius, 2007 [475–221 BCE]. The Analects of Confucius. Columbia University Press, New York.

Dahl, Robert A., 1977. On removing certain impediments to democracy in the United States. Political Science Quarterly 92 (1), 1–20.

De Tocqueville, Alexis, 1945 [1830]. Democracy in America. Vintage.

Debreu, Gerard, 1984. La superiorite du liberalisme est mathématiquement demontree. Le Figaro 10, 80.

Durham, William H., 1991. Coevolution: Genes, Culture, and Human Diversity. Stanford University Press, Stanford.

Dvorak, Fabian, Fischbacher, Urs, Sator, Georg, Schmelz, Katrin, 2026. Public moral agreement can overstate shared values: intrinsic and strategic conformity. Available at SSRN: https://papers.ssrn.com/abstract=7161240.

Dvorak, Fabian, Fischbacher, Urs, Schmelz, Katrin, 2024. Strategic conformity or anticonformity to avoid punishment and attract reward. The Economic Journal.

Dworkin, Ronald, 1985. A Matter of Principle. Harvard University Press, Cambridge.

Edgerton, Robert B., 1992. Sick Societies: Challenging the Myth of Primitive Harmony. The Free Press, New York.

Edwards, Richard C., 1976. Individual traits and organizational incentives: what makes a "good" worker? The Journal of Human Resources, 51–68.

Edwards, Richard C., 1977. Personal traits and 'success' in schooling and work. Educational and Psychological Measurement 37, 125–138.

Enke, Benjamin, 2019. Kinship, cooperation, and the evolution of moral systems. The Quarterly Journal of Economics 134 (2), 953–1019.

Enke, Benjamin, 2023. Market exposure and human morality. Nature Human Behaviour 7 (1), 134–141.

Eshel, I., Cavalli-Sforza, L.L., 1982. Assortment of encounters and evolution of cooperativeness. Proceedings of the National Academy of Sciences of the United States of America 79, 1331–1335.

Falk, Armin, Becker, Anke, Dohmen, Thomas, Enke, Benjamin, Huffman, David, Sunde, Uwe, 2018. Global evidence on economic preferences. The Quarterly Journal of Economics 133 (4), 1645–1692.

Falk, Armin, Kosfeld, Michael, 2006. The hidden costs of control. American Economic Review 96 (5), 1611–1630.

Fehr, Ernst, Charness, Gary, 2024. Social preferences: fundamental characteristics and economic consequences. Also published as URPP Equality of Opportunity Discussion Paper No. 44. https://www.zora.uzh.ch/id/eprint/255996/.

Fehr, Ernst, Fischbacher, Urs, 2003. The nature of human altruism. Nature 425 (6960), 785–791.

Fehr, Ernst, Fischbacher, Urs, 2004. Third-party punishment and social norms. Evolution and Human Behavior 25 (2), 63–87.
Fehr, Ernst, Gächter, Simon, 2000a. Cooperation and punishment in public goods experiments. American Economic Review 90 (4), 980–994.
Fehr, Ernst, Gächter, Simon, 2000b. Fairness and retaliation: the economics of reciprocity. The Journal of Economic Perspectives 14 (3), 159–181.
Fehr, Ernst, Klein, Alexander, Schmidt, Klaus M., 2007. Fairness and contract design. Econometrica 75 (1), 121–154.
Fehr, Ernst, Rockenbach, Bettina, 2003. Detrimental effects of sanctions on human altruism. Nature 422 (6928), 137–140.
Fischbacher, Urs, Gächter, Simon, Fehr, Ernst, 2001. Are people conditionally co-operative? Evidence from a public goods experiment. Economics Letters 71 (3), 397–404. http://www.sciencedirect.com/science/article/B6V84-42VV88K-J/2/a10343e2ec9404a699db48705378abcd.
Fochesato, Mattia, Bowles, Samuel, 2015. Nordic exceptionalism? Social democratic egalitarianism in world-historic perspective. Journal of Public Economics 127, 30–44. http://www.sciencedirect.com/science/article/pii/S0047272714000504.
Gächter, Simon, Herrmann, Benedikt, Thöni, Christian, 2010. Culture and cooperation. Philosophical Transactions of the Royal Society B-Biological Sciences 365 (1553), 2651–2661.
Gächter, Simon, Schulz, Jonathan F., 2016. Intrinsic honesty and the prevalence of rule violations across societies. Nature 531 (7595), 496–499.
Gellner, Ernest, 1983. Nations and Nationalism. New Perspectives on the Past. Cornell University Press, Ithaca.
Gibbard, Allan, 1973. Manipulation of voting schemes: a general result. Econometrica 41 (4), 587–601.
Gintis, Herbert, 1972. A radical analysis of welfare economics and individual development. The Quarterly Journal of Economics 86 (4), 572–599.
Giuliano, Paola, Nunn, Nathan, 2021. Understanding cultural persistence and change. The Review of Economic Studies 88 (4), 1541–1581.
Gneezy, Uri, Rustichini, Aldo, 2000. A fine is a price. The Journal of Legal Studies 29 (1), 1–17.
Greif, A., Tabellini, G., 2010. Cultural and institutional bifurcation: China and Europe compared. American Economic Review 100 (2), 135–140.
Güth, Werner, Schmittberger, R., Schwarze, B., 1982. An experimental analysis of ultimatum bargaining. Journal of Economic Behavior & Organization 3 (4), 367–388.
Habermas, Jürgen, 1975. Legitimation Crisis. Beacon Press, Boston.
Hamilton, W.D., 1964. The genetical evolution of social behaviour. Journal of Theoretical Biology 7 (1), 1–52.
Henrich, J., Boyd, R., Bowles, S., Camerer, C., Fehr, Ernst, Gintis, H., McElreath, R., 2001. In search of homo economicus: behavioral experiments in 15 small-scale societies. American Economic Review 91 (2), 73–78.
Henrich, Joseph, Boyd, R., 1998. The evolution of conformist transmission and the emergence of between-group differences. Evolution and Human Behavior 19 (4), 215–242.
Herlihy, David, Klapisch-Zuber, Christiane, 1985. Tuscans and Their Families: a Study of the Florentine Catasto of 1427. Yale University Press, New Haven.
Herrmann, Benedikt, Thöni, Christian, Gächter, Simon, 2008. Antisocial punishment across societies. Science 319 (5868), 1362–1367.
Hirschman, Albert O., 1985. Against parsimony: three easy ways of complicating some categories of economic discourse. Economics and Philosophy 1 (1), 7–21.
Hobbes, Thomas, 1949 [1642]. De Cive or The Citizen. Appleton-Century-Crofts, New York.
Hobbes, Thomas, 2005 [1651]. Leviathan, vol. 2. Continuum, London.
Holden, C., Mace, R., 1997. Phylogenetic analysis of the evolution of lactose digestion in adults. Human Biology 69, 605–628.

Houser, Daniel, Xiao, Erte, McCabe, Kevin, Smith, Vernon, 2008. When punishment fails: research on sanctions, intentions, and non-cooperation. Games and Economic Behavior 62, 509–532.
Hume, David, 1898 [1742]. Essays: Moral, Political and Literary, vol. I. Longmans, Green, and Co., London.
Hwang, Sung-Ha, Bowles, Samuel, 2015. Altruism, bargaining power, and Pareto efficiency in bilateral trading.
Inglehart, Ronald, Welzel, Christian, 2005. Modernization, Cultural Change, and Democracy: The Human Development Sequence, vol. 333. Cambridge University Press, Cambridge.
Jones, P., 1989. The Neutral State. Routledge, London.
Jürgens, Ulrich, 2002. Corporate governance, innovation and economic performance: a case study on Volkswagen.
Kaplan, Hillard, Hill, Kim, 1985. Food sharing among ache foragers: tests of explanatory hypotheses. Current Anthropology 26 (2), 223–246.
Kerr, Benjamin, Godfrey-Smith, Peter, Feldman, Marcus, 2004. What is altruism? Trends in Ecology & Evolution 19 (3), 135–140.
Kohn, M.L., Naoi, A., Schoenbach, C., Schooler, C., Slomczynski, K.M., 1990. Position in the class-structure and psychological functioning in the United States, Japan, and Poland. American Journal of Sociology 95 (4), 964–1008.
Kohn, Melvin L., 1983. On the transmission of values in the family: a preliminary formulation. Research in Sociology of Education and Socialization 4 (1), 1–12.
Kosse, Fabian, Deckers, Thomas, Pinger, Pia, Schildberg-Hörisch, Hannah, Falk, Armin, 2020. The formation of prosociality: causal evidence on the role of social environment. Journal of Political Economy 128 (2), 434–467.
Kreps, David M., 2023. Arguing about tastes: modeling how context and experience change economic preferences. In: Kenneth J. Arrow Lecture Series. Columbia University Press.
Laffont, Jean-Jacques, Maskin, Eric, 1979. A Differentiable Approach to Expected Utility-Maximizing Mechanisms. North Holland, Amsterdam, pp. 289–308.
Lane, Tom, Nosenzo, Daniele, Sonderegger, Silvia, 2023. Law and norms: empirical evidence. American Economic Review 113 (5), 1255–1293.
Lee, Jun-Hyung, Hwang, Sung-Ha, Bowles, Samuel, 2026. One-sided altruism and efficient mechanisms in bilateral trading. Unpublished paper presented at the Econometric Society Meeting, Seoul, 2025.
Levy, Reuben, 1957. The Social Structure of Islam. Cambridge University Press, Cambridge.
Loehlin, John C., 2005. Resemblance in personality and attitudes between parents and their children. In: Bowles, Samuel, Gintis, Herbert, Groves, Melissa Osborne (Eds.), Unequal Chances: Family Background and Economic Success. Princeton University Press, pp. 192–207.
Loewenstein, George F., Thompson, Leigh, Bazerman, Max H., 1989. Social utility and decision making in interpersonal contexts. Journal of Personality and Social Psychology 57 (3), 426–441.
Lonner, Walter J., Berry, John W., Hofstede, Geert, 1980. Culture's consequences: international differences in work-related values. In: University of Illinois at Urbana-Champaign's Academy for Entrepreneurial Leadership Historical Research Reference in Entrepreneurship.
Lowes, S., Nunn, N., Robinson, J.A., Weigel, J.L., 2017. The evolution of culture and institutions: evidence from the Kuba kingdom. Econometrica 85 (4), 1065–1091.
Lucas, Robert E., 1976. Econometric policy evaluation: a critique. In: Brunner, Karl, Meltzer, Allan H. (Eds.), The Phillips Curve and Labor Markets Carnegie-Rochester Conference Series on Public Policy, vol. 1. North-Holland, Amsterdam, pp. 19–46.
Machiavelli, Niccolò, 1984. Discorsi sopra la prima deca di Tito Livio. Rizzoli, Milano (first published in 1513–1517, translation by the present authors).
Mandeville, Bernard, 1988. A Search into the Nature of Society, vol. I. Indianapolis. Liberty Fund, pp. 323–370.
Martinsson, P., Medhin, H., Persson, E., 2019. Minimum levels and framing in public good provision. Economic Inquiry 57 (3), 1568–1581.

Mattauch, Linus, Hepburn, Cameron, Spuler, Fiona, Stern, Nicholas, 2022. The economics of climate change with endogenous preferences. Resource and Energy Economics 69, 101312.
Meyer, Peter J., 1972. Schooling and the Reproduction of the Social Division of Labor. Thesis.
Miettinen, Topi, Kosfeld, Michael, Fehr, Ernst, Weibull, Jörgen, 2020. Revealed preferences in a sequential prisoners' dilemma: a horse-race between six utility functions. Journal of Economic Behavior & Organization 173, 1–25.
Mill, John Stuart, 1965 [1848]. Principles of Political Economy with Some of Their Applications to Social Philosophy, Collected Works of John Stuart Mill, vol. 2. University of Toronto Press, Toronto.
Mill, John Stuart, 1994 [1844]. On the Definition and Method of Political Economy. In: Hausman, Daniel (Ed.), The Philosophy of Economics: An Anthology. Cambridge University Press, Cambridge, pp. 52–68.
Mill, John Stuart, 1998 [1859]. On Liberty and Other Essays. Oxford University Press, USA.
Miu, Elena, Rendell, Luke, Bowles, Sam, Boyd, Rob, Cownden, Daniel, Enquist, Magnus, Eriksson, Kimmo, Feldman, Marcus W., Lillicrap, Timothy, McElreath, Richard, et al., 2024. The refinement paradox and cumulative cultural evolution: complex products of collective improvement favor conformist outcomes, blind copying, and hyper-credulity. PLoS Computational Biology 20 (9), e1012436.
Mokyr, Joel, 2016. A Culture of Growth: The Origins of the Modern Economy. Princeton University Press.
Myerson, Roger B., Satterthwaite, Mark A., 1983. Efficient mechanisms for bilateral trading. Journal of Economic Theory 29, 265–281.
Naidu, Suresh, Hwang, Sung-Ha, Bowles, Samuel, 2010. Evolutionary bargaining with intentional idiosyncratic play. Economics Letters 109 (1), 31–33.
Nowak, Stefan, 1981. Values and attitudes of the Polish people. Scientific American 245 (1), 45–53.
Nunn, Nathan, 2021. History as evolution. In: Bisin, Alberto, Federico, Giovanni (Eds.), The Handbook of Historical Economics. Elsevier, pp. 41–91. Chap. 3.
Nunn, Nathan, Wantchekon, Leonard, 2011. The slave trade and the origins of mistrust in Africa. American Economic Review 101 (7), 3221–3252.
Nuti, Domenico M., 2011. Industrial relations at FIAT: Dr Marchionne's class war. Transfer: European Review of Labour and Research 17 (2), 251–254.
Nyborg, Karine, Anderies, John M., Dannenberg, Astrid, Lindahl, Therese, Schill, Caroline, Schlüter, Maja, Neil Adger, W., Arrow, Kenneth J., Barrett, Scott, Carpenter, Stephen, Chapin, F. Stuart, Crépin, Anne-Sophie, Daily, Gretchen, Ehrlich, Paul, Folke, Carl, Jager, Wander, Kautsky, Nils, Levin, Simon A., Madsen, Ole Jacob, Polasky, Stephen, Scheffer, Marten, Walker, Brian, Weber, Elke U., Wilen, James, Xepapadeas, Anastasios, de Zeeuw, Aart, 2016. Social norms as solutions. Science 354 (6308), 42–43.
Ober, J., 2008. Democracy and Knowledge: Innovation and Learning in Classical Athens. Princeton University Press, Princeton.
Odling-Smee, F.J., Laland, Kevin N., Feldman, Marcus, 2003. Niche Construction: The Neglected Process in Evolution. Monographs in Population Biology, vol. 37. Princeton University Press, Princeton.
Ostrom, Elinor, 2000. Crowding out citizenship. Scandinavian Political Studies 23 (1), 3–16.
Persson, Torsten, Tabellini, Guido, 2021. Culture, institutions, and policy. In: Bisin, Alberto, Federico, Giovanni (Eds.), The Handbook of Historical Economics. Elsevier, pp. 463–489. Chap. 16.
Posner, Eric, 2000. Law and Social Norms. Harvard University Press, Cambridge.
Rawls, John, 1971. A Theory of Justice. Harvard University Press, Cambridge.
Robson, A.J., Samuelson, L., 2026. The Evolutionary Foundations of Preferences. Cambridge University Press, Cambridge.
Rowthorn, Robert, 2006. The evolution of altruism between siblings: Hamilton's rule revisited. Journal of Theoretical Biology 241 (4), 774–790.
Royal Swedish Academy of Sciences, 2007. Mechanism Design Theory.

Rozin, Paul, 1991. Family resemblance in food and other domains: the family paradox and the role of parental congruence. Appetite 16 (2), 93–102.

Rustagi, Devesh, 2024. Historical self-governance and norms of cooperation. Econometrica 92 (5), 1473–1502.

Schmelz, Katrin, 2021. Enforcement may crowd out voluntary support for COVID-19 policies, especially where trust in government is weak and in a liberal society. Proceedings of the National Academy of Sciences of the United States of America 118 (1).

Schmelz, Katrin, Bowles, Samuel, 2021. Overcoming COVID-19 vaccination resistance when alternative policies affect the dynamics of conformism, social norms, and crowding out. Proceedings of the National Academy of Sciences of the United States of America 118 (25). https://www.pnas.org/content/pnas/118/25/e2104912118.full.pdf.

Schmelz, Katrin, Bowles, Samuel, 2022. Opposition to voluntary and mandated COVID-19 vaccination as a dynamic process: evidence and policy implications of changing beliefs. Proceedings of the National Academy of Sciences of the United States of America 119 (13).

Schmelz, Katrin, Bowles, Samuel, 2026. An empirically based dynamic approach to sustainable climate policy design. Nature Sustainability 9 (2), 212–221.

Schmelz, Katrin, Bowles, Samuel, Ziegelmeyer, Anthony, 2026. The effect of liberal-democratic and authoritarian institutions on the preference for autonomy. Working paper.

Schulz, Jonathan F., 2022. Kin networks and institutional development. The Economic Journal 132 (647), 2578–2613.

Schulz, Jonathan F., Bahrami-Rad, Duman, Beauchamp, Jonathan P., Henrich, Joseph, 2019. The church, intensive kinship, and global psychological variation. Science 366 (6466), eaau5141.

Schumpeter, Joseph A., 1950. The March into socialism. The American Economic Review 40 (2), 446–456.

Slotwinski, Michaela, Stutzer, Alois, 2023. Women leaving the playpen: the emancipating role of female suffrage. The Economic Journal 133 (650), 812–844.

Smith, Adam, 1937 [1776]. The Wealth of Nations. Modern Library, New York. (Originally published in 1776).

Stigler, George J., Becker, Gary S., 1977. De Gustibus Non Est Disputandum. American Economic Review 67 (2), 76–90.

Sunstein, Cass R., 1996. On the expressive function of law. University of Pennsylvania Law Review 144 (5), 2021–2053.

Tabellini, Guido, 2008a. Institutions and culture: presidential address. Journal of the European Economic Association 6 (2–3), 255–294.

Tabellini, Guido, 2008b. The scope of cooperation: values and incentives. The Quarterly Journal of Economics 123 (3), 905–950.

Taylor, Michael, 1987. The Possibility of Cooperation. Cambridge University Press, New York.

The Economist, 2007. Intelligent design. https://www.economist.com/finance-and-economics/2007/10/18/intelligent-design. (Accessed 22 September 2024).

Tilly, Charles, 1990. Coercion, Capital, and European States, AD 990–1990. B. Blackwell, Cambridge, Mass., USA.

Truelove, Heather Barnes, Carrico, Amanda R., Weber, Elke U., Toner Raimi, Kaitlin, Vandenbergh, Michael P., 2014. Positive and negative spillover of pro-environmental behavior: an integrative review and theoretical framework. Global Environmental Change 29, 127–138. https://www.sciencedirect.com/science/article/pii/S0959378014001599.

Weber, Eugen, 1976. Peasants into Frenchmen: The Modernization of Rural France, 1870–1914. Stanford University Press, Stanford.

Weizsäcker, Carl Christian von, 2024. Freedom and adaptive preferences. Routledge, Milton Park.

Wood, Elisabeth, 2003. Insurgent Collective Action and Civil War In El Salvador. Cambridge University Press, Cambridge.

Wu, Sherry Jueyu, Paluck, Elizabeth Levy, 2020. Participatory practices at work change attitudes and behavior toward societal authority and justice. Nature Communications 11 (1), 2633. https://doi.org/10.1038/s41467-020-16383-6.

Ziegelmeyer, Anthony, Schmelz, Katrin, Ploner, Matteo, 2012. Hidden costs of control: four repetitions and an extension. Experimental Economics 15 (2), 323–340.

Chapter 7

Identity economics and the economics of culture☆

George Akerlof[a] **and Rachel Kranton**[b]
[a]*McCourt School of Public Policy, Georgetown University, Washington, DC, United States,*
[b]*Department of Economics, Duke University, Durham, NC, United States*

In classic economic models, people are principally concerned with their own individual welfare; with this objective, they choose their consumption of goods and services and also their time spent in work and leisure. But real people are more complex. We have names and families; we live in neighborhoods, communities, and nations; we have religious and moral beliefs; we think of each other; and we think of ourselves in terms of gender, race, and ethnicity. These descriptors of self and others describe the structure of our social—and, also, our business—world. Moreover, all these features and designations are associated with norms of how people *should* look, sound, and behave, and who belongs and who does not belong to our many different groups. These designations and these norms are all part of the culture of a society and of most organizations. Many chapters in this volume are devoted to understanding how such notions come about.

Identity economics develops a framework to capture these features of society and how these features impact individual behavior. An identity framework focuses on people and motivations for their minute-by-minute, day-to-day, year-by-year decisions. It also focuses on their interactions, which will be influenced by the norms of the groups with which they identify (or disidentify), and even by the norms and actions of those who identify with other groups, with their different norms.

These observations about people, as social beings with identities and norms, are the basis for much of the social sciences outside of economics—including sociology, anthropology, psychology, and history. The project of identity economics is to bring these features into economic analysis. Identity economics relies, therefore, on the extensive literature outside of economics on

☆ We are grateful to the editors, Benjamin Enke, Paola Giuliano, Nathan Nunn, and Leonard Wantchekon, for their excellent work in arranging and editing this Handbook. We especially thank Jacopo Ballabio, Elisabetta Campagna, Paola Giuliano, and Yujing Huang for their insightful and helpful comments.

Handbook of Culture and Economic Behavior, Volume 1, ISSN 3051-1682
https://doi.org/10.1016/bs.hceb.2026.02.002

people, culture, communities, and norms. We discuss below that the ingredients of identity models—the relevant social categories and norms for a given situation—should be drawn from data such as ethnographies which provide detailed descriptions of how people live their lives. While such data is perhaps not standard in economics, detailed descriptions of people and how they live their lives and what motivates their choices are precisely the type of information needed to incorporate the motivations of real people into economic models. This chapter considers in-depth two such ethnographies—of the United States Military Academy, West Point, and of the investment bank Goldman Sachs—and how the deliberate formation of norms and culture shape these organizations and those who study and work there, respectively.

By advancing the framework of identity, we aim for economic models of decision-making and of interaction that are more realistic and more robust. These identity-based models allow a more general—and richer—set of motivations than traditional economics models. Therefore, the identity-based models give a more general—and often a more realistic—picture of how people think of themselves, and how they think of, and interact with one another. With models attentive to cultural and social settings, identity economics often yields new and different predictions than standard economic models. As a result, it provides a better understanding of behavior, and, consequently, a better guide for analysis and policy.

The applications of the identity framework also go well beyond the triumvirate of gender, race, and ethnicity. Just to give one example, consider the designations of nuclear and then extended families, as they designate brother, sister, mother, father, grandmother, and grandfather, aunts, uncles, and so on. These designations not only describe the relation, they also evoke cultural and social norms and expectations of behavior. These norms not only guide people's actions; the norms themselves are topics of debate. As one illustration, the norms for what is considered a good mother are contested, and the contestation is the subject of movies (e.g. "Bad Moms" (2016)). The essential feature of identity economics is the emphasis on the actual concerns of the decision-maker rather than the concerns which the economist assumes for the decision-maker. As illustration, consider how identity changes the modeling of education, described classically by Gary Becker (1962) as the "acquisition of human capital." In a standard model of schooling, the decision-maker trades off the cost of effort against the future benefits from the extra skills obtained (such as increased wages). An identity framework puts the spotlight on the motivations of the students themselves and their concerns to fit into their social setting; these motivations are shaped by the students' own backgrounds and by the cultural environment of their school.

With this imperative of capturing real decision makers and their concerns, the identity model captures features of culture. In the example of schooling, an identity framework would introduce the position of education and work in the culture of the diverse children and their families, following the definition of culture as the "customary beliefs, social forms, and material traits of a racial, religious, or social group." And an identity framework would bring in the culture of the school, following a second meaning of culture as: "the set of shared attitudes, values, goals, and practices that characterizes an institution or organization" (Merriam Webster dictionary definitions).[1] We will also return to such features of culture in our later exposition of the economics of organization.

While much of what we review in this chapter considers people with primary motivating identities which relate to the setting at hand, we emphasize that people are multifaceted, with possibly multiple identities. People's different identities could be salient to decisions at different points in time and in different settings. A person can feel like a professional at work but a parent at home, and the choices they make in each domain can involve tradeoffs among identities themselves (as indeed reflected in the debates over what it means to be a good mother mentioned above). In experimental work, Benjamin et al. (2010) show that identities can be "cued"; Asian American subjects make more patient choices when their ancestry is evoked. Within social categories, people can adhere more or less strongly to norms, and iterative adjustment of the group membership and the norms can lead to multiplicity and break-out groups, as in Carvalho and Sacks (2024) theory of radicalization.

We note that many scholars have studied norms and the desire of people to conform to the actions of others. For example, Bernheim (1994) considers conformity as a way of signaling one's desirable attributes to others. Young (1993) considers how conventions emerge in a society, and Brock and Durlauf (2001) study social interactions and the influence of other people's choices on one's own. Manski (1993) considers empirical strategies of identifying such impacts. More recently, Bursztyn et al. (2020) find that people can hold incorrect beliefs about what peers consider to be appropriate behavior, and correcting these beliefs can lead to behavior change.

Ongoing work on identity in different contexts, some of which we review below, considers how norms and values, which can be understood as parts of culture, emerge and evolve through mutual interactions. Charness and Chen (2020) review the theoretical and experimental literature which has followed on Akerlof and Kranton (2000), and Shayo (2020) provides a comprehensive review of empirical work. In this chapter, we show how to combine an identity framework and empirics in particular domains that relate to culture, and we demonstrate the power of detailed ethnographies as data when considering the interplay between identity, culture and economics.

This chapter, "Identity economics and the economics of culture," is organized as follows. Section 1 presents the basic framework of identity economics and illustrates by applying the framework to the economics of

[1] Slightly differently, Guiso et al. (2006, p. 23) have defined "culture" as "those customary beliefs and values that ethnic, religious and social groups transmit fairly unchanged from generation to generation." They acknowledge that they have adopted this "fairly narrow" definition for the purpose of "identify[ing] a causal link from culture to economic outcomes."

schooling. Section 2 considers the identity economics of labor supply and occupational choice and gender. This section summarizes the original models; it also showcases empirical research which has followed from our first treatments in Akerlof and Kranton (2000) and Akerlof and Kranton (2010). Section 3 considers the creation of specific organizational identities, as forms of organizational culture. It especially focuses on two examples: at West Point and at Goldman Sachs. Section 4 concludes with a summary, a discussion of the identity framework applied to falling male labor market participation in the United States, and suggestions for future research.

1 Identity economics overview and application to the economics of schooling

In this section we give an overview of the identity economics framework and relate this framework to culture in economics; we then sketch an application to the case of schooling (Akerlof and Kranton, 2002). The application draws on anthropological and sociological accounts of children and adolescents in American schools. These studies highlight the importance of students' social groups and their norms. The identity framework captures the descriptions of such groups and norms as part of students' motivations for their choices and interactions. The framework further shows how schools, as institutions, can affect those norms, and, ultimately, shape the culture of the school and possibly beyond.

1.1 Summary of the identity economics framework and culture

Identity economics aims to capture how social and cultural contexts shape individual decision making and people's interactions with one another. The framework considers how people's understanding of "who they are" and "how they and others should behave," affect, more or less consciously, people's motivations and ultimately their choices. In this way, identity economics incorporates cultural norms into models of individual behavior. Beyond the basic model which we outline below, further analysis captures the interaction between each other's identities. An identity framework thus highlights the limitations in economic thinking (and in economic outcomes) of classical, individualistic assumptions about people's motivations.

Identity economics proposes an expanded utility function and provides a roadmap for how to build such a utility function based on the empirical observations of the setting at hand. With such utility functions, people have the standard preferences for goods and services—as in a classic economic model. But people *also* have motivations for their actions from norms, which describe appropriate and inappropriate choices and behaviors for themselves and for others. Importantly, these actions reflect the beliefs people hold about themselves, others, and the state of the world. By including both a standard model and the identity ingredients, the identity framework can help identify how norms change the conclusions of economic analysis. The initial step in building an identity framework is to identify the behaviors and choices to be studied and to specify a standard economic model. The framework then adds the identity ingredients as follows.

The first step in adding identity is to determine the relevant *social categories*. The social categories specify how the people at hand think of themselves and others, perhaps in relation to each other. These categories would depend on the particular setting of interest. In a study of labor market participation, the relevant categories could include gender, as will be discussed at length below. In a study of choice of occupation, gender could again be relevant, as might be ethnicity, or caste, as will also be discussed below. In a study of organizations, the relevant categories might be workers and management. In schooling and education, the relevant categories could include the ethnic groups within the community and the corresponding social groupings of students, or the social groups of the students themselves.

As discussed in the Introduction, we emphasize that specifying the social categories for the setting is not an arbitrary exercise, but, like all ingredients of an identity economics model, it should draw on empirical observations, including non-traditional sources of data such as ethnographies. The key is that the researcher specifies how people understand and see themselves and others based on anthropological, sociological, historical or other evidence.

The second step in formulating an identity framework is to specify the norms for the categories and the impact on individual payoffs from abiding by the norms. These norms include the ideal traits and characteristics and the prescriptions for how people in the categories should behave. These norms would again depend on the setting of interest. In a study of labor market participation, the gender norms could be different in different historical or cultural contexts. In a study of occupation choice, the association of gender, caste, or ethnicity to jobs would depend on the setting at hand. In a study of organizations, the relevant categories might be workers and management, which could depend not only on the wider societal context, but also on the norms of a particular workplace. In schooling and education, norms for academic achievement and engagement in school could be both local and national. As in the specification of the categories themselves, the specification of the norms should rely on evidence. With the norms well-defined, the utility function would include the impact of abiding by the norms on the utility of individuals.

To fix ideas, we spell out all these moving parts of such a utility function. For a population of individuals, from a set of possible actions for each person, let a_j be individual j's (vector of) actions and let a_{-j} represent the (vectors of) actions of all agents other than j. In a standard economic model, individual j has preferences over own actions and others' actions, which can be represented by a utility function $W_j(a_j, a_{-j})$. This function includes the possibility of externalities of other peoples' action on j as well as strategic interaction between j and other people. This model allows for the possibility that each person has a different utility function, which could depend, for example, on an individual's idiosyncratic tastes and on an individual's idiosyncratic attributes. We think of individual traits as including height, weight, talent, birthplace, and other attributes which are typically given rather than choices of an individual. The notation ε_j would summarize individual j's traits.

To this model we add the identity ingredients: the set of social categories C, the norms that indicate which actions and which attributes are ideally associated, N, and an identity function which captures the impact of how own actions and others' actions will affect j's utility $I_j(a_j, a_{-j}; c, N, \varepsilon_j)$ where c is the particular assignment of j and others to categories and ε_j represents j's given traits and characteristics. This function gives the "identity utility" which derives from the extent to which j's and others' actions match the norms for their respective categories and the extent to which j's individual attributes match the ideal for j's category.

The overall utility function would include a standard impact of actions on utility as well as these identity payoffs: $U_j(a_j, a_{-j}, I_j())$. In this way, the identity model captures the standard impact of the own action a_j on utility as well as the impact on utility through the identity function $I_j()$.

The identity framework rests on the distinction between the *preferences* for actions represented in the utility function U_j and the impact of actions on the identity function I_j. The impact of j's and other's actions have direct effects on utility as in a standard model; people like certain actions and dislike others, and they have direct benefits or costs from other peoples' actions. These preferences can be summarized as what people *like* to do and what people *like* other people to do. In contrast, the identity function and the norms capture what people think they *should* do and what they think others *should* do. The norms give prescriptions for actions for self and others. What people think they and others *should* do is fundamentally connected to who a person is. The differences between *like* and *should* are thus at the heart of the identity framework.

Once the utility function is specified, j's choice over actions then depends on the standard returns to actions and on the identity payoffs that accrue to j through the identity function $I_j()$. These payoffs come from, first, acting as one should, that is, the match between own, others' actions and norms N for categories. The payoffs further come from the extent to which a person fits their category, which is given by the match (or distance) between a person's individual set of characteristics ε_j and ideal of category specified by N. Finally, an individual has identity payoffs which derive from the status of their category, which is given the specification of the function $I_j()$. In the short run, an individual makes this decision, taking as given the categories, the norms, and own attributes, which all follow the semi-colon in the identity function $I_j(a_j, a_{-j}; c, N, \varepsilon_j)$.

In the long run, however, these elements are not fixed, but can be changed; and, indeed, they can even be changed by individual actions. People may act to change the norms; they may act to change the categories themselves; and they may act in many ways that will change their own identity and also change others' perception of that identity. Third parties can have incentives to create categories and change norms. People argue, rally, protest, and die for changes to categories and norms. Thus, identity economics allows for a more realistic view of preferences. In contrast to the classic theory in which preferences are fixed and not to be disputed (Stigler and Becker, 1977), the norm-based prescriptions in identity models are, on the contrary, very much in dispute (see also Kreps (2023)).

Such a model does not just allow for choice of identities by the individual. It also allows for the effects of a person's actions, beliefs, and values on others, which, in turn, may interactively affect the choice of identity and actions by others, thus resulting in equilibria, which can be considered as the "culture." Those cultural equilibria can occur at many levels: for the individual, as well as for all kinds of groups of individuals. Those groups are then associated with particular attributes, norms, and identity categories.[2]

In this way, the identity framework incorporates statics and the dynamics of cultural elements into economics. In the short run, a fixed utility function captures the effects of how people in a given culture think of themselves, the groups, religions, communities, and other social designations and identities, as well as the norms for inclusion, exclusion, and behavior. In the long run, the utility formulation includes the possibility that people's own actions themselves—and also their own values and beliefs—play major roles not only in determining their own actions and identities, but also in determining the norms that are associated with those identities. As new norms become established, there is cultural change. This change can be at the level of the school or the firm or the society. In the examples that follow in this chapter, we will discuss how the work in identity economics has captured both the statics and the dynamics of cultural norms.

1.2 Illustration of an identity model: schooling

Schooling provides a straightforward, and important, example of how an identity framework incorporates features of culture in people's day-to-day lives, with clear consequences for economic decisions, identities, and outcomes. Here we provide a model where students are the decision-makers; as in a standard economic model, they care about labor market consequences of their effort in school, but they also want to feel good about themselves, and to fit in with their peers. The details are found in Akerlof and Kranton (2002).

2 Carvalho's article "Veiling" (2013) gives an excellent example of such interactions at work, elaborating how prohibition of veiling can hamper Muslim women's labor market participation. Carvalho (2017) captures how "cultural constraints" can inhibit coordination which would be economically valuable.

As discussed above, the initial step in formulating an analysis of how identity affects behavior is to posit a standard economic model. We posit a simple model of individual effort in school, which is an investment in human capital for future returns on the labor market. Consider individuals who each have a characteristic represented by a positive real number n_i uniformly distributed on [0, 1], which we call "ability." For each individual, the attainment of marketable skills comes from combining this ability with effort in school, which we denote e_i which is also a positive real number. The effort in school entails a personal cost of $k(e_i)$. A standard utility function for a student i, denoted $v_i(e_i; n_i)$, would specify the costs and benefits of effort in school given ability level n_i. A simple specification would be $v_i = n_i e_i - k(e_i)$ where the benefits of effort, such as the future wages, are increasing in the ability of the student, and the function $k(e_i)$ is the effort cost to the student, which is positive. A student who maximizes utility would choose e_i to balance the benefits relative to the costs of effort.

But this model does not necessarily capture well the motivations of students. In particular, the model we specify considers the students' social lives. It considers their social groups: the norms for who is in and who is out of such groups, and the norms for and against effort. The students then make decisions about effort in school in this context.

The treatment below follows the many ethnographies and sociological studies of schools in the United States (see Akerlof and Kranton (2002) for review). We capture the culture of schools in the United States as described in these studies. We emphasize that this attentiveness to cultural particularities is critical to an identity model. While students may prioritize interacting with and fitting in with their peers, the model elaborated below specifies typical social groupings found in American contexts. We do not argue that this specific model of social categories and norms for students would apply universally. Rather, an identity framework requires that the model specify the relevant social groupings and norms for a particular setting. Indeed, the model we specify below could be further refined for particular contexts in the United States, with its diversity of schooling environments. In this sense, an identity model can capture the intricacies of a local culture. In the model of schools we specify, the culture is not just that of the larger society, the model is inclusive of school cultures within their larger society. (Following Coleman's (1961) classic study, the cultures of the observed schools are distorted reflections of adult culture.)

Proceeding as described above to build an identity economics model, we specify the social categories and the norms which are relevant to the context at hand. For schooling in the American context, we articulate three social categories C: the "cool kids" denoted by L, the "nerds" denoted by R, and the "burnouts" denoted by B. In addition to the attribute of "ability" n_i, each student also has an attribute l_i which we call "looks," which are uniformly distributed on [0, 1]. This latter attribute could be a physical characteristic such as stature or hair color or their parents' income. These are just some attributes that are important for being part of social groups. The norms specify that the ideal "cool kid" has attribute $l = 1$ and the ideal "nerd" has attribute $n = 1$.

The norms further give the ideal effort levels in school for each category, which we denote $e(C)$. We specify that the nerds are supposed to exert the most effort in school, and the burnouts exert the least effort, which gives the following ordering $e(R) > e(L) > e(B)$.

The school social setting itself also involves status: following the ethnographies, we specify that the students in the cool kids' group have the highest status.

We next specify a simple identity utility function for an individual who is in category c. A student has identity utility from (i) the status of belonging to the group c, (ii) the extent to which the student's individual attributes fit the ideal of group c, and (iii) the extent to which effort in school conforms to the ideal effort for the category. We specify a fixed amount of identity utility (related to status) from being in a group, such that $I_L > I_R > I_B$ and a simple specification for the other elements of utility such as

$$u_i\,(e_i; c, \varepsilon_i) = I_c - t\,(1 - \varepsilon_i; c) - \frac{1}{2}(e_i - e\,(c))^2$$

where $\varepsilon_i = n_i$ for $c = R$, and $\varepsilon_i = l_i$ for $c = L$. Overall, then, an individual's utility is the sum of the standard utility and the identity utility:

$$U_i\,(e_i; c) = n_i e_i - k\,(e_i) + I_c - t\,(1 - \varepsilon_i; c) - \frac{1}{2}(e_i - e\,(c))^2.$$

In the short run, each student i chooses effort, e_i, to maximize utility given their category c. Given the norms for the effort level for the category, this choice in general departs from the economically optimal level. For students with the same ability n, the chosen effort will be lower for someone who is a burnout and higher for someone who is a nerd. This short-run decision captures the effect of the school culture on individual behavior.

With the definitions of the social groups and the associated norms fixed, we can study how students might choose their category, c, to maximize their utility along with their effort level in school. In this case, the student faces a new tradeoff, between the status of the category and fitting in with the category. A student might want to be part of the high-status cool-kids category, for example, and earn I_L, but their attribute l_i could be far from the ideal of 1, which would entail a loss of $t(1 - l_i)$. This identity trade-off is in addition to the consideration of higher or lower marketable skills from more or less effort; and it is also in addition to the loss from exerting effort levels different from the norms for a chosen category.

These considerations lead to further differences between students' efforts in school and the economically optimal levels. A student who has both high ability n_i and high looks l_i, might choose to be a "cool kid" to gain higher status, which would also entail lower effort in school than otherwise. On the other hand, a student with a high n_i and low l_i could choose to be a "nerd" with higher effort in school than otherwise, and indeed perhaps higher effort than is economically optimal, depending on the magnitude of the norms $e(R)$. The following section reviews recent theoretical treatments of students' choice of social groups in school, where the ideals of each group are endogenous.

Thus far in our description, the identity framework for schooling only accounts for individual student choices given social categories and norms, but the identity framework also gives a basis for understanding how third parties and policies can change individual choices by manipulating the social categories and norms. These decisions effectively change the school culture. A ubiquitous policy in the United States, for example, is easily incorporated into the model. The school can introduce another social category to the students' social environment which can affect students' efforts in school. By sponsoring sports teams, a school can add "jocks" to the social setting. The model would specify for each student an additional characteristic, athletic ability a_i i.i.d. in $[0, 1]$, and the norms specify an ideal for the jock category of $a_i = 1$, and a status level I_J which would be at least as high as, if not higher than the identity status that accrues to the "cool kids." Following the ethnographies, the effort norms for jocks in schools would be below that of nerds, but above those of burnouts.

The introduction of the additional social category of jocks and of the associated norms would change students' choices. Students with high athletic ability a_i but with low n_i or low l_i would choose to be jocks rather than burnouts. The introduction of the jocks social category thus provides an avenue to increase skill acquisition through providing another identity for students who otherwise would have been low-achievement burnouts. On the other hand, the introduction of the jocks category could also suppress the effort of those who otherwise would have chosen to be nerds. As we emphasize above, beyond the economic returns to effort in school, the tradeoffs the students face regarding fitting in with the different groups ultimately affect their educational attainment.

This model can be extended to consider students in a society with different ethnic and social identities where the curriculum is understood to favor different categories, such as a dominant cultural or ethnic group. The marketable skills could depend on effort at mastering this curriculum, which itself has an identity association. Mastering the curriculum then has different identity payoffs for the students in the different groups. The students in the dominant group suffer no loss in identity utility from effort in school. However, students who are outside the dominant group could suffer such a loss, and, to avoid this loss, they could eschew mastering the curriculum. Obvious examples are the language used in the school and the permissibility of using local languages or dialects in the classroom and schoolwork. Such a model suggests that curricula which reflected different students' ethnicities could lead to higher school involvement, and also higher academic achievement for students in various groups. We discuss these outcomes further below when we present recent theoretical and empirical work on school curricula associated with particular social categories. We see below how associated norms and languages can lead to backlash from students and families; as we will also see the opposite side of the spectrum: that curricular reforms can lead to greater school engagement of diverse students.

1.3 Identity literature on schooling and identity: new theoretical work

The original work on identity and schooling largely considered individual students' decisions in a static context. The students choose their effort and group, taking social categories and norms as given. School policies could adjust or amend the norms and social groups within a school. Two prominent theoretical papers have now considered how interactions among the students themselves, and how parents and students can shape the social categories and the norms and thus shape the culture of a school.

R. Akerlof (2017) proposes a foundation for the utility in the identity model of schooling. In this theory, individuals (who in this case are the students) have a desire for *esteem*. (Models by Bénabou and Tirole (2002) and (2011) introduced esteem as individual motivation for actions.) Students each have idiosyncratic individual ability to perform one of two different activities: one of these is related to academic achievement while the other relates to some other activity like athletics. Students can choose how much effort to exert at each of these activities. The key assumption is that students want to perform well at their chosen task, which will result in *self esteem*, and students desire *peer esteem* which reflects their relative achievement in the activity of their chosen identity group.

With desire for both *self-esteem* and for *peer-esteem*, students choose their *values*, which here means the activities from which they will derive both types of esteem. An individual who only cared about self-esteem would value the activity for which they have the greatest ability and they would exert effort only at that activity. The desire for peer-esteem adds another dimension of choice; students also choose with whom to interact and thereby from whom they will derive peer-esteem. Students possibly face a tradeoff between wanting to value the same activity as other students, to garner peer-esteem, and wanting to value the activity at which they have the highest ability. In equilibrium, students will focus their efforts on the activity which has the highest overall esteem returns to effort and value those activities for which their performance is sufficiently high. In equilibrium, they tend to choose to interact with those who have the same values.

Several insights into identity and culture, and particularly local culture and social groups, emerge from R. Akerlof's (2017) study. In the school, the overall choice set of activities is fixed, but the student culture, as in "the set of shared attitudes, values, goals, and practices that characterizes an institution or organization," is the result of social interactions among the students. In equilibrium, some students value some activities and other students value other activities. The model provides micro foundations for the division of these students into sets of students with different values, and the social categories and norms of an identity framework.

R. Akerlof (2017) also endogenizes the composition of the social groups; that is, who is in what group depends on who else is in that group. This model then captures nuanced tradeoffs in students' identity choices—to which groups the student will choose to belong—and thereby their effort in school.

The model can thus explain some initially puzzling findings in the peer-effects literature, which posits positive spillovers from peers' efforts on others' performance. Here, if peers' ability in an activity is sufficiently high, a student will gain less peer esteem if they engage in that same activity. So, while there might be peer complementarities in effort in such an activity, a relatively low-ability student might choose to value a different activity. This student and others could then form a subgroup: i.e., another social category. As an empirical example, evaluating a policy to induce spillovers among students in the US Air Force Academy, Carrell et al. (2013) found that low-ability students eschewed interactions with higher ability students. Instead, they formed a more homogeneous low-ability group, with overall lower academic performance than those placed in a more heterogeneous mixed-ability squadron.

Carvalho et al. (2024) consider a school's explicit efforts to shape the identity of students, and thereby of society. The paper provides a model of education whose purpose, alongside the development of marketable skills, is the transmission of cultural values. The study provides a review of the history of public education in Europe and in the United States—whose purpose was to create a homogeneous society, sharing the same language and a national, or local, loyalty. The Akerlof and Kranton (2002) identity framework described above would predict that students in such schools who are from minority groups in society would identify less with the school and therefore have lower academic achievement.

Following Bisin and Verdier (2000; 2001), Carvalho et al. (2024) bring in the parents as decision makers as well, and they consider how parents and children could react to such efforts. The parents can engage in alternative strategies in the face of curricula which run counter to a family's beliefs and values. These efforts can stymie the efforts of the educational system to effect cultural change in the society. First, parents and students could individually "drop out," which is essentially equivalent to the choice presented in the identity framework; parents and children do not partake of the education provided by the school, and, therefore have both lower academic achievement and lower exposure to the acculturating material. Second, parents and children could individually "tune out" the acculturating content of the curriculum. These students would still exert effort in school and enjoy the labor market benefits of the human capital acquired *per se*, but they and their parents engage on the side in alternative cultural and social activities which promote their individual values. These efforts prevent the full spread of the schools' values within the population. The schools then strive to moderate the strength of the acculturation efforts so that this "tuning out" does not become full "backlash," in which case the acculturation efforts backfire, leading to less adoption than would have taken place in the absence of the curriculum.

Carvalho et al. (2024) also model a third strategy. "exit/opting out" is a collective effort on the part of students and parents to actively oppose the acculturating educational project of the schools. This collective effort is an even stronger form of backlash. The minority population exits the official school system altogether and establishes alternative schools which emphasize the minority values. These schools will serve the minority population when the cost of their establishment is not too high, and when the quality of the human capital obtained and the strength of the acculturation project is sufficient that parents prefer to send their children to these schools.

1.4 Empirical evidence of identity and schooling

Along with the new theoretical treatments of identity and schooling, a set of papers demonstrates the empirical validity of the identity framework and the importance of considering identity in the context of schooling and the acquisition of human capital.

First, the identity economic theories of schooling and education suggest that student achievement in school depends not only on the anticipated future wages, but also on the association of the curriculum with majority or minority groups. While introducing an acculturating curriculum can lead to lower academic achievement, on the flip side, as discussed in Akerlof and Kranton (2002), schools could possibly increase academic achievement by introducing curricular reforms and courses which allow students to engage in effort in schooling without losses in identity utility. In the United States, ethnic studies courses, which focus on historically marginalized communities and social justice, as well as curricula which are culturally relevant to different students, have been promoted as ways to engage students in school (Bonilla et al., 2021).

Empirical tests of the efficacy of such reforms would be subject to all the difficulties of identifying causal impacts of a policy change. In this case, the policies themselves of course could reflect some attentiveness to students or other quality of the personnel or leadership of the school or school district, which could affect student achievement. Studies show that students who opt into culturally relevant courses, such as a Mexican American Studies program in Tucson, Arizona (Cabrera et al., 2014), have higher academic achievement, but the analysis is subject to selection bias.

A recent study of San Francisco schools, however, employs a regression discontinuity design to identify a long-term causal impact of such a curricular innovation (Bonilla et al., 2021). The study considers low-performing students who are just at the grade-point cut-off for eligibility for a 9th grade ethnic studies course. Students assigned to the ethnic studies course had significantly higher rates of attendance, probability of high school graduation, and of pursuing post-secondary education. The data involves schools with diverse student bodies, and the study finds little evidence of heterogeneous treatment effects. As the discussion of the study notes, the timing of the course at the transition of high school and at a critical age in child development could also affect its impact.

Studying assimilationist educational policies in the United States, Fouka (2020) finds evidence of the response to policies emphasized by Carvalho et al. (2024). After World War I, English-only policies were instituted in schools in Indiana and Ohio, with explicit mention of outlawing use of German in schools. The paper considers how these policies affected the assimilation of students of German descent, comparing those on the borders of Indiana and Ohio with those across the borders in adjacent states. The main findings from the difference-in-differences design are that students exposed to compulsory schooling which prohibited use of German were more likely to marry others of German descent; less likely to volunteer to serve in World War II; and more likely to give their children a first name of German origin. This study does not consider the educational attainment of these children, but it does show evidence of "tuning out".

Empirical studies of Germany and of Spain indicate that educational policies which promote the majority culture can be effective. Clots-Figueras and Masella (2013) consider educational policies in Catalonia after the 1983 educational reform. Spanish was no longer the *official* language for schools in the region; both Catalan and Spanish were taught. The authors compare students with different exposure (in number of years) to Catalan in compulsory school. Students with greater exposure later expressed more support for Catalan-focused political parties, and also more support for separatist parties in other regions. These results held even for students with non-Catalan parents. In Germany—more than fifty years after the fact—Voigtländer and Voth (2015) have also found long-term effects of schooling on positions vis a vis other groups. Children and adolescents exposed to the Nazi ideology in schools and extracurricular activities have stronger anti-Semitic views than other age cohorts.

2 Identity and gender

2.1 Labor supply and occupational choice—overview

This section reviews how identity economics captures implications of gender and other norms in day-to-day labor market decisions and in decisions surrounding division of labor in the household, marriage, and divorce.

The identity framework thus complements work in this volume which studies the historical antecedents of gender norms. This volume provides comprehensive reviews of the compelling work on the historical determinants of gender norms. In a now classic study, Alesina et al. (2013) have found that people with origins in societies where the plough was central to agriculture have less egalitarian gender norms. Grosjean and Khattar (2019) have identified gender norms, in particular those that emphasize masculinity, from historical settlement patterns in Australia which involved imbalances in male-female sex ratios.

This section of our chapter considers how those gender norms can play out in people's lives and decisions of whether to work or not, where to work, whether to be married or not, whether to divorce, and who does the dishes. This section of our chapter also considers empirical evidence that the norms are mutable. History is not necessarily destiny for gender norms. Rather, institutions and interventions can change how boys and girls, and men and women, view work and marriage. Indeed, even the current backdrop of "traditional" gender norms in the United States, and pink vs. blue-collar jobs, was not inherited from early days of the country, but is a more recent phenomenon related to industrialization (Goldin, 2006). The identity framework gives a way to understand the impact of fixed cultural norms on the very microeconomic decisions about when and where to work in the short run. The framework also allows for actors and institutions to change the norms, in the longer run.

We first discuss how to add identity to models of labor supply and then summarize several empirical studies that demonstrate the impact of gender identity on people's decisions.

2.2 An identity model of labor supply

In a classic model of labor supply, individuals have preferences over labor (which garners consumption goods) and leisure. An individual would choose how much to work depending on this tradeoff. An embellished model could include preferences over tasks or jobs: some people might like to work in a hospital but not like to work in a coal mine. The labor-leisure tradeoff can include such preferences, and workers might need compensating wage differentials to work in a job they otherwise dislike.

An identity model would specify the social categories and the norms for which jobs and tasks are appropriate for people in each social category. Gender is an obvious application. The categories would be men and women, and the norms would specify which jobs and tasks are appropriate for men, and which are appropriate for women. The identity utility function would specify the individual gains and losses from abiding by the gender norms. The identity utility would also specify the externalities: in particular the losses from others not abiding by the norms such as a woman working in a "man's" job. Individuals would choose jobs and their labor supply more generally, considering the labor-leisure trade off, but augmented with such identity considerations.

Labor supply decisions are often made in the context of a family or marriage. In our original article (Akerlof and Kranton, 2000), we considered how identity would impact the household division of labor—including how much each partner would work in the home, or outside of it. As described above, the first step in the construction of an identity model is the specification of a standard economic model. Here, we start with a model of a marriage where each partner has utility over a public good in the marriage, as well as their hours worked inside, and outside, the home, which contribute to this public good. (See Lundberg and Pollak (1996) for a review of different model specifications of households.) Each partner may have different abilities for the respective types of work. The household is assumed to maximize the sum of partners' utility subject to a constraint that each partner has the same level of utility, which represents equal bargaining power. This tends to yield a model of comparative advantage: the prediction is that whoever works more *outside* the home will work less *inside* the home, whether it be the husband or the wife.[3]

However, this is not the historically observed pattern at least for the American households we considered from the Panel Study of Income Dynamics (PSID) (Akerlof and Kranton, 2000), nor in Hochschild's (2012) study *The Second Shift*. Women who worked *less than half* of the total outside hours, contributed *more than half* of the total hours inside the home. In contrast, men who worked *less than half* of the total outside hours, contributed *less than half* of the hours worked in the home. *The Second Shift* provides insights into such asymmetries and how working wives essentially take on another shift of work when arriving home. In one of Hochschild's couples, the husband took care of the dog and the basement; the wife took care of the child and the remaining housework.

An identity model of the household comfortably explains such patterns. Following the formula above, the first step to building an identity model is to specify the social categories, which here are "men" and "women," or "husbands" and "wives." The model would then specify the norms, with housework being appropriate for women, but not for men. The norms could further specify that a wife should not earn more than her husband. When a woman works more hours outside of the home or when a woman earns more, this leads to disutility for the husband. To meet the constraint of equal utility, the husband contributes less to housework (including child-care/dog-care) than the wife.

2.3 Empirical evidence—labor market participation and marriage norms

Since we wrote our original article, there have been a growing number of studies which empirically engage with the identity model of labor supply and occupational choice, with striking results.

Fortin (2005) was one of the first papers to directly test for relationships between individual attitudes toward gender and labor market participation. The study considers responses in the World Values Survey regarding labor

[3] If, as specified by Hersch and Stratton (1994) and others, the party who earns more has greater bargaining power, the effect of bargaining would lead to a further reduction of hours worked in the household for the partner who works more outside the household.

market participation and relative earnings in 25 OECD countries. She found direct relationships between survey answers and labor market patterns. The attitude that "scarce jobs should go to men first" has the most significant effect on women's employment rates (p. 431), and agreement with statements such as "being a housewife is just as fulfilling as working for pay" predicts women's lower employment. Fortin also finds a negative relationship between labor market participation and what she calls "mother's guilt," measured by disagreement with the statement "a working mother can establish just as warm and secure a relationship with her child as a mother who does not work."

Bertrand et al. (2015) find evidence of three predictions of the Akerlof and Kranton (2000) model of gender and marriage. First, they consider the relationship between earnings and the gender gap in time spent on work in the household for married male-female couples. Using data from the American Time Use Survey (ATUS) and the Current Population Survey (CPS), for 2003 to 2011, they find that this gender gap is higher for women who earn more than their husbands. Analysis of data from the Panel Study of Income Dynamics (PSID) shows a similar pattern: when a wife begins to earn more than her husband, she takes on more housework and her husband takes on less, though the first effect is larger. These findings mirror those of Bittman et al. (2003) who, using data from the Australia National Time Use Survey, found a non-monotonicity in women's share of the housework. When women earn less income than their husbands, their contribution to household production falls as their income increases. But when women earn more income than their husbands, their contributions to household production increase as their income increases.

Second, Bertrand et al. (2015) find predicted patterns in the relative earnings of men and women. Examining United States administrative data, they find a discontinuity in relative income of husbands and wives. The distribution is increasing and then there is a sharp drop at one-half. That is, couples appear to be making decisions about labor market participation so that the wives do not earn more than their husbands.

Finally, Bertrand et al. (2015) find impacts of relative earnings on the marriage itself. In the identity model of the household, there is a loss in utility when the wife earns more than the husband. To restore equality of utility, the couple could respond to a woman's higher earning power by adjusting the household labor, as discussed, or by cutting back on her labor market participation and keeping the ratio of earnings within the gender norm bounds. As another outcome, the marriage could dissolve. Using data from the National Survey of Families and Households (NSFH), Bertrand et al. (2015) find that in couples where the wife earns more than the husband, the partners report being less happy in the marriage, are more likely to have discussed separation, and more likely to report trouble in the marriage. Furthermore, the likelihood of divorce is about six percentage points higher when the wife earns more than the husband (Bertrand et al., 2015, p. 602).

Folke and Rickne (2020) provide causal evidence for the impact on divorce rates when women are promoted or win top positions. Based on thirty years of Swedish data, the study follows male and female job candidates over time and employs a difference-in-differences approach. For elections to high-level political positions such as mayor or parliamentarian in Sweden, three years after winning such promotions, the women who won were seven percentage points less likely to remain married to their spouse at the time of the election than the women who lost in such elections (Folke and Rickne, 2020, p. 261). They also found similar patterns for women vs. men who are promoted to CEO.

Recent empirical research studies possible further implications of the norm that husbands should earn more than their wives: violence in the marriage. A model of the household could incorporate violence directly into the utility functions of the husband and wife. Aizer (2010) considers the predictions of a bargaining model where men gain—and women lose—from violence against the wife, and the extent of the violence depends on relative bargaining power. When women have increased earning potential, their bargaining power increases, since the threat to leave the relationship is more credible, and intimate-partner-violence is predicted to decrease. In data from California, Aizer (2010) finds that local increases in relative wages from female-dominated vs. male-dominated occupations are correlated with lower hospitalization rates for women from domestic abuse. Similarly, Anderberg et al. (2016) consider relative risk of unemployment of men and women. Their survey evidence finds that reported incidence of domestic violence against women falls when the unemployment rates relatively favor women's employment.

However, an identity framework which includes norms for women's and men's relative income would have different predictions, which would depend on the specific context; the increase in wife's income relative to her husband leads to reduction in utility for the husband, which then must be restored, here through "backlash" violence against his spouse. A series of empirical studies in developing countries find exactly this pattern. Using a household survey in India, Dhanaraj and Mahambare (2022) find that women who work outside the home are subject to more interpersonal violence than those who do not. These women are also more likely to excuse the violence. In a longitudinal study in Bangalore, Krishnan et al. (2010) find that women who were unemployed and then began employment faced significantly higher incidence of violence compared to women whose employment status did not change. Similarly, women whose husbands faced instability in employment also faced higher odds of violence compared to women whose husbands were steadily employed. Guarnieri and Rainer (2021) exploit a historical division in Cameroon to compare women in former British and French colonies. They find that relative to women in territories previously controlled by France, women in former British territories have greater opportunities for paid work outside the home, but are also more likely to experience spousal abuse.

2.4 Experimental evidence—labor market participation

Researchers have also been testing the predictions of the identity framework using experimental methods in the field. In a study of gender norms, Bursztyn et al. (2017) show that the norms concerning marriage and relative earnings of men and women are operative, even among MBA students in the United States. Their experimental design exploits settings where women's answers to career objectives can be observed—or not—by unmarried male peers. Among their findings, relative to women with partners, single women underperform in coursework where the graded tasks are publicly observed. Single women also profess less desire for salary and for jobs with travel in a real-stakes questionnaire when it is expected that unmarried male peers will see their answers relative to private answers.

Moving from gender to caste, Oh (2023) shows in an experiment in India that caste membership and related caste norms directly determine labor supply in an experimental context. The setting matches the labor market model described above except that, instead of men and women, the social categories are castes and certain jobs are associated with certain castes. In the experiment, participants choose whether to undertake tasks that are associated with different castes. A control setting involves a task which is not associated with a caste. The decision to undertake the task is either publicly observed or not. The experiment also varies the wage rate and the time spent on the task. Overall, the main finding was that subjects were willing to forgo up to a month's wages to avoid undertaking a task which was contrary to their caste norms. This choice was often made even when those tasks would have been undertaken privately and would have taken subjects less than an hour to complete.

2.5 Change in gender and labor market norms

These studies give a sense of how cultural norms play out in people's everyday lives and life histories. The identity framework, however, also allows for the possibility that norms can change. Norms are human creations and are constantly being adjusted and challenged, by people with convictions about social justice and, also, by people seeking power or profits.

In a prominent example, Goldin (2002) describes the changes in gender norms and work in the United States over the 20th century. Certain occupations took on "auras of gender" in the early part of the century; that is, jobs were labeled "female" or "male." One might say that jobs took on "secondary gender characteristics." White collars faded into "pink" collars (p. 32). These notions are currently in decline. Because such processes often occur in conjunction with other trends, such as changes in technology, it can be difficult to determine the causal effects of changes in norms on behavior.

In a comprehensive study, Lippmann et al. (2020) demonstrate that the East German state did effectively change gender norms and behavior, as seen in the post-reunification attitudes and behavior of people with East German roots. They exploit the 41-year division of Germany after World War II. The East German state promoted and endorsed policies and norms of equal right and obligation to work; the state also instituted programs such as childcare, which eased women's entry into the labor force. Such programs were not instituted in West Germany. By the time of unification in 1990, women's participation in the labor market in East Germany was among the highest in the world, about thirty percentage points higher than in West Germany (p. 1664).

The causal argument considers the legacy of East German policies after reunification. The study considers data from the German Socio-Economic Panel from 1991 to 2012. The findings essentially give a flipped mirror image of those of Bertrand et al. (2015). The "male breadwinner" norm was prevalent in West Germany, but not in the East. Women in East Germany also express similar preferences to men about paid work, in contrast to women in West Germany. Women who earn more than their husbands do not contribute more hours to housework; instead, as their contribution to household income rises, women in East Germany decreased the hours spent on housework. In contrast, in West Germany higher earning women increase their housework hours. The probability of divorce is higher in West Germany when the husband earns less than the wife, but not in East Germany. Nor do East German women withdraw from the labor force when their earning potential becomes higher than their husbands' earnings; the opposite occurs in West Germany.

In a field experiment, Dhar et al. (2022) show that direct intervention into gender norms can have short-term and long-term effects. The paper considers a randomized controlled trial of a secondary-school program in Haryana, India. Implemented by a non-profit organization, the program involved adolescents in discussions about gender equality over two and a half school years. The sessions promoted gender equality and discussions of gender roles and stereotypes, including girls' education, labor market participation, and harassment. The program significantly increased views of gender equality. The changes were apparent even five years after the start of the program. The behavior change was most evident for boys, who increased their contribution to household chores, and also encouraged their sisters' education.

Norms and values are transmitted within families and communities, as studied extensively by Bisin and Verdier (2000) and others. In the theoretical models, parents are assumed to have values, and they prefer their children to share them. Parents are willing to incur costs to this end, and they tradeoff their own economic success for the transmission of these values. For gender norms, a set of empirical studies test for the congruence of gender norms and behaviors across generations within families and communities. Using the U.S. National Longitudinal Survey of Youth, Farre and Vella (2013) find that children's views toward women who work reflect the views of their mothers. They also find that these attitudes relate to actual labor market participation; daughters of mothers with less traditional views of women's roles are more likely to work.

3 Identity and organizations

In 1776 Adam Smith wrote: "It is not from the benevolence of the butcher, the brewer, or the baker that we expect our dinner, but from their regard to their own interest" (Smith, 1937, Chapter 2, p. 14). We agree with Smith. We also agree with Milton Friedman: that free trade undertaken for people's own purposes plays a major role in modern capitalist economic systems. But this is not the whole story.

A very large number of economic transactions in these economies are not pursued in free trade with the decisions of both sides of the transaction pursued for narrow self-interest (as described by Smith). Instead, a very large number, and volume, of transactions take place within organizations and firms (Coase, 1937). Within most effective organizations, actions are not just taken to narrowly maximize the welfare of the individuals on either side of a transaction. Instead, people are placed into different "jobs" with stated responsibilities. Alongside these formal designations, there are understandings—we might call them "norms"—regarding what the holders of those jobs should or should not do.

Those norms then greatly mitigate (even if they do not completely solve) problems of coordination that cannot be addressed more formally. Principal-agent theory is a classic formulation of such coordination problems. In the model of Steven A. Ross (1973), a *principal* has their own objective function; likewise, the *agent* who works for the principal has their own objectives. However, the agent has information that is not available to the principal, and as a result of this asymmetry of information, the principal cannot directly observe, or pay, the agent for work effort. Moreover, there will be problems if agents base their decisions on their own self-interest, which is unlikely to align perfectly with the interest of the principal. In Ross's solution to this problem, the principal gives monetary incentives to the agent, designed so that the agent's choice of actions will be closer to the principal's goals.

However, such incentives—based solely on monetary considerations on observed actions—are likely to result in serious distortions (for instance, see Holmstrom and Milgrom (1991) and Prendergast (1999)). The simplest example illustrates: rewarding teachers for their students' test performance gives incentives "to teach to the test" rather than to teach what is in the students' best interest, which presumably, is the principal's objective.

To show the importance of norms in organizations and the possible molding of organizational culture, we intentionally elaborate this discussion by referring to detailed participant-observer accounts of two organizations. These studies show how the leadership influences their employees to align their identities with the goals of the organization—for which the framework has been specified in Akerlof and Kranton (2008, 2010). In the endeavor to incorporate identity (i.e., features of culture) into economics, it is often useful to rely on such, perhaps untraditional, sources of data. We need accounts of how people interact day-today—and even minute-by-minute—in different social contexts, and how people understand each other's motives and reactions. In this section of our chapter, ethnographies of two organizations give detailed windows on the leadership's intentional shaping of the norms and identities to better serve the mission of the organization. R. Akerlof et al. (2020) have described such organizations as fostering "stories at work": with the stories purposefully chosen to change the agents' identities. Their paper also gives a useful review of the significant literature on this subject.

With this preface, let's turn to our two examples: West Point and Goldman Sachs.

3.1 West Point

We chose the first of these examples, The United States Military Academy, West Point, for two reasons. Identity plays a special role in the education of future military officers, and the book, *Absolutely American* by David Lipsky (2003), is an excellent source of fine-grained information regarding identity in action. Lipsky followed a cohort of cadets during their four years at West Point; his account describes how the military academy imbues its cadets with a special identity, as it is training them to be future leaders of the United States Army. The book further gives detailed description of the cadets' responses.

Lipsky especially seeks the answer to the question: why, despite the strictness and exactitude of the demands placed on these cadets (nonstop for four years), they imbibe the values that West Point seeks to give them. Those values place special emphasis on willing acceptance of (legitimate) commands coming from those—usually of higher rank—with the authority to give them. Such willingness is itself a major part of what is expected of students at West Point.

Let's give a very specific example. If there are episodes which most cadets would almost uniformly remember as important to their time at West Point, it would be the events of their very first day.[4] Called "R-Day," this is just the beginning of West Point's deliberate program to imbue its students with a special identity. At West Point, probably *the major goal* is to mold the cadets' identity: to be appropriate for their future leadership in the Army.

R-Day begins as the new cadets arrive with their families at West Point's football field, where they are divided into groups of forty. On the R-Day described by Lipsky, after a few introductory remarks, an older cadet, who is addressing the large audience tells the assembled families: "All right. At this time I will now ask parents to prepare their final goodbyes. You will be moving out in 90 seconds."

---

4 Described in the chapter on R-Day, Lipsky (2003).

Such precise timing—90 seconds to depart from one's family—gives a foretaste of cadet-life at West Point for the next four years. Lipsky then describes a series of steps over the next few hours that drive home the message.

1. Tags on the bags: The groups of forty are first taken to a room where they must put tags on their bags. "Hurry up you have places to be!"
2. Short trip on bus: With "twenty seconds to board." Getting off the bus: "head and shoulders will remain straightforward at all times." (Lipsky side-comments regarding "heads [only facing] straightforward": "West Point now has dominion on what you will see.")
3. Lipsky immediately follows up, with the beginning of the next paragraph: "At R-Day you surrender yourself in stages." Lipsky's implication: just as the key notes of R-Day are "surrender" of self, that will be the dominant key of almost every moment for the next four years.
4. Uniforms: The cadets strip off down to their underwear. Whatever they were wearing before is replaced by uniforms. The same for every new cadet.
5. Skin examination: Cadets' skin is examined for tattoos, which might be potentially offensive.
6. Eyeglasses: Exchange of eye-glasses from home for West-Point issue—as described by Lipsky as unusually unattractive.
7. Medicine from home: Seized and replaced by medicine from the West Point Pharmacy.
8. Signing contract with West Point: Including "that you have read, understand and will abide by the Statement of Policies."
9. Affirmation of vital statistics (such as name, home address).
10. Haircut. Lipsky comment: "and the Army takes your hair."
11. The Capstone of the Day: "[coming] up to the Cadet in the Red Sash's Line." The incoming cadets must salute the Cadet in the Red Sash in precisely the right way, and say: "Sir, New Cadet Doe reports to the Cadet in the Red Sash for the first time as ordered." One might think this would be easy. But the Cadet in the Red Sash is hard to please. He or she looks for the tiniest errors: in wording, in posture, in place and way to stand, etc., etc. The Cadet in the Red Sash demands immediate fix of these "errors." The instructions are issued as strict commands, which the new cadets strive to obey. The orders are given without civilian *please*'s; nor with civilian *thank you*'s.

Such treatment is not some unusual quirk of that very first day. On the contrary, it is a well-designed prelude to every day at West Point prior to graduation, four years in the future.

Lipsky, who was *Rolling Stone's* leading expert on college-age students, writes that the cadets at West Point were "happier than students almost anywhere else." (Lipsky, 2003, p. 34) He explains why he thinks this could be possible. The cadets understand that the demands on their lives are unusually exacting. As just one example of the ubiquitous becks-and-calls which echo R-Day, cadets were required to wear full uniform when out of their rooms, even including on a middle-of-the-night trip down the hall to the bathroom (which, if seen, could be reported by other cadets as a violation of rules (Lipsky, 2003, p. 9)). But the cadets deeply identify with West Point; they take great pride in being a member of a team, which is being trained to be of service to their country. Following our identity model, that means that they also get "identity utility" from adherence to the West Point norms, however demanding those norms may be.

Another element that accounts for the "happiness" is cadets' friendships with one another. And Lipsky says that those friendships are especially deep because they are buttressed by the mutuality of the values themselves and by the cadets' similarity of experience. The mutuality of marching together, and even the mutuality of wearing exactly similar clothes—appropriately called "*uniforms*"—reinforce the reasons for acceptance of the same identity.

West Point, as described by Lipsky, gives its students an identification as "good" people, with "good" values.[5] And, especially for the hardy people who gain admission, the strictness and discipline has its own logic: the aim of West Point, and the aim of getting the cadets to subscribe to these values, are to produce young men and women who will be good leaders. The adoption of such norms as part of their identity also accords with the cadets' commitment to the United States, and to its Armed Forces. Furthermore, because their classmates who surround them also share these principles, the cadets have further reason to adopt these values. Thus, for a variety of reasons, the West Point values appeal to the cadets' own aspirations of identity. Such identities and such attachment, in turn, legitimate the strict commands and strict rules that dictate the lives of the cadets at West Point.

So far, this part of the essay has not emphasized the relation between culture and identity. But the relation between the two at West Point enforces the relation, as we will discuss further in the Concluding Summary. In sum, as we see it, Lipsky's ethnography of West Point gives a perfect example of how an identity framework can capture culture in the daily lives and interactions of people: Identity determining what each individual is thinking; and culture being inclusive of the identities of the different people, and how they interact in concert. The culture of West Point consists of people's identities; how those identities affect their actions and beliefs; and how, in turn, those actions and beliefs of others in turn reciprocally affect the identities and actions of those others.

3.2 Goldman Sachs

Our second example, Goldman Sachs, is based on the account by a former employee: Steven Mandis (2013), *What Happened to Goldman Sachs*. This

5 In the Preface (p. xii) Lipsky says: "I could feel the basic goodness of the place": this theme keeps reappearing throughout the book, as it is also a central feature of West Point identities.

book—taken from his PhD dissertation in sociology at Columbia University—is based on Mandis' previous 12-year personal experience at Goldman Sachs, supplemented with interviews with current employees and others with special knowledge of the firm. The central theme concerns whether—and, if so, why—there has been change in the "culture" of Goldman Sachs. Mandis' view is *yes*: "A firm that had largely upheld a higher ethical standard shifted to a more legal standard" (Mandis, 2013, p. 13). Beginning with a description of the culture when he was first employed by Goldman Sachs in 1992, Mandis explains how and why such a change occurred.

Mandis bases his description of the initial culture on a statement in 1979 by John Whitehead, who was co-head and co-senior partner of the firm. Up to that time, the Goldman Sachs "culture" had been passed on to new employees by word-of-mouth, with individual mentors playing a major role. But Whitehead worried that, with the rapid growth of the firm then occurring, such a person-to-person approach to passing on the culture was highly fragile. To meet these concerns, at home one Sunday afternoon, Whitehead scribbled out 12 "principles". Those principles described the basis of the culture that he wanted to protect. A copy of them was sent to each employee.

A summary of the most important of these principles gives an indication of the ideals of Goldman Sachs as an organization, including its expectations of individuals. Principle 1, which is the most important, states: "Our clients' interests always come first. Our experience shows that if we serve our clients well, our own success will follow." Principle 2 gives an economic explanation regarding why "serving our clients well" is of such importance: "Our assets are our people, capital, and reputation. If any of these are ever lost, the last is the most difficult to regain." Principle 12[6] describes how to "serve the clients well" and to preserve and to enhance our "reputation": "Integrity and honesty are the heart of our business. We expect our people to maintain high ethical standards in everything they do, both in their work for the firm and in their personal lives." The Principles also emphasize cooperation and teamwork, as expressed in Principle 7[7]: "We stress *teamwork* in *everything* we do. While individual creativity is always encouraged, we have found that *team* effort often produces the best results. *We have no room for those who put their personal interests ahead of the interests of the firm and its clients*." (italics added)

Mandis focuses on three applications of the Goldman Sachs principles. The first of these examples occurred close to the time of his initial employment. In the fall of 1987, there had been a freak event in stock markets. In the week of October 12 to October 16, the Dow Jones fell by approximately 10 percent; then, yet worse, on the following Monday, the decline continued, with a 22.6 percent further decline. This drop in stock prices then spread internationally. This spread entailed a further shock for Goldman Sachs. At the time, in the

[6] Which is now Principle 14.

[7] Now Principle 8.

process of de-nationalization under Margaret Thatcher, the British government had agreed with an assortment of investment banks to sell their remaining holdings of stock in British Petroleum.[8] Goldman Sachs along with three other American underwriters had agreed to pay 3.3 British pounds per share—or about $5.48—for its part of the pie.[9] Fast forward then to two days after the Black Monday, and just two days before the underwriters were to honor their commitment. British Petroleum stock had fallen to $4.47, entailing a loss to the American underwriters of approximately 18 percent below what they had agreed to pay. For Goldman Sachs alone, the loss was estimated at the time as $100 million.[10]

As Mandis tells the story, Goldman Sachs dealt with this problem by adherence to Principle 1: "Our clients' interests always come first."[11] It did join the three other American underwriters in asking whether the force majeure clause of their contract might allow them some relief; but, when their requests were rejected by the British Chancellor of the Exchequer and the Parliament, Goldman Sachs "stood firm in honoring its commitment."[12] That contrasted with "[the] other investment banks, [which were] trying to analyze their legal liability and their legal rights to nullify their commitments…[while Goldman] stood firm in honoring [its] commitment."[13] Goldman Sachs was also honoring Principle 12: "Integrity and honesty are the heart of our business. We expect our people to maintain high *ethical* standards in everything they do."

A second Mandis tale illustrates further Goldman's adherence to its principles. Early in his career at Goldman Sachs, Mandis worked with Henry Paulson to give financial advice to the Sara Lee Corporation. Mandis does not describe the subject of their advice[14]; but he does describe the dedication of his group in giving the best possible report: 100-hour work weeks, with Froot Loops for breakfast, and McDonalds hamburgers and fries for dinner; and "financial analysis on every possible alternative and issue" resulting in a 50-to-70 page report accompanied by a 100-page appendix. All with the expectation of "perfection."[15]

The verbal report, on completion of the work, took place in the Sara Lee boardroom. The five assistants sat across the table from the Sara Lee CEO, John Bryan. Paulson sat beside him. First Paulson, and then the assistants gave their explanations, with everyone—and especially Paulson—taking their views "very

8 These holdings were 32 percent of the stock of the company (Mandis, 2013, p. 34).

9 That was to yield an underwriting fee of about 6 percent, since British Petroleum stock had been trading at about 3.5 pounds per share.

10 Mandis (2013, p. 34).

11 Mandis (2013, p. 34).

12 Mandis (2013, p. 34).

13 Mandis (2013, p. 34).

14 Following what is now listed as Principle 12: that "breach[ing] a confidence or to use confidential information improperly or carelessly would be unthinkable." See Goldman Sachs (2019).

15 Mandis (2013, p. 35).

seriously."[16] Furthermore, beyond these arrangements, more usually, it would have been the client's job to ask the questions; the advisors' jobs to answer them.

But that is not what happened in this case, according to Mandis. Instead, Paulson inserted himself as an equal. It's not just where he had placed himself physically: beside Bryan, rather than across the table with his own Goldman-Sachs team. Nor tellingly, did Paulson position himself verbally, as just the "deliverer of the report". Instead Paulson behaved as Bryan's co-equal; that is especially shown as Paulson led the discourse, especially with supplementary questions that "he felt should be on Bryan's mind." Mandis summarizes what is really going on: "I wondered, which one is the client—Bryan or Paulson.... They were one and the same.... To Paulson, Bryan was not a client; rather he was a friend.... This [being a friend]," Mandis continues, "was Goldman's first business principle in action."[17]

A third example of the changes at Goldman Sachs concerned the hiring and firing of employees. The market for skilled employees became much more competitive. When Mandis was first hired, Goldman Sachs would interview candidates at the so-called "best colleges", with offers to only about one percent of the interviewees. Hires at more advanced lateral levels from outside firms were all but nonexistent. This meant that most Goldman Sachs employees had started there at the beginning of their careers; thus greatly easing the transference of the culture from one generation to the next.[18] (We note parenthetically that, in this respect, Goldman Sachs was not that different from West Point.)

A further aspect of employment indicates the expectations of the Goldman-Sachs "We, Not I". There were intransigent norms against solicitation, or even the consideration, of outside job offers—though such offers might be for considerably better pay, and they might also be much more family-friendly than the Goldman-Sachs 100-hour weeks.

A story from Mandis' own experience illustrates how strictly such norms against outside offers were enforced. An employee in Mandis' Acquisitions and Mergers unit told one of the department heads of a potential job-offer from another firm. The response was not a salary raise, or even a smile. Instead, the senior partner involved immediately told security to obtain the offender's "suit jacket" from his cubicle, and to escort him off the floor. Later, such intransigent response to outside offers was relaxed as Goldman addressed the competing pressures it faced in hiring. It even responded in salary and workload to workers that it wanted to keep. And it also took some recruits from outside firms at more advanced levels.

16 Mandis (2013, p. 36).

17 Mandis (2013, p. 36).

18 Mandis (2013, Section: "Rehiring People and Making Counteroffers", pp. 134-135).

In summary, Mandis' view of Goldman Sachs has given us a second example of the central role of culture in an important organization. "The Whitehead Principles" describe what employees and their superiors should—and should *not*—do. Adherence to those norms—and their passage from one generation to the next—plays a major role in the identities of the "We's" of Goldman Sachs; as, in turn, those identities play a major role in their motivation. Thus, we have seen how norms and internalized identities served to shape people at two very different types of institutions.

4 Concluding remarks

This volume contains many examples of historical sources of culture; norms for behavior today are traced to primitives in the past. Identity economics provides a framework to study how such historical norms play out in individual lives. A primary example is gender norms. The seminal study of Alesina et al. (2013) shows that current gender norms track agricultural settings where the plough was a dominant technology. In these areas, men were the primary workers in agricultural production since upper-body strength is an advantage for controlling a plough. Their study finds that the norms concerning gender and women's participation in the labor market exhibit less equality in regions where the plough was dominant. In this chapter, we have shown how identity economics brings such norms into individual decision-making on marriage, household divisions of labor, labor supply, and occupational choice; the identity framework captures how norms shape the large and small decisions and interactions in people's lives. Schooling, as elaborated above, is another primary example of the day-to-day, week-to-week interactions which identity economics captures as instantiations of cultural norms.

In the conclusion of this chapter, we would like to discuss emerging current implications of both gender norms and schooling in the case of men in the United States. The example is both important in the real-world of people's lives and policy; and the example illustrates the possibility of the change in norms and the possibility of equilibrium dynamics in norm change. Much of the literature on gender considers the norms and effects on women. Recently, scholarly and policy concern has turned to the norms for men. Baranov et al. (2023) consider the historical emergence of norms for men, and, particularly, the possibility of notions of masculinity that involve behaviors which are detrimental to physical and mental health. Recently, and increasingly in the United States, researchers and policy makers are concerned with a "crisis of masculinity," as both well-summarized and elaborated in Richard Reeves' *Of Boys and Men* (2022).

An identity framework highlights the problems that can arise when there is a disconnect between the traditional norms for men and what they can accomplish in the labor force. Traditional norms would posit men to earn an independent living and to marry and support a family. With changes in technology and the workplace, however, less-educated men have become less able to fulfill traditional roles and norms as husbands and breadwinners. As before, the phenomena we discuss here could have similar patterns in other societies, but we focus on the United States for specificity, which is key to an identity economics analysis. We will describe three different sets of statistics in the United States, especially for men with low levels of education (that is, no schooling beyond graduation from high school) which pinpoint this crisis. The statistics serve to highlight the day-to-day and week-by-week lives of men and women and families.

Statistics on Marriage. Historically, men with no more than a high school degree would get married at an early age. According to the gender norms of traditional families, and following our model of Section 2 above, marriage would contribute positively to men's identity utility in at least three ways: they are married, they are the prime wage earner, and they are head of household. But over the past five decades, marriage in the United States has been much diminished. Between 1970 and 2015, marriage rates of 35-to-45-year-old male white high school graduates without further education fell from 90 percent to 58 percent; for white high school "dropouts" (i.e. those without high-school completion), from 86 percent to 51 percent. For Blacks of the same age and with high school degrees but no college, the fall was from 70 percent to 38 percent; for the "dropouts," from 66 percent to 27 percent (Binder and Bound, 2019, Table 4, p. 182).

Statistics on Nonparticipation in Labor Force. In the traditional family, as prime earners, men's identity utility would especially depend on holding a job. However, for low-education men there has been a significant increase in the fraction who do not participate in the labor market (Krueger, 2017, Fig. 5, p. 18). Between 1977 and 2017 the rate of labor force "nonparticipation" of low-education prime age males (25 to 54) more than doubled: from approximately 7 percent to approximately 16 percent. That means, that even in 2017, which was a time of almost full employment, 16 percent of these men not only did not hold a job; they were not even seeking one (which would have classified them as in the labor force, although unemployed). A 2016 report by the Council of Economic Advisers further suggests that the time freed from neither holding a job nor seeking one, was not being used to take care of others (such as children and older people). Prime-age male labor-force nonparticipants were spending the same amount of time taking care of others as those who were in the labor force: in both cases an average of just 36 minutes per day. What were they doing instead? On average, the whole sample of prime-age men were spending an average of 154 minutes per day watching TV; in contrast the subsample of nonparticipants were spending 335 minutes (Council of Economic Advisers, 2016, Table 1).

Statistics on Incarceration. Over the forty years from 1972 to 2012, the United States rate of incarceration more than quadrupled: from 161 per 100,000 in 1972 to 706 per 100,000 in 2012 (Travis et al., 2014, p. 13). About 90 percent of incarcerates are men.[19] And about 85 percent of incarcerates are without education beyond high school[20] (see Harlow, 2003, Table 1, p. 3). Hence, the huge increase in incarceration almost surely has had its main direct effect on men with no more than high school or GED education. (We also add that, according to the 2016 census of inmates, the fraction of prisoners currently married and not separated was only 14.9 percent (Beatty and Snell, 2021, Table 2, p. 6).)

An identity framework considers how low rates of marriage and of labor force participation, and the high rate of incarceration, indicate low levels of self-esteem and low levels of peer esteem. In more advanced treatments, such a framework considers the reinforcing dynamics of such outcomes on values and norms of particular subsets of a population (R. Akerlof, 2017). For example, low levels of self-esteem play a major role in a long list of addictions to computer games, to the internet, to alcohol, to opioids, to drugs, and to television which would reinforce the inability to participate in the labor force. The inability, or unwillingness, to find remunerative jobs leads to an erosion of a traditional narrative of marriage (R. Akerlof and Rayo, 2020). The problems of the men, for example, make the women reluctant to marry (Edin and Kefalas, 2011). The women then not only become the prime wage earners, but also, they are the residual caretakers of the children and the elderly, as well as being caretakers for the troubled men themselves—including their unmarried partners, their brothers, their nephews, and even their fathers. R. Akerlof and Rayo (2020) further consider the dynamic reinforcement of the collapse of traditional marriage norms.

The identity economics framework provides a way to see how norms affect individual people's lives, and a primary direction for further study is how norms can change and evolve. While historical circumstances give a legacy of gender norms, for example, gender norms have changed dramatically in many societies, as likewise, conceptions of gender itself have changed. Arguably, with the decline in marriage and the crisis in masculinity described above, gender norms are currently going through another transformation. Race is a similar social category whose definition and norms for behavior have evolved dramatically over time and continue to evolve. These changes have also occurred rapidly, in the past sixty years. Several studies cited earlier, including R. Akerlof (2017) and Carvalho and Sacks (2024), provide theoretical underpinnings of such transformations based on interactions among people and their desire to be part of groups which share their values. Further theoretical research could elaborate such social dynamics and incorporate technological change and other forces which appear to be empirically important drivers of this transformation. An emerging theoretical literature considers the dynamics of politics and

[19] Combining Zeng (2023, Table 2, p. 8) on inmates in jails with Beatty and Snell (2021, Table 1, p. 3) on inmates in prisons.

[20] Harlow (2003, Table 1, p. 3) reports on education levels of both prisons and jails combined. The 85 percent includes those with a GED degree but also no further education beyond high school.

identity, and the relationship with redistribution (Shayo, 2009; Bonomi et al., 2021). Of course, further empirical work could seek to document and identify these processes. An identity economics framework would suggest emphasizing people's personal attachments to political parties and movements.

Future research could engage how norms can change and emerge not only through social interaction but through individual actions and institutional and government policy. Empirical and experimental evidence presented earlier (East Germany, India, West Point, Goldman Sachs) indicates that people act to change norms, and those actions can effectively change people's opinions and their actions. Studies could consider the motivations of these agents of change, and the predictors of their success. As emphasized throughout this chapter, such research should be based on data concerning the specificities of each situation, such as can be found in the work of anthropologists and other social scientists. This research endeavor likely will require efforts from many types of scholars, those who study the large macro determinants of culture and those who study the day-to-day, week-by-week behavior of individuals whose actions are shaped by the norms but whose actions also shape the norms.

References

Aizer, Anna, 2010. The gender wage gap and domestic violence. American Economic Review 100 (4), 1847–1859.

Akerlof, George A., Kranton, Rachel E., 2000. Economics and identity. The Quarterly Journal of Economics 115 (3), 715–753.

Akerlof, George A., Kranton, Rachel E., 2002. Identity and schooling: some lessons for the economics of education. Journal of Economic Literature 40 (4), 1167–1201.

Akerlof, George A., Kranton, Rachel E., 2008. Identity, supervision, and work groups. American Economic Review 98 (2), 212–217.

Akerlof, George A., Kranton, Rachel E., 2010. Identity Economics: How Our Identities Shape Our Work, Wages, and Well-Being. Princeton University Press.

Akerlof, Robert, 2017. Value formation: the role of esteem. Games and Economic Behavior 102, 1–19.

Akerlof, Robert, Matouschek, Niko, Rayo, Luis, 2020. Stories at work. AEA Papers and Proceedings 110, 199–204.

Akerlof, Robert, Rayo, Luis, 2020. Narratives and the Economics of the Family. Working paper. Warwick Economics, No. 1299.

Alesina, Alberto, Giuliano, Paola, Nunn, Nathan, 2013. On the origins of gender roles: women and the plough. The Quarterly Journal of Economics 128 (2), 469–530.

Anderberg, Dan, Rainer, Helmut, Wadsworth, Jonathan, Wilson, Tanya, 2016. Unemployment and domestic violence: theory and evidence. The Economic Journal 126 (597), 1947–1979.

Baranov, Victoria, De Haas, Ralph, Grosjean, Pauline, 2023. Men. Male-biased sex ratios and masculinity norms: evidence from Australia's colonial past. Journal of Economic Growth 28 (3), 339–396.

Beatty, Lauren G., Snell, Tracy L., 2021. Profile of prison inmates, 2016. US Department of Justice, Office of Justice Programs, Bureau of Justice Statistics.

Becker, Gary S., 1962. Investment in human capital: a theoretical analysis. Journal of Political Economy 70 (5, Part 2), 9–49.

Bénabou, Roland, Tirole, Jean, 2002. Self-confidence and personal motivation. The Quarterly Journal of Economics 117 (3), 871–915.

Bénabou, Roland, Tirole, Jean, 2011. Identity, morals, and taboos: beliefs as assets. The Quarterly Journal of Economics 126 (2), 805–855.
Benjamin, Daniel J., Choi, James J., Strickland, A. Joshua, 2010. Social identity and preferences. American Economic Review 100 (4), 1913–1928.
Bernheim, Douglas, 1994. A theory of conformity. Journal of Political Economy 102 (5), 841–877.
Bertrand, Marianne, Kamenica, Emir, Pan, Jessica, 2015. Gender identity and relative income within households. The Quarterly Journal of Economics 130 (2), 571–614.
Binder, Ariel J., Bound, John, 2019. The declining labor market prospects of less-educated men. Journal of Economic Perspectives 33 (2), 163–190.
Bisin, Alberto, Verdier, Thierry, 2000. Beyond the melting pot: cultural transmission, marriage, and the evolution of ethnic and religious traits. Quarterly Journal of Economics 115 (3), 955–988.
Bisin, Alberto, Verdier, Thierry, 2001. The economics of cultural transmission and the dynamics of preferences. Journal of Economic Theory 97 (2), 298–319.
Bittman, Michael, England, Paula, Sayer, Liana, Folbre, Nancy, Matheson, George, 2003. When does gender trump money? Bargaining and time in household work. American Journal of Sociology 109 (1), 186–214.
Bonilla, S., Dee, T.S., Penner, E.K., 2021. Ethnic studies increases longer-run academic engagement and attainment. Proceedings of the National Academy of Sciences 118 (37).
Bonomi, Giampaolo, Gennaioli, Nicola, Tabellini, Guido, 2021. Identity, beliefs, and political conflict. The Quarterly Journal of Economics 136 (4), 2371–2411.
Brock, William A., Durlauf, Steven N., 2001. Discrete choice with social interactions. The Review of Economic Studies 68 (2), 235–260.
Bursztyn, Leonardo, Fujiwara, Thomas, Pallais, Amanda, 2017. 'Acting wife': marriage market incentives and labor market investments. American Economic Review 107 (11), 3288–3319.
Bursztyn, Leonardo, González, Alessandra L., Yanagizawa-Drott, David, 2020. Misperceived social norms: women working outside the home in Saudi Arabia. American Economic Review 110 (10), 2997–3029.
Cabrera, Nolan L., Milem, Jeffery F., Jaquette, Ozan, Marx, Ronald W., 2014. Missing the (student achievement) forest for all the (political) trees empiricism and the Mexican American studies controversy in Tucson. American Educational Research Journal 51, 1084–1118.
Carrell, Scott, Sacerdote, Bruce I., West, James Edward, 2013. From natural variation to optimal policy? The importance of endogenous peer group formation. Econometrica 81 (3), 855–882.
Carvalho, Jean-Paul, 2013. Veiling. Quarterly Journal of Economics 128 (1), 337–370.
Carvalho, Jean-Paul, 2017. Coordination and culture. Economic Theory 64 (3), 449–475.
Carvalho, Jean-Paul, Koyama, Mark, Williams, Cole, 2024. Resisting education. Journal of the European Economic Association 22 (6), 2549–2597.
Carvalho, Jean-Paul, Sacks, Michael, 2024. Radicalisation. The Economic Journal 134 (659), 1019–1068.
Charness, Gary, Chen, Yan, 2020. Social identity, group behavior, and teams. Annual Review of Economics 12 (1), 691–713.
Clots-Figueras, I., Masella, P., 2013. Education, language and identity. The Economic Journal 123 (570), F332–F357.
Coase, Ronald H., 1937. The nature of the firm. Economica 4 (16), 386–405.
Coleman, James S., 1961. The Adolescent Society. Greenwood Press.
Council of Economic Advisers, 2016. The long-term decline in prime-age male labor force participation. Report. White House, Washington. https://obamawhitehouse.archives.gov/sites/default/files/page/files/20160620_cea_primeage_male_lfp.pdf.
Dhanaraj, Sowmya, Mahambare, Vidya, 2022. Male backlash and female guilt: women's employment and intimate partner violence in urban India. Feminist Economics 28 (1), 170–198.
Dhar, Diva, Jain, Tarun, Jayachandran, Seema, 2022. Reshaping adolescents' gender attitudes: evidence from a school-based experiment in India. American Economic Review 112 (3), 899–927.

Edin, Kathryn, Kefalas, Maria, 2011. Promises I Can Keep: Why Poor Women Put Motherhood Before Marriage. Univ of California Press.

Farre, Lidia, Vella, Francis, 2013. The intergenerational transmission of gender role attitudes and its implications for female labor force participation. Economica 80, 219–247.

Folke, Olle, Rickne, Johanna, 2020. All the single ladies: job promotions and the durability of marriage. American Economic Journal: Applied Economics 12 (1), 260–287.

Fortin, Nicole M., 2005. Gender role attitudes and the labour-market outcomes of women across OECD countries. Oxford Review of Economic Policy 21 (3), 416–438.

Fouka, Vasiliki, 2020. Backlash: the unintended effects of language prohibition in US schools after World War I. The Review of Economic Studies 87 (1), 204–239.

Goldin, Claudia, 2006. The quiet revolution that transformed women's employment, education, and family. American Economic Review 96 (2), 1–21.

Goldin, Claudia, 2002. The rising (and then declining) significance of gender. NBER Working Paper 8915.

Goldman Sachs, 2019. Goldman Sachs introduces 14 business principles that define the firm. https://www.goldmansachs.com/our-firm/history/moments/1979-business-principles.

Grosjean, Pauline, Khattar, Rose, 2019. It's raining men! Hallelujah? The long-run consequences of male-biased sex ratios. The Review of Economic Studies 86 (2), 723–754.

Guarnieri, Eleonora, Rainer, Helmut, 2021. Colonialism and female empowerment: a two-sided legacy. Journal of Development Economics 151, 102666.

Guiso, Luigi, Sapienza, Paola, Zingales, Luigi, 2006. Does culture affect economic outcomes? Journal of Economic Perspectives 20 (2), 23–48.

Harlow, Caroline Wolf, 2003. Education and correctional populations. Bureau of Justice Statistics Special Report, NCJ 195670.

Hersch, Joni, Stratton, Leslie S., 1994. Housework, wages, and the division of housework time for employed spouses. The American Economic Review 84 (2), 120–125.

Hochschild, Arlie, 2012. The Second Shift: Working Families and the Revolution at Home. Penguin Books.

Holmstrom, Bengt, Milgrom, Paul, 1991. Multitask principal–agent analyses: incentive contracts, asset ownership, and job design. The Journal of Law, Economics, and Organization 7 (special issue), 24–52.

Kreps, David, 2023. Arguing About Tastes: Modeling How Context and Experience Change Economic Preference. Columbia University Press.

Krishnan, Suneeta, Rocca, Corinne H., Hubbard, Alan E., Subbiah, Kalyani, Edmeades, Jeffrey, Padian, Nancy S., 2010. Do changes in spousal employment status lead to domestic violence? Insights from a prospective study in Bangalore, India. Social Science & Medicine 70 (1), 136–143.

Krueger, Allan B., 2017. Where have all the workers gone? An inquiry into the decline of the U.S. labor force participation rate. Brookings Papers on Economic Activity 48 (2), 1–87.

Lippmann, Quentin, Georgieff, Alexandre, Senik, Claudia, 2020. Undoing gender with institutions: lessons from the German division and reunification. The Economic Journal 130 (629), 1445–1470.

Lipsky, David, 2003. Absolutely American: Four Years at West Point. Houghton Mifflin, Boston.

Lundberg, Shelly, Pollak, Robert A., 1996. Bargaining and distribution in marriage. Journal of Economic Perspectives 10 (4), 139–158.

Mandis, Steven, 2013. What Happened to Goldman Sachs: An Insider's Story of Organizational Drift and Its Unintended Consequences. Harvard Business Review Press, Boston. Kindle edition.

Manski, Charles F., 1993. Identification of endogenous social effects: the reflection problem. The Review of Economic Studies 60 (3), 531–542.

Oh, Suanna, 2023. Does identity affect labor supply? American Economic Review 113 (8), 2055–2083.

Prendergast, Canice, 1999. The provision of incentives in firms. Journal of Economic Literature 37 (1), 7–63.
Reeves, Richard V., 2022. Of Boys and Men: Why the Modern Male Is Struggling, Why It Matters, and What to do About It. Brookings Institution Press.
Ross, Stephen A., 1973. The economic theory of agency: the principal's problem. The American Economic Review 63 (2), 134–139.
Shayo, Moses, 2009. A model of social identity with an application to political economy: nation, class, and redistribution. American Political Science Review 103 (2), 147–174.
Shayo, Moses, 2020. Social identity and economic policy. Annual Review of Economics 12 (1), 355–389.
Smith, Adam, 1937. An Inquiry into the Nature and Causes of the Wealth of Nations (1776). Modern Library Edition.
Stigler, George J., Becker, Gary S., 1977. De gustibus non est disputandum. The American Economic Review 67 (2), 76–90.
Travis, Jeremy, Western, Bruce, Redburn, F. Stevens, 2014. The Growth of Incarceration in the United States: Exploring Causes and Consequences. National Research Council (U.S.), Committee on Law and Justice, National Academies Press.
Voigtländer, Nico, Voth, Hans-Joachim, 2015. Nazi indoctrination and anti-semitic beliefs in Germany. Proceedings of the National Academy of Sciences 112 (26), 7931–7936.
Young, H. Peyton, 1993. The evolution of conventions. Econometrica 61 (1), 57–84.
Zeng, Zhen, 2023. Jail inmates in 2022–Statistical tables. US Department of Justice Bureau of Justice Statistics, Washington, DC.

Chapter 8

Biological foundations of economic behavior☆

Arthur J. Robson[a] **and Nikolaus Robalino**[b]
[a]*Department of Economics, Simon Fraser University, Burnaby, BC, Canada,* [b]*Department of Economics, Rochester Institute of Technology, Rochester, NY, United States*

1 Introduction

The traditional economic approach to preferences is "creationist". That is, a set of abstract axioms is proposed, evaluated in terms of their inherent plausibility, and the logical implications for choice behavior of the axioms are derived.[1] An evolutionary approach considers instead how particular preferences might realistically have been the product of Darwinian natural selection, so outcompeting and displacing the alternatives.

The evolutionary approach does not inevitably contradict the axiomatic approach but suggests modifications that might not otherwise suggest themselves. For example, an essentially demographic theory of the evolution of attitudes to risk implies classical expected utility when gambles are statistically independent across individuals. That is, individuals whose choices maximize the appropriate form of expected utility will numerically swamp those whose choices do not. When gambles are correlated, however, the favored risk attitudes may no longer be consistent with expected utility, but might instead entail interdependent preferences. This latter possibility arises specifically due to the demographic nature of the model and might seem implausible outside of an evolutionary context.

The evolutionary approach takes little for granted. It is not merely the properties of utility that are subjected to the forge of natural selection, but aspects of decision making that are often taken for granted. Indeed, Section 2 begins by asking the basic question—Why might we have utility functions in

☆ We thank Ben Enke, Nathan Nunn, Larry Samuelson, and participants at the conference at Northwestern University on the Economics of Culture for helpful comments. We thank Babak Sahragard for research assistance. Robson thanks the Social Sciences and Humanities Research Council of Canada for financial support. The authors' names were randomized by the AEA author randomization tool, https://www.aeaweb.org/journals/random-author-order.

[1] For example, von Neumann and Morgenstern (1944) derive expected utility theory from a small set of reasonable axioms on choice in the presence of uncertainty. Savage (1954) extends this work to account for subjective probabilities.

Handbook of Culture and Economic Behavior, Volume 1, ISSN 3051-1682
https://doi.org/10.1016/bs.hceb.2026.02.003

the first place? The answer given is that the possession of a utility function allows the individual free agency, so individuals can take full advantage of local information.

Given a basic rationale for utility functions, we then move on to ask what properties they might have. Robson and Samuelson (2024), for example, argue that neuroscience provides evidence that utility is not merely a pale reflection of choice as in the theory of revealed preference but is "substantive"—a term defined by them to mean represented as quantifiable neural activity in the brain, where this activity drives choice rather than simply reflecting it.

This neural perspective is the first of two evolutionary approaches considered here.[2] Neuroscientific evidence first implicates hard-wired cognitive structures as underlying decision-making. These then suggest features to be incorporated in models of utility that are ultimately biological in origin. This approach is not maximally reductionist, but is built on a solid foundation of direct observation.

Since all neural processes are irreducibly noisy, this implies that utility should adapt to circumstances. In this chapter, we review a model of this adaptation and its empirical implications—a preference for growth, the "hedonic treadmill" and the Easterlin paradox, among these. The rich implications constitute the "proof of the pudding" for the adaptive model.

The resulting model of adaptive substantive utility indeed has some kinship to the large literature on habit formation in economics. For example, Campbell and Cochrane (1999) apply a simple model of habit formation to address anomalies arising in dynamic asset pricing. The agent evaluates present consumption relative to a stock representing the level of habit, where this level is itself built up from the history of consumption. However, the details of the present formulation are new; further, the dependence on history here is a result rather than an assumption.

The second approach to the evolutionary basis of behavior examined in this chapter is explicitly evolutionary and essentially demographic in nature. This considers the effect of various choices on population growth rates, using demographic models of the implications for growth rates of lifetime profiles of fertility and mortality. The type having the lifetime profiles that induce the fastest growth will then be selected since it will ultimately dominate a population that starts with any mixture of the types. This represents a Darwinian methodology in a straightforward manner. A systematic, explicitly evolutionary approach like this to preferences seems largely new in economics.

Section 3 investigates the implications of this demographic approach for attitudes to idiosyncratic risk and time preference. It first shows that an individual should be risk neutral with respect to idiosyncratic risk concerning offspring, which translates readily into the expected utility theorem. We argue for the plasticity of attitudes to risk so that the choice of gamble might adjust

[2] The second approach taken in this chapter was informally applied already in this introduction. More formally, it relies on demographic modeling and an explicit analysis of evolutionary dynamics. We discuss this second approach in greater detail in Sections 3 and 4.

appropriately to the environment, given this can be observed by the individual. Such plasticity arises as the careful tailoring of utility to current circumstances rather than a capricious change in attitudes to risk.

This demographic approach generates the simplest standard form of time preference, where an intertemporal consumption stream is evaluated as a sum of flow utilities weighted by a geometrically growing discount factor. A geometrically growing contribution to the discount factor arises from a new source—population growth. There is also a contribution from mortality to discounting, which is a well-known effect, being described by Fisher (1930).

Such time preference might have been exercised in hunter-gatherer societies despite the lack of opportunities to borrow or save, involving instead the substantial intergenerational transfers then prevalent. The pure rate of time preference found theoretically is shown to be capable of accounting for moderate modern observations. This rate of time preference may also be plastic—adjusting appropriately to variation in the observed environment. Furthermore, the model suggests testable hypotheses concerning how the ancestral environment of a particular country would influence modern rates of time preference.

Section 4 then shows how this second demographic approach generates a greater aversion to aggregate risk than to idiosyncratic risk. In the model of Robson (1996), individuals who, in each generation, experience a distribution of offspring independently of others do better in the long run than do individuals who experience the same distribution but where the outcomes are correlated across individuals. This greater aversion to aggregate risk than to idiosyncratic risk is not an hypothesis that seems to have arisen previously in just that guise.

Robson (1996) has generated a small but persistent literature. The role of the discrete time basis of the effect was illuminated by Robatto and Szentes (2017) who show that, in a continuous time framework where the birth rate and mortality are age independent, the contrast between attitudes to aggregate and idiosyncratic risk disappears. Robson and Samuelson (2019) show that the contrast generally reappears in a continuous time framework in which fertility and mortality are age dependent, although it is not inevitable that idiosyncratic risk is preferred. Robson and Samuelson (2024) present an extensive discussion of this theoretical debate.

Here, we consider theoretical arguments that are helpful in framing the contrast empirically—and review work by Oprea and Robalino (2024) showing that such a distinction can be seen in experiments. These experiments show that a significant distinction arises even in a laboratory setting where aggregate risk entails outcomes that are shared only by the subjects actually present.

This surprising prediction concerning a differential response to aggregate risk drawn from an evolutionary perspective dramatizes the scientific value of this approach.

The focus so far has been on the individual. Ultimately, however, it is crucial to consider human social interactions, which are often the central concern. We take a step in this direction in Section 5 by looking at "theory of mind" (ToM) as in psychology where agents recognize the agency of themselves and others. Individuals have only a "theory" of another individual's preferences and beliefs, for example, since they must infer these from behavior. This is perhaps the central component of human social intelligence. Here we consider, in particular, the implications of recognizing that others have preferences that may differ from one's own.

Using Robalino and Robson (2016) and Kimbrough et al. (2017), we discuss theoretically why the attribution of payoffs to others would promote evolutionary success. This applies essentially the demographic approach. We then look at relevant experiments from Kimbrough et al. (2017) that examine how well individuals predict the choices of others in strategic interactions. If you have observed another agent's choice between various alternatives in previous plays of a game, you may be able to predict their choice in future plays. The game is constructed so that this prediction can be made with varying degrees of sophistication. We correlate performance in such strategic settings with measures of autism, a key component of which is thought to be a lack of theory of mind.

2 A biological rationale for utility

We start with a broad evolutionary rationale for a fundamental economic concept—that of utility—a rationale that might apply to distant ancestral species of humans as well. The basic framework we propose is that of the principal-agent problem, where evolution is the principal and the individual is the agent.[3]

A typical application in economics for the principal-agent model is to the interaction between an owner of a firm and the manager. The manager knows much more about the day to day operation of the firm, and knows how hard he himself works, in particular. The owner observes the profits of the firm which are only a noisy signal of the manager's effort, and designs a contract to best incentivize the manager to maximize the net profit of the owner.

As in that model, there is a gain from evolution devolving partial control to the individual because the individual has information about current local conditions that evolution does not. More precisely, this is because current local conditions are so novel that evolution would not have been able to program an optimal response, to build an automaton that responds appropriately to these local conditions.

Why would it make sense for evolution to devolve only some control over the actions of the individual? The wrinkle here is that evolution also knows things that the individual does not. These might concern the long-run evolutionary consequences of outcomes attained. This consideration means that it might well be optimal for evolution to convey such information by means of a utility

[3] This analogy to the principal-agent model was proposed by Binmore (1994). The principal agent model in economics is outlined in Mas-Colell et al. (1995, Chapter 14).

function. For example, the fitness advantages of a balanced diet might not be immediately apparent to an individual, who only has limited direct data available. However, if the appropriate utility function were embedded in the agent, the experience of many generations of ancestors concerning a balanced diet could be effectively taken into account.

Consider a simple model to illustrate this argument concerning dietary diversity. Suppose an individual must first choose one of I foods to forage for, and then one of J locations at which to forage. Choosing good $i = 1, ..., I$ and location $j = 1, ..., J$ means the individual has probability $p^i_j \in [0, 1]$ of obtaining 1 unit of this i-th good in one period.[4] We will consider two cases—either that these probabilities are known by evolution or—if they are not—that they are instead known to the individual.

To simplify the calculations, suppose draws for these goods at these locations are taken frequently, so that there are r draws per unit of time, with the quantities of the various goods scaled accordingly by $1/r$ to keep the overall level of consumption comparable. As $r \to \infty$, the choice of good i at location j then generates a deterministic flow of that good at rate p^i_j, by the strong law of large numbers.

Dietary diversity is introduced by supposing the individual can apportion her time across the possible goods and locations. Suppose the proportion of time the individual chooses good i is π_i for each i, where $\sum_i \pi_i = 1$ and suppose that the location used if good i is chosen is j_i.[5] Suppose the arrival rate of offspring is then given by the function

$$\lambda\left(\pi_1 p^1_{j_1}, \pi_2 p^2_{j_2}, ...\right)$$

which reflects how flow fitness depends on the flow rates of goods. This function λ is assumed to be strictly increasing in each argument.

Let us first suppose that the various probabilities p^i_j are known to evolution, as is the utility function λ, meaning more precisely just that this entire problem has persisted in its current form for a long time. Then evolution's design problem is straightforward—solve

$$\max_{\pi} \lambda\left(\pi_1 \max_j p^1_j, \pi_2 \max_j p^2_j, ...\right),$$

since choosing j_i to maximize p^i_j for each i is uniformly best, regardless of π. That is, in this case, evolution can reduce the role of the individual, making the evolutionarily appropriate choices on his behalf of time allocation π_i and of location conditional on the good chosen. The assumption that evolution knows all these probabilities, or that there has been sufficient time for the appropriate optimal choices to have been selected, is not generally plausible, however.

4 Obtaining a good i at date t is independent of obtaining other goods $j \neq i$ and over t.

5 Mixing over locations would not be difficult to allow.

Suppose now, more plausibly, that evolution does not know the probabilities p^i_j. The entire problem is too transient for evolution to exploit. In particular, there has not been time for the optimal choice of good and location to have been directly prescribed by evolution. The probabilities can, however, be observed by the individual, who is familiar with local idiosyncrasies.

This situation creates an opportunity for a mechanism of partial devolution of control to be evolutionarily optimal. Since evolution does not know the probabilities, it is desirable to allow the individual to make use of her knowledge of these. One way to achieve the optimum is to embed evolution's function λ—flow fitness—as the utility function in each agent. In addition, agents should be given the motivation to maximize this utility function. The agent is then responsible for picking the best location for each good and for choosing the right weights for each good given the utility.

A conceptually related model is in Robson (2001b). In that model the individual faces a two armed bandit that becomes degenerate with many repetitions. It then pays for evolution to dictate the von Neumann-Morgenstern utility of the various outcomes, while leaving the individual to learn the appropriate probabilities.

Why does the optimal decentralization of control from evolution to the individual stop here? Why give the individual a utility function that depends on consumption? Why wouldn't the appropriate utility be simply offspring? Why not have the individual simply observe the actual offspring produced as a consequence of any choice of consumption? Offspring, after all, are only the final good, and consumption is just a means to an end, an intermediate good. Why do we care about food, sex, and so on, when these are only biologically advantageous for the offspring they help produce?

One answer is as follows. The problem is that there is only a small number of offspring produced in each lifetime. If a population were in steady state, each parthenogenetic (asexual) individual would produce one offspring on average. With sex, each couple would produce two, in the steady state. Not many, in any event. If an individual relied on observing the actual number of offspring produced, there would necessarily be a significant probability of making the wrong choice. Relying on the right utility would reduce the probability of such mistakes to zero.

Suppose, for example, that an individual faces two options, to strip the problem to the bare minimum. Option A has higher expected offspring than option B and hence should be chosen. In particular, option A generates 1 offspring with probability $1/3$ and 2 offspring with probability $2/3$ and option B generates 1 offspring with probability $2/3$ and 2 with probability $1/3$.[6] The individual does not know this and has no reason to prefer either option over the other, but can observe one independent draw of each option and then has to commit to one of them. If one option generates more offspring in the

6 These offspring numbers are only meant to capture the issue in a simple way.

trial, that option is chosen; if they generate the same number, choice is made on a 50-50 basis. The probability of committing to A is then $(2/3)(2/3) + 2(1/2)(1/3)(2/3) = 2/3$ which is the probability of observing 2 offspring from A and 1 from B plus a half the probability of observing the same number from A and B. Hence the probability of committing to B is $1/3 > 0$ which is less than the probability of committing to A, but still positive.

Building a preference for A into the individual's utility, on the other hand, can be accomplished by using the evolutionary experience of a large number of ancestors and ensures the correct choice can be always made. More precisely, the individuals who give a higher utility to A than to B have expected offspring $1/3 + 4/3 = 5/3$ and hence grow faster than the individuals who give a higher utility to B than to A and have expected offspring $2/3 + 2/3 = 4/3$. Clearly, the type that prefers A does better than the type that experiments, since B is chosen by 1/3 of these types. In this sense, evolution is wise to things that the individual is not.

2.1 The neural representation of utility

In the previous subsection, we sketched a basic rationale for the existence of utility functions, as part of an evolutionary mechanism to shift partial control from evolution to the individual in order to exploit the individual's familiarity with idiosyncratic current circumstances. We turn now to a more detailed account of the implementation of utility in the brain. We argue that neural processes represent utility in a concrete and quantifiable fashion and that this drives choice rather than being merely a ghostly reflection of it.

Robson and Samuelson (2024) propose a three way nested classification of possible notions of utility:

1) Representational utility. This is the standard view that utility is merely an analytical device used to describe behavior, but without any independent existence. Utility is then described as "preferences" to emphasize the weakness of the notion. The culmination of this notion is the theory of revealed preference, which involves a set of axioms that constitute the irreducible nub of demand theory, so that further simplification must have observable consequences for demand.[7]

2) Substantive utility. Robson and Samuelson (2024) use this term to denote utility that has a concrete existence, as neural activity in the brain, and is the form of utility advocated here. Further, utility does not merely reflect choice but drives it and so it is representational and more. The payback from adopting this perspective is that it suggests properties of utility that would not be as compelling under revealed preference. Once utility is seen as neural activity, in particular, it is natural to consider how the prevalence of neural noise leads

7 Revealed preference theory is outlined in Mas-Colell et al. (1995, Chapter 1).

to possibly erroneous choice, making adaptation a central feature.[8] We sketch these implications here; they are developed further by Robson and Samuelson (2024).

3) Hedonic utility. In a more tentative spirit, Robson and Samuelson suggest that utility is not merely substantive but can be interpreted in terms of affect or pleasure. This notion of utility has a lineage stretching back to Bentham (2007) who advocated a notion of cardinal and hedonic utility. Bentham was mainly preoccupied with social welfare. In order to make social trade-offs, utility must be cardinally comparable in some fashion across individuals; Bentham thought the hedonic element would provide a basis for this. The modern revealed preference approach was the culmination of the reaction against such earlier views, a reaction that came to be organized around "Occam's Razor"—the principle that redundant hypotheses should be dropped.[9] An hedonic view of utility is involved in modern discussions of "life satisfaction"—see Clark et al. (2018), for example.

We turn now to evidence that buttresses the notion of utility as substantive at least and derive the implications. We briefly mention the more incomplete evidence bearing on hedonic utility.

Stauffer et al. (2014) (SLS) provide evidence that utility is directly represented in the brain and apparently drives choice. The evidence concerns primates and some of it involves direct observation of neural activity.

Two monkeys, A and B, are offered juice rewards. By finding the certainty equivalents to various binary gambles, SLS first derive von Neumann-Morgenstern (vNM) utility for each monkey, using a familiar procedure that is purely behavioral. As might be found for human subjects using a similar procedure, the resulting vNM utility function is S-shaped. SLS check that this vNM utility function predicts choices between the certainty equivalent and various out-of-sample gambles. This construction is represented in Fig. 1.

They now show that vNM utility is realized in the brain by dopamine-producing neurons. Most basically, perhaps, a burst of activity of the dopamine neurons is associated with an unanticipated physical reward. Indeed, these unanticipated neural firing rates are quantitatively similar to behavioral vNM utility. See Fig. 2.

The precise role of dopamine in shaping behavior remains controversial, despite a backdrop consensus that dopamine has some connection to both behavior and emotion. On the one hand, Schultz (2015), for example, stresses that dopamine plays a central role in inducing learning. On the other hand, Berridge (2007, 2009) is a leading proponent of the view that dopamine reflects the desire for something, and is not tied rigidly to learning. He buttresses his argument by pointing to instances where learning occurs without the aid of dopamine.

8 Glimcher (2011) advocates a related concept of utility as generated by neural processes and subject to inescapable error.

9 Kahneman et al. (1997) is a modern revival of some of Bentham's views.

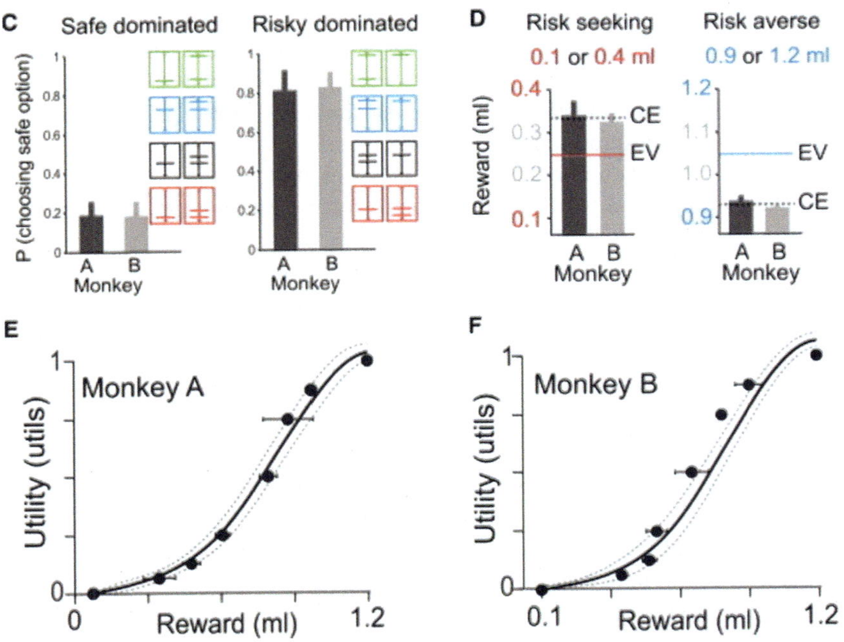

FIGURE 1 This describes the purely behavioral construction of von Neumann-Morgenstern (vNM) utility for each of two monkeys presented with a choice between a binary 50-50 gamble over juice rewards and a certain outcome. This experiment requires a huge number of repetitions in order that the monkeys appreciate what the gambles involve. This figure excerpts Stauffer et al.'s (2014) Fig. 1. Used under Creative Commons.

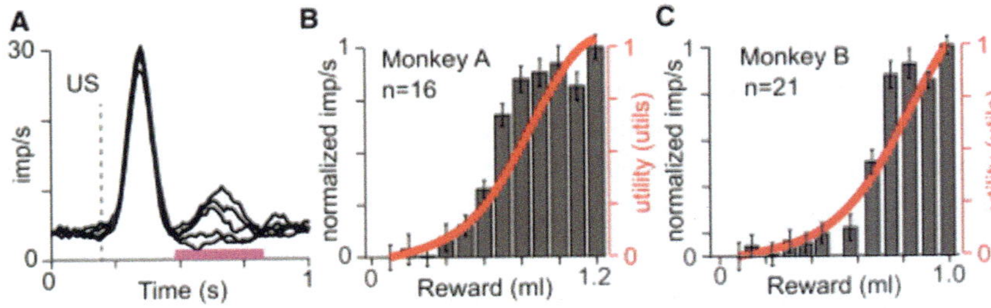

FIGURE 2 This reports the results of presenting each subject monkey with various, unanticipated quantities of the reward. The bar graphs depict the firing rates of dopamine neurons in response to the reward; the (red) superimposed curve is the vNM utility obtained behaviorally as in Fig. 1. The firing rates used derive from the region in the first panel that is underlined, which is where the effect of the differing amounts of juice is seen. This is Stauffer et al.'s (2014) Fig. 4. Used under Creative Commons.

A typical current view is that pleasure often arises from a few small neural sites that are spatially distributed in the brain. These sites involve so-called opioid receptors. Recent progress (e.g., Kragel et al. (2023)) has been made in recognizing a characteristic pattern of activation that can be associated with pleasure, where such pleasure summarizes multiattribute rewards. Berridge and Kringelbach (2015) provide a recent survey of research on the neural foundation and function of pleasure. They describe the similarity of the circuitry switched on in diverse pleasures ranging widely from food to music. Such a system apparently uses a common currency of pleasure, permitting a flexible response to novel stimuli, so a wide variety of options can be evaluated, compared and chosen among.

The consumption of food is an illuminating example of how behavior may be driven by hedonic utility, as represented by opioid receptor activity. Tuulari et al. (2017) find experimentally that food causes a significant surge in endogenous opioids in humans, after consumption of either a palatable or a non-palatable meal.

Altogether, a tentative picture that emerges for the mechanism behind feeding behavior is that (i) dopamine either helps control learning about cues leading to food acquisition (as described by Stauffer et al. (2014)) or orchestrates "wanting" food (as hypothesized by Berridge (2009), for example), or both, while (ii) opioid receptors, for example, generate a pleasurable response to the actual consumption of food.

With respect to either dopamine or opioid receptors the evolutionary history is deep, going back well beyond hunting and gathering, to ancestral non-human species. Dopamine has a huge variety of functions, many of which appear unrelated to the present focus. Costa and Schoenbaum (2022) provide a summary account of both the functions of dopamine and its evolutionary antiquity, as evidenced by its being currently found in fruit flies and sea snails. Dreborg et al. (2008) trace opioid receptors back at least 450 million years to the first vertebrates with jaws. However, it is plausible that hunting and gathering refined the mechanisms implementing utility.

Freed (2022, Chapter 11) is a compelling and clear textbook treatment of current knowledge of the neuroscientific basis of motivation and choice. He provides an engaging account of the roles of dopamine and opioid receptors, in particular.

2.2 A model of adaptive substantive utility

The previous subsection outlined evidence for noisy and adaptive substantive utility. We now consider two models of how substantive utility is realized in the brain, the first of these is in the limelight in Sections 2.2.1-2.2.6 and the second is sketched in Section 2.3. These models share a common motivation and differ only in the details as to how they capture this.

As a simile, consider the issue of measuring a voltage in physics. With many voltmeters, it is necessary to first guess the right range in which the unknown voltage lies. If you guess a range that is too high, the needle might not budge, and so no useful information is obtained; if you guess a range that is too low,

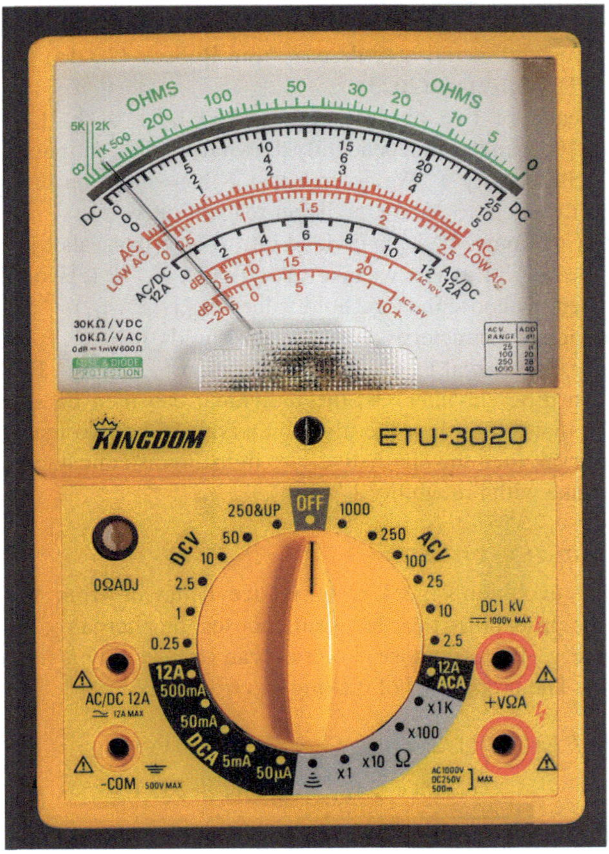

FIGURE 3 Voltmeter with various ranges for voltages. Creative Commons. A.M. Felicisimo.

the needle will peg against the stop at the top, or the meter will blow out, and again no information can be obtained (Fig. 3).

Analogously, we propose that bundles of goods are only perceived with imprecision, and that this imprecision leads to errors in choice that can be offset by adaptation of perception. In Section 2.1 we summarized evidence that von Neumann-Morgenstern utilities correspond to measurable events in the brain, firing rates of dopamine neurons, in particular. Given that utility is concrete and noisy like this, there will be an evolutionary advantage in designing utility functions that shift with the circumstances. That is, it will pay to have more precise perception where the traffic is heavy and less precise perception where the traffic is light. If traffic patterns shift, then it will pay for perception to shift in response. There is an advantage in putting the "steep part" of the utility function where it counts.

2.2.1 A threshold model

This basic threshold model here derives from Robson (2001a) which is much elaborated in Robson et al. (2023).

Suppose each of two alternatives, denoted by $i \in \{1,2\}$, generates an outcome $y_i \in [0, 1]$ that is independently drawn from the continuous distribution function F with density f. We assume that F has values on $[0, 1]$. Evolution would prefer the agent to secure the larger realization y_i.

The set of outcomes $[0, 1]$ is divided into $N + 1$ intervals by N thresholds $0 < x_1 < .... < x_N < 1$, where we take $x_0 = 0$ and $x_{N+1} = 1$. Evolution's design problem is then to choose the threshold values of $\{x_1, \ldots x_N\}$.[10]

The individual characterized by the thresholds $0 < x_1 < .... < x_N < 1$ observes only the interval to which the realization y_i belongs. Faced with two realizations in different intervals, the individual can then be sure the higher realization is that falling into the higher interval. If the two realizations lie in the same interval, then the alternatives are indistinguishable and the individual makes a mistake with probability $1/2$.

2.2.2 Minimizing error

Suppose that evolution's goal is to induce behavior from the agent that minimizes the probability that the agent chooses the alternative with the lower realized value y_i. First, suppose evolution can choose only a single threshold, denoted by x. The probability of making an error is

$$\begin{aligned} PE(1) &= (1/2)\Pr\{y_1, y_2 < x\} + (1/2)\Pr\{y_1, y_2 > x\} \\ &= (1/2)(F(x))^2 + (1/2)(1 - F(x))^2 \\ &= (1/2)\xi^2 + (1/2)(1 - \xi)^2, \end{aligned}$$

where y_1 and y_2 are the outcomes of the two arms and $\xi = F(x)$. That is, an error occurs if and only if y_1 and y_2 are either both below or both above x, when the probability of an erroneous decision is $1/2$.

This objective function is a convex function of ξ, so the first-order condition is sufficient:

$$\frac{dPE(1)}{d\xi} = \xi - (1 - \xi) = 0,$$

and hence $\xi = F(x) = \frac{1}{2}$. Thus x should be the median of the distribution described by F.

Evolution's preferred utility function then depends on the distribution F generating realizations.

---

10 Evolution must also choose the number of thresholds, N, given the costs and benefits of N. Whatever N is chosen, however, the thresholds should be optimally allocated.

What if the agent is able to identify multiple thresholds? Suppose there are N thresholds

$$0 = x_0 < x_1 < x_2 < ... < x_N < x_{N+1} = 1.$$

The probability of error is now

$$\begin{aligned} PE(N) &= (1/2)(F(x_1))^2 + ... + (1/2)(F(x_{n+1}) - F(x_n))^2 + ... \\ &\quad + (1/2)(1 - F(x_N))^2 \\ &= (1/2)(\xi_1)^2 + ... + (1/2)(\xi_{n+1} - \xi_n)^2 + ... + (1/2)(1 - \xi_N)^2, \end{aligned}$$

where $\xi_n = F(x_n)$ for $n = 1, ..., N$. Each term is the probability that y_1 and y_2 both fall between the same pair of threshold values, times the probability $1/2$ that an erroneous decision then occurs.

It follows readily that the optimal allocation of thresholds, the one that minimizes $PE(N)$, is given by

$$\xi_n = F(x_n) = \frac{n}{(N+1)}, \quad \text{for } n = 1, ..., N.$$

The thresholds that minimize the probability of error are thus equally spaced in terms of probability. If $N = 9$, the thresholds should be at the deciles of the distribution.

The probability of error $PE(N)$, when the thresholds are (optimally) evenly spaced in terms of probability, is

$$PE(N) = \overbrace{\frac{1}{2(N+1)^2} + ... + \frac{1}{2(N+1)^2}}^{N+1 \text{ terms}} = \frac{1}{2(N+1)} \to 0, \text{ as } N \to \infty.$$

Each term is the probability that y_1 and y_2 both fall between a common pair of thresholds, multiplied by the probability of one half of then making an error. Additional thresholds are advantageous—evolution prefers larger values of N. Increasing N sharpens the agent's perceptual precision. The optimal number of thresholds balances the benefits of better decision making against the cost of more precise perception.

In the limit as N gets arbitrarily large, the limiting density of thresholds is the density function f. The simplest utility function, which corresponds to counting thresholds in the finite N case, would assign the realization y to y's percentile rank in the distribution of thresholds. For a given distribution f of thresholds, the utility of realization y is then

$$U(y) = \int_0^y f(z)dz.$$

Having an infinite number of thresholds ensures that the agent never makes a mistake. We appeal to this limiting case mainly to shed light on the shape of the utility function. This shape remains, even in the limit when there are no mistakes, serving to illustrate what will happen for large finite N.

Robson et al. (2023) discuss the important alternative that the thresholds are chosen to maximize the fitness of the alternative chosen. Although maximizing fitness is an appealing criterion, we confine ourselves here to the more tractable case of minimizing the probability of error.

2.2.3 Dynamic adaptation

The implication of the previous discussion is that evolution would like to tailor the utility thresholds to the distribution F from which outcomes are drawn. Intuitively, the thresholds are optimally concentrated "where the heavy traffic is." In regions where the density f is large and hence realizations are likely, thresholds should be relatively prevalent, giving a utility function that is relatively steep and hence capable of finely distinguishing alternatives. In regions where the density f is small and hence realizations rare, thresholds are sparse, giving a relatively flat utility function that permits more mistakes, conditional on being in these regions in the first place.

This generates a need for utility to adapt rapidly. Consider then the following simple adaptive learning process. We focus here on the case of the probability of error criterion.[11] For a fixed distribution F, this learning process converges to an approximation of the optimal configuration of thresholds. The process is simple and requires no parametric information about F. As long as this adjustment process can proceed relatively rapidly, compared to the rate at which the environment fluctuates, with new F's being introduced, the agent will most of the time employ a utility function that is nearly optimal.

Suppose that the thresholds must be chosen on a finite grid $\mathcal{G} = \{0, \varepsilon, 2\varepsilon, ..., G\varepsilon, 1\}$, for an integer G such that $(G+1)\varepsilon = 1$. Evolution must provide a rule that chooses N elements from this set to comprise the thresholds in the individual's choice rule. It is technically convenient to have a finite number of possible thresholds. We will consider the limiting case as ε approaches zero.

We let $x_n^t \in \mathcal{G}$, where $0 < x_1^t < ....x_N^t < 1$, at time $t = 1, 2, ...$, denote the various thresholds at time t. Consider the following rule for adjusting the thresholds:

Suppose the period t outcome y_t is in $[x_{n-1}^t, x_n^t)$. Then:
If x_{n-1}^t is not $x_0 = 0$, then $x_{n-1}^{t+1} = x_{n-1}^t + \varepsilon$, and if x_n^t is not $x_{N+1} = 1$, then $x_n^{t+1} = x_n^t - \varepsilon$.

The basic motivation for the rule is that intervals shrink when realizations land in them. This ensures that, in regions where outcomes are relatively likely, the intervals are small, allowing the agent to discriminate finely between outcomes that occur there.

[11] See Robson et al. (2023) for a detailed treatment of a generalized model that treats the maximizing fitness case in a limiting sense as $N \to \infty$.

In response to this learning rule, the values of the thresholds will constantly fluctuate. This fluctuation will continue even if the distribution F from which realizations are drawn is permanently fixed. These fluctuations have the upside of creating the ability to adjust to changes in the distribution F.

More formally, this adjustment process induces a Markov chain whose state space consists of vectors of thresholds. The Markov chain is "irreducible"—so that there is a time T such that, given any initial vector of thresholds, there is a positive probability of reaching any other vector at T. It follows that there is a unique "invariant distribution" and that the distribution of state vectors converges to this from any initial state.

In the limit with small ε, the thresholds adjust so as to minimize the probability of error. That is, Robson et al. (2023, Theorem 3.1) prove:

Proposition. *Fix N. In the limit as $\varepsilon \to 0$, the invariant distribution of the nth threshold x_n^t converges to a point mass at x_n^*, where $F(x_n^*) = n/(N+1)$, for $n = 1, ..., N$.*

Hence, as the grid of possible values becomes finer, the adjustment rule generates thresholds arbitrarily close to the equally-spaced-in-terms-of-probability rule that is optimal for minimizing the probability of error.

We do not claim that this learning *process* is optimal. If the distributions F the agent encounters are drawn from some parametric class, then the efficient mechanisms should exploit this restriction. To talk about optimal learning, in general, one would specify the stochastic process governing the evolution of the distribution F, equip the agent with Bayesian beliefs over the identity of the current distribution, and solve a discounted expected utility maximization problem. This might be beyond evolution's power to implement.

The current exercise confirms just that there exists a simple process leading the agents to an ultimately approximately optimal response to any fixed distribution F. There are undoubtedly many other ultimately approximately optimal behavioral rules.

2.2.4 Preference for growth

Consider now a dynamic application of adaptive utility, involving preferences over income profiles. The motivating empirical background here is a clear tendency for wages to increase with a worker's tenure at a firm. For example, Dustmann and Meghir (2005) provide evidence of the returns to tenure, finding that skilled workers enjoy substantial wage gains with experience, with strong gains from staying with the same firm. Unskilled workers' wages grow even more strongly early in their tenure.[12]

A well-known explanation (for example, Becker (1964)) for rising wage profiles is that firms invest in workers early in their careers, and then pay wages

[12] This material on a preference for growth is drawn from Robson et al. (2023), which also presents simulations. See also Robson and Samuelson (2024).

that increase with tenure as an inducement for the workers to remain with the firm, allowing the firm to reap the return on its investment. This investment may take the form of explicit training or education, but may also be implicit—if worker productivity increases with tenure, no matter what the reason, then the early years of employment are effectively an investment, with the subsequent higher wages reflecting the importance of retaining workers who have longer tenures and are hence more productive.

Frank and Hutchens (1993), on the other hand, argue persuasively that conventional preferences are unable to fully explain the ubiquity of increasing remuneration streams. They show that intercity bus drivers and commercial airline pilots both earn wages that increase with tenure. They argue that in the case of airline pilots, most of their training consists of prior experience in the military, so that there is little explicit investment to be recouped by an airline. In the case of intercity bus drivers, there seems to be little room for improved performance with a long tenure. Frank and Hutchens then argue that increased wage profiles should be partly explained by including a primitive preference for a growing rate of consumption in the utility function. We propose an evolutionary derivation of such preferences.

Let us consider a scenario in which an agent faces a steadily increasing income stream. It can be shown that the agent's utility evaluations will adapt, converging to a constant level arising from the sequence of increasing consumption. Furthermore, this constant level is raised by the increasing nature of the sequence.

If the agent makes choices among such increasing (or decreasing) income streams, we assume that she correctly anticipates how her utility function will evolve with the consumption stream, and evaluates a consumption stream according to its induced average utility.

Take the model of Section 2.2.1, with N thresholds, whose values are adjusted according to the process introduced in Section 2.2.3. To capture a trend in incomes, we fix a distribution F^0, and suppose that rewards at time $t \geq 0$ are drawn from the distribution F^t, satisfying

$$F^t(x) = F^0(x - \alpha t).$$

Hence, the distribution from which rewards are drawn shifts at a constant rate α. The distribution F^0 has support on a unit interval $[x_0, x_0 + 1]$, while F^t has support on $[x_0 + \alpha t, x_0 + \alpha t + 1]$. We allow the case of $\alpha > 0$, so that the distribution is shifting upward, as well as $\alpha < 0$ and a downward shifting distribution.

Let x_n^t denote the value of the nth threshold at time t. Define

$$\hat{x}_n^t = x_n^t - \alpha t.$$

We refer to $\hat{x}_n^t$ as the detrended value of the nth threshold at time t, and refer to x_n^t as a raw threshold.

The distribution of the raw thresholds y^t will steadily increase or decrease in response to the shift in F^t. In contrast, the detrended thresholds converge within the unit interval. That is, the argument of Robson et al. (2023, Lemma 7.1) shows:

Proposition. *Fix the number of thresholds N. For sufficiently small α, there exists an interior invariant distribution of the detrended thresholds $\hat{y}_n^t$. In the limit as $\varepsilon \to 0$, the invariant distribution of detrended thresholds converges to the distribution that assigns a point mass to the vector with components $\hat{y}_n^*$, $n = 1, ..., N$ that are the unique solutions to*

$$(F^0(\hat{y}_{n+1}^*) - F^0(\hat{y}_n^*)) = (F^0(\hat{y}_n^*) - F^0(\hat{y}_{n-1}^*)) + \alpha \tag{2.1}$$

for $n = 1, ..., N$.

This implies that average utility is raised by increasing realizations and lowered by falling realizations. The intuition is that with increasing realizations, the thresholds are constantly lagging behind the distribution of realizations. This lagging behind means that the raw thresholds x_n^* are being constantly tugged upward, as they need to be. On average, the realizations are then good news. With decreasing realizations, the thresholds are again constantly lagging behind the realizations, but this time the realizations are, on average, bad news.

Robson and Samuelson (2024) examine a more dramatic version of this phenomenon, for an adjustment rule that does well, in a limiting sense, in terms of expected fitness rather than the probability of error, which we focused on in this chapter. They show that people might prefer *time-varying* income streams over comparable constant streams. The setting itself is quite special, and the result holds for a specific adjustment rule. The example nevertheless illustrates how a mechanism that is only approximately optimal in typical situations might generate startling choices in rather different circumstances.

2.2.5 Hedonic treadmill

We discussed how a preference for rising income might arise from adaptive utility. The evidence in favor of adaptive utility is compelling—both evidence concerning its neuroscientific basis and evidence of its predicted effects. A less clear picture emerges for hedonic utility, which is not merely substantive but associated with reported pleasure or happiness. In a more tentative spirit, then, we turn to the most well-known of phenomena that concern adaptive pleasure—the so-called "hedonic treadmill".

Schkade and Kahneman (1998) found that students in Ann Arbor and Los Angeles reported similar levels of life satisfaction. However, students in Ann Arbor predicted significantly higher levels of life satisfaction for those living in LA. Schkade and Kahneman describe this as a "focusing illusion". For them, there is a distinction between "decision utility"—which would be the basis of a decision to move to LA—and "experienced utility"—what you actually experience once there, and the "hedonic honeymoon" is over.

It is not surprising somehow that students in Michigan would predict greater life satisfaction for those living in LA, or for themselves, if they would move there. Suppose, for example, you compare surfing in the winter in Michigan (Fig. 4) ...

FIGURE 4 Surfing in the winter on Lake Michigan. Image generated by Google Gemini.

... with surfing in the winter in California (Fig. 5) ...

FIGURE 5 Surfing in the winter in Encinitas, California. Image generated by Google Gemini.

Since realized long term life satisfaction in LA does not match this rosy prediction, Schkade and Kahneman assert that decision utility is then *wrong*—that you might well make a mistake in deciding to move to LA.

Robson and Samuelson (2011) use the Rayo and Becker (2007) model to generate distinct decision and experienced utilities, so agreeing with Schkade and Kahneman up to a point, but crucially argue that there is no suboptimality here. That is, decision utility is the basis of the best possible choice about moving, and experienced utility the basis of the best possible decisions once in LA. That is, far from being a problem, adaptation represents the biologically optimal response to limited perceptual accuracy.

2.2.6 Treadmill—simulations

Reconsider the preference for growth model of Section 2.2.4 with the parametric class of cumulative distribution functions $F(x) = x^{\gamma}$ and probability density functions $f(x) = \gamma x^{\gamma-1}$, for all $x \in [0, 1]$, with parameter $\gamma > 0$. Suppose the grid size is $\varepsilon = 0.0005$. Set $N = 9$ and take 100,000 periods, where $\gamma = 1$ for the first 20,000 periods and $\gamma = 5$ thereafter up to 100,000.

Fig. 6 demonstrates how, assuming that substantive utility induces experienced and reported pleasure, the adaptive utility model illuminates the phenomenon of the hedonic treadmill.

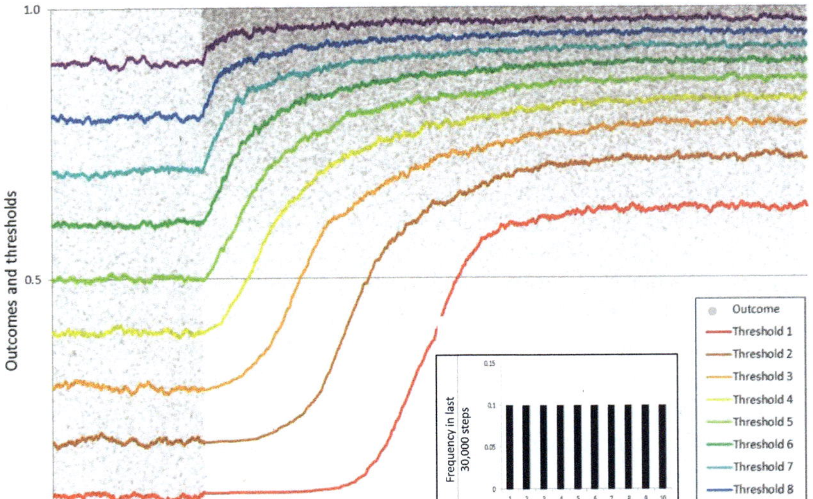

FIGURE 6 Simulations of the hedonic treadmill. The thresholds move to the new deciles, as shown by the ultimately equal probabilities of each interval for the new distribution. Average utility rises sharply at first, with the shift to a first-order stochastically dominant distribution, but then subsides to its original level, despite the permanence of the shift.

2.2.7 Variants

Variants of the model can also shed light on phenomena that directly involve variation across individuals rather than across the outcomes of a gamble. This could involve hypothesizing that the choices that an individual needs to make scale with the distribution of wealth or income.

Consider, for example, the Easterlin paradox, as described originally in Easterlin (1974), which is the observation that, although reported life satisfaction typically increases within a nation, or across nations, with greater income, there is less evidence of a secular rise in life satisfaction with generally rising incomes.[13]

Consider the hedonic treadmill in this light. There is steady progress—a positive secular trend—in the distribution of income and hence steady progress in the outcomes of the relevant decisions faced by an individual. The growth process induces a higher level of happiness but not happiness that grows over time. Contemporaneously, happiness is higher for higher outcomes, as is all consistent with Easterlin. The hedonic treadmill model presumes that the decisions faced involve purely contemporaneous tradeoffs, which might be a plausible approximation.

A further related application would be to the concern with status, especially the life satisfaction deriving from that. Such a concern is often associated with Veblen (2017). Duesenberry (1949), for example, showed that the fraction of income that is consumed depends largely on one's relative position in the wealth distribution. That is, for example, someone at the lower quintile, say, of the wealth distribution currently consumes a similar fraction of income to someone at the same relative position 20 years ago and not someone with the same real income, who would then have been relatively richer.

Robson (1992) argues that hypothesizing a concern with status in the sense of the position in the wealth distribution accounts for the observations made by Friedman and Savage (1948) concerning the taking and avoidance of risk. That is, the avoidance of gambles involving moderate gains and losses, but the taking of lotteries involving small losses with high probabilities and large gains with small probabilities suggests that von Neumann-Morgenstern utility might be concave at first but then become convex. If this utility were a function of wealth alone, the large gains with small probability should decrease with growth, contrary to observation. Hypothesizing an additional concern with relative position can account for large gains that increase with growth, as is actually observed.[14]

---

[13] The Easterlin paradox generated a vast literature. Easterlin and O'Connor (2022) is a recent paper that addresses some of the criticisms it has attracted.

[14] See Ray and Robson (2012) for a dynamic version of this model.

2.3 Encoding and decoding noisy signals

The threshold model that is the main focus here arranges outcomes into bins, with utility constant within a bin and taking jumps from one bin to another. We could view this as a simple model of a just-noticeable difference rather than a literal description of utility functions. Netzer et al. (2025) (NRSK) present a model of noisy perception that smooths some of the lumpiness of the threshold model.

The model of NRSK endows the individual with a continuous set of perceived outcomes. The individual perceives the realized value of each outcome, transformed by a nonlinear encoding function and perturbed by an added noise term. For tractability, NRSK focus on the limiting case where there are many observations on each outcome. If the individual has a correct view of the statistical relationship among the various outcomes, the individual will draw the appropriate inferences about each observation and will then make appropriate risk-neutral choices.

Matters become more interesting when the individual misperceives this statistical relationship, perhaps mistakenly coalescing outcomes. Such misperceptions might arise because it is beyond the power of evolution to endow the agent with a perfect understanding of the environment. In this case, even with a large number of observations, individuals will choose in a way that reflects the nonlinear encoding function. If there are just two outcomes, for example, which the individual believes must have the same realization, the individual evaluates the binary gamble in terms of the expectation of the encoding function, where the expectation reflects the sampling rates on the two outcomes.

This model avoids awkward conceptual issues concerning the sharp edges of the threshold model. That is, at each threshold there is a discontinuous jump in the signal the individual obtains. On the other hand, the continuous model is less tractable. It is more difficult to analyze even the static case, but the difficulties are exacerbated in the dynamic case. The threshold model allows one to describe the process of dynamic adjustment in terms of how a finite number of thresholds shift with experience. In a continuous model, on the other hand, adjustment concerns the much less tractable problem of adaptation of an encoding *function*.

In the current section, we considered utility as instantiated by neural activity in the brain. We circled the wagons most tightly about this notion of utility as substantive, where such neural activity drives choice. The inevitable neural noise then makes adaptation desirable and we derived the observable consequences. We also considered more tentatively the implications for hedonic utility—so reported pleasure or life satisfaction would exhibit adaptation. We now switch gears, adopting an approach founded on a literally evolutionary perspective. We take a theoretical view of how different time preferences and different attitudes to risk would have different long run demographic success, thus selecting favored time preferences and risk attitudes. We investigate the empirical implications.

3 Evolution of attitudes to idiosyncratic risk and time preference

Two basic attributes of preferences are attitudes to risk and time preference. It is also quite plausible that these two attributes were shaped by natural selection in hunter-gatherer societies. In particular, time preference has a dimensionless quality that could have retained its precise meaning in widely different circumstances.

We first consider the straightforward fashion in which evolution shapes attitudes to idiosyncratic risk. This straightforward attitude derives from the biological criterion for success in this setting—expected offspring. This is a building block in all that follows—including, for example, results on time discounting, as well as the results concerning aggregate risk presented in Section 4. We show that attitudes to idiosyncratic risk might have evolved to reflect the environment, to be "plastic". That is, an evolutionary approach does not force everyone into a straitjacket of identical preferences.

We then consider how the pure rate of time preference might have evolved in a hunter-gatherer society. We consider how the receipt of resources at different ages would have a differential effect on biological success. This demographic approach derives time preference from age rather than from time into the future, which distinguishes this approach from the conventional one. Even when this demographic approach generates rates of time preference that vary with age, this does not imply preference reversals. We show how time preference may also exhibit plasticity with a time-varying environment and how it might reflect geographic variation in evolutionary history.

3.1 Attitudes to idiosyncratic risk

Consider a population that reproduces parthenogenetically, that is, without sex. Each of individuals $n = 1, ..., N$ has a distribution of offspring given by an independent draw $\tilde{x}_n$ of the random variable $\tilde{x}$ with mean $\bar{x}$.[15] It follows that the growth rate of the population is

$$\frac{\sum_n \tilde{x}_n}{N} \rightarrow \bar{x},$$

as $N \rightarrow \infty$, with probability 1, by the strong law of large numbers.

That is, individuals evaluate options in terms of the expected offspring they generate. For example, suppose that resources $r \geq 0$ translate into expected offspring according to the function $x = f(r) \geq 0$, where the random variable representing offspring conditional on r is independent across individuals. Then, gambles over r, given as the random variable $\tilde{r}$, that are also independent across individuals are evolutionarily evaluated as $E(f(\tilde{r}))$. That is, they are evaluated

[15] That is, the probability of $i \geq 0$ offspring under $\tilde{x}$ is $p_i \geq 0$ for some p_i where $\sum_i p_i = 1$.

in terms of expected utility where the role of von Neumann-Morgenstern utility is played by the function f that connects resources to expected offspring.

3.1.1 Plasticity of attitudes to idiosyncratic risk

We now illustrate the general point that it is generally advantageous for behavior to be "plastic"—to respond to the environment—showing that evolution is readily capable of generating a spectrum of behavior, adapted to time varying circumstances.

We first consider attitudes to risk. Suppose then that the expected offspring generated by a random allocation of resources $\tilde{r}$ depends on the environment ξ as $Ef(\tilde{r}, \xi)$, say. Suppose ξ has two possible realizations ξ_1 and ξ_2.[16] Conditional on ξ_1, expected offspring for a particular gamble $\tilde{r}_1$ exceeds that for another gamble $\tilde{r}_2$, but conditional on ξ_2, the reverse is true. That is,

$$Ef(\tilde{r}_1, \xi_1) > Ef(\tilde{r}_2, \xi_1)$$

but

$$Ef(\tilde{r}_2, \xi_2) > Ef(\tilde{r}_1, \xi_2).$$

Suppose that the environment is independently drawn each period, with the probability of state ξ_i being p_i for $i = 1, 2$, where $p_1 + p_2 = 1$.[17]

Suppose the large total population at date T is now given by $P(T)$, where $P(0) = 1$. If there is no information about the state, the gamble chosen cannot depend on the state. If gamble $\tilde{r}_i$ is taken throughout, then the population at date T is

$$P(T) = (Ef(\tilde{r}_i, \xi_1))^{T_1} (Ef(\tilde{r}_i, \xi_2))^{T-T_1}$$

where T_1 is the random variable giving the number of times that state ξ_1 is in effect, so that $T - T_1$ is the number of times ξ_2 is in effect. The limiting growth rate of population this choice of gamble induces is then

$$\begin{aligned}\frac{\ln P(T)}{T} &= \frac{T_1}{T} \ln (Ef(\tilde{r}_i, \xi_1)) + \frac{T - T_1}{T} \ln (Ef(\tilde{r}_i, \xi_2)) \\ &\to p \ln (Ef(\tilde{r}_i, \xi_1)) + (1 - p) \ln (Ef(\tilde{r}_i, \xi_2)) = R_i,\end{aligned}$$

say, with probability one, as $T \to \infty$, by the strong law of large numbers. This limiting growth rate characterizes the evolutionary success of a type that takes gamble r_i always.

These calculations consider aggregate uncertainty concerning the environment $\xi_i; i = 1, 2$, and presage the treatment of attitudes to aggregate risk in

16 A particular case might be that the individual becomes more or less risk averse with the change in the environment.

17 The i.i.d. nature of the environment can readily be significantly generalized. For example, it could be a Markov chain with limiting probabilities p_1 and p_2.

Section 4. The choices available here are different idiosyncratic gambles *conditional* on the aggregate state $\xi_i, i = 1, 2$. The focus in Section 4 is to compare gambles that involve aggregate risk with those that involve idiosyncratic risk. The most general gamble there involves a random aggregate state with i.i.d. gambles conditional on each state. Choice among these gambles expresses a differential concern with aggregate risk.

Suppose now the shift in the environment is signaled so that an individual can condition on the signal. The type that will do best will then maximize expected offspring conditional on the environment. That is, the total population at T is now

$$P(T) = (Ef(\tilde{r}_1, \xi_1))^{T_1} (Ef(\tilde{r}_2, \xi_2))^{T-T_1}$$

with a limiting growth rate

$$p \ln (Ef(\tilde{r}_1, \xi_1)) + (1 - p) \ln (Ef(\tilde{r}_2, \xi_2)) = R^*,$$

say, where it follows immediately that $R^* > R_i$, $i = 1, 2$. Hence the type that adapts to the environment outperforms either type that does not, eventually dominating the population.

This argument demonstrates the advantage of behavioral plasticity, where the optimal choice to be made is conditional on the environment, and where such choice can be made rapidly. There might be an underlying genetically controlled predisposition to detect and apply information that induces such rapid adaptation, but the predisposition itself might have arisen by the much slower process of natural selection, given repeated exposure to the various environments.

Such behavioral plasticity is a familiar phenomenon in biology. For example, female North American red squirrels responded to the abundance of white spruce cones created by global warming by advancing their average age at the first birth of offspring by 18 days (see Réale et al. (2003)). Such plasticity is not confined to behavior. For example, many species of turtle change sex depending on the temperature of the water (see Bull (1980), for example).

3.2 Time preference[18]

We sketch now an account of the evolution of the rate of time preference, based on the demographic variables of survival to each age and fertility at each age.[19]

For simplicity, although the results here hold more generally, agents live three periods, producing x_i expected offspring at ages $i = 1, 2, 3$. Three periods is the minimum life span needed to consider any variation in the rate of time preference with age. However, most of the results found here extend straightforwardly to more periods.

[18] A fuller treatment of the material in Sections 3.2-3.2.2 is in Robson and Samuelson (2024).

[19] This material is drawn from Robson and Samuelson (2007).

The probability of survival from age i to age $i+1$ is S_i for $i = 0, 1, 2$. Suppose there is a large population described by the vector $N_a(t)$ for ages $a = 1, 2, 3$ and dates $t = 0, 1, \ldots$. Given that survival and fertility are independent risks, this population evolves deterministically as

$$N_1(t+1) = S_0\left(N_1(t)x_1 + N_2(t)x_2 + N_3(t)x_3\right).$$

That is, there are $N_1(t)x_1 + N_2(t)x_2 + N_3(t)x_3$ newborns at t given the numbers and fertility of the three adult ages and these newborns survive with probability S_0 to $t+1$.[20] The evolution of the older ages is very simple. Each cohort comes from the cohort one period ago that was then one period younger, allowing for interim mortality:

$$N_2(t+1) = S_1 N_1(t), \tag{3.1}$$

$$N_3(t+1) = S_2 N_2(t), \tag{3.2}$$

for $t = 0, 1, \ldots$ Using (3.1) and (3.2) for $N_2(t)$ and $N_3(t)$,

$$N_1(t+1) = S_0 N_1(t)x_1 + S_0 S_1 N_1(t-1)x_2 + S_0 S_1 S_2 N_1(t-2)x_3, \quad \text{for } t = 2, \ldots \tag{3.3}$$

In steady state growth, the proportions of each age class remain constant over time, so that each age class grows with the same factor. If there is steady state growth with growth factor λ, then, in particular, $N_1(t+1) = \lambda N_1(t)$, for all t. It follows from (3.3) for $N_1(t+1)$ that

$$1 = \frac{S_0 x_1}{\lambda} + \frac{S_0 S_1 x_2}{\lambda^2} + \frac{S_0 S_1 S_2 x_3}{\lambda^3}, \tag{3.4}$$

which is the Euler-Lotka equation. This equation determines λ from the discounted value of expected offspring at each adult age, $S_0 S_1 x_2$ at age 2, for example. The discount factor λ is raised to a power corresponding to age.

Although this equation cannot be solved in closed form, whenever the maximum age is more than a few periods, it is readily seen to always have a unique real positive solution for the growth factor λ.

Perron-Frobenius Theorem. *Given any initial population vector, the population settles down into steady state growth with growth factor given by the unique positive solution of the Euler-Lotka equation.*[21]

---

[20] The notation suppresses, explicitly, the number of newborns.

[21] The first-order difference equations describing the evolution of the population given by (3.3), (3.1) and (3.2) can be compactly represented in matrix notation as $N(t+1) = N(t)L$, where $N(t+1)$ is the population 3-vector at date $t+1$ and L is the 3×3 "Leslie matrix". The unique positive solution of the Euler-Lotka equation is the so-called "dominant eigenvalue" or "Frobenius root" of L. Frauenthal (1986) is a careful treatment of this result and its implications for demography.

The main content of this theorem is convergence to steady-state growth from arbitrary initial conditions. That is, once that is given, it is generally straightforward to derive the Euler-Lotka equation, basically as we did in this example.

Consider now the set of the x_i that yield the same value of λ and are thus on an evolutionary indifference surface. These surfaces are linear functions of the x_i and are thus hyperplanes (Fig. 7).

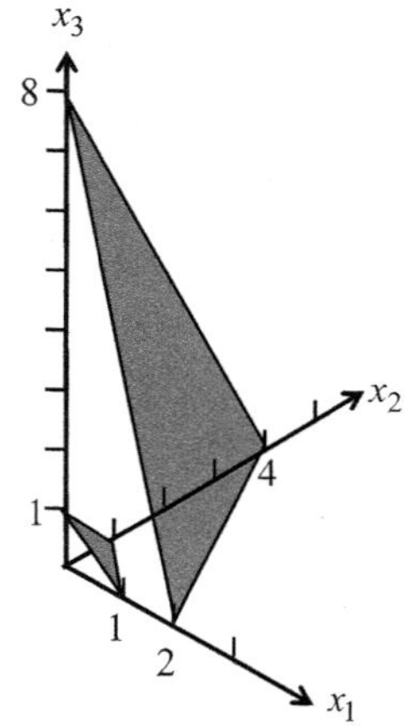

FIGURE 7 Hyperplanes on which λ is constant. This is Fig. 1 from Robson and Samuelson (2007). [Copyright American Economic Association; reproduced with permission of the American Economic Review].

Since λ is constant, the Euler-Lotka equation implies the tradeoff between any two adjacent x_i as follows:

$$0 = \frac{S_0 \ldots S_{i-1} dx_i}{\lambda^i} + \frac{S_0 \ldots S_i dx_{i+1}}{\lambda^{i+1}} \text{ so that } -\frac{dx_{i+1}}{dx_i} = \frac{\lambda}{S_i}.$$

3.2.1 Preferences over intertemporal consumption

We now translate the above purely demographic account to come closer to the conventional intertemporal model of preferences.

The simplest way to connect resources to the demographic account is to suppose $x_i = f_i(c_i)$ gives age-i fertility as a function of age-i consumption c_i. The f_i are strictly increasing and concave.

For any consumption vector c, then,

$$1 = \frac{S_0 f_1(c_1)}{\lambda} + \frac{S_0 S_1 f_2(c_2)}{\lambda^2} + \frac{S_0 S_1 S_2 f_3(c_3)}{\lambda^3}, \tag{3.5}$$

where $\lambda > 0$ is constant on an indifference surface. $\lambda(c_1, c_2, c_3)$ is readily seen to be strictly increasing and can also be shown to be strictly quasi-concave in c. Hence the biological utility function λ generates indifference curves of the conventional type.

3.2.2 Relationship to conventional model with geometric discounting

Choosing the optimal consumption bundle (c_1, c_2, c_3) that maximizes the growth factor λ implies that the right hand side of the Euler-Lotka equation is maximized given the optimal λ. That is, suppose (c_1, c_2, c_3) is the optimal consumption profile and let λ^* be the associated maximal feasible growth rate. Then

$$1 = \frac{S_0 f_1(c_1)}{\lambda^*} + \frac{S_0 S_1 f_2(c_2)}{(\lambda^*)^2} + \frac{S_0 S_1 S_2 f_3(c_3)}{(\lambda^*)^3},$$

If (c_1', c_2', c_3') is a suboptimal profile generating growth factor $\lambda' < \lambda^*$ then

$$\begin{aligned}\frac{S_0 f_1(c_1')}{\lambda'} + \frac{S_0 S_1 f_2(c_2')}{(\lambda')^2} + \frac{S_0 S_1 S_2 f_3(c_3')}{(\lambda')^3} &= 1 \\ &> \frac{S_0 f_1(c_1')}{\lambda^*} + \frac{S_0 S_1 f_2(c_2')}{(\lambda^*)^2} + \frac{S_0 S_1 S_2 f_3(c_3')}{(\lambda^*)^3}.\end{aligned}$$

That is, the individual should maximize

$$\frac{S_0 f_1(c_1')}{\lambda^*} + \frac{S_0 S_1 f_2(c_2')}{(\lambda^*)^2} + \frac{S_0 S_1 S_2 f_3(c_3')}{(\lambda^*)^3}$$

given the *maximal* λ^*.

Mathematically, this is not very useful, because you need to know λ^* before you can use this observation to find the optimal c_1, c_2, c_3. But finding λ^* involves first finding the optimal c_1, c_2, c_3.

Nonetheless, this seems potentially relevant. That is, reasonable estimates of the modern pure rate of time preference often exceed estimates of mortality; certainly estimates of modern mortality away from the very beginning and end of life, but even mid-range estimates of hunter-gatherer mortality. So an extra source of impatience might help close the gap. We return to this issue below in Section 3.2.4.

3.2.3 Time preference in hunter gatherers

An issue that arises with considering the evolutionary basis of time preference in hunter-gatherers is: Why would time preference have mattered if the technology did not permit borrowing or lending? That is, most food acquired by foragers must be consumed right away or it will be wasted.

A salient feature of hunter-gatherer societies, however, one that sets humans apart from chimpanzees, for example, is intergenerational transfer of resources. This is exhibited in Figs. 8 and 9 which contrast male and female production and consumption of food. The enormous loan given by adults to the young is evident in the large initial excess of consumption over production followed by a counterbalancing excess of production over consumption. Chimpanzees, our closest living relatives, are close to autarky. This intergenerational transfer to the young is an enormous investment in skill acquisition, an investment that is amply rewarded by the adults' ultimate productivity. For this enormous investment to be worthwhile, it is also crucial that humans have low enough mortality. This is illustrated in Fig. 10 which shows how combining human consumption with chimpanzee mortality would be catastrophic.[22]

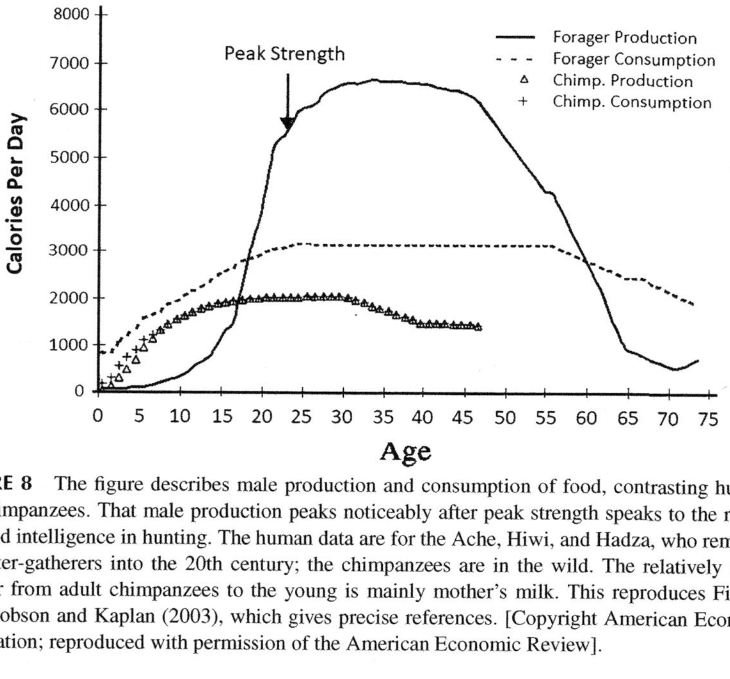

FIGURE 8 The figure describes male production and consumption of food, contrasting humans and chimpanzees. That male production peaks noticeably after peak strength speaks to the role of skill and intelligence in hunting. The human data are for the Ache, Hiwi, and Hadza, who remained as hunter-gatherers into the 20th century; the chimpanzees are in the wild. The relatively minor transfer from adult chimpanzees to the young is mainly mother's milk. This reproduces Fig. 2A from Robson and Kaplan (2003), which gives precise references. [Copyright American Economic Association; reproduced with permission of the American Economic Review].

These intergenerational transfers are not confined to immediate relatives. Sharing across all members of a band is most evident for meat obtained by collaborative hunting, usually by the males. One function of this sharing is risk-management, given that large animals are not inevitably successfully hunted. It may be that especially proficient hunters get the choicest parts, and it may be that larger families get somewhat less per child, but these effects arise as perturbations around largely equal division.[23] From an economics perspective, it is not at all obvious how such wide sharing could be sustained in equilibrium

---

[22] See Robson and Kaplan (2006) for further discussion of the interaction between longevity and intelligence. The question of why aging occurs at all is addressed in Kaplan and Robson (2009).

[23] There is much less sharing of plants that are gathered.

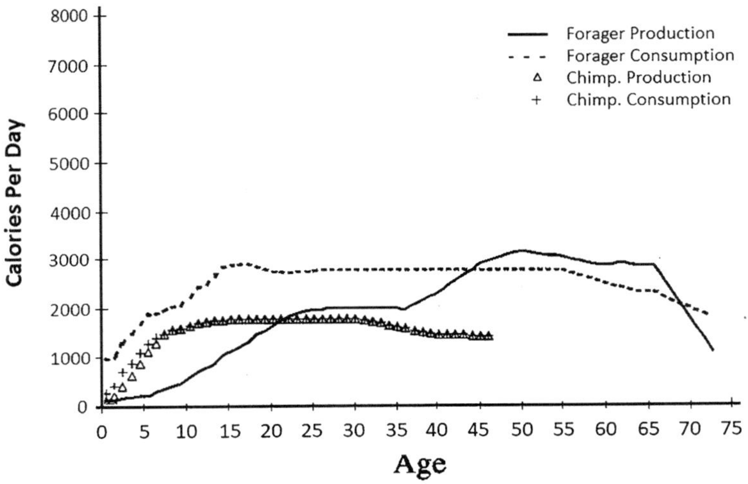

FIGURE 9 The figure describes female production and consumption of food, contrasting humans and chimpanzees. Compare with the male schedules. The significant contribution by females in rearing children is missing from this picture. This reproduces Fig. 2B from Robson and Kaplan (2003). [Copyright American Economic Association; reproduced with permission of the American Economic Review].

by selfish individuals.[24] But the brute fact is that it did happen. Hill and Hurtado (1996) provide a detailed account of food production and sharing among the Ache of Paraguay.[25]

In order to model these transfers, consider a hunter-gatherer society in steady state when all classes grow at the same factor λ^*. Consider the three adult age class example of the previous subsection. The steady state relative sizes of the three adult age classes are $\left(\frac{S_0}{\lambda^*}, \frac{S_0 S_1}{(\lambda^*)^2}, \frac{S_0 S_1 S_2}{(\lambda^*)^3}\right)$. Assume the population is large so that idiosyncratic risks of fertility or survival have essentially determinate effects.[26] That is, each age $a = 1, 2, 3$ class comes from an age 0 class a periods ago. Older age classes then stem from smaller age 0 classes as reflected in λ^*, and the size of the class is also deflated by survival. There is a social budget constraint at each time given by

$$\frac{S_0 c_1}{\lambda^*} + \frac{S_0 S_1 c_2}{(\lambda^*)^2} + \frac{S_0 S_1 S_2 c_3}{(\lambda^*)^3} = Y, \tag{3.6}$$

24 Another mostly hidden incentive might have been that proficient hunters were especially desirable mates.

25 See also Robson and Kaplan (2003) for discussion of this issue.

26 Finite group sizes would make the problem substantially more awkward. Hunter gatherer groups were typically around 30, which would make the resulting stochasticity of transfers small but still possibly important.

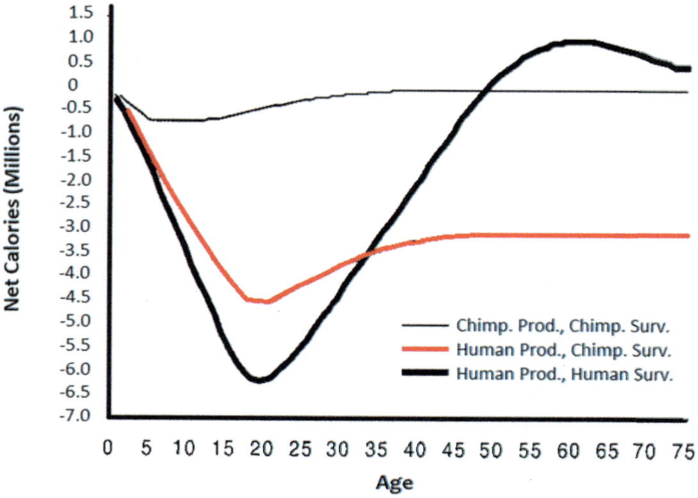

FIGURE 10 This describes cumulated expected net production of food by age, contrasting humans and chimpanzees. At each age, the difference between production and consumption, weighted by the probability of the individual still being alive, is added to the running total, which was initialized at zero. This calculation corresponds to finding the net social surplus in a society with free transfers across ages in a steady state with no growth. Human adults are able to cover the expected deficits of the young in the steady-state, as is revealed by this cumulated excess converging to a small positive level, which would actually permit moderate growth. This requires low mortality. To dramatize this, suppose human net production is combined with chimpanzee mortality. In this hypothetical case, the cumulated expected excess remains well below zero. In the steady state, such a deficit could only be accommodated with a catastrophic population decline. This reproduces Fig. 4 from Robson and Kaplan (2003). [Copyright American Economic Association; reproduced with permission of the American Economic Review].

where

$$Y = \frac{S_0 y_1}{\lambda^*} + \frac{S_0 S_1 y_2}{(\lambda^*)^2} + \frac{S_0 S_1 S_2 y_3}{(\lambda^*)^3},$$

say. Although transfers over time are taken to be impossible, transfers between age cohorts at each point in time are unrestricted.

As we argued in Section 3.2.2, it is necessary that the optimal (c_1, c_2, c_3) (that maximize λ) should maximize the right hand side of Eq. (3.5) subject to Eq. (3.6) given the optimal λ^*. This particular case is simplified because the weights on the fertility function f in Eq. (3.5) are the same as the weights on consumption c_a for $a = 1, 2, 3$, in Eq. (3.6). In the case that $f_i = f$, for example, this implies that the c_1, c_2, c_3 that maximize the right hand side of Eq. (3.5) subject to Eq. (3.6) are equal.

The evolutionarily optimal allocation of resources is then simply described. Pool all the resources contributed by all the living representatives of each age cohort and reallocate them equally.

It is as if the individual were maximizing a conventional lifetime utility function subject to a conventional lifetime budget constraint, one that allows borrowing and saving, and then choosing a substantially different consumption pattern from the production pattern. These intertemporal preferences entail a pure rate of time preference that arises from survival and from the population growth rate, and are as derived earlier in Section 3.2.2.

In this sense, hunter-gatherer economics generates two key features of conventional intertemporal preferences that otherwise seem arbitrary—additive separability and a constant discount factor, once mortality is netted out. These key features trace back to the application of the Euler-Lotka equation.

These preferences might have been explicitly expressed among hunter-gatherers if individuals were able to make small individual changes in consumption levels at various ages. There were suitable privately owned assets—bows and arrows, for example—even among the Ache, who were among the more egalitarian of hunter gatherer societies. These assets would have permitted modest intertemporal transfers that parallel those available in modern societies.[27]

3.2.4 The effect of population growth on time preference

The present approach provides a basis for the usual simple model of time preferences. There is a component of the pure rate of time preference, involving population growth, which entails a *constant* rate of discount of the future, justifying what seems an arbitrary assumption made in the simplest model of intertemporal preferences in economics.

The influence of mortality on time preference is well-appreciated in economics (see Fisher (1930), for example). Although the usual approach does not emphasize age-varying time preference, a possibly age-related effect of mortality is then as expected. What the present derivation points out is that there is an age-constant influence of the rate of population growth on time preference.

However, the average λ over the 1.8 million years of our evolutionary history must be very close to 1, as a matter of arithmetic necessity. It follows then that the pure rate of time preference, $\ln\lambda - \ln S = \ln\lambda + \delta$, is simply mortality δ. So population growth would seem unable to contribute to an explanation of

27 The results sketched here can be substantially generalized. Robson and Samuelson (2022, Section 5) consider endogenous fertility and mortality when intergenerational transfers are freely permitted, but all social intertemporal transfers are ruled out. Mortality can be reduced by resources devoted to that purpose. Fertility is assumed to be subject to a threshold effect that makes zero fertility optimal at very young and old ages. It is then optimal to invest resources in people who have no future fertility as long as they retain future output, as in the "grandmother effect". Each individual trades off resources available at various ages with the same pure rate of time preference as found here. These results are part of an examination of the effect of occasional aggregate shocks, but this involves a complete treatment of the case with no such shocks. Robson and Kaplan (2003) consider investment in somatic capital and in mortality reduction given that neural capital, in particular, facilitates learning to forage and thus generates a rich payback substantially later in life. The optimality of these twin investments is evaluated using a rate of time preference analogous to that here.

the pure rate of time preference. The puzzle of the remaining gap between the biological prediction of the rate of time preference and the rate that is observed is the motivation for Robson and Samuelson (2009), which we take up next.

This closing of the gap invokes aggregate risk concerning survival. The differential effect of idiosyncratic and aggregate risk is examined in greater detail in the subsequent Section 4.

Reconsider the three age population model of Sections 3.2.3 and 3.2.4. There is a population structure at t given by $(N_1(t), N_2(t), N_3(t))$. All survival probabilities are subject to an *aggregate* shock[28] so that, with three adult ages,

$$N_1(t+1) = \tilde{S}\{N_1(t)x_1 + N_2(t)x_2 + N_3(t)x_3\}$$
$$N_2(t+1) = \tilde{S}N_1(t)$$
$$N_3(t+1) = \tilde{S}N_2(t),$$

where $\tilde{S}$, the survival factor, is i.i.d.

Consider also the evolution of the population stripped of all *interim* mortality

$$M_1(t+1) = M_1(t)x_1 + M_2(t)x_2 + M_3(t)x_3$$
$$M_2(t+1) = M_1(t)$$
$$M_3(t+1) = M_2(t).$$

Suppose that the stripped population has steady state growth factor λ. The stripped population is in steady state growth if and only if the original population is in steady state growth. This is because the imposition of a uniform survival factor does not shift the age structure of the population. Think of the original population as first growing without mortality followed by the imposition of mortality. Then, in the first period, the growth factor is just

$$\lambda\tilde{S},$$

so that the growth of the original population is the stripped growth factor multiplied by the random survival factor.

Consider the exponential rate at which i.i.d. products of the survival factor $\tilde{S}$ shrink. Suppose, to take a simple case, that $\tilde{S} = S_1$ with probability p and $\tilde{S} = S_2$ with probability $1-p$ independently over time. Hence the overall survival factor after T periods is $\tilde{S}(T) = S_1^{T_1} S_2^{T-T_1}$, where T_1 is the number of times $\tilde{S} = S_1$. Hence $\frac{1}{T}\ln\tilde{S}(T) = \frac{T_1}{T}\ln S_1 + \frac{T-T_1}{T}\ln S_2 \to p\ln S_1 + (1-p)\ln S_2 = E\ln\tilde{S}$, as $T \to \infty$. This result readily generalizes to any number of outcomes and to continuous distributions.

28 It is easy to allow arbitrary idiosyncratic risk as well.

The results of Robson and Samuelson (2009) can then be given in a highly simplified form as follows. The growth rate of the factor $\lambda \tilde{S}$ is now

$$\Lambda = E \ln \tilde{S}\lambda(x),$$

so that

$$-\frac{dx_{i+1}}{dx_i} = \frac{\frac{d\Lambda}{dx_i}}{\frac{d\Lambda}{dx_{i+1}}} = \frac{\frac{d\lambda}{dx_i}}{\frac{d\lambda}{dx_{i+1}}} = \lambda.$$

Thus the discount rate is the growth rate that arises with no mortality. (This is equivalent to the claim that the discount rate is the sum of the actual growth rate plus the mortality rate.)

The current approach with aggregate survival can accommodate realistic pure rates of time preference if it is first possible to construct a comparable growth rate in a hypothetical case where mortality is set to zero. Secondly, it should be possible to incorporate plausible aggregate mortality capable of bringing the realized growth rate back to zero.

We then need an idea of how fast a population would grow in the absence of any mortality. Consider the following example. Suppose that individuals start reproducing at age 15 and stop at age 45, with no risk of death before age 45. The Hill and Hurtado (1996, Chapter 8, especially Table 8.3) study of the Ache suggests a prime-age birth probability of 0.15 per year. (This cuts the birth probabilities reported there in half. The 0.15 then represents the probability of a female birth, providing a valid comparison with the model of asexual reproduction.)

Since individuals start reproducing at age 15 and stop at age 45, and the probability of giving birth in a given year is 0.15, the dominant eigenvalue solves $1 = \sum_{\tau=15}^{45} \frac{(.15)}{\lambda^t}$, so $\lambda = 1.05675$ and $\ln \lambda = 0.055$. If the growth rate is zero,

$$0 = \Lambda = \ln \bar{\lambda} + E \ln \tilde{S} = 0.055 + E \ln \tilde{S}.$$

Suppose further that, with probability $1 - p$, the death rate is about two percent, reflecting the idiosyncratic risk of dying from accidents and disease. With remaining probability p, an aggregate catastrophe with survival rate of $S^\dagger$ appears. Then $E \ln \tilde{S} = p \ln S^\dagger + (1 - p)(-0.02) = -0.055$. Thus if $S^\dagger = 0.50$, then $p = 0.05$ works for example. Alternatively, if $p = 0.01$ then $S^\dagger = 0.03$.

It could easily be that events with probabilities of only 1% would entirely escape notice in the geological record of humans. This would mean that human populations could generate a pure rate of time preference as high as 5.5% despite the necessity of a long run rate of growth near zero and an apparent mortality rate of perhaps only 2%. Even if the possibility of such events were recognized, it would add only about 1% to the raw probability of an individual dying each year. (The 1% is an upper bound, arising from estimating that the catastrophe kills everyone.) The aggregate nature of the catastrophe leads to an exaggerated effect of about 3.5% on the long run growth rate. With no recognition of this effect, that is, there would still be 2.5% unaccounted for. The lower the probability of the catastrophe, the greater the exaggeration, assuming the catastrophe remains severe enough to keep the overall long run growth rate at zero. It is essentially this exaggeration that we explore further in Section 4, where we examine the differential evaluation of aggregate and idiosyncratic risk in preferences.

The catastrophe described in the preceding paragraph sounds suspiciously severe, but there is amazing evidence, drawn from the DNA of modern humans, that, somewhat less than a million years ago, an event occurred in which only about one percent of the population of human ancestors survived, reducing the population from about 100,000 to about 1000, with the population remaining at the latter level for about 100,000 years—see Hu et al. (2023). Such an event would have made our ancestral line teeter on the brink of extinction. The event seems to have driven a marked reduction in human genetic diversity and the creation of a new human species. The period apparently experienced an unfavorable climate shift and coincides with a substantial gap in the fossil record.[29]

That is, this argument is readily capable of generating a pure rate of time preference of about 5% which covers most of the non-experimental empirical observations on the pure rate of time preference. It covers, for example, the moderate values used by Nordhaus (1994) in his analysis of global warming. Such moderate values are enough to tilt global warming away from being a dire problem to being more tractable. Stern (2006) derives the dire consequences of taking the pure rate of time preference to be near zero. The issue for Stern, however, is not so much to estimate the pure private rate of time preference but to argue, on philosophical grounds, that the public rate should be near zero.

It is true that even carefully done experiments may produce substantially higher estimates of time preference than 5%—see Harrison et al. (2007), for example. The rates of time preference derived experimentally, however, often do not seem credible outside the laboratory. Oprea (2024) suggests that experimental measurement of risk aversion might actually be measurement of aggregation frictions. Perhaps the experimental measurement of time preference is also subject to an alternative interpretation in terms of cognitive or perceptual frictions.

3.2.5 *Plasticity of time preference*

The argument concerning adaptation of attitudes to risk in Section 3.1.1 can be extended to time preference. That is, if a shift in the environment leads to a change in the demographic variables, and this shift is signaled, individuals should make different intertemporal trade-offs, reflecting the pure rate of time preference suited to each environment. Modeling time preference entails a

29 The prolonged nature of this episode illustrates the need to investigate environmental shocks that are *not* i.i.d.

nontrivial population structure and this makes the argument less straightforward now, however, because the process of converging to a new steady state—one in which the pure rate of time preference applies—will take time. Nevertheless, at least if the shift in the environment is rare, the advantage of adaptation is clear.

To see this, consider the simplest possible demography, with just two adult ages $a = 1, 2$. Suppose survival from age 0 to 1, or from age 1 to 2 is certain, for further simplicity. There are two states, $s = 1, 2$, and two actions, $a = 1, 2$. Fertility at either adult age if action a is taken in state s is $u(a, s) > 0$, which is the expectation of idiosyncratic risk conditional on the aggregate state s and action a. Suppose that action a is optimal in state a for $a = 1, 2$, so that $u(1, 1) > u(2, 1)$ and $u(2, 2) > u(1, 2)$. The long run growth factor from action a in state s is then λ_{as} which is the unique positive solution for λ of

$$1 = \frac{u(a, s)}{\lambda} + \frac{u(a, s)}{\lambda^2}.$$

That is, using the quadratic formula,

$$\lambda_{as} = \frac{u(a, s) + \sqrt{u(a, s)^2 + 4u(a, s)}}{2}.$$

Of course, it follows that $\lambda(1, 1) > \lambda(2, 1)$ and $\lambda(2, 2) > \lambda(1, 2)$. Suppose without much loss of generality that $u(1, 1) > u(2, 2)$, so that taking the appropriate action in state 1 outperforms taking the appropriate action in state 2 and hence the pure rate of time preference is higher.

Suppose now the state is driven by a simple Markov process in continuous time with a continuous time probability rate $\pi > 0$ of making a transition either from state 1 to 2 or vice versa. It follows that the limiting probability of either state is $1/2$. Consider now the further limit as $\pi \to 0$.[30] Since transitions are then rare, the population has time to settle down to grow at rate $\ln \lambda_{as}$ if action a is taken in state s. If the state cannot be seen by individuals then the limiting overall growth rate from choosing action $a = 1, 2$ is[31]

$$\frac{\ln \lambda_{a1} + \ln \lambda_{a2}}{2}.$$

If the state can be observed, the individual can and should choose the matching action, generating overall limiting growth rate

$$\frac{\ln \lambda_{11} + \ln \lambda_{22}}{2}$$

[30] This assumption goes beyond those to obtain the plasticity of risk aversion in Section 3.1.1. There was no need there to allow the population structure to settle down.

[31] The mathematics needed to show this claim rigorously are as in Robson and Samuelson (2019).

which is clearly higher than either limiting growth rate attainable when the state is not observed.[32]

Hence, it is advantageous for time preference—which is reflected in the factor λ here—to be plastic and adapt rapidly to the environment. The genetic mechanism that enables such rapid choice of the matching action might itself be subject to slow natural selection, and would require repeated exposure to the various environments. That is, natural selection does not amount to a straitjacket that limits the range of observable time preferences.

3.2.6 *Ancestral environment and modern time preference*

Estimates of the pure rate of time preference vary substantially by region and country. Falk et al. (2018) report and analyze an extensive survey of economic attributes including time preference and risk preference from 80,000 people in 76 countries. They relate these attributes to contemporaneous variables such as geography, culture, language, and religion. Becker et al. (2020) look back in time, and show that populations that diverged genetically due to earlier migration exhibit more pronounced differences in economic attributes.[33]

What does the current evolutionary argument imply about how the ancestral environment would shape the genes that influence modern time preference? In particular, what ancestral demography might indirectly generate high modern pure rates of time preference?

To address this, consider the three-adult-age-class model under the additional simplifications that all adult fertility levels are identical at f and that all survival probabilities are also identical at $S \in (0, 1)$.[34] The Euler-Lotka equation is then

$$1 = \frac{Sf}{\lambda} + \frac{S^2 f}{\lambda^2} + \frac{S^3 f}{\lambda^3}.$$

The factor reflecting the pure rate of time preference, which discounts fertility, is then $\frac{\lambda}{S}$. If there were data on these parameters for the ancestral environment, it would be possible to verify whether high estimates of $\frac{\lambda}{S}$ were associated with high modern pure rates of time preference.

Even if estimates of ancestral population growth are missing, a rough estimate of population growth follows as a matter of arithmetic necessity. That is, over any long period of time, thousands of years, say, the ancestral population

---

32 Again, the treatment of the aggregate states 1, 2 here anticipates the treatment of aggregate gambles in Section 4. The options here involve intertemporal tradeoffs derived from idiosyncratic risk *conditional* on each aggregate state.

33 Galor and Özak (2016) also look back in time to test their hypothesis that agriculture, in particular, shaped the pure rate of time preference.

34 These assumptions can be considerably relaxed. The simplicity here is meant to capture the central effect of mortality, for example, on time preference, as might be investigated empirically.

could only have grown at a low rate, so that $\lambda = 1$, approximately.[35] If $\lambda = 1$, a higher pure rate of time preference would then arise from lower survival S or, equivalently, from higher mortality. This would necessitate higher fertility f.[36] Hence an ancestral regime that would lead eventually to high modern pure rates of time discount might have had high fertility and high mortality.

In the data presented by Falk et al. (2018, Fig. 1, for example), Sweden is one of the most patient countries that have been settled for a long time. Did Sweden experience the low mortality and low fertility that would induce high patience? Did Egypt, which is an old country that features as impatient, experience high mortality and high fertility?

4 Attitudes to aggregate risk

In the preceding section, we dug into the evolutionary foundations of attitudes to idiosyncratic risk and time preference, applying a demographic model of literal natural selection. We anticipated there the asymmetry between the effect of idiosyncratic risk and that of aggregate risk. We now focus further on this asymmetry. In particular, using a demographic model, we examine the prediction that individuals have different attitudes to aggregate risk—where a single giant coin is flipped to decide an outcome for everyone—versus idiosyncratic risk—where individuals flip their own personal coins.

We thus derive preferences that are not purely selfish—to evaluate an agent's preferences, it is not enough to know the distribution of that agent's offspring alone. The correlation with other agents' offspring outcomes is also important. This interdependence arises despite a resolutely selfish gene perspective. Success is inevitably measured in an evolutionary sense by a large number of adherents, but a large number of adherents passes through the filter composed of a sequence of aggregate states to an extent that cannot be captured by selfish preferences. This is an intriguing challenge to providing an evolutionary basis for purely independent preferences in all circumstances.

The results of Robson (1996), which frames the question in discrete time, can be illustrated with a simple example. Individuals of Type I have either $f_1 > 0$ or $f_2 > 0$ expected offspring each with probability $1/2$. If all this risk is idiosyncratic, and there is a large number of individuals, the population grows according to the mean. That is, if $x(T)$ is the number of Type I at period $T = 1, 2, \ldots$, with a population of size 1 initially, then

$$x(T) = \left(\frac{f_1 + f_2}{2}\right)^T, \text{ so } \frac{\ln x(T)}{T} \to \ln\left(\frac{f_1 + f_2}{2}\right) \text{ as } T \to \infty,$$

with probability 1, in the light of the strong law of large numbers.

---

[35] A complete account of fertility and mortality would incorporate population as an argument so that $\lambda \to 1$ as the population approaches carrying capacity.

[36] Indeed, in this case, $f = \frac{1}{S+S^2+S^3}$.

Suppose, on the other hand, individuals of Type II experience the same distribution of outcomes, but as aggregate risk. That is, if $y(T)$ is the number of Type II's at date $T = 1, 2, ...,$ then $y(T) = f_1^{n(T)} f_2^{T-n(T)}$, where $n(T)$ is the random number of heads in T flips of a fair coin. Hence

$$\frac{\ln y(T)}{T} = \frac{n(T)}{T} \ln f_1 + \frac{T - n(T)}{T} \ln f_2 \to \frac{\ln f_1 + \ln f_2}{2}, \text{ as } T \to \infty,$$

with probability 1.

Since $\frac{\ln f_1 + \ln f_2}{2} < \ln \left(\frac{f_1 + f_2}{2} \right)$, by concavity of the log function, individuals exposed to aggregate risk experience lower growth rates than those exposed to precisely comparable idiosyncratic risk. That is, individuals should be more averse to aggregate risk than they are to idiosyncratic risk.

Robatto and Szentes (2017) cast the question in continuous time instead and obtain contrasting results. Consider now Type III, say, that produces offspring either at a rate of $r_1 > 0$, which applies in State 1, or $r_2 > 0$, which applies in State 2. The state is governed by a continuous time Markov process with a probability of $\pi \in (0, 1)$ per unit time of making a transition in either direction. The limiting probability of being in either state is then $1/2$. If $z(T)$ is the number of Type III at time T, and there is a population of size 1 initially, then

$$z(T) = e^{r_1 T_1} e^{r_2 (T - T_1)}$$

where $T_1 \in [0, T]$ is the length of time that State 1 is in effect. It follows that

$$\frac{\ln z(T)}{T} = r_1 \frac{T_1}{T} + r_2 \frac{T - T_1}{T} \to \frac{r_1 + r_2}{2} \text{ as } T \to \infty,$$

with probability one.

Hence individuals exposed to this aggregate risk experience a random growth rate, but one generating the same limiting growth rate as the mean of the random growth rates. Individuals then should be indifferent to the choice between the aggregate gamble over growth rates and a deterministic growth rate that is the mean of the random growth rates.

The demographic structure of the Robatto and Szentes model is stark. All individuals regardless of age experience the same underlying fertility and mortality rates. Robson and Samuelson (2019) show that this stark structure lies behind the risk-neutrality obtained. Once age affects fertility or mortality rates, there is generally an evolutionary distinction between the effects of aggregate and idiosyncratic risk. Usually, but not always, idiosyncratic risk is preferred to comparable aggregate risk. If there is an age gap before fertility begins, as seems only realistic, this gap arising from age dependent demography has effects roughly comparable to the gap formally created in the discrete time model. In the simplest case, individuals reproduce as a spike at one particular age, in which case the continuous time model generates essentially the same results as the discrete model.[37]

In the final analysis, the issue cannot be resolved on a purely theoretic basis. Rather, it is: which of the models best approximates reality? That is, do people exhibit a preference for idiosyncratic risk over comparable aggregate risk? This is the question we look at in the present section.

In environments where agents freely choose reproductive gambles, any effect on the population growth rate of aggregate risk will be reflected in individual attitudes to aggregate risk. Curry (2001), for example, considers a discrete time model (as in Robson (1996)), but where each individual chooses a gamble that is a best response to the distribution of gambles of the others in the population. The evolutionarily dominant type is shown to be one that maximizes relative numbers of own offspring, that is, own offspring divided by offspring per individual for the remainder of the population. Evolutionarily dominant preferences are interdependent, and importantly, individuals are averse to correlation in own offspring and average offspring of the rest of the population.[38]

Correlation aversion here is in the sense of Epstein and Tanny (1980), as follows. Consider joint distributions f and g over a pair of variables (x, y). Define f as inducing more correlation than g if f and g imply the same marginal distributions over x and y, but under f it is more likely to observe pairs (x, y) where x and y are both low, or both high.[39] An individual is then averse to correlation in x and y if she prefers the distribution g to f whenever f induces more correlation than g. Epstein and Tanny (1980) show that an individual with utility over pairs, (x, y), is averse to correlation in x and y if, and only if, her marginal utility of x decreases in y. Aversion to correlation in offspring then follows immediately in Curry (2001), since there the marginal utility of own offspring decreases in the average number of offspring of the others in the population.

---

37 Robson and Samuelson (2024) include an extensive discussion of this debate.

38 Heller and Nehama (2023) provide another utility based implementation of the evolutionary optimum in a discrete time set-up. In their dual-utility approach individuals use one utility function to assess idiosyncratic gambles over offspring, and another more risk averse utility function to assess gambles entailing aggregate risk, where there is heterogeneity in preferences over correlated gambles.

39 More formally, f induces more correlation in x and y than g if they imply the same marginal distributions, and for all $\alpha, \alpha' \geq 0$,

$$f(\{x \geq \alpha, y \geq \alpha'\}) \geq g(\{x \geq \alpha, y \geq \alpha'\}),$$

and

$$f(\{x \leq \alpha, y \leq \alpha'\}) \geq g(\{x \leq \alpha, y \leq \alpha'\}).$$

These inequalities, holding for all α, and α', mean that under f it is more likely to observe pairs (x, y) where x and y are both high, or both low, hence f *induces more correlation* than g.

Oprea and Robalino (2024) use the evolutionary theory to generate testable hypotheses regarding attitudes to correlation in consumption. As in Robson (1996), consider a biological population where consumption is mapped to offspring as follows. If an individual consumes x, then she has j offspring with probability $p(j, x)$. Assume realized own offspring is independent across individuals and independent of the state, conditional on own consumption. Assume more consumption unambiguously improves the distribution of offspring, in the sense of first-order stochastic dominance.

The following is then proved by Oprea and Robalino (2024). If aggregate risk in offspring is evolutionarily disadvantageous (as in the model of Robson (1996)), then this will be reflected in individuals having an aversion to correlation of own and others' consumption. On the other hand, if aggregate risk in offspring is evolutionarily neutral (as in the model of Robatto and Szentes (2017)), then this will be reflected in individuals being indifferent to correlation of own and others' consumption. Finally, if aggregate risk in offspring is evolutionarily advantageous, then this will be reflected in individuals having an affinity for correlation of own and others' consumption.

In a large population the effect of correlation in own consumption and the consumption of a small number of others is negligible. Hence the results here describe preferences for correlations between own consumption and that of a large number of others. Whatever attitude is evolutionarily appropriate might, however, be reflected in corresponding attitudes in the small. For example, if aversion to correlation is evolutionarily advantageous, a heuristic might arise to be averse to correlation in own consumption and the consumption of a small group of others. Oprea and Robalino (2024) test correlation attitudes in small groups.

4.1 Experimental evidence

Oprea and Robalino (2024) experimentally test the implications of the evolutionary theory. Their test is based on the bomb risk elicitation task by Crosetto and Filippin (2013). The bomb task offers an intuitive method for measuring risk attitudes. A subject decides how many boxes to stack, $b \in \{0, 1, 2, \ldots, 50\}$. A laser then fires, randomly and uniformly, from a vertical position $s \in \{0, 1, 2, \ldots, 50\}$. If the laser misses the subject's stack, then she earns some amount m for each box stacked. If the laser strikes the subject's stack, then she earns zero. Subjects that are more risk averse (loving) will stack fewer (more) boxes. A risk neutral subject will choose $b = 25$. Risk averse subjects will stack $b < 25$ boxes, and risk loving subjects will choose $b > 25$. The test allows between subject comparisons. If subject A is more risk averse than B, in the sense of everywhere having a higher Arrow-Pratt coefficient of risk aversion, then A stacks fewer boxes than B.

In the ID (idiosyncratic) task each subject makes a choice in the bomb task, alone, in order to measure risk preferences in an uncorrelated environment. Each subject also faces one of three social bomb tasks. In the LEAD social task the subject chooses a stack height for herself, and this choice determines the stack height of 30 other subjects. All 31 subjects then face the same laser. Hence, payoffs are perfectly correlated—all the subjects involved in the task earn zero, or the payment implied by the decision maker's choice.

Importantly, for each given box choice, the distribution of the subject's payoff is the same in ID and LEAD. An indifference to correlated payoffs (as in conventional expected utility theory) implies the same choice in the two tasks. A greater aversion to aggregate risk than to commensurate idiosyncratic risk implies a less risky choice in the LEAD than in ID.[40]

Results from ID fall within the normal range of measured risk aversion in the prior literature. The mean subject chooses $b = 19.5$, which corresponds to a CRRA parameter of 0.738, given the utility specification $u(x) = x^r$. In LEAD, however, the implied CRRA parameter decreases by 0.0118. The drop is statistically significant, and compares in magnitude to the difference in risk aversion recorded between men and women. Hence, the resulting decrease in risk taken in LEAD relative to ID is consistent with greater aversion to aggregate risk than to commensurate idiosyncratic risk.

The difference in risk taking observed between LEAD and ID, however, might also be explained by some other type of interdependent preferences, rather than aversion to aggregate risk. For example, subjects might have felt uncomfortable taking risks for others. They might have then tailored their choices in LEAD to accommodate what they believed were the risk preferences of the other subjects. If this were the case, then the reduced risk taking observed in LEAD relative to ID, would not be due to correlation aversion. Two other treatments are carried out in order to address such a concern. In each of these, a subject only chooses for herself, but her payoffs are correlated with the payoffs of other subjects (positive correlation in POS and negative correlation in NEG). We discuss these in detail below.

In the POS (positive correlation) social task, the decision maker chooses her own stack height, but is shown the box height choices of 30 other subjects. All the subjects face the same bomb, as in LEAD. Payoffs in POS are thus positively correlated (see Fig. 11). In POS, however, in contrast to LEAD, the subjects' choice has no implications for the payoffs of the others.

Again, if a subject is indifferent to correlation in own payoff and the payoffs of the others, as in the conventional theory, then her choices in POS and ID will be the same. If the subject is averse to correlation in own and others' payoffs, then she will make a less risky choice in POS than in her ID task (this is proved in Oprea and Robalino (2024)). On the other hand, an affinity for such correlation implies a more risky choice in POS than in ID. Results from the POS treatment are in line with those from LEAD, suggesting an aversion to correlated payoffs.

40 The proof is given by Oprea and Robalino (2024).

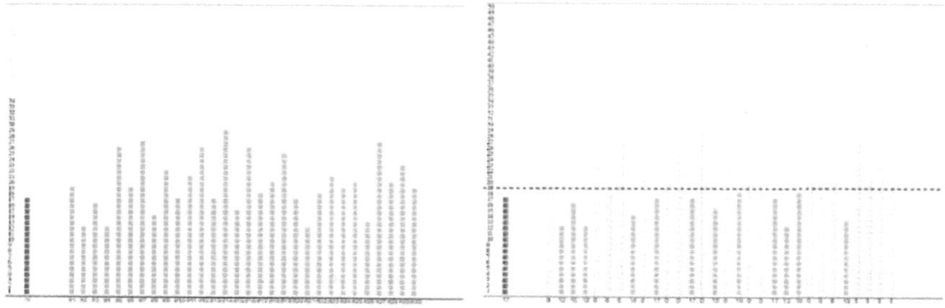

(e) POS Screenshot (During Task) (f) POS Screenshot (After Task)

FIGURE 11 On the left is the view of a subject in the POS task. The dark (green) stack to the far left is the subject's stack. The other stacks are stacks of the other subjects. The subject's choice does not affect the payoffs of the others. On the right is the subject's view after the laser has been fired. Subjects with stacks struck by the laser (faded stacks) get zero. The others are paid according to their chosen box heights.

A third treatment, NEG, controls for possible social imitation in POS. In NEG, the set-up is as in POS (Fig. 11), except that the decision maker's stack is hung from the ceiling. The situation is identical to POS except that the subject's payoffs are now negatively correlated with the payoffs of the 30 other subjects. Again, the conventional theory predicts the same choice in NEG and ID. An aversion to (affinity for) correlated payoffs implies a more (less) risky choice in NEG than in ID. Subjects do make slightly more risky choices in NEG than in ID, in line with aversion to correlation, though the difference is not statistically significant. In any case, negative correlation eliminates the increased risk aversion observed when payoffs are positively correlated, suggesting it is positively correlated payoffs that produce more risk aversion in POS than in ID.

Results for all treatments are summarized in Figs. 12 and 13. They contradict conventional expected utility theory, where individuals care only about the marginal distribution of own payoffs. In particular, positively correlated payoffs induce more risk averse choices, and the effect is shut down when payoffs are negatively correlated. Hence, more risk averse choices in LEAD and POS appear to be driven by positively correlated payoffs. This is consistent with a greater aversion to aggregate risk than to commensurate idiosyncratic risks, and with a corresponding aversion to correlation in own and others' consumption, in line with the model from Robson (1996).

Fig. 12 shows the average ID choice is riskier than the average choices in the LEAD and POS task. Risk taking is higher in NEG than in ID, but the difference is not statistically significant. Importantly, within-subject comparisons are consistent with correlation aversion, which is implied by the biological theory that aggregate risk in offspring is disadvantageous (Robson (1996)). Fig. 13 shows the difference, averaged across subjects, between an individual's choice in ID and her corresponding choice in the social task (LEAD, POS, or NEG). The mean subject makes a riskier choice in ID than in LEAD and POS. The

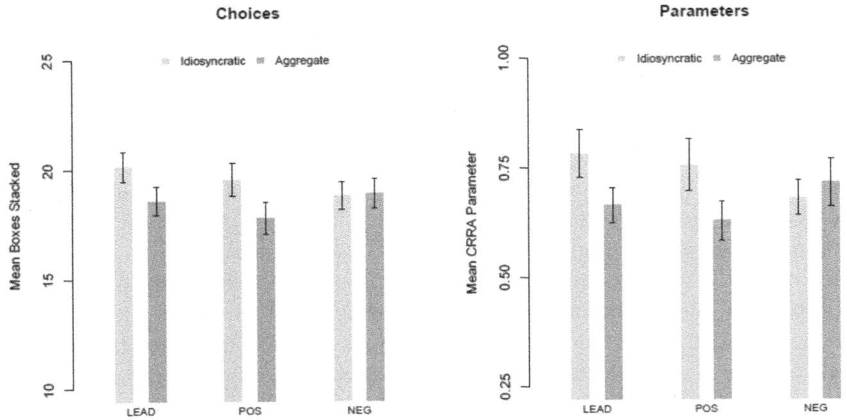

FIGURE 12 On the left are box heights observed in each ID task and in the corresponding LEAD/POS/NEG task. On the right is the implied CRRA parameter in each ID task and the corresponding LEAD/POS/NEG task.

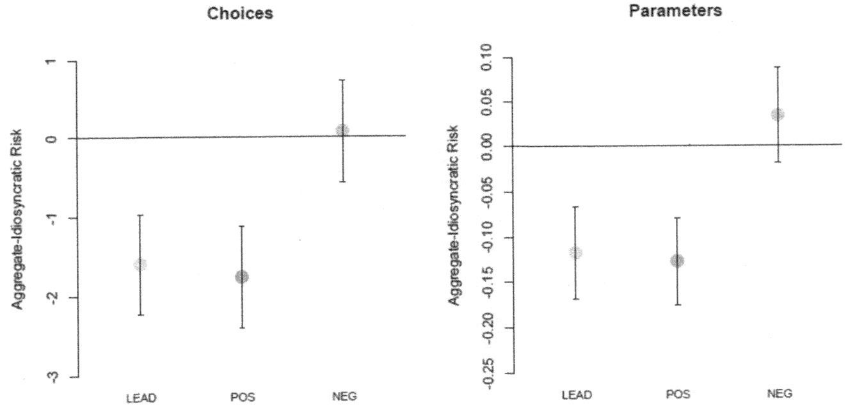

FIGURE 13 On the left is the within-subject difference in box height between the ID task and LEAD/POS/NEG. On the right is the inter-subject difference in implied CRRA parameter between ID and LEAD/POS/NEG.

difference is significant. Again, the mean subject makes a riskier choice in NEG than in ID, though the difference is not statistically significant.

Age-structured models predict interesting patterns of attitudes to correlation in offspring and mortality across different age cohorts (for example, see Robson and Samuelson (2019)), suggesting further experimental work is needed.

This section has sketched how a striking theoretical prediction of the current evolutionary approach—that individuals are more averse to aggregate risk than to idiosyncratic risk—finds empirical validation. That this prediction came from left field—would not otherwise have been readily foreseen—reinforces the scientific merit of the approach.

5 Theory of mind

We have so far discussed the evolution of utility, and some of its key properties, thereby providing a biological basis for economic decision-making in non-strategic situations. Humans are highly social, however. Many important choices involve interaction with others. In conventional game theory we are assumed to be fully sophisticated. Individuals in a game attribute motives and intentions to others, and they fully understand the implications of these mental states. This is, moreover, understood by all the players in the game—that is, player 1 is intentional, knows that player 2 is intentional, knows that player 2 knows that player 1 is intentional, and so on. There are alternatives to this fully strategic conception of social interaction. An agent in a game need not be aware at all of others' mental states, but instead might learn the appropriate choice through reinforcement learning, for example. There is good evidence, however, that humans are strategic, at least to some extent—that they reason about the motives and beliefs of others. We now explore the evolution of this strategic sophistication.

Theory of mind (ToM) refers to the ability to impute mental states to oneself and to others. An individual with ToM can conceive of others as intentional beings that are motivated by internal states. She can infer these states from observed behavior, and can use these inferences to predict behavior in the future. The term "theory of mind" was first used by Premack and Woodruff (1978)—we have a 'theory' of another mind because mental states cannot be directly observed, but must be inferred from behavior.

The ability to reason about mental states from observed behavior is called mind-reading. Mind-reading and ToM are manifest in humans beyond infancy. They form perhaps the central component of human social intelligence. Whether humans are alone in possessing this ability remains the subject of debate. However, it is commonly accepted that the ToM component is present, and most fully developed, in the human species.

ToM is assumed in game theory without apology. Agents in a game are often automatically assumed to share common knowledge about various aspects of the situation—preferences, the structure of the game, the rationality of the players, etc. The most general cases involve hierarchies of beliefs—beliefs about others' preferences, beliefs about others' beliefs about beliefs, and so on.[41]

Although the suite of cognitive mechanisms supporting ToM appear to be innate in humans, ToM emerges ontogenetically throughout development. An early illustration of this emergence is provided by Wimmer and Perner (1983). They tested children's understanding of two sketches. Each sketch involved a protagonist in a room storing an object in a location, and then leaving the scene, only to have an antagonist move the object to a different location. The child subject observes the surreptitious move of the object, and must know the

[41] Harsanyi (1967, 1968a,b) develops an equilibrium notion that finesses the often unwieldy hierarchical description.

protagonist could not have observed it. The child then has to indicate where the protagonist would look for the object when returning to the room. Subjects ranged in age from 3 to 9 years. No subject less than 4 years old guessed the correct answer—that the protagonist would look for the object where she hid it. Less than 57% of 4-6 year olds guessed correctly, but 86% of 6-9 year olds guessed correctly.

A second sketch involved the protagonist either helping a friend find the object, or undermining a foe that wants the object. Fully 85% of the older children inferred that the protagonist would lead his friend to where the object was hidden originally, and that he would lead the foe to the other location. Hence, around age 4, there emerges an ability to attribute beliefs to others that differ from one's own, and, moreover, to predict the corresponding behavior.[42]

Baron-Cohen et al. (1985) develop the 'Sally-Anne Test', in which children observe a puppet-play version of the Wimmer and Perner (1983) scenario. In line with Wimmer and Perner, they find that attribution of false belief emerges around age 4. Interestingly, they find that only 20% of subjects diagnosed with autism give the correct answer in the false-belief task, suggesting that autism involves a ToM deficit.[43]

Following Wimmer and Perner, several attempts have been made to push back the age at which false-belief reasoning emerges. The cutoff has subsequently been the subject of intense debate (Scott and Baillargeon (2017)). For example, Onishi and Baillargeon (2005) test false-belief understanding in infants using a design based on the tendency of infants to gaze longer at events that violate their expectations. Their non-verbal test suggests that 15 month-olds can understand false-beliefs.

Further tests suggest that other components of ToM emerge already in preverbal infants. Repacholi and Gopnik (1997), for example, find that, around 18 months, infants begin to differentiate their own desires from the desires of others. In their test, children observe an individual (non-verbally) expressing disgust when tasting one food and pleasure when tasting another food. The children then had an opportunity to offer the individual the two types of food. Whereas 14 month-old subjects offered the food they themselves preferred, 18 month-olds offered the individual the food that induced a happy reaction initially, even when this was their own less preferred option.

There is evidence of cultural variation in several aspects of ToM (Lillard (1998)). But some basic components appear to be universal. For example, Avis and Harris (1991) find that, among the children of the Baka, a group of hunter-gatherers, older children (mean age 5) pass a version of the Sally-Anne test, while most younger children (mean age 3.5) do not.

---

42 The Wimmer and Perner test—and many others based on it that followed—are known as 'false-belief' tests.

43 The notion that autism might entail a ToM deficit was later criticized. For example, it has been suggested that the Sally-Anne results with autistic children might result from a language deficit rather than diminished ToM ability (Bloom and German (2000)).

ToM in other species

Premack and Woodruff (1978) first asked, "Does the chimpanzee have a theory of mind?" Answers to such questions might help identify the evolutionary preconditions for this ability. Heyes and Frith (2014), for example, argue that the sophisticated expression of ToM that is observed in humans requires uniquely human cognitive byproducts, such as language and culture. ToM in non-verbal species would imply verbal language is not needed for this ability, although it might enhance it. For a survey of ToM animal studies see Krupenye and Call (2019). Several species of great apes direct their gaze to where an agent falsely believes an object is hidden, even though the apes know the object is located somewhere else (Krupenye et al. (2016)).

The presence of ToM in non-human animals has been debated since Premack and Woodruff (1978). For non-human species, a test for ToM must be non-verbal. Any display of the ability must also be non-verbal. This makes identification challenging. For example, a deceptive action by an animal—such as hiding food—could be interpreted as evidence of ToM. However, the deceptive strategy might have plausibly arisen via adaptive learning, requiring no reasoning at all about others' mental states. (See Whiten (1996), Heyes (2015), and Krupenye and Call (2019) for discussions of the difficulties involved in ToM animal studies.)

Hunter gatherers and ToM

Whiten and Erdal (2012) argue that ToM is a key pillar in the development of a socio-cognitive niche that facilitated hunter-gatherer social structure, and led to its success and predominance.

Dunbar (1992) argues that human intelligence is driven by the social environment (the social intelligence hypothesis). Group size in primates correlates with relative neocortex volume. Ecological problem solving seems to have played a smaller role. For example, there is no relationship between relative neocortex size and range size. Dunbar (2003) reviews evidence for the social intelligence hypothesis and for alternative explanations of primate intelligence.

5.1 The evolution of ToM

We now address the question of why ToM might have evolved. Although ToM is clearly advantageous in social situations, its supporting cognitive components are likely to be biologically costly (Dunbar (1992, 1998)). The question then is, what evolutionary edge does ToM confer over less sophisticated approaches to strategic interaction, such as, for example, adaptive learning?

The basic issue might be illustrated with an example of deception in animals. Scrub-jays prefer to hide food in a distant location when another jay is observing, but are equally likely to hide food at a near or distant location when the observer's view is occluded by an opaque barrier (Dally et al. (2005)). How do we explain this behavior? A ToM based explanation is that the deceptive jay understands her observer's mental states and understands their behavioral implications. The ToM jay hides her food in order to intentionally thwart her observer. Another explanation doesn't involve reasoning about others' mental states at all. The jay might have had her cache raided before, and has learned this happens less often whenever she stores food far from other jays. The hiding strategy is met with success and thus reinforced.

Robalino and Robson (2016) study the evolution of a key component of ToM, which they christen "theory of preferences" (ToP). ToP refers to the ability to impute preferences to others, to learn these preferences in strategic situations, and to use this knowledge to predict behavior in novel circumstances. The key result is that ToP has a sharp evolutionary edge over naivety when the strategic environment is characterized by persistent strategic novelty. A naive approach, such as reinforcement learning, might do well when novelty is introduced sufficiently slowly. However, agents with ToP can adapt to a higher rate of arrival of novelty than any reasonably specified naive type. The advantage to ToP is that it confers an ability to extrapolate knowledge about preferences across games.

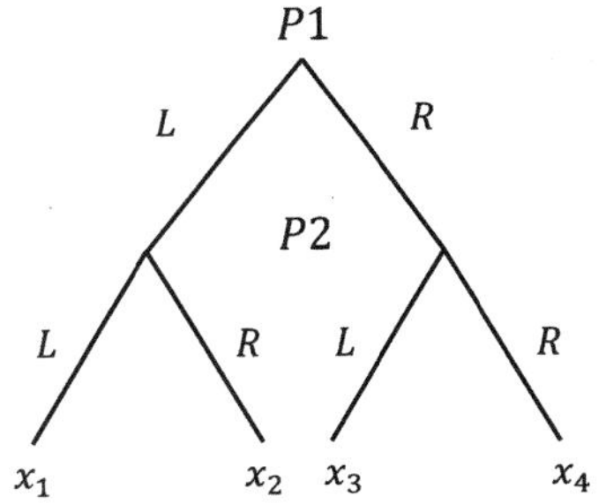

FIGURE 14 The game played by $P1$ and $P2$ in period t. The outcomes x_1, x_2, x_3, x_4 are drawn uniformly from the set of outcomes, X_t.

Consider a dynamic environment where, in each period, a perfect information game is generated by drawing outcomes from a set, X_t, that grows over time. At each date, a large population of individuals is matched to play the realized game. The situation where the game has two players is displayed in Fig. 14. Suppose all players know their own preferences over the outcomes, and that they choose a dominant action whenever one is available.[44]

Robalino and Robson (2016) consider a horse-race between two types of individuals in this environment. A naive type is essentially a reinforcement learner. This type learns how to behave in a game through repeated exposure to the specific game. When a game is new, the naive type maps the game to an arbitrary choice. On the other hand, a ToP type knows that her opponents'

[44] Suppose there are no super-game effects because in each period the $P1/P2$ pairs are randomly matched.

choices are motivated by preferences, endeavors to learn these preferences, and can extrapolate to novel games what has been learned in previous circumstances.

The naive type is thus characterized by an insensitivity, or blindness, to others' preferences. Such blindness might, nevertheless, appear sophisticated, in a limited sense. In Fig. 14, for example, a salient naive strategy for $P1$ is, in each novel game, to choose the action that yields the highest 50-50 average of the payoffs that follow the action. For example, in Fig. 14, $P1$ will choose L if

$$u_1(x_1) + u_1(x_2) > u_1(x_3) + u_1(x_4).$$

Actually, this would be the fully Bayesian optimal choice for $P1$ in the first round, given only that $P2$'s preferences are symmetrically distributed, so that the two choices that $P2$ might make after either choice by $P1$ are equally likely. Of course, this rule yields the appropriate choice whenever $P1$ has a dominant action.

The key difference is the rate at which the two types learn after the first round—while the naive type only learns game by game, the ToP type learns preferences. If a ToP type of $P1$ had previously observed $P2$ choose x_1 over x_2, and x_3 over x_4, perhaps in separate games, then she can predict $P2$'s choice in the game from Fig. 14 even if this particular game has never arisen before.

Robalino and Robson (2016) prove the following. If the set of outcomes grows very slowly, then both the naive type and the ToP type can keep up with the arrival of novel outcomes, and thus both types can learn effectively. If outcomes arrive too fast, then neither type can keep up. Although the ToP is able to learn more efficiently, neither type can keep up with the arrival rate of novelty. In an intermediate range of the arrival rate of novelty, however, the naive type is swamped, essentially facing a new game each period, while the ToP type can acquire her opponent's preferences and thus learn to play appropriately in every circumstance in the long run.

This key intermediate range of the arrival rate of strategic novelty thus provides the necessary impetus for ToP—a low enough arrival rate so the ToP type can learn, but sufficiently high to swamp the naive types. In this range, the ToP type will have a sharp advantage over the naive individuals even if there is a cost to ToP, arising perhaps from the required cognitive resources, provided this cost is sufficiently small. The reason the ToP type can cope with a higher arrival rate is because it needs to track far less information than the naive type. The set of 2-by-2 games, when there are N outcomes, is of the order of N^4, while the binary choices the ToP must learn are of the order of N^2.

Kimbrough et al. (2017) further develop this idea, establishing a precise sense in which the set of 2-by-2 games that can be generated from a set of N outcomes is more complex than the set of complete binary relations over the outcomes, which in turn is more complex than the set of transitive orderings of the outcomes. A sophisticated ToP type that knows her opponents' preferences are transitive will then learn faster than a simple ToP type that learns via binary choices. In turn, simple ToPs will beat a naive type that endeavors to learn games. Kimbrough et al. (2017) further design and execute an experiment to test the ability to learn others' preferences in one strategic setting and to extrapolate this knowledge to novel games.

As in Section 5.1 consider a two-stage, two-action, perfect information game tree. Player 1 (P1) moves first, then Player 2 (P2). Each player has preferences over a fixed finite set of outcomes, X, and each player knows his own preferences. Let G be the set of all extensive form games as just described with outcomes from X. Suppose $P1$ and $P2$ are to play a randomly drawn game, $g \in G$. Before $P1$ and $P2$ play the game, however, suppose $P1$ observes a 'training' history h informing $P1$ of $P2$'s subgame perfect strategy in M games, where each of these is independently drawn from G with replacement.

In all of the games $P2$'s problem is straightforward. The question is, how does $P1$ condition his choice in g on the training history h? We consider three types of $P1$, differing in how they incorporate information across games.

Definition 5.1. A naive type of $P1$ makes an arbitrary choice in g if the game is not observed along h. Otherwise, the naive type chooses a best response to the known SPE choices of $P2$ in the game.

As in Robalino and Robson (2016), this naive type considers each game an independent circumstance, and thus requires direct exposure to each particular game in order to learn the appropriate choice. The naive player, by luck, might get it right in a novel game; however, for any reasonable specification of naivete, she will initially make a suboptimal choice in some of the games.

This specification gives the naive types generous credit, in the sense that they need only *one* exposure to a given game to learn how to play it. This only strengthens the results since we will show that, even in this case, there is a marked edge to the ToP types.

A ToP type understands that $P2$'s choices along h are motivated by a complete binary relation over the set of outcomes. If a ToP type observes $P2$ choosing an outcome x when y was available, then she will know that $P2$ prefers x to y, and can predict this choice when it arises in any circumstance. Hence, the ToP type is sure to choose optimally in g whenever both corresponding binary choices of $P2$ have been observed along the training history, even if the game itself has not been seen before.

Definition 5.2. If $P2$'s choice in a subgame of g is revealed along the training history, then the ToP type of $P1$ uses this to formulate her best response in g. Otherwise, the ToP type attributes an arbitrary strategy to $P2$ in the subgame and best responds to this.

The ToP ignores the implications of transitivity, having to directly observe a binary choice in order to infer the corresponding preference. A more sophisticated ToP understands that $P2$ has transitive preferences and can apply this to correctly predict her opponent's choice in a subgame that may not have been seen previously.

Definition 5.3. A ToP* type of $P1$ chooses a best response in g to an arbitrary $P2$ strategy implied by a transitive ordering of X, where this ordering is consistent with the $P2$ strategies observed along the training history.

The key issue is now how effective the various types are in using the training history to learn about G. Clearly, the ToP* extracts more useful information from a given history than does the ToP, and this is also true for the ToP relative to the naive type. For instance, if a ToP learns the appropriate choice in g by observing h, then so must the more sophisticated ToP* that understands transitivity. At the same time there are cases where the ToP* learns but the ToP does not. Intuitively then, the ToP* is the most efficient learner, and the naive type the least.

The edge to sophistication can be made precise by considering a sufficiently large set of games. Recall that h entails M examples of uniformly drawn games from G, and their corresponding $P2$ strategies. Consider a notion of learning in the current circumstance:

Definition 5.4. A type $\tau \in$ {naive, ToP, ToP* } can $(1 - \epsilon)$-learn G after M examples if the following holds. For any transitive preference ordering of $P2$, $P1$'s choice in g after observing a randomly drawn history h is the subgame perfect choice with probability no less than $1 - \epsilon$, uniformly in the $P2$ preference ordering.

That is, M examples suffice for $P1$ to learn $P2$'s preferences in any G with probability $(1 - \epsilon)$. Given an arbitrary preference relation of his opponent, training on M examples ensures $P1$ will get it right in at least a fraction $(1 - \epsilon)$ of the games. This notion of learning—probably approximately correct learning, (PAC-learning)—is due to Valiant (1984).[45]

Clearly, the number of examples required for a $P1$ type to learn about G will depend on the parameter ϵ, however, it will also depend on the complexity of what the type is really trying to learn. PAC-learning theory makes a tight connection between the complexity of the concept being learned and the number of training examples required (see Kalai (2003) for a detailed discussion of the theory). Recall that the naive type is learning a set of games, while the ToP type is learning binary choices, and the ToP* type is learning a linear ordering. The set of games is the most complex, and the transitive ordering the least, in a way that can be made precise in PAC-learning theory. We have the following result, which is proved in Kimbrough et al. (2017):

Theorem 5.1. *Suppose there are at least 4 outcomes. There are positive continuous functions, $L(\epsilon)$, and $U(\epsilon)$ with $L(\epsilon) < U(\epsilon)$, such that the following*

45 See Kalai (2003) also, where the theory is applied to the related problem of the learnability of rational preference orderings.

holds. (1) *A naive type of* $P1$ *is sure to* $1-\epsilon$ *learn G after M examples if* $M \geq |X|^4 \cdot U(\epsilon)$, *but not if* $M < |X|^4 \cdot L(\epsilon)$. (2) *A ToP type of* $P1$ *is sure to* $1-\epsilon$ *learn G after M examples if* $M \geq |X|^2 \cdot U(\epsilon)$, *but not if* $M < |X|^2 \cdot L(\epsilon)$. (3) *A ToP* type of* $P1$ *is sure to* $1-\epsilon$ *learn G after M examples if* $M \geq |X| \cdot U(\epsilon)$, *but not if* $M < |X| \cdot L(\epsilon)$.

That is, the ToP* learns the fastest, requiring the least number of examples, and the naive type learns the slowest. The differences in speeds of learning are, moreover, stark, and reveal a sharp edge for ToP* over ToP, and for ToP over the naive type. As in Robalino and Robson (2016), the sophisticated types learn more efficiently because they can extrapolate to a novel game information that was acquired in a different circumstance.

The above results show that an increase in the number of strategic problems might lead to a transition where there is a sharp edge to ToM. This is in line with theory and evidence from other disciplines regarding the evolutionary growth of human intelligence—for example, a central argument there is that the transition from an arboreal niche to the more complex circumstances in the savannah led to an increase in human intelligence. (For discussion see, for example, Robson and Kaplan (2003).)

5.2 Theory of preferences: experimental evidence

Kimbrough et al. (2017) further design an experiment testing the ability to learn others' preferences and to exploit this knowledge strategically. The design is based on the simple theoretical learning model discussed in the previous section.

As in the above theoretical model the experiments involve two-stage two-action games of perfect information. In each experimental session, an even number of subjects are assigned the roles of $P1$ and $P2$, where these roles are fixed throughout the session. There is a fixed set of outcomes, X, where each $x \in X$ induces a unique monetary payoff for each player role, $Pi, i = 1, 2$. All Pi's, $i = 1, 2$, obtain the same monetary payoff from each given $x \in X$. Hence, each subject in a given role has the same induced preferences over X. Each subject knows her own preferences, but not the preferences of players in the other role.

In each period, $t = 1, \ldots, T$, of a session, a game is formed by uniformly drawing 4 outcomes from X and appending these to a 2-by-2 extensive form. $P1$'s and $P2$'s are then randomly and anonymously matched to play the game. At the end of the period, all the $P1$ subjects observe the choices of all the $P2$s at any nodes that were reached by any $P2$ during the period of play. As in the theoretical model, if a $P1$ subject has ToP, she can learn about $P2$'s preferences. If the likelihood of SPE play by $P1$s varies with the history of play, this might reveal the extent to which subjects have ToP and properly apply it.

The overall trend of play suggests substantial learning. This is displayed in Fig. 15 which shows the fraction of $P1$s making the SPE choice in each period. An upward trend indicates learning. The pool of games is restricted over time.

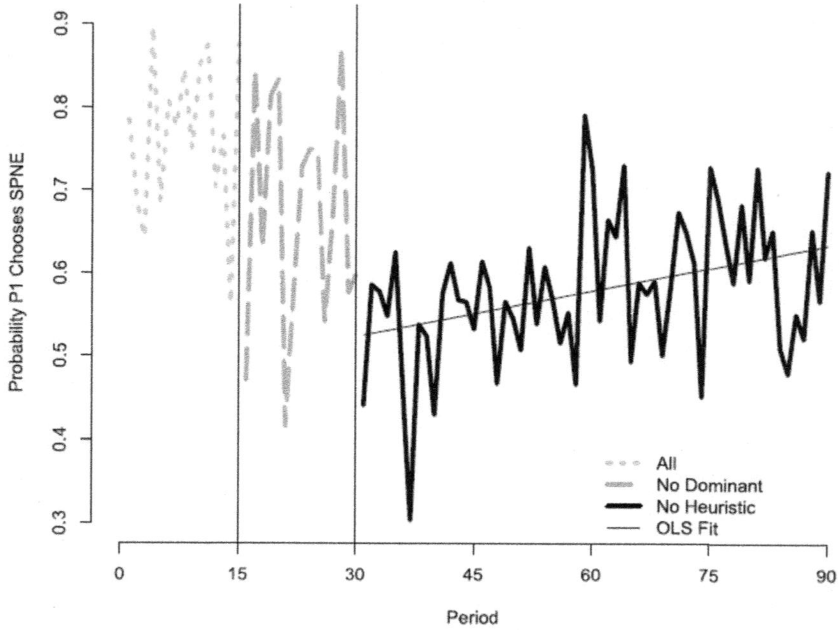

FIGURE 15 Learning an opponent's preferences. This is Fig. 2 from Kimbrough et al. (2017). Reuse of this Elsevier material is permitted under STM guidelines.

The goal was to observe learning but, for some games, the SPE choice could too easily be inferred. Specifically, in each session, after period 15, no game gave the $P1$s a dominant choice; after period 30, no SPE choice of $P1$ was consistent with a 50-50 heuristic, where this involved choosing the action with the highest 50-50 mean payoff for $P1$ in the resulting subgame.

To determine the type of learning observed—naive, ToP, or ToP*—the probability of SPE choice in a game is regressed on indicators of (1) whether the game was played previously (naive learning), (2) whether the pairwise choices of $P2$ in the game had been observed (ToP learning), (3) whether the pairwise choices of $P2$ in the game are implied by the history of play, given that the $P2$s have transitive preferences (ToP* learning).

Results from two main regressions are presented in Table 1. The first column examines how $P1$s use the public history of play. The second column examines how a $P1$ conditions choice on histories involving own opponents only. The results suggest a bias in the use of information. Subjects tend to focus more on their own personal histories, seeming to pay less attention to the public history. ToP learning appears to be better established than ToP* learning. Overall, there is evidence that subjects endeavor to infer others' preferences and that they apply knowledge of preferences appropriately to make optimal choices. Subjects also completed two well-known survey instruments that are used in psychology

TABLE 1 **Learning an opponent's preferences in circumstances that would enable naive, ToP, or ToP* learning. Clustered standard errors in parentheses. Under a one-tailed hypothesis test, * means $p < 0.10$, ** means $p < 0.05$, and *** means $p < 0.01$. This is an excerpt from Table 1 from Kimbrough et al. (2017). Reuse of this Elsevier material is permitted under STM guidelines.**

P1 makes the SPE choice	**Public histories**	**Own history**
Period	0.002*** (0.001)	0.002*** (0.001)
P1 has a dominant choice	0.482*** (0.026)	0.483*** (0.024)
50-50 heuristic implies P1's SPE choice	0.371*** (0.025)	0.370*** (0.023)
Game played previously	0.007 (0.018)	0.050** (0.020)
Fraction of all prior P2 choices that are optimal	0.451** (0.249)	
ToP knows the SPE from the public history	0.025 (0.019)	
ToP* knows the SPE from the public history	0.012 (0.033)	
Fraction of all prior P2 choices that are optimal		0.274*** (0.087)
ToP knows the SPE from own history		0.089*** (0.020)
ToP* knows the SPE from own history		0.045* (0.034)
Constant	−0.045 (0.228)	0.115* (0.078)
Observations	7743	7743
R^2	0.235	0.240

to measure ToM (Hurley et al. (2007)). Interestingly, ToP ability as measured by the game experiments correlates with responses on the ToM surveys from psychology. Hence, the notion of ToP examined experimentally corresponds with ToM as understood by psychologists.

5.3 Related papers on ToM in economics

In addition to the papers discussed above, there is a small literature in economics that covers several aspects of ToM. We now outline some of this relevant work.

5.3.1 Theoretical papers

A small number of papers examine the evolutionary emergence of strategic intelligence. A key question is whether sophistication is evolutionarily inevitable—that is, does it confer a sufficient advantage over more simple, and perhaps less costly, approaches? Foremost among these is Stahl (1993), which considers a cognitive hierarchy of types, ranging in levels of sophistication. A smart$_0$ player does not reason about the game at all, automatically choosing an arbitrary strategy instead. For $n \geq 1$, a smart$_n$ type can reason about which choices are n-level rationalizable, and knows that no smart$_{n-1}$ player would use a strategy that is not $(n-1)$-level rationalizable. A key result of Stahl is that, in a stationary strategic environment, it does not always pay to be smart. In particular, smart$_0$ players that happen to choose the right strategy cannot be driven out by more sophisticated agents. In some cases, when sophistication entails a cost, the smart$_0$ will drive the smart types to extinction.

In a similar vein, Mohlin (2012) studies the closely related level-k approach in a more general model allowing for multiple games, learning, and partial observability of type. It remains true, however, that low reasoning types coexist in the long run with higher types. In a Bayesian game setting, Gauer and Kuzmics (2020) show that, in conflict games, the probability that a player will pay a small cost to acquire her opponent's preferences is bounded away from both zero and one. The result holds given an arbitrary positive cost of sophistication. All of the above works examine a stationary strategic environment. On the other hand, the Robalino and Robson (2016) result in favor of sophistication is driven by persistent strategic novelty.

5.3.2 Experimental papers

On the experimental front there is a large literature examining learning in games. Although deviations from classic rationality are well-known and often observed, there is substantial evidence that learning is more sophisticated than in simple adaptive learning. An important paper is Erev and Roth (1998) which compares the predictive performance of various adaptive learning models. They show that a simple reinforcement model fits the data better than assuming equilibrium is instantly reached. An even better fit is attained when experimentation and forgetting are added to the basic setup. A model where players condition on beliefs about others' strategies yet further improves predictive performance, suggesting individuals reason about other players, as in ToM.

Camerer et al. (2002) develop an elaboration of reinforcement learning called experience weighted attraction (EWA). EWA combines elements of reinforcement learning with the more sophisticated fictitious play. The basic model is extended to incorporate sophisticated learning, where a player understands her opponent might be adaptive, or perhaps, may likewise be a sophisticated learner. Such sophistication improves predictive power relative to an EWA model with only unsophisticated agents.

Knoepfle et al. (2009) use eye-tracking technology to show that subjects examine others' payoffs carefully, further supporting elements of strategic sophistication. In another study using eye-tracking, Polonio et al. (2015) show that there is heterogeneity in the pattern of information acquisition used by subjects in games, but that subjects' patterns are stable across games, and that these patterns predict behavior. Some of these information acquisition patterns correspond to ones discussed here. For example, some individuals in the study systematically neglect the payoffs of their opponents like our naive individuals. Interestingly, these individuals' eye-movements are consistent with searching for a dominant choice, or the strategy yielding the highest mean payoff. Other subjects performed saccades that alternated fixation on own and others' payoffs, appearing to consider the rationality of their opponents, akin to our ToP types. Related is the question of whether subjects are even aware they are in a strategic situation, and that their choices ought to depend on what they believe about others. Fehr and Huck (2016) show that some subjects are strategically unaware, and that awareness is correlated with cognitive ability.

A key element of ToM is recursive rationality. Although, in principle, there is no limit on the number of recursive embeddings that are possible, in practice, people most often operate at one or two levels (Camerer et al. (2004), Bosch-Domènech et al. (2002)). Kneeland (2015) examines the prevalence and depth of recursive rationality in experimental subjects using a novel application of ring games. In a ring game, player 1's payoff depends on player 2's choice, player 2's payoff depends on player 3's choice, ..., player $(n - 1)$'s payoff depends on player n's choice; and player n's payoff depends on player 1's choice. This ring structure allows higher order payoff to vary independently of lower order payoffs, and thus allows the identification of an individual's depth of recursive rationality. About 6 percent of the subjects are not rational at all. The remaining pool of subjects consists of first-order through fourth-order rationals, with approximately equal shares of each.

In an interesting study involving children, Fe et al. (2022) find that level-k depth correlates with both ToM ability and cognitive ability. Older children incorporate information about their opponents' cognitive ability in a manner suggestive of strategic sophistication. There is some evidence, however, that observed depth of sophistication, as in level-k, depends on the circumstance. Georganas et al. (2015), for example, find in a test of level-k that an individual's level of reasoning will vary across games. Moreover, it was not possible to rank subjects by depth of reasoning—the most sophisticated subjects in one circumstance were not always the most sophisticated in another case.

6 Future directions

Of all the topics covered in this chapter, perhaps the leading candidate for extension is theory of mind. All that was sketched here was one aspect of that—the imputation of utility to others as relevant in particular sequential strategic interactions. This merely gathers the lowest-hanging fruit concerned with this issue.

Firstly, it would be worth examining how theory of mind could be evolutionarily advantageous in other strategic interactions. A leading example here would be simultaneous-move games. These would again involve imputing utility to others but also considering the evolutionary advantages of understanding that an opponent would not choose a dominated strategy, as the first step in iterated elimination of dominated strategies. Such games could be examined in the laboratory.

Another interesting aspect of theory of mind is the imputation of beliefs to others as also relevant in strategic interactions, especially when beliefs have effects distinct from those of utility.

Promising empirical work derived from this chapter concerns the transmission of a genetic component to time preference. How would the ancestral environment of various countries shape the time preference seen there now? Section 3.2.6 argues that low ancestral mortality and low ancestral fertility might be reflected in high modern patience. If ancestral mortality and fertility for the last few thousand years could be estimated, the prediction could be checked against the data in Falk et al. (2018, Fig. 1, for example).

From a big picture viewpoint, it seems desirable for future research to develop and test integrated genetic and cultural models for the transmission of economic preferences. Such dual transmission mechanisms could feature the possibility that copying other individuals promoted evolutionary success. The coevolution of genes and culture is intrinsically plausible. The reason for confining attention here at first to purely genetic inheritance is for parsimony and simplicity but also as part of a conservative methodological approach. Biological evolution is the obvious candidate for justifying the conventional assumption in economics that preferences are exogenous and fixed, at least in the short run.

7 Conclusions

Staying within the ambit of genetically based preferences, the literature surveyed in this chapter still reflects a deliberate reluctance to make wholesale changes to economic theory. For time preference as considered in Sections 3.2-3.2.6, for example, the central model of intertemporal preferences is a standard model based on additively separable flow utility, mortality and a constant discount factor. The novel twist is just that this criterion is a result rather than an assumption, where a constant component of the discount factor deriving from population growth is augmented by mortality. It is argued that such a discount factor might have originated in hunter-gatherer societies despite the apparent paucity of opportunities to make large intertemporal tradeoffs and that this discount factor might be appreciable despite the arithmetic impossibility of substantial growth in human populations over the long run.

Section 4 describes how the predictions of an evolutionary approach based on demography can come from left field, despite the reluctance to make wholesale changes. These predictions are that individuals should be more averse to aggregate risk than to idiosyncratic risk. If such left field predictions are borne out anyway, they boost greatly the inherent appeal of the approach. We describe work by Oprea and Robalino (2024) that corroborate that such a distinction can be seen in experiments.

Section 2 adopted a different evolutionary approach. Rather than considering a Darwinian battle for the numerical supremacy of various rates of time preference and various attitudes to risk, we draw inspiration from direct neuroscience observations. We sketch how utility is apparently directly represented as noisy neural firing rates, so creating the need for utility to adapt to where the heavy traffic is. We present a model of adaptive utility and show it makes predictions—about a preference for growth, for example—that are substantiated. We delve into the possibility that utility might further be reflected as pleasure which then provides an explanation for the hedonic treadmill and raises thorny questions about happiness economics.

These results demonstrate the power of an evolutionary approach to buttress economic theory, to suggest novel hypotheses, to extend its application. The link to neuroscience, in particular, holds out the promise of eventually better integrating economics and other sciences that study the same human beings.

References

Avis, Jeremy, Harris, Paul L., 1991. Belief-desire reasoning among Baka children: evidence for a universal conception of mind. Child Development 62 (3), 460–467.

Baron-Cohen, Simon, Leslie, Alan M., Frith, Uta, 1985. Does the autistic child have a "theory of mind"? Cognition 21 (1), 37–46.

Becker, Anke, Enke, Benjamin, Falk, Armin, 2020. Ancient origins of the global variation in economic preferences. AEA Papers and Proceedings 110, 319–323.

Becker, Gary S., 1964. Human Capital. Columbia University Press, New York.

Bentham, Jeremy, 2007. An Introduction to the Principles of Morals and Legislation. Dover Publications, Mineola, New York.

Berridge, Kent C., 2007. The debate over dopamine's role in reward: the case for incentive salience. Psychopharmacology 191, 391–431.

Berridge, Kent C., 2009. Wanting and liking: observations from the neuroscience and psychology laboratory. Inquiry 52 (4), 378–398.

Berridge, Kent C., Kringelbach, Morten L., 2015. Pleasure systems in the brain. Neuron 86 (3), 646–664.

Binmore, Kenneth George, 1994. Game Theory and the Social Contract Volume I: Playing Fair. MIT Press.

Bloom, Paul, German, Tim P., 2000. Two reasons to abandon the false belief task as a test of theory of mind. Cognition 77, B25–B31.

Bosch-Domènech, Antoni, Montalvo, José G., Nagel, Rosemarie, Satorra, Albert, 2002. One, two, (three), infinity, ...: newspaper and lab beauty-contest experiments. American Economic Review 92 (5), 1687–1701.

Bull, James J., 1980. Sex determination in reptiles. The Quarterly Review of Biology 55 (1), 3–21.

Camerer, Colin F., Ho, Teck-Hua, Chong, Juin-Kuan, 2002. Sophisticated experience-weighted attraction learning and strategic teaching in repeated games. Journal of Economic Theory 104 (1), 137–188.

Camerer, Colin F., Ho, Teck-Hua, Chong, Juin-Kuan, 2004. A cognitive hierarchy model of games. Quarterly Journal of Economics 119 (3), 861–898.

Campbell, John Y., Cochrane, John H., 1999. By force of habit: a consumption-based explanation of aggregate stock market behavior. Journal of Political Economy 107 (2), 205–251.

Clark, Andrew E., Flèche, Sarah, Layard, Richard, Powdthavee, Nattavudh, Ward, George, 2018. The Origins of Happiness: The Science of Well-Being over the Life Course. Princeton University Press, Princeton.

Costa, Kauê Machado, Schoenbaum, Geoffrey, 2022. Dopamine. Current Biology 32 (15), R817–R824.

Crosetto, Paolo, Filippin, Antonio, 2013. The "bomb" risk elicitation task. Journal of Risk and Uncertainty 47 (1), 31–65.

Curry, Philip A., 2001. Decision making under uncertainty and the evolution of interdependent preferences. Journal of Economic Theory 98 (2), 357–369.

Dally, Joanna M., Emery, Nathan J., Clayton, Nicola S., 2005. Cache protection strategies by western scrub-jays, Aphelocoma californica: implications for social cognition. Animal Behaviour 70 (6), 1251–1263.

Dreborg, Susanne, Sundström, Görel, Larsson, Tomas A., Larhammar, Dan, 2008. Evolution of vertebrate opioid receptors. Proceedings of the National Academy of Sciences 105 (40), 15487–15492.

Duesenberry, James S., 1949. Income, Saving, and the Theory of Consumer Behavior. Cambridge University Press, Cambridge.

Dunbar, R.I.M., 1992. Neocortex size as a constraint on group size in primates. Journal of Human Evolution 22 (6), 469–493.

Dunbar, R.I.M., 1998. The social brain hypothesis. Evolutionary Anthropology 6 (5), 178–190.

Dunbar, R.I.M., 2003. The social brain: mind, language, and society in evolutionary perspective. Annual Review of Anthropology 32 (1), 163–181.

Dustmann, Christian, Meghir, Costas, 2005. Wages, experience and seniority. Review of Economic Studies 72 (1), 77–108.

Easterlin, Richard A., 1974. Does economic growth improve the human lot? Some empirical evidence. In: Nations and Households in Economic Growth: Essays in Honor of Moses Abramovitz.

Easterlin, Richard A., O'Connor, Kelsey J., 2022. The Easterlin paradox. In: Handbook of Labor, Human Resources and Population Economics. Springer, pp. 1–25.

Epstein, Larry, Tanny, Stephen, 1980. Increasing generalized correlation: a definition and some economic consequences. Canadian Journal of Economics 13 (1), 16–34.

Erev, Ido, Roth, Alvin, 1998. Predicting how people play games: reinforcement learning in experimental games with unique, mixed strategy equilibria. American Economic Review 88 (4), 848–881.

Falk, Armin, Becker, Anke, Dohmen, Thomas, Enke, Benjamin, Huffman, David, Sunde, Uwe, 2018. Global evidence on economic preferences. Quarterly Journal of Economics 133 (4), 1645–1692.

Fe, Eduardo, Gill, David, Prowse, Victoria, 2022. Cognitive skills, strategic sophistication, and life outcomes. Journal of Political Economy 130 (10), 2643–2704.

Fehr, Dietmar, Huck, Steffen, 2016. Who knows it is a game? On strategic awareness and cognitive ability. Experimental Economics 19 (4), 713–726.

Fisher, Irving, 1930. The Theory of Interest, as Determined by Impatience to Spend Income and Opportunity to Invest It. MacMillan, New York.

Frank, Robert H., Hutchens, Robert M., 1993. Wages, seniority, and the demand for rising consumption profiles. Journal of Economic Behavior & Organization 21 (3), 251–276.

Frauenthal, James C., 1986. Analysis of age-structure models. In: Mathematical Ecology: An Introduction. Springer, pp. 117–147.
Freed, William J., 2022. Motivation and Desire: A New Way to Think About Why We Do Everything and Its Basis in Neuroscience. Springer Nature.
Friedman, Milton, Savage, Leonard J., 1948. The utility analysis of choices involving risk. Journal of Political Economy 56 (4), 279–304.
Galor, Oded, Özak, Ömer, 2016. The agricultural origins of time preference. American Economic Review 106 (10), 3064–3103.
Gauer, Florian, Kuzmics, Christoph, 2020. Cognitive empathy in conflict situations. International Economic Review 61 (4), 1659–1678.
Georganas, Sotiris, Healy, Paul J., Weber, Roberto A., 2015. On the persistence of strategic sophistication. Journal of Economic Theory 159, 369–400.
Glimcher, Paul W., 2011. Foundations of Neuroeconomic Analysis. Oxford University Press, New York.
Harrison, Glenn W., Lau, Morten I., Rutström, E. Elisabet, 2007. Estimating risk attitudes in Denmark: a field experiment. Scandinavian Journal of Economics 109 (2), 341–368.
Harsanyi, John C., 1967. Games with incomplete information played by 'Bayesian' players I. Management Science 14, 159–182.
Harsanyi, John C., 1968a. Games with incomplete information played by 'Bayesian' players II. Management Science 14, 320–334.
Harsanyi, John C., 1968b. Games with incomplete information played by 'Bayesian' players III. Management Science 14, 486–502.
Heller, Yuval, Nehama, Ilan, 2023. Evolutionary foundation for heterogeneity in risk aversion. Journal of Economic Theory 208, 105617.
Heyes, Cecilia M., 2015. Animal mindreading: what's the problem? Psychonomic Bulletin and Review 22, 313–327.
Heyes, Cecilia M., Frith, Chris D., 2014. The cultural evolution of mind reading. Science 344 (6190), 1357.
Hill, Kim, Hurtado, A. Magdalena, 1996. Ache Life History: The Ecology and Demography of a Foraging People. Aldine de Gruyter, New York.
Hu, Wangjie, Hao, Ziqian, Du, Pengyuan, Di Vincenzo, Fabio, Manzi, Giorgio, Cui, Jialong, Fu, Yun-Xin, Pan, Yi-Hsuan, Li, Haipeng, 2023. Genomic inference of a severe human bottleneck during the early to middle Pleistocene transition. Science 381 (6661), 979–984.
Hurley, Robert S.E., Losh, Molly, Parlier, Morgan, Reznick, Stephen J., Piven, Joseph, 2007. The broad autism phenotype questionnaire. Journal of Autism and Developmental Disorders 37 (9), 1679–1690.
Kahneman, Daniel, Wakker, Peter P., Sarin, Rakesh, 1997. Back to Bentham? Explorations of experienced utility. Quarterly Journal of Economics 112 (2), 375–406.
Kalai, Gil, 2003. Learnability and rationality of choice. Journal of Economic Theory 113 (1), 104–117.
Kaplan, Hillard S., Robson, Arthur J., 2009. We age because we grow. Proceedings of the Royal Society B: Biological Sciences 276 (1663), 1837–1844.
Kimbrough, Erik O., Robalino, Nikolaus, Robson, Arthur J., 2017. Applying "theory of mind": theory and experiments. Games and Economic Behavior 106 (1), 209–226.
Kneeland, Terri, 2015. Identifying higher-order rationality. Econometrica 83 (5), 2065–2079.
Knoepfle, Daniel T., Camerer, Colin F., Wang, Joseph T., 2009. Studying learning in games using eye-tracking. Journal of the European Economic Association 7 (2–3), 388–398.
Kragel, Philip A., Treadway, Michael T., Admon, Roee, Pizzagalli, Diego A., Hahn, Emma C., 2023. A mesocorticolimbic signature of pleasure in the human brain. Nature Human Behaviour, 1–12.
Krupenye, Christopher, Call, Josep, 2019. Theory of mind in animals: current and future directions. Wiley Interdisciplinary Reviews: Cognitive Science 10 (6), 1–25.
Krupenye, Christopher, Kano, Fumihiro, Hirata, Satoshi, Call, Josep, Tomasello, Michael, 2016. Great apes anticipate that other individuals will act according to false beliefs. Science 354 (6308), 110–114.

Lillard, Angeline, 1998. Ethnopsychologies: cultural variations in theories of mind. Psychological Bulletin 123 (1), 3–32.

Mas-Colell, Andreu, Whinston, Michael, Green, Jerry, 1995. Microeconomic Theory. Oxford University Press, New York.

Mohlin, Erik, 2012. Evolution of theories of mind. Games and Economic Behavior 75 (1), 299–318.

Netzer, Nick, Robson, Arthur, Steiner, Jakub, Kocourek, Pavel, 2025. Risk perception: measurement and aggregation. Journal of the European Economic Association 23 (4), 1309–1349.

Nordhaus, William D., 1994. Managing the Global Commons: the Economics of Climate Change, vol. 31. MIT Press, Cambridge, MA.

Onishi, Kristine H., Baillargeon, Renée, 2005. Do 15-month-old infants understand false beliefs? Science 308 (8), 255–258.

Oprea, Ryan, 2024. Decisions under risk are decisions under complexity. American Economic Review 114 (12), 3789–3811.

Oprea, Ryan, Robalino, Nikolaus, 2024. Are humans more averse to aggregate risk? Testing an evolutionary economic theory. Working Paper.

Polonio, Luca, Di Guida, Sibilla, Coricelli, Giorgio, 2015. Strategic sophistication and attention in games: an eye-tracking study. Games and Economic Behavior 94 (1), 80–96.

Premack, David, Woodruff, Guy, 1978. Does the chimpanzee have a theory of mind? Behavioral and Brain Sciences 1 (4), 515–526.

Ray, Debraj, Robson, Arthur J., 2012. Status, intertemporal choice, and risk taking. Econometrica 80 (4), 1505–1531.

Rayo, Luis, Becker, Gary S., 2007. Evolutionary efficiency and happiness. Journal of Political Economy 115 (2), 302–337.

Réale, Denis, McAdam, Andrew G., Boutin, Stan, Berteaux, Dominique, 2003. Genetic and plastic responses of a northern mammal to climate change. Proceedings of the Royal Society of London. Series B: Biological Sciences 270 (1515), 591–596.

Repacholi, Betty M., Gopnik, Alison, 1997. Early reasoning about desires: evidence from 14- and 18-month-olds. Developmental Psychology 33 (1), 12–21.

Robalino, Nikolaus, Robson, Arthur J., 2016. The evolution of strategic sophistication. American Economic Review 106 (4), 1046–1072.

Robatto, Roberto, Szentes, Balázs, 2017. On the biological foundation of risk preferences. Journal of Economic Theory 172, 410–422.

Robson, Arthur J., 1992. Status, the distribution of wealth, private and social attitudes to risk. Econometrica 60 (4), 837–857.

Robson, Arthur J., 1996. The evolution of attitudes to risk: lottery tickets and relative wealth. Games and Economic Behavior 14 (2), 190–207.

Robson, Arthur J., 2001a. The biological basis of economic behavior. Journal of Economic Literature 39 (1), 11–33.

Robson, Arthur J., 2001b. Why would nature give individuals utility functions? Journal of Political Economy 109 (4), 900–914.

Robson, Arthur J., Kaplan, Hillard S., 2003. The evolution of human life expectancy and intelligence in hunter-gatherer economies. American Economic Review 93 (1), 150–169.

Robson, Arthur J., Kaplan, Hillard S., 2006. The economics of hunter-gatherer societies and the evolution of human characteristics. Canadian Journal of Economics/Revue canadienne d'économique 39 (2), 375–398.

Robson, Arthur J., Samuelson, Larry, 2007. The evolution of intertemporal preferences. American Economic Review 97 (2), 496–500.

Robson, Arthur J., Samuelson, Larry, 2009. The evolution of time preference with aggregate uncertainty. American Economic Review 99 (5), 1925–1953.

Robson, Arthur J., Samuelson, Larry, 2011. The evolution of decision and experienced utilities. Theoretical Economics 6 (3), 311–339.

Robson, Arthur J., Samuelson, Larry, 2019. Evolved attitudes to idiosyncratic and aggregate risk in age-structured populations. Journal of Economic Theory 181, 44–81.

Robson, Arthur J., Samuelson, Larry, 2022. The evolution of risk attitudes with fertility thresholds. Journal of Economic Theory 205, 105552.
Robson, Arthur J., Samuelson, Larry, 2024. The evolutionary foundations of preferences. Book manuscript.
Robson, Arthur J., Whitehead, Lorne A., Robalino, Nikolaus, 2023. Adaptive utility. Journal of Economic Behavior & Organization 211, 60–81.
Savage, Leonard J., 1954. The Foundations of Statistics. John Wiley and Sons, London.
Schkade, David A., Kahneman, Daniel, 1998. Does living in California make people happy? A focusing illusion in judgments of life satisfaction. Psychological Science 9 (5), 340–346.
Schultz, Wolfram, 2015. Neuronal reward and decision signals: from theories to data. Physiological Reviews 95 (3), 853–951.
Scott, Rose M., Baillargeon, Renée, 2017. Early false-belief understanding. Trends in Cognitive Sciences 21 (4), 237–249.
Stahl, Dale O., 1993. Evolution of smart$_n$ players. Games and Economic Behavior 5 (4), 604–617.
Stauffer, William R., Lak, Armin, Schultz, Wolfram, 2014. Dopamine reward prediction error responses reflect marginal utility. Current Biology 24 (21), 2491–2500.
Stern, Nicholas, 2006. Stern Review on the Economics of Climate Change. Her Majesty's Treasury. London.
Tuulari, Jetro J., Tuominen, Lauri, de Boer, Femke E., Hirvonen, Jussi, Helin, Semi, Nuutila, Pirjo, Nummenmaa, Lauri, 2017. Feeding releases endogenous opioids in humans. Journal of Neuroscience 37 (34), 8284–8291.
Valiant, L.G., 1984. A theory of the learnable. Communications of the ACM 27 (11), 1134–1142.
Veblen, Thorstein, 2017. The Theory of the Leisure Class. Routledge, New York.
von Neumann, John, Morgenstern, Oskar, 1944. Theory of Games and Economic Behavior. Princeton University Press, Princeton, NJ.
Whiten, Andrew, 1996. When does smart behavior-reading become mind-reading. In: Carruthers, P., Smith, P.K. (Eds.), Theories of Theories of Mind. Cambridge University Press, Cambridge, UK, pp. 277–292.
Whiten, Andrew, Erdal, David, 2012. The human socio-cognitive niche and its evolutionary origins. Philosophical Transactions of the Royal Society B. Biological Sciences 367 (1599), 2119–2129.
Wimmer, Heinz, Perner, Josef, 1983. Beliefs about beliefs: representation and constraining function of wrong beliefs in young children's understanding of deception. Cognition 13 (1), 103–128.

Chapter 9

Economic models of cultural transmission

Alberto Bisin[a,b,c] and Thierry Verdier[d,e,c]
[a]*Department of Economics, New York University, New York, NY, United States,* [b]*NBER, Cambridge, MA, United States,* [c]*CEPR, London, United Kingdom,* [d]*Paris School of Economics and Ecole des Ponts-Paris Tech, Paris, France,* [e]*PUC-Rio, Rio de Janeiro, Brazil*

1 Introduction

In this chapter we survey recent advances in the economic theory of cultural transmission, demonstrating that cultural explanations of socio-economic phenomena are not tautological "residual" explanations as long as theoretical and empirical restrictions are imposed and tested on what culture is and on how it evolves.

While it is well recognized that the social sciences do not rely on a well-agreed upon abstract definition of culture, the existing definitions – 164 of them were classified already in the 1950s[1] – are actually very closely related when projected into an actionable formal space. For our purposes, we let culture represent:

> *those components of behavioral traits, preferences, attitudes, and beliefs which depend upon the capacity for social learning and transmission across generations.*

While the economic theory of cultural transmission draws on the influential work in evolutionary biology and anthropology from the 1980s – notably Cavalli-Sforza and Feldman (1981) and Boyd and Richerson (1985) – it has gone much further by developing a coherent set of models which leverage economic theory to understand the dynamics of culture and its determinants. Importantly, economic models of cultural transmission successfully disentangle socio-economic and political characteristics that may affect (and interact with) cultural evolution mechanisms. Furthermore, this literature, by developing testable models with a wealth of empirical implications, has inspired numerous empirical studies exploring the role of culture in shaping socio-economic and political contexts, contributing e.g., to a better understanding of conditions

1 See Alfred Kroeber and Clyde Kluckhohn's "Culture: a critical review of concepts and definitions" (Kroeber and Kluckhohn, 1952).

Handbook of Culture and Economic Behavior, Volume 1, ISSN 3051-1682
https://doi.org/10.1016/bs.hceb.2026.02.010

under which cultures persist over time and vary across geographical areas and to the identification of the main mechanisms which favor such persistence.[2]

The basic structure of an economic model of cultural transmission may be construed as a map from preferences and technologies onto rates of cultural transmission – that is, onto a transmission mechanism for a set of cultural traits. Cultural transmission can be inter-generational, from parents and other parental figures to children, or it can be intra-generational, capturing various identity formation mechanisms by children. Cultural traits are represented by preferences, which in turn determine the children's actions in their lifetime. Most importantly, the parental transmission process is modeled as the result of parental choices, altruistically evaluating the children's actions and anticipating the socio-economic environment they (the children) will inhabit.

As a consequence, in economic models cultural transmission depends on socialization preferences, opportunity costs, resource constraints, information structures, policies, as well as social connectivity and group structures, spatial and ecological elements, and institutional dimensions that regulate economic, political and social interactions. In such a set-up, these factors jointly shape the relative success for traits to diffuse and be transmitted more effectively across individuals. Importantly, these factors rely on forward-looking choice and expectation formation mechanisms. This is in contrast to cultural transmission models in evolutionary anthropology, centered on backward-looking social learning processes driven by past socio-economic success (and various proxies for it when success is not directly observable).

In Section 2 we pursue a novel detailed analysis of the distinct approaches to the study of cultural transmission and evolution in evolutionary anthropology and in economics, identifying the main conceptual differences and their implications.

In Section 3 we concentrate on the economic approach to cultural transmission. We demonstrate that the choice theoretic formulation of socialization in economics opens up these models to a rich set of extensions – which allow for a varied class of models, addressing a large set of new questions, well-defined enough that they can be tackled empirically. We find it useful to categorize these extensions as driven by either preferences or technology. On the preference side, we first introduce (a novel analysis of) complementarity and substitutability between consumption and socialization. We then survey contributions in the literature which focus on parental preferences for socialization which are endogenously depending on the socio-economic environment children will inhabit; on cultural leaders and collective transmission mechanisms. On the technology side, we survey the literature studying cultural transmission mechanisms that rely on the composition of parental effort as well as other

2 We concentrate on the theory of cultural transmission in this chapter. But see Bisin and Verdier (2010) for an early survey of empirical work and, recently, Bisin and Verdier (2023) and Nunn (2021).

parental choices, like fertility or marriage; that display various forms of complementarity between parental and societal transmission mechanisms; that allow for e.g., network effects and bias due to parental choices or identity formation choices on the part of the children.

In Section 4 we survey a recent literature which, departing from the relationship between cultural evolution and social interactions, focuses on the two-way interactions between cultural and institutional environments. The models in this literature generally have the distribution of cultural traits in the population affecting the institutional and political structure of society and, on the other hand, the institutional and political structure of society affecting the distribution of cultural traits in the population. They offer a novel approach to growth and development. Unlike traditional studies that try to isolate the causal impact of each factor on contemporary outcomes, these models can study how historical shocks propagate through their joint dynamics, and analyze how these interactions may have magnified or mitigated effects on long-run socioeconomic outcomes. We discuss a series of interesting applications of this literature, to the study of the relationship between culture and various specific institutions – market, political, environmental institutions – and to the study of the cultural and institutional determinants of long-run growth.

We end the chapter – in Section 5 – with a brief discussion of several areas of research – within the theory of cultural transmission – which in our opinion merit further attention in the future.

We believe that the literature surveyed in this chapter serves as clear evidence of the substantial advances in the economic theory of cultural transmission. This theory has generated significant insights on how cultural diversity evolves and how it may persist. It can help provide better understanding of e.g., economic growth and development, political economy, and long-run historical phenomena.

2 The canonical model of cultural transmission

The purpose of this section is to review the structure and logic of cultural transmission models in the social sciences. With this aim we constrain ourselves to a simple abstract environment. We consider a population constituted by a continuum of agents. Agents are characterized by the cultural trait they are associated to. We assume for simplicity the trait to be binary, i, j.[3] Let $0 \leq q^i \leq 1$ denote the fraction of the population with trait i. Cultural traits are transmitted inter-generationally, from parents to children. Under the simple abstract specification we shall introduce next, the dynamics of the cultural distribution in the population – that is, the dynamics of q^i over generations –

3 In Appendix A, we outline extensions of cultural transmission models with traits taking $n > 2$ discrete values or a continuum of values in an interval.

will satisfy the following *logistic* equation:

$$\dot{q}^i = q^i(1 - q^i)f^i. \quad (1)$$

By analogy with evolutionary biology, this same equation – called *replicator dynamics* in evolutionary biology – drives the selection of genetic traits, where f^i is a measure of the relative fitness of trait i (Taylor and Jonker, 1978; Hofbauer and Sigmund, 1998; Weibull, 1995). Then, in the canonical cultural transmission model of Eq. (1), f^i is interpreted as the *relative cultural fitness* of trait i. The conceptualization of f^i is what distinguishes genetic and cultural transmission – as well as different models of cultural transmission – in this abstract context.

2.1 Transmission technology

The first mathematical models of intergenerational cultural transmission were pioneered by Cavalli-Sforza and Feldman (1981) in evolutionary biology. The simple abstract cultural transmission technology proposed in this paper has become canonical in the literature and provides a micro-foundation for the general logistic equation (1) and for relative cultural fitness f^i.

Let population size be stationary – and normalized to 1 – by having each parent give birth asexually to one child. Cultural transmission operates via two distinct channels occurring in stages. The first channel – called *direct vertical* or *parental* transmission – has each parent with trait i socialize his/her child to trait i with probability d^i. With the residual probability $1 - d^i$, the second channel – called *oblique* or *social* transmission – comes into operation. In the social transmission stage the child is matched randomly to a member of the parent's generation and is socialized to his/her trait.[4] Therefore, conditionally on reaching this stage (with probability $1 - d^i$), the child is socialized to trait i with probability q^i (since matching is random). Notably, a child of a parent with trait i can be socialized to trait i either by parental transmission or by social transmission, while he/she can be socialized to trait $j \neq i$ only by social transmission.

Formally, letting P^{ij} denote the transition probability that a child from a parent with trait i is socialized to trait j, this cultural transmission technology is represented by the following system of equations:

$$P^{ii} = d^i + (1 - d^i)q^i, \quad P^{ij} = (1 - d^i)(1 - q^i). \quad (2)$$

Using the Law of Large Numbers, this process of cultural socialization results in a dynamics of the distribution of trait i in the population,

$$\dot{q}^i = q^i(1 - q^i)(d^i - d^j),$$

4 Transmission can also be *horizontal*, within the children's generation. We avoid horizontal transmission here for simplicity but we shall introduce it later in the survey.

which is a specification of the general logistic equation (1), where the relative cultural fitness f^i is represented by the difference in parental transmission rates:

$$f^i = d^i - d^j. \tag{3}$$

2.2 Cultural fitness in the social sciences

The canonical technology of cultural transmission introduced in the previous section, from Cavalli-Sforza and Feldman (1981), constitutes the initial building block for the study of the population dynamics of culture in the social sciences. Distinct theories of cultural transmission – in the simple context of the canonical model of cultural transmission represented by Eqs. (1)–(3) – can be synthetically identified along two lines, i) the definition of a cultural trait i, and ii) the determination of parental transmission d^i (and hence of relative cultural fitness f^i). In this section we abstractly distinguish two different classes of such theories, developed respectively in evolutionary anthropology and in economics. We introduce the simplest barebone models in either case – the most direct projections of the canonical model of cultural transmission.

Evolutionary anthropology. The earliest cultural transmission model in evolutionary anthropology is in Boyd and Richerson (1985), building on the analysis of Cavalli Sforza and Feldman. Generally, in this literature, cultural traits are represented by behavioral traits: to a trait i is associated directly an action/behavior x^i. Furthermore, fitness is interpreted literally as an indicator of reproductive success. Behavioral traits are transmitted inter-generationally via a process of social learning. Relative fitness is then generally biased toward the trait which – in previous periods – was more successful in the population – *direct bias* – and/or more associated to a proxy for relative success, like wealth or social prestige – *indirect bias*.

Formally, the transmission rate of trait i will then be frequency-dependent, that is, a function of the relative size of group i, q^i. More specifically, direct and indirect bias will (be modeled so as to) induce a characterization of social learning displaying some form of *conformity*, so that transmission rates will be as follows:

$$d^i = d(q^i), \text{ where } d(.) \text{ is increasing and (for regularity) } d^i(0) = 0. \tag{4}$$

Economics. The economic approach to the theory of cultural transmission has been developed by Bisin and Verdier (2001a,b). While building closely on Cavalli-Sforza and Feldman as well as on Boyd and Richerson, their analysis develops along radically different conceptual lines from evolutionary anthropology. First of all, cultural traits are represented by preference traits: to a trait i is associated a utility function u^i, which in turn determines an action x^i as a choice of the agent. Secondly, cultural fitness is not interpreted literally, as reproductive success, but it generally encodes a cultural socialization mechanism built on the distinction between parental and social transmission in the canonical technology of Cavalli-Sforza and Feldman. Most importantly, the parental transmission process is modeled as the result of parental choices, which anticipate the possible occurrence of the social transmission stage. Relative cultural fitness therefore will not only be frequency-dependent, but it will also depend on parental preferences regarding the cultural socialization of children.

Formally, the transmission rate of trait i is modeled as the solution of a parental socialization choice problem. A parent with trait i obtains a payoff of V^{ij} if her child acquires trait j. Assume that $V^{ii} > V^{ij}$ whenever $i \neq j$, that is, parents have a preference to transmit their own cultural trait to their own children. A rational parent chooses the transmission rate d^i – facing a socialization effort cost $c(d^i)$ – to maximize the expected parental payoff from socialization, $P^{ii}V^{ii} + P^{ij}V^{ij}$, where P^{ii}, P^{ij} satisfy the transmission technology in Eq. (2) at the chosen d^i. But $P^{ii}V^{ii} + P^{ij}V^{ij} = V^{ij} + P^{ii}\Delta V^i$, where $\Delta V^i = V^{ii} - V^{ij}$ encodes parental preferences over their child's cultural trait, the *cultural intolerance* of parents i. The socialization problem therefore reduces to

$$\max_{d^i} P^{ii}\Delta V^i - c(d^i) \qquad (5)$$

$$s.t.\ P^{ii} = d^i + (1 - d^i)q^i$$

where $c(d^i)$ is assumed increasing and convex for regularity. At the solution, the transmission rate is

$$d^i = d(q^i, \Delta V^i), \qquad (6)$$

where $d(.)$ is increasing in ΔV^i, decreasing in q^i, and $d^i(1) = 0$.[5]

We can now compare the canonical models of cultural transmission in evolutionary anthropology and in economics along three important dimensions: i) the object of cultural transmission, i; ii) the determinants of relative fitness f^i; and iii) the population dynamics of the distribution of cultural traits q^i. With respect to the object of cultural transmission – that is, the implicit definition of culture – the conceptual distinction between evolutionary anthropology and economics is quite stark. In evolutionary anthropology, cultural traits are construed as agents' actions – they are to be interpreted as lifetime behavioral patterns of actions – independent of intra-generational changes in the environment – or as broad social norms of behavior.[6] In economics, cultural traits are instead defined as (parameters of) preferences and attitudes, in turn determining behavior which is well-adapted to changing environments. As a

5 Under (the often adopted simplification with) quadratic socialization costs, $d^i = (1 - q^i)\Delta V^i$.

6 Examples of such patterns include cooperating (Boyd and Richerson, 1982, 1988a; Henrich and Boyd, 2001), favoring kin altruistically (Fehr and Fischbacher, 2003; Lehmann and Feldman, 2008; McElreath et al., 2003), reciprocating favors (Boyd and Richerson, 1988a), punishing altruistically (Guzmán et al., 2007).

consequence, the objects of cultural transmission can be represented both by fundamental dimensions of human preferences (and hence behavior) as well as by historically determined characteristics of preferences.[7]

With respect to their transition mechanisms – that is, the determinants of the transmission rates d^i, d^j and hence of the relative cultural fitness f^i – both approaches produce formulations of cultural fitness which are frequency-dependent; but they result in orthogonally different implications: the transmission rate of cultural trait i is increasing in the frequency of the trait q^i in the evolutionary anthropology model and decreasing in the economic model; compare Eqs. (4) and (6).[8] Most importantly, in the economic model, the transmission rate of cultural trait i depends on parental preferences ΔV^i.[9] Parental preferences in turn generally depend on the socio-economic environment in which parents and children live and make choices. In particular, to evaluate their preferences ΔV^i and to choose upon them parents need to form expectations about the future socio-economic environment, its realization and equilibrium behavior. This dependence opens up cultural transmission and social learning to a rich set of socio-economic determinants – to forward-looking behavior in particular – with important theoretical (and interesting empirical) implications. In evolutionary anthropology, on the other hand, social learning is generally a backward-looking process and so is agents' behavior in socio-economic environments.[10]

The third important dimension of comparison between the canonical models of cultural transmission in evolutionary anthropology and in economics refers to the distinct implications of the two models with regard to the population

---

7 Economic cultural transmission of fundamental preferences includes e.g., time-discounting, risk-aversion, attitude toward social status and toward cooperation (Bisin and Verdier, 1998, 2010, Bisin et al., 2004a, for a survey; Zakharenko, 2016). Cultural transmission of historical preferences includes, instead, ethnic and religious traits (Bisin and Verdier, 2000; Bisin et al., 2004b), or civic and social capital (Francois and Zabojnik, 2005; Bidner and Francois, 2011; Guiso et al., 2008; Tabellini, 2008; Okada, 2020; Acemoglu and Robinson, 2025; Bisin et al., 2024; Bisin and Verdier, 2024; and several of the papers collected in Bisin and Federico, 2021). Relatedly, an interesting literature in economics – referred to as *Indirect evolutionary approach* and introduced by Güth and Yaari (1992a,b) and Güth (1995) – also aims at providing an evolutionary foundation for fundamental preferences by assuming that agents' choices are rational given preferences whose change is driven by an evolutionary process depending on the relative success of individuals endowed with these preferences (Koçkesen et al., 2000; Ely and Yilankaya, 2001; Ok and Vega-Redondo, 2001).

8 This is not the case, obviously, in less canonical models in either approaches. The fundamental distinct "forces" we are identifying in this section are meant to characterize the core mechanisms of these models.

9 Their foundation on rational or behavioral choice gives these models a solid bedrock on which e.g., to select assumptions about preferences and psychological attitudes – validated by the whole theoretical and empirical corpus of the economic discipline.

10 Even when modeling social learning and social behavior as the result of agents' interactions – the game theoretic constructs adopted in the literature rely on backward-looking equilibrium concepts (Henrich, 2021; and Smaldino, 2023, survey this literature). This is the case, for instance, in the analysis of cooperative behavior, with no reference, e.g., to the classic folk-theorem results in repeated games (Bisin, 2024, for a review of Smaldino, 2023).

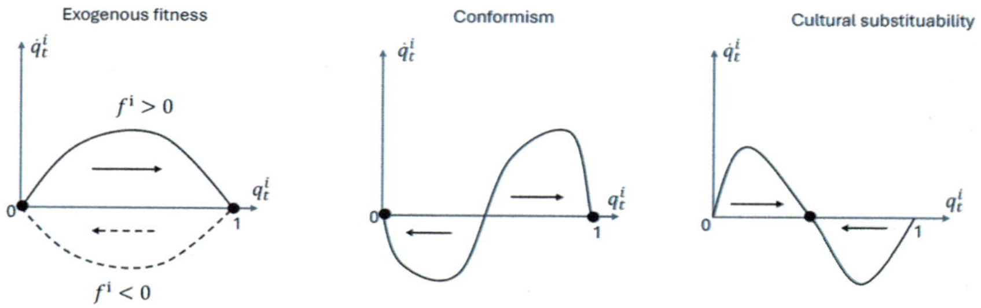

FIGURE 1 Cultural dynamics.

dynamics of culture in the limit, that is, the stationary states of the distribution of culture and their stability properties. This is important because the "massive diversification of human cultures" contrasts with the fact that "humans are a species with low genetic diversity" (Boyd and Richerson, 2024, p. 7/10); and because cultural resilience and fractionalization – e.g., in the context of ethnic and religious traits – motivate a large fraction of the theoretical and empirical literature on culture in the social sciences (Bisin and Verdier, 2010). In this respect, we study and compare the dynamics of Eq. (1) in three different cases: i) when cultural fitness $f^i = d^i - d^j$ is exogenous; ii) when social learning induces conformity, due to direct or indirect bias, in the canonical model in evolutionary anthropology; iii) when parental socialization results from parental choice, in the economic model. Fig. 1 represents graphically the dynamical equations in the three distinct cases.

The results of this comparison are striking: Within the confines of the canonical model, the differential implications of these models with respect to frequency-dependence of relative cultural fitness imply that only parental socialization choice manifests a "force" leading to cultural heterogeneity by means of the resilience of cultural traits across generations. Formally,

i) With exogenous fitness, the population converges to cultural homogeneity with

$$q^i = 1 \text{ if } f^i > 0 \text{ and } q^i = 0 \text{ if } f^i < 0.$$

Trivially, population is constant if $f^i = 0$.

ii) With conformity in social learning, the population also converges monotonically to cultural homogeneity, where

$$q^i = 0 \text{ or } q^i = 1, \text{ depending on the initial condition.}$$

A stationary state $0 < q^i < 1$ such that $f(q^i) = 0$ exists but is unstable.

iii) With parental socialization choice the population converges monotonically to cultural heterogeneity, that is, to a stationary state

$$0 < q^i < 1 \text{ such that } f^i(q^i) = 0.$$

The culturally homogeneous states $q^i = 0$ and $q^i = 1$ are also stationary states but they are unstable.[11]

The dynamics in the economic model are a consequence of the property that d^i is decreasing in q^i – which Bisin and Verdier (2001a,b) call *cultural substitution*. It implies that parents with the minoritarian trait socialize their children relatively more than parents with the majoritarian trait, to overcome the effect of social transmission, which favors majorities. On the other hand, it is the complementarity built into the evolutionary dynamics – via conformity in the social learning process – that induces cultural homogeneity. While of course the canonical cultural evolutionary model can be extended in several dimensions to obtain richer dynamics, the complementarity in social learning tends to reduce the explanatory power of the model with respect to cultural heterogeneity, at least at relatively short time scales – say at historical (as opposed to evolutionary) frequencies. Henrich (2021), for instance, suggests that "the variation (in cultural traits) we observe around the world and back into history represents different stable equilibria or cultural evolutionary trajectories toward different equilibria." But multiple equilibria of un-coupled population dynamics in evolutionary times are not natural determinants of e.g., the wide variation of ethnic and cultural traits at the historical frequencies at which socio-economic environments and institutional set-ups vary within and across interacting populations.

2.2.1 Genetic and cultural evolution

Our comparison of models of cultural evolution in evolutionary anthropology and economics in the previous section has taken as given the process controlling cultural dynamics: social learning and parental socialization, respectively. But evolutionary anthropologists also study gene-culture coevolution theory, modeling genes and cultural traits co-evolving and influencing each other over time measured at evolutionary time-scale. In our context, most relevant is the class of models pertaining to the *Dual inheritance theory* developed by Boyd and Richerson (1976, 1985) and Richerson and Boyd (1978) (and then, e.g., Richerson and Boyd, 2005; Henrich and McElreath, 2007; Boyd et al., 2011), which study the joint dynamics of both cultural traits and (specific aspects of) the cultural evolution process – identified with social learning. This literature produces various interesting theoretical predictions regarding evolutionary adaptations of the social learning process, e.g., a general bias toward social conformity (Boyd and Richerson, 1985; Rogers, 1988; Perreault et al., 2012; Derex and Boyd, 2015); a bias in favor of prestige, or social status (Henrich and Gil-White, 2001 and Jiménez and Mesoudi, 2019); and a bias in

[11] With quadratic costs, the stationary state is

$$0 < q^i = \frac{\Delta V^i}{\Delta V^i + \Delta V^j} < 1.$$

favor of observable costly displays (Henrich, 2009; 2016). Most importantly, this literature identifies the cumulative capacity of cultural evolution – via high-fidelity transmission – as a fundamental property of human culture (Boyd and Richerson, 1988b; Tomasello, 2010; Boyd et al., 2011; Mesoudi, 2011; Muthukrishna et al., 2018; Mesoudi and Thornton, 2018; Richerson and Boyd, 2022).[12] Along these lines, Bisin and Verdier (2001a,b) and Giuliano and Nunn (2021) study how the characteristics of social learning mechanisms which are evolutionarily selected – specifically, how persistent are transmitted traits within families across generations – depend on the stochastic processes driving the environment agents face.[13]

From the point of view of economists, what is striking in this literature in evolutionary anthropology is the lack of any attempt to identify theoretically conditions under which evolutionary adaptations would favor some form of rationality in the social learning process. Rational choice – even when restricted by various behavioral limitations rooted in psychological evidence – introduces both flexibility with respect to environmental change and forward-looking considerations which could provide an evolutionary advantage to human populations and hence be adaptively selected. Indeed, a small but fascinating literature in economics has developed which aims to endogenously derive elements of rational choice – including the assumption that cultural evolution operates on preferences rather than on actions – from social learning processes as selected by genetic evolution.[14] Robson's (2001) aptly titled paper – *Why would nature give individuals utility functions?* – is the foundational paper in this literature. A wealth of results in this literature pertains generally to identifying conditions under which time-discounting – whether exponential or quasi-hyperbolic (with present-bias) – and expected utility representations – whether on linear or concave utility functions (with risk-neutrality or risk-aversion) – are endogenously obtained as evolutionary adaptations; see Robson and Samuelson (2011; 2026), Robalino and Robson (2019; 2026, in this Handbook) and Bisin and Verdier (2026) for exhaustive surveys. Even with

[12] The collection of papers in Fogarty et al. (2024) – including Boyd and Richerson (2024) – and Boyd and Richerson (2026)'s contribution to this Handbook provide surveys of these and other related results in the literature. Several other interesting papers along these lines also include Feldman and Laland (1996), Strimling et al. (2009), McElreath and Strimling (2006), Richerson and Boyd (2005), Richerson et al. (2010), Chudek and Henrich (2011), Ghirlanda and Enquist (2007), Enquist et al. (2011), Derex et al. (2018).

[13] See for instance Strimling et al. (2009); Enquist et al. (2011); Ghirlanda and Enquist (2007); Derex et al. (2018).

[14] The ideological divide in the social sciences along the rational choice line might in part explain – but not justify – why only economists tend to consider rational forward-looking models in the study of cultural evolution. In this sense – admittedly with some liberty of interpretation – we read Morgan and Feldman's (2025) call for the theory of cultural evolution in anthropology and biology to recognize *open-endedness* as the defining feature of human culture, as a prominent suggestion that (the flexibility induced by) rational choice may help explain the "scope [...] of what can be acquired and transmitted in human culture" across varying socio-economic and environmental conditions.

respect to the cumulative character of human culture, the role of strategic rationality and greater recall memory in particular has been shown to represent an evolutionarily adaptive foundation for it (the *Red Queen effect*, in Robson, 2003).

One of the main manifestations of the lack of rational choice in the theory of cultural transmission in evolutionary anthropology is the absence of parental socialization choice. But evolution might select parental preferences for socialization whereby, other things equal, parents have a preference to transmit their own cultural trait to their children (Bisin and Verdier, 2001a,b, 2026). In economic cultural transmission models, parental socialization choice allows for social learning mechanisms which are well-adapted to a moving socio-economic environment. As such, cultural transmission can be represented by relatively high-frequency processes – within and across ethnic and religious traits – driving e.g., family values and gender roles (Escriche et al., 2004; Hiller and Baudin, 2016; Alesina et al., 2015); attitudes toward work/leisure (Senik and Verdier, 2011; Sáez-Martí and Zenou, 2012; Michau, 2013); preferences for fertility (Baudin, 2010; Bar-Gill and Fershtman, 2016; Melki et al., 2024); preferences for autonomy (Hiller, 2011); preferences for lifestyle (Ponthiere, 2010).

3 Economic models of cultural transmission

In this section we concentrate on the economic approach to cultural transmission. Our aim is to demonstrate that the choice theoretic formulation of socialization in economics opens up these models to a rich set of extensions – which allow for a varied class of models, addressing a rich set of novel questions, well-defined enough that they can be tackled empirically.[15] Socialization and cultural transmission are modeled as the outcome of different individuals' and institutions' choices: parents, children themselves e.g., via peer effects, role models, on one side; schools, churches, nations, cultural leaders, on the other. Relative cultural fitness will therefore depend on parental preferences but also on children attitudes toward cultural identity, and on various institutional characteristics of society, the present and future socio-economic conditions affecting these choices. Furthermore, being integrated in the specific present and future socio-economic conditions of a society, cultural transmission will generally rely on a varied set of direct and indirect mechanisms, as technologies for socialization and identity formation, including e.g., fertility, marriage, social segregation, identity formation and so on. Importantly, in this class of economic models, parental socialization preferences generally depend – via some form of altruism – on the socio-economic outcomes of their children. As a conse-

15 While outside of the scope of the present chapter, we note here that the economic theory of cultural transmission – after the early theoretical contribution following Bisin and Verdier (2001a,b) – has developed into a substantial and vivid empirical field. Several chapters of this Handbook survey this literature.

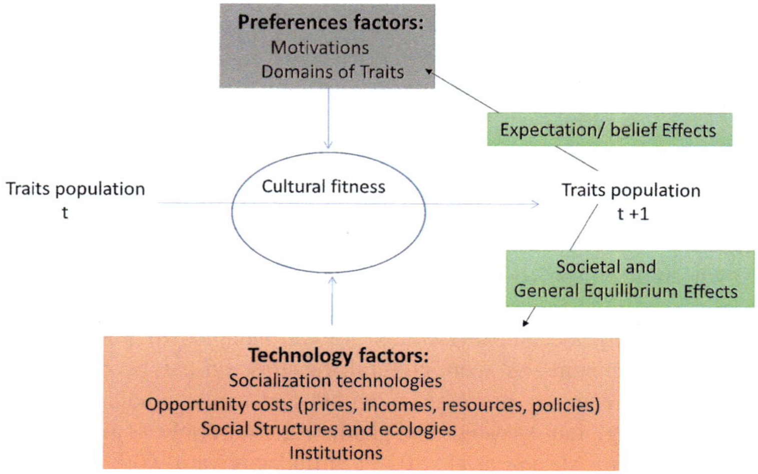

FIGURE 2 Economics and cultural fitness.

quence, socialization and cultural transmission are forward-looking equilibrium processes in the economics literature, a substantial difference with respect to the processes studied in evolutionary anthropology, which greatly expands the space of applications and the interest of the analysis.[16] Finally, focusing on cultural phenomena at higher time frequencies than evolutionary anthropology models, the economic approach to cultural transmission has a precise focus on the socio-economic determinants of cultural transmission and their selective implications for cultural dynamics, resulting from costly and purposeful socioeconomic actions by socializing agents. This perspective typically generates cultural transmission rates that are affected by important socio-economic factors such as prices, incomes, resources and more generally institutional contexts.

Along these dimensions, the theory of cultural transmission in economics has built on the canonical model along a series of very interesting dimensions. We categorize them in this paper as follows – see also Fig. 2 – distinguishing extensions on preferences from those on technology.

Preferences. In the canonical economic cultural transmission model parental preferences for socialization are encoded by exogenous *cultural intolerances* ΔV^i and are assumed separable from preferences for consumption $u^i(x^i)$. More generally, in this section we shall study models where:

16 This is not the case in the simple canonical model we introduced in this section, but it will be in most of the theoretical analyses of cultural transmission we shall present in the following sections. Forward looking models require some theoretical sophistication to handle the different formal representations of the dynamic equations.

1. The separability between socialization and consumption choice is relaxed by assuming that socialization requires resources, both in terms of income and time.
2. Parental preferences for socialization are endogenous: cultural intolerance ΔV^i depends on the socio-economic environment children will inhabit.
3. Collective transmission mechanisms – like cultural leaders through various institutions – act to affect parental preferences for socialization.

Technology. In the canonical economic cultural transmission model the socialization technology is determined by the composition of a direct parental effort d^i and oblique transmission in the form of random matching. More generally, in this section we shall study models where:

4. Relative cultural fitness f^i is modeled as a socio-economic mechanism structured as the composition of parental effort as well as other parental choices, like fertility or marriage.
5. Parental transmission has a more general form than implied by cultural substitution.
6. Oblique transmission has a more general form than random matching, allowing e.g., for network effects and bias due to parental choices or identity formation choices on the part of the children.

3.1 Parental transmission and consumption

In the canonical economic model of cultural transmission the consumption and the socialization problems of the agents are assumed separable. Relaxing this assumption allows us to characterize how the socialization choice of parents depends on their resources – like income and time – and on prices, including wages. By simply allowing for socialization costs to be derived implicitly from the agents' budget constraint, we present a version of this model which emphasizes how, in its basic form, cultural transmission i) fits rightly into the standard simple model of consumer's choice in microeconomics; and therefore ii) has comparative statics driven by basic income and substitution effect.

Formally, let parental transmission d^i represent the outcome of a production function with resources m^i and time l^i as factors in the socialization process of the child: $d^i = d(f(m^i, l^i))$, where the function $d(.)$ is an increasing function defined on the interval $[0, \infty[$ such that $d(0) = 0$, $d(\infty) = 1$ and $f(m^i, l^i)$ satisfies the usual properties of production function: increasing concave in each argument and homogeneous of degree 1.[17] Assume that parents of cultural type i are endowed with an exogenous endowment of the resource R and an amount of time $L = 1$ that they can share between producing resources at wage w and socializing their child.

[17] This specification ensures that d^i remains a probability between 0 and 1.

Now, the choice problem of each agent is

$$\max_{x^i, m^i, l^i} u^i(x^i) + P^{ii} \Delta V^i$$
$$s.t.\ d^i = d(f(m^i, l^i))$$
$$x^i + m^i = R + w(1 - l^i).$$

Solving this problem we obtain a transmission rate of the form

$$d^i(q^i, \Delta V^i; R, w),$$

that is, depending on total resources R and on the wage w – besides $q^i, \Delta V^i$ as in the canonical model. The relevant comparative statics correspond to those of the canonical model: $\frac{\partial d^i}{\partial \Delta V^i} > 0$; $\frac{\partial d^i}{\partial q^i} < 0$. An increase in ΔV^i leads to more effective parental socialization by increasing the marginal utility of socialization, other things equal; while a change in the state of the cultural population q^i also affects the marginal rate of substitution between x^i and d^i and its effect depends on cultural substitution. But, when embedding the socialization problem and the consumption problem, we have further interesting novel effects:

$$\frac{\partial d^i}{\partial R} > 0; \frac{\partial d^i}{\partial w} \gtrless 0.$$

In fact, an increase in R has a positive income effect.

Conversely, an increase in w leads to a change in the budget constraint that can be decomposed in an income and a substitution effect: as the wage increases, the opportunity cost of socialization increases but so do the total available resources, other things equal.

These comparative statics with respect to d^i map directly into comparative dynamics on the distribution of traits in the population – via Eq. (1). In particular, the analysis can be naturally extended to the case where socio-economic fundamentals such as R and w are different across cultural groups. For instance, it is easy to see that the relative cultural fitness $d^i - d^j$ is an increasing (resp. decreasing) function of R^i (resp. R^j). If the difference between R^i and R^j is not too large, there will exist an interior steady state q^i increasing in R^i. Thus the cultural trait group having access to more economic resources is more likely to prevail in the long run. Correspondingly, consider what happens when work productivities w^i and w^j are different. In that case the differential effect of these economic fundamentals on the cultural selection process will depend on the relative strength of the income and the substitution effects; the opportunity cost of vertical socialization may increase or decrease. It could in particular be the case that the trait associated to the group with higher productivity is less likely to be culturally selected if the substitution effects are stronger than the income effects for both groups.

Interestingly, this framework also allows us to analyze the effect of economic heterogeneity within cultural trait groups. Consider an environment in which resources R are heterogeneously distributed within groups. Let the cumulative distribution of R for group i be $F_i(R)$. Let i be the group with more equally distributed resources R, in that $F_j(.)$ is a mean-preserving spread of $F_i(.)$. We show that, ceteris paribus, the trait associated to a more equal distribution of resources is more likely to prevail in the long run cultural dynamics of the population.[18]

3.2 (Endogenous) preferences for cultural transmission

In canonical cultural transmission models, parental socialization depends on the exogenous value of having a child with the same cultural trait, ΔV^i (the *paternalistic or cultural intolerance* motive of trait i). While this assumption is useful to illustrate the main elements of an abstract model of cultural transmission – how to formulate cultural fitness and how to derive the population dynamics – in general ΔV^i have to be modeled as endogenous, influenced by various environments. For example, in markets, individuals' utility may depend on economic variables like prices, incomes, or policy outcomes shaped by the prevailing distribution of cultural traits. Similarly, in strategic interactions, matching, political economy, and public choice contexts, an individual's payoffs are likely affected by the population's cultural trait distribution. In this section we allow for cultural intolerance to represent (indirect utilities) determined at a socio-economic equilibrium of interest. While the implications of the endogeneity of ΔV^i for socialization and population dynamics need to be derived case-by-case, a reduced form analysis is useful, to clarify what to look for in the applications.

Consider each individual (parent or child) choosing some action x to maximize $u^i(x, q^i)$. The action x can be interpreted e.g., as a lifetime pattern of choices. Assume parental preferences display a form of imperfect altruism – called *imperfect empathy* (Bisin and Verdier, 2001a,b): parents evaluate their children actions with their own (the parents') preferences. In this case, parental socialization preferences for types i depend on

$$\Delta V^i(q^i) = u^i(x^i, q^i) - u^i(x^j, q^i).$$

The socio-economic interaction between agents determines, at equilibrium, the endogenous *cultural intolerance* $\Delta V^i(q^i)$, as a transformation of the agents' indirect utilities – depending on child's choices in the future, in the future socio-economic environment (prices, policies, social interactions, political economy).[19] The socialization problem then determines $d^i\left(q^i, \Delta V^i(q^i)\right)$ so

18 This result follows by Jensen's inequality from concavity of parental socialization d^i with respect to R; see Appendix A for details and proofs.

19 Note that in this context paternalism does not now necessarily imply that $\Delta V^i(q^i) \geq 0$. In fact, socialization to the parents' trait might put the children at a disadvantage in the child social

that:

$$\frac{d}{dq_t^i} d^i\left(q^i, \Delta V^i(q^i)\right) = \underbrace{\frac{\partial d^i}{\partial q_t^i}}_{\text{direct effect}} + \underbrace{\frac{\partial d^i}{\partial \Delta V^i} \frac{\partial \Delta V^i}{\partial q_{t+1}^i}}_{\text{feedback effect}} \underbrace{\frac{dq_{t+1}^i}{dq_t^i}}_{\text{expectations effect}}.$$

A negative direct effect follows from cultural substitution; while a positive (resp. negative) feedback effect corresponds to a strategic social complementarity (resp. substitution).

When paternalistic motivations are endogenous, the dynamic system for the evolution of cultural traits can be written as:

$$\dot{q}^i = q^i(1-q^i)\left[d^i(q^i, \Delta V^i(q^i)) - d^j(1-q^i, \Delta V^j(1-q^i))\right].$$

In this case, a sufficient set of conditions to obtain a heterogeneous cultural distribution in the limit, requires cultural substitution as well as an additional condition on $\Delta V^i(q^i)$ – called *strategic substitution* in Bisin and Verdier (2001a,b):

$$\frac{\partial}{\partial q^i} \Delta V^i(q^i) < 0.$$

In words, *strategic substitution* ensures that cultural minorities face relatively larger gains from socialization, independently of the socialization mechanism. It is then easy to see that, when the social environment is characterized by strategic substitution and that moreover direct and oblique socialization mechanisms are cultural substitutes, then from any interior state $q \in (0, 1)$, the cultural dynamics converge to cultural heterogeneity, that is, a $0 < q^i < 1$. In the case of strategic complementarity (i.e., $\frac{\partial}{\partial q^i} \Delta V^i(q^i) > 0$), cultural minorities face smaller (even possibly negative) socialization gains. Depending on the strength of cultural substitution, therefore, in this case cultural heterogeneity might or might not be preserved.

In summary, i) cultural substitution and strategic substitution tend to induce cultural heterogeneity as stable stationary state; while ii) social strategic complementarity tends to induce cultural homogeneity – that is, corners – as stable stationary states. The way $\Delta V^i(q^i)$ might be frequency dependent and vary with q^i depends on the circumstances. In many social contexts, an increase in q^i can reduce social and economic discrimination against individuals with that trait. More individuals sharing trait i means more opportunities for interaction within that group, reducing reliance on others and the impact of socio-economic discrimination. As discrimination decreases, the perceived

environment, represented by q^i. While imperfect empathy reflects parents' preferences for sharing their cultural traits with their children, these preferences are also influenced by the economic and social conditions parents anticipate for their children. Consequently, different conditions might lead parents to socialize their children to adopt traits different than their own (or to not socialize them).

economic cost of transmitting the trait intergenerationally also drops, thereby increasing the parents' paternalistic motive $\Delta V^i(q^i)$ to pass on their trait. Conversely, an increase in the frequency of a cultural group q^i may also induce a lower paternalistic motive $\Delta V^i(q^i)$, when discrimination has an endogenous taste or identity component. For instance, a higher value of q^i may increase the frequency of intergroup contacts which might trigger negative reactions of other groups to reaffirm their differences, leading to more discrimination and social segmentation against group i. This reduces the paternalistic motive $\Delta V^i(q^i)$ to transmit the trait. This *strategic substitution* effect gives smaller minority groups higher incentives to preserve their traits, thus promoting cultural diversity.

3.2.1 Endogenous preferences in specific applications of interest

A large strand of the economic literature on cultural transmission has explored the transmission of various distinct cultural traits in contexts where parental socialization choices anticipate the socio-economic environment which the children will inhabit with the preferences they will be socialized to. The resulting models are specific applications of the general set-up exposed in the previous section. They are generally laid out as such: i) the specific socio-economic interactions of the children are modeled; ii) a reduced form for $\Delta V^i(q^i)$ is obtained; iii) the induced properties of the transmission rates d^i – and hence of fitness f^i are characterized; iv) the implications about the dynamics of cultural traits in the population are derived. We now introduce some relatively new and interesting theoretical contributions along these lines.[20]

General patterns of strategic interaction and matching. Della Lena and Dindo (2022) study the implications for cultural intolerance $\Delta V^i(q^i)$ of general patterns of strategic interactions across the generation of children. In particular, they show that strategic complementarity (resp. substitutability) in the structure of such interactions maps into strategic complementarity (resp. substitutability) in cultural intolerance and hence in the cultural transmission process – leading the cultural dynamics to homogeneity (resp. heterogeneity).[21]

20 A first wave of examples include Hauk and Saez-Marti (2002) for attitudes toward corruption; Olcina and Penarrubia (2004) for other-regarding preferences in hold-up contexts; Escriche et al. (2004) for family-related preferences and gender labor market discrimination; Francois (2002), Francois and Zabojnik (2005) and Estrella López (2003) for social capital; Bisin and Verdier (2005) for the transmission of work ethic and redistributive policies, Sáez-Martí and Zenou (2012) and Senik and Verdier (2011) for work values and ethnic labor market discrimination; Bidner and Francois (2011), for the evolution of informal institutions; Hiller (2011) for preferences for autonomy and work organization; Hiller and Verdier (2014) for pro-social preferences and corporate culture; Baudin (2010) for fertility; Ponthiere (2010) for lifestyles transmission and longevity; Melindi Ghidi (2009) for political ideology; Correani et al. (2010) for tolerance; Michau (2013) for work values and social/unemployment insurance, Pichler (2008) and Panebianco (2009) for general analyses on endogenous cultural distance and oblique socialization.

21 In more specific strategic contexts, Della Lena et al. (2021) study parental transmission of guilt aversion in a society where agents' interactions are centered on a trust game (with or without incomplete information). Delli Gatti et al. (2022) analyze parental incentives to transmit patience

Wu (2017; 2021) studies instead the implications for cultural intolerance $\Delta V^i(q^i)$ of different matching interactions across the generation of children. More precisely, in Wu (2017) political institutions regulate the hierarchical structure of matching interactions between a majority and a minority with distinct cultural traits. High hierarchical status is obtained differentially across institutional environments which differ by their degree of inclusiveness toward minorities, and cultural transmission has stronger selective power under more inclusive political institutions. Wu (2021) instead studies a more decentralized setting where children interact in production, comparing the cultural transmission process under different rules governing surplus sharing in matching interactions. In particular, two types of matching mechanisms are compared: i) *bargaining in match* (BIM) – which induces a stable matching a la Gale and Shapley (1962), depending on the outside option under no match; and ii) *binding agreement in the matching market* (BAMM) – which induces equilibrium matches a la Shapley and Shubik (1971) and Becker (1973). It turns out that cultural transmission tends to lead to cultural homogeneity under BIM – favoring the cultural group with the highest outside option – and to cultural heterogeneity under BAMM – which induces a sort of cultural substitution which increases the socialization effort of minorities as in Bisin and Verdier (2001a,b).[22]

Olivier et al. (2008) and Bisin and Verdier (2014) study instead competitive market interactions. Strategic substitution – and hence heterogeneity of preferences in the cultural transmission limit – obtains in the case of standard Walrasian price effects on the demand side. Indeed, the larger the predominance in the population of a trait i, associated to a preference for a specific class of commodities, the higher is total demand for this class of commodities, and hence the higher its relative market price at equilibrium. As a consequence, the relative parental preference for socialization of the children to this trait is lower, $\Delta V^i(q^i)$ is decreasing and strategic substitutability obtains. In Olivier et al. (2008), however, some of the commodities also generate group identity externality effects – a la Akerlof and Kranton (2000) – for those who identify with the group. In this case, the strategic substitution effects on ΔV^i arising from the Walrasian price effects are compensated by strategic complementarity effects due to the group externality associated to identity. Strategic complementarity typically also arises in market interactions involving social increasing returns, positive market size, or market matching thickness effects, fostering long-term cultural homogeneity. Maystre et al. (2014) provide an example where a specific differentiated commodity is traded in a monopolistically competitive environment. As the size of the cultural group with a preference bias for the commodity increases, so does the market size and entry of firms producing differentiated varieties. This makes it more attractive

across different economic environments. Goto (2022) centers on the transmission of an egalitarian culture in an environment where high productivity is rewarded only under meritocratic institutions.

22 See also Ellis et al. (2020) for an analysis on labor markets.

to acquire and transmit preferences for the commodity, resulting in strategic complementarity, that is, to an increasing $\Delta V^i(q^i)$.

Preferences for cooperative behavior in the Prisoner's Dilemma. The population dynamics of preferences for cooperative behavior, within the context of the economic theory of cultural transmission is studied by Bisin et al. (2004a). Consider preferences which induce a psychological gain when playing cooperatively in situations like e.g., the Prisoner's Dilemma.[23] More precisely, the population is composed of two groups of agents, Non-Cooperators and Cooperators, who are distinguished by their preferences (their actions being Nash equilibrium actions given their preferences): the payoffs of Non-Cooperators are the Prisoner's Dilemma's; while the payoffs of Cooperators are the Prisoner's Dilemma's to which however they add $d > 0$ utils when cooperating. Cooperators are in fraction q^C of the population. In this context, it is natural to distinguish environments with complete or incomplete information, that is environments where agents do or do not observe each other's preferences (adherence to the norms) before playing the Prisoner's Dilemma. Consider complete information first. Agents are randomly matched to play a Prisoner's Dilemma. In an environment where agents are matched randomly to play the Prisoner's Dilemma, the gains to transmit norms of pro-sociality tend to be higher when many individuals in the population share the norms.

Let $V^{NC}(q^C)$, $V^C(q^C)$ denote the expected payoff of the non-cooperators and the cooperators. Bisin et al. (2004a) show that cultural transmission leads to a heterogeneous stationary state $q^c > 0$ when the payoffs of the game are such that Cooperators cooperate unconditionally (independently of whether they are matched with a Cooperator or not). On the other hand the dynamics converge to the cultural homogeneous stationary state $q^C = 1$ when Cooperators cooperate conditionally (only with Cooperators). The first case occurs, e.g., when the psychological gain h is high enough. This is an important result in that it contrasts with what is generally obtained in models of cultural transmission where the cultural trait is the action and the intensity of transmission is linked to fitness defined as the Prisoner's Dilemma payoff.[24]

Relatedly, Tabellini (2008) examines norms that i) impose a psychological cost on individuals who fail to cooperate in situations like the Prisoner's Dilemma and are such that ii) this cost decreases with the cultural distance of the opponent. The cultural traits in the population separate individuals with more or

23 The evolutionary selection of cooperative behavior is a central issue in the social sciences. More related to the approach surveyed here – where it is preferences for cooperation rather than behavior which is selected – see e.g., Bowles and Gintis (2002) who study cultural evolutionary models of norms of cooperation, but in contexts with exogenous cultural transmission and standard replicator dynamics.

24 Bisin et al. (2004a) also characterize conditions on the payoff of the game under which incomplete information hinders or favors the transmission of Cooperation, that is, under which q^C is higher or smaller in the limit.

less "limited" morality, that is, with higher or lower steepness of the dependence of the cost with respect to distance. In equilibrium individuals cooperate only with culturally close opponents, the more so the more limited is their morality. Building on Bisin et al. (2004a,b), Tabellini (2008) embeds this structure into an economic model of cultural transmission. A higher anticipated fraction of individuals in the children's generation with relatively general – less limited – morality makes cooperation less costly and more beneficial in psychological terms. Consequently, the gains from socializing children to preferences of general morality are higher in societies where such preferences prevail and strategic complementarity obtains.

Institutions and political economy. In several interesting contexts, the gains from socialization to a trait i are affected by a collective choice/action in the children's generation, that in turn may depend on the size of the respective cultural groups. For instance, in Tabellini's (2008) study of local and general morality norms, gains from socialization depend on voting decisions about the structure of the legal enforcement system. Under majority rule, minority traits may suffer, leading to inefficient legal systems that hinder cultural transmission of norms of general morality. This in turn reinforces the political support for an inefficient legal system. Similarly, Bisin and Verdier (2000) explore cultural transmission of preferences for a public good determined by voting, revealing a two-way causality between culture and political decision-making. Parents' gains from socialization hinge on expectations of political aggregation, while voting outcomes depend on the present trait distribution, influenced by past socialization. Under perfect foresight, initial conditions shape preference and political outcome dynamics, leading to either homogeneous long-run preferences or multiple equilibrium paths for balanced initial distributions.

In the same vein, Bisin and Verdier (2005) examine the interaction between the transmission of work ethic and support for redistributive policies. The paper highlights how welfare state policies may weaken incentives to pass on work ethic norms, leading to sustained political support for redistribution, but ultimately causing its own decline as work ethic norms fade. Along the perfect foresight path of preferences evolution in the society, redistribution fosters cultural homogenization toward a preference structure that is initially strongly majoritarian in society. However, if the initial distribution of work ethic preferences is sufficiently balanced, cultural and political dynamics can generate multiple paths, depending on the type of expectations individuals are coordinated on. These different trajectories have long-term consequences for cultural values and policy outcomes. Crucially, steady-state politico-cultural equilibria are shaped by self-fulfilling expectations, highlighting the role of ideologies as programmatic coordination expectation devices that help to select a particular path of cultural values and political power structure in society.

3.3 Collective transmission mechanisms

In the canonical economic model of cultural transmission, traits are transmitted individually from parent to child. Recent economic literature has expanded the cultural transmission process to consider collective mechanisms like schools, churches, parties, and community institutions. We refer to these collective mechanisms as *cultural leaders*.

Leaders have their motivations regarding specific cultural traits, influencing their promotion or discouragement within society. They can manipulate individuals' paternalistic motives, impacting cultural dynamics. Moreover, through centralized actions, leaders can internalize group-related effects of cultural transmission, incentivizing collective action and taking a forward-looking perspective on cultural evolution and the dynamic externalities associated with the diffusion of cultural attributes. Lastly, cultural leaders may compete across or within communities to maintain their positions, shaping the supply side of cultural transmission alongside decentralized parental and oblique motives. From a conceptual perspective, the process of cultural transmission is therefore not only determined by decentralized parental and social transmission motives but also by the competitive context in which cultural leaders and organizations design incentives and motivations for cultural transmission.

Following Verdier and Zenou (2018), consider a leader of the cultural group i, who can – possibly at a cost – affect or manipulate the paternalistic motives ΔV^i of parents. For instance, the cultural leader can provide the members of group i with a public good G^i which increases the paternalistic motive of parents of type i to transmit their trait, so that $V^{ii} = V^{ii}(G^i)$. Assume that the cultural leader is intrinsically motivated by proselytism, i.e., to maximize the number of people socialized to their cultural trait. Assume also that the leader only cares about the steady states of the cultural dynamics. Then, with a linear cost of providing the public good cG^i and quadratic costs of parental socialization, a proselytizing leader of group i solves the following problem:

$$\max_{G^i} \frac{\Delta V^i(G^i)}{\Delta V^i(G^i) + \Delta V^j(G^j)} - cG^i,$$

given G^j. If both groups have a cultural leader, the equilibrium is the Nash equilibrium of the game.

Relatedly, Hauk and Mueller (2015) extend this analysis by considering both cultural leaders intrinsically motivated by proselytism, or alternatively by rents associated to the overall level of socialization effort exerted in their group. With quadratic socialization costs, a rent-seeking leader maximizes

$$q^i d^i = q^i(1 - q^i)\Delta V^i = \left(\frac{\Delta V^i}{\Delta V^i + \Delta V^j}\right)^2 \Delta V^j.$$

In either case, the cultural leader is allowed to affect the paternalistic values of members of his/her group i, V^{ii}, V^{ij}, as well as the perceptions members of group j hold regarding group i, V^{ji}. Clearly, the cultural leader has an incentive to raise the perception of cultural differences ΔV^i, the *cultural intolerance*, of in-group members. This can be achieved through the provision of cultural values, that is, raising V^{ii}; or through claims of "cultural superiority" making the alternative trait appear inferior, that is, lowering V^{ij}. Furthermore, suppose the cultural leader has some influence on the intolerance of the members of the out-group toward the in-group, ΔV^j, for instance through manipulation of V^{ji}. Then a proselytizing leader from group i would have an incentive to increase V^{ji}, to reduce in turn ΔV^j. Interestingly, this is not necessarily the case for a rent-seeking leader, who might find it optimal to manipulate the cultural perception of the out-group toward the in-group so as to increase ΔV^j by lowering V^{ji} – going for *cultural alienation,* in the terminology of Hauk and Mueller (2015). This results from *cultural substitution.* As ΔV^j rises, out-group members intensify socialization efforts to maintain their traits, reducing the in-group's population and q^i. In response, the in-group enhances its own socialization (d^i). This may offset the shrinking in-group size, potentially increasing the leader's rents (proportional to $q^i d^i$). Thus, leaders may prefer a smaller, highly active in-group, the source of their rents. Consequently, leaders may amplify cultural intolerances, which may not benefit the population or even their own group members.[25]

The transitional dynamics effect of forward-looking cultural leaders is studied by Verdier and Zenou (2018) and Almagro and Andrés-Cerezo (2020). In both these studies leaders provide community public goods that affect positively the paternalistic motive of their members to transmit their trait to their children. In Verdier and Zenou (2018), when the provision of G^i is allowed to be time-varying, the cultural leader is perfectly forward-looking and his utility is a discounted sum of instantaneous utilities linear in q^i, the solution has a bang-bang property. The optimal cultural trajectory has the property that it approaches as rapidly as possible some interior point q^i and stays there forever. The characterization of q^i (and the associated time-varying control function $G^i(t)$) clearly depends on the initial state q_0^i of the population. When q_0^i is small, the cultural leader might find it too costly to promote more socialization than in-group parents already do, so the system remains at q_0^i. Conversely, when q_0^i is large, parental socialization may be intense enough that the leader doesn't need to stimulate further cultural transmission. It's only when q_0^i takes

[25] Prummer and Siedlarek (2017) study cultural leaders who care about the economic wellbeing of their cultural group members and who influence the beliefs and attitudes of community members, by establishing rules and social norms. Carvalho (2016) studies organizations – cultural clubs – dealing with various externalities associated to cultural transmission by (i) imposing rules of participation in cultural activities and (ii) excluding non-members from social interactions. Carvalho et al. (2024) analyze group level socialization efforts interacting with an education system transmitting a mainstream cultural trait.

intermediate values that it may be optimal for the leader to push cultural dynamics toward a higher steady state. Interestingly, short-term parameter shifts have different effects on socialization activity compared to long-term effects, leading to potential over- or under-shooting. These transitional dynamics hold significant policy implications for minority cultural community associations. Extending the framework to strategic forward-looking leaders in either of the cultural groups, equally patient leaders set the same level of public goods, neutralizing therefore their cultural influence. When however time discount rates are different, the more patient leader dominates, while the less patient remains inactive. As differences in time discount factors may reflect variations in institutional stability, this suggests that leaders from stable organizations shape cultural diffusion at the expense of less stable outgroups.[26]

Almagro and Andrés-Cerezo (2020) explore a similar problem in the context of nation-building, studying how a forward looking leader, i.e., a central state, may promote the diffusion of a cultural trait like national identity on its territory. The key control variable in this context is the share of a fixed resource that is allocated to the provision of a public good specifically attached to the national identity trait. Differently from Verdier and Zenou (2018), the zero-sum character of the conflict over resources pushes the cultural dynamic toward homogeneous steady states and extreme levels of allocations of the public good.

Forward looking leaders are also the focus of Carvalho and Sacks (2024), who study the conditions under which such a leader would be willing and able to radicalize a cultural group/community, transitioning it from an inclusive and liberal state to an exclusive and strict club. Two mechanisms are critical to radicalization: *prestige-biased* cultural transmission and *niche construction*.[27] Prestige bias occurs when active community members with higher visibility and prestige exert disproportionate influence on cultural transmission. Niche construction involves a leader inducing blanket discrimination against community members, shielding the club from external pressures. In both cases, leaders start with a small extreme club, radicalizing the community over time through cultural transmission and niche construction. However, competition between clubs prevents these dynamic radicalization strategies.

Finally a series of papers centers on public education and media in their role in collectively transmitting cultural values within a community. In this vein, Gradstein and Justman (2002; 2005) analyze how education can promote a common culture, emphasizing the importance of school curricula convergence to prevent excessive polarization. Similarly, Dixit (2009) explores how norms of pro-sociality, transmitted through majority-funded schools, can impact a country's economic success. Taking a more information-based mechanism approach of cultural transmission, Dessi (2008) investigates collective socialization through intergenerational transmission of collective

[26] See also Verdier and Zenou (2015) for a simpler model of competition between cultural leaders.

[27] See Henrich and Gil-White (2001) and Odling-Smee et al. (2003) for the study of prestige bias and niche construction in models of cultural evolution.

memory, highlighting how younger generations' investment decisions are influenced by beliefs inherited from older generations. Carvalho et al. (2024) model an education system which transmits a mainstream cultural trait, while the minority group may culturally react at the individual level or as a coordinated group. Hauk and Immordino (2014) study cultural dynamics in an environment where the media industry plays a role in socialization and provides coverage to cultural traits.

3.4 Relative cultural fitness as a socio-economic mechanism

In the canonical economic cultural transmission model direct vertical transmission is modeled as a parental effort choice to socialize children. More generally, however, socialization is the outcome of a combined series of parental choices. In this section we shall study models where parental socialization results directly from parental effort and fertility or marriage.

3.4.1 Fertility

In this section we introduce endogenous fertility choices and investigate how they interact with cultural socialization. Consider, for instance, the canonical model of cultural transmission, and extend it to allow for some parental choice of reproductive pattern. Specifically let $n_i \geq 0$ denote the number of children chosen by parents with trait i, at cost $\mu \cdot n_i$ (where μ is the cost of raising one child). Parents of type i choose d^i, n^i to maximize

$$n^i(P^{ii}V^{ii} + P^{ij}V^{ij}) - n^i c(d^i) - \mu \cdot n^i \tag{7}$$

with P^{ii}, P^{ij} as in (2). Relative cultural fitness encodes both parental socialization and fertility:

$$f^i = \frac{d^i \nu^i - d^j \nu^j}{\nu^i q^i + (1-\nu^i)\left(1-q^i\right)}.$$

The dynamics of the distribution of traits in the population is then determined by

$$\dot{q}^i = q^i(1-q^i)\frac{d^i \nu^i - d^j \nu^j}{\nu^i q^i + (1-\nu^i)\left(1-q^i\right)},$$

where $\nu^i = \frac{n^i}{n^i+n^j}$.

As noted by Bisin and Verdier (2001a,b), the choice of reproduction patterns tends to introduce a cultural complementarity force in the cultural transmission process, in that $n^i(q^i)$ is increasing in q^i. Indeed, parents endowed with a more frequent trait have a higher chance, everything else being equal, to get their children sharing their trait through society's socialization. Such an outcome is perceived by paternalistic parents as increasing the "quality" of children, motivating higher fertility rates and consequently more effective cultural transmission of their trait in the population. When more generally fertility interacts with direct socialization, total socialization costs increase with the number of children, and hence parents, when choosing direct children socialization, incur a classic quantity/quality (of children) trade-off. In such a case, the quantity/quality trade-off is sufficient to re-establish the dynamics associated to cultural substitution, over-riding the cultural complementarity due to endogenous fertility.[28]

In summary, under some regularity conditions: i) there exists an interior locally stationary state; ii) either the interior stationary state is globally stable or it is locally stable and then there exist intervals in initial q^i which are basins of attraction for each of the corner stationary states. Essentially, cultural substitutions tend to induce dynamics converging toward the interior, while the quality/quantity trade-off in fertility tends to induce dynamics converging to the corner stationary states (majority children – with high socialization rates at little cost – have higher quality).

More recently, Bar-Gill and Fershtman (2016) provide an extension of the Bisin and Verdier model with endogenous fertility to the case where paternalistic preferences for transmitting one's own trait are not separable across children: the nature of the cultural trait adopted by one child affects the paternalistic motives to transmit one's own trait to another child. In this context, the analysis highlights two opposite situations: one in which the emphasis is on having at least one child remaining loyal to the parents' cultural trait (described as a "survivalist type"). In the other, the emphasis is on having all the children maintaining the group's cultural trait (described as a "zealot type"). Individuals' fertility decision and their direct socialization effort therefore crucially depend on their degree of zealousness. Interestingly in such a case, integration cultural policies aimed at promoting the cultural conversion of minority groups to the trait of the majority may be ineffective, and even result in more resilient and larger minority groups. Indeed, whenever individuals are of the "survivalist" type, an integration policy may induce higher fertility rates as individuals may switch from a one child strategy with a high (and costly) direct socialization level to a two children strategy with much lower direct socialization levels. This change may result in a larger minority size whenever the effect of higher fertility is stronger than the effect of lower direct socialization.

3.4.2 *Marriage*

Earlier models in Bisin and Verdier (2000) and Bisin et al. (2004a,b) study the marriage mechanism as a component of cultural transmission, where the preferences in marriage are endogenous, and reflect the indirect preferences of the expected outcomes of the marriage match. Specifically, they assume

---

28 Bar-El et al. (2013) provide numerical simulations of a version of this fertility model to investigate the evolution of secularization in a society. In their framework, the presence of both cultural complementarity and cultural substitution effects eventually leads to multiple steady state levels of secularization in the population.

that the only relevant characteristic of marriage matches consists in whether they are homogamous or heterogamous, in that homogamous marriages are valued because they are more effective socialization mechanisms. In the extreme case, for illustration purposes, only homogamous marriages have the option to directly transmit their trait to their children at a rate d^i. In this case, the probability that a child in a homogamous marriage of type i is socialized to trait i is $P^{ii,hom} = d^i + (1 - d^i)q^i$; while the probability that a child in a heterogamous marriage is socialized to trait i is $P^{i,het} = q^i$. Letting the probability of homogamous marriage of such type i be π^{ii}, the population dynamics take the form:

$$\dot{q}^i = q^i(1 - q^i)\left(d^i\pi^{ii} - d^j\pi^{jj}\right). \tag{8}$$

We discuss next two different models for the determination of π^i, π^j.

Restricted pool. Consider a marriage mechanism where each individual can affect, at a cost, the probability to be married homogamously by entering a restricted pool in which marriages, if they occur, are homogamous.[29]

The probability of marrying homogamously is:

$$\pi^i(\alpha^i, A^i, A^j, q^i) = \alpha^i + (1 - \alpha^i)\frac{(1 - A^i)q^i}{(1 - A^i)q^i + (1 - A^j)(1 - q^i)}$$

where $\alpha^i \in [0, 1]$ is the probability of being married homogamously in the restricted pool entered at a cost (convex in α^i); and A^i, A^j are the fractions of agents from group i, j in the restricted pool. The ex ante probability that a parent of group i has a child of type i is

$$P^i(\alpha^i, q^i) = \pi^i(\alpha^i, A^i, A^j, q^i)P^{ii,hom} + (1 - \pi^i(\alpha^i, A^i, A^j, q^i))P^{i,het}.$$

Socialization entails the choice of d^i, α^i given A^i, A^j:

$$\max_{d^i,\alpha^i} P^i(\alpha^i, q^i)V^{ii} + \left(1 - P^i(\alpha^i, q^i)\right)V^{ij}.$$

At equilibrium $A^i = \alpha^i$, $A^j = \alpha^j$.

Under convexity and regularity assumptions, Bisin and Verdier (2000) show the existence of a unique symmetric Nash equilibrium of this marriage game, where all individuals of type i choose the same marital segregation effort. At equilibrium, cultural substitution is satisfied, that is $d^i\pi^{ii}$ is decreasing in

[29] Churches, ethnic clubs, and various other cultural institutions may serve for instance this purpose.

q^i, and the population dynamics (8) induce a stationary distribution which is culturally heterogeneous.[30]

Frictionless matching. Bisin and Tura (2019) extend this class of models, where the preferences in marriage represent the indirect preferences of the expected outcomes of the marriage match, by i) allowing for the cultural transmission of heterogamous households; and by ii) allowing for fertility and divorce choices in the marriage match.

Agents are characterized by binary gender and dichotomous cultural type i. A household where the male has type h and the female j is hj. A household type composed of a single male with type h is $h0$ and the one composed of a single female with type j is $0j$. Matching is frictionless with transferable utility (TU) across spouses. Expected utility is constructed rationally anticipating future choices as a household (fertility, divorce, socialization, ...). It also accounts for an idiosyncratic component – observed before marriage – capturing residual idiosyncratic returns from marriage. Homogamy has a socialization advantage (as above): $P^{ii,hom} \geq P^{i,het}$ for the same effort d^i and for any q^i.

Given expected marital utility U_t for all different potential types of matches $t \in T$ (including those composed of single individuals), μ_t is the fraction of marriages of type $t \in T$ and m_h and f_j are males and females with trait h and j, respectively. Under separability and appropriate distributional assumptions, the optimal stable assignment μ_t solves[31]:

$$\begin{aligned} &\max_{(\mu_t \geq 0)_{t \in T}} \quad \textstyle\sum_{t \in T} \mu_t U_t - \varepsilon(\mu), \\ &s.t. \\ &\textstyle\sum_j \mu_{hj} + \mu_{h.} = m_h \quad \forall h \in C, \\ &\textstyle\sum_h \mu_{hj} + \mu_{.j} = f_j \quad \forall j \in C. \end{aligned} \tag{9}$$

The cultural dynamics are characterized computationally in a structurally estimated model, giving rise to long run distributions by trait which converge to homogeneity – whereby immigrants assimilate to the trait of natives – and interesting comparative dynamics results about the speed of assimilation.[32]

30 Hiller et al. (2022) study marriage markets with either homophilic or heterophilic preferences. When marriage preferences are homophilic and parental transmission is more efficient – indeed perfect – in homogamous families, cultural heterogeneity prevails as a stationary state. However, the presence of a small mass of heterophilic individuals is enough to break that result and to lead to cultural homogeneity in the long-run.

31 $\varepsilon(\mu)$ is the generalized entropy of the matching, which captures the dispersion of individual preferences with respect to the aggregate preferences, conditional on spouses' attributes (Chiappori et al., 2017; Galichon and Salanié, 2022).

32 See also Guirkinger et al. (2026) analyzing the intergenerational conflict on marriage decisions in migrants' families with a bargaining game between parents, brides and grooms, in the context of the transmission of cultural values to future grandchildren. Similarly, Farahzadi (2024) investigates the issue of "migration by marriage", using a matching model involving the choice of marrying a partner from the country of origin, because of a preference for cultural endogamy.

Gender effects. In the canonical model of cultural transmission socialization is the choice of one parent, that is, of two parents treated as a unitary household. Even in the marriage models in this section it is the cultural composition of the household – whether it's homogamous or heterogamous – that determines socialization at the first order.

Several papers study instead environments where parental socialization is mediated by the gender. In Bisin and Tura (2019) maternal and paternal socialization are endogenously different through an equilibrium effect. It is assumed in fact that upon divorce it is only mothers that socialize their children. Through an anticipation effect of a divorce shock, therefore, the parents face distinct socialization problems. For either of the parents, however, socialization is gender neutral.[33] In Wu and Zhang (2021) and Wu (2021), instead, parental socialization is mediated by the gender of the child. Interesting results are obtained leveraging the interaction between gender-specific parental transmission rates and degrees of assortativeness in the marriage market. Finally, while in Wu and Zhang (2021) gender-specific transmission rates are exogenous, Hiller and Baudin (2016) and Baudin and Hiller (2019) consider an environment where parents may endogenously socialize their sons and daughters differently, studying the evolution of cultural traits within male and female populations distinctly. On the other hand, they restrict the marriage market to random matching.[34]

3.5 Parental transmission: complementarities and information

A series of recent papers has studied more general models of parental transmission, incorporating interesting forms of interaction between direct parental transmission and the cultural composition of society as well as informational limits and constraints in the parental socialization problem.

3.5.1 Cultural complementarity

In the canonical economic model of cultural transmission, d^i has the cultural substitution property, that is d^i is decreasing in q^i. Considering more general

[33] In Bezin et al. (2022) maternal and paternal socialization operate differently: socialization depends on the presence of the father in the household, as children from broken families are more influenced by peers.

[34] Bezin et al. (2022) is another example illustrating how family composition, influenced by economic factors, impacts cultural evolution. Specifically, they examine an environment where traits like honesty depend on the father's presence. Children from broken families are more influenced by peers, increasing their likelihood of engaging in crime. Imprisoning criminal fathers leads to more single-parent families, which are less effective at transmitting honesty than two-parent families. The study shows that intense crime repression can backfire by increasing the likelihood that criminals' sons also become criminals. This model aligns with sociological disorganization theories of crime, and explains the emergence and persistence of urban ghettos, where high crime rates and broken families are prevalent, further perpetuating criminal behavior through negative community influences.

socialization technologies $P^{ii}(q^i)$ than in (2), it can be shown that cultural substitution follows when $\frac{\partial^2 P^{ii}}{\partial d^i \partial q^i} < 0$. Intuitively, the property of *cultural substitution* indicates that role models inside the family (direct vertical transmission) act as *cultural substitutes* to role models outside the family (oblique or horizontal transmission). In such a case, parents have less incentives to socialize their children the more widely dominant are their values in the population. Formally, with *cultural substitution*, the cultural fitness of trait i is a continuous, strictly decreasing function of q^i and, moreover, $f(d^i) = 0$ when $q^i = 1$. In this case, it is easy to see that the cultural dynamics are away from the boundaries $q = 0$ and $q = 1$. Conversely, when $\frac{\partial^2 P^{ii}}{\partial d^i \partial q^i} > 0$ vertical and oblique transmission are complements, a case Bisin and Verdier (2001a,b) call *cultural complementarity*. In this case, the population dynamics of culture leads to homogeneity – either $q^i = 1$ or $q^i = 0$ depending on the initial condition. As an illustration of cultural transmission mechanisms in which complementarities arise consider the following cultural transmission technology where direct and oblique transmission are not sequentially separated: Any child is first exposed simultaneously to the parent's trait and to the trait of a role model from the population with which he or she is matched randomly; if the parent and the role model are culturally homogeneous, the child is directly socialized to their common trait; otherwise the child is matched a second time randomly with a role model from the population, and adopts his or her trait. In this case, indeed,

$$P^{ii} = d^i q^i + (1 - d^i q^i) q^i$$

and $\frac{\partial^2 P^{ii}}{\partial d^i \partial q^i} > 0$.

3.5.2 Parental information

In the canonical cultural transmission model parental information plays no role. Recently however, more detailed technologies for cultural transmission have been studied which leverage parental information to produce important insights.

Learning and persuasion. Adriani et al. (2018) consider parental socialization as an explicit process of information transmission.[35] Children do not have full information about their own preferences – that is, about the payoffs associated to their actions. They then observe an action taken by the parents, form beliefs about the desirability of that action, and choose their own optimal action. Parents have better information about the payoff of each action and have a

35 A small emerging economic literature tackles the issue of parenting styles. For instance, Lizzeri and Siniscalchi (2008) investigate the trade-off between sheltering the child from mistakes and encouraging learning from experience. Similarly, Doepke and Zilibotti (2008; 2014; 2017) analyze the trade-off between direct parental intervention (authoritarian parenting) and respecting the child's autonomy (authoritative parenting). More recently, Seror (2022) presents a model where parent-child interactions create a complementarity in the formation of cognitive and non-cognitive skills. As the child learns from the parent, he forms cognitive skills.

paternalistic attitude toward their children. In this context, parental choices convey information to children, thus generating an information externality. Moreover, as informed parents are aware that their own choices set relevant examples to their children, they may use this signal strategically. In the context of the paper, parents might exert for instance self-restraint to avoid setting a negative example to the next generation. Embedding this information mechanism into a dynamic model of cultural transmission, Adriani et al. (2018) investigate the implications of the signaling distortion for the long run distribution of traits in the population. Interestingly, in this model some form of cultural heterogeneity may persist even in the absence of cultural substitution.[36]

Incomplete information. In the benchmark cultural transmission model, parents have perfect information in terms of how they perceive their interactions with their children and with society. Della Lena and Panebianco (2021) extend this framework to an environment where parents have incomplete information regarding the effects of their socialization practices, via their interactions with children and with society. Specifically, consider an environment where parents may not have full information on the distribution of the cultural traits in the population.[37] While the population dynamics of culture is unchanged with respect to the canonical model in (1), cultural fitness now depends on the parents' conjectures about population shares, denoted $\hat{q}^i$. The analysis highlights how incomplete information in the technology of transmission affects both parental socialization efforts and long-run population dynamics. In particular, it shows how cultural heterogeneity might not be sustained in the limit even under conditions of cultural substitution. The rationale for this result relates directly to the structure of perceptions bias from the minority and the majority groups about the actual distribution of the population. Consider for instance the steady state with $q^i = 0$. In the neighborhood of this point, agents of type i – the minority group – can only have non-negative biases, whereby $\hat{q}^i - q^i \geq 0$. Because of this, under cultural substitution, agents with trait i choose an average effort that is lower than the average optimal effort under complete information. This reduces the probability that, in the next period, the trait of type i is transmitted, and it negatively affects the dynamics of q^i. Similarly, agents of type j – the majority group – cannot overestimate their population share, generally inducing a higher effort than with complete information. This also negatively affects the dynamics of the minority trait i. When the negative average bias of the majority group is large enough, its average socialization effort is strong enough to dominate the average socialization effort of the minority group. As a consequence, the minority trait i cannot survive for

36 Adriani and Sonderegger (2018) also consider an extension of this framework to analyze how the desire to conform to peer pressure or to a social norm interacts with parents' signaling distortion, and affects cultural transmission.

37 Della Lena and Panebianco (2021) also study an environment where the incomplete information regards the effectiveness of their own parental socialization technology.

small values of q^i and the steady state $q^i = 0$ is stable and long-run cultural homogeneity prevails.

3.6 Social transmission: networks, identity, segregation

A series of recent papers has studied novel mechanisms of social transmission, extending the random matching mechanism exploited in the canonical model. In this section we first study models where social transmission is the result of the children's interaction with a culturally biased subset of society. The bias can be exogenous – for instance a pre-determined network of parental relationships – or endogenous. In this last case it could be the result of parental socialization choice – e.g., segregating the space of interactions of their children in the social transmission stage – or the results of the children's themselves *identity* choices.

3.6.1 Network effects

In the canonical model of cultural transmission, oblique transmission occurs via random matching. Finite networks and social structures through which individuals are connected have however been emphasized in several recent contributions to the literature; see Vaughan (2013), Büchel et al. (2014), Panebianco (2014), Verdier and Zenou (2017). In order to ensure long run cultural convergence, these models impose enough structure on the interacting social network matrix Γ. Panebianco and Verdier (2017) consider the case of complex random social networks, merging therefore insights from the epidemiological literature on large scale networks (Pastor-Satorras and Vespignani, 2003) and the cultural transmission literature. Specifically, consider a society of agents located on a large random network, with links formed according to a standard degree-based sampling process, and a degree distribution $(\xi(k))_k$ among neighboring nodes. The socialization rate of parents of type i, dk^i, depends on their network connectivity, i.e., on the degree k in the network. Let q_k^i denote the share of individuals of type i in the subset of agents with degree k; and let $\tilde{q}^i$ be the expected fraction of neighbors of cultural type i in the network, $\tilde{q}^i = \sum_{k=0}^{\infty} \xi(k) q_k$. In the mean-field approximation, the dynamics of q_k^i are the natural extension of those in (1):

$$\dot{q}_k^i = \left[-q_k^i(1 - d_k^i)(1 - \tilde{q}^i) + (1 - q_k^i)(1 - d_k^j)\tilde{q}^i \right] \tag{10}$$

where $-(1 - d_k^i)(1 - \tilde{q}^i)q_k^i$ represents how many children of i parents with degree k become of type j; and $(1 - q_k^i)(1 - d_k^j)\tilde{q}^i$ represents how many children of j parents with degree k become of type i. Under quadratic degree dependent socialization costs, the socialization rates are obtained as $d_k^i = c_k(1 - \tilde{q}^i)\Delta V^i$, and satisfy the *cultural substitution* property. The dynamics therefore converge to a set of cultural heterogeneous steady states $\left(q_k^i\right)_k$, characterized by the fixed point conditions:

$$q_k^i = \frac{(1-d_k^j)\tilde{q}^i}{(1-d_k^i)(1-\tilde{q}^i)+(1-d_k^j)\tilde{q}^i},$$

where

$$\tilde{q}^i = \sum_{k=0}^{\infty} \xi(k) \frac{(1-d_k^j)\tilde{q}^i}{(1-d_k^i)(1-\tilde{q}^i)+(1-d_k^j)\tilde{q}^i}.$$

3.6.2 *Segregation and isolation*

Sociologists and social psychologists have widely acknowledged the fact that people have significant contacts with others like themselves, and that social interactions are characterized by homophily (that is the fact that contact between similar people occurs at a higher rate than among dissimilar people) (McPherson et al., 2001). From a cultural transmission perspective, this feature implies that socialization at large with society is unlikely to be fully random. In particular, the matching process through which children get socialized may be partly controlled by their parents (or other role models) through their choice of schools, neighborhood where to live, associations or clubs where to go, and so on. As well, children themselves may also choose peer connections in a non random way, reinforcing or mitigating the bias that parents produced in the first place.

In the benchmark model, oblique transmission occurred through random matching with society at large. One may however extend this framework to include the possibility that the cultural composition of society children get exposed to is at least partly under the control of parents. Abstracting from specific details of the contact process, the transmission probabilities could be generally written as,

$$P^{ii} = d^i + (1-d^i)Q^i, \tag{11}$$

$$P^{ij} = (1-d^i)(1-Q^i), \tag{12}$$

where the composition of the social environment of the child, Q^i, is itself a function of the population shares q^i and a costly parental intervention, say s^i. In such a case, the effective "technology" of parental socialization is multidimensional, involving various margins of transmission: time effort, and social or spatial segregation decisions.

A simple example may take the following form:

$$Q^i = Q^i(s^i, q^i) = s^i + (1-s^i)q^i$$

with $s^i \in [0, 1]$ the oblique bias chosen by the parent. Typically when $s^i = 0$, there is random matching for oblique transmission and $Q^i(0, q^i) = q^i$. There is a positive bias to match toward a model similar to parent i when $s^i > 0$. Indeed when $s^i = 1$, oblique transmission is completely biased toward the cultural variant of the parent and the child is only exposed to that specific type. After substitution, the dynamics of change across generations become:

$$\dot{q}^i = q^i(1-q^i)\left[\varphi^i - \varphi^j\right]$$

with $\varphi^i = d^i + (1-d^i)s^i$ reflecting the "effective" rate of cultural transmission of type i. This is the sum of the socialization direct parental bias d^i plus the oblique socialization bias $(1-d^i)s^i$. Again the difference between these "effective" transmission rates across the two cultural variants is what creates a cultural selective force in the population.

The cost of the socialization of a parent of type i can be now denoted as $C(d^i, s^i)$. The optimal direct socialization rates d^i and degree of oblique transmission bias s^i are then the solution of the following problem:

$$\max_{(d^i, s^i)} -C(d^i, s^i) + \left[P^{ii}(d^i, s^i)V^{ii} + P^{ij}(d^i, s^i)V^{ij}\right].$$

Assuming that socialization costs satisfy some standard regularity assumptions, it can be shown that when vertical transmission and biased oblique transmission reinforce each other in the socialization process – that is, when the two dimensions appear as complements in the socialization technology and $\frac{\partial^2 C^i}{\partial d^i \partial s^i} < 0$ – then cultural substitution prevails, namely the optimal socialization choices $d^i\left(q^i, \Delta V^i\right)$ and $s^i\left(q^i, \Delta V^i\right)$ are decreasing in the frequency of the parent trait q^i. As a result the "effective" rate of cultural transmission of type i, φ^i, is also decreasing in the frequency q^i. The long run state of the population dynamics is culturally heterogeneous.

Several other models of endogenous biased oblique transmission are analyzed for instance in Bisin and Verdier (2001a,b) and Sáez-Martí and Sjögren (2008). The marriage segmentation model analyzed in Bisin and Verdier (2000) is also an example of segregation strategies that affect cultural transmission. More recent examples consider explicitly a social network structure and analyze how the topology of social connections matters for the cultural dynamics (Büchel et al., 2014; Panebianco, 2014; Patacchini and Zenou, 2016; Panebianco and Verdier, 2017; Verdier and Zenou, 2017).

3.6.3 Identity formation

While parents directly make various socialization choices to influence the preference formation of their children, vertical socialization is nonetheless in general limited by the children's pro-active motivations in choosing their own preferences and cultural traits, and forming their *identity* in the jargon of social psychology. In this respect, the economic model of cultural transmission can easily be extended to incorporate insights from the economics of identity formation (Akerlof and Kranton, 2000).[38] Typically, the formation of social identity (race, gender, religious or political) can be analyzed through two somewhat opposite lenses. A first perspective argues that group identity is driven by a motive for inclusiveness and *cultural conformity*, and therefore that identity is reduced by assimilation and contact across cultures.[39] The alternative view suggests that cultural minorities are motivated in keeping their own distinctive heritage to generate a sense of positive *distinctiveness* or *cultural distinction*[40] from individuals who are not part of that group.[41] When identity formation is characterized by cultural distinction, social interactions across groups might induce the formation of oppositional or radical identities on the part of specific groups.

Several economic models of cultural transmission account for children taking conscious actions toward their own cultural *identity formation*. In these models, the technology of cultural socialization is predicated on the interactions between vertical socialization processes (e.g. parental effects) and horizontal socialization (e.g., peer pressure effects). In this respect, parents attempt in various ways to mitigate or control the peer pressure their children are exposed to. For instance they may prevent interactions with other kids, provide counter-balancing values, or be more closely engaged with their children. Such parental internalization of peer pressure effects contributes to the long run dynamics of culture.

As a first step along those lines, Bisin et al. (2011) present a framework where individuals, after being socialized by their families to a particular trait, choose the intensity of their identification with that trait. High intensity is seen as a *cultural distinction* process. Parents invest in socializing their children to their ethnic trait, anticipating the children's identity formation.

Socialization technology allows for parents to bias the social set of contacts the child is exposed to when not directly socialized.

The probability of drawing a contact of type i in the oblique transmission component of cultural transmission is

$$Q^i(s^i, q^i)$$

---

38 See, for instance, Darity et al. (2006) for an exogenous replicator dynamics mechanism of identity formation.

39 *Assimilation theories*, in political science and sociology (Gordon, 1964; Moghaddam and Solliday, 1991), *contact theory* in social psychology (Allport, 1953) are the prominent theories of this line of thought.

40 *Cultural distinction*, as defined here, is a property of individual preferences. It is related but distinct from *cultural substitution*, which is a property of socialization mechanisms.

41 These ideas have been expressed by the theories of *multiculturalism* (Glazer and Moynihan, 1970). At a broader level, this view is also related to the *social identity theory* in social psychology (Tajfel, 1979; Tajfel et al., 1979; and Abrams and Hogg, 1988).

with $s^i \in [0, 1]$ and $Q^i(s^i, q^i)$ as before. Identity formation requires that oblique transmission involves the choice of the child, so that the probability that the child adopts trait i is $T^i(s^i, q^i)$.

We can consider two distinct child adoption rules:

By conformity: drawing an (odd) number N of contacts and picking the type of the majority, so that the (Binomial) probability the child is of type i is:

$$T^i(s^i, q^i) = \binom{N}{\frac{N+1}{2}} \left(Q^i(s^i, q^i)\right)^{\frac{N+1}{2}} \left(1 - Q^i(s^i, q^i)\right)^{N - \frac{N+1}{2}}.$$

By extreme conformity ("It takes a village," when the village is a minority): picking the type i only if all the contacts are i:

$$T^i(s^i, q^i) = \left(Q^i(s^i, q^i)\right)^N.$$

The parental socialization problem is

$$\max_{(\tau^i, s^i) \in [0,1]^2} \quad -c(\tau^i) - C(s^i) + P^{ii}(\tau^i, s^i, q^i)V^{ii} + (1 - P^{ii}(\tau^i, s^i, q^i))V^{ij}$$

where $P^{ii}(\tau^i, s^i, q^i) = \tau^i + (1 - \tau^i)T^i(s^i, q^i)$. Under regularity assumptions, cultural substitution is maintained.

Another interesting recent contribution along the same lines is Giavazzi et al. (2019). In this paper, as in Bisin et al. (2011), parents first choose the family socialization rates and then children choose their own cultural identity.[42] Agents in the children generation match randomly and obtain a payoff for the match. Let V denote the value of a match between agents in the children generation with the same cultural trait. Let θ^M (resp. θ^m) denote the fraction of the value of the match lost when a child keeps (resp. switches from) the parental identity and meets with an individual of the other group. While parents derive utility from transmitting their own cultural trait, they also care about the value of that trait for their own child in society and they anticipate the child's own choice problem, knowing the distribution of the switching costs he/she will face but not the realization.

Specializing the model to one where the cultural choice is only on the part of the minority group – say group i – where switching identity may be interpreted as assimilating – the socialization rate d^i is increasing in ΔV^i, decreasing in the cost of the effort and, most interestingly, decreasing in θ^M and increasing in θ^m. Altruistic parents in fact internalize the cost their socialization choice imposes

[42] See also Lazear (1999) and Konya (2005). Relatedly, Michaeli and Wu (2022) – building on Cheung and Wu (2018) cultural transmission model of a continuum of traits – explore the roles of peer pressure and show that strong paternalistic parents, ignoring peer pressure's social costs on their children, adopt more extreme socialization to counteract their children's conformity away from the parent's preference.

on their children and reduce their socialization effort d^i the larger is θ^M and decrease it the smaller is θ^m.

Two types of equilibria may emerge in this model: one where all dynamical paths converge to assimilation of the minority, and another where the minority group does not assimilate. The occurrence of complete assimilation depends upon a set of parameters such as the payoffs and switching costs from assimilating, the degree of cultural intolerance of parents, the technology of parental socialization, and finally on how much parents account for their child's utility payoff, that is, their altruism.[43]

4 The joint evolution of culture and institutions

The literature we survey in the previous sections is centered on models of the dynamics of the distribution of cultural traits in the population. These models have highlighted the relationship between cultural evolution and social interactions. In several instances, these models capture the role that social and political institutions play in these dynamics.

A recent line of research explicitly focuses on the two-way interactions between cultural and institutional environments: the distribution of cultural traits in the population affects the institutional and political structure of society and, on the other hand, the institutional and political structure of society affects the distribution of cultural traits in the population.[44] These models are typically formally represented by a system of (two) dynamic equations: one describing cultural evolution and the second describing institutional change. They offer a novel approach to growth and development. Unlike traditional studies that try to isolate the causal impact of each factor on contemporary outcomes, these models can discuss how historical shocks propagate through their joint dynamics, and analyze how these interactions may have magnified or mitigated effects on long-run socioeconomic outcomes. Moreover, they often generate non-linear transitory trajectories with a host of interesting implications such as non-ergodicity, path dependence, and hysteresis effects – challenging the neo-classical view of development as fully determined by initial conditions and monotonic accumulation processes.

In a simple two political groups society set-up, let β^i denote a structural parameter characterizing the institutional structure of society, e.g., capturing the relative political power of group i. Parental preferences for socialization – depending on the cultural and institutional environment their children inhabit – take the form $\Delta V^i(q^i, \beta^i)$. Cultural evolution is then modeled as an application of the economics cultural transmission we have introduced in the previous sections: it follows Eq. (1), with the relative cultural fitness term represented

43 Furthermore, Giavazzi et al. (2019) obtain interesting results about the speed of convergence as a function of the parameters of the environment, identifying the characteristics of traits which are likely to spread quickly across generations.

44 See Alesina and Giuliano (2015) for an empirical survey.

by

$$\left[d^i(q^i, \Delta V^i(q^i, \beta^i)) - d^j(1-q^i, \Delta V^j(1-q^i, 1-\beta^i))\right].$$

Institutional change characterizes instead the evolution of the structural parameter β^i, in a game that determines policies and outcomes in society.[45] In a political economy perspective, β^i summarizes the power structure across, e.g., two political groups. Institutional change then may take different forms, from incremental changes in the institutional bargaining structure, to open conflicts and abrupt changes in the political system.[46] In general though, the forces of motion of β^i will reflect the fact that the institutional system imperfectly and indirectly internalizes various externalities and commitment issues which plague social choice problems.

Bisin and Verdier (2024) provide a simple abstract set-up that illustrates the core structure of the institutional bloc of these models. Each period t, a societal policy game is played between private individuals and a hierarchical public policy authority (the state) controlling socio-economic policies. Individuals in each group i are characterized by an objective function $U^i(a^i, p, A)$ that depends on private actions a^i, a policy vector p, and some measure of socio-economic outcomes A, capturing the aggregate society-wide outcomes of the interactions between private agents and public authorities. These aggregate outcomes naturally depend on the vector $a = [a^1, a^2]$ of actions by individuals of the two groups, the public policy vector p, and the cultural distribution q^i in society: $A = A\left(a, p, q^i\right)$.

Policies are the outcome of a (collective) decision problem, in accordance with the distribution of political power between the groups encoded and represented by institutions. Institutions can then be abstractly defined and parametrized by the (Pareto) weight $\beta^i = 1 - \beta^j$ in the decision making problem regarding the policy vector p. Specifically, we could have the objective of the public policy authority identified by a social welfare function

$$W = \beta^i U^i(a^i, p, A) + (1-\beta^i) U^j(a^j, p, A). \tag{13}$$

Given institutions β^i, a set of policies $p = p\left(\beta^i, q^i\right)$ and actions $a = a\left(\beta^i, q^i\right)$, characterize the equilibrium of the societal policy game between individuals and the public authority. Importantly, the equilibrium outcomes $p = p\left(\beta^i, q^i\right)$ and $a = a\left(\beta^i, q^i\right)$ also depend on the distribution of cultural traits q^i prevailing in the population.

It should be noted that the policy game is in general characterized by several economic and political externalities that are not fully accounted for by private and public decisions. Externalities typically arise because of socio-economic or political imperfections associated with the existence of various frictions

---

45 See Acemoglu et al. (2006), and Acemoglu et al. (2021) for surveys.

46 Acemoglu and Robinson (2000; 2006) typically consider discrete phenomena like democratization, revolutions and coup regime changes.

going from asymmetric/incomplete information, matching problems, limited rationality and cognitive biases, strategic behaviors associated with market power, private opportunism and lack of political commitment. The equilibrium outcomes $a(\beta^i, q^i)$ and $p(\beta^i, q^i)$ of the societal policy game do not fully internalize their impacts on aggregate social outcomes $A(a, p, q^i)$, and as a result inefficient policies and social allocations are implemented.

The core element is then the mechanism driving institutional change. A society characterized by a power structure β_t^i at any point in time t, might have an incentive to change the distribution of political power in the future, to internalize the externalities responsible for the inefficiencies at equilibrium.

For instance, Bisin and Verdier (2024) consider institutions as general mechanisms operating on the distribution of political power to internalize externalities due to some form of lack of commitment on the part of the public policy decision maker. This is consistent with earlier political economy work on institutional change such as Acemoglu and Robinson (2000; 2006). Allowing for smooth changes $\beta^i \in [0, 1]$,[47] institutional change takes a relatively simple form:

$$\beta_{t+1}^i \in \arg\max \beta_t^i U^1(\beta_{t+1}^i, q_{t+1}^i) + (1 - \beta_t^i) U^2(\beta_{t+1}^i, q_{t+1}^i)$$

where $U^i(\beta_{t+1}, q_{t+1}^i) = U^i(a^i(\beta_{t+1}^i, q_{t+1}^i), p(\beta_{t+1}^i, q_{t+1}^i), A(\beta_{t+1}^i, q_{t+1}^i))$ is the utility for members of group $i \in \{1, 2\}$ evaluated at future equilibrium choices with institution β_{t+1}^i.[48] Institutional change takes the form of delegation of power from the current institutional structure (as reflected by the power weight β_t^i) to a new institutional setup (as reflected by a power weight β_{t+1}^i). The direction of institutional change relates to the general principle that the political group most likely to internalize the externality is the group receiving more residual decision rights along the institutional dynamics.[49] Power weights therefore change continuously, according to an endogenous dynamic law, $\dot{\beta}^i = \phi(\beta^i, q^i)$ (in the continuous time approximation).[50]

The second part of the framework concerns the cultural transmission block, while various cultural selection mechanisms may be considered,[51] in the Bisin-

[47] This captures incremental institutional changes (Mahoney and Thelen, 2010) rather than more extreme phenomena like democratization or revolutions and coup regime changes as in Acemoglu and Robinson (2000; 2006).

[48] For convenience we denote $A(\beta_{t+1}^i) = A\left(p(\beta_{t+1}^i)\right), a(\beta_{t+1}^i), q_{t+1}^i)$.

[49] The stationary state of such process is not generally efficient, see for instance Acemoglu et al. (2010), Bisin and Verdier (2024).

[50] Acemoglu and Robinson (2001; 2006) were the first to formally study institutional change, focusing on power delegation by elites to avoid social conflict rather than to internalize externalities. In this case the dynamics of β is effectively discrete and hence it cannot be represented by a dynamic law. Besley and Persson (2009; 2011a; 2011b) also explore related aspects of institutional change.

[51] For instance Besley (2017), Besley and Persson (2019b; 2020a; 2020b) use the indirect evolutionary approach of cultural change from Güth and Yaari (1992a,b), while Bidner and Francois (2011), Bisin and Verdier (2024), or Bezin (2019) use economic cultural transmission models.

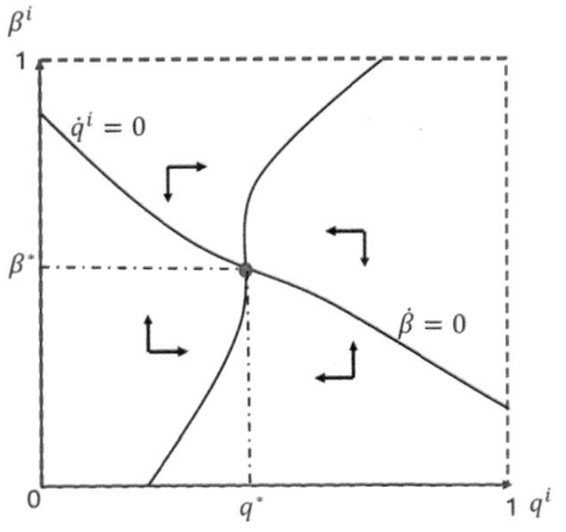

FIGURE 3 Joint evolution of culture and institutions.

Verdier set-up, the important feature is the fact that paternalistic motivations for cultural transmission now depend on the equilibrium outcome of the societal policy game $\Delta V^i = \Delta V^i(a, p)$. Under cultural substitution, parental socialization is generally stronger for cultural minorities and, ceteris paribus, for the group which is relatively favored at the equilibrium outcome (a, p) of the policy game.

These considerations determine the cultural dynamic of the profile of society q_t over time. Given that (a, p) are themselves function of the institutional weights β_t^i, the diffusion of cultural traits across generations is consequently also influenced by the status of the institutional system, β_t^i. This mechanism induces a cultural dynamic $\dot{q}^i = q^i(1 - q^i)G(\beta^i, q^i)$ (in the continuous time approximation).

The politico-economic and cultural structures of society are then characterized by the joint dynamics of institutions and culture $\left(\beta^i, q^i\right)$ as described in Fig. 3. This system eventually reaches a long run steady state (β^*, q^*).

A major theme across the literature is to highlight whether the joint dynamics between culture and institutions reinforce or hinder each other, depending on whether culture and institutions are dynamic complements or substitutes. Typically, a key complementarity between institutions and the dynamics of preferences would occur when having more of a certain cultural trait in the population is likely to induce an institutional equilibrium with an outcome that benefits more individuals endowed with such trait. In turn, the induced payoff outcomes are likely to facilitate the cultural diffusion of the trait in the population.[52]

52 A stylized model illustrating such a situation is Salazar and Szentes (2021) which considers a population game in which selfish agents and unconditional cooperators play the Prisoner's Dilemma repeatedly against random opponents, and there is institutional capital promoting cooperation among players. Both the type distribution and capital evolve according to a myopic best-response

4.1 Culture and various specific institutions

We turn to briefly discuss several papers in the literature that highlight the idea of a bi-directional relationship between culture and institutions in more specific contexts.

4.1.1 Culture and market institutions

An interesting line of research considers the relationship between culture, growth and market institutions. Earlier on, Doepke and Zilibotti (2008) already pointed at the role played by the development of an entrepreneurial culture in the industrialization process, and emphasized the relative importance of bourgeois cultural values compared to aristocratic cultural values as the roots of Britain's industrialization process. Along this line and using the Bisin and Verdier (2001a,b) approach, Bidner and Francois (2011) considered the interaction between honesty norms and institutions encouraging trading, while other papers investigated the connections between cultural values and labor market institutions (Aghion et al., 2011; Michau, 2013 and Alesina et al., 2015). Hiller (2011) analyzed the reciprocal interplay between the cultural evolution of workers' autonomy and the industrialization process. More recently, Chakraborty et al. (2016) and Klasing (2014) consider the interaction between an entrepreneurship culture, measured by agents' risk attitudes, and the process of economic development, while Gorodnichenko and Roland (2017) investigate the existence of mutual reinforcement between the culture of individualism, growth and protection against the risk of expropriation.

Eruchimovitch et al. (2024) also explore the coevolution between individualism/collectivism and market-supporting institutions. In this setup, individuals join one of two types of social organizations: "market" or "clan", depending on the relative productivity in the market, the strength of individualistic inclinations, and the quality of market-supporting institutions. Statically, market size depends on individualism and institutional quality. When the quality of market institutions and the prevalence of the individualistic trait become endogenous, the model exhibits two stable long run equilibria: one with high individualism, strong institutions, and a thriving market organization, and the other one with collectivism, no institutions, and a weak market.

4.1.2 Culture and political institutions

A set of papers focus more specifically on the connections between culture and political institutions. For instance, Besley (2017) shows how the interplay between the dynamics of preferences for aspirations and the politics of income redistribution creates a feedback loop, which allows for the possibility of an aspirational poverty trap in which countries are locked into a low aspirations culture which inhibits development. Similarly, Besley (2020) discusses the idea

dynamics. The system exhibits complementarity between cultural types and institutional capital with eventually multiple equilibria which can be Pareto-ranked.

of government as a reciprocal social contract between the state and its citizens: the citizens pay taxes and the state provides public goods. A strong civic culture, evolving in the society according to the relative payoffs of civic-minded and materialist citizens, manifests itself as high tax revenues sustained by high levels of voluntary tax compliance and provision of public goods. In the same vein, the complementarity between political institutions and culture is also investigated in Ticchi et al. (2013), and Besley and Persson (2019b), to study the coevolution between democratic values and democratic institutions.[53] Finally, Besley and Persson (2021) discuss the dynamics of identity politics and the two-way relationship between politics and nationalism. They consider a context where voters have multidimensional cleavages and policies: redistribution along a rich/poor dimension and immigration control along a nationalist/cosmopolitan identity dimension that evolves over time. The model exhibits political hysteresis, with large enough shocks to class polarization and immigration salience having long-run consequences on nationalism and immigration policy.

Taking a different angle, Alesina et al. (2021) explore national identity formation through "nation-building," where policies like mass education or indoctrination shape the divergence of preferences among citizens. Their analysis, though lacking explicit dynamics of cultural homogenization, compares the incentives for homogenization in dictatorships versus democracies, considering government type and borders as endogenous. A key finding is that the threat of democratization strongly incentivizes preference homogenization, consistent with historical episodes in the nineteenth century and correlations from 1925-2014 data.[54]

4.1.3 Culture and political-economic institutions

Touré (2021) examines how culture interacts with market and political institutions. Specifically, as in Bisin and Verdier (2017, 2024), political power is divided between workers and elites, with elites further split into entrepreneurs (who have a strong work ethic) and nonentrepreneurs. Culture evolves based on the relative utility of these traits. Public goods, such as infrastructure, that promote industrialization, are determined by a political process reflecting the balance of power between the different social classes. It suffers from suboptimal provision due to commitment issues. Importantly, these elements are embodied in a general equilibrium model of market interactions with a final good competitively produced using both labor and intermediate inputs in a complementary way. In this context, workers prefer the highest level of public investment, as it boosts labor productivity. Entrepreneurs support an intermediate level, benefiting from labor's complementarity with their intermediate goods, while nonentrepreneurs favor the lowest level, as they gain little from industrialization. Following the logic of Bisin and

53 See Bisin (2020) for a discussion.

54 See also Iyigun et al. (2021) for the connection between cultural revivals and Elite power.

Verdier (2017, 2024), institutional change corrects the suboptimal provision of public infrastructure by shifting power toward workers, especially when policy externalities are large. A politically powerful elite limits the scope of public investment, weakening productivity, and consequently the diffusion of the entrepreneurial trait is weak. Conversely, when entrepreneurship is rare, intermediate goods production remains low, reducing the marginal impact of the public policy. As the policy externality to be corrected is small, this makes an institutional shift toward workers less likely.

Together these elements generate a coevolution between culture and political and economic institutions with strong complementarities. An economy where entrepreneurial culture is not widespread and/or workers have little power is trapped in a regime without industrialization and in which institutions and culture do not evolve. Conversely, an economy with enough entrepreneurial culture and/or workers' empowerment is likely to take off, and along its trajectory, industrialization will follow jointly with an ever expanding diffusion of the entrepreneurial culture and increasing workers' empowerment. The author discusses historical evidence suggestive of this mechanism in the case of British history.

4.1.4 *Culture and environmental institutions*

Key complementarities have also been identified in the diffusion of environmental culture, and its interactions with markets and political institutions. In this respect, Bezin (2015) considers an overlapping generations model of environmental externalities and capital accumulation where private contributions to environmental quality are motivated by a desire to socialize others into environmental attitudes. Along the equilibrium path of capital-accumulation some, but not all, green agents contribute to the environment and effectively transmit a green culture intergenerationally.[55] Furthermore, Bezin (2019) considers the coevolution between a green consumer culture and sustainable technological change. Importantly, the set-up has now three state variables: culture, technology and the environment. Green preferences evolve according to the Bisin and Verdier (2001a,b) model of cultural transmission, while innovation is endogenously directed toward green or brown sectors depending on culture through market size effects. Finally, pollution accumulates depending on the production level of the brown sectors. Because of dynamic complementarities between technological change and cultural evolution, the model exhibits path dependency, an important feature of sustainable innovation processes. Also, when taxes on dirty production are decided by majority voting of the mature generation, a politically sustainable environmental tax exists only when the cost of socialization to green preferences is low enough. This highlights the key role for

55 In the same vein, Schumacher (2015) analyzes a dynamic model with Leontief preferences such that environmental quality and consumption are perfect complements, and investing in the formation of an environmental culture is costly. An environmental culture emerges only after the society has reached a critical level of economic development.

non-monetary interventions ("green" education) to foster the political sustainability of economic instruments (tax and subsidies).

Relatedly, Besley and Persson (2019a; 2019b; 2020b; 2021) also highlight the complementarity between value adaptation and policy choice in environmental policy. Their model features two types of citizens: materialists and environmentalists. Political outcomes are determined by a two-party competition model with probabilistic voting, where the policy reflects the average swing voter's interests, leading to a Pigouvian-like outcome. As environmental values evolve based on relative payoffs, policy choices drive society toward either environmentalism or materialism. The complementarity between expected policy and preference evolution stems from political externalities in majoritarian policymaking, which prevents optimal long-term welfare outcomes. As the political system does not internalize value dynamics induced by policies, institutional changes may be needed that delegate decision rights on environmental policies to political structures favoring environmentalist preferences, aligning therefore with Bisin and Verdier's (2017, 2024) perspective.

4.2 Cultural and institutional determinants of long-run growth

Dynamic complementarities between culture and institutions facilitate the emergence of different long-run social organizational forms and divergent institutional and cultural trajectories. Some papers explicitly emphasize this dimension to model critical historical junctures in specific comparative historical contexts.

Greif and Tabellini (2017) compare social organizations such as clans and corporations that sustain cooperation through different enforcement methods. Clans rely on kin-based loyalty and reciprocal obligations, while corporations (e.g., cities or guilds) depend on generalized moral obligations and impersonal enforcement. Individuals with different cultural traits (personalized or generalized morality) choose to affiliate with either clans or corporations. The population's cultural trait distribution determines the equilibrium size of these organizations, as different traits provide advantages to each. This structure in turn affects the evolution of cultural traits, leading to multiple steady states based on initial conditions. The model is used to compare the organizational dynamics in China and Europe over the last millennium.

The same logic is applied by Bisin et al. (2024) to examine the role of religious legitimacy in political economy. Legitimacy enables secular elites to affirm their authority and lower the transaction costs of implementing policies. However, clerics' ability to supply legitimacy depends on how well religious values are disseminated in society. This dissemination is facilitated by institutions granting more political power to clerics. Drawing on Bisin and Verdier's (2017, 2024) institutional change mechanism, if the legitimacy effect is strong enough, institutional change shifts power toward clerics, internalizing the social externalities of religious activities.[56] Clerics then exercise this power by providing religious activities in larger quantities, in turn propagating cultural values within the population that justify the ruling and extractive capacity of the political elite. Culture and institutions are then complementary. As in Greif and Tabellini (2017), these effects give rise to multiple stationary states with joint diverging dynamic trajectories, converging toward a *religious state* or alternatively, a *secular state.* The model formally compares the historical institutional and cultural trajectories of the Christian West and the Muslim East at the end of medieval times.

4.2.1 Substitutability between culture and institutions

While complementarity between culture and institution is a feature of most models of their dynamics, dynamic substitutability also plays a role in this literature. Early on in this literature, Tabellini (2008) notes that legal systems based on localized external enforcement are likely to undermine the transmission of cooperative cultural values. Similarly, Aghion et al. (2010) highlight the fact that trust and entry regulation can be substitutes, as low-trust economies demand entry regulation to prevent entrepreneurs with limited civic values from imposing negative externalities on the market. In the same vein, Carlin et al. (2009) consider the functioning of financial markets and suggest that trust and regulation are substitutes or complements depending on the extent of social capital in the society. More recently, Bisin and Verdier (2024) provide an example of dynamics between civic culture, corruption and political empowerment of the civil society that suggest that the relationship between culture and institutional structures can be complements or substitutes depending on technological fundamentals of the social environment.

Migliaccio and Verdier (2018) provide an example where the degree of complementarity/substitutability between culture and institutions is time varying. Specifically, they analyze how cooperative cultural traits spread spatially and lead to social segregation institutions shaped by political processes at the level of local communities. In their set-up, local cultural transmission is influenced by parental efforts and a random spatial noise. Assortative matching allows cooperators to partially segregate, but its degree is endogenous and costly. Using reaction-diffusion equations on a continuum space, the analysis shows how cooperation spreads via a *traveling wave*, enabling localized clusters to expand and influence broader spatial populations.[57] The equilibrium assortativity level evolves non-monotonically during spatial diffusion. In places where cooperators and segmentation are absent, an assortative matching

---

[56] See Benabou et al. (2015) and Seror (2018) for a discussion of these externalities.

[57] Technically, this approach differs from agent-based simulations models analyzing cooperation in discrete spatial environments such as lattice or networks frameworks. Considering spatial diffusion on a continuum space, allows the application of mathematical techniques and results from partial differential reaction-diffusion equations theory, with the derivation of analytical results on the spatial evolution of cooperation and assortative matching institutions.

mechanism emerges and spreads. However, as cooperators grow locally in number, it eventually fades away. Culture and institutions initially complement each other, but later become substitutes, shaping the diffusion dynamics of cooperative behavior.

Asano (2022) also exhibits an example where the relationship between cultural and institutional dynamics can be time varying. He examines the coevolution of trust and legal institutions in competitive credit markets. Entrepreneurs can be civic (productive) or uncivic (cheating), with their true intentions being private information, and enforcement quality shaping their incentives. Strong enforcement benefits civic entrepreneurs by reducing cross-subsidization of uncivic ones but harms uncivic entrepreneurs. Voting dynamics determine enforcement: high-trust economies (with many civic entrepreneurs) support strong enforcement, while low-trust economies prefer weak enforcement. Civic values evolve according to a transmission process a la Bisin and Verdier (2001a,b). This influences long-term institutional quality, potentially leading to an underdevelopment trap with weak enforcement and distrust. Interestingly, long-term complementarity between trust and enforcement contrasts with short-term substitutability. Indeed, during transitions where uncivic entrepreneurs are pivotal political agents, higher trust improves the long run establishment of civic entrepreneurs who support enforcement, but it also leads in the short run, uncivic ones to vote for weaker enforcement to exploit the benefits of cheating.

5 Future avenues for research

As testified by the literature reviewed above, substantial advances have been made in the economic theory of cultural transmission. This has generated significant insights on how cultural diversity evolves and how it may persist. Furthermore, cultural transmission processes have been embedded into models aimed at better understanding e.g., economic growth and development, political economy, long-run historical phenomena, and environmental sustainability issues. In this last section, we conclude by briefly discussing three areas that, in our opinion, merit further attention in future research.

5.1 Cumulative culture and the transmission of cultural systems

Most economic theories of cultural transmission focus on the evolution of individual cultural traits. However, culture typically consists of packages of traits, suggesting an "extensive margin" alongside the "intensive margin" of trait frequency in the population. This conceptualization of culture aligns well with the notion of *cumulative culture* in evolutionary anthropology and biology, which we discuss in Section 2. When culture is cumulative, information accumulates over time to create complex artifacts and knowledge beyond the capability of a single generation. Research in this area explores how the amount and complexity of culture evolve dynamically, often examining constraints on cumulative cultural evolution, and identifying its determinants.[58]

Cultural systems of multiple traits have been studied with the help of graph-theory and agent-based models (Buskell et al., 2019; Jansson et al., 2021), but they lack explicit socio-economic context modeling.[59] Recently, Acemoglu and Robinson (2025) propose a hierarchical cultural framework with various attributes, building upon the insights from cultural sociology which sees culture as a "toolkit" of attributes that individuals use to shape and justify their actions (Swidler, 1986; Alexander, 2003; DiMaggio and Markus, 2010). They discuss how the fluidity of the cultural system depends on the nature of the attributes, their connectivity, and specific social and political contexts. They do not however explore population-level cultural transmission or diffusion, which remains a significant challenge.

Population dynamics of cultural systems can bring new and interesting insights on the dynamics of culture and its interactions with socio-economic contexts. It may identify conditions for the emergence of cultural clusterings, self-organization, and path dependency. It may also illustrate how connections between traits contribute to modulating rates of cultural change, in turn providing a better understanding of slow-moving cultural change (Roland, 2004) as opposed to fast-moving fads and fashions.[60]

5.2 The economic geography of cultural transmission

Cultural specificities persist and differ significantly across space, e.g., neighborhoods or cities. At the same time, cultural traits also tend to spatially diffuse, whether directly through cultural contacts of the population carrying the trait, or indirectly through trade and exchange of goods implicitly embodying cultural information. Few economic models of cultural transmission focus explicitly on these spatial and geographic dimensions.

As already mentioned, Migliaccio and Verdier (2018) is an example applying the theory of reaction-diffusion models to analyze the spatial transmission and diffusion of a cooperative cultural trait. In this set-up, the spatial dispersal of the trait evolves according to a simple random walk process. This leaves

---

58 For instance, Henrich (2004) and Kobayashi and Aoki (2012) analyze how larger populations directly facilitate cumulative cultural evolution through biased cultural transmission models. Derex and Boyd (2016) and Derex et al. (2018) show that population structure critically affects cumulative culture, Smolla and Akçay (2023) consider the co-evolution of cumulative culture and social networks.

59 See as well Enquist et al. (2011) for a general formal framework to study stepwise modification, differentiation or combination of elements in cultural systems.

60 In the terminology of Acemoglu and Robinson (2025), cultural sets may be expanding or contracting at low frequency, while cultural attributes may be wired and rewired at higher frequency; enriching the span of plausible responses to changes in the socio-economic environment, at different time scales.

aside any relevant economic aspect related to geographic mobility or location decisions. Specifically, an important insight from economic geography and urban economics has been to identify the source of agglomeration and diffusion forces which affect the spatial distribution of socio-economic activities and their associated amenities and opportunity costs. In economic models of cultural transmission, such elements are likely to impact cultural socialization strategies and the dynamics of the spatial distribution of cultural traits. These features have started to be illustrated in Bezin and Moizeau (2017) and Bezin et al. (2022) in the context of education and crime, respectively. They provide examples of models of neighborhood formation and cultural transmission, showing how the tension between culture preservation and socioeconomic integration drives the pattern of segregation in the city.[61]

More generally, a promising area for future research might be to construct spatial models that incorporate explicitly the two dimensions of agglomeration/dispersion forces related to the location of socio-economic activities, and the transmission of cultural traits that are functional (or not) to these activities. Such an approach is expected to generate an economic geography theory of the emergence/persistence of cultural clusters and their association to specific markets and spatial infrastructures. Given the feedback effects and externalities that exist in spatial economic contexts, this can also be useful to derive interesting policy implications.

5.3 Equilibrium models of culture, institutions, and growth

As we noted in Section 4, a recent literature has successfully embedded cultural transmission and institutional change to study the dynamics of several important long-run historical phenomena. With regards to specific comparative historical contexts of differential growth, Greif and Tabellini (2017) and Bisin et al. (2024) are the main examples of this approach. More generally, however, after the large literature on endogenous growth theory,[62] studies of the determinants of long-run growth and development in economics i) have widened in focus, to account for various relevant socio-economic activities characterizing economic development – like the formation of democratic and autocratic institutions, voting participation, public health, gender and racial equality, ethnic fractionalization; ii) are searching for explanatory factors of long-run growth in persistent cultural and institutional factors.[63]

61 In the context of international labor mobility, Rapoport et al. (2020) also present a theoretical model of migration-based cultural change that investigates how migration affects cultural proximity between home and host countries.

62 See e.g., Aghion and Howitt (2008) and Acemoglu (2009) for book-length treatments of the subject.

63 Inspiration for these analyses is found, e.g., in the early work of Douglass North (North and Thomas, 1973) and Avner Greif (Greif, 1989; 1993). But this literature in its current form has its origin in Acemoglu et al. (2001) and the subsequent work of Daron Acemoglu, James Robinson and coauthors; see Bisin and Federico (2021) for detailed analyses and discussions of this approach.

In this context, theoretical models that center on institutional change and on the interaction of culture and institutions are a first step toward a novel theory of long-run growth and development. So far, these models lack however a fully integrated analysis of culture, institutions, and the various relevant socio-economic activities that contribute to economic development. Theoretical contributions along these lines are challenging, due to the high degree of heterogeneity and dimensionality of the dynamical system to be studied. However, these technical aspects have been at the center of the macroeconomic literature with heterogeneous agents (Krusell and Smith, 2006; Achdou et al., 2022) and dynamic political macroeconomic models (Hassler et al., 2003). Adapting the tools developed in this literature to study general equilibrium models of growth with cultural and institutional change could provide interesting qualitative insights, aligned with historical narratives. It will also generate quantitative implications clarifying the total and relative influence of culture and institutions on development, beyond the standard focus of first-order causal effects which are at the core of the wealth of recent *persistence studies*.[64]

Appendix A Extensions

In this appendix we indicate several extensions of interest.

A.1 Within cultural group heterogeneity and cultural socialization

We consider the effect of economic heterogeneity within cultural trait groups on the cultural dynamics. For this assume now that all the socioeconomic parameters $u^i(.)$ and ΔV^i are the same across members of the two cultural groups, but the resource R is heterogeneously distributed within group i according to a cumulative distribution $F_i(.)$.

First, denote for convenience the minimum economic cost $C(w, d)$ for a parent to reach a given level of socialization rate $d = d(f(m_i, l_i))$ where $d(.)$ is an increasing concave function such that $d(0) = 0$ and $d(\infty) = 1$, and $f(m_i, l_i)$ is a standard production function concave in each argument and with constant returns to scale:

$$C(w, d) = \min_{m_i, l_i} m_i + wl_i, \tag{14}$$
$$d(f(m_i, l_i)) = d.$$

Standard properties of the socialization production function provide that $C(w, d)$ can be rewritten as $C(w, d) = c(w)\varphi(d)$ with $c(w)$ an increasing concave function of the productivity w and $\varphi(d)$ an increasing convex function

64 See Bisin and Moro (2021), Voth (2021), and several other contributions in Bisin and Federico (2021) for overviews of the literature on persistence studies.

of d such that $\varphi(0) = 0$ and $\varphi(1) = +\infty$. Using the budget constraint, the socialization problem of a typical parent of type i can then be stated as

$$\max_{d^i} u^i(R + w - c(w)\varphi(d^i)) + P^{ii}(d^i, q^i)V^{ii} + P^{ij}(d^i, q^i)V^{ij}.$$

Then the socialization rate of that parent with trait i and resource R is given by $d^i\left(R, q^i\right) = d^*(R, w, q^i, \Delta V)$ solution of the equation

$$c(w)\varphi'(d^*) \cdot u'(R + w - c(w)\varphi(d^*)) = (1 - q^i)\Delta V.$$

It is easy to see that the dynamic evolution of the cultural population therefore is then given by:

$$\dot{q_t^i} = q_t^i(1 - q_t^i)\left[\int d^i\left(R, q_t^i\right) dF_i(R) - \int d^j\left(R, q_t^j\right) dF_j(R)\right].$$

Consider then the fact that the resource R is more unequally distributed across individuals with trait j than across individuals with trait i, in the sense that the distribution $F_j(.)$ is a mean-preserving spread of $F_i(.)$. By Jensen's inequality, it is easy to see that the effect of such distributional difference on the dynamics of culture will depend on whether the individual vertical socialization rate $d^i\left(R, q_t^i\right)$ is a convex or a concave function of R. When it is convex, then the trait where the resource is more unequally distributed has a relatively higher cultural fitness than the other trait. The converse holds when the vertical socialization rate $d^i\left(R, q_t^i\right)$ is concave in R. In particular, at a second order approximation of the concave utility function $u(.)$, and when the socialization rate function $d^i\left(R, q_t^i\right)$ is also concave in R, we easily prove the following result:

Result. *Assume that the functions $u(.)$ and $\varphi(.)$ are such that $u''' \geq 0$ and $2\varphi''^2 < \varphi'\varphi'''$. Then the socialization rate $d^i\left(R, q_t^i\right)$ is concave in R, and, ceteris paribus, the trait associated to a more equal distribution of resources R is more likely to prevail in the long run cultural dynamics of the population.*

Indeed from the FOC, one gets that $d^*(R, w, q^i, \Delta V)$ is satisfying:

$$c(w)\varphi'(d^*) \cdot u'(R + w - c(w)\varphi(d^*)) = (1 - q^i)\Delta V$$

and thus differentiation provides (with obvious notations):

$$\frac{\partial d^*}{\partial R} = \frac{-u''\varphi'}{\varphi'' \cdot u' - c\left[\varphi'\right]^2 \cdot u''} > 0.$$

Observe as well that

$$1 - c\varphi'\frac{\partial d^*}{\partial R} = \frac{\varphi'' \cdot u'}{\varphi'' \cdot u' - c\left[\varphi'\right]^2 \cdot u''} > 0.$$

Differentiating another time provides that the sign of $\frac{\partial^2 d^*}{\partial R^2}$ is the same as the sign of

$$A = \begin{array}{c} \left[-u'''\varphi'\left(1-c\varphi'\frac{\partial d^*}{\partial R}\right)-u''\varphi''\frac{\partial d^*}{\partial R}\right]\left[\varphi''\cdot u'-c\left[\varphi'\right]^2\cdot u''\right] \\ +u''\varphi'\left[\begin{array}{c} \varphi'''\frac{\partial d^*}{\partial R}\cdot u'+\varphi''\cdot u''\left(1-c\varphi'\frac{\partial d^*}{\partial R}\right) \\ -2c\varphi''\varphi'\frac{\partial d^*}{\partial R}\cdot u''-c\left[\varphi'\right]^2\cdot u'''\left(1-c\varphi'\frac{\partial d^*}{\partial R}\right) \end{array}\right] \end{array}.$$

Note that A can be decomposed into two terms:

$$B = -u'''\varphi'\left(1-c\varphi'\frac{\partial d^*}{\partial R}\right)\left[\varphi''\cdot u'-c\left[\varphi'\right]^2\cdot u''\right] - u''\varphi'c\left[\varphi'\right]^2\cdot u'''\left(1-c\varphi'\frac{\partial d^*}{\partial R}\right)$$

and

$$C = -u''\varphi''\frac{\partial d^*}{\partial R}\left[\varphi''\cdot u'-c\left[\varphi'\right]^2\cdot u''\right] + u''\varphi'\left[\varphi'''\frac{\partial d^*}{\partial R}\cdot u'+\varphi''\cdot u''\left(1-3c\varphi'\frac{\partial d^*}{\partial R}\right)\right].$$

The sign of B is negative when $u''' \geq 0$ (recalling that $1-c\varphi'\frac{\partial d^*}{\partial R} > 0$ and $\varphi'' > 0$) as B rewrites as:

$$B = u'''\left(1-c\varphi'\frac{\partial d^*}{\partial R}\right)\left[-\varphi'\varphi''\cdot u'\right] < 0.$$

The sign of C is the same as the sign of

$$D = \frac{\partial d^*}{\partial R}\left(\varphi''^2-\varphi'\varphi'''\right)\cdot u' + \frac{\partial d^*}{\partial R}2c\varphi'^2\varphi''u'' - \varphi'\varphi''\cdot u''.$$

Substituting the value of $\frac{\partial d^*}{\partial R}$ and rearranging terms after tedious but straightforward calculations provides that

$$D = \frac{-\varphi'\left(\varphi''^2-\varphi'\varphi'''\right)\cdot u'u''}{\varphi''\cdot u'-c\left[\varphi'\right]^2\cdot u''} - \varphi'\varphi''\cdot u''\left[\frac{\varphi''\cdot u'+cu''\varphi'^2}{\varphi''\cdot u'-c\left[\varphi'\right]^2\cdot u''}\right].$$

Thus $D < 0$ when

$$\left[-\varphi'\left(\varphi''^2-\varphi'\varphi'''\right)\cdot u'u''\right] - \varphi'\varphi''\cdot u''\left[\varphi''\cdot u'+cu''\varphi'^2\right] < 0$$

or

$$\left(-u''\right)\left[\left(2\varphi''^2-\varphi'\varphi'''\right)\varphi'u'+\varphi''cu''\varphi'^3\right] < 0.$$

Thus when $2\varphi''^2 - \varphi'\varphi''' < 0$, we have $D < 0$.

Collecting these results we see that $2\varphi''^2 < \varphi'\varphi'''$ and $u''' \geq 0$ are sufficient conditions for $\frac{\partial^2 d^*}{\partial R^2} < 0$. □

A.2 The domain of cultural traits

A first line of research has been to expand the domain of the cultural traits transmitted across generations, allowing in particular for multiple (more than 2) discrete traits and for a continuum of traits. This extension is important as it naturally introduces a topology over cultural traits.

Multiple (discrete) traits

An important contribution along these lines has been the extension of the cultural transmission model in Bisin and Verdier (2001a,b) (from now on BV), pursued by Bisin et al. (2009) and Montgomery (2010), to a domain of $n > 2$ discrete trait values. Consider for instance the direct extension of the dynamics in Eq. (1) to n cultural traits:

$$\dot{q}^i = q^i\left[d^i - \sum_j q^j d^j\right], \text{ for all } i = 1, \dots n. \tag{15}$$

Clearly, when the transmission rates d^i's are exogenous, the dynamic converges from every interior state to a homogeneous distribution centered on trait $i \in \arg\max_i \{d^i\}_{i=1}^n$. Allowing for endogenous parental socialization à la BV, we obtain instead the following dynamics:

$$\dot{q}^i = q^i\left[C'^{-1}(\sum_j q^j \Delta V^{ij}) - \sum_j q^j C'^{-1}(\sum_k q^k \Delta V^{jk})\right], \text{ for all } i = 1, \dots n. \tag{16}$$

When the cost function $C(d)$ takes a simple quadratic form $C(d) = c\frac{d^2}{2}$, Eq. (16) rewrites as

$$\dot{q}^i = q^i\left[\sum_j q^j \frac{\Delta V^{ij}}{c} - \sum_j \sum_k q^j q^k \frac{\Delta V^{jk}}{c}\right], \text{ for all } i = 1, \dots n,$$

which represents the replicator dynamics of an $n \times n$ random matching evolutionary game with matrix payoffs $\mathbf{\Delta V} = \left(\Delta V^{ij}/c\right)_{ij \in [1,n]^2}$, once $\Delta V^{ij}/c$ is interpreted as the payoff from playing strategy i against j.[65]

There is therefore a formal connection between cultural transmission and other evolutionary game theory processes. This allows the application of a

65 These replicator dynamics can arise from natural selection, imitation, and reinforcement learning (see Young (1998) and Sandholm (2010)).

large body of results about the replicator dynamics to study cultural evolution. Specifically, suppose for instance that $\Delta V^{ij} = \Delta V^i$ for all $j \neq i$ (and $\Delta V^{ii} = 0$); that is, suppose that each group's *cultural paternalism* does not depend on the identity of the other group. Then the evolutionary game structure associated to the cultural transmission model is a *strictly stable* game. There is a unique distribution of traits, $q^i = \frac{1}{n}$, which is globally asymptotically stable and every trajectory of the replicator dynamics in the interior of the n-dimensional simplex converges to this state. Importantly, this implies, again, persistent cultural diversity in the limit.[66]

Continuous traits

A well established tradition in evolutionary biology and anthropology considers continuous traits models of cultural transmission. These models postulate a dynamic of cultural traits which is driven by exogenous linear mixing (Cavalli Sforza and Feldman (1973); Otto et al. (1994)).

Formally, consider a finite population of N dynasties. Each representative individual of dynasty i at time t is characterized by the intensity of a cultural trait $H_t^i \in (0, \infty)$ that he/she holds during his/her lifetime. Transmission from one generation to the next results from vertical and oblique transmission. Specifically, let $d^i \in (0, 1)$ represent vertical socialization by parents of type i and let oblique transmission be represented as a weighted average of various role models in society, $G_t^i = \sum_{j=1}^{j=N} \phi^{ij} H_t^j$; where $\Phi = \left[\phi^{ij}\right]_{i,j}$ is a row stochastic matrix reflecting the social connectivity of oblique influence across the different dynasties. Cultural dynamics then is postulated to follow the process

$$\dot{H}^i = (1 - d^i)(G^i - H^i). \tag{17}$$

Let $H = \left(H^j\right)_{i=1,N}$ denote the population N-dimensional vector of the cultural trait, I the identity matrix of dimension N, and T a diagonal matrix of dimension N where the ith diagonal element is d^i. The cultural dynamics can then be written in matrix form:

$$\dot{H} = (Z - I) \cdot H, \quad Z = T + (I - T)\Phi.$$

The matrix Z is a row stochastic matrix reflecting the force of the cultural inheritance blending process resulting from the interaction between vertical and oblique transmission. When the vertical influence weights d^i are exogenous, and the matrix Z is irreducible and noncyclic, the evolutionary process induces

66 A recent interesting application of this general multiple-trait transmission model is Wu and Zhang (2022), which specializes the *cultural paternalism* structure to analyze conditions for the emergence of polarization of ideologies, exploiting the implied topology of traits.

homogeneity of the trait, leading to a "melting-pot" equilibrium, in which the value of the cultural trait is the same across the population.[67]

With a proper probabilistic structure of cultural transmission, however, cultural diversity may still be obtained in the limit, once again as a consequence of *cultural substitution*. Indeed, this is the main result obtained by Cheung and Wu (2018), in an elegant extension of BV along these lines. Specifically, consider a population of unit mass, where each agent in the population has a trait from set $H = [0, 1]$. Denote by $\Delta V^{zy} := V^{zz} - V^{zy}$ the *cultural paternalistic motive* of a z-parent toward trait $y \in H$, with $\Delta V^{zy} \geq 0$, $= 0$ only if $y = z$. A population state over H is described by its probability distribution μ. Denoting by $d^z(\mu)$ the socialization rate exerted by a z-parent at population state μ, the cultural evolutionary dynamic is characterized by a differential equation for all (integrable) subset of traits $J \subseteq H$ of the following form:

$$\dot{\mu}(J) = \underbrace{\int_{y\in J}\int_{z\in H\setminus J}(1 - d^z(\mu))\mu(dz)\mu(dy)}_{\text{inflows}} - \underbrace{\int_{y\in J}\int_{z\in H\setminus J}(1 - d^y(\mu))\mu(dy)\mu(dz)}_{\text{outflows}}. \tag{18}$$

Intuitively, $\dot{\mu}(J)$, the change in the mass of agents with traits in set J, is equal to the "inflow" of children whose parents' traits are not in set J, minus the "outflow" of children whose parents' traits are in set J. In this context, *cultural substitutability* is defined by the socialization rate $d^z(\mu)$ being an increasing function of the average intolerance of group z at population state μ, $\Delta V^z(\mu) = \int_{y\in H} \Delta V^{zy}\mu(dy)$. As in Bisin and Verdier (2001a,b) *cultural substitution* is satisfied by this cultural transmission process μ and the cultural dynamics with continuous traits satisfy the following:

$$\dot{\mu}(J) = \int_{y\in J} \Delta V^y(\mu)\mu(dy) - \mu(J)\int_{z\in H} \Delta V^z(\mu)\mu(dz). \tag{19}$$

As Montgomery (2010) for discrete traits, Cheung and Wu (2018) note a formal connection with evolutionary game dynamics: the cultural dynamics of continuous traits in Eq. (19) is equivalent to a continuous strategy type replicator dynamics (Oechssler and Riedel, 2001). Using sophisticated measure theory tools for such dynamic systems, they show that cultural substitutability is again essential for the preservation of long run cultural heterogeneity. Furthermore, when an agent's cultural paternalistic motive toward another agent ΔV^{zy} is an increasing convex function of their cultural distance $|z - y|$, Cheung and Wu

67 On the other hand, Brueckner and Smirnov (2007; 2008) show that cyclicity of the matrix Z preserves the possibility of long term heterogeneity.

(2018) show that only the most extremely polarized state distribution with mass points at the extreme traits $z=0$ and $z=1$ is a stable limit point of the cultural dynamics, replicating the results for discrete traits transmission found in Wu and Zhang (2022).

A.3 Dynastic forward looking cultural transmission

An implicit assumption of most economic models of cultural transmission is the fact that parents, when socializing their children, do not take into account how children themselves will raise their grandchildren. While there may be cognitive reasons for the existence of such myopia, parents might also take a more "dynastic" perspective of the transmission of their cultural traits across generations. One key aspect that arises in such a context, is the fact that parents need to take into account that their children will solve a similar problem as themselves, problem which replicates itself at each generational level. This creates a proper dynamic game between all generations. Spiro (2020) presents a simple linear-quadratic framework analyzing such decisions of multigenerational transmission of culture.

The basic model consists of a dynasty with an infinite sequence of overlapping generations indexed by $i \in \mathbb{N}$. Each generation consists of one individual referred to as i, who is "the parent" of individual $i+1$ referred to as "the child". Each i in the dynasty is associated with a type $t_i \in \mathbb{R}$ and takes an action $s^i \in \mathbb{R}$. The game is sequential so that i takes her action before $i+1$, who in turn takes her action before $i+2$, and so on. The socialization problem of parent i is the following:

$$\min_{s^i} L(s^i, t^i) = \min_{s^i} \left[\frac{\left(t^i - s^i\right)^2}{2} + \sum_{h=1}^{h=\infty} \beta^h \frac{\left(t^i - \widetilde{s}^{i+h}\right)^2}{2} \right] \tag{20}$$

under the constraints:

$$t^{i+h} = \alpha \widetilde{s}^{i+h-1} + (1-\alpha)\overline{s}^{i+h-1}, \tag{21}$$

$$\widetilde{s}^{i+h} = \arg\min_{s^{i+h}} L(s^{i+h}, t^{i+h}). \tag{22}$$

Eq. (20) states that parent i gets a disutility loss when taking an action s^i that differs from her bliss point type t^i, and when also all future generations' optimal actions $\widetilde{s}^{i+h}$ differ from her type. The parent discounts this utility loss at a rate $\beta \in]0,1[$ the further away the generation. (21) states that the type of an individual t^{i+h} is determined by a weighted average of her parent's action $\widetilde{s}^{i+h-1}$ (the vertical transmission channel) and some other action in society $\overline{s}_{i+j-1}$ (the oblique transmission channel). $\alpha \in]0,1[$ captures the relative importance of the vertical channel. In the simplest version of the model, $\overline{s}_{i+j-1}$ is assumed to be constant in all generations and normalized to zero. Finally, the last Eq. (22) reflects the fact that each subsequent generation $i+h$ solves the same problem as the parent, taking her own preferences type t^{i+h} into account.

Taking into account this chain of intergenerational transmission of preferences when trying to affect future generations, the first-order condition for the parent writes as:

$$-\left(t^i - s^i\right) - \sum_{h=1}^{h=\infty} \beta^h \left(t^i - \widetilde{s}^{i+h}\right) \frac{d\widetilde{s}^{i+h}}{ds^i} = 0 \tag{23}$$

where the transmission to future generations is captured by the derivatives $\frac{d\widetilde{s}^{i+h}}{ds^i}$. Given the quadratic nature of the objective function, it is natural to focus on linear Markov Perfect Equilibria of the form $s^{i*}(t^i) = C \cdot t^i$ for all $i \geq 0$ where C is a constant to be determined. Assuming this form of intergenerational strategy, the equilibrium value C^* is characterized by a fixed point equation derived from (21) and (23).[68]

Solving this equation, it can be seen that $C^* > 1$, namely agents behave more extremely than their own type, and that the more extreme a type is the more she extremizes (i.e. $s^{i*}(t^i) - t^i$ is increasing in t^i). Still, there is dynastic integration as $t^{i+1} = \alpha C^* t^i < t^i$. Intuitively, forward looking parents anticipate that over their dynasty, their own trait will converge toward the external trait $\overline{s} = 0$. To fight against this process, they "overshoot" the trait they transfer to their child. Still, this is not enough to prevent convergence, and the best they can do is to reduce the speed of convergence toward $\overline{s} = 0$.[69]

References

Abrams, D., Hogg, M.A., 1988. Comments on the motivational status of self-esteem in social identity and intergroup discrimination. European Journal of Social Psychology 18 (4), 317–334.

Acemoglu, D., 2009. Introduction to Modern Economic Growth. Princeton University Press, Princeton.

Acemoglu, D., Egorov, G., Sonin, K., 2010. Political selection and persistence of bad governments. Quarterly Journal of Economics 125 (4), 1511–1575.

Acemoglu, D., Egorov, G., Sonin, K., 2021. Institutional change and institutional persistence. In: Bisin, A., Federico, G. (Eds.), Handbook of Historical Economics. Elsevier North Holland, Amsterdam, pp. 365–389.

Acemoglu, D., Johnson, S., Robinson, J.A., 2001. The colonial origins of comparative development: an empirical investigation. American Economic Review 91 (5), 1369–1401.

68 (21) implies $s^{i+h} = (C\alpha)^h s^i$. Substitution in (23) and manipulations yields that C^* is the solution of

$$C^* = \frac{1 - \beta\left(C^*\alpha\right)^2}{1 - \beta\left(C^*\alpha\right)}.$$

69 The model can be extended to the case with two groups influencing each other, that is where the child's type of a given group is influenced both by her own parent's behavior (with weight α), but also by the behavior of the parent in the other group (with weight $1-\alpha$).

Acemoglu, D., Johnson, S., Robinson, J.A., 2006. Institutions as the fundamental cause of long-run growth. In: Aghion, P., Durlauf, S. (Eds.), Handbook of Economic Growth, vol. 1A. Elsevier North Holland, Amsterdam, pp. 386–472.

Acemoglu, D., Robinson, J.A., 2000. Why did the West extend the franchise? Democracy, inequality, and growth in historical perspective. Quarterly Journal of Economics 115 (4), 1167–1199.

Acemoglu, D., Robinson, J.A., 2001. A theory of political transitions. American Economic Review 91 (4), 938–963.

Acemoglu, D., Robinson, J.A., 2006. Economic Origins of Dictatorship and Democracy. Cambridge University Press, Cambridge.

Acemoglu, Daron, Robinson, James A., 2025. Culture, institutions, and social equilibria: a framework. Journal of Economic Literature 63 (2), 637–692.

Achdou, Y., et al., 2022. Income and wealth distribution in macroeconomics: a continuous-time approach. Review of Economic Studies 89 (1), 45–86.

Adriani, F., Matheson, J.A., Sonderegger, S., 2018. Teaching by example and induced beliefs in a model of cultural transmission. Journal of Economic Behavior and Organization 145, 511–529.

Adriani, F., Sonderegger, S., 2018. Signaling about norms: socialization under strategic uncertainty. Scandinavian Journal of Economics 120 (3), 685–716.

Aghion, P., Algan, Y., Cahuc, P., 2011. Civil society and the state: the interplay between cooperation and minimum wage regulation. Journal of the European Economic Association 9 (1), 3–42.

Aghion, P., Algan, Y., Cahuc, P., Shleifer, A., 2010. Regulation and distrust. Quarterly Journal of Economics 125 (3), 1015–1049.

Aghion, P., Howitt, P.W., 2008. The Economics of Growth. MIT Press, Cambridge, MA.

Akerlof, G.A., Kranton, R.E., 2000. Economics and identity. Quarterly Journal of Economics 115 (3), 715–753.

Alesina, A., Algan, Y., et al., 2015. Family values and the regulation of labor. Journal of the European Economic Association 13 (4), 599–630.

Alesina, A., Giuliano, P., 2015. Culture and institutions. Journal of Economic Literature 53 (4), 898–944.

Alesina, A., Giuliano, P., Reich, B., 2021. Nation-building and education. Economic Journal 131 (638), 2273–2303.

Alexander, J.C., 2003. The Meanings of Social Life: A Cultural Sociology. Oxford University Press, New York.

Allport, G.W., 1953. The psychological nature of personality. The Personalist 34 (4), 347–357.

Almagro, M., Andrés-Cerezo, D., 2020. The construction of national identities. Theoretical Economics 15, 763–810.

Asano, K., 2022. Trust and law in credit markets. Economica 89 (354), 332–361.

Bar-El, R., et al., 2013. The evolution of secularization: cultural transmission, religion and fertility—theory, simulations and evidence. Journal of Population Economics 26, 1129–1174.

Bar-Gill, S., Fershtman, C., 2016. Integration policy: cultural transmission with endogenous fertility. Journal of Population Economics 29, 105–133.

Baudin, T., 2010. A role for cultural transmission in fertility transitions. Macroeconomic Dynamics 14 (4), 454–481.

Baudin, T., Hiller, V., 2019. On the dynamics of gender differences in preferences. Oxford Economic Papers 71 (3), 503–527.

Becker, G.S., 1973. A theory of marriage: Part I. Journal of Political Economy 81 (4), 813–846.

Benabou, R., Ticchi, D., Vindigni, A., 2015. Religion and innovation. American Economic Review 105 (5), 346–351.

Besley, T., 2017. Aspirations and the political economy of inequality. Oxford Economic Papers 69, 1–35.

Besley, T., 2020. State capacity, reciprocity, and the social contract. Econometrica 88 (4), 1307–1335.

Besley, T., Persson, T., 2009. The origins of state capacity: property rights, taxation, and politics. American Economic Review 99 (4), 1218–1244.
Besley, T., Persson, T., 2011a. Pillars of Prosperity: The Political Economics of Development Clusters. Princeton University Press, Princeton.
Besley, T., Persson, T., 2011b. The logic of political violence. Quarterly Journal of Economics 126 (3), 1411–1445.
Besley, T., Persson, T., 2019a. JEEA-FBBVA lecture 2017: the dynamics of environmental politics and values. Journal of the European Economic Association 17, 993–1024.
Besley, T., Persson, T., 2019b. Democratic values and institutions. American Economic Review: Insights 1, 59–76.
Besley, T., Persson, T., 2020a. Escaping the climate trap? Values, technologies, and politics. Stockholm University. Mimeo.
Besley, T., Persson, T., 2020b. The joint dynamics of organizational culture, design, and performance. LSE. Mimeo.
Besley, T., Persson, T., 2021. The rise of identity politics: policy, political organization, and nationalist dynamics. Stockholm University. Mimeo.
Bezin, E., 2015. A cultural model of private provision and the environment. Journal of Environmental Economics and Management 71, 109–124.
Bezin, E., 2019. The economics of green consumption, cultural transmission and sustainable technological change. Journal of Economic Theory 181, 497–546.
Bezin, E., Moizeau, F., 2017. Cultural dynamics, social mobility and urban segregation. Journal of Urban Economics 99, 173–187.
Bezin, E., Verdier, T., Zenou, Y., 2022. Crime, broken families, and punishment. American Economic Journal: Microeconomics 14 (4), 723–760.
Bidner, C., Francois, P., 2011. Cultivating trust: norms, institutions and the implications of scale. Economic Journal 121 (555), 1097–1129.
Bisin, A., 2020. A comment on: State capacity, reciprocity, and the social contract by Timothy Besley. Econometrica 88 (4), 1345–1349.
Bisin, A., 2024. Review of: Modeling Social Behavior: Mathematical and Agent-Based Models of Social Dynamics and Cultural Evolution, by P. Smaldino.
Bisin, A., Federico, G., 2021. The Handbook of Historical Economics. Academic Press.
Bisin, A., Moro, A., 2021. LATE for history. In: Bisin, A., Federico, G. (Eds.), Handbook of Historical Economics. Elsevier North Holland, pp. 269–296.
Bisin, A., Patacchini, E., et al., 2011. Formation and persistence of oppositional identities. European Economic Review 55 (8), 1046–1071.
Bisin, A., Rubin, J., et al., 2024. Culture, institutions and the long divergence. Journal of Economic Growth 29 (1), 1–40.
Bisin, A., Topa, G., Verdier, T., 2004a. Cooperation as a transmitted cultural trait. Rationality and Society 16 (4), 477–507.
Bisin, A., Topa, G., Verdier, T., 2004b. Religious intermarriage and socialization in the United States. Journal of Political Economy 112 (3), 615–664.
Bisin, A., Topa, G., Verdier, T., 2009. Cultural transmission, socialization and the population dynamics of multiple-trait distributions. International Journal of Economic Theory 5 (1), 139–154.
Bisin, A., Tura, G., 2019. Marriage, fertility, and cultural integration in Italy. Tech. Rep. W26303. National Bureau of Economic Research.
Bisin, A., Verdier, T., 1998. On the cultural transmission of preferences for social status. Journal of Public Economics 70 (1), 75–97.
Bisin, A., Verdier, T., 2000. Beyond the melting pot: cultural transmission, marriage, and the evolution of ethnic and religious traits. Quarterly Journal of Economics 115 (3), 955–988.
Bisin, A., Verdier, T., 2001a. Agents with imperfect empathy may survive natural selection. Economics Letters 71 (2), 277–285.

Bisin, A., Verdier, T., 2001b. The economics of cultural transmission and the dynamics of preferences. Journal of Economic Theory 97 (2), 298–319.
Bisin, A., Verdier, T., 2005. Work ethic and redistribution: a cultural transmission model of the welfare state. NYU. Mimeo.
Bisin, A., Verdier, T., 2010. The economics of cultural transmission and socialization. In: Benhabib, J., Bisin, A., Jackson, M. (Eds.), Handbook of Social Economics. Elsevier North Holland, pp. 339–416.
Bisin, A., Verdier, T., 2014. Trade and cultural diversity. In: Ginsburgh, V.A., Throsby, D. (Eds.), Handbook of the Economics of Art and Culture. Elsevier North Holland, pp. 439–484.
Bisin, A., Verdier, T., 2017. On the joint evolution of culture and institutions. No. w23375. National Bureau of Economic Research.
Bisin, A., Verdier, T., 2023. Advances in the economic theory of cultural transmission. Annual Reviews 15, 63–89.
Bisin, A., Verdier, T., 2024. On the joint evolution of culture and political institutions: elites and civil society. Journal of Political Economy 132 (5), 1485–1564.
Bisin, A., Verdier, T., 2026. Culture as nature's mechanism. NYU. Mimeo.
Bowles, S., Gintis, H., 2002. The puzzle of prosociality. Santa Fe Institute. Mimeo.
Boyd, R., Richerson, P.J., 1982. Cultural transmission and the evolution of cooperative behavior. Human Ecology 10, 325–351.
Boyd, R., Richerson, P.J., 1985. Culture and the Evolutionary Process. University of Chicago Press, Chicago.
Boyd, R., Richerson, P.J., 1988a. The evolution of reciprocity in sizable groups. Journal of Theoretical Biology 132 (3), 337–356.
Boyd, R., Richerson, P.J., 1988b. Culture and the Evolutionary Process. University of Chicago Press.
Boyd, R., Richerson, P.J., 2024. Cultural evolution: where we have been and where we are going (maybe). Proceedings of the National Academy of Sciences 121 (48), e2322879121.
Boyd, R., Richerson, P.J., 2026. The nature of culture. In: Enke, B., et al. (Eds.), Handbook of the Economics of Culture. Elsevier North Holland.
Boyd, R., Richerson, P.J., Henrich, J., 2011. The cultural niche: why social learning is essential for human adaptation. Proceedings of the National Academy of Sciences 108 (Suppl. 2), 10918–10925.
Boyd, Robert, Richerson, Peter J., 1976. A simple dual inheritance model of the conflict between social and biological evolution. Zygon: Journal of Religion and Science 11 (3).
Brueckner, J., Smirnov, O., 2007. Workings of the melting pot: social networks and the evolution of population attributes. Journal of Regional Science 47 (2), 209–228.
Brueckner, J., Smirnov, O., 2008. Social networks and the convergence of population attributes: a generalization. Journal of Regional Science 48 (2), 359–365.
Büchel, B., Hellmann, T., Pichler, M.M., 2014. The dynamics of continuous cultural traits in social networks. Journal of Economic Theory 154, 274–309.
Buskell, A., Enquist, M., Jansson, F., 2019. A systems approach to cultural evolution. Palgrave Communications 5 (1), 1–15.
Carlin, B.I., Dorobantu, F., Viswanathan, S., 2009. Public trust, the law, and financial investment. Journal of Financial Economics 92 (3), 321–341.
Carvalho, J.P., 2016. Identity-based organizations. American Economic Review 106, 410–414.
Carvalho, J.P., Koyama, M., Williams, C., 2024. Resisting education. Journal of the European Economic Association 22 (6), 2549–2597.
Carvalho, J.P., Sacks, M., 2024. Radicalization. Economic Journal 134 (659), 1019–1068.
Cavalli Sforza, L.L., Feldman, M.W., 1973. Cultural versus biological inheritance: phenotypic transmission from parent to children. American Journal of Human Genetics 25, 618–637.
Cavalli-Sforza, L.L., Feldman, M.W., 1981. Cultural Transmission and Evolution: A Quantitative Approach. Princeton University Press, Princeton.
Chakraborty, S., Thompson, J.C., Yehoue, E.B., 2016. The culture of entrepreneurship. Journal of Economic Theory 163, 288–317.

Cheung, M.W., Wu, J., 2018. On the probabilistic transmission of continuous cultural traits. Journal of Economic Theory 174, 300–323.
Chiappori, P.A., Salanié, B., Weiss, Y., 2017. Partner choice, investment in children, and the marital college premium. American Economic Review 107 (8), 2109–2167.
Chudek, M., Henrich, J., 2011. Culture–gene coevolution, norm-psychology and the emergence of human prosociality. Trends in Cognitive Sciences 15 (5), 218–226.
Correani, L., Di Dio, F., Garofalo, G., 2010. The evolutionary dynamics of tolerance. Theoretical and Practical Research in Economic Fields 1 (2), 218.
Darity, W., Mason, P., Stewart, J.B., 2006. The economics of identity: the origin and persistence of racial identity norms. Journal of Economic Behavior and Organization 60 (3), 283–305.
Della Lena, S., Dindo, P., 2022. An economic model of acculturation under strategic complements and substitutes. Monash University. Mimeo.
Della Lena, S., Manzoni, E., Panebianco, F., 2021. On the transmission of guilt aversion and the evolution of trust. SSRN WP 3997787.
Della Lena, S., Panebianco, F., 2021. Cultural transmission with incomplete information. Journal of Economic Theory 198, 105373.
Delli Gatti, D., et al., 2022. The impact of growth on the transmission of patience. CESifo Working Paper No. 9829.
Derex, M., Boyd, R., 2015. The foundations of the human cultural niche. Nature Communications 6 (1), 8398.
Derex, M., Boyd, R., 2016. Partial connectivity increases cultural accumulation within groups. Proceedings of the National Academy of Sciences 113, 2982–2987.
Derex, M., Perreault, C., Boyd, R., 2018. Divide and conquer: intermediate levels of population fragmentation maximize cultural accumulation. Philosophical Transactions of the Royal Society B 373, 2171–2180.
Dessi, R., 2008. Collective memory, identity, and cultural investments. American Economic Review 98, 534–560.
DiMaggio, P., Markus, H.R., 2010. Culture and social psychology: converging perspectives. Social Psychology Quarterly 73, 347–352.
Dixit, A., 2009. Governance institutions and economic activity. American Economic Review 99 (1), 5–24.
Doepke, M., Zilibotti, F., 2008. Occupational choice and the spirit of capitalism. Quarterly Journal of Economics 123 (2), 747–793.
Doepke, M., Zilibotti, F., 2014. Culture, entrepreneurship, and growth. In: Aghion, P., Durlauf, S. (Eds.), Handbook of Economic Growth. Elsevier North Holland, pp. 1–48.
Doepke, M., Zilibotti, F., 2017. Parenting with style: altruism and paternalism in intergenerational preference transmission. Econometrica 85 (5), 1331–1356.
Ellis, C., Thompson, J.C., Wu, J., 2020. Labor market characteristics and cultural choice. Journal of Public Economic Theory 22, 1584–1617.
Ely, J.C., Yilankaya, O., 2001. Nash equilibrium and the evolution of preferences. Journal of Economic Theory 97 (2), 255–272.
Enquist, M., Ghirlanda, S., Eriksson, K., 2011. Modelling the evolution and diversity of cumulative culture. Philosophical Transactions of the Royal Society B 366, 412–423.
Eruchimovitch, I., Michaeli, M., Sarid, A., 2024. On the coevolution of individualism and institutions. Journal of Economic Growth 29 (3), 391–432.
Escriche, L., Olcina, G., Sanchez, R., 2004. Gender discrimination and intergenerational transmission of preferences. Oxford Economic Papers 56 (3), 485–511.
Estrella López, O.C., 2003. Social capital and government in the production of public goods. Unpublished.
Farahzadi, S., 2024. Migration for marriage. Available at SSRN: https://ssrn.com/abstract=4982438.
Fehr, E., Fischbacher, U., 2003. The nature of human altruism. Nature 425 (6960), 785–791.
Feldman, M.W., Laland, K.N., 1996. Gene-culture coevolution. In: Evolutionary Ecology and Human Behavior, pp. 139–163.

Fogarty, L., et al., 2024. Half a century of quantitative cultural evolution.

Francois, P., 2002. Social Capital and Economic Development. Routledge.

Francois, P., Zabojnik, J., 2005. Trust, social capital and the process of economic development. Journal of the European Economic Association 3 (1), 51–94.

Gale, D., Shapley, L.S., 1962. College admissions and the stability of marriage. American Mathematical Monthly 69 (1), 9–15.

Galichon, A., Salanié, B., 2022. Cupid's invisible hand: social surplus and identification in matching models. The Review of Economic Studies 89 (5), 2600–2629.

Ghirlanda, S., Enquist, M., 2007. Cumulative culture and explosive demographic transitions. Quality and Quantity 41, 581–600.

Giavazzi, F., Petkov, I., Schiantarelli, F., 2019. Culture: persistence and evolution. Journal of Economic Growth 24, 117–154.

Giuliano, P., Nunn, N., 2021. Understanding cultural persistence and change. The Review of Economic Studies 88 (4), 1541–1581.

Glazer, N., Moynihan, D.P., 1970. Beyond the Melting Pot: The Negroes, Puerto Ricans, Jews, Italians, and Irish of New York City, vol. 63. MIT Press, Cambridge, MA.

Gordon, M.M., 1964. Assimilation in American Life: The Role of Race, Religion, and National Origins. Oxford University Press.

Gorodnichenko, Y., Roland, G., 2017. Culture, institutions, and the wealth of nations. Review of Economics and Statistics 99 (3), 402–416.

Goto, H., 2022. Belief in egalitarianism and meritocracy. International University of Japan. Mimeo.

Gradstein, M., Justman, M., 2002. Education, social cohesion, and economic growth. American Economic Review 92 (4), 1192–1204.

Gradstein, M., Justman, M., 2005. The melting pot and school choice. Journal of Public Economics 89 (5–6), 871–896.

Greif, A., 1989. Reputation and coalitions in medieval trade: evidence on the Maghribi traders. Journal of Economic History 49 (4), 857–882.

Greif, A., 1993. Contract enforceability and economic institutions in early trade: the Maghribi traders' coalition. American Economic Review 83 (3), 525–548.

Greif, A., Tabellini, G., 2017. The clan and the corporation: sustaining cooperation in China and Europe. Journal of Comparative Economics 45 (1), 1–35.

Guirkinger, C., Platteau, J.P., Wahhaj, Z., 2026. Behind the veil of cultural persistence: marriage and divorce in a migrant community. Economic Journal 136 (674), 813–827.

Guiso, L., Sapienza, P., Zingales, L., 2008. Social capital as good culture. Journal of the European Economic Association 6 (2–3), 295–320.

Güth, W., 1995. An evolutionary approach to explaining cooperative behavior by reciprocal incentives. International Journal of Game Theory 24 (4), 323–344.

Güth, W., Yaari, M., 1992a. An evolutionary approach to explain reciprocal behavior in a simple strategic game. In: Witt, U. (Ed.), Explaining Process and Change—Approaches to Evolutionary Economics. University of Michigan Press, pp. 23–34.

Güth, W., Yaari, M., 1992b. Explaining reciprocal behavior in simple strategic games: an evolutionary approach. In: Explaining Process and Change: Approaches to Evolutionary Economics, pp. 23–34.

Guzmán, R.A., Rodríguez-Sickert, C., Rowthorn, R., 2007. When in Rome, do as the Romans do: the coevolution of altruistic punishment, conformist learning, and cooperation. Evolution and Human Behavior 28 (2), 112–117.

Hassler, J., Storesletten, K., Zilibotti, F., 2003. Dynamic political choice in macroeconomics. Journal of the European Economic Association 1 (2–3), 543–552.

Hauk, E., Immordino, G., 2014. Parents, television and cultural change. Economic Journal 124 (579), 1040–1065.

Hauk, E., Mueller, H., 2015. Cultural leaders and the clash of civilizations. Journal of Conflict Resolution 59 (3), 367–400.

Hauk, E., Saez-Marti, M., 2002. On the cultural transmission of corruption. Journal of Economic Theory 107, 311–335.

Henrich, J., 2004. Demography and cultural evolution: how adaptive cultural processes can produce maladaptive losses—the Tasmanian case. American Antiquity 69 (2), 197–214.

Henrich, J., 2009. The evolution of costly displays, cooperation and religion: credibility enhancing displays and their implications for cultural evolution. Evolution and Human Behavior 30 (4), 244–260.

Henrich, J., 2016. The Secret of Our Success: How Culture Is Driving Human Evolution, Domesticating Our Species, and Making Us Smarter. Princeton University Press.

Henrich, J., Boyd, R., 2001. Why people punish defectors: weak conformist transmission can stabilize costly enforcement of norms in cooperative dilemmas. Journal of Theoretical Biology 208 (1), 79–89.

Henrich, J., Gil-White, F.J., 2001. The evolution of prestige: freely conferred deference as a mechanism for enhancing the benefits of cultural transmission. Evolution and Human Behavior 22 (3), 165–196.

Henrich, J., McElreath, R., 2007. Dual-inheritance theory: the evolution of human cultural capacities and cultural evolution.

Henrich, Joseph, 2021. Game theory in cultural evolution. In: Nobel Symposium.

Hiller, V., 2011. Work organization, preferences dynamics and the industrialization process. European Economic Review 55 (7), 1007–1025.

Hiller, V., Baudin, T., 2016. Cultural transmission and the evolution of gender roles. Mathematical Social Sciences 84, 8–23.

Hiller, V., Verdier, T., 2014. Corporate culture and identity investment in an industry equilibrium. Journal of Economic Behavior & Organization 103, 93–112.

Hiller, V., Wu, J., Zhang, H., 2022. Heterophily, stable matching, and intergenerational transmission in cultural evolution. Paris 2. Mimeo.

Hofbauer, J., Sigmund, K., 1998. Evolutionary Games and Population Dynamics. Cambridge University Press.

Iyigun, M., Rubin, J., Seror, A., 2021. A theory of cultural revivals. European Economic Review 135, 103734.

Jansson, F., et al., 2021. Modelling cultural systems and selective filters. Philosophical Transactions of the Royal Society of London. Series B, Biological Sciences 376 (1828).

Jiménez, Á.V., Mesoudi, A., 2019. Prestige-biased social learning: current evidence and outstanding questions. Palgrave Communications 5 (1).

Klasing, M.J., 2014. Cultural change, risk-taking behavior and implications for economic development. Journal of Development Economics 110, 158–169.

Kobayashi, Y., Aoki, K., 2012. Innovativeness, population size and cumulative cultural evolution. Theoretical Population Biology 82 (1), 38–47.

Koçkesen, L., Ok, E.A., Sethi, R., 2000. The strategic advantage of negatively interdependent preferences. Journal of Economic Theory 92 (2), 274–299.

Konya, I., 2005. Minorities and majorities: a dynamic model of assimilation. Canadian Journal of Economics 38 (4), 1431–1452.

Kroeber, A., Kluckhohn, C., 1952. Culture: a critical review of concepts and definitions. Papers of the Peabody Museum of American Archaeology and Ethnology 47 (1).

Krusell, P., Smith Jr., A.A., 2006. Quantitative macroeconomic models with heterogeneous agents. In: Blundell, R., Newey, W.K., Persson, T. (Eds.), Advances in Economics and Econometrics: Theory and Applications. Cambridge University Press, pp. 298–340.

Lazear, E.P., 1999. Culture and language. Journal of Political Economy 107 (6), 95–126.

Lehmann, L., Feldman, M.W., 2008. The co-evolution of culturally inherited altruistic helping and cultural transmission under random group formation. Theoretical Population Biology 73 (4), 506–516.

Lizzeri, A., Siniscalchi, M., 2008. Parental guidance and supervised transmission. Journal of Economic Theory.

Mahoney, J., Thelen, K., 2010. A theory of gradual institutional change. In: Explaining Institutional Change: Ambiguity, Agency, and Power, vol. 1.
Maystre, N., et al., 2014. Product-based cultural change: is the village global? Journal of International Economics 92 (2), 212–230.
McElreath, R., Boyd, R., Richerson, P., 2003. Shared norms and the evolution of ethnic markers. Current Anthropology 44 (1), 122–130.
McElreath, R., Strimling, P., 2006. When natural selection favors imitation of parents. Proceedings of the Royal Society of London. Series B, Biological Sciences 273 (1582), 2107–2113.
McPherson, M., Smith-Lovin, L., Cook, J.M., 2001. Birds of a feather: homophily in social networks. Annual Review of Sociology 27 (1), 415–444.
Melindi Ghidi, P., 2009. A Model of Ideological Transmission with Endogenous Paternalism. Tech. Rep.. UCL-Université Catholique de Louvain.
Melki, M., et al., 2024. Cultural remittances and modern fertility. Tech. Rep. 32990. National Bureau of Economic Research.
Mesoudi, A., 2011. An experimental comparison of human social learning strategies: payoff-biased social learning is adaptive but underused. Evolution and Human Behavior 32 (5), 334–342.
Mesoudi, A., Thornton, A., 2018. What is cumulative cultural evolution? Proceedings of the Royal Society B 285 (1880). https://doi.org/10.1098/rspb.2018.0712.
Michaeli, M., Wu, J., 2022. Fighting polarization with (parental) internalization. Journal of Economic Behavior and Organization 194, 124–138.
Michau, J.B., 2013. Unemployment insurance and cultural transmission: theory and application to European unemployment. Journal of the European Economic Association 11 (6), 1320–1347.
Migliaccio, E., Verdier, T., 2018. On the spatial diffusion of cooperation with endogenous matching institutions. Games 9 (3), 58. https://doi.org/10.3390/g9030058.
Moghaddam, F.M., Solliday, E.A., 1991. Balanced multiculturalism and the challenge of peaceful coexistence in pluralistic societies. Psychology and Developing Societies 3 (1), 51–72.
Montgomery, J.D., 2010. Intergenerational cultural transmission as an evolutionary game. American Economic Journal: Microeconomics 2 (4), 115–136.
Morgan, Thomas J.H., Feldman, Marcus W., 2025. Human culture is uniquely open-ended rather than uniquely cumulative. Nature Human Behaviour 9 (1), 28–42.
Muthukrishna, Michael, et al., 2018. The cultural brain hypothesis: how culture drives brain expansion, sociality, and life history. PLoS Computational Biology 14 (11), e1006504.
North, D.C., Thomas, R.P., 1973. The Rise of the Western World: A New Economic History. Cambridge University Press.
Nunn, N., 2021. History as evolution. In: Bisin, A., Federico, G. (Eds.), The Handbook of Historical Economics. Elsevier North Holland, pp. 41–91.
Odling-Smee, F.J., Laland, K.N., Feldman, M.W., 2003. Niche Construction: The Neglected Process in Evolution. Princeton University Press.
Oechssler, J., Riedel, F., 2001. Evolutionary dynamics on infinite strategy spaces. Economic Theory 17, 141–162.
Ok, E.A., Vega-Redondo, F., 2001. On the evolution of individualistic preferences: an incomplete information scenario. Journal of Economic Theory 97 (2), 231–254.
Okada, Akira, 2020. The cultural transmission of trust and trustworthiness. Journal of Economic Behavior and Organization 169, 53–69.
Olcina, G., Penarrubia, C., 2004. Hold-up and intergenerational transmission of preferences. Journal of Economic Behavior and Organization 54, 111–132.
Olivier, J., Thoenig, M., Verdier, T., 2008. Globalization and the dynamics of cultural identity. Journal of International Economics 76, 356–370.
Otto, S.P., Christiansen, F.B., Feldman, M.W., 1994. Genetic and cultural inheritance of continuous traits. Tech. Rep. Stanford University, Morrison Institute for Population and Resource Studies, Working Paper 0064.
Panebianco, F., 2009. "Driving while black": a theory for interethnic integration and evolution of prejudice. Tech. Rep. University Ca'Foscari of Venice, Dept. of Economics Research Paper Series No. 10.

Panebianco, F., 2014. Socialization networks and the transmission of interethnic attitudes. Journal of Economic Theory 150, 583–610.

Panebianco, F., Verdier, T., 2017. Paternalism, homophily and cultural transmission in random networks. Games and Economic Behavior 105, 155–176.

Pastor-Satorras, R., Vespignani, A., 2003. Epidemics and immunization in scale-free networks. In: Bornholdt, S., Schuster, H.G. (Eds.), Handbook of Graphs and Networks: from the Genome to the Internet. Wiley-VCH, pp. 111–130.

Patacchini, E., Zenou, Y., 2016. Racial identity and education in social networks. Social Networks 44, 85–94.

Perreault, C., Moya, C., Boyd, R., 2012. A Bayesian approach to the evolution of social learning. Evolution and Human Behavior 33 (5), 449–459.

Pichler, M.M., 2008. Culture formation and endogenous cultural distance. Tech. Rep. 403. Working Papers.

Ponthiere, G., 2010. Unequal longevities and lifestyles transmission. Journal of Public Economic Theory 12 (1), 93–126.

Prummer, A., Siedlarek, J.P., 2017. Community leaders and the preservation of cultural traits. Journal of Economic Theory 168, 143–176.

Rapoport, H., Sardoschau, S., Silve, A., 2020. Migration and cultural change. Tech. Rep. CESifo Working Paper No. 8547.

Richerson, P.J., Boyd, R., 2005. Not by Genes Alone: How Culture Transformed Human Evolution. University of Chicago Press.

Richerson, P.J., Boyd, R., 2022. What sort of mind/brain is compatible with cultural adaptation? Journal of Cognition and Culture 22 (5), 390–405.

Richerson, P.J., Boyd, R., Henrich, J., 2010. Gene-culture coevolution in the age of genomics. Proceedings of the National Academy of Sciences 107 (Suppl. 2), 8985–8992.

Richerson, Peter J., Boyd, Robert, 1978. A dual inheritance model of the human evolutionary process I: basic postulates and a simple model. Journal of Social and Biological Structures 1 (2), 127–154.

Robalino, N., Robson, A.J., 2019. The biological foundations of economic preferences. In: Oxford Research Encyclopedia of Economics and Finance.

Robalino, N., Robson, A.J., 2026. The biological foundations of economic behavior. In: Enke, B., et al. (Eds.), Handbook of the Economics of Culture. Elsevier North Holland.

Robson, A.J., 2001. Why would nature give individuals utility functions? Journal of Political Economy 109 (4), 900–914.

Robson, A.J., 2003. The evolution of rationality and the Red Queen. Journal of Economic Theory 111 (1), 1–22.

Robson, A.J., Samuelson, L., 2011. The evolutionary foundations of preferences. In: Benhabib, J., Bisin, A., Jackson, M. (Eds.), Handbook of Social Economics, pp. 221–310.

Robson, A.J., Samuelson, L., 2026. The Evolutionary Foundations of Preferences. Econometric Society Monograph Series. Cambridge University Press. Forthcoming.

Rogers, A.R., 1988. Does biology constrain culture? American Anthropologist 90 (4), 819–831.

Roland, G., 2004. Understanding institutional change: fast-moving and slow-moving institutions. Studies in Comparative International Development 38, 109–131.

Sáez-Martí, M., Sjögren, A., 2008. Peers and culture. Scandinavian Journal of Economics 110 (1), 73–92.

Sáez-Martí, M., Zenou, Y., 2012. Cultural transmission and discrimination. Journal of Urban Economics 72 (2–3), 137–146.

Salazar, V., Szentes, B., 2021. On the coevolution of cooperation and social institutions. Tech. Rep. LSE. Mimeo.

Sandholm, W.H., 2010. Population Games and Evolutionary Dynamics. MIT Press, Cambridge.

Schumacher, I., 2015. The endogenous formation of an environmental culture. European Economic Review 76, 200–221.

Senik, C., Verdier, T., 2011. Segregation, entrepreneurship and work values: the case of France. Journal of Population Economics 24, 1207–1234.

Seror, A., 2018. A theory on the evolution of religious norms and economic prohibition. Journal of Development Economics 134, 416–427.

Seror, A., 2022. Child development in parent-child interactions. Journal of Political Economy 130 (9), 2462–2499.

Shapley, L.S., Shubik, M., 1971. The assignment game I: the core. International Journal of Game Theory 1, 111–130.

Smaldino, Paul, 2023. Modeling social behavior: Mathematical and agent-based models of social dynamics and cultural evolution.

Smolla, M., Akçay, E., 2023. Pathways to cultural adaptation: the coevolution of cumulative culture and social networks. Evolutionary Human Sciences 5, 1–20.

Spiro, D., 2020. Multigenerational transmission of culture. Journal of Economic Theory 188, 105037.

Strimling, P., Enquist, M., Eriksson, K., 2009. Repeated learning makes cultural evolution unique. Proceedings of the National Academy of Sciences 106 (33), 13870–13874.

Swidler, A., 1986. Culture in action: symbols and strategies. American Sociological Review 51, 273–286.

Tabellini, G., 2008. The scope of cooperation: norms and incentives. Quarterly Journal of Economics 123, 905–950.

Tajfel, H., 1979. Individuals and groups in social psychology. British Journal of Social and Clinical Psychology 18 (2), 183–190.

Tajfel, H., et al., 1979. An integrative theory of intergroup conflict. In: Organizational Identity: A Reader. Oxford University Press, pp. 56–65.

Taylor, P.D., Jonker, L.B., 1978. Evolutionary stable strategies and game dynamics. Mathematical Biosciences 40 (1–2), 145–156.

Ticchi, D., Verdier, T., Vindigni, A., 2013. Democracy, dictatorship and the cultural transmission of political values. Tech. Rep. 7441. IZA Discussion Papers.

Tomasello, M., 2010. Origins of Human Communication. MIT Press.

Touré, N., 2021. Culture, institutions and the industrialization process. Journal of Economic Behavior and Organization 186, 481–503.

Vaughan, D., 2013. Nurture versus nurture: endogenous parental and peer effects and the transmission of culture. Tech. Rep. Banco de México, Working Paper 2013-04.

Verdier, T., Zenou, Y., 2015. The role of cultural leaders in the transmission of preferences. Economics Letters 136, 158–161.

Verdier, T., Zenou, Y., 2017. The role of social networks in cultural assimilation. Journal of Urban Economics 97, 15–39.

Verdier, T., Zenou, Y., 2018. Cultural leaders and the dynamics of assimilation. Journal of Economic Theory 175, 374–414.

Voth, H.J., 2021. Persistence – myth and mystery. In: Bisin, A., Federico, G. (Eds.), Handbook of Historical Economics. Elsevier North Holland, pp. 243–267.

Weibull, J., 1995. The mass-action interpretation of Nash equilibrium. In: Dynamic Evolutionary Game Theory in Biology and Economics, vol. 427. Industrial Institute for Economic and Social Research (Industriens Utredningsinstitut), pp. 1–18.

Wu, J., 2017. Political institutions and the evolution of character traits. Games and Economic Behavior 106, 260–276.

Wu, J., 2021. Matching markets and cultural selection. Review of Economic Design 25, 267–288.

Wu, J., Zhang, H., 2021. Preference evolution in different matching markets. European Economic Review 137, 103804.

Wu, J., Zhang, H., 2022. Polarization, antipathy, and political activism. Economic Inquiry 60 (3), 1005–1017.

Young, H.P., 1998. Individual Strategy and Social Structure: An Evolutionary Theory of Institutions. Princeton University Press, Princeton.

Zakharenko, Roman, 2016. Nothing else matters: evolution of preference for social prestige. Mathematical Social Sciences 80, 58–64.

Chapter 10

Modeling social institutions☆

Jean-Paul Carvalho
Department of Economics, University of Oxford, Oxford, United Kingdom

> *"But nobody can be a great economist who is only an economist—and I am even tempted to add that the economist who is only an economist is likely to become a nuisance if not a positive danger." (Hayek, 1967, p. 123)*

1 The socially-embedded economy

In March 2023, I gave a talk titled 'The Socially-Embedded Economy' at New College, Oxford, where I am a Fellow. One of the remarkable features of an Oxford college is the interaction among scholars drawn from the full spectrum of disciplines in a university. Perplexed by the title of my talk, one of the lecturers in French asked me, 'Where would I find an economy that is not socially embedded?' My answer was, 'In our models'. That is not to say that economics is entirely oblivious to social institutions. Indeed, this chapter will review some of the major contributions made by economists to the study of such institutions. Instead, the point is that mainstream economics remains underpinned by a worldview which separates human interaction into two independent domains—economy and society—with the latter deemed of minor interest to the discipline. This artificial construction was considered eccentric even by the standards of a French literary scholar.

One reason for the neglect of social institutions is that when economics was mathematized in the late nineteenth and early twentieth centuries, the mathematical and conceptual tools needed to incorporate the 'soft' social and psychological factors that interested the classical economists were simply unavailable. Since then, two important developments have paved the way for the incorporation of social institutions into standard economics. The first is game theory, especially in its evolutionary form (e.g. Maynard Smith and Price, 1973; Young, 1998; Newton, 2018). The second is the emergence of an empirical literature on the role of culture in economics which makes use of new data sources and empirical methods (Spolaore and Wacziarg, 2013;

☆ I am grateful for comments and suggestions by seminar participants at New College, Oxford. Research assistance was provided by Grok and ChatGPT. All errors are mine.

Handbook of Culture and Economic Behavior, Volume 1, ISSN 3051-1682
https://doi.org/10.1016/bs.hceb.2026.02.011

Nunn, 2014). This chapter presents a framework for modeling social institutions that synthesizes the two bodies of work—theoretical and empirical. In doing so, it provides a guide for incorporating social institutions into the standard economics found in textbooks.

Institutions have been defined as "the rules of the game in a society or, more formally, are the humanly devised constraints that shape human interaction" (North, 1990, p. 3). Formal political institutions are structured, legally established entities with defined roles, rules, and authority, such as legislatures, courts, and electoral systems. Such institutions have received a considerable amount of attention in economic history and political economy. The 2024 Nobel Memorial Prize in Economics was awarded to Daron Acemoglu, Simon Johnson, and James Robinson for their pioneering work on the role of formal institutions in long-term development (Acemoglu et al., 2001, 2002; Acemoglu and Robinson, 2012). The literature on social institutions is less well developed and integrated into mainstream economics. Informal social institutions are behavioral regularities that emerge at the population level through social interaction. They can be codified or tacit and include social norms and the cultural preferences, values, and beliefs that underpin them. These social institutions can be thought of as adaptive software for navigating 'large worlds', that is to say, complex environments that are beyond the understanding of any one individual. They structure social and economic life, balance stability and adaptability, and encode a lot of information about the local cultural and historical context.

The neglect of social institutions in economics is not a problem *per se*. Models are by definition simplifications of reality and many things have to be left out. The problem is that the social-embeddedness of markets is critical to their functioning. Without incorporating social institutions such as norms, customs, and conventions, the basic analysis of markets in economics is incomplete, and possibly even misleading. That is why George Akerlof (2020) has described the disregard in economics for such 'soft' factors as 'sins of omission'. If one were auctioning Russian art in London in the 1990s, it would be more important to approach oligarch *A* and convince him that his rival oligarch *B* is interested in the item than to choose the optimal auction format. Understanding the social ecology of the market is key. The following examples further illustrate the link between social institutions and market behavior.

1. Long-term development. Social institutions such as norms of literacy, work, corruption, trust, and civic engagement impact long-term economic development by influencing investment, human capital formation, and innovation (e.g. Platteau, 2000; Becker and Woessmann, 2009; Tabellini, 2010; Nunn and Wantchekon, 2011). For example, Nunn and Wantchekon (2011) find that the slave trade had a deleterious long-term effect on economic development by lowering trust, both within and across African ethnic groups.

2. Labor markets. Collectivist, gender, and caste-based norms influence educational attainment and labor force participation (Gorodnichenko and

Roland, 2017; Fernández and Fogli, 2009; Alesina et al., 2013; Iyer, 2018; Oh, 2023). For example, in conservative Muslim communities, veiling can reduce the stigma from working outside the home and thereby boost female labor force participation (Carvalho, 2013; Shofia, 2024).

3. Organizational behavior. Norms of cooperation and fairness shape wage compression, decentralization, and firm size and performance (e.g. Akerlof, 1982; Card et al., 2012; Bloom et al., 2012). For example, Bloom et al. (2012) show that firms headquartered in high-trust regions can achieve greater decentralization and scale.

4. Consumer behavior. Consumption decisions, including the consumption of status goods and cultural products, are not based on fixed, universal preferences but rather shaped by the socio-cultural environment (e.g. Akerlof and Kranton, 2000; Guiso et al., 2006; Falk et al., 2018; Atkin, 2016; Bursztyn et al., 2020a). For example, Atkin (2016) shows that interstate migrants in India pay a significant caloric cost to consume staple foods from their region of origin.

5. Financial markets. Firm valuation, investment fads, analyst forecasts, earnings guidance, and the value of fiat money, gold, and cryptocurrency are a function of norms and narratives (e.g. Menger, 1892; Trueman, 1994; Hong et al., 2000; Shiller, 2000, 2019). For example, Trueman (1994) and Hong et al. (2000) show that analysts herd in their forecasts partly due to norms of performance evaluation under which it is better to be wrong when everybody else is wrong.

6. Political risk. Political events such as revolutions, civil conflict, and international war, which have a first-order effect on economic growth and development, are influenced by norms of accountability, expression, and tolerance, as well as the cultural compatibility between groups (e.g. Kuran, 1991; Waldinger, 2024; Iyigun, 2008; Cederman et al., 2010; Gartzke and Gleditsch, 2006). For example, Cederman et al. (2010) show that norms of exclusion and discrimination against ethnic groups can lead to rebellion and civil conflict.

These examples illustrate why a model of the world divided into separate economic and social domains is incomplete and misleading.

The systematic incorporation of social institutions into mainstream economics is an ongoing program. For example, the CORE (Curriculum Open-access Resources in Economics) program initiated by Wendy Carlin and Samuel Bowles aims to broaden the scope of economics curricula to include elements such as human psychology, social institutions, and historical context (The CORE Team, 2017). This chapter contributes to this program by presenting a framework for modeling social institutions based on evolutionary game theory, and in particular the work of Peyton Young (e.g. Young, 1998, 2015, forthcoming), and showing how this framework can guide the growing empirical literature in economics on norms, culture, identity, and religion.

First and foremost, social institutions can be viewed as behavioral regularities, or norms. In addition to formal institutions and laws, norms structure and regulate markets. For example, they simplify certain aspects of decision-making (e.g., contractual forms), enabling participants in a market to focus on other aspects of a transaction (e.g., prices). This is a form of dimensional reduction in decision-making that shapes production and exchange in important ways. Unlike classical game theory, with its assumptions of common knowledge of the structure of the environment and equilibrium knowledge, evolutionary game theory enables us to understand how these norms emerge. Players are myopic, forming expectations of play based on currently available information and their memory of the history of play. They are not continuous optimizers, but revise their strategies from time to time for idiosyncratic reasons and based on environmental cues. This model of economic and social systems places little burden on the reasoning of individual agents. Behavioral regularities, or norms, emerge in a bottom-up manner from the decentralized actions of many individuals in a system.

There are three key properties of norms identified by this evolutionary game-theoretic model (Young, 2015, forthcoming). First, coordination, conformity, and learning effects lead to *behavioral compression*, reducing behavioral diversity within groups of individuals who interact frequently. For example, landlords and tenants in certain regions may coordinate on particular divisions in sharecropping contracts, such as 50-50 (Burke and Young, 2011). Of course, this does not rule out divergence in behavior between groups. Second, patterns of behavior can remain in place for long periods of time despite environmental changes and shifts in incentives, being locked in by the various coordination, conformity, and learning effects that produce behavioral compression. Equally so, long-established norms could be disrupted and shift abruptly without any apparent change in fundamentals. In biology, long periods of stasis followed by abrupt change are called *punctuated equilibrium*. Such behavior is also observed in economic and social systems. Consider the following question: "Is religion a source of stasis, or does it produce rapid societal change?" Punctuated equilibrium tells us that the answer is both, with the same mechanisms behind both stasis and change. Third, it is not straightforward to infer which norms will emerge from the details of an environment and individual incentives. This disconnect between the microscopic components of a system and its macroscopic behavior is called *emergence*. The concept was first understood in physics, especially thermodynamics and statistical mechanics, and later explored in the social sciences (Schelling, 1978; Young, 1998). Emergence cautions against bold attempts at social engineering, including many of the norm interventions that have recently been proposed by economists.

I suggest three ways to extend this model of norms and connect it to the growing empirical literature in economics on culture, identity, and religion. The process of norm formation, operating through individual adjustments in behavior in response to what other members of a population are doing, could be shaped by slower-moving cultural processes going on 'under the hood'. First, how individuals respond to others' behavior depends on the distributions of values, beliefs, shared memories, and ways of viewing the world in a population, which are themselves the product of cultural evolution (Bisin and Verdier, 2000a, 2001). Second, interactions in populations tend to be structured based on various identity markers, including ethnicity, gender, religion, and kinship groups. This identity-based population structure shapes the process of norm formation and can lead to significant diversity between groups, even as behavior becomes compressed within groups (Akerlof and Kranton, 2000, 2010; McElreath et al., 2003). Finally, norms form not only through decentralized bottom-up processes but are also subject to top-down attempts at cultural control. For example, norm entrepreneurs can significantly affect norm formation by shaping preferences and beliefs about right and wrong behavior in groups (e.g., religious organizations) or through the state. These cultural interventions may be resisted or contested by subpopulations who wish to hold onto different views (Carvalho and Sacks, 2024; Carvalho et al., 2024). Both cultural interventions and the response to them could be incorporated into models of norm formation. More broadly, more attention needs to be devoted to integrating the cultural factors underpinning norms into the standard evolutionary game-theoretic model.

The remainder of this chapter is structured as follows. Section 2 presents a survey of economic thought on social institutions from Ancient Athens and India to today. Section 3 sets out the leading model of norms based on evolutionary game theory. Section 4 suggests three extensions of this model to (i) the internalization of norms, (ii) identity-dependence, and (iii) contestation of norms. Section 5 concludes with lessons from our analysis of social institutions for designing empirical studies and interpreting results. It also cautions against norm interventions without deep institutional knowledge of the society in question.

2 Economic thought on social institutions

2.1 Classical origins

Unlike their great achievements in philosophy, politics, geometry, and other fields, the ancient Athenians are not known for their contributions to economics. Thinkers such as Xenophon, Plato, Aristotle, and Hesiod wrote about specialization, money, trade flows, wealth accumulation, and inequality.[1] Historians such as Thucydides and Herodotus wrote about trade networks, tribute systems, and resource conflicts.[2] However, their theories and observations were not broken out and formalized into a separate field called 'economics'. That is remarkable because the term 'economics' comes from the Greek *oikonomike*, that is, from *oikos* meaning 'house' and *nomos* meaning 'law'. Hence, the ancients used the

1 See Xenophon (2002/c. 362 BCE), Plato (2012/c. 380 BCE), Aristotle (2014/c. 340 BCE*a*), Aristotle (2013/c. 350 BCE*b*), and Hesiod (2008/c. 700 BCE).

2 See Thucydides (2013/c. 410 BCE) and Herodotus (2014/c. 440 BCE).

term 'economics' to refer to small-scale 'household management' (Xenophon, 2002/c. 362 BCE). Their understanding of production and exchange on a larger scale, what we call 'economics' today, was woven into a broad intellectual vision and inextricably connected to politics, historical dynamics, and philosophical ideals.

In 4th century BCE India, a more systematic study of economics grounded in political and social institutions was written by Kautilya, a key advisor to Emperor Chandragupta Maurya. The *Arthashastra* was a practical guide to statecraft. Its policy prescriptions ranged from optimal taxation and monetary policy to how to weaken the economies of rivals and boost military capacity, administrative efficiency, and social stability (Kautilya, 2012/c. 300 BCE). In the mid-18th century, French scholars with similar interests in managing the affairs of state combined the term *économie* with *politique* to denote the study of public administration. Adam Smith used the term 'political economy' in this sense in *The Wealth of Nations* (Smith, 2008/1776). He was of course familiar with the work of Quesnay (2009/1758) and the Physiocrats, having met Quesnay during his travels in France. *The Wealth of Nations* owes a debt to these French political economists, especially its laissez-faire orientation and rejection of mercantilism.

Smith's monumental work ushered in the classical period of economics. During this time, the use of the term 'political economy' expanded to encompass everything we deem to be 'economics' today, beyond public administration to the operation of markets, firms, and households. The classical economists were motivated by the economic and social revolution taking place (Hicks, 2001/1969). The revolution was not limited to the creation of a market economy, but also a 'market society' in which "[i]nstead of the economy being embedded in social relations, social relations are embedded in the economic system" (Polanyi, 2001/1944). Examples include the replacement of traditional feudal obligations (*noblesse oblige*) and barter transactions by employment contracts, the emergence of urban slum communities around newly created factories, and the rise of a consumer class and culture. Thus, political economy took a broad view of markets as embedded in social and political institutions.

Many of the subjects that concerned the classical economists would surprise readers of modern textbooks in economics. In *The Theory of Moral Sentiments*, Adam Smith wrote about how human psychology shapes decision-making, especially empathic feelings beyond self interest (Smith, 2002/1759). David Ricardo was concerned with the role of class-based institutions in the economy (Ricardo, 1817). John Stuart Mill distinguished between "higher" (intellectual, moral) and "lower" (physical) pleasures and was deeply interested in concepts of conformity and freedom (Mill, 1848, 1861). David Hume, Adam Smith, and Adam Ferguson, key figures in the Scottish Enlightenment, wrote about the evolution of property rights which govern markets (Hume, 2000/1739; Ferguson, 2001/1767; Smith, 2008/1776). In Book V of *The Wealth of Nations*, Smith writes:

"It is in the age of shepherds, in the second period of society, that the inequality of fortune first begins to take place, and introduces among men a degree of authority and subordination which could not possibly exist before. It thereby introduces some degree of that civil government which is indispensably necessary for its own preservation: and it seems to do this naturally, and even independent of the consideration of that necessity. The consideration of that necessity comes no doubt afterwards to contribute very much to maintain and secure that authority and subordination." (Smith, 2008/1776, p. 689)

In this passage, Smith describes an unconscious process of societal adaptation in which technological changes produce formal and informal institutions that entrench the new forms of inequality. It reflects a broad economic perspective by emphasizing the role of ideas, norms, and political institutions. Smith's point has recently been taken up by Thomas Piketty in *Capital and Ideology* which argues that rising inequality in OECD countries is supported by an ideological system—the modern intellectual framework—that legitimizes the *status quo* distribution of power and wealth (Piketty, 2020). A key part of this modern intellectual framework is a narrow, neoclassical approach to economics that neglects the role of power and institutions.

2.2 Narrow mathematization

In the 1870s, economists sought deeper insights into the operation of markets through the application of mathematics. This was the so-called marginal revolution led by William Stanley Jevons (2013/1871), Carl Menger (2007/1871), and Léon Walras (2014/1874). As part of the mathematization of the subject and the effort to create a 'hard science', the term 'economics' began to be used, entirely replacing the term 'political economy' during the early 20th century. As part of this process, the 'soft' political and social institutions that had interested the classical economists were stripped out. This neoclassical economics is the mainstream economics of today.

Mainstream economics was shaped by the particular course that mathematization took, a course inspired by philosophy and physics. Firstly, the foundational models were not grounded in empirical facts about human decision-making. Data were scarce and empirical evidence limited. Instead, models were built on a set of theoretical axioms (discussed below) motivated more by the pursuit of elegance, rationality, and tractability than reality. Hence, economics followed in the footsteps of Descartes and the French Enlightenment thinkers in imagining an abstract and idealized world and formulating policy based on it (Descartes, 1998/1637). Another legacy of the French Enlightenment and its emphasis on reason, individual autonomy, and rejection of traditional authorities is the primacy of the individual in economics. 'Methodological individualism' in which the fundamental decision-making unit is the individual (or household) is so ingrained in mainstream economics as to be unconsciously accepted. Thus, neoclassical economics was, from its inception, a liberal enterprise.

The second source of inspiration came from physics, in particular the deterministic and mechanistic approach then dominant in physics that was used to predict the motion of planets. As with celestial mechanics, the equations describing human interaction were assumed to be the same everywhere and at all times. Economic laws were supposed to exist and had to be universal to be meaningful. That meant all societies had to be fundamentally the same. This theoretical orientation made economics a liberal universalist enterprise and profoundly shaped economic thinking and policy. A prime example is the one-size-fits-all program of structural adjustment, known as the Washington Consensus, which was imposed on economies as diverse as the UK's and Thailand's.

To shoe-horn highly complex markets into a mathematical framework inspired by Newtonian mechanics required many simplifying assumptions. Individuals were (i) atomized, mainly interacting with each other through large, competitive markets and the impersonal price system, (ii) small, with an absence of large traders who could move markets, (iii) anonymous, without individual reputation or group identity, and (iv) smart, with a great deal of computational power and knowledge about their environment. In addition, smooth, concave utility and profit functions, along with constant returns to scale, often ruled out multiple equilibria and a role for historical path dependence. Property rights were assumed to be enforced and the role of power in economic affairs grossly underestimated.

Thus, mainstream economics came to reflect little of the classical economists' understanding of the role of political and social institutions in the economy. One can see remnants of the broader classical perspective even in Alfred Marshall's *Principles of Economics*, the text that popularized the demand and supply diagrams familiar to generations of undergraduate students (Marshall, 2013/1890). In the opening paragraphs of his *Principles*, Marshall writes about the social and economic forces governing preference formation:

> *"Political Economy or Economics is a study of mankind in the ordinary business of life; it examines that part of individual and social action which is most closely connected with the attainment and with the use of the material requisites of wellbeing.*
>
> *Thus, it is on the one side a study of wealth; and on the other, and more important side, a part of the study of man. For man's character has been moulded by his every-day work, and the material resources which he thereby procures, more than by any other influence unless it be that of his religious ideals; and the two great forming agencies of the world's history have been the religious and the economic."*
> *(Marshall, 2013/1890, p. 1)*

But Marshall's *Principles*, and economics with it, went on to focus on a narrow form of interaction between people, through large competitive markets, thus ignoring the role of social institutions.

This narrowing of the scope of economics was perhaps necessary. Mathematization was already an incredible feat and the social institutions that had concerned earlier generations of economists could not be incorporated into the models given the mathematical and conceptual tools available at the time. The narrowing was also useful. It produced many of the models (i.e., lenses) through which we view the world today and conferred on economists considerable influence. Unfortunately, some economists started to view their models not as simplified and useful maps, but rather as representations of the ideal and/or empirical world, even blurring the distinction between the two. Thus, after squinting at one part of the picture, economics became largely blind to the rest. In particular, the social institutions that were left out of the models were now considered beyond the scope of economics.

2.3 The role of the rational actor

By the mid-1950s, the Chicago economist Gary Becker had begun to vastly expand the scope of economics, venturing into non-traditional domains such as discrimination, crime, human capital, addiction, and the family. According to Becker, economics is not defined by its subject matter, but by its approach. This view gave him license to roam beyond the neoclassical boundaries of economics, a venture criticized as 'economic imperialism' by other social scientists. Instead of importing concepts from disciplines such as sociology and psychology, Becker simply applied standard economic methods wherever he roamed, and with great impact. This rational choice theory even became influential in political science and sociology for some time. In *The Economic Approach to Human Behavior*, Becker wrote, "The combined assumptions of maximizing behavior, market equilibrium, and stable preferences, used relentlessly and unflinchingly, form the heart of the economic approach as I see it" (Becker, 1976, p. 5). In dealing with social institutions, this economic approach has several limitations. At the root of the problems is the so-called 'rational actor', which is built from Becker's notion of maximizing behavior based on well-defined and stable preferences. These assumptions atomize and isolate the rational actor, stripping it of its place in society.

Consider the assumption of stable preferences. By stability, Becker meant several things at once. Firstly, an individual's preferences are fixed over time, so that behavioral changes can be attributed solely to economic factors, by which he means (generalized) prices and incomes, not changing tastes (Stigler and Becker, 1977). Secondly, and relatedly, preferences are 'exogenous', meaning that they are not shaped by one's environment, but presumably given directly by God or nature. Thirdly, preferences are context-free. For example, they are independent of social cues and conventions, allowing the economist to generalize from behavior in one context to another. In practice, it is typically assumed that individuals are also purely self-regarding. David Hume's maxim that "every man must be supposed a knave" is well known (Hume, 1987/1741,

p. 313). What is less well known is Hume's immediate qualification: "Though at the same time it appears somewhat strange that a maxim should be true in politics, which is false in fact". That is, context matters. Fourthly, preferences are assumed to be the same everywhere. As Becker writes, preferences are assumed not to be "very different between wealthy and poor persons, or even between persons in different societies and cultures" (Becker, 1976, p. 5). Hence, Becker's economic approach rules out (or at least deemphasizes) roles for history and culture in shaping beliefs and preferences and for thereby producing observed patterns of behavioral diversity.

Uncertainty places even greater demands on the rational actor. Let me focus on one of these demands, which I call 'structural knowledge'. When Leonard Savage developed the framework for decision-making under uncertainty, he warned that the model should only be applied to "small worlds", in which individuals know a great deal about the structure of their environment (Savage, 1954; Binmore, 2009). But every economic decision that we care about, from what occupations we choose to whom we marry to how we invest our pensions, involves 'radical uncertainty' about the structure of the environment (Knight, 1921; King and Kay, 2020). The decisions an economist typically cares about are made in large worlds.

This point was understood by Friedrich Hayek and economists of the Austrian School. In 'The Use of Knowledge in Society', Hayek writes:

> *"If we possess all the relevant information, if we can start out from a given system of preferences and if we command complete knowledge of available means, the problem which remains is purely one of logic. [...] This, however, is emphatically not the economic problem which society faces. And the economic calculus which we have developed to solve this logical problem, though an important step toward the solution of the economic problem of society, does not yet provide an answer to it. The reason for this is that the "data" from which the economic calculus starts are never for the whole society "given" to a single mind which could work out the implications, and can never be so given." (Hayek, 1945, pp. 519–520)*

These "data" are collected and transmitted not only through the price system of markets. No individual knows the structure of the economy, not even the component that is relevant to them. It is through human interaction and social institutions that this fragmented knowledge is shared, integrated, and stored. From this socially compiled body of knowledge, individuals learn and make economic decisions. Through the accumulation of these decisions, the economy evolves and the stock of knowledge is updated. Thus, rationality does not reside at the individual level, but at the population level. The collective creation and transmission of knowledge through interactions and institutions that transcend individual cognition was recognized by Kenneth Arrow, one of the most influential figures in neoclassical economics (Arrow, 1994). This form of networked intelligence has also been described as 'the collective brain' (Muthukrishna and Henrich, 2016; Henrich and Muthukrishna, 2024).

By focusing on the individual rationally updating their beliefs using Bayes rule based on signals from the environment, the rational actor model ignores the role of social institutions in shaping knowledge and choice under incomplete information.

Thus, while making important contributions, rational choice theory did not adequately incorporate social institutions into the study of the economy. By ruling out roles for history and culture in shaping preferences and beliefs, as well as social institutions for transmitting knowledge, the rational choice approach drew a sharp line between the economy and society. No such line was apparent to the ancient thinkers or the classical economists.

2.4 Beyond behavioral economics

By the 1970s, evidence against the rational decision-maker of neoclassical economics had piled up. These "Anomalies" were catalogued by Richard Thaler in a famous series of short articles published by the *Journal of Economic Perspectives* in the 1980s and 1990s (Thaler, 1992). To fix the many problems, it appeared that the rational actor needed a more realistic psychology. At the time, cognitive psychology was dominant. It focused on the individual functioning of the brain, including memory, attention, and language. Cognitive psychologists such as Duncan Luce, Amos Tversky, and Daniel Kahneman laid the mathematical and conceptual foundations for the integration of psychology into economics. Thus, Behavioral Economics was born.

Being a direct response to the rational actor model, behavioral economics inherited many of its limitations. There was no attempt to rework mainstream economics. Camerer and Loewenstein (2004) write that behavioral economics "does not imply a wholesale rejection of the neoclassical approach" [p. 3]. Rather, the method is "to modify one or two assumptions in standard theory in the direction of greater psychological realism" [p. 7]. This approach lies behind the extraordinary success of behavioral economics. Minimal departures from the rational actor model made it immediately intelligible to economists, as well as the much larger educated population who had swum in the sea of mainstream economics.

In contrast, Herb Simon proposed a different approach to bounded rationality which took human cognitive limitations as its starting point, not the ideal decision-making benchmarks of rational choice theory (Simon, 1947, 1955, 1956, 1957). Rather than precisely optimizing by evaluating all possible choices, Simon treated individuals as 'satisficing', only changing behavior when payoffs fall below a target payoff (or aspiration level). This adaptive behavior includes trial-and-error and social learning, which connect individuals in an organization or society via learning feedback loops. For example, Simon drew on concepts from sociology and social psychology to understand the role of routines, which are standardized, repetitive decision-making processes that individuals and organizations follow to simplify complex tasks. He viewed routines as a form of 'organizational memory', allowing firms to replicate successful practices over time and avoid unsuccessful ones. Thus, firms are viewed not as efficient units for limiting transaction costs (Coase, 1937; Williamson, 1975, 1985) and aligning incentives (Grossman and Hart, 1986; Hart and Moore, 1990), but rather as experimental ecosystems and stores of know-how and knowledge.

A more direct attempt to explore the social bases for economic production and exchange was made by George Akerlof. Akerlof's incorporation of concepts from sociology and social psychology into economic models stands in contrast to both Becker's unflinching application of the economic approach and the individualistic orientation of behavioral economics, which is drawn from cognitive psychology. The concepts explored by Akerlof include the role of custom and norms in market behavior (Akerlof, 1980, 2005), gift exchange and fairness in the labor market (Akerlof and Yellen, 1988, 1990), social psychological factors in driving booms and busts (Akerlof, 2002; Akerlof and Shiller, 2009), and the role of identity in shaping individual behavior and market outcomes (Akerlof and Kranton, 2000, 2010). Akerlof's approach brought economists' attention to the inseparability of economy and society and paved the way for a wave of innovative work on culture, identity, religion, norms, and narratives, which would have previously been considered beyond the scope of economics.

With notable exceptions (e.g. Burke and Young, 2011; Giuliano and Nunn, 2021; Bergeron et al., 2024), theoretical and empirical work in this area has remained largely separate. Evolutionary game theory has developed powerful mathematical techniques and models of population dynamics which can be applied to the formation of social norms and institutions. Meanwhile, empirical studies in cultural economics have made excellent use of new sources of data and used creative methods to test theories developed by anthropologists, historians, and sociologists. They have not, however, been guided by an explicit theoretical framework. The aim of this chapter is to provide a step toward a synthesis of evolutionary game theory and empirical work on norms, culture, and identity.

3 Modeling social institutions as norms

Unlike (formal) political institutions, which are structured, legally established entities with defined roles, rules, and authority, (informal) social institutions are behavioral regularities that emerge at the population level through social interaction. Examples include customs, conventions, and traditions, all of which fall under the umbrella of behavioral norms. In modeling social institutions as norms, we can draw on the large theoretical literature on the evolution of norms (e.g. Young, 2015, forthcoming) and the cultural preferences and beliefs underpinning this process (e.g. Bisin and Verdier, 2000a; Bergeron et al., 2024). In particular, this section will set out an evolutionary game-theoretic approach to the emergence and persistence of norms developed by Young (1993a, 1998, forthcoming) and Sandholm (2010).

3.1 Game theory and evolution

Game theory is a mathematical language and set of predictive tools for studying strategic interaction. It was pioneered (mainly) by mathematicians such as Cournot (1838), Zermelo (1913), Borel (1921), von Neumann (1928); von Neumann and Morgenstern (1944), and Nash (1950a). Its incorporation into economics was made possible by the development of Nash equilibrium, defined by mutual best responses, as a tool for predicting interactive behavior (Nash, 1950a). Nash (1950a) showed that such an equilibrium exists in a large class of games, so the concept is widely applicable. However, for Nash equilibrium to be a reasonable prediction of play, the following conditions must be met.

1. Players are *rational*: They can formulate strategies that maximize their payoff given what everyone else is doing.
2. Players have some level of mutual *knowledge* of the game they are playing, e.g. they know the strategy set and the payoffs generated by each strategy profile.
3. Players have *equilibrium knowledge*: They can correctly anticipate what other players will do.

Each of these conditions is restrictive and not satisfied in complex real-world settings.

Another problem is that of multiple equilibria. While the Nash theorem guarantees equilibrium existence in a large class of games, it does not generally make a unique prediction of play. When there are multiple equilibria, how does one make a prediction? Game theory was initially silent on this matter, leaving a great deal of indeterminacy. Eventually, the equilibrium refinements program emerged to address this question by placing further restrictions on reasoning in an attempt to arrive at a unique equilibrium (e.g. Cho and Kreps, 1987). But these refinements of Nash equilibrium placed unreasonable burdens on the rationality of players.

Thomas Schelling took a different, empirical approach to the problem of multiple equilibria. He asked his students at Yale to independently name where and when they would meet in New York City if separated and unable to communicate (Schelling, 1960). Pairs of subjects were rewarded if they chose the same time and place. To Schelling's surprise, subjects were able to coordinate despite the massive choice set (and set of Nash equilibria). Most chose under the clock at Grand Central Station at noon. Schelling concluded that some choices are 'focal points' due either to natural salience (e.g. noon, the clock) or precedent (Grand Central station). Grand Central Station was a focal location because students from New England usually met up in New York City, traveling by train. All routes from New Haven (and other college towns) took them to Grand Central Station.

Game theory initially lacked a framework for modeling the alignment of strategic beliefs and behavior over time. According to von Neumann and Morgenstern (1944):

We repeat most emphatically that our theory is thoroughly static. A dynamic theory would unquestionably be more complete and preferable. [pp. 44-45]

In his PhD thesis, Nash (1950c) briefly sketched an evolutionary approach that could form the basis for the kind of dynamic theory von Neumann and Morgenstern (1944) had in mind:

We shall now take up the "mass-action" interpretation of equilibrium points [...] It is unnecessary to assume that the participants have full knowledge of the total structure of the game, or the ability and inclination to go through any complex reasoning processes. But the participants are supposed to accumulate empirical information on the relative advantages of the various pure strategies at their disposal. [p. 21]

It was, however, evolutionary biologists, not mathematicians or economists, who would develop the dynamic, evolutionary approach to strategic interaction (e.g. Lewontin, 1961; Maynard Smith, 1972; Maynard Smith and Price, 1973; Hamilton, 1967). In this original version of evolutionary game theory, organisms are programmed with a strategy. (Players are essentially strategies.) Strategies that do better, given what everyone else is doing, proliferate. In particular, payoffs are interpreted as reproduction rates of strategies or *fitness*. This extends Darwin's notion of survival of the fittest from an exogenous environment to an interactive setting. Equilibrium states can be perturbed by random shocks. To be stable, an equilibrium must be resistant to invasion by 'mutant strategies'. Hence, participants do not themselves "accumulate empirical information on the relative advantages of the various pure strategies", as Nash suggested. Instead, the job is done by natural selection.

Evolutionary game theory was then imported back into economics to give bounded rationality and spontaneous order a firm theoretical foundation. To capture the behavior of individual humans and organizations, it expanded the set of rules for updating strategies beyond natural selection to include imitation, reinforcement learning, Bayesian social learning, myopic best responses, and cultural transmission. That is, modern evolutionary game theory studies populations of boundedly rational agents who may learn or evolve their way into equilibrium by gradually revising simple, myopic rules of behavior. This is a model of bounded rationality in which knowledge and computation are distributed and learning takes place at the population level. The learning process is self-referential, because as an individual learns about the behavior of others and responds accordingly, the other players react, altering what the individual is learning about. By specifying an explicit dynamic process of adjustment (i.e., out-of-equilibrium dynamics), models of evolution and learning in games enable us to address the following questions:

- Are equilibria stable in the face of random shocks? (*local stability*)
- Does evolution/learning lead to an equilibrium from any initial state? (*global convergence and nonconvergence*)

- To which equilibria, if any, does an evolutionary dynamic lead? (*equilibrium selection*)

An evolutionary game consists of two primary ingredients, a population game and a revision protocol that describes how strategies are updated. Together, these elements give rise to an evolutionary dynamic which describes the evolution of behavior in the population over time. I will start with the first element and introduce the second in Section 3.3.

3.2 Population games

A population game consists of (i) a population of individuals, (ii) an underlying game played by these individuals, and (iii) a matching structure governing who interacts with whom.[3] The following exposition follows Sandholm (2010).

The population is a set of agents (possibly a continuum). The set of (pure) strategies is $S = \{1, \ldots, n\}$, with typical members i, j, and k. The mass of agents choosing strategy i is m_i, where $\sum_{i=1}^{n} m_i = m$. Let $x_i = \frac{m_i}{m}$ denote the share of players choosing strategy $i \in S$. The set of population states (or strategy distributions) is the unit simplex in $\mathbb{R}^n$: $X = \{x \in \mathbb{R}^n_+ : \sum_{i \in S} x_i = 1\}$. The set of vertices of X is the pure population states—those in which all agents choose the same strategy. These are the standard basis vectors in $\mathbb{R}^n$:

$$e_1 = (1, 0, 0, \ldots), e_2 = (0, 1, 0, \ldots), e_3 = (0, 0, 1, \ldots), \quad \ldots$$

Payoffs are given by a *continuous* payoff function $F : X \to \mathbb{R}^n$ that assigns to each population state a vector of payoffs, consisting of a real number for each strategy. $F_i : X \to \mathbb{R}$ denotes the payoff function for strategy i. The precise form of the payoff function will depend on the underlying game and the matching structure in the population.

For now, we will focus on uniform random matching. Consider the expected payoff to strategy i if i is matched with another strategy drawn uniformly at random from the population to play the following *two-player* game:

	1	2	...	n
i	$u(i, 1)$	$u(i, 2)$	...	$u(i, n)$

The expected payoff to strategy i in state x is:

$$F_i(x) = x_1 u(i, 1) + x_2 u(i, 2) \ldots + x_n u(i, n)$$
$$= \sum_{j=1}^{n} x_j u(i, j)$$

[3] I focus here on a single *ex ante* homogeneous population. For the multi-population analysis, see Sandholm (2010). I will examine a two-population setting in Section 3.5.2 when considering bargaining.

$$= \sum_{j=1}^{n} x_j F_i(e_j),$$

which depends *linearly* on the population state.[4]

x^* is a Nash equilibrium of the population game if

$$(x^* - x)' F(x^*) \geq 0 \text{ for all } x \in X.$$

Nash equilibria can be *monomorphic* in which case only one strategy is present in the population: $x^* = e_i$. Alternatively, they can be *polymorphic*: $x^* \neq e_i$ for $i \in S$.[5]

Theorem 1. *Every population game with a continuum of agents admits at least one Nash equilibrium.*

This can be proved in the usual manner using Kakutani's fixed point theorem.

For some evolutionary dynamics, we will need to keep track of the average payoff in the population:

$$\overline{F}(x) = x_1 F_1(x) + x_2 F_2(x) \ldots + x_n F_n(x)$$
$$= \sum_{i=1}^{n} x_i F_i(x).$$

Note that this is the same as the payoff from playing the mixed strategy x against itself.

3.3 Revision protocols

I will now introduce the concept of a revision protocol, before characterizing the properties of evolutionary dynamics generated by their operation in population games. As a benchmark, let us first consider the basic biological mechanism of natural selection in which payoffs represent *fitness* (rates of reproduction) such that strategies with higher payoffs proliferate. When reproduction takes place in continuous time, this yields a continuous-time evolutionary dynamic called *the replicator dynamic* (Taylor and Jonker, 1978). The replicators here are pure strategies that are copied without error from parent to child. As the population state x changes, so do the payoffs and thereby the fitness of each strategy. The replicator dynamic is formalized as a (deterministic) system of ordinary differential equations without mutation.

4 Under more general matching structures, interactions could depend non-linearly on x.

5 As with mixed Nash equilibria of a normal-form game, an indifference condition is required for polymorphic equilibria of a population game: $F_i(x^*) = F_j(x^*) \geq F_k(x^*)$ for all i, j in support of x^* and k not in the support of x^*.

The interpretation of payoffs as fitness can be formalized as follows. Let the rate of growth of strategy i be

$$\frac{\dot{m}_i}{m_i} = [\beta - \delta + F_i(x)],$$

where β and δ are background birth and death rates (which are independent of payoffs). The rate of growth in strategy i's population share x_i is then computed as follows. Recall that $x_i = \frac{m_i}{m}$, so $\ln(x_i) = \ln(m_i) - \ln(m)$. Therefore,

$$\begin{aligned}\frac{\dot{x}_i}{x_i} &= \frac{\dot{m}_i}{m_i} - \frac{\dot{m}}{m}\\ &= \frac{\dot{m}_i}{m_i} - \sum_{j=1}^{n} \frac{\dot{m}_j}{m}\\ &= \frac{\dot{m}_i}{m_i} - \sum_{j=1}^{n} \frac{m_j}{m_j}\frac{\dot{m}_j}{m}\\ &= [\beta - \delta + F_i(x)] - \sum_{j=1}^{n} x_j[\beta - \delta + F_j(x)]\\ &= F_i(x) - \overline{F}(x).\end{aligned}$$

Hence, the growth rate of a strategy equals the excess of its payoff over the average payoff. The following results are immediate. Those subpopulations that are associated with better than average payoffs grow and *vice versa*. The subpopulations associated with pure best replies to the current population state $x \in X$ have the highest growth rate. Finally, a strategy that goes extinct cannot reproduce. Hence, the dynamic exhibits *support invariance*: $\dot{x}_i = x_i[F_i(x) - \overline{F}(x)]$, so that if $m_i = 0$ at some T, then $m_i = 0$ for all t.

Following Sandholm (2010), let us now extend the concept of a revision protocol beyond the basic biological approach to encompass a variety of boundedly rational learning and decision-making processes used by humans.

Definition 1. Sandholm (2010) A revision protocol ρ is a map $\rho : R^n \times X \to R^{n \times n}$.

The scalar $\rho_{ij}(\pi, x)$ is called the conditional switch rate from strategy $i \in S$ to strategy $j \in S$ given payoff vector π and population state x.

A population game F, a population size N, and a revision protocol ρ define a continuous-time evolutionary process on the state space $\chi = X \cap \frac{1}{N}\mathbb{Z}^n = \{x \in X : Nx \in \mathbb{Z}^n\}$, i.e., a discrete grid embedded in the original state space X.

There are two forms of bounded rationality here. First, agents are *myopic*: choices depend only on current behavior and payoffs, not on beliefs about the future trajectory of play. Second, there is *inertia* in that agents do not consider revising their strategies at every point in time. Rather than individuals continuously optimizing, revisions occur at random intervals as follows. Let each agent be equipped with a (Poisson) alarm clock. When the alarm clock rings the agent has one opportunity to revise its strategy. The time between rings is independent across agents and follows a rate 1 exponential distribution. Then the number of rings during time interval $[0, t]$ follows a Poisson distribution with mean t. Strategy choices are made independently of the clocks' rings. An i player faced with a revision opportunity switches to strategy j at rate $\rho_{ij}(\pi, x)$.

When each agent uses such a revision protocol, the state x follows a stochastic process $\{X_t\}$ on the state space χ. The expected motion of $\{X_t\}$ can be described by a deterministic process called *the mean dynamic*, which is a good approximation of the stochastic dynamic over finite time horizons when the population size is large (Benaïm and Weibull, 2003). Given the current state x, the number of revision opportunities received by agents currently playing i over the next dt time units is approximately $Nx_i dt$.[6] Therefore, the number of $i \to j$ switches in the next dt time units is approximately $Nx_i\rho_{ij}dt$. Hence, the expected change in the use of strategy i is:

$$N\left(\sum_{j\in S} x_j\rho_{ji} - x_i\sum_{j\in S}\rho_{ij}\right)dt,$$

that is, the 'inflow' minus the 'outflow'.

Dividing by N and eliminating the time differential yields:

$$\dot{x}_i = \sum_{j\in S} x_j\rho_{ji} - x_i\sum_{j\in S}\rho_{ij},$$

which is the mean dynamic corresponding to the revision protocol ρ and population game F.

Now consider the following specific protocols:

Reinforcement Learning. A revising agent abandons their current strategy with probability linearly decreasing in their current payoff, then imitates the strategy of a randomly chosen opponent:

$$\rho_{ij}(\pi, x) = (K - \pi_i)x_j,$$

where K is an aspiration level.[7] This protocol requires minimal information. In fact, agents need not even know they are in a game.

Imitation of Success. A revising agent is exposed to a randomly chosen opponent and imitates their strategy, say j, with probability linearly increasing in the current payoff to strategy j:

$$\rho_{ij}(\pi, x) = x_j(\pi_j - K).$$

6 Because x_i may change between time 0 and dt, this is an approximation. It is a good approximation for dt small, however.

7 Note that K must be sufficiently large for switch rates to always be positive.

Pairwise Proportional Imitation. An agent is paired at random with an opponent and imitates the opponent if the opponent's payoff is higher than their own, doing so with probability proportional to the payoff difference:

$$\rho_{ij}(\pi, x) = x_j[\pi_j - \pi_i]_+,$$

where $[a]_+ = \max\{a, 0\}$.

The evolutionary dynamic generated by each of these protocols is simply the replicator dynamic. That is, various forms of social learning generate the same population-level behavior as natural selection (e.g. Schlag, 1998; Benaïm and Weibull, 2003). The proof is in the Appendix. Of course, not every revision protocol generates the replicator dynamic at the population level. For example, the *best-response protocol* in which agents choose among the set of myopic best responses to the current population state x generates qualitatively different behavior.

The set of possible rest points for the replicator dynamic, and other imitative dynamics that exhibit support invariance, is the set of *restricted equilibria*:

$$RE(F) = \{x \in X : x_i > 0 \implies F_i(x) = \max_{j \in S: x_j > 0} F_j(x)\}.$$

These are the Nash equilibria of a restricted version of F in which only strategies in the support of x can be played.

When it comes to the best response dynamic, any strategy can be chosen regardless of whether it is present in the population. Hence, the set of rest points is the set of Nash equilibria:

$$NE(F) = \{x \in X : x_i > 0 \implies F_i(x) = \max_{j \in S} F_j(x)\}.$$

3.4 Norm formation

This model of evolutionary dynamics is very different from the standard game-theoretic focus on small groups of forward-looking individuals with equilibrium knowledge and common knowledge of the interactive environment. Here, members of a large population respond to information about others' behavior by gradually revising their actions according to simple, myopic adjustment rules. In large populations, interactions tend to be anonymous—considerations such as reputation and other sources of forward-looking behavior in repeated games are less relevant. In addition, each agent is 'small', so they do not have to consider how their behavior will affect the trajectory of play. When such an evolutionary dynamic converges to a pattern of behavior, we can call this behavioral regularity a *norm*. Thus, norms form from the bottom up out of the decentralized actions of individuals.

To see how this evolutionary framework can be used to model norm formation, consider the following game. An individual with a revision

TABLE 1 Coordination game without coercion.

Pure Coordination

	1	2
1	1, 1	0, 0
2	0, 0	2, 2

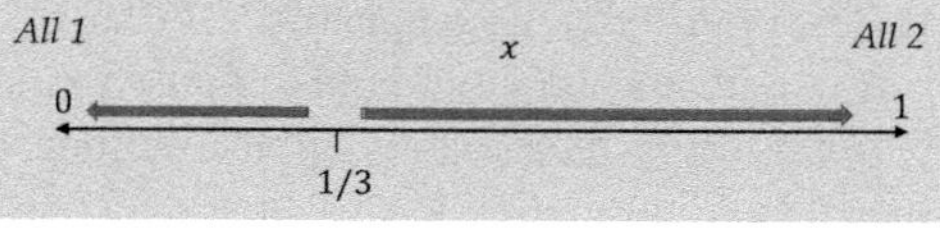

opportunity is paired uniformly at random with another member of the population. Once paired, they engage in conversation. They can either truthfully express what they believe about a controversial topic (action 2) or falsely express a neutral, uncontroversial opinion (action 1). Due to their desire to be agreeable and conform to each other's opinions, they only receive a payoff when they choose the same action. Conditional on coordination, however, the truth still matters: they receive two points for coordinating on the truth and one point for coordinating on the uncontroversial opinion. This pure coordination game is represented in Table 1. Also included are the basins of attraction of the truthful (*All 2*) and untruthful (*All 1*) equilibria under both the replicator and best-response dynamics, where x is the population share playing action 2.

Notice that there are multiple rest points of the evolutionary dynamics considered which correspond to the pure Nash equilibria of the underlying coordination game. If the population starts out with few truth-tellers, behavior in the population will converge to the untruthful (and inefficient) All-1 norm, and *vice versa*. The precise basins of attraction of each norm are defined by the mixed Nash equilibria of the underlying coordination game. In the pure coordination game, we see that only 1/3 of the population need to be truth-tellers for the dynamic to converge to the truth-telling norm. That is good news in that the efficient norm is more 'attractive'.

Now suppose that the government imposes a penalty of 3 for expressing a controversial opinion (action 2). When a player expresses 2 and their opponent expresses the uncontroversial opinion 1, the player is reported to the government by their opponent and receives the penalty. This yields the game in Table 2, which is the canonical Stag Hunt game. Coercion means that we now need 2/3 or more of the population to be truth-tellers for the dynamic to converge to the truth-telling norm. The untruthful equilibrium has a larger basin of attraction and is thus 'more likely' in a sense to be formalized.

TABLE 2 Coordination game with coercion.

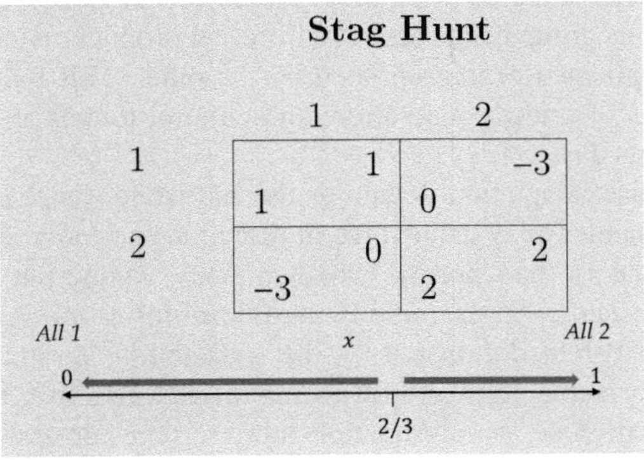

This brings us to various fundamental properties of norm dynamics. For a more comprehensive treatment of these properties, see Young (1998, 2015, forthcoming).

First, there are important implications for behavioral diversity. Locally, norms generate compression in behavior compared to outcomes predicted by standard models of markets. Examples of compression include coordination on certain forms of contract (Bernstein, 1992; Greif, 1993) and contracting terms (Burke and Young, 2011), as well as compressed wage distributions within organizations (Card et al., 2012; Breza et al., 2018). Combined with norm persistence, which creates behavioral regularity over time, this local conformity effect provides greater certainty about market behavior. Globally, however, the existence of multiple equilibria means that two societies or groups in the same interactive environment may arrive at very different norms. To get sharp predictions for testing, applied economists sometimes try to refine or assume away this multiplicity. However, this kind of indeterminacy and behavioral diversity is a fundamental feature of the social and economic world and should be studied, not ignored. Another form of behavioral diversity occurs within populations. A population playing the coordination games studied so far will converge to a *monomorphic* equilibrium, i.e., one strategy drives out all others. In contrast, a single population playing an anti-coordination game such as the canonical Hawk-Dove game (Maynard Smith and Price, 1973) will converge to a *polymorphic* equilibrium with aggressive (*hawk*) and passive (*dove*) types coexisting.

Second, the importance of initial conditions over short-medium horizons tells us about path dependence in norm formation. A basic theme in economic history is that history casts a long shadow (North, 1981, 1990; Allen, 2009; Kuran, 2012). There is also a considerable body of evidence in cultural economics on the path dependence and persistence of norms. For example, Jha (2013) uses historical trade port data and modern violence records to show that medieval Indian port towns are less likely to experience Hindu-Muslim conflict today, even though some of these ports are no longer in operation. Jha argues that each religious group had access to a different production technology, which could not be replicated or expropriated by the other. This mutual dependence stabilized norms of trade, cooperation, and cultural tolerance which locked in and persist to this day.

Third, because adaptation occurs at the individual level in a myopic and decentralized manner, play can evolve in directions no individual intends. One possible outcome is 'bad norms' which nobody wants, but from which no individual can escape. An example is the untruthful norm (All-1) in Tables 1 and 2 which is Pareto dominated by the truth-telling norm. Nevertheless, it remains a locally stable norm and is possibly more 'attractive' than the efficient truth-telling norm. Due to coordination motives (e.g., desire for conformity), it can be difficult to tell whether people like the norm in place or would prefer to collectively deviate to another norm. 'Pluralistic ignorance' occurs when individuals privately reject a norm but conform to it publicly because they mistakenly believe others accept it, thus perpetuating the norm (Bicchieri, 2006). Bursztyn et al. (2020b) present evidence of pluralistic ignorance about gender norms in Saudi Arabia, where there are conservative norms against female employment. Through an anonymous survey of 500 men, they found that 87% privately supported their wives working outside the home, while 72% underestimated the level of support among other men, believing only 63% shared this view. This kind of misperception of injunctive norms can lock in unwanted behavioral (or descriptive) norms.

3.5 Stochastic dynamics

Even more can be learned about the evolution of norms by turning our attention from the deterministic approximation studied so far to the exact stochastic process $\{X_t\}$ governing norm formation. The stochastic dynamic introduces two new properties of norms: punctuated equilibrium and emergence.

3.5.1 Punctuated equilibrium

Deterministic evolutionary dynamics tell us about norm formation and persistence. History, however, is marked by periods of rapid, dramatic change. Examples include the spread of Christianity and Islam, the Reformation, the Enlightenment, and the French Revolution. Both social stasis and change can be accommodated in our framework. Recall that the deterministic process studied so far is only a good approximation to the stochastic dynamic over finite horizons. In the long run, norm shifts will occur taking the process toward a new equilibrium, far from the earlier one. In evolutionary biology, this is known as *punctuated equilibrium*. The fossil record indicates that species experience long periods of stasis interrupted by bursts of evolutionary change (Eldredge and Gould, 1972). An example is the Cambrian Explosion around 540 million years ago as seen in the fossils found in the Burgess Shale which indicate a sudden emergence of complex organisms after a very long period of simpler life forms.

Social institutions such as money, religion, standards of dress, and rules of deference exhibit similar punctuated dynamics. Revolutions, for example, are explosive events that upset longstanding norms of self-censorship and acquiescence to authoritarian control. Kuran (1991) provides an explanation for the abrupt and unforeseen revolutions in Eastern Europe in 1989 based on preference falsification. Suppression of dissent makes it difficult to predict when a critical mass of people will publicly voice their opposition and trigger a norm shift that leads to revolution. Another example is the rapid shift in American public opinion toward greater acceptance of gay rights over recent decades. Fernández et al. (2024) link this norm shift to the increased visibility of the gay community during the AIDS epidemic which triggered political and cultural changes driven by media representation.

We can capture the sudden disruption of long periods of stasis by studying the precise stochastic dynamic introduced in Section 3.3. In our formulation, $\{X_t\}$ is a continuous-time (time-homogeneous) *Markov process* on the finite state space $\mathcal{X}$. The process is fully characterized by its transition probabilities $P = \{P_{xy}\}_{x,y \in \mathcal{X}}$, where P_{xy} is the probability of transiting from state x to y in exactly one revision. Over finite-horizons, the focus is on the deterministic mean dynamic. In the long run, however, the process can move around the state space at random with transition paths constrained by P. While we cannot precisely predict the motion of the evolutionary dynamic, we can say quite a bit about its long-run behavior through its *stationary distribution* μ. A stationary distribution of a Markov process $\{X_t\}$ is a probability distribution over the state space χ, i.e., μ is a $|\chi|$-dimensional vector with each element being a probability placed on a state. The stationary distribution is an important description of long-run behavior because it is the frequency distribution of visits to each state as $t \to \infty$, i.e. almost surely the process spends proportion $\mu(x)$ of the time in state x (Kemeny and Snell, 1960).

Let us follow the definitive approach of Young (1993a, 1998) to determine which states the stationary distribution places weight on. A *closed communication class* C is a set of states in which each state x in C is accessible from a state y if and only if y is also in C. An *absorbing state* is a singleton closed set. If a state is part of a closed communication class, it is *recurrent*. Otherwise, it is *transient*.

Theorem 2. *Let $\{X_t\}$ be a Markov Process on a finite set $\mathcal{X}$. Starting from any state x_0, the frequency distribution of visits to states converges to a stationary distribution μ, which solves*

$$\mu P = \mu.$$

In such a vector, $\mu(x) = 0$ for all transient states.

That is why closed communication classes are commonly called recurrence classes.

There exists at least one stationary distribution because every non-negative row stochastic matrix has at least one left eigenvector with eigenvalue one, i.e., there exists a μ such that $\mu P = \mu$. Under certain conditions, this stationary distribution is unique. For example, a Markov Process is *irreducible* if there is a positive probability path from each state to every other, or equivalently if the entire state space χ forms a closed communication class.

Theorem 3. *If the Markov process $\{X_t\}$ is irreducible then it has a unique stationary distribution, which is the long run frequency distribution of visits to states independently of the initial state.*

In this case, we say that the process $\{X_t\}$ is *ergodic*, i.e., its long-run behavior does not depend on initial conditions. If there are multiple stationary distributions, then the long run frequency distribution is among these, and can be any one of them. When there is randomness in individual choice, due to experimentation, errors, or idiosyncratic payoff shocks, such that all strategies are chosen with positive probability, then the Markov process produced is irreducible and therefore ergodic. Let us now consider two such protocols.

Best response with mutations. A revising agent switches to its current best response with probability $1-\varepsilon$, and chooses a strategy uniformly (mutates) with probability $\varepsilon > 0$. Let us refer to this protocol as $BRM(\varepsilon)$.[8]

Logit Choice. Switch rates are as follows:

$$\rho_{ij}(\pi) = \frac{exp(\eta^{-1}\pi_j)}{\sum_{k\in S} exp(\eta^{-1}\pi_k)}.$$

We can define $\varepsilon^{-1} = \exp(\eta^{-1})$, where ε is an increasing function of η. As $\eta \to 0$, $\varepsilon \to 0$. In this way, we can rewrite the revision protocol as

$$\rho_{ij}(\pi) = \frac{\varepsilon^{-\pi_j}}{\sum_{k\in S} \varepsilon^{-\pi_k}}.$$

This is a smoothed version of the $BRM(\varepsilon)$ protocol with the feature that agents tend to avoid more costly errors. In both cases, the noise level is given by ε.

Even though these revision protocols generate an irreducible Markov process and thereby yield a unique stationary distribution, two problems remain. First, it may not be possible to compute the stationary distribution explicitly. Second, even if it is possible to do so, the stationary distribution may spread weight widely over the state space and fail to yield sharp predictions. The leading solution to this problem is provided by the concept of *stochastic stability*, which can drastically reduce the number of states which attract positive weight in

8 In case of best response ties, it is often assumed that a non-mutating agent sticks with its current strategy if it is a best response; otherwise it chooses at random from among the set of best responses.

the stationary distribution. In particular, as we take the limit $\varepsilon \to 0$ (the small noise limit) or as $N \to \infty$ (the large population limit) or both, the stationary distribution concentrates weight on a small set of states, and often a single state. There are different ways of defining stochastic stability depending on which limits are taken and in what order. Results can differ depending on the definition used. I focus here on the small noise limit:

Definition 2. A state x is *stochastically stable* if $\lim_{\varepsilon \to 0} \mu^{\varepsilon, N}(x) > 0$ (Foster and Young, 1990).

In other words, for ε small, the process spends virtually all the time (as $t \to \infty$) in the stochastically stable set of states. While long periods of stasis are disrupted by abrupt shifts in norms, the stochastically stable states tell us which norms will dominate in the long run. Thus, curiously, the introduction of noise enables us to say more about norm dynamics, because it makes long-run behavior independent of initial conditions. In contrast, behavioral economics tends to take a micro-focus and highlight the problems caused by noisy decision-making, while ignoring its systemic effects on norm dynamics (Kahneman et al., 2021). Young (1998) focuses on the following class of noise structures.

Definition 3. For each $\varepsilon \in [0, \varepsilon^*]$, let $\{X_t^\varepsilon\}$ be a Markov process.

$\{X_t^\varepsilon\}$ is a *regular perturbed Markov process* if it is (a) irreducible for all $\varepsilon \in (0, \varepsilon^*]$ and (b) if for every $x, x' \in X$, $P_{xx'}^\varepsilon$ approaches $P_{xx'}^0$ at an exponential rate, i.e.

$$\lim_{\varepsilon \to 0} P_{xx'}^\varepsilon = P_{xx'}^0,$$

and if $P_{xx'}^\varepsilon > 0$ for $\varepsilon > 0$, then $0 < \lim_{\varepsilon \to 0} P_{xx'}^\varepsilon / \varepsilon^{r(x,x')} < \infty$ for some $r(x, x') \geq 0$.

$r(x, x')$ is a real number measuring the *resistance* (or cost) of the transition $x \to x'$. There cannot be two distinct exponents that satisfy the last condition, so $r(x, x')$ is uniquely identified. Note that $r(x, x') = 0$ if and only if $P_{xx'}^0 > 0$, i.e., transitions that occur under the unperturbed process ($\varepsilon \to 0$) have zero resistance. It is straightforward to show that the BRM(ε) and logit choice protocols generate regular perturbed Markov processes.

To compute the stochastically stable states, let $E_1, E_2, \ldots, E_K$ be recurrence classes of the unperturbed process ($\varepsilon = 0$). A jk-path is a sequence of states $\zeta = (x_1, x_2, ..., x_q)$ that begins in recurrence class E_j and ends in E_k. The resistance is the sum of the resistances of its edges, i.e. $r(\zeta) = r(x_1, x_2) + r(x_2, x_3) + ... + r(x_{q-1}, x_q)$. Let $r_{jk} = \min r(\zeta)$ be the least resistance over all jk paths. By the definition of a recurrence class, $r_{jk} > 0$ for all $j \neq k$.

Next construct a complete directed graph of K vertices, one for each recurrence class. The weight on the directed edge $j \to k$ is r_{jk}. A tree rooted at vertex j (a j-*tree*) is a set of $K - 1$ directed edges such that from every vertex different to j there is a unique directed path in the tree to j. The resistance of a rooted tree is the sum of the resistances of its edges. The *stochastic potential* of E_j is the minimum resistance over all trees rooted at j.

Theorem 4. *(Young, 1993a) Let $\{X_t^\varepsilon\}$ be a regular perturbed Markov process and let μ^ε be the unique stationary distribution of $\{X_t^\varepsilon\}$ for each $\varepsilon > 0$. Then $\lim_{\varepsilon \to 0} \mu^\varepsilon = \mu^0$ exists, and μ^0 is a stationary distribution of the unperturbed process $\{X_t^0\}$.*

The stochastically stable states are precisely those states that are contained in the recurrence classes of $\{X_t^0\}$ having minimum stochastic potential.

To illustrate, consider a 2×2 coordination game played by a single population. There are two recurrence classes E_1 (All-1) and E_2 (All-2). With a certain sequence of nonbest responses, the perturbed process can transit between recurrence classes. Let $r(E_1, E_2)$ be the resistance of the transition $E_1 \to E_2$. Under the $BRM(\varepsilon)$ protocol, this is the minimum number of errors required for the process to transit from state E_1 to state E_2. In addition, let x^* be the weight on strategy 2 in the mixed-Nash equilibrium of the underlying coordination game. The corresponding trees are:

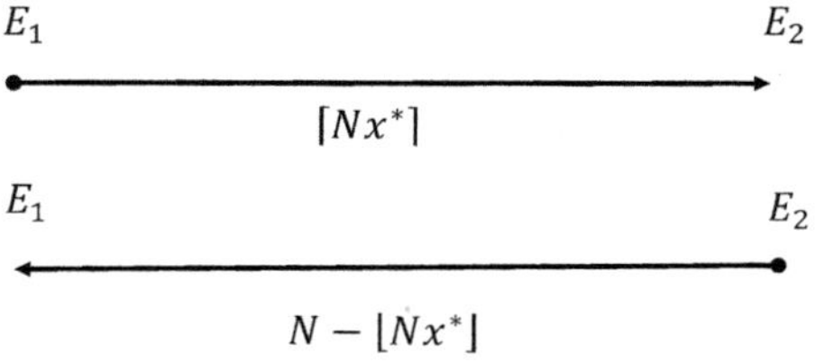

For N sufficiently large, E_1 is stochastically stable if and only if $Nx^* > N - Nx^*$ or $x^* > \frac{1}{2}$. For a symmetric 2×2 game, this is equivalent to the *risk dominance* criterion (Harsanyi and Selten, 1988). That is, the stochastically stable norm is not necessarily the payoff dominant norm, but the risk dominant one. Returning to our expression game in Table 1, $x^* = \frac{1}{3}$. Hence, in the long run, without coercion, society will spend almost all of the time in the truth-telling norm. When coercion is introduced, however, as in Table 2, $x^* = \frac{2}{3}$. Hence, coercion drives society to spend almost all of the time in the untruthful norm.[9]

When there are many recurrence classes of the unperturbed Markov process $\{X_t^0\}$, the spanning tree method of finding a stochastically stable state can *sometimes* be difficult to implement. Consider the following method due to Ellison (1993) that provides a sufficient condition for stochastic stability (the spanning tree method provides a necessary and sufficient condition). Once again, let $r(E, E_\ell)$ be the resistance (or cost) of the transition $E \to E_\ell$. Define the *radius* of recurrence class E by

$$R(E) = min_\ell \; r(E, E_\ell)$$

9 Similarly, see Carvalho (2017) on the effect of cultural taboos on social coordination.

and the *coradius* of E by

$$CR(E) = max_\ell \; r(E_\ell, E).$$

Theorem 5. *(Ellison, 1993) If* $R(E) > CR(E)$*, then* E *is the unique stochastically stable class of* $\{X_t^\varepsilon\}$.

The intuition for this result is as follows. A lower bound on the probability of exiting recurrence class E is on the order of $\varepsilon^{R(E)}$. An upper bound on the probability of entering recurrence class E is on the order of $\varepsilon^{CR(E)}$. As $\varepsilon \to 0$, $\varepsilon^{R(E)-CR(E)} \to 0$ iff $R(E) > CR(E)$. In this case, the proportion of time spent in E is far, far greater than the proportion of time spent outside of E as the noise level becomes vanishingly small.

Therefore, stochastic norm dynamics generate the long periods of stasis punctuated by abrupt shifts in behavior observed historically. Moreover, these punctuated dynamics allow us to say quite a lot about the social norms that prevail in the long run, with norms that are easy to establish but hard to escape being in place almost all of the time. Despite the noise in the process (or rather because of it), the predictions are sharp in the sense that they are independent of initial conditions.

3.5.2 Emergence

The second property of norm formation that comes out of the stochastic analysis is *emergence*. Emergence is a concept first developed in physics to describe systems whose behavior at a macroscopic level cannot be straightforwardly deduced from the properties of their individual components at a microscopic level. The concept took shape in thermodynamics and statistical mechanics during the nineteenth century, where macroscopic properties such as temperature and pressure arise from the collective behavior of countless microscopic particles (Boltzmann, 1877; Maxwell, 1860). From the twentieth century onward, advances in nonlinear dynamics, chaotic dynamics, and complex systems deepened our understanding of emergence, producing applications to cosmology, quantum field theory, superconductivity, and many other areas (Pines et al., 2023).

We have already seen flashes of emergent behavior in the selection of risk-dominant over payoff-dominant equilibria in 2×2 games. Though somewhat surprising, there is, however, an intuitive explanation for this. Strategies that form part of a payoff-dominant equilibrium perform better in equilibrium (by definition). However, for an evolutionary dynamic to converge to such an equilibrium, these strategies must also perform well out-of-equilibrium. Where the risk-dominant equilibrium and payoff-dominant equilibrium diverge, it is the strategies that form part of the risk-dominant equilibrium that perform better out-of-equilibrium. Hence, it is these 'strategically safer' strategies that are favored by evolution. The fact that there is an intuitive explanation for the stochastic stability of risk-dominant equilibria in 2×2 games means that it is not the best example of emergence.

Deeper insights into emergence in economic and social systems are provided by Schelling (1978) in his seminal book, *Micromotives and Macrobehavior*. Schelling shows how individual decision-making can lead to unintended and complex outcomes at the societal level. The leading example is Schelling's model of residential segregation. Suppose individuals are located on squares of a checkerboard (representing a neighborhood) and are one of two types, black or white. They have preferences over the types of their immediate neighbors and can relocate accordingly. In agent-based simulations, Schelling found that individuals need only have mild preferences for being near others of the same type (e.g., they only want one immediate neighbor of their own type) for full residential segregation to be the most likely outcome, with all the black pieces on one side of the board and all the white pieces on the other side. An analyst viewing such an extreme outcome may infer high levels of intolerance in this population. Instead, residential segregation here is an emergent phenomenon weakly linked to individual motives. Young (1998) provides a formal analysis of Schelling's model and demonstrates that the fully segregated states are indeed stochastically stable.

Another important example of emergence is bargaining norms as studied by Young (1993b). Consider the Nash demand game. Two players simultaneously announce demands, x_1 and x_2 respectively, from a pot of size one. If their demands sum to one or less, each player receives their demand. The associated utilities are $u(x_1)$ and $v(x_2)$. Otherwise, both players get zero. Every set of demands that sum to one is a Nash equilibrium of this game (and there are more). That is, there is a continuum of Nash equilibria. How then can we formulate a prediction of the bargaining outcome? Classical game theory does not provide a method for doing so. But Young's evolutionary analysis does.

What I will present now is a simplified version of the analysis in Young (1993b). Even then, we will need to embellish the simple framework we have been working with by introducing two populations of agents, a new revision protocol called *adaptive play*, and some change in notation. Consider two disjoint populations, rows and columns (e.g., buyers and sellers; workers and bosses) of equal size N. Every revision opportunity, the selected player is matched with a player from the other population to play a Nash demand game. Their utility functions u (row) and v (column) are strictly increasing, concave, and continuously differentiable. To keep the strategy set finite, consider a discretized set of demands $\Delta \equiv \{\delta, 2\delta, 3\delta, ..., 1\}$. Every division $(x, 1-x)$, such that $0 < x < 1$, constitutes a *strict Nash equilibrium* of the demand game. We shall call such a division a *bargaining norm*.

Let us introduce the adaptive play protocol. The history of play is a vector $h^t = \left((x_1^{t-m}, x_2^{t-m}), \ldots (x_1^{t-1}, x_2^{t-1})\right)$, where x_1^{t-1} is the most recent demand made by a row player and m is the memory length. A *convention* is a history of the form $h^* = \left((x, 1-x), \ldots (x, 1-x)\right)$, which is simply m instances of a norm. A revising row player at time t draws a random sample of size am (an integer) from h^t, the m previous plays by members of the column population. A revising column player at time t draws a random sample of size bm from the m previous plays by members of the row population. The revising player computes the frequency $p(x)$ of each demand x in their sample. With high probability $1-\varepsilon$, a revising player best responds to their sample. With low probability ε, they choose a demand x within δ of a best response to their sample.[10]

Proposition 1. *The unperturbed process converges almost surely to a convention from any initial state and locks in.*

The proof is in the Appendix.

Again, there is a large number of potential bargaining norms. Which ones are stochastically stable? The answer is not straightforward, *a priori*. To answer this question, we need to analyze transitions between conventions under the perturbed dynamic.

Suppose that the process is in convention $(x, 1-x)$. Recall that all transitions are 'local'. What is the probability of a 'downward' transition to convention $(x-\delta, 1-x+\delta)$? Suppose there are i consecutive plays of $1-x+\delta$ by column players, so that the next revising row player can draw a sample with i instances of $1-x+\delta$. By reducing their demand to $x-\delta$, the row player gets $u(x-\delta)$ for certain. By retaining their demand x, the row player estimates getting $u(x)$ with probability $1-\frac{i}{am}$, and zero otherwise. Hence row players retain their demand if

$$(1-\tfrac{i}{am})u(x) \geq u(x-\delta).$$

The critical value of i is

$$i^*(x) = am\frac{u(x)-u(x-\delta)}{u(x)}.$$

Similarly, a column player retains their demand of $1-x$ (rather than increasing it to $1-x+\delta$) when drawing a sample of j instances of $x-\delta$ if

$$v(1-x) \geq \tfrac{j}{bm}v(1-x+\delta).$$

The critical value of j is

$$j^*(x) = bm\frac{v(1-x)}{v(1-x+\delta)}.$$

Therefore it takes a minimum number of errors $\lceil i^*(x)\rceil \wedge \lceil j^*(x)\rceil$ to induce a downward transition. When δ is sufficiently small, the first term is the smaller of the two (as the loss from sticking to x is large relative to the loss of δ from reducing demand, for δ small). Therefore the resistance of a downward transition is

$$r(x, x-\delta) = \left\lceil am\frac{u(x)-u(x-\delta)}{u(x)}\right\rceil.$$

10 'Local errors' are not required in the paper, but are assumed here for the purpose of illustration.

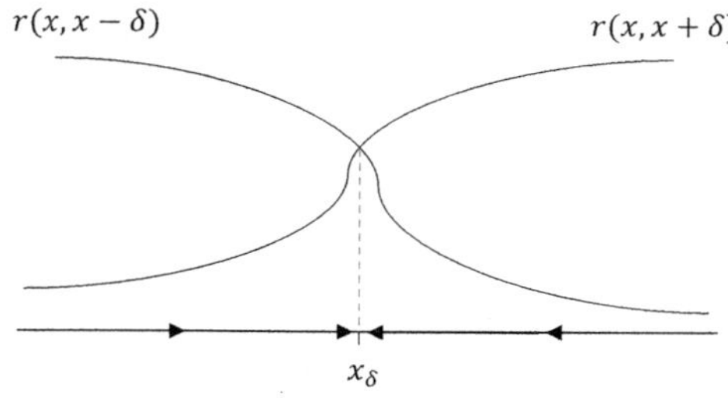

FIGURE 1 Resistance of downward and upward transitions in evolutionary bargaining model.

By an analogous argument, the resistance of an upward transition is

$$r(x, x+\delta) = \left\lceil bm \frac{v(1-x) - v(1-x-\delta)}{v(1-x)} \right\rceil.$$

For δ sufficiently small, the resistances are well approximated by

$$r(x, x-\delta) \approx \left\lceil am \frac{\delta u'(x)}{u(x)} \right\rceil,$$
$$r(x, x+\delta) \approx \left\lceil bm \frac{\delta v'(1-x)}{v(1-x)} \right\rceil.$$

Define the function:

$$f_\delta(x) = \min\{r(x, x+\delta), r(x, x-\delta)\}.$$

Note that $r(x, x+\delta)$ is an increasing function of x, whereas $r(x, x-\delta)$ is a decreasing function of x. Therefore, $f_\delta(x)$ is unimodal as shown in Fig. 1.

Let x_δ be a maximizer of $f_\delta(x)$. The tree rooted at x_δ is the least resistant rooted tree. Hence the stochastically stable state(s) correspond to the convention(s) that maximize(s) $f_\delta(x)$. When δ is small and m is large relative to δ (so that there are no integer issues), any maximum of $f_\delta(x)$ lies close to the point x^* at which the two curves intersect:

$$a \frac{u'(x^*)}{u(x^*)} = b \frac{v'(1-x^*)}{v(1-x^*)}. \tag{1}$$

Several remarks are in order. First, it cannot be straightforwardly deduced from the primitives of the model that the bargaining norm that prevails in the long-run x^* satisfies this condition. In other words, this is a case of emergence. Second, notice that under symmetry, $a = b$ and $u = v$, the bargaining outcome is equal shares. Hence, bargaining norms have an emergent egalitarian property. Third, Eq. (1) is not just any condition. It is the first-order condition that defines the asymmetric Nash bargaining solution. Nash (1950b) tried to solve the bargaining problem using an entirely different approach to Young. He stated three axioms—Pareto efficiency, invariance to equivalent utility representations (scale invariance), and independence of irrelevant alternatives—which can be interpreted as conditions that a 'reasonable' bargaining solution should satisfy. Nash demonstrated that there is a unique bargaining solution that satisfies these conditions which is given precisely by the solution x^* to condition (1). Nash interpreted a and b as the bargaining power of each agent. In Young's evolutionary model, bargaining power is determined by sample size—the more information one has, the greater one's share of the surplus. The result is formally stated as follows.

Theorem 6. *(Young, 1993b) Consider random matching from two populations to play the discrete Nash demand game using the adaptive play protocol with memory m and sample sizes am and bm. As δ becomes small, the stochastically stable division(s) converge to the asymmetric Nash (1950b) bargaining solution.*

Therefore, norms have important emergent properties: precisely which norms arise and persist over the long run is not easily deducible from the incentives of the individuals involved. This fact should call for epistemic humility when it comes to understanding social institutions. In particular, policymakers should be highly cautious with regard to norm interventions. The emergent properties of norms mean that the role of incentives in shaping behavior could be poorly understood.

4 Agenda: cultural factors underpinning norms

The model of norm formation examined so far can be extended to incorporate various cultural factors underpinning norms, including the cultural evolution of preferences, the role of identity in shaping behavior, and top-down attempts to shift norms by shaping preferences and beliefs. This section examines these cultural factors and sets out an agenda for incorporating them into the standard model of norm formation:

- Internalization of norms,
- Identity-dependence of norms,
- Contestation of norms.

The mechanisms governing preference formation, in particular, can be viewed as parallel cultural evolutionary processes operating over longer time scales. For example, Nunn and Wantchekon (2011) combine historical data on slave exports and ethnographic records with modern survey data from the Afrobarometer to study the long-term effects of the slave trade. They find that African ethnic groups with greater exposure to the slave trade exhibit lower participation in market transactions, civic activities, mutual support networks, informal lending, community projects, and long-term ventures requiring trust. Accordingly, these groups have lower levels of trust today, both within and across groups. Their explanation is that slave raids taught individuals to be wary of betrayal by neighbors and kin, and this mistrust was culturally transmitted across generations and encoded in behavioral norms.[11] Therefore, it is important to incorporate cultural evolutionary processes into our framework for modeling norms.

4.1 Norm internalization

According to the leading model of norms in economics, individuals form beliefs about others' behavior based on the history of play and, given these strategic beliefs, choose behavior to maximize a payoff function (e.g., Young, 1998). In this model, individual preferences (i.e., payoff functions) are fixed and, in particular, unaffected by the patterns of behavior that emerge. That is, people abide by norms because they expect others to abide by the norm. According to this view, if you place a person in a new environment, they will fairly rapidly adjust to the new system of norms. There is, however, substantial evidence that norms are internalized and ported to contexts in which they no longer apply. Once a norm is in place, people either unconsciously follow the norm, experience some form of internal punishment (e.g., guilt, anxiety) when violating the norm, and/or pass on a preference for the norm to their children.

For example, Fernández and Fogli (2009) show that second-generation immigrants whose parents come from countries with higher fertility and lower female labor force participation have more children and are less likely to work outside the home. Blau et al. (2013) and Salari (2018) present evidence that this is due to intra-household transmission of cultural preferences from mother to daughter. Atkin (2016) finds that interstate migrants in India pay a significant caloric cost to consume staple foods from their region of origin, most likely due to internalization of norms relating to food preparation and consumption. Finally, Fisman and Miguel (2007) show that parking fines incurred by UN diplomats in Manhattan (all of whom had diplomatic immunity) are higher for those from high-corruption countries. This suggests that culture runs deeper than social coordination and is encoded in preferences. Naturally, such cultural processes can lock in norms to various degrees and thereby affect their stability. Thus, norm internalization should be incorporated into the framework for modeling social institutions.

In economics, the leading model of the evolution of preferences and other cultural traits is the cultural transmission model of Bisin and Verdier (2000a, 2001), which I will now briefly describe. (See Bisin et al. (2023) for a review.)[12]

---

[11] See Algan and Cahuc (2010) for further evidence of intergenerational transmission of trust.

[12] An alternative model is the indirect evolutionary approach developed by Frank (1987), Güth and Yaari (1992), Heifetz et al. (2007), and Dekel et al. (2007) in which individuals make decisions based on a subjective payoff function determined by their cultural traits. In turn, the cultural traits that proliferate are the ones that maximize an objective fitness function, which may differ from the subjective payoff function which individuals have in mind. See Bergeron et al. (2024) for an application of this approach to the cultural evolution of demotivating traits.

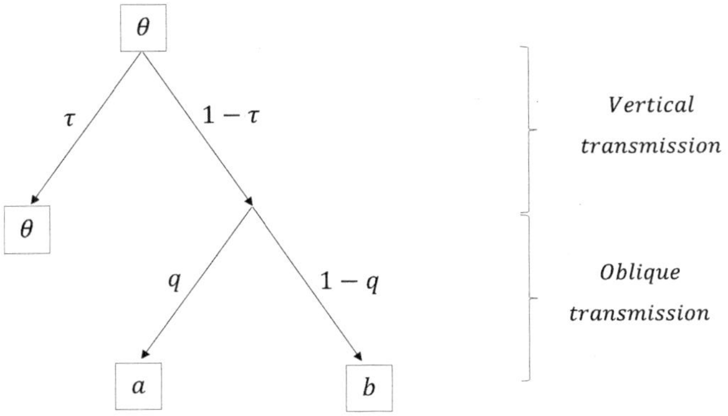

FIGURE 2 $\tau \in [0, 1]$ is parental socialization effort, and q is the (adult) population share of trait a.

Consider a large population, formally a continuum of unit mass. Each individual possesses a cultural trait a or b. Let q be the population share of trait a. Each parent (asexually) produces one child, socializes them, then dies. Following Cavalli-Sforza and Feldman (1981), there are two forms of socialization in this model:

- *Vertical transmission*: with probability τ_θ, a parent with trait $\theta \in \{a, b\}$ passes on trait θ to their child.
- *Oblique transmission*: with probability $1 - \tau_\theta$, a child is matched at random with someone from their parent's generation and acquires their trait.

This process of cultural transmission is depicted by Fig. 2 for an individual born to a parent with trait θ. Hence, the likelihood that an individual with trait b has a child with trait a is $P_{ba} = (1 - \tau_b)q$. The likelihood that an individual with trait a has a child with trait b is $P_{ab} = (1 - \tau_a)(1 - q)$. In continuous time, the resulting dynamic is:

$$\begin{aligned} \dot{q} &= \underbrace{(1-q)\,P_{ba}}_{inflow} - \underbrace{q\,P_{ab}}_{outflow} \\ &= (1-q)(1-\tau_b)q - q(1-\tau_a)(1-q) \\ &= (\tau_a - \tau_b)q(1-q). \end{aligned} \tag{2}$$

With exogenous levels of socialization τ, the evolutionary dynamic converges to a *monomorphic* cultural equilibrium. In particular:

- $q = 1$ is asymptotically stable if $\tau_a > \tau_b$,
- $q = 0$ is asymptotically stable if $\tau_b > \tau_a$.

How then do we get cultural diversity? Bisin and Verdier's contribution is to introduce a choice of socialization effort, for example teaching within the home, school choice, residential choice, and homogamy. To model socialization choice, parents need to have preferences over the traits that their children can acquire. Bisin and Verdier assume *imperfect empathy*: parents evaluate their children's behavior based on their own preferences. That is, a parent with trait θ gets a payoff of $V_{\theta\theta'}$ if their child acquires trait θ', where $V_{\theta\theta} > V_{\theta\theta'}$ whenever $\theta \neq \theta'$. Hence, a parent with trait a in state q has the following payoff function:

$$U^a(q) = \underbrace{[\tau_a + (1-\tau_a)q]}_{P_{aa}} V_{aa} + \underbrace{(1-\tau_a)(1-q)}_{P_{ab}} V_{ab} - c(\tau_a).$$

They choose socialization effort τ_a at cost $c(\tau_a)$ to maximize this function. A parent with trait b in state q has the following payoff function:

$$U^b(q) = \underbrace{[\tau_b + (1-\tau_b)(1-q)]}_{P_{bb}} V_{bb} + \underbrace{(1-\tau_b)q}_{P_{ba}} V_{ba} - c(\tau_b).$$

Define 'cultural intolerances' $\Delta_a = V_{aa} - V_{ab}$ and $\Delta_b = V_{bb} - V_{ba}$. The first-order condition for an a-trait parent is

$$(1-q)\Delta_a = c'(\tau_a).$$

The first-order condition for a b-trait parent is

$$q\Delta_b = c'(\tau_b).$$

Thus, optimal socialization effort varies as follows:

(i) τ_i is strictly increasing in 'cultural intolerance' Δ_i,
(ii) τ_a is strictly decreasing in q,
(iii) τ_b is strictly increasing in q,
(iv) $\tau_a > \tau_b$ if and only if $q < \frac{\Delta_a}{\Delta_a + \Delta_b}$.

Hence, people with intolerant cultural traits socialize more intensively. Likewise, 'minorities' expend more effort on socialization, consistent with evidence on religious participation by Catholic minorities in the United States (Bisin et al., 2004). This socialization behavior has the following long-term effect:

Proposition 2. *(Bisin and Verdier, 2001) The cultural dynamic converges to the interior steady state* $q^* = \frac{\Delta_a}{\Delta_a + \Delta_b}$ *from any* $q \in (0, 1)$.

Hence, a *polymorphic* cultural distribution emerges from almost every initial state and the share of each trait in this distribution equals its relative intolerance.

This model is extended to n traits by Montgomery (2010). Moreover, Montgomery shows that when the cultural intolerance of trait i toward j, i.e., Δ_{ij}, is interpreted as the payoff from playing strategy i against j, the Bisin-Verdier cultural dynamic is the same as the replicator dynamic operating on uniform matching to play the $n \times n$ game composed of the payoffs Δ_{ij}. Thus, standard results from evolutionary game theory on the replicator dynamic can be applied to the study of cultural transmission.

To model internalization of norms in the Bisin-Verdier model, we need to abandon imperfect empathy and make the payoffs to having a child with trait θ dependent on the pattern of behavior in society, i.e., the population state x. For example, the closer society is to consensus (i.e., x is to a pure population state), the more a parent may want their child to acquire a preference for the prevailing behavioral norm. How much so may depend on the particular norm, thereby altering which norms are stochastically stable. Hence, norm internalization should be incorporated into the framework for modeling social institutions, including applications of stochastic stability. An early attempt to make cultural transmission dependent on the distribution of behavior was Bisin and Verdier (2000b). A more systematic analysis is conducted by Della Lena and Dindo (2024), but how internalization shapes stochastic dynamics and equilibrium selection remains to be studied.

4.2 Identity-dependence

Population structure in models of norms is usually captured by a network specifying the strength of pairwise links between individuals (Jackson, 2008; Goyal, 2023). These links tell us who interacts with whom and how frequently. Identity is a different form of population structure. Fictitious communities form around markers such as ethnicity, religion, gender, and kinship group (Anderson, 2006; Desmet and Wacziarg, 2021). People may care about, imitate, and learn from members of their identity group even if they never directly interact with them. Hence, the role of identity in norm formation is not captured by network-based models of local interaction.

Social identity can shape preferences and norms in a number of ways. The mechanism that has attracted most attention is ingroup bias. Chen and Li (2009) split experimental subjects into two groups based on their preferences for paintings by Wassily Kandinsky and Paul Klee. They find that average earnings are significantly higher when participants are matched with an ingroup rather than an outgroup member due to greater generosity, greater likelihood of a social welfare maximizing choice, and positive reciprocity among ingroup members. Subjects are also more likely to forgive less generous behavior of ingroup members. Similar findings of ingroup bias are observed in the field. For example, Shayo and Zussman (2011) analyze data from Israeli small claims courts between 2000 and 2004, where the assignment of cases to Arab or Jewish judges is effectively random. They find that judges were significantly more likely to favor individuals from their own group and the salience of group membership (e.g., Arab vs. Jewish) and ingroup bias in judicial decisions heightens around the time of terrorist attacks.

More relevant for our purposes is the seminal work by Akerlof and Kranton (2000, 2010) on the economics of identity. Their main idea is that each identity group (chosen or ascriptive) has a distinct set of prescriptive norms, which are internalized and socially enforced. The identity-dependence of norms explains a range of anomalous behavior, including group differences in labor supply and occupational choice, disengagement with education, and frictions within organizations. However, this raises the question: Where do these identity-specific norms come from?

Oh (2023) examines the extent to which norms of occupational choice are shaped by historical categories and roles. In a field experiment on caste and labor supply in rural India, casual daily-wage laborers were asked to evaluate various real job offers. Workers were significantly less willing to take up offers that required them to spend as little as ten minutes on tasks associated with other castes. The effect was larger for castes lower in the caste hierarchy than a subject's own, but also present for higher castes. The effects persisted when decisions were made in private, reflecting internalized identity norms. In addition, Carvalho (2013) studies veiling among Muslim women and shows how the historical meaning of the veil as a religious symbol can be used to navigate conservative gender norms. Due to its acquired meaning, veiling serves as a commitment device for abiding by the conservative norms of the community even while outside its monitoring range. This allows women to take up educational and labor market opportunities without losing community esteem. There is now considerable empirical support for this theory (Aksoy and Gambetta, 2016; Abdelgadir and Fouka, 2020; Shofia, 2024). An appeal to historical identity-specific norms, however, simply pushes the question back a level. Ultimately, we would like to understand how these historical categories and roles emerge and persist over centuries.

Work by Carvalho and Pradelski (2022, 2024) on the evolution of identity-specific norms of economic participation (e.g., education, employment) makes progress in this direction (see also Akerlof, 2017).[13] They propose a 'representation dynamic' governing the evolution of identity norms in which the larger a group's representation in an economic activity, the more the activity is deemed 'normal' or 'appropriate' for its members. Since representation is a rival good, representation concerns induce rivalry between groups, alongside increasing returns within groups. To understand the representation dynamic, consider two (fixed) groups N_A and N_B. Each individual i can choose to participate in an economic activity ($e_i = 1$) or not ($e_i = 0$). Examples of participation ($e_i = 1$) include college education, labor force participation, and choice of a high-skilled occupation. The participation rate for group A, p_A, is the share of group A members choosing $e_i = 1$. The representation of group A, R_A, is the share of participants from group A. p_B and R_B are defined similarly for group B. The key supposition made by Carvalho and Pradelski (2022, 2024)

[13] Another mechanism is screening by identity groups. When identities are chosen, groups (especially, religious organizations) design behavioral requirements for membership to promote cooperation and efficient matching (Iannaccone, 1992; Carvalho et al., 2019; Carvalho, 2020; Carvalho and Sacks, 2021).

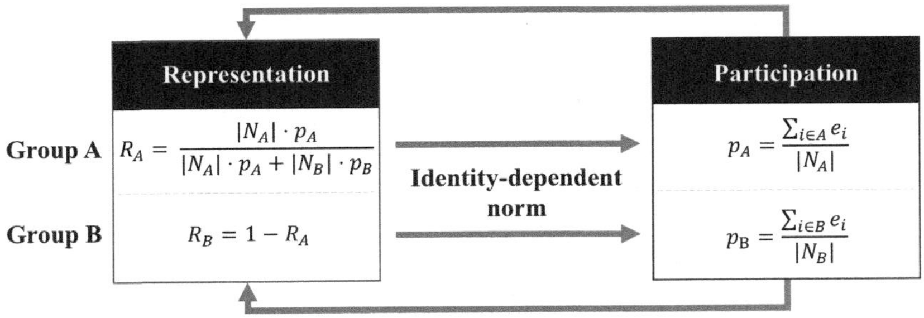

FIGURE 3 The representation dynamic.

is that higher representation in an activity makes individuals feel that the activity is more 'normal' or congruent with their identity. Thus, there is a feedback loop in which low representation of a group reduces participation by its members, which further lowers the group's representation, and so forth. This process is depicted by Fig. 3.

Embedded in this representation feedback loop is a rivalry between groups, as is apparent from the definition of R_A. This rivalry produces more severe and robust inequality between identity groups than found in prior work (e.g., Coate and Loury, 1993; Borjas, 1993; Benabou, 1996). Generically, equal opportunity almost never produces equal outcomes, even among equally productive groups. In addition, inequality emerges in every equilibrium, not just some bad equilibria. There is path dependence across cohorts and the career life cycle as underrepresentation becomes normalized and locked in. The process of norm formation also exhibits majority bias. Nevertheless, minorities that are more productive can become dominant as identity-specific norms amplify intrinsic group differences.

A natural extension of this model is to multi-dimensional identities, where the basic unit of analysis is the intersectional group (i.e., the identity vector). While almost all of the literature has focused on uni-dimensional notions of identity, individuals may care about multiple identity dimensions, including race, gender, socioeconomic status, and sexual orientation (Sen, 2006). Carvalho and Pradelski (2022) study the evolution of norms with multi-dimensional identities showing that 'sterilized' norm interventions are generically impossible in such settings. That is, reducing underrepresentation along one dimension can worsen underrepresentation along other dimensions. To eliminate underrepresentation altogether, interventions need to be connected across identity dimensions and based on the intersectional groups (see also Carvalho et al., 2025). The next generation of work on social institutions should incorporate such identity-dependent processes into the standard evolutionary model of norms.

4.3 Contestation of norms

Norms not only emerge from the bottom-up as a product of the decentralized decisions of individuals. They are also contested by policymakers, corporations, religious leaders, and cultural influencers. A leading example is norm interventions to end footbinding in China and female genital cutting (FGC) in Northeast Africa (Mackie, 1996; Gulesci et al., 2025). Less directly, norm entrepreneurs can attempt to shift a whole complex of norms (e.g., gender norms) by changing the culture of a society or organization. Often this takes the form of attempts to shift injunctive norms, that is, beliefs about right and wrong. Cultural change is important to such actors because culture affects consumption and investment decisions (Guiso et al., 2006), labor force participation and fertility (Fernández and Fogli, 2009), entrepreneurship and productivity (Doepke and Zilibotti, 2008), corruption and legal compliance (Besley and Persson, 2014), state formation (Sambanis and Shayo, 2013), and political legitimacy (Rubin, 2017). Cultural change is not always passively accepted, however. In many cases, it is resisted by subpopulations that want to retain existing ways of thinking and doing things.

An example of a cultural program aimed at shifting a whole complex of norms is Mustafa Kemal Atatürk's cultural revolution in Turkey (Hanioğlu, 2011). In 1924, Islamic schools were banned. In 1925, veiling was prohibited in public schools, universities, and government institutions. The fez was banned outright and the Islamic Hijra calendar replaced by the Gregorian calendar. In 1928, the Arabic script was replaced by the Latin script. In 1925, the weekly holiday was switched from Friday to Sunday and sharia law was replaced by the Swiss civil code and the Italian penal code. Of course, this program of cultural change was eventually contested and partially reversed (e.g. Meyersson, 2014).

Carvalho et al. (2024) analyze the contest between top-down attempts at cultural control and bottom-up resistance in the context of education. An immediate question is: Can a policymaker eliminate an unfavored cultural trait from a population using the education system? If not, how far can they go? As we shall see, cultural resistance places limits on cultural control. In particular, individuals can resist the cultural content of education in three ways. They could drop out, tune out by engaging with other forms of cultural content (e.g., parental socialization), or turn out to collectively change the cultural content of education (e.g., by establishing new schools). I will focus here on the first two forms of resistance.

Carvalho et al. (2024) build on the model of Bisin and Verdier (2000a, 2001) by adding cultural transmission through the education system. In particular, individuals can choose whether to invest in their child's education ($e = 1$) or not, on top of their choice of socialization effort τ. A policymaker favors trait A, which is called the mainstream trait, and disfavors trait B, called the alternative trait. It chooses how strongly to transmit the mainstream trait through the education system by altering the cultural content of education.

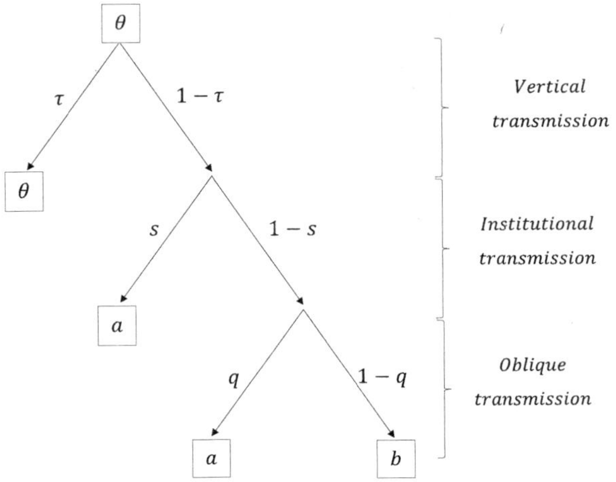

FIGURE 4 $\tau \in [0, 1]$ is parental (or self) socialization effort, $s \in [0, 1]$ is the strength of institutional transmission, and q is the (adult) population share of trait a.

The chosen strength of institutional transmission is denoted by s. Specifically, if parental socialization fails, an educated child acquires the mainstream trait a with probability s. Fig. 4 depicts the cultural transmission process for an educated individual ($e = 1$) born to a θ-type parent. For an uneducated child, the process is the same as in the Bisin-Verdier model depicted by Fig. 2.

Carvalho et al. (2024) find the following. First, the policymaker always chooses $s > 0$. Hence, cultural control is always exerted. However, the policymaker cannot eliminate the alternative trait because parental socialization ramps up in response to stronger institutional transmission. Nevertheless, the share of mainstream types is always larger than when education is culturally neutral ($s = 0$). Therefore, cultural control does work to some degree. Most importantly, however, the policymaker can go too far. Increasing the strength of institutional transmission s beyond some threshold can reduce the share of the mainstream trait a in the population. Hence, Carvalho et al. (2024) provide a theoretical foundation for empirical studies of cultural backlash (e.g., Fouka, 2020; Bazzi et al., 2020). For further work on the role of cultural leaders, see Hauk and Mueller (2015), Carvalho (2016), Prummer and Siedlarek (2017), Verdier and Zenou (2018), and Carvalho and Sacks (2024).

Returning to the example of Turkey, Meyersson (2014) presents evidence of a backlash to Kemalist secularization policies. He finds that where Islamist mayors were elected in the 1994 municipal elections, rates of female high school education increased, especially among the poor and religious. These mayors financed Islamic 'add-ons' to the public education system, such as Quranic study groups and dorms in which girls could wear headscarves. The unwinding of secularization policies in this way made parents from conservative families more likely to send their daughters to school. Moreover, the treated students ended up becoming more secular, being less likely to be married in adolescence and express Islamic political preferences. This suggests that there are limits to top-down cultural control and that, in particular, more secularization could be achieved with a lighter touch.

Overall, this section examines various cultural factors that underpin norms and recommends that these factors be integrated into evolutionary game-theoretic models of norms. I believe this synthesis would provide a powerful analytic framework for studying social institutions.

5 Lessons for empirical work and policy

Let me conclude with some lessons for the design of empirical studies and policy interventions. The framework for modeling social institutions in this chapter points to certain limitations in what we can know about real-world economic and social systems. First, it suggests limits to how much we can learn from average treatment effects in empirical studies of exogenous shocks and policy interventions. The magnitude (and possibly direction) of behavioral responses depends on the stability of the norms in place in that society. Responses could be muted if norms are strong, but exaggerated if norms are weak as the treatment induces a cascade in behavior toward a new norm. Responses to an intervention may also be delayed, appearing only slowly over time as the intervention weakens the *status quo ante* norm.

Second, the mapping between a treatment that changes individual incentives and new patterns of behavior may be complex and difficult to understand without deep institutional knowledge of the society. In addition to the issue of emergence—the disconnect between micro-motives and macro-behavior—a policymaker will have to account for whether a norm intervention is consistent with the identities of the treated individuals, and the extent to which these individuals may object to and resist the intervention. There is also the problem of second-best institutions (Carvalho, 2019). An existing norm may be inefficient and harmful in an ideal system, but in reality may be compensating for other inefficiencies in the system. 'Correcting' this norm could lead to even worse outcomes overall. For example, banning veiling in the pursuit of more progressive gender norms could reduce education and labor force participation among Muslim women (Carvalho, 2013; Abdelgadir and Fouka, 2020).

Finally, norm interventions raise difficult ethical issues. For example, female genital cutting (FGC) is typically performed by mothers and grandmothers who have undergone the procedure themselves (Gulesci et al., 2025). Ending the FGC norm requires convincing them that the procedure is not purifying or enhancing, but damaging. That is, a norm shift requires a psychological sacrifice by the older generation. Are economists equipped to decide whether such a sacrifice is worth it, whether such an intervention is ethical? Therefore, our framework suggests that norm interventions may be fraught with unintended consequences. That is not to say that they are entirely inadvisable (see for example Mackie (1996) on footbinding), but rather that we should be cautious about bold moves to remake other societies. At the very least, deep institutional knowledge of the society in question is required.

Appendix A Mathematical appendix

Proof of equivalence to the replicator dynamic. The following is based on Sandholm (2010).

(a) ***Reinforcement learning***. The mean dynamic is:

$$\begin{aligned}\dot{x}_i &= \sum_{j\in S} x_j\rho_{ji}\big(F(x),x\big) - x_i\sum_{j\in S}\rho_{ij}\big(F(x),x\big)\\ &= \sum_{j\in S} x_j\big(K - F_j(x)\big)x_i - x_i\big(K - F_i(x)\big)\\ &= x_i\left(K - \sum_{j\in S} x_j F_j(x) - K + F_i(x)\right)\\ &\equiv x_i\big(F_i(x) - \overline{F}(x)\big),\end{aligned}$$

which is the replicator dynamic.

(b) ***Imitation of success***. Again, the mean dynamic is:

$$\begin{aligned}\dot{x}_i &= \sum_{j\in S} x_j\rho_{ji}\big(F(x),x\big) - x_i\sum_{j\in S}\rho_{ij}\big(F(x),x\big)\\ &= \sum_{j\in S} x_j x_i\big(F_i(x) - K\big) - x_i\sum_{j\in S} x_j\big(F_j(x) - K\big)\\ &= x_i\big(F_i(x) - K\big) + x_i K - x_i\sum_{j\in S} x_j F_j(x)\\ &\equiv x_i\big(F_i(x) - \overline{F}(x)\big).\end{aligned}$$

(c) ***Pairwise proportional imitation***. Again, the mean dynamic is:

$$\begin{aligned}\dot{x}_i &= \sum_{j\in S} x_j\rho_{ji}\big(F(x),x\big) - x_i\sum_{j\in S}\rho_{ij}\big(F(x),x\big)\\ &= \sum_{j\in S} x_j x_i\big[F_i(x) - F_j(x)\big]_+ - x_i\sum_{j\in S} x_j\big[F_j(x) - F_i(x)\big]_+\\ &= x_i\sum_{j\in S} x_j\big[F_i(x) - F_j(x)\big]\\ &= x_i\big(F_i(x) - \sum_{j\in S} x_j F_j(x)\big)\\ &\equiv x_i\big(F_i(x) - \overline{F}(x)\big).\end{aligned}$$

□

Proof of Proposition 1. For convergence, we need to show there is a positive probability path from any state to a convention.

With positive probability, the next m revisions are by row players and each revising row player draws the same sample, playing the same best response x. There is also a positive probability that the subsequent m revisions are by column players. They must each draw a sample consisting solely of demands equal to x and choose the best response $1 - x$.

Second, each convention is an absorbing state of the unperturbed process. To see this, consider m instances of the norm $(x, 1 - x)$. All possible samples for a row player consist of am plays of $1 - x$ to which the unique best response is x. Similarly for column players.

Thus the convention is perpetuated. □

References

Abdelgadir, A., Fouka, V., 2020. Political secularism and Muslim integration in the West: assessing the effects of the French headscarf ban. American Political Science Review 114 (3), 707–723.

Acemoglu, D., Johnson, S., Robinson, J.A., 2001. The colonial origins of comparative development: an empirical investigation. American Economic Review 91 (5), 1369–1401.

Acemoglu, D., Johnson, S., Robinson, J.A., 2002. Reversal of fortune: geography and institutions in the making of the modern world income distribution. The Quarterly Journal of Economics 117 (4), 1231–1294.

Acemoglu, D., Robinson, J.A., 2012. Why Nations Fail: The Origins of Power, Prosperity, and Poverty. Crown Business, New York, NY.

Akerlof, G.A., 1980. A theory of social custom, of which enforced norms are special cases. The Quarterly Journal of Economics 94 (4), 749–775.

Akerlof, G.A., 1982. Labor contracts as partial gift exchange. The Quarterly Journal of Economics 97 (4), 543–569.

Akerlof, G.A., 2002. Behavioral macroeconomics and macroeconomic behavior. American Economic Review 92 (3), 411–433.

Akerlof, G.A., 2005. Explorations in Pragmatic Economics. Oxford University Press, Oxford, UK.

Akerlof, G.A., 2020. Sins of omission and the practice of economics. Journal of Economic Literature 58 (1), 405–418.

Akerlof, G.A., Kranton, R.E., 2000. Economics and identity. The Quarterly Journal of Economics 115 (3), 715–753.

Akerlof, G.A., Kranton, R.E., 2010. Identity Economics: How Our Identities Shape Our Work, Wages, and Well-Being. Princeton University Press, Princeton, NJ.

Akerlof, G.A., Shiller, R.J., 2009. Animal Spirits: How Human Psychology Drives the Economy, and Why It Matters for Global Capitalism. Princeton University Press, Princeton, NJ.

Akerlof, G.A., Yellen, J.L., 1988. Fairness and unemployment. American Economic Review 78 (2), 44–49.

Akerlof, G.A., Yellen, J.L., 1990. The fair wage-effort hypothesis and unemployment. The Quarterly Journal of Economics 105 (2), 255–283.

Akerlof, R., 2017. Value formation: the role of esteem. Games and Economic Behavior 102, 1–19.

Aksoy, O., Gambetta, D., 2016. Behind the veil: the strategic use of religious garb. European Sociological Review 32 (6), 792–806.

Alesina, A., Giuliano, P., Nunn, N., 2013. On the origins of gender roles: women and the plough. The Quarterly Journal of Economics 128 (2), 469–530.

Algan, Y., Cahuc, P., 2010. Inherited trust and growth. American Economic Review 100 (5), 2060–2092.

Allen, R.C., 2009. The British Industrial Revolution in Global Perspective. Cambridge University Press, Cambridge.

Anderson, B., 2006. Imagined Communities: Reflections on the Origin and Spread of Nationalism. Verso, London.

Aristotle, 2013/c. 350 BCE*b*. Politics. Hackett Publishing Company, Indianapolis.

Aristotle, 2014/c. 340 BCE*a*. Nicomachean Ethics. Cambridge University Press, Cambridge.

Arrow, K.J., 1994. Methodological individualism and social knowledge. American Economic Review 84 (2), 1–9.

Atkin, D., 2016. The caloric costs of culture: evidence from Indian migrants. American Economic Review 106 (4), 1144–1181.

Bazzi, S., Hilmy, M., Marx, B., 2020. Religion, education, and the state. National Bureau of Economic Research working paper.

Becker, G.S., 1976. The Economic Approach to Human Behavior. University of Chicago Press, Chicago.

Becker, S.O., Woessmann, L., 2009. Was Weber right? A human capital theory of protestant economic history. The Quarterly Journal of Economics 124 (2), 531–596.

Benabou, R., 1996. Equity and efficiency in human capital investment: the local connection. The Review of Economic Studies 63 (2), 237–264.

Benaïm, M., Weibull, J.W., 2003. Deterministic approximation of stochastic evolution in games. Econometrica 71 (3), 873–903.

Bergeron, A., Carvalho, J.-P., Henrich, J., Nunn, N., Weigel, J., 2024. Zero-sum environments, the evolution of effort-suppressing beliefs, and economic development. Working paper.

Bernstein, L., 1992. Opting out of the legal system: extralegal contractual relations in the diamond industry. The Journal of Legal Studies 21 (1), 115–157.

Besley, T., Persson, T., 2014. Why do developing countries tax so little? The Journal of Economic Perspectives 28 (4), 99–120.

Bicchieri, C., 2006. The Grammar of Society: The Nature and Dynamics of Social Norms. Cambridge University Press, Cambridge.

Binmore, K., 2009. Rational Decisions. Princeton University Press, Princeton.

Bisin, A., Carvalho, J.-P., Verdier, T., 2023. Cultural transmission and religion. In: Sauer, R.M. (Ed.), The Economics of Religion. World Scientific Publishing, pp. 1–62. Chapter 1.

Bisin, A., Topa, G., Verdier, T., 2004. Religious intermarriage and socialization in the United States. Journal of Political Economy 112 (3), 615–664.

Bisin, A., Verdier, T., 2000a. Beyond the melting pot: cultural transmission, marriage, and the evolution of ethnic and religious traits. The Quarterly Journal of Economics 115 (3), 955–988.

Bisin, A., Verdier, T., 2000b. A model of cultural transmission, voting and political ideology. European Journal of Political Economy 16 (1), 5–29.

Bisin, A., Verdier, T., 2001. The economics of cultural transmission and the dynamics of preferences. Journal of Economic Theory 97 (2), 298–319.

Blau, F.D., Kahn, L.M., Liu, A.Y.-H., Papps, K.L., 2013. The transmission of women's fertility, human capital, and work orientation across immigrant generations. Journal of Population Economics 26 (2), 405–435.

Bloom, N., Sadun, R., Van Reenen, J., 2012. The organization of firms across countries. The Quarterly Journal of Economics 127 (4), 1663–1705.

Boltzmann, L., 1877. Über die beziehung zwischen dem zweiten hauptsatze der mechanischen wärmetheorie und der wahrscheinlichkeitsrechnung respektive den sätzen über das wärmegleichgewicht. Wiener Berichte 76, 373–435.

Borel, É., 1921. La théorie du jeu et les équations intégrales à noyau symétrique. Comptes Rendus de L'Académie Des Sciences 173.

Borjas, G.J., 1993. The intergenerational mobility of immigrants. Journal of Labor Economics 11 (1, Part 1), 113–135.

Breza, E., Kaur, S., Shamdasani, Y., 2018. The morale effects of pay inequality. The Quarterly Journal of Economics 133 (2), 611–663.

Burke, M.A., Young, H.P., 2011. Social norms, custom, and contract: the evolution of informal cooperation in repeated interactions. American Economic Review 101 (3), 108–113.
Bursztyn, L., Ferman, B., Fiorin, S., Kanz, M., Rao, G., 2020a. Status goods: experimental evidence from platinum credit cards. The Quarterly Journal of Economics 135 (3), 1561–1595.
Bursztyn, L., González, A.L., Yanagizawa-Drott, D., 2020b. Misperceived social norms: women working outside the home in Saudi Arabia. American Economic Review 110 (10), 2997–3029.
Camerer, C.F., Loewenstein, G., 2004. Behavioral economics: past, present, future. In: Camerer, C.F., Loewenstein, G., Rabin, M. (Eds.), Advances in Behavioral Economics. Princeton University Press, Princeton, NJ, pp. 3–51.
Card, D., Mas, A., Moretti, E., Saez, E., 2012. Inequality at work: the effect of peer salaries on job satisfaction. American Economic Review 102 (6), 2981–3003.
Carvalho, J.-P., 2013. Veiling. The Quarterly Journal of Economics 128 (1), 337–370.
Carvalho, J.-P., 2016. Identity-based organizations. The American Economic Review: Papers and Proceedings 106, 410–414.
Carvalho, J.-P., 2017. Coordination and culture. Economic Theory 64 (3), 449–475.
Carvalho, J.-P., 2019. Religious clubs: the strategic role of religious identity. In: Advances in the Economics of Religion. Springer.
Carvalho, J.-P., 2020. Sacrifice and sorting in clubs. Forum for Social Economics 49 (4), 357–369.
Carvalho, J.-P., Iyer, S., Rubin, J. (Eds.), 2019. Advances in the Economics of Religion. Palgrave Macmillan.
Carvalho, J.-P., Koyama, M., Williams, C., 2024. Resisting education. Journal of the European Economic Association.
Carvalho, J.-P., Pradelski, B.S., 2022. Identity and underrepresentation: interactions between race and gender. Journal of Public Economics 216, 104764.
Carvalho, J.-P., Pradelski, B.S., 2024. The representation dynamic and the "normalization" of group differences. Journal of Law, Economics, & Organization, ewae014.
Carvalho, J.-P., Pradelski, B.S., Williams, C., 2025. Intersectionality: affirmative action with multidimensional identities. Management Science 71 (5), 4495–4509.
Carvalho, J.-P., Sacks, M., 2021. The economics of religious communities. Journal of Public Economics 201, 104481.
Carvalho, J.-P., Sacks, M., 2024. Radicalisation. The Economic Journal 134 (659), 1019–1068.
Cavalli-Sforza, L.L., Feldman, M.W., 1981. Cultural Transmission and Evolution: A Quantitative Approach, vol. 16. Princeton University Press.
Cederman, L.-E., Wimmer, A., Min, B., 2010. Why do ethnic groups rebel? New data and analysis. World Politics 62 (1), 87–119.
Chen, Y., Li, S.X., 2009. Group identity and social preferences. American Economic Review 99 (1), 431–457.
Cho, I.-K., Kreps, D.M., 1987. Signaling games and stable equilibria. The Quarterly Journal of Economics 102 (2), 179–221.
Coase, R.H., 1937. The nature of the firm. Economica 4 (16), 386–405.
Coate, S., Loury, G.C., 1993. Will affirmative-action policies eliminate negative stereotypes? American Economic Review, 1220–1240.
Cournot, A.A., 1838. Recherches sur les principes mathématiques de la théorie des richesses. L. Hachette, Paris.
Dekel, E., Ely, J.C., Yilankaya, O., 2007. Evolution of preferences. The Review of Economic Studies 74 (3), 685–704.
Della Lena, S., Dindo, P., 2024. An economic model of acculturation under strategic complements and substitutes. Available at SSRN: https://ssrn.com/abstract=4786867 or https://doi.org/10.2139/ssrn.4786867, 2024.
Descartes, R., 1998/1637. Discourse on the Method of Rightly Conducting One's Reason and of Seeking Truth in the Sciences. Hackett Publishing Company, Indianapolis.
Desmet, K., Wacziarg, R., 2021. The cultural divide. The Economic Journal 131 (637), 2058–2088.

Doepke, M., Zilibotti, F., 2008. Occupational choice and the spirit of capitalism. The Quarterly Journal of Economics 123 (2), 747–793.

Eldredge, N., Gould, S.J., 1972. Punctuated equilibria: an alternative to phyletic gradualism. In: Schopf, T.J.M. (Ed.), Models in Paleobiology. Freeman, Cooper & Co., San Francisco, pp. 82–115.

Ellison, G., 1993. Learning, local interaction, and coordination. Econometrica 61 (5), 1047–1071.

Falk, A., Becker, A., Dohmen, T., Enke, B., Huffman, D., Sunde, U., 2018. Global evidence on economic preferences. The Quarterly Journal of Economics 133 (4), 1645–1692.

Ferguson, A., 2001/1767. An Essay on the History of Civil Society. Cambridge University Press, Cambridge.

Fernández, R., Fogli, A., 2009. Culture: an empirical investigation of beliefs, work, and fertility. American Economic Journal. Macroeconomics 1 (1), 146–177.

Fernández, R., Parsa, S., Viarengo, M., 2024. Coming out in America: thirty years of cultural change. Journal of Law, Economics, & Organization.

Fisman, R., Miguel, E., 2007. Corruption, norms, and legal enforcement: evidence from diplomatic parking tickets. Journal of Political Economy 115 (6), 1020–1048.

Foster, D.P., Young, H.P., 1990. Stochastic evolutionary game dynamics. Theoretical Population Biology 38, 219–232.

Fouka, V., 2020. Backlash: the unintended effects of language prohibition in US schools after World War I. The Review of Economic Studies 87 (1), 204–239.

Frank, R.H., 1987. If homo economicus could choose his own utility function, would he want one with a conscience? American Economic Review, 593–604.

Gartzke, E., Gleditsch, K.S., 2006. Identity and conflict: ties that bind and differences that divide. European Journal of International Relations 12 (1), 53–87.

Giuliano, P., Nunn, N., 2021. Understanding cultural persistence and change. The Review of Economic Studies 88 (4), 1541–1581.

Gorodnichenko, Y., Roland, G., 2017. Culture, institutions, and the wealth of nations. Review of Economics and Statistics 99 (3), 402–416.

Goyal, S., 2023. Networks: An Economics Approach. MIT Press, Cambridge, MA.

Greif, A., 1993. Contract enforceability and economic institutions in early trade: the maghribi traders' coalition. American Economic Review 83 (3), 525–548.

Grossman, S.J., Hart, O.D., 1986. The costs and benefits of ownership: a theory of vertical and lateral integration. Journal of Political Economy 94 (4), 691–719.

Guiso, L., Sapienza, P., Zingales, L., 2006. Does culture affect economic outcomes? The Journal of Economic Perspectives 20 (2), 23–48.

Gulesci, S., Jindani, S., La Ferrara, E., Smerdon, D., Sulaiman, M., Young, H.P., 2025. A stepping stone approach to norm transitions. Technical report. National Bureau of Economic Research.

Güth, W., Yaari, M., 1992. An evolutionary approach to explain reciprocal behavior in a simple strategic game. In: Witt, U. (Ed.), Explaining Process and Change—Approaches to Evolutionary Economics. University of Michigan Press.

Hamilton, W.D., 1967. Extraordinary sex ratios. Science 156 (3774), 477–488.

Hanioğlu, M.Ş., 2011. Atatürk: An Intellectual Biography. Princeton University Press, Princeton, NJ.

Harsanyi, J.C., Selten, R., 1988. A General Theory of Equilibrium Selection in Games. MIT Press, Cambridge, MA.

Hart, O., Moore, J., 1990. Property rights and the nature of the firm. Journal of Political Economy 98 (6), 1119–1158.

Hauk, E., Mueller, H., 2015. Cultural leaders and the clash of civilizations. The Journal of Conflict Resolution 59 (3), 367–400.

Hayek, F.A., 1945. The use of knowledge in society. American Economic Review 35 (4), 519–530.

Hayek, F.A., 1967. Studies in Philosophy, Politics and Economics. University of Chicago Press, Chicago.

Heifetz, A., Shannon, C., Spiegel, Y., 2007. What to maximize if you must. Journal of Economic Theory 133 (1), 31–57.
Henrich, J., Muthukrishna, M., 2024. What makes us smart? Topics in Cognitive Science 16 (2), 322–342.
Herodotus, 2014/c. 440 BCE. The Histories. Penguin Classics, London.
Hesiod, 2008/c. 700 BCE. Theogony and Works and Days. Harvard University Press, Cambridge, MA.
Hicks, J., 2001/1969. A Theory of Economic History. Oxford University Press, Oxford.
Hong, H., Kubik, J.D., Solomon, A., 2000. Security analysts' career concerns and herding of earnings forecasts. The Rand Journal of Economics 31 (1), 121–144.
Hume, D., 1987/1741. Essays, Moral, Political, and Literary. Liberty Fund, Indianapolis.
Hume, D., 2000/1739. A Treatise of Human Nature. Oxford University Press, Oxford.
Iannaccone, L.R., 1992. Sacrifice and stigma: reducing free-riding in cults, communes, and other collectives. Journal of Political Economy 100 (2), 271–291.
Iyer, S., 2018. The Economics of Religion in India. Harvard University Press, Cambridge, MA.
Iyigun, M., 2008. Lessons from the Ottoman Empire: religious diversity, institutions, and the longevity of empire. The Journal of Economic History 68 (4), 1128–1176.
Jackson, M.O., 2008. Social and Economic Networks. Princeton University Press, Princeton, NJ.
Jevons, W.S., 2013/1871. The Theory of Political Economy. Palgrave Macmillan, Basingstoke.
Jha, S., 2013. Trade, institutions, and ethnic tolerance: evidence from south Asia. American Political Science Review 107 (4), 806–832.
Kahneman, D., Sibony, O., Sunstein, C.R., 2021. Noise: A Flaw in Human Judgment. Little, Brown Spark, New York, NY.
Kautilya, 2012/c. 300 BCE. The Arthashastra. Penguin Books India, New Delhi.
Kemeny, J.G., Snell, J.L., 1960. Finite Markov Chains. D. van Nostrand Company, Princeton, NJ.
King, M., Kay, J., 2020. Radical Uncertainty: Decision-Making Beyond the Numbers. W.W. Norton & Company, New York.
Knight, F.H., 1921. Risk, Uncertainty and Profit. Houghton Mifflin Company, Boston.
Kuran, T., 1991. Now out of never: the element of surprise in the East European revolution of 1989. World Politics 44 (1), 7–48.
Kuran, T., 2012. The Long Divergence: How Islamic Law Held Back the Middle East. Princeton University Press.
Lewontin, R.C., 1961. Evolution and the theory of games. Journal of Theoretical Biology 1 (3), 382–403.
Mackie, G., 1996. Ending footbinding and infibulation: a convention account. American Sociological Review, 999–1017.
Marshall, A., 2013/1890. Principles of Economics. Palgrave Macmillan, Basingstoke.
Maxwell, J.C., 1860. Illustrations of the dynamical theory of gases. Philosophical Magazine 19 (126), 19–56.
Maynard Smith, J., 1972. Game theory and the evolution of fighting. In: On Evolution. Edinburgh University Press, Edinburgh, pp. 8–28.
Maynard Smith, J., Price, G.R., 1973. The logic of animal conflict. Nature 246 (5427), 15–18.
McElreath, R., Boyd, R., Richerson, P.J., 2003. Shared norms and the evolution of ethnic markers. Current Anthropology 44 (1), 122–129.
Menger, C., 1892. On the origin of money. The Economic Journal 2 (6), 239–255.
Menger, C., 2007/1871. Principles of Economics. Ludwig Von Mises Institute, Auburn, AL.
Meyersson, E., 2014. Islamic rule and the empowerment of the poor and pious. Econometrica 82 (1), 229–269.
Mill, J.S., 1848. Principles of Political Economy with Some of Their Applications to Social Philosophy. John W. Parker, London.
Mill, J.S., 1861. Utilitarianism. Parker, Son, and Bourn, London.
Montgomery, J.D., 2010. Intergenerational cultural transmission as an evolutionary game. American Economic Journal. Microeconomics 2 (4), 115–136.

Muthukrishna, M., Henrich, J., 2016. Innovation in the collective brain. Philosophical Transactions - Royal Society. Biological Sciences 371 (1690), 20150192.
Nash, J., 1950a. Equilibrium points in n-person games. Proceedings of the National Academy of Sciences of the United States of America 36 (1), 48–49.
Nash, J.F., 1950b. The bargaining problem. Econometrica 18 (2), 155–162.
Nash, J.F., 1950c. Non-Cooperative Games. PhD thesis. Princeton University, Princeton, NJ.
Newton, J., 2018. Evolutionary game theory: a renaissance. Games 9 (2), 31.
North, D.C., 1981. Structure and Change in Economic History. W.W. Norton & Company, New York.
North, D.C., 1990. Institutions, Institutional Change and Economic Performance. Cambridge University Press, Cambridge.
Nunn, N., 2014. Historical development. In: Aghion, P., Durlauf, S.N. (Eds.), Handbook of Economic Growth, vol. 2, pp. 347–402.
Nunn, N., Wantchekon, L., 2011. The slave trade and the origins of mistrust in Africa. American Economic Review 101 (7), 3221–3252.
Oh, S., 2023. Does identity affect labor supply? American Economic Review 113 (8), 2055–2083.
Piketty, T., 2020. Capital and Ideology. Harvard University Press.
Pines, D., Laughlin, R.B., Wolynes, P.G., 2023. Emergence and complexity in modern physics. Nature Reviews Physics 5 (7), 393–404.
Plato, 2012/c. 380 BCE. Republic. Cambridge University Press, Cambridge.
Platteau, J.-P., 2000. Institutions, Social Norms and Economic Development. Harwood Academic Publishers, Amsterdam.
Polanyi, K., 2001/1944. The Great Transformation: The Political and Economic Origins of Our Time. Beacon Press, Boston.
Prummer, A., Siedlarek, J.-P., 2017. Community leaders and the preservation of cultural traits. Journal of Economic Theory 168, 143–176.
Quesnay, F., 2009/1758. The Economic Table (Tableau Économique). Palgrave Macmillan, London.
Ricardo, D., 1817. On the Principles of Political Economy and Taxation. John Murray, London.
Rubin, J., 2017. Rulers, Religion, and Riches: Why the West Got Rich and the Middle East Did Not. Cambridge University Press.
Salari, M., 2018. The impact of intergenerational cultural transmission on fertility decisions. Economic Modelling 70, 1–10.
Sambanis, N., Shayo, M., 2013. Social identification and ethnic conflict. American Political Science Review 107 (2), 294–325.
Sandholm, W.H., 2010. Population Games and Evolutionary Dynamics. MIT Press.
Savage, L.J., 1954. The Foundations of Statistics. John Wiley & Sons, New York.
Schelling, T.C., 1960. The Strategy of Conflict. Harvard University Press, Cambridge, MA.
Schelling, T.C., 1978. Micromotives and Macrobehavior. W.W. Norton & Company, New York, NY.
Schlag, K.H., 1998. Why imitate, and if so, how? A boundedly rational approach to multi-armed bandits. Journal of Economic Theory 78 (1), 130–156.
Sen, A., 2006. Identity and Violence: The Illusion of Destiny. Norton.
Shayo, M., Zussman, A., 2011. Judicial ingroup bias in the shadow of terrorism. The Quarterly Journal of Economics 126 (3), 1447–1484.
Shiller, R.J., 2000. Irrational Exuberance. Princeton University Press, Princeton, NJ.
Shiller, R.J., 2019. Narrative Economics: How Stories Go Viral and Drive Major Economic Events. Princeton University Press, Princeton, NJ.
Shofia, N., 2024. The economic and social drivers of veiling: Evidence from Indonesia. Working paper. National University of Singapore.
Simon, H.A., 1947. Administrative Behavior: A Study of Decision-Making Processes in Administrative Organizations. Macmillan, New York.
Simon, H.A., 1955. A behavioral model of rational choice. The Quarterly Journal of Economics 69 (1), 99–118.

Simon, H.A., 1956. Rational choice and the structure of the environment. Psychological Review 63 (2), 129–138.
Simon, H.A., 1957. Models of Man: Social and Rational. John Wiley & Sons, New York.
Smith, A., 2002/1759. The Theory of Moral Sentiments. Cambridge University Press, Cambridge.
Smith, A., 2008/1776. An Inquiry into the Nature and Causes of the Wealth of Nations. Oxford University Press, Oxford.
Spolaore, E., Wacziarg, R., 2013. How deep are the roots of economic development? Journal of Economic Literature 51 (2), 325–369.
Stigler, G.J., Becker, G.S., 1977. De gustibus non est disputandum. American Economic Review 67 (2), 76–90.
Tabellini, G., 2010. Culture and institutions: economic development in the regions of Europe. Journal of the European Economic Association 8 (4), 677–716.
Taylor, P.D., Jonker, L.B., 1978. Evolutionary stable strategies and game dynamics. Mathematical Biosciences 40 (1–2), 145–156.
Thaler, R.H., 1992. The Winner's Curse: Paradoxes and Anomalies of Economic Life. Princeton University Press, Princeton, NJ.
The CORE Team, 2017. The Economy: Economics for a Changing World. Oxford University Press, Oxford, UK. https://www.core-econ.org/the-economy/book/text/0-3-contents.html.
Thucydides, 2013/c. 410 BCE. The Peloponnesian War. Oxford University Press, Oxford.
Trueman, B., 1994. Analyst forecasts and herding behavior. The Review of Financial Studies 7 (1), 97–124.
Verdier, T., Zenou, Y., 2018. Cultural leader and the dynamics of assimilation. Journal of Economic Theory 175, 374–414.
von Neumann, J., 1928. Zur theorie der gesellschaftsspiele. Mathematische Annalen 100 (1).
von Neumann, J., Morgenstern, O., 1944. Theory of Games and Economic Behavior. Princeton University Press, Princeton, NJ.
Waldinger, M., 2024. 'Let them eat cake': drought, peasant uprisings, and demand for institutional change in the French revolution. Journal of Economic Growth 29 (1), 41–77.
Walras, L., 2014/1874. Elements of Pure Economics: Or the Theory of Social Wealth. Routledge, London.
Williamson, O.E., 1975. Markets and Hierarchies: Analysis and Antitrust Implications. Free Press, New York, NY.
Williamson, O.E., 1985. The Economic Institutions of Capitalism. Free Press, New York, NY.
Xenophon, 2002/c. 362 BCE. Oeconomicus: A Social and Historical Commentary. Oxford University Press, Oxford.
Young, H.P., 1993a. The evolution of conventions. Econometrica 61, 57–84.
Young, H.P., 1993b. An evolutionary model of bargaining. Journal of Economic Theory 59 (1), 145–168.
Young, H.P., 1998. Individual Strategy and Social Structure: An Evolutionary Theory of Institutions. Princeton University Press.
Young, H.P., 2015. The evolution of social norms. Annual Review of Economics 7 (1), 359–387.
Young, H.P., forthcoming. The Dynamics of Social Norms. Oxford University Press.
Zermelo, E., 1913. Über eine anwendung der mengenlehre auf die theorie des schachspiels. In: Proceedings of the Fifth International Congress of Mathematicians, vol. 2.

Chapter 11

A stairway to success: how parenting shapes culture and social stratification☆

Francesco Agostinelli[a], Matthias Doepke[b], Giuseppe Sorrenti[c], and Fabrizio Zilibotti[d]
[a]*University of Pennsylvania, Philadelphia, PA, United States,* [b]*London School of Economics, London, United Kingdom,* [c]*University of Lausanne, Lausanne, Switzerland,* [d]*Yale University, New Haven, CT, United States*

1 Introduction

Culture can be defined as a set of widely shared values, preferences, and beliefs that characterize a particular group or society. Parenting, in turn, is one of the primary mechanisms through which culture is transmitted across generations. Parents shape not only their children's skills and preferences, but also their broader worldviews and social behavior. As such, parenting plays a fundamental role in preserving and transforming cultural traditions over time. Conversely, cultural norms influence parenting practices by shaping expectations about child-rearing and parent-child relationships. Beyond culture, economic conditions, social institutions, and peer influences also shape how parents raise their children. The feedback loop between parenting, culture, and the economy that arises from these reciprocal influences is the focus of this chapter.

We propose an economic approach to parenting that clarifies these connections by examining how parenting both reflects and reshapes cultural norms, and how economic and institutional forces influence this process. A central feature of our framework is that parenting decisions respond to economic incentives. Parents adapt their socialization strategies based on anticipated future payoffs for their children, which are shaped by labor market conditions, technological change, educational opportunities, neighborhood effects, and social mobility.

☆ We thank UK Research and Innovation (Horizon Europe ERC Guarantee Grant EP/Y027671/1) and the National Science Foundation (grant SES-1949228) for financial support and Paola Giuliano for helpful suggestions that greatly improved the chapter. We also thank Carmen Arbaizar Mazas and James Symons-Hicks for excellent research assistance. Zilibotti thanks the University of Copenhagen and the Danmarks Nationalbank for generous hospitality.

Handbook of Culture and Economic Behavior, Volume 1, ISSN 3051-1682
https://doi.org/10.1016/bs.hceb.2026.04.002

This perspective helps explain why parenting norms differ across countries, time, and socioeconomic environments, and how they evolve in response to changing economic landscapes.

For instance, in societies experiencing rising economic inequality, parents may feel increasing pressure to instill work ethic and discipline to secure their children's future prospects. Where success is closely tied to performance in standardized academic tests, they may invest heavily in structured education and intensive tutoring, while also cultivating values of discipline and achievement. In contrast, in economies where entrepreneurial skills or creativity yield high returns, parenting may prioritize fostering independence and risk-taking. A key driver of these responses is parental altruism: parents love their children and aim to provide them with a "stairway to success" by preparing them for the world they will enter as adults.

Beyond altruism, paternalism also shapes parenting decisions. The key distinction is that, when acting paternalistically, parents base their choices on what they believe is best for their children, even when this conflicts with the children's own preferences. In other words, parents may override their children's desires and induce or impose choices they believe to be ultimately beneficial for them, or simply the morally right thing to do. This paternalistic dimension is particularly important in the persistence of traditional values such as religious beliefs or political ideologies, where parents often seek to transmit their own convictions rather than encourage independent thinking. Altruism and paternalism coexist in parenting decisions—sometimes reinforcing each other, sometimes pulling in opposite directions.

We incorporate these ideas into an economic framework by drawing on the developmental psychology literature on parenting styles (Baumrind, 1967), as adapted in our recent research (Doepke and Zilibotti, 2017, 2019; Doepke et al., 2019; Agostinelli et al., 2022, 2026). Whereas psychology typically treats parenting styles as stable personality traits, our approach interprets them as strategic choices that respond to economic and cultural conditions. We focus on the three parenting styles identified by Baumrind: authoritarian, authoritative, and permissive.[1] Authoritarian parents impose strict control, ensuring compliance with their values and, possibly, punishing deviation. Authoritative parents aim to shape preferences so that children internalize the desired behavior. Permissive parents, by contrast, prioritize self-expression and independence, and refrain from imposing specific values or preferences on their children.

The choice of parenting style depends on both parental preferences and external conditions. In rigid social environments where success depends on conformity, authoritarian parenting may dominate. Conversely, in dynamic

1 We exclude the neglecting parenting style (Maccoby and Martin, 1983), which is typically associated with problematic family situations beyond the scope of our analysis.

economies where adaptability and innovation are rewarded, parents may favor authoritative or permissive styles that encourage independence.

Parenting styles also respond to external influences such as peer groups, schools, and the media—factors that can either reinforce or undermine the values parents seek to instill. When parents perceive these influences as misaligned with their own values, they may respond by intensifying their efforts to shape their child's preferences. We refer to this strategic response as *defensive parenting*: parents take active measures to shield their children from potentially disruptive social forces and assert tighter control.

For instance, religious parents in highly secular societies may respond by segregating their children from mainstream culture and redoubling efforts at religious socialization (Bisin and Verdier, 2000). This pattern is evident in the rise of homeschooling and religious schooling among devout families in secular environments, where parents actively seek to control curricular content and peer influence. In contrast, secular parents in the same setting may exert little effort in cultural transmission, trusting that societal influences reflect their own values. Our model captures this mechanism formally, emphasizing how parental decisions depend on trust in social institutions and perceived external risks. Cultural transmission thus interacts dynamically with the broader environment, generating complementarities—or tensions—between parenting and culture.

Parental perceptions of their immediate community are no less important. In neighborhoods characterized by cooperative norms and high interpersonal trust, parents are more likely to promote openness, autonomy, and engagement with broader society. These strategies facilitate the intergenerational transmission of trust, as shown, among others, by Algan and Cahuc (2010). In contrast, when the local environment is perceived as risky or hostile, parents often adopt more protective strategies that emphasize caution, conformity, and limited openness to unfamiliar individuals or ideas. These responses reinforce parochial norms and constrain the accumulation of social capital, with long-run consequences for a society's cooperative capacity.

A central implication of our analysis is that the mutual interactions between culture, parenting, and the economy can generate endogenous stratification along both cultural and economic dimensions. For instance, cultural traits such as thrift or risk tolerance have particularly high returns in specific occupations. This complementarity contributes to the emergence of distinct social classes, where families sharing a common set of cultural values dominate occupations that rely on these values. Stratification may also stem from non-economic cultural attributes—such as religious beliefs—when these values affect economic behavior and outcomes. The potential for stratification is further amplified when residential choices respond to cultural preferences, as resulting patterns of residential segregation reinforce disparities in both the cultural and economic environments faced by children.

A second important insight is that the effectiveness of policy interventions aimed at reducing disparities depends crucially on how parents respond.

In a world where parenting decisions play a central role in fostering or hindering social mobility, policies that ignore these behavioral responses may fail to achieve their intended goals. Addressing persistent inequalities therefore requires a careful understanding of how incentives and environments shape parenting behavior.

In the following sections, we develop these insights through a series of illustrative models. In Section 2, we introduce a general framework to analyze parental choice over parenting styles. Section 3 applies this model to examine how the formation of economic preferences interacts with economic conditions, shaping cultural stratification and the endogenous formation of social classes. Section 4 extends the analysis to the transmission of non-economic values, with a particular focus on religion. Section 5 explores the relationship between residential and cultural segregation within a framework of parenting and location choices. Throughout these sections, we also present historical and empirical evidence consistent with our theoretical predictions.

The research program outlined in this chapter is still in its early stages. In Section 6, we discuss avenues for future research, including the need for more empirical evidence, quantification of channels of influence, policy analysis, and expanding connections to research in other social sciences that touch on similar issues of stratification and social inequality. Section 7 concludes with a summary of our main findings.

2 A framework for the interaction of parenting and culture

We begin by outlining a general framework for analyzing the mutual interactions between economic conditions, parenting, residential choices, and cultural transmission. We consider a population of dynasties in which each parent has a child, followed by a grandchild, and so forth. The model combines features of the economic literature on child development (Heckman and Mosso, 2014, Attanasio, 2015) with the literatures on the economics of culture (Guiso et al., 2006; Fernández, 2008; Fernández and Fogli, 2009; Bisin and Verdier, 2010; Enke, 2019; Giuliano and Nunn, 2021) and the economics of parenting.

2.1 The parent's decision problem

The circumstances of a given parent are characterized by two state variables, H and X. H represents economic state variables; in the applications discussed below, H typically denotes human capital, though it may also include other factors such as wealth. The variable X captures the preferences, attitudes, and values that represent culture in our analysis. X can encompass economic preferences such as work ethic, patience, or risk tolerance; broader social attitudes such as trust and altruism; and distinct cultural elements, including religious beliefs. The child's state variables, shaped by the parent, are denoted as H' and X'.

A parent derives utility from consumption and cares about their child's well-being. Specifically, the preferences of a parent with state variables H and X are described by the value function:

$$V(H,X) = \max_{\{Y,P,N\}} \left\{ E\left[U(C,P) + z\left(\lambda\, \tilde{v}(H',X'|X,N) + (1-\lambda)\, v(H',X')\right)\right]\right\}. \tag{1}$$

The maximization is subject to a set of feasibility constraints, which may include budget and time constraints; the technologies governing human capital accumulation and preference transmission that jointly determine the child's state variables H' and X'; as well as the influence of neighborhood choice N, which may affect both parent and child.

The parent makes choices across multiple dimensions: Y encompasses standard economic decisions such as occupational choice; P represents parenting decisions; and N denotes residential location.

The parent's felicity is represented by a standard utility function that depends on consumption and the parenting style adopted, $U(C,P)$, where both consumption and the cost of different parenting styles may depend on H.[2] The overall weight assigned to the child's welfare is captured by the parameter $z > 0$. The concern for the child is a linear combination of an altruistic and a paternalistic component. With the altruistic weight $1-\lambda$, the parent values the child's actual lifetime utility, $v(H',X')$, defined as:

$$v(H',X') = u(X') + \beta\, V(H',X').$$

During childhood, the child derives utility $u(X')$ from their values X'. As an adult, the child's lifetime utility is given by the value function $V(H',X')$, discounted by β.[3]

If $\lambda = 0$, the parent is fully altruistic, and no conflict arises between parent and child: the parent's utility is aligned with the child's preferences. When $\lambda > 0$, the parent's utility includes a paternalistic component—a judgment about what is best for the child that may differ from the child's own preferences.

Paternalism implies that the parent holds independent views about the child's well-being, irrespective of the child's own utility. It can manifest along several dimensions. Earlier work on the economics of parenting has emphasized potential disagreements between parent and child over the tradeoff between present enjoyment and future investment. For instance, forward-looking parents may encourage academic effort and discourage risk-taking during adolescence, even if these choices conflict with the child's immediate preferences.

2 The nature and relative cost of different parenting styles may vary across applications. An authoritarian style may strain family relationships by prioritizing strict control over open communication. An authoritative style may require significant time and effort to shape the child's preferences. A permissive approach also carries costs, as it involves expanding the child's choice set and accepting the potential consequences of a more liberal upbringing.

3 In more general economic models of parenting, the child's utility during childhood may depend on additional choices and state variables. Here, we restrict attention to cultural factors.

In this study, we focus on a broader cultural dimension of paternalism, emphasizing potential disagreement over the child's attitudes and values, encapsulated in X'. The paternalistic utility function is given by:

$$\tilde{v}(H', X'|X, N) = \tilde{u}(X'|X, N) + \beta\, V(H', X').$$

This formulation retains the same future utility term $V(H', X')$ as in the altruistic case but replaces the child's own evaluation $u(X')$ with the parent's assessment $\tilde{u}(X'|X, N)$. For instance, a parent may prefer that the child adopts the parent's religious beliefs, even if doing so does not maximize the child's own utility, as in the model we study in Section 4. The parent's evaluation $\tilde{u}(X'|X, N)$ may also depend on neighborhood characteristics N, as explored in Section 5.

2.2 Parenting styles

The potential conflict between parent and child arising from paternalism gives rise to the concept of parenting styles. A parenting style describes how conflict is managed and control is exercised in the child's upbringing.

In developmental psychology (Baumrind, 1967), the standard classification of parenting styles consists of permissive, authoritative, and authoritarian types. These categories have also been adopted by Doepke and Zilibotti (2017), who reinterpret them through the lens of parental control and belief formation. Their model emphasizes the extent to which parents restrict their children's choice set and seek to influence their values and preferences. Broadly, permissive parents grant their children significant freedom and refrain from intervening in their choices. Authoritative parents actively shape their children's values in order to guide both present and future decisions. In contrast, authoritarian parents impose restrictions and demand obedience without necessarily justifying their decisions or attempting to persuade the child.

In our model, parenting styles influence the formation of the child's values, X', which unfolds in two stages. Let $X_P^\star$ denote the parent's preferred values for the child. In the first stage, the parent decides whether to exert effort to instill these values. In the second stage, the parent chooses whether to allow the child to express their own preference, $X_C^\star$, or to suppress it. The child forms this preference by maximizing their own utility, resulting in:

$$X_C^\star = \arg \max_{X' \in \mathbb{X}(X_P^\star, P)} \left\{ E\left[u(X') + \beta\, V(H', X') \right] \right\},$$

where the expectation is taken over the realization of H' given the state variables.

The set $\mathbb{X}(X_P^\star, P)$ denotes the set of feasible values available to the child, which may depend on the parent's prior choices. In particular, some values X' become attainable only if the parent first invests effort in shaping them. For example, a child may be unable to choose to be patient and future-oriented on their own but may come to value these traits if they are first modeled or encouraged by the parent.

The three parenting styles emerge from the parent's choices at the two stages described above. If the parent neither attempts to instill specific values nor intervenes in the child's decision, the parenting style is permissive: the child determines X' autonomously. If the parent seeks to instill particular values but ultimately allows the child to express their own preference, the style is authoritative. Finally, if the parent suppresses the child's preference and enforces their own, the style is authoritarian. Formally, we express X' as a function of the parent's and child's preferred values, the parenting style P, and potential random shocks ϵ:

$$X' = f\left(\sigma(P)X_P^\star + (1-\sigma(P))X_C^\star, \epsilon\right). \tag{2}$$

We can now define parenting styles in our model.

Definition 1 (Parenting style). The function $\sigma(P)$ characterizes the parenting style as follows:

(i) If $\sigma(P) = 0$, the parent does not interfere with the child's choice of X'; the parenting style is *permissive*.
(ii) If $0 < \sigma(P) < 1$, the parent molds the child's preferences but also allows the child to influence X'; the parenting style is *authoritative*.
(iii) If $\sigma(P) = 1$, the parent suppresses the child's influence on X'; the parenting style is *authoritarian*.

This definition aligns with the axiomatic framework of Doepke and Zilibotti (2017), who characterize parenting styles based on how parents restrict their child's choice set and shape preferences. The parametric formulation introduced here serves to operationalize these distinctions and is tailored to the applications developed in the following sections.

The setup implies that authoritative parenting can vary in intensity. A parent who shapes the child's preferences and also exerts substantial influence over the final choice (i.e., sets $\sigma(P)$ close to one) adopts an authoritative style that leans toward authoritarian. Conversely, when the parent shapes the child's preferences but allows greater autonomy in the final decision (i.e., sets $\sigma(P)$ close to zero), the authoritative style approaches the permissive style.

The value of $\sigma(P)$ may reflect the parent's own disposition—whether more liberal or strict—but it can also be shaped by external constraints on the parent's ability to intervene. For example, once the child leaves home to attend college, the parent may no longer be able to influence their academic effort directly. In such cases, a low value of $\sigma(P)$ may be imposed by circumstances, prompting the parent to invest more heavily in shaping the child's preferences at an earlier stage.

The parenting style may have implications beyond the determination of X'. For example, suppressing the child's choices may require a degree of control that also inhibits independence and creativity, thereby affecting the development of the child's human capital H'.

2.3 General predictions

Even at this level of generality, our framework yields insights into the interplay between parenting, culture, and economic conditions. For instance, if the parent is fully altruistic ($\lambda = 0$), they will never choose an authoritarian style, as parent and child are fully aligned in their preferred value of X'.

By contrast, when parents are paternalistic ($\lambda > 0$), a tradeoff arises between enforcing their own values and responding to the implications of specific values X' for the child's future utility $V(H', X')$. If economic conditions evolve in such a way that certain values yield high returns for the child—regardless of the parent's own preferences X—there will be a tendency toward greater uniformity in children's values, independent of parental culture.

At the same time, multiple mechanisms in the model contribute to the stratification of preferences and culture in society. These include the role of parental values X in paternalistic utility, complementarities between specific values X' and human capital formation H', and interactions with neighborhood choice N.

2.4 Relationship with the literature

The model outlined in this section builds on our recent research on the economics of parenting (Doepke and Zilibotti, 2017, 2019; Doepke et al., 2019; Agostinelli et al., 2022, 2026). The intellectual roots of this approach to the link between parenting and culture lie in the seminal work of Becker (1981). In Becker's approach, as in ours, parents maximize a family utility function that includes weight on children's well-being. While preferences are exogenous in Becker (1981), subsequent work by Becker and Mulligan (1997) provides a foundation for understanding intergenerational preference formation, particularly in shaping time preferences (patience) through parental investment. The role of patience as a cultural asset was further developed in Doepke and Zilibotti (2008).

Our research is also closely related to the work of Bisin and Verdier (2000, 2001), who develop models of cultural transmission in which parents actively shape their children's preferences while also being influenced by external social interactions (oblique transmission). Relative to their framework, we emphasize an explicit utilitarian approach in which we separate the role of altruism and paternalism. This distinction allows us to study a dynamic interaction where parents enforce values they believe to be beneficial for the child, even against the child's preferences. Moreover, we explicitly incorporate into our analysis the notion of parenting style.

Another closely related theory is that of Hauk and Sáez Martí (2002), who analyze cultural transmission through the lens of strategic complementarities, where parents invest in shaping their children's preferences based on expectations about the broader social environment. Their work emphasizes how cultural traits persist when individual incentives to conform reinforce or oppose existing social norms. A similar theme is developed by Sáez Martí and Zenou (2012), who analyze the relationship between cultural transmission and racial discrimination. In their work, cultural persistence arises primarily due to strategic complementarity effects, where parents transmit values that they expect to be advantageous given prevailing social norms. Our analysis in Section 5 is especially close to theirs.

Finally, our work is related to Lizzeri and Siniscalchi (2008). They propose a theoretical model where parents act as supervisors, guiding their children's learning processes by providing information and shaping their beliefs. In this framework, children learn about the world through observations and signals from their parents, who serve as carriers of information, influencing the development of the child's preferences and decision-making strategies. While Lizzeri and Siniscalchi emphasize parents as conveyors of information, our work studies the motivations behind parental guidance.[4]

2.5 Outlook

To examine the forces at play in the general model, we consider three applications that highlight specific mechanisms shaping the interaction between economic conditions and culture. In the analysis below, we simplify the general framework by replacing the child's dynastic value function, $V(H', X')$—which accounts for the future utility of grandchildren, great-grandchildren, and subsequent generations—with a value function, $V_C(H', X')$, that considers only the child's own felicity. This simplification allows for fully analytical results without altering the main insights.

In each of the models below, the cultural variable X corresponds to a specific dimension of preferences or values: work ethic A in Section 3, religion R in Section 4, and trust T in Section 5. The models emphasize different tradeoffs and different aspects of cultural transmission. The first model focuses on the tradeoff between permissive and authoritative parenting. In the model on religion, we introduce authoritarian parenting into the analysis. Finally, the model on trust examines the role of neighborhood interactions and residential sorting.

4 Other recent contributions in economics that also focus on parenting decisions include Lundberg et al. (2009), Zhang and Ikeda (2016), and Cobb-Clark et al. (2019).

3 Economic incentives and cultural stratification

Cultural heterogeneity is reflected in a wide range of attitudes and preferences. Some of these have direct economic relevance, such as risk tolerance, patience, or work ethic, while in other cases, like religious or political beliefs, the implications for economic behavior are more indirect.

In this section, we abstract from the broader cultural spectrum and focus on a setting where preferences directly influence economic choices. Specifically, we consider how variation in work ethic shapes occupational choice, and how this interaction gives rise to cultural stratification and patterns of social mobility. Because the trait under consideration has clear consequences for individual outcomes, we observe meaningful links between parenting, economic conditions, and the intergenerational transmission of culture—even in the absence of paternalistic motives.

To highlight these forces more clearly, we focus on the case of fully altruistic parents ($\lambda = 0$). Under this assumption, parenting style reduces to a binary choice: whether or not to invest in molding the child's preferences—that is, whether to adopt an authoritative or a permissive approach.

3.1 The origin of work ethic

Consider an economy where production requires the input of workers in two occupations: managers and laborers. The wage per efficiency unit of labor supply for managers is denoted by w_M, while the wage for laborers is w_N, with $w_N < w_M$. In general equilibrium, these wages would depend on the labor supply in each occupation (see, e.g., Doepke and Zilibotti, 2014); here, for simplicity, we take w_M and w_N as given.

The efficiency units a worker can supply in each occupation depend on both their talent for that occupation and a preference trait, A, which we interpret as "work ethic." In this framework, work ethic A serves as the cultural variable X described in the general model above. The economic state variable H represents an individual's talent for the managerial occupation. Specifically, a worker with talent H for the managerial occupation and work ethic $A \in \{0, 1\}$ can supply:

$$L_M(H, A) = H + \rho A$$

efficiency units of managerial labor. The talent variable H is uniformly distributed on the interval $[0, 1]$ among workers. The parameter $\rho > 0$ captures the economic return to the work ethic trait A, which may vary depending on technology and production methods.

In contrast, the effective labor supply of laborers is independent of both preferences and talent and is fixed at unity:

$$L_N(H, A) = 1.$$

The key assumption here is that the return to the preference trait A differs across occupations.

Given free occupational choice, a worker selects the occupation that offers the higher return. A worker will, therefore, choose to become a manager if:

$$w_M(H + \rho A) \geq w_N,$$

which is equivalent to:

$$H \geq \frac{w_N}{w_M} - \rho A \equiv \tilde{H}(A). \quad (3)$$

Thus, individuals with a strong work ethic ($A = 1$) are more likely to become managers.

Next, we examine the origins of work ethic. A child's work ethic is shaped by their parent, who can choose either to instill this trait or to refrain from doing so. This decision is captured by the variable $P \in \{0, 1\}$, where $P = 1$ denotes that the parent actively instills a work ethic, and $P = 0$ corresponds to no intervention. We interpret $P = 1$ as authoritative parenting, since the parent actively shapes the child's preferences, whereas $P = 0$ reflects a permissive style.

The effort cost associated with authoritative parenting is denoted by $D(A) > 0$, where A represents the parent's own work ethic. This cost captures the time and effort the parent invests in transmitting values to the child. We assume $D(0) > D(1) > 0$: the cost is lower when the parent has a strong work ethic, since leading by example facilitates transmission.

While the child always benefits from having a work ethic, they are unable to acquire one without the parent's active involvement. If $P = 0$, the child lacks exposure to this trait and defaults to $A_C^{\star} = 0$. By contrast, if $P = 1$, the child has access to a work ethic and strictly prefers it, so $A_C^{\star} = 1$.

If the parent invests in instilling a work ethic, the child develops $A' = 1$ with high probability p_1 from the combined effect of the parent aiming to instill $A' = 1$ and the child reaffirming this choice. Conversely, without investment ($P = 0$), this probability is reduced to p_0, where $0 < p_0 < p_1 < 1$.[5]

Both parents and children derive linear felicity from consumption. In addition, parents care about their children's utility. The value function of a parent with talent H and work ethic A, choosing between occupations $i \in \{M, N\}$, is given by:

$$V(H, A) = \max_{i \in \{M,N\},\ P \in \{0,1\}} \left\{ w_i L_i(H, A) - D(A)P + z\, E\left[V_C(H', A')\right] \right\}.$$

The value function is a special case of the general decision problem in (1), under the assumptions $\lambda = 0$ (no paternalism), $u(A) = 0$ (children do not derive utility from work ethic during childhood), and $\beta = 1$.

5 An authoritarian parenting style would force the child to make a particular occupational choice. We do not discuss this option because it would not be ex-post desirable from the perspective of an altruistic parent.

The first term captures the parent's own utility from labor income, net of any effort cost associated with parenting style P. The second term reflects the parent's concern for the child's future well-being, defined here by the child's adult utility $V_C(H', A')$. The expectation is taken over both the realization of the child's talent H' and their preference A', which in turn depends on the parent's choice of $P \in \{0, 1\}$.

The adult utility of a child with preference A' is determined by their labor income[6]:

$$V_C(H', A') = \max\left\{w_M L_M(H', A'),\ w_N L_N(H', A')\right\}.$$

3.2 Occupational and cultural stratification in equilibrium

We now characterize the equilibrium outcomes. Our primary interest lies in the potential for complementarities between specific occupations and preferences to drive cultural stratification and the endogenous formation of social classes in society.

Consider the parent's evaluation of the child's utility, $V_C(H', A')$. We focus on the case where $\rho < w_N/w_M$, which ensures that the threshold $\tilde{H}(A')$ for selecting the managerial occupation remains strictly between zero and one, regardless of A'. Given that talent H follows a uniform distribution, the child's expected income for a given A' is:

$$E\left[V_C(H', A')\right] = (1 - \tilde{H}(A'))\left(\frac{1 + \tilde{H}(A')}{2} + \rho A'\right) w_M + \tilde{H}(A') w_N.$$

The first term represents the probability that $H' \geq \tilde{H}(A')$, implying that the child chooses to become a manager. The second term corresponds to the expected productivity in the managerial occupation, conditional on $H' \geq \tilde{H}(A')$. Using Eq. (3), we can simplify the expression as:

$$E\left[V_C(H', A')\right] = \frac{1}{2}(w_M + w_N^2/w_M) + \rho A'(w_M - w_N) + \frac{1}{2}\rho^2 (A')^2 w_M.$$

The benefit derived from the child acquiring a work ethic $A' = 1$ is given by:

$$E\left[V_C(H', 1)\right] - E\left[V_C(H', 0)\right] = \rho(w_M - w_N) + \frac{1}{2}\rho^2 w_M. \tag{4}$$

If $D(0)$ is prohibitively large, parents without a work ethic will never invest in their children's work ethic, as they may not fully understand what it entails. In

6 As noted above, one simplification relative to the general framework in Section 2 is that the parent evaluates only the child's expected income, rather than the full continuation value $V(H', A')$, which would incorporate the child's own concern for their offspring (i.e., the parent's grandchild). This assumption simplifies the analysis without affecting the main results.

contrast, the decision of parents with a strong work ethic ($A = 1$) depends on the return ρ to a work ethic in the managerial occupation.

We can now characterize how social stratification and social mobility depend on economic conditions.

Proposition 1 (Classless society). *If the return ρ to a strong work ethic is sufficiently low such that $\rho < \tilde{\rho}$, where*

$$\tilde{\rho} = \frac{w_M - w_N}{w_M}\left(\sqrt{1 + \frac{2w_M D(1)}{z(p_1 - p_0)(w_M - w_N)^2}} - 1\right),$$

then:

- *No parents invest in their children's work ethic;*
- *The children of managers and laborers have an equal likelihood of becoming managers.*

Proof. The parent's decision problem implies that no parent will invest in the child's work ethic if:

$$z(p_1 - p_0)\left(E\left[V_C(H', 1)\right] - E\left[V_C(H', 0)\right]\right) \leq D(1).$$

Using (4), this yields the threshold $\tilde{\rho}$ at which this expression holds as an equality. If $\rho < \tilde{\rho}$, there will be no persistence in economic status across generations because the distribution of children's preferences is identical across occupations, and the distribution of skill is independent of the parent's skill or occupation. □

In a society where $\rho < \tilde{\rho}$, the returns to specific economic preferences are not strong enough to induce social stratification. The distribution of preferences remains identical among the children of managers and laborers, and children from both groups are equally likely to enter the managerial profession. The only observable social distinction is that managers are more likely to have a strong work ethic, as a higher work ethic lowers the ability threshold for managerial entry. Additionally, managers earn a higher income than laborers, as most exceed the ability threshold and, therefore, receive a wage premium over laborers.

Next, we consider the case where the return to work ethic in the managerial occupation is sufficiently high to generate intergenerationally persistent social stratification of preferences.

Proposition 2 (Stratified society). *If the return ρ to work ethic is sufficiently high such that $\rho \geq \tilde{\rho}$, then the steady state of the economy exhibits the following properties:*

- *Parents with a work ethic ($A = 1$) invest in their children's work ethic, while other parents do not;*

- *The children of managers have a higher likelihood of becoming managers than the children of laborers;*
- *The difference in average work ethic between managers and laborers increases with ρ;*
- *Intergenerational persistence in occupation and income increases with ρ.*

The proof for the proposition is given in the appendix.

When the return to work ethic is sufficiently high, parental socialization decisions, combined with variation in the return to specific traits across occupations, lead to cultural stratification in society, where individuals in different occupations are characterized by distinct preferences and values. The degree of stratification increases with the economic return to work ethic, ρ.

Moreover, the mutual complementarity between working in a given occupation and possessing suitable preferences generates persistence in social status and limits intergenerational mobility. This occurs despite the fact that our illustrative model abstracts entirely from the direct transmission of human capital or ability; the sole source of persistence is that a parent with a specific preference trait finds it easier to endow their child with the same trait.

3.3 Separated social classes

In our baseline model, there are no formal barriers to social mobility; persistence in status arises solely from endogenous preference transmission. Historically, however, many societies have reinforced class distinctions through institutional mechanisms such as hereditary aristocracies, caste systems, or legal restrictions on occupational mobility. These structures impose exogenous constraints on social mobility, preventing individuals from freely transitioning across economic roles, regardless of their abilities or preferences.

We next examine how the forces shaping cultural differences evolve in our model when such rigid class boundaries are present. Specifically, we consider how restricting mobility affects the intergenerational transmission of economic preferences, the stability of cultural stratification, and the persistence of inequality over time.

Proposition 3 (Stratified society with exogenous class boundaries). *Consider an environment with a strict separation between two social classes. That is, all members of the managerial class become managers, as do their children, while all members of the laboring class remain confined to the laborer occupation. The steady state exhibits the following properties:*

- *Members of the laboring class never invest in work ethic.*
- *The threshold $\tilde{\rho}_{CB}$ above which managerial-class parents with a work ethic invest is lower than the threshold in a society without fixed class boundaries, $\tilde{\rho}_{CB} < \tilde{\rho}$.*

Proof. Laborers have no incentive to invest in work ethic, as it yields returns only in the managerial occupation, from which their children are excluded. For managers, the child's expected utility is given by:

$$E\left[V_C(H', A')\right] = \left(\frac{1}{2} + \rho A'\right) w_M.$$

Thus, the benefit from investing in work ethic is:

$$z(p_1 - p_0)\left(E\left[V_C(H', 1)\right] - E\left[V_C(H', 0)\right]\right) = z(p_1 - p_0)\rho w_M.$$

The threshold $\tilde{\rho}_{CB}$ at which a manager is indifferent to investing in work ethic satisfies

$$D(1) = z(p_1 - p_0)\tilde{\rho}_{CB} w_M,$$

which yields:

$$\tilde{\rho}_{CB} = \frac{D(1)}{z(p_1 - p_0) w_M} < \tilde{\rho}. \qquad \square$$

The threshold for investing in work ethic is lower in a society with fixed class boundaries because parents in the managerial class know that a strong work ethic will benefit their children with certainty, rather than only if the child also possesses sufficient talent to enter the managerial occupation. If $\rho > \tilde{\rho}_{CB}$ and, in addition, $p_1 - p_0$ is sufficiently large, differences in culture—measured here by the average work ethic—are amplified relative to an economy with class mobility. This result follows because the fixed nature of occupational inheritance strengthens parents' incentives to transmit preferences and values that align with their child's predetermined occupation. The effect is particularly strong when $p_1 - p_0$ is large, meaning that parents exert a strong influence on shaping their children's preferences.

Another important force at play is self-selection: in a mobile society, children with a strong work ethic self-select into the managerial occupation, whereas in an immobile society, this selection effect is absent. As a result, self-selection increases occupational differences in preferences in a mobile society. However, the parental transmission effect dominates when parents have a sufficiently strong impact in shaping their children's preferences.

3.4 Extensions

The baseline model can be extended in several directions. Allowing for a continuous choice in shaping children's preferences does not alter the main conclusions, as it leaves the fundamental mechanism—complementarity between specific occupations and specific preferences—unchanged. Introducing diminishing marginal utility in consumption would amplify class distinctions in the economy, as investing in children's work ethic becomes more costly (in utility terms) for laborers due to their lower earnings. The model can be applied to other aspects of economic preferences that offer different returns in different occupations. For example, Doepke and Zilibotti (2014) consider an environment in which parents can transmit patience and risk tolerance, attributes that matter for entrepreneurship. Doepke and Zilibotti (2014) show that an environment similar to what is described here can generate multiple growth paths, where faster-growing countries are characterized by a larger share of the population displaying an "entrepreneurial spirit" of patient and risk-tolerant preferences.

General equilibrium

General equilibrium effects can further reinforce some of the mechanisms described above. Consider an environment in which the labor supply of each occupation is aggregated through a production function with diminishing returns to each factor. If parents from one group invest more heavily in developing their children's occupation-specific preferences, more children from that group will enter the corresponding occupation, thereby reducing its average return. This, in turn, will discourage parents from other groups from preparing their children for that occupation, further entrenching occupational stratification.

Financial markets

Incentives to endow children with occupation-specific preferences may also depend on the development of financial markets. This is particularly relevant for occupations in which patience and risk tolerance yield high returns.

Consider, for instance, an occupation that requires substantial investment during early adulthood—whether monetary, as in capital-intensive professions, or in time, as in highly-skilled careers involving prolonged training—followed by high returns later in life. If financial markets are underdeveloped and borrowing constraints are severe, only highly patient individuals who can forgo consumption for an extended period will enter such professions. In this case, parents who wish their children to pursue these careers have strong incentives to instill patience as a core value.

Conversely, if financial markets function well and allow individuals to borrow and smooth consumption over the life cycle, patience becomes less critical. As a result, parents will invest less in fostering patience, and cultural distinctions between occupations will weaken.

A similar logic applies to risk tolerance and entrepreneurship. If entrepreneurship involves bearing large, undiversifiable risks, parents who want their children to become entrepreneurs will be incentivized to cultivate risk tolerance. However, if financial markets facilitate risk-sharing—through mechanisms such as limited liability, public capital markets, or private equity funding—risk tolerance becomes less important. Consequently, entrepreneurs may become less culturally distinct over time, at least in terms of their risk preferences.

Interaction of work ethic and patience

Up to this point, we have considered a model in which the parent is fully altruistic, and both parent and child agree that possessing a strong work ethic is desirable. In this setting, work ethic functions as a form of human capital: while not directly tied to knowledge or technical skills, it is a child characteristic in which parents can invest, yielding returns in the form of higher future income.

The main insights from this analysis extend to a richer framework involving multiple preference traits and potential parent-child conflict. Consider a scenario in which acquiring a work ethic requires effort by the child, and the parent and child differ in their time preferences: the parent favors long-term preparation, while the child prefers present enjoyment. In this case, attempts to instill work ethic may fail if the child is unwilling to exert the necessary effort. For transmission to succeed, the parent must resort to additional strategies—either authoritarian (e.g., compelling the child to comply) or authoritative (e.g., instilling patience alongside work ethic). The core mechanism remains intact: parental effort is motivated by the future economic returns for the child. This logic holds not only in fully altruistic settings but also in models with some degree of parent-child conflict, provided that at least a minimal level of altruism is present.

Doepke and Zilibotti (2008) develop a dynamic model closely related to this extension, focusing on the joint transmission of patience and work ethic within the family. Their theory offers a historical application by providing an economic explanation for cultural differences across social classes in preindustrial societies, as well as explaining cultural and economic shifts that followed the British Industrial Revolution. As in our extended framework, parents face a tradeoff between children's present-oriented preferences and the long-term returns of instilling forward-looking traits. Differences in parenting strategies, shaped by economic incentives, lead to heterogeneous cultural outcomes across social classes.

A general feature of this type of model is the role of economic conditions in reinforcing cultural and occupational persistence across generations. Doepke and Zilibotti (2008) suggest that cultural attitudes toward patience and hard work are complementary to occupational characteristics, leading to self-reinforcing patterns of wealth accumulation and inequality. Our model shares this fundamental mechanism: when the return to work ethic is sufficiently high, parents from managerial backgrounds disproportionately invest in transmitting work-oriented values, resulting in stratified social classes. Conversely, in an environment where work ethic has low returns, parental investment in cultural transmission weakens, and intergenerational mobility increases.

3.5 Historical applications

The forces that lead to cultural stratification in the model outlined in this section are particularly powerful in a society that has high barriers to mobility across occupations and social classes and where financial markets are underdeveloped. The theory, therefore, lends itself to historical applications in a preindustrial world. The arguments developed here are consistent with the work of historians such as de Vries (2008) and Mokyr (2018), who examine the cultural and economic transformations in early modern Europe that paved the way for the Industrial Revolution.

Before the mechanized transformation of production in the late 18th century, profound changes occurred in work habits, consumption preferences, and attitudes toward effort—a phenomenon that de Vries terms the *Industrious Revolution.* This period saw households increasing their labor supply, reallocating time from leisure to market-oriented work, and intensifying production in response to expanding consumer demand.

Beyond these changes, Mokyr (2018) highlights a broader cultural transformation. He argues that the rise of scientific inquiry, technological progress, and a pro-innovation culture fostered by the European Enlightenment played a critical role in setting the stage for sustained economic growth. The interplay between changing work ethics, economic incentives, and the diffusion of knowledge created an environment conducive to industrialization, reinforcing the long-term cultural and technological shifts that underpinned the modern economy. The models developed in this chapter suggest a mutual interdependence between technological and institutional changes and the cultural shifts described by economic historians. For example, a strong work ethic contributes to industriousness, and the formation of the work ethic responds to the return to effort and labor supply in a given technological and institutional environment.

In Doepke and Zilibotti (2008), the economic characteristics of preindustrial society result in cultural segregation along occupational lines. The landowning aristocracy had incentives to promote a leisure-oriented mindset in their children, because they lived on income derived from land rather than labor. The landless poor did rely on hard work but lived a hand-to-mouth existence, with little in terms of investment opportunities in human capital or other investments. These conditions fostered a working-class culture that placed little value on future orientation and far-sighted behavior. By contrast, the artisan middle class endogenously cultivated both patience and a strong work ethic.

The middle-class emphasis on patience emanated from the central role of human capital in this group. From apprenticeship to journeymanship to ultimately qualifying as a master in a trade, urban artisans and craftsmen underwent a long period of human capital investment. During training, future artisans would live on limited income, but, if successful, they had a bright future ahead of them. In this sense, the careers of preindustrial artisans and craftsmen were akin to modern-day graduate and professional students (e.g., in medicine). The resulting culture provided a clear contrast to the leisure-oriented upper class of landowners and the short-sighted working class. Hence, the endogenous transmission of cultural values from parents to children in a preindustrial society leads to the emergence of class-based cultures, with a leisure-oriented upper class, a short-sighted working class, and a hard-working and future-oriented middle class of artisans and craftsmen. These endogenous class-based cultures in Doepke and Zilibotti (2008) match well with the characteristics that historians and authors have long ascribed to the members of different social classes in the preindustrial world.

Doepke and Zilibotti (2008) show that class-based traits played a central role in the transformation of the income distribution and the social hierarchy following the onset of the Industrial Revolution. The middle-class combination of hard work and future orientation proved especially valuable once industrialization created new opportunities for enrichment through entrepreneurship and capital investment. This alignment between economic opportunity and class-based culture allowed the middle class to thrive as technological change unfolded. The authors document that urban artisans, craftsmen, and merchants—core segments of the middle class—provided the vast majority of entrepreneurs during the industrialization period. By the end of the 19th century, entrepreneurial families with middle-class origins had caught up with the landowning class, and by the early 20th century they had come to dominate Britain's wealth elite. Conversely, many aristocratic families experienced economic decline, accumulated debt, and were eventually forced to sell off their estates. In the authors' model, the divergent trajectories of social classes reflect the compatibility—or lack thereof—between inherited cultural traits and the demands of a changing economic environment.

The model of Doepke and Zilibotti (2008) also predicts that class-based cultures will continue to evolve as industrialization alters the economic environment faced by each group. In particular, as economic growth advances, parenting styles within the entrepreneurial bourgeoisie undergo a transformation—from a culture centered on patience and a strong work ethic to one increasingly oriented toward leisure and consumption (as emphasized by Veblen, 1899). Initially, an ethos of diligence and perseverance defined the early captains of industry. But as successful entrepreneurs gradually transitioned into rentiers, relying less on their own labor, the incentives for parents to instill the virtues of thrift and hard work weakened.

Beyond cultural differences across social classes and occupations, the framework developed here can also be fruitfully applied to understanding how alternative modes of social organization shape cultural values. A number of authors, including Greif (2006) and Greif and Tabellini (2010), have emphasized the institutional distinctions between clan-based and nuclear-family-based societies. In clan-based systems, social organization revolves around extended kinship networks, with loyalty and control within the clan taking precedence. In contrast, in societies where the influence of clans waned—such as in Western Europe—alternative institutions such as cities, guilds, and corporations became central.

These institutional differences can have far-reaching economic consequences. For instance, de la Croix et al. (2018) argue that clan-based structures impeded the diffusion of knowledge across family boundaries, thereby slowing technological progress and productivity growth. From the perspective of the current framework, such differences in social organization would also lead to persistent cultural divergence. In a clan-based society, values such as respect for authority and deference to elders may be particularly salient. These values, in turn, can generate economic frictions—especially when technological change pits young innovators against older elites invested in the status quo. Empirical work by Alesina and Giuliano (2014) documents a strong association between the strength of family ties and particular cultural attitudes, but formal models of how such values form and persist—and how they interact with economic development—remain scarce.

A more recent application of similar ideas concerns the contrast between the formation of culture and preferences in open versus authoritarian or totalitarian societies. Alesina and Fuchs-Schündeln (2007) document persistent differences in the cultural and political attitudes of West and East Germans who were socialized under distinct economic and political systems. Doepke and Klasing (2025) study the formation of economic preferences in the same context, using a framework similar to the one developed here, but incorporating competing influences from parents, state indoctrination, and biological transmission.

3.6 Taking stock

The stylized model outlined in this section provides a framework for understanding how economic incentives shape the intergenerational transmission of cultural traits, particularly economic preferences such as work ethic. We provide an explicit link between occupational choice and cultural stratification, showing that, when economic conditions favor traits like work ethic, parents actively invest in shaping their children's values, leading to persistent cultural differences across social classes. Conversely, when these traits yield lower economic returns, cultural stratification diminishes, and intergenerational mobility increases.

Our model sheds light on the mechanisms that sustain inequality across generations. Even in the absence of direct transmission of human capital or wealth, cultural complementarities between occupational choice and preferences create persistent social divisions. This highlights a channel through which economic structures reinforce class stratification. In our model, culture is not merely an outcome of economic conditions but an active force that shapes economic opportunities.

The theory makes contact with classic ideas on the relationship between culture and the economy, tracing back to the work of Karl Marx and Max Weber. Marx and Weber each discussed the link between cultural and economic factors, albeit with opposing views regarding the main causal direction.

Marx viewed culture as a byproduct of material conditions, arguing that the function of the dominant ideology is to provide legitimacy to the prevailing economic system (Marx, 1859). Specifically, the economic base (the structure of production and class relations) determines the cultural superstructure, including values, beliefs, and institutions. In contrast, Weber maintained that culture can be an independent driver of economic behavior and success (Weber, 1905). A prime example is Weber's concept of the capitalist spirit, which he argued emerged from the Protestant ethic, which emphasizes discipline, frugality, and hard work. According to Weber, these values encouraged entrepreneurship and led groups endowed with such values to economic prosperity and a distinct class identity. Still, Weber also allowed for a role of economic factors. In the concluding paragraph of Weber (1905), he explicitly cautioned against substituting "for a one-sided materialistic an equally one-sided spiritualistic causal interpretation of culture and history."

Our theory provides a synthesis of these two classic perspectives. Economic returns, measured by the parameter ρ, shape the evolution and stratification of culture in society, where culture is represented by economic preferences. Higher returns to specific values, such as work ethic, reinforce the transmission of these values across generations, leading to the emergence of culturally distinct social classes. At the same time, cultural values influence economic decisions, occupational choices, and patterns of social mobility and inequality. By allowing for bidirectional causality, the model highlights how cultural and economic forces reinforce one another, contributing to the persistence of economic and cultural divisions across generations.[7]

4 The transmission of non-economic cultural traits

We now turn to a central facet of culture, namely religion. Religious creeds often include prescriptions relevant to economic outcomes, such as endorsements of frugality and hard work. In other cases, religious tenets intersect with economic behavior only tangentially. However, even when religious beliefs do not directly shape economic decision-making, their transmission remains influenced by the tradeoffs emphasized in the economics of parenting.

Paternalism plays a central role in this process. Unlike economic preferences such as work ethic or risk aversion, which parents may strategically encourage to promote their children's economic success, religious beliefs are often transmitted because of deeply held normative convictions. Accordingly, while the previous section assumed purely altruistic parental concerns, here we allow for paternalism. Specifically, religious parents derive utility from their children adopting the same faith, viewing their creed as intrinsically right.

Introducing paternalism into the analysis has important implications. Parenting choices driven by paternalism may not always align with a child's economic interests. Religious parents may encourage beliefs or practices that restrict career options, shape occupational choices, or influence attitudes

7 A more comprehensive discussion of the relationship between economic models of parenting and the intellectual perspectives of Marx and Weber can be found in Sáez Martí and Zilibotti (2008).

toward wealth accumulation. Some religious norms promote behaviors that reduce economic engagement—such as prioritizing community service over professional advancement—while others reinforce economically beneficial traits, including trust, work ethic, or long-term planning.

The degree of parental enforcement also matters. Highly paternalistic parents may impose strict socialization strategies to ensure adherence to religious values, whereas more permissive parents allow greater individual choice. These variations contribute to differences in how religious identity interacts with economic behavior across families and social groups. More generally, religion often persists across generations through cultural transmission mechanisms. Even when it does not directly influence economic decision-making, parental investment and socialization shape how religious values interact with broader economic attitudes, including work, consumption, and societal participation.

The discussion in this section could be extended beyond religion to encompass political ideologies and moral doctrines that parents transmit for their intrinsic worth rather than for their economic utility. This perspective resonates with Kant's categorical imperative, which asserts that moral principles should be upheld as ends in themselves, irrespective of consequences or context (Kant, 1785).

4.1 A model of religious preferences and economic returns

To analyze the implications of paternalism in religious socialization, consider an economy where individuals adopt religious beliefs R from a finite set. Here R represents the cultural variable X in our general model. Religious affiliation may encompass broad traditions such as Christianity or Islam, specific denominations within these faiths, or secular alternatives, including atheism and agnosticism.

For simplicity, we categorize beliefs into three groups, $R \in \{F, M, S\}$: fervent believers (F), who adhere strictly to religious doctrine; moderate believers (M), who take a more flexible approach to faith; and the secular group (S), consisting of non-believers. This classification allows us to examine how religious transmission varies across parents with different levels of religiosity and the tradeoffs they face in passing on their beliefs to their children.

Parenting style

Parents derive a paternalistic utility flow, $\tilde{u}(R, R')$, depending on whether their child's religion R' matches their own. In contrast, a child's utility from religion, $u(R')$, is independent of the parent's beliefs and is maximized when $R' = S$, meaning secular beliefs provide the greatest enjoyment for the child. Parents are assumed to be fully paternalistic ($\lambda = 1$), implying that religious parents will attempt to transmit their own faith to their child.

The choice of parenting style is binary, $P \in \{0, 1\}$. If the parent adopts an authoritarian approach ($P = 1$), they restrict the child's exposure to individuals with different beliefs.[8] If the parent is permissive ($P = 0$), the child is free to choose their religion based on their own inclinations.

Parenting style affects the probability that the child adopts the parent's religion. Under permissive parenting, the child leans toward secular beliefs, which they adopt with probability $p > 0.5$. Under authoritarian parenting, the child adopts the parent's religious faith with probability $p > 0.5$. In both cases, random shocks may influence the outcome: with probability $1 - p$, the child adopts one of the two remaining options with equal probability. Specifically, under permissive parenting, the child has a $(1 - p)/2$ probability of adopting either $R' = F$ or $R' = M$, while under authoritarian parenting, they have the same probability of adopting one of the two beliefs different from the parent's. This randomness reflects external influences beyond parental control. A child may encounter a particularly persuasive believer, or an authoritarian parent's efforts may fail, leading to deviations from the intended outcome.

Choosing authoritarian parenting increases the probability that the child adopts R from $(1 - p)/2$ to p, while reducing the probability of secular beliefs from p to $(1 - p)/2$. We define the resulting increase in the probability of successful religious transmission under authoritarian parenting as $\Delta p = p - \frac{1-p}{2}$.

Costs and benefits of authoritarian parenting

Imposing an authoritarian parenting style on the child requires costly effort, denoted by ξ, on the part of the parent. This effort cost varies across parents and follows a uniform distribution, $\xi \sim U(0, 1)$. Beyond the direct cost ξ, authoritarian parenting also imposes an indirect cost by restricting the child's freedom and independence, which may have economic consequences. For instance, a child raised in an authoritarian manner may have fewer opportunities to explore their talents and interests or may develop weaker critical thinking skills, both of which can affect future earnings. These broader implications establish a connection between religious transmission and economic conditions.

We model this economic cost of authoritarian parenting by introducing an economic return to independence such that the child's earnings capacity is given by:

$$H' = W + \rho(1 - P),$$

[8] One could, in principle, distinguish between an authoritative strategy, where parents attempt to persuade the child of their beliefs while ultimately allowing them to choose, and a stricter authoritarian approach. Under our assumption, parents strictly prefer the authoritarian strategy, using any available means to maximize the likelihood that their child adopts their faith. A weaker version of this result could arise if persuasion were less costly than restricting choice, leading some parents to prefer persuasion over coercion. While this scenario introduces richer dynamics, it ultimately leads to similar conclusions.

where W represents the wage of a child raised under authoritarian parenting, and ρ captures the additional income earned by a child who was raised with a permissive parenting style ($P = 0$).

The parent's value function

The full value function of a parent with human capital H and religion R is given by:

$$V(H, R) = E\left[\max_{P}\left\{H - \xi P + zE\left[\tilde{u}(R, R') + \beta V_C(H', R')\right]\right\}\right].$$

Here, the outer expectation is taken over the realization of the parenting cost ξ, while the inner expectation is over the realization of the child's religion R'. The value function incorporates the parent's felicity, here solely determined by consumption, along with a concern for the child, weighted by z.

The parental concern includes a paternalistic component, $\tilde{u}(R, R')$, which depends on the parent's religion R and the child's religion R'. This term reflects the notion that religious parents seek to transmit their beliefs to their children. Specifically, $\tilde{u}(R, R')$ takes the following form:

$$\tilde{u}(R, R') = -\mu_F\,\chi(R = F, R' \neq F) - \mu_M\,\chi(R = M, R' \neq M),$$

where $\chi(\cdot)$ is an indicator function that equals one if both conditions are met and zero otherwise. Here, $\mu_F > 0$ represents the disutility experienced by fervent believers ($R = F$) if their child does not adopt the same religion, while μ_M captures the corresponding disutility for moderate believers. We assume $\mu_F > \mu_M$, meaning that fervent believers care more about religious transmission than moderate believers, whereas secular parents remain indifferent with respect to their child's religious choices, $\mu_S = 0$. This implies that secular parents always adopt a permissive parenting style.

The child's problem

The child's utility function is given by:

$$v(H', R') = u(R') + \beta V_C(H', R').$$

Here, the child's immediate felicity, $u(R')$, is maximized when $R' = S$, indicating that children raised under permissive parenting are naturally drawn to secular beliefs. The child's adult utility is determined solely by their consumption-based utility:

$$V_C(H', R') = H'.$$

As in the previous section, we consider a simplified framework where the child's concern for their own offspring is omitted. This assumption simplifies the analysis while preserving the key insights.

4.2 The interaction between economic conditions and religiosity

Our primary focus is on how the transmission of R is influenced by the economic return to independence, ρ. We analyze steady-state equilibria in which each generation of children encounters the same decision problem in raising their own offspring as their parents did.

The following proposition characterizes the role of ρ in shaping both cultural and economic stratification within the model economy.[9]

Proposition 4 (Returns to independence and religiosity). *The return to independence ρ determines equilibrium outcomes as follows:*

1. *If*

$$\rho < \frac{\mu_M \, \Delta p - z^{-1}}{\beta},$$

then all religious parents with $R \in \{F, M\}$ adopt an authoritarian parenting style. In the steady state, each group $R \in \{F, M, S\}$ constitutes one-third of the population.

2. *If*

$$\frac{\mu_M \, \Delta p - z^{-1}}{\beta} \leq \rho < \frac{\mu_M \, \Delta p}{\beta},$$

all fervent parents ($R = F$) are authoritarian, while the proportion of authoritarian parents among moderates ($R = M$) decreases with ρ. In steady state, the share of moderates decreases, whereas the share of secular individuals increases with ρ.

3. *If*

$$\frac{\mu_M \, \Delta p}{\beta} \leq \rho < \frac{\mu_F \, \Delta p - z^{-1}}{\beta},$$

only fervent parents ($R = F$) are authoritarian, while all other parents adopt a permissive parenting style. In steady state, the fervent group ($R = F$) makes up one-third of the population, the moderate group ($R = M$) shrinks to a share of $(1 - p)/2$, and the secular group ($R = S$) becomes the largest, accounting for a share of $\frac{p}{2} + \frac{1}{6}$.

4. *If p is sufficiently high, the income ratio between secular and fervent individuals increases with ρ.*

The proposition demonstrates that, although religion itself does not have direct economic consequences in this model, the constraints imposed by a parenting style focused on religious transmission create an interaction between economic conditions and cultural persistence.

9 The proof of this proposition is provided in the appendix. Note that, for sufficiently large values of ρ, even (some) fervent parents abandon the authoritarian parenting style, leading to a more secular society.

First, as the economic returns to independence increase, the cost of transmitting religion rises. Since parents vary in their tolerance for the effort required to enforce an authoritarian parenting style, this results in a gradual process of secularization as the benefits of independence grow. Notably, secularization disproportionately affects moderate religious groups, as they place a lower priority on ensuring religious continuity across generations.

Second, within religious groups that strongly prioritize transmission (here, the fervent group), the burden of maintaining religious adherence becomes more pronounced when the returns to independence are high. Consequently, highly insular religious communities, such as the Amish or Ultra-Orthodox Jews, must forgo relatively more economic opportunities to sustain their way of life in environments where independence is increasingly rewarded. This suggests a tradeoff: societies with strict religious transmission of norms may survive only by remaining economically isolated or by developing institutional mechanisms that compensate for the economic disadvantages of authoritarian parenting.

4.3 Religiosity and economic development

In our model, parenting decisions respond to economic incentives: parents choose strategies based on their own values and the expected returns to specific traits. Historically, authoritarian parenting was the dominant mode. Doepke and Zilibotti (2019) argue that a key reason for its prevalence in preindustrial societies was the economic value of obedience. When children were expected to follow their parents' profession, direct control and learning by example were effective, while independence and creativity had limited relevance. Religious traditions have historically justified strict discipline. Biblical and Islamic sources, along with cultural proverbs, often present corporal punishment as a moral imperative.

As economies evolved—with industrialization, rising occupational mobility, and the expansion of human-capital-intensive sectors—the appeal of authoritarian parenting declined. This shift aligns with our argument that strict upbringing and the transmission of religious principles tend to persist in environments where stability is rewarded, and fade when the economic return to independence rises.

Doepke and Zilibotti (2019) further show that economic modernization—particularly the spread of higher education and the growing demand for flexible skills—eroded the value of rigid child-rearing strategies. Our model captures a similar mechanism: when specific cultural traits become less valuable, parents reduce their effort to instill them through strict methods.

Empirical evidence also supports the prediction that cultural stratification weakens in more fluid economies. Authoritarian parenting remains prevalent in settings characterized by low mobility and high economic insecurity—for example, in Brazil, where persistent inequality reinforces both strict parenting and religious commitment. In contrast, in dynamic economies with developed financial systems, the incentives for rigid value transmission are weaker.

4.4 Empirical evidence on parenting and religiosity from the World Values Survey

We now present empirical evidence supporting our theoretical predictions regarding religion and parenting using data from the World Values Survey (WVS) (Haerpfer et al., 2022). The WVS enables us to examine parenting styles in contemporary societies and their correlation with cultural attitudes. Our analysis primarily draws on the seventh and most recent wave of the WVS, focusing on the United States.[10] Concentrating on the United States helps minimize cross-country confounding factors, though we also include some international comparisons.[11]

Following our previous work, we proxy parenting styles using respondents' answers to the question: *"Here is a list of qualities that children can be encouraged to learn at home. Which, if any, do you consider to be especially important?"* We focus on four specific responses: obedience, hard work, imagination, and independence.[12] Additionally, we consider responses to the question: *"Please tell me for each of the following actions whether you think it can always be justified, never be justified, or something in between... Parents beating children."* Respondents rate their opinion on a scale from one ('Never justifiable') to ten ('Always justifiable').

We classify parents as authoritarian if they mention obedience as an important value for children to learn at home or if they assign a score higher than three to the justification of beating children.[13] We classify parents as authoritative if they are not authoritarian but consider hard work an important value to instill in children. Finally, we define parents as permissive if they are neither authoritarian nor authoritative but emphasize imagination or independence as key values for children to learn at home. We exclude the small share of respondents (ca. 3% of the sample) who do not fall into any of these categories.

Fig. 1 presents the distribution of parenting styles in the data. Half of respondents are classified as authoritative parents, while 33% fall into the

10 In the United States, the seventh wave of the WVS was collected in 2017.

11 More extensive cross-country analyses of parenting styles based on earlier waves of the WVS can be found in Doepke and Zilibotti (2017) and Doepke et al. (2019).

12 Each respondent can select up to five options. Other available choices include: good manners; feeling of responsibility; tolerance and respect for other people; thrift, saving money and things; determination, perseverance; religious faith; and unselfishness.

13 Our empirical results remain robust to alternative definitions of authoritarian parenting, such as requiring both the mention of obedience and a score greater than one to the justifiability of beating children.

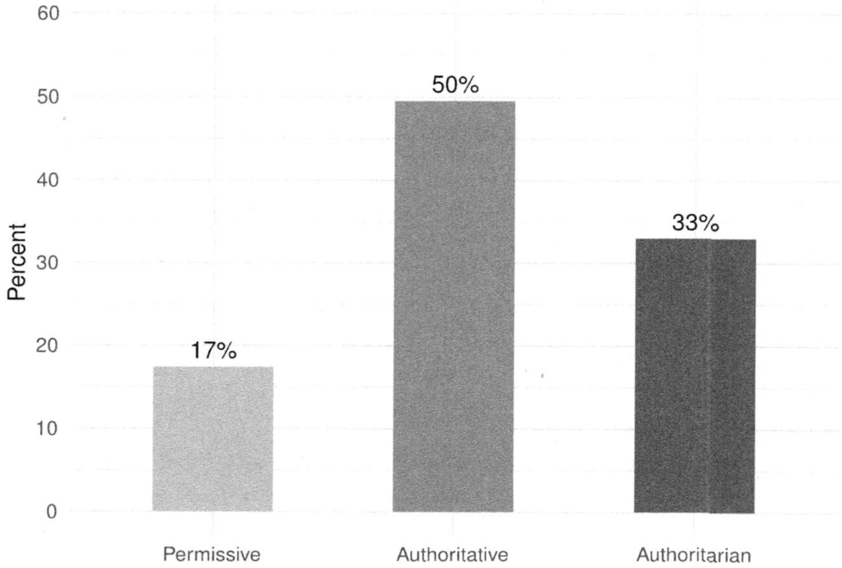

FIGURE 1 Parenting style.
Notes: This figure displays the proportions of permissive, authoritative, and authoritarian parenting styles in the sample. See the text for details on how these parenting styles are defined.

authoritarian category. As shown in Doepke and Zilibotti (2019), the permissive parenting style is the least common in the United States, with fewer than one in five respondents classified as permissive parents.

Given this data on parenting, let us now turn to the issue of religion. Our model suggests that religious parents place greater emphasis on paternalistically transmitting their own values and faith to their children. As a result, we expect them to exhibit a stronger tendency toward adopting an authoritarian parenting style while being less inclined toward permissive parenting.

The WVS contains information about individuals' attitudes toward religion. We classify a respondent as religious if they select 'A religious person' in response to the question: *"Independently of whether you attend religious services or not, would you say you are…?"* Those who choose '…not a religious person' or '…an atheist' are classified as non-religious. In our sample, 55% of respondents are classified as religious.

Fig. 2 presents the distribution of parenting styles by religiosity. The figure shows that religious parents are more likely to adopt an authoritarian parenting style (+11 percentage points, henceforth pp) and less likely to adopt a permissive style (−10 pp). The authoritative parenting style is about equally prevalent among religious and non-religious parents.

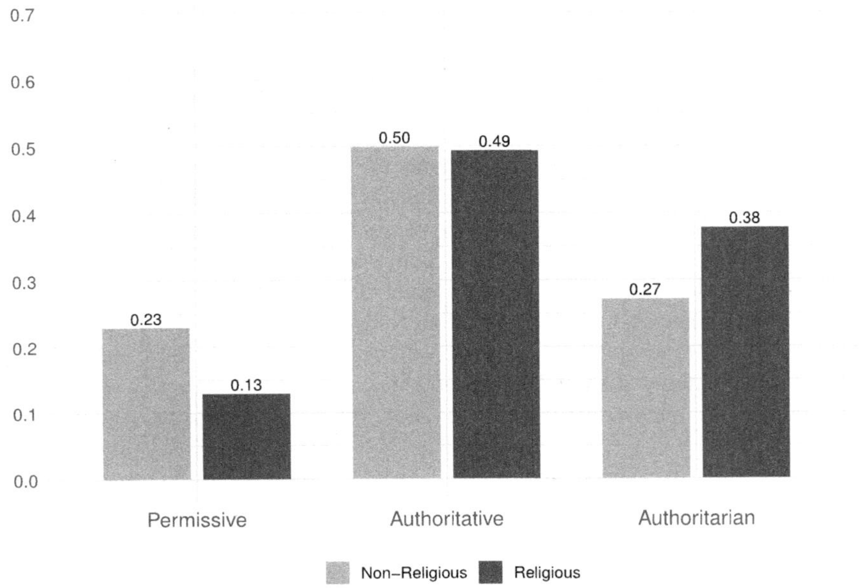

FIGURE 2 Parenting style and religiosity.
Notes: This figure shows the distribution of parenting styles by religiosity. Respondents are classified as religious if they answer 'A religious person' to the question: "*Independently of whether you attend religious services or not, would you say you are... ?*". Respondents who answer 'Not a religious person' or 'An atheist' are classified as non-religious. See the text for further details.

Regression analysis

To address potential confounding factors, we estimate multiple regressions controlling for socioeconomic characteristics, including education, race, gender, and age.[14] All results we report should be interpreted as correlations rather than causal effects.

We treat the dependent variables as follows:

1. The first set of regressions (columns 1–3) estimates the effect of religiosity on the likelihood of adopting a permissive parenting style relative to any of the alternatives.
2. The second set of regressions (columns 4–6) estimates the effect of religiosity on the likelihood of adopting an authoritarian parenting style relative to any of the alternatives.
3. The third set of regressions (columns 7–9) defines a dependent variable that orders the three parenting styles by increasing levels of parental control:

[14] In some specifications, we also include variables capturing neighborhood quality and trust in other people. A detailed discussion of these variables follows in the next section. However, it is important to highlight here that the inclusion of neighborhood quality and trust does not affect the conditional correlation between religiosity and parenting style.

1 for permissive parents, 2 for authoritative parents, and 3 for authoritarian parents. This approach reflects the idea that authoritative and authoritarian parenting represent varying degrees of parental influence over children's values. We label this dependent variable intensity of parenting.

Table 1 presents the key coefficients of interest, including that for *High education*, a binary indicator for respondents with at least a bachelor's degree or equivalent education (ISCED 6). The full set of coefficients is reported in Appendix Table B.1. We report the results for OLS regressions.[15]

The results reveal that there is a clear association between religiosity and parenting styles even after socioeconomic differences between religious and non-religious respondents are controlled for. Religious respondents are 9 to 10 pp less likely to adopt a permissive parenting style and 10–11 pp more likely to adopt an authoritarian style, with both effects highly statistically significant. Religiosity is uncorrelated with the adoption of an authoritative parenting style.[16]

The table also shows that highly educated respondents are more likely to adopt permissive or authoritative parenting styles and less likely to be authoritarian. Appendix Table B.1 with the full set of coefficients further reveals that Black and Hispanic respondents have a higher likelihood of adopting an authoritarian parenting style, and women are less likely to be authoritarian.

International evidence

While the empirical analysis so far has focused on the United States, we can also examine whether the relationship between parenting styles and religiosity holds more broadly across countries. The seventh wave of the WVS makes this possible, providing data on 84,046 respondents across 64 countries.[17] According to our classification, 61% of respondents are religious, while 39% are non-religious.

Fig. 3 presents the results. Consistent with the US findings, religious parents are more likely to adopt an authoritarian parenting style (+12 pp) and less likely to adopt a permissive style (−10 pp). The share of authoritative parents is similar across religious and non-religious respondents.

These international patterns are consistent with findings from earlier waves of the WVS, as discussed in Doepke and Zilibotti (2019).[18] Their analysis similarly finds a systematic association between religiosity and parenting styles,

[15] Given the nature of the intensity of parenting variable, which takes three values ranging from 1 to 3, Appendix Table B.2 also reports estimates from a multinomial probit model. The results are consistent with those presented in Table 1.

[16] This follows from the fact that the coefficients for permissive and authoritarian parenting styles have similar magnitudes but opposite signs, and that the three parenting styles are mutually exclusive.

[17] See Appendix C for the full list of countries included.

[18] Doepke and Zilibotti (2019) classify respondents as religious if they consider religion to be 'Very' or 'Rather Important,' and as non-religious otherwise.

TABLE 1 The determinants of parenting style.

	Permissive			Authoritarian			Intensity of parenting		
	(1)	(2)	(3)	(4)	(5)	(6)	(7)	(8)	(9)
Religious	−0.09***	−0.09***	−0.10***	0.10***	0.10***	0.11***	0.20***	0.19***	0.21***
	(0.02)	(0.02)	(0.02)	(0.02)	(0.02)	(0.02)	(0.03)	(0.03)	(0.03)
High neighbor. quality		0.06***			−0.07**			−0.12***	
		(0.02)			(0.03)			(0.04)	
Trust in people		0.04***			−0.07***			−0.12***	
		(0.02)			(0.02)			(0.03)	
Neighbor. quality (Factor)			0.02**			−0.02			−0.03**
			(0.01)			(0.01)			(0.02)
Trust (Factor)			0.02*			−0.03**			−0.05***
			(0.01)			(0.01)			(0.02)
High education	0.06***	0.04***	0.04**	−0.11***	−0.09***	−0.09***	−0.17***	−0.13***	−0.13***
	(0.02)	(0.02)	(0.02)	(0.02)	(0.02)	(0.02)	(0.03)	(0.03)	(0.03)
Observations	2,466	2,455	2,405	2,466	2,455	2,405	2,466	2,455	2,405

Notes: This table shows the relationship between religiosity, neighborhood quality, trust, and parenting style. The dependent variables are: an indicator for a permissive parenting style (columns 1–3); an indicator for an authoritarian parenting style (columns 4–6); and a measure of intensity of parenting, coded as 1 for permissive, 2 for authoritative, and 3 for authoritarian (columns 7–9). *High neighborhood quality* is an indicator for respondents who answer 'Not frequently' or 'Not at all frequently' to the question: *"How frequently do the following things occur in your neighborhood? Street violence and fights"*. *Trust in people* is an indicator for respondents who answer 'Most people can be trusted' to the question: *"Generally speaking, would you say that most people can be trusted or that you need to be very careful in dealing with people?"*. *Neighborhood quality (Factor)* is derived from factor analysis based on responses to questions about the frequency of specific behaviors at the neighborhood level. *Trust (Factor)* is derived from factor analysis based on responses to questions about trust in different groups of people. *High education* is an indicator for respondents with at least a bachelor's degree or equivalent education (ISCED 6). All regressions control for race, gender, age, and age squared. See the text for further details. Robust standard errors are reported in parentheses. $^{*}p < 0.10$, $^{**}p < 0.05$, $^{***}p < 0.01$.

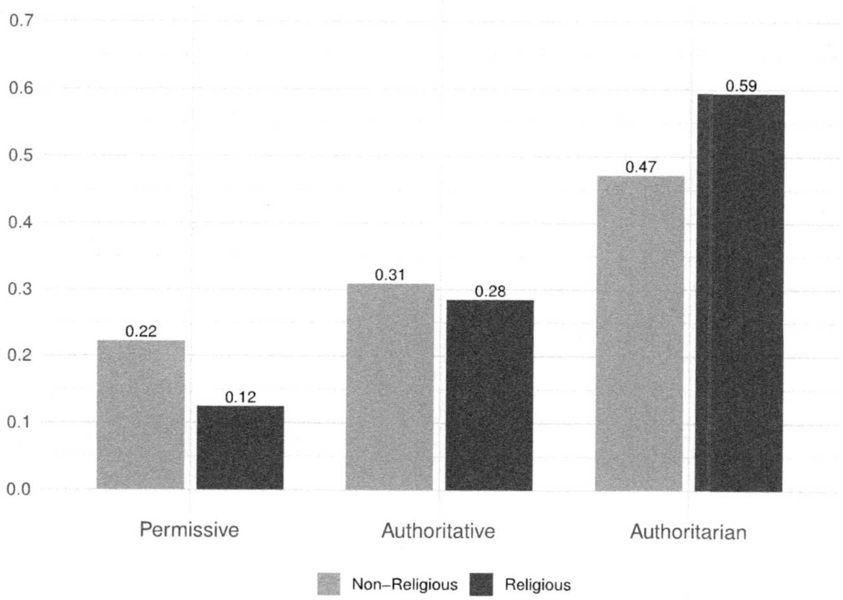

FIGURE 3 Parenting style and religiosity—cross-country sample.
Notes: This figure replicates Fig. 2 using the full set of countries from WVS Wave 7. See the main text and Appendix C for further details and for the list of countries included in the analysis.

with religious individuals overrepresented among authoritarian parents and underrepresented among permissive ones.

Overall, the empirical evidence aligns with our theoretical prediction that religious parents are more inclined toward authoritarian parenting and less likely to adopt a permissive approach. These patterns hold consistently across multiple data sources and remain robust after accounting for heterogeneity in socioeconomic characteristics.

4.5 Relationship with the literature

Our stylized model captures only one aspect of the complex interactions between economics and religion. Bisin and Verdier (2000) emphasize the interaction of the transmission of religion with the composition of the local population, an issue we will discuss in the following section. More broadly, religious beliefs and doctrines can exert direct economic effects, which, in turn, shape the incentives for parents to adopt different parenting styles.

We have already reviewed Max Weber's thesis that Protestant ethics—particularly the emphasis on hard work and frugality—played a key role in fostering the development of capitalism in Western societies.[19] Recent economic research has investigated the Weberian hypothesis from an empirical perspective. Specifically, Becker and Woessmann (2009) analyze 19th-century Prussian counties to assess the economic impact of Protestantism. They find that Protestant regions exhibited greater economic prosperity, though the primary mechanism appears to be an increase in literacy rather than a distinct Protestant work ethic. Their interpretation is that Protestantism encouraged individual Bible reading, which led to higher literacy rates and, in turn, supported economic development through enhanced human capital.

Conversely, Cantoni (2015) investigates the long-term economic consequences of the Protestant Reformation across German cities from 1300 to 1900. His findings indicate no significant growth differences between Protestant and Catholic cities, challenging the notion that Protestantism inherently spurred economic development.

Andersen et al. (2017) suggest that some of the cultural values associated with the Protestant work ethic—such as diligence and thrift—may indeed have religious roots, but these predate the Reformation. Their study finds that medieval European regions with a historical presence of Cistercian monasteries exhibited higher levels of productivity and long-term economic success. These monasteries, which emphasized disciplined labor and resource management, may have helped instill values that later aligned with Protestant teachings. These findings support the idea that religion played a role in shaping economically relevant cultural values, but challenge the view that such values were unique to Protestantism or originated with the Reformation.

Another important contribution to this debate comes from Botticini and Eckstein (2005, 2012), who argue that the Jewish transition from agriculture to urban professions and the formation of the diaspora were influenced by a religious mandate for male literacy. Following the destruction of the Second Temple in 70 CE, Jewish religious leaders emphasized Torah study, making education a religious obligation. This emphasis on literacy led Jews to gravitate toward occupations that valued reading and writing skills, such as trade and finance, particularly as these skills became economically advantageous under Muslim rule during the Middle Ages. Their perspective offers an intriguing parallel to Weber's hypothesis, though their analysis shifts the focus from religious ethics to the role of religiously motivated education in economic specialization and success.

The Weberian debate has been equally prominent in sociology. In a classic contribution, Lenski (1961) argued that Protestant communities generally outperformed Catholic ones in terms of economic development, due to Protestantism's encouragement of individualism and independent reasoning. He suggested that these traits fostered advancements in science and technology

19 See Weber (1905). Weber (1920) extends the analysis to other world religions, examining how their beliefs shape economic behavior and societal development.

by promoting critical thinking and individual responsibility.[20] While Lenski's thesis has been debated and criticized (see, e.g., Calhoun, 2004), it remains a noteworthy attempt to explain how specific religious values may foster or hinder economic development through their effects on individual autonomy and intellectual independence.

The secularization hypothesis has been examined extensively, including by Inglehart (1990), who argues that economic development drives cultural change, leading to declining religiosity. His main argument is about the perception of economic security rather than the economic return to independence. Specifically, he argues that, in preindustrial and low-income societies, religion functions as a coping mechanism for existential insecurity stemming from poverty, illness, and instability. As economies develop, improvements in living standards and social welfare systems mitigate these risks, thereby reducing the need for religious belief. In line with Inglehart's hypothesis, Becker and Woessmann (2013) document a negative relationship between rising incomes and Protestant church attendance in a panel of 175 Prussian counties between 1886 and 1911. Viewed through the lens of our economic theory of parenting, this evidence suggests that, as economies develop, parents reduce their investment in religious socialization when its perceived value diminishes.

The interplay between religion and economic development is also central to the work of Barro and McCleary (2003), who use international survey data to investigate the causal effects of religious beliefs and practices on economic outcomes. Using an instrumental variables strategy, they find that beliefs in concepts such as heaven and hell are positively associated with growth, whereas frequent church attendance is negatively associated with it. These findings support the idea that certain religious beliefs may foster economic activity—for example, by promoting a strong work ethic—while more intense religious practice may hinder economic performance. In a more recent and comprehensive study, McCleary and Barro (2019) examine how variations in religious beliefs and practices intersect with both economic performance and political institutions. Their analysis explores how different dimensions of religiosity affect productivity, long-run growth, and the stability of democratic governance.

Religious beliefs also play a role in shaping social norms and social capital, both of which are known to influence economic development. The empirical study by Guiso et al. (2003), based on World Values Survey data, examines how religiosity affects individual attitudes toward a range of economic and social issues, including cooperation, the role of government, gender norms,

[20] The role of individualism in economic development is further highlighted in recent economics research by Gorodnichenko and Roland (2011, 2017). Their studies suggest that individualistic cultures, which emphasize personal freedom and achievement, tend to generate higher rates of innovation and, in turn, greater economic growth. To the extent that religious values cultivate either individualism or collectivism, they can influence economic outcomes by shaping cultural attitudes toward innovation and autonomy.

legal institutions, thrift, and perceptions of market fairness. On the one hand, the authors find that religious individuals tend to report greater trust in others, more confidence in government and legal institutions, a lower willingness to break the law, and a stronger belief in the fairness of market outcomes. These patterns are consistent with higher levels of social capital and institutional trust. On the other hand, religiosity is also associated with more conservative views on gender roles—particularly regarding women's participation in the workforce—as well as higher levels of social intolerance.

4.6 Taking stock

In this section, we developed a simple model in which parents transmit religious principles to their children because they regard those principles as intrinsically valuable, even when doing so may come at the expense of their children's economic success. The key takeaway is not that religion and economic achievement are inherently in conflict, but that they are interconnected through cultural transmission and evolving economic incentives. In our model, this connection operates through parenting style; yet even within this specific channel, we observe meaningful interactions between economic conditions, cultural change, and social stratification.

More broadly, parents adjust the emphasis they place on religious values based on how those values are expected to shape their children's future economic prospects. This suggests that the intergenerational transmission of religiosity is not static, but responsive to broader societal forces including technological change, labor market dynamics, and the evolving demands of human capital formation in a modern economy.

5 Social interactions and the transmission of trust

Culture shapes how people interact, and these interactions are influenced by parenting. Norms of cooperation and trust, often transmitted from parents to children, guide individual behavior and form a central component of social capital.[21] Cultural attitudes such as trust both shape and respond to local social environments. As a result, residential segregation and neighborhood composition play a central role in the choice of parenting styles and the intergenerational transmission of cultural values.

In this section, we incorporate social interactions into our analysis, focusing on trust. Trust governs interpersonal cooperation, local economic exchange, and civic engagement. For example, in high-trust communities, small businesses

---

21 The notion of social capital dates back to Hanifan (1916), who described the value of social networks in improving education and civic life. The concept has become central in modern sociology—see, e.g., Bourdieu (1986), Coleman (1988), and Putnam (1993, 2000). Contributions in economics include Knack and Keefer (1997), Glaeser et al. (2002), Guiso et al. (2004, 2016), Durlauf and Fafchamps (2004), and Algan and Cahuc (2010).

can flourish through informal arrangements: local shopkeepers extend credit, neighbors pool resources, and community ties support mutual aid. An example is tightly knit ethnic enclaves such as Chinatowns or Jewish merchant communities where intra-group trust facilitated trade, investment, and the transmission of economic practices across generations (Greif, 1994).

These examples underscore how trust, once established, can become self-sustaining and economically valuable. But trust is not evenly spread: it varies across neighborhoods and social groups. Its origins lie not only in local institutions, but also in cultural attitudes passed down within families. To capture these patterns, we extend our framework to model trust formation as an endogenous outcome. Parents choose neighborhoods based on income and expectations about the local social environment. These choices give rise to residential segregation, which in turn affects the cultural and economic landscape children grow up in.

Building on insights from Rohner et al. (2013), we emphasize the role of strategic complementarity in trust formation: when more parents in a neighborhood instill trust in their children, others are more likely to do the same.[22] This dynamic generates a feedback loop that links neighborhood composition, parenting strategies, and the social fabric of communities.

In affluent neighborhoods, where interactions are generally safe and predictable, parents are more likely to instill trust, reinforcing social cohesion and contributing to collective economic success. In contrast, in disadvantaged neighborhoods marked by crime and juvenile problems, peer effects are often negative, prompting parents to adopt a defensive posture. In these contexts, instilling caution and distrust becomes a strategy to protect children. These divergent parenting styles reinforce underlying inequalities: high-income, high-trust neighborhoods evolve into cohesive and prosperous communities, while low-income, low-trust neighborhoods remain trapped in cycles of stagnation and exclusion. The process is driven by the intergenerational transmission of cultural attitudes shaped by local conditions.

By linking trust formation to parenting and residential choice, we show how cultural values evolve alongside economic conditions. Just as differences in work ethic shape occupational outcomes, and religious beliefs influence moral views, trust matters for the accumulation of social capital and the strength of communities. Parenting strategies—shaped by neighborhood context—can reinforce or reduce persistent gaps across social groups.

5.1 A model of trust and neighborhoods

We develop a stylized theory where parents make a residential choice and, through the choice of their parenting style, influence their children's trust in

22 Rohner et al. (2013) examine how trade and conflict influence intergroup trust, showing that cooperative behavior is reinforced when trust is reciprocated and eroded when it is not. Their model highlights strategic complementarities in the accumulation (or breakdown) of trust.

other people. The state variables for a given parent consist of human capital H and trust $T \in \{0, 1\}$, where trust represents the cultural variable X in the general model in Section 2. There are three levels of human capital, $H \in \{H_1, H_2, H_3\}$, with $H_1 < H_2 < H_3$, and each group makes up one-third of the population.

Trust

Parents can shape the trust $T' \in \{0, 1\}$ of their children, and we aim to examine how the intergenerational transmission of trust interacts with economic decisions and neighborhood effects. Trust has dual implications for a child's outcomes. First, children interact with others in their local neighborhood, and the level of trust they develop influences how these interactions affect their development. Second, trust has long-term economic consequences, as it may enhance a child's ability to thrive in occupations that rely on cooperation, reputation, and social capital.

As in the previous section, we focus on the case of $\lambda = 1$, i.e., parents are fully paternalistic. The value function of a parent with human capital H and trust T is given by:

$$V(H, T) = \max_{N,P} \left\{C + zE\left[\tilde{u}(T', T'(N)) + \beta V_C(H', T')\right]\right\}.$$

Here $\tilde{u}(T', T'(N))$ represents the parent's paternalistic evaluation of the child's local interactions during childhood, which depends on both the child's own trust level T' and the average trust level in the local neighborhood, $T'(N)$. The term $V_C(H', T')$ captures the child's future adult utility as a function of skill H' and trust T', which is determined by adult income:

$$V_C(H', T') = Y(H', T').$$

In adulthood, trust is valuable, and especially so for a child with more human capital. To capture this in a simple way, we assume that returns are independent of human capital for a mistrusting individual, $Y(H_1, 0) = Y(H_2, 0) = Y(H_3, 0) = \bar{Y}$, but increasing in human capital for trusting individuals, $\bar{Y} < Y(H_1, 1) < Y(H_2, 1) < Y(H_3, 1)$.

The parent's maximization problem is subject to the budget constraint:

$$C = Y(H, T) - D(N).$$

Here $D(N)$ denotes the rent required to reside in neighborhood N. The child's human capital H' evolves stochastically as a function of the parent's human capital H, capturing either direct ability transmission or, in reduced form, the higher returns to human capital investment among highly skilled parents. For simplicity, we initially assume perfect transmission, so that $H' = H$. We will later relax this stark assumption.

Similar to the religion model, the child's trust is shaped by both parental influence and the child's own choices. The child selects their preferred trust level by maximizing utility:

$$v(H', T') = u(T') + \beta V_C(H', T').$$

Here, we assume that $u(1) > u(0)$, implying that children have a natural inclination for trusting other people. Since we also assume $V_C(H', 1) \geq V_C(H', 0)$, reflecting the economic returns to trust later in life, children will always opt for $T' = 1$ if they are given free choice. The parent then faces a decision: whether to accept the child's choice or to overrule it. Thus, as in the religion model, the choice reduces to selecting between two parenting styles: permissive ($P = 0$) or authoritarian ($P = 1$). Under a permissive approach, the child's preference prevails, and $T' = 1$. However, an authoritarian parent can override this choice, enforcing $T' = 0$. This imposition may involve indoctrination, restrictions on the child's social interactions (e.g., forbidding interactions with strangers, enforcing curfews), or other protective measures.

From the parent's perspective, limiting the child's trust may prevent harmful interactions, a concern captured by the paternalistic utility function $\tilde{u}(T', T'(N))$. Intuitively, the parent may view the child's natural preference for trust as naive and seek to correct it. However, the parent also recognizes that enforcing mistrust ($T' = 0$) affects the child's future utility, given the economic benefits of trust embedded in $V_C(H', T')$.

Residential choice

A second key parental decision concerns the choice of neighborhood. We consider a setting with two neighborhoods, $N \in \{G, B\}$, which may differ in the rent $D(N)$ required to live there. The neighborhood plays a crucial role because it shapes local interactions, which, in turn, influence the parent's paternalistic evaluation, $\tilde{u}(T', T'(N))$. Specifically, parents may perceive trust as more problematic in an environment where many peers are distrusting. As a result, the neighborhood choice interacts with the transmission of trust, influencing both parental strategies and children's socialization experiences.

Local interactions

Next, we turn to the impact of local interactions. Children may be influenced by interactions with other individuals in their neighborhood, and the outcomes of these interactions depend both on the child's cultural attitudes and on the distribution of attitudes in the surrounding environment. Specifically, if a child is trusting ($T' = 1$) but frequently encounters distrusting individuals, parents may perceive that the child risks being exploited or harmed. We capture the parent's perception of these interactions through the paternalistic utility $\tilde{u}(T', T'(N))$, where $T' \in \{0, 1\}$ represents the child's level of trust, and $T'(N) \in [0, 1]$ denotes the average trust in neighborhood N. We assume utility satisfies the following properties.

Assumption 1. *The paternalistic utility* $\tilde{u}(T', T'(N))$ *is such that:*

1. *Parents always prefer their children to be cautious:* $\tilde{u}(0, T'(N)) > \tilde{u}(1, T'(N))$*, meaning that, in terms of local interactions alone, parents favor distrust over trust.*
2. *Higher neighborhood trust is always beneficial:* $\tilde{u}(T', T'(N))$ *is strictly increasing in* $T'(N)$*, implying that living in a more trusting neighborhood is preferable.*
3. *The risk of being trusting diminishes in more trusting environments: The difference* $\tilde{u}(0, T'(N)) - \tilde{u}(1, T'(N))$ *is strictly decreasing in* $T'(N)$*, indicating that trust becomes less harmful when more people around the child are also trusting.*

This formulation captures the idea that children interact with others in the neighborhood, some of whom may have different levels of trust. If a trusting child encounters a distrusting individual, they might be taken advantage of, leading to lower utility. Since the probability of meeting a distrusting individual depends on the overall composition of the neighborhood, being trusting is relatively safer in an environment where a high share of individuals are also trusting.

We can interpret this paternalistic function as capturing the parent's belief that a trusting child is naive and does not fully comprehend the risks associated with interacting with distrusting individuals. The parent, recognizing these risks, may, therefore, attempt to shield the child by discouraging trust.

We abstract from parenting costs beyond the rent paid for residing in a particular neighborhood. Thus, the choice between permissive and authoritarian parenting (and, hence, between $T' = 1$ and $T' = 0$) solely depends on the paternalistic utility from local interactions $\tilde{u}(T', T'(N))$ and from the child's future utility as an adult $V_C(H', T')$.

Simplifying assumptions

To simplify the analysis and focus on the core mechanisms, while avoiding a taxonomic presentation, we impose the following additional assumptions:

Assumption 2. *The function* $\tilde{u}$ *is such that the following conditions are satisfied:*

1. *If the child has high skill,* $H' = H_3$*, the parent prefers the child to be trusting even if no one in the neighborhood is trusting* ($T'(N) = 0$)*:*

$$\tilde{u}(0, 0) - \tilde{u}(1, 0) < \beta \left(V_C(H_3, 1) - V_C(H_3, 0)\right).$$

2. *If the child has low skill,* $H' = H_1$*, the parent prefers the child to be distrusting even if everyone in the neighborhood is trusting* ($T'(N) = 1$)*:*

$$\tilde{u}(0, 1) - \tilde{u}(1, 1) > \beta \left(V_C(H_1, 1) - V_C(H_1, 0)\right).$$

3. *If the child has mid-level skill, $H' = H_2$, there is a threshold level $\bar{T}$ of neighborhood trust, where $0 < \bar{T} < 1$, such that the parent prefers the child to be trusting if $T'(N) \geq \bar{T}$ and distrusting otherwise, i.e.:*

$$\tilde{u}(0, \bar{T}) - \tilde{u}(1, \bar{T}) = \beta \left(V_C(H_2, 1) - V_C(H_2, 0) \right).$$

Hence, for parents of a high-skill child, the returns to trust in the child's future life always outweigh other considerations. Although this predetermines their decision to instill trust in their child, the parent still cares about the neighborhood; in fact, given that the child will be trusting, such a parent has a particularly strong desire to live in a neighborhood with many trusting individuals, which ensures a safer environment for local interactions. In contrast, parents of low-skill children perceive a lower return to trust in the future, and instill distrust in their offspring. For the middle group with $H' = H_2$, the decision to foster trust depends on the prevailing level of trust within their chosen neighborhood. This decision exhibits strategic complementarity: the higher the proportion of parents who instill trust in their children within a neighborhood, the more inclined each parent is to do the same.

5.2 Residential and cultural segregation in equilibrium

We now characterize possible equilibria in terms of neighborhood and socialization choices. There are two neighborhoods, ex-ante identical, denoted by $N \in \{G, B\}$. However, these locations will differ ex-post as families with different skill levels endogenously sort into distinct neighborhoods. We assume a fixed capacity for each neighborhood, ensuring that both G and B house an equal number of families. Consequently, half of all families must reside in G and the other half in B. When demand for one location exceeds its capacity, rents $D(N)$ adjust accordingly and are paid to a group of rentiers who play no other role in the economy.

An equilibrium that always exists is a fully segregated equilibrium, in which neighborhoods become sharply distinguished by their local culture. In this scenario, families with similar cultural traits and trust levels cluster together, reinforcing distinct socialization patterns across locations.

Proposition 5 (Segregated equilibrium). *There exists an equilibrium in which all high-skill families $H' = H_3$ and half of the mid-skill families $H' = H_2$ reside in neighborhood G. In this neighborhood, all parents are permissive ($P = 0$), and all children are trusting ($T' = 1$). All other families live in neighborhood B, where all parents are authoritarian ($P = 1$) and all children are distrusting ($T' = 0$).*[23]

[23] An alternative equilibrium that also exists is a fully symmetric equilibrium, in which the two neighborhoods are perfectly identical in all respects. Such an equilibrium would not be stable: a small perturbation in beliefs toward more trusting individuals in one neighborhood would unravel the equilibrium and lead to sorting. Given its fragility, we do not discuss this equilibrium.

The rent in neighborhood B is zero ($D(B) = 0$), while the rent in neighborhood G is determined such that mid-skill individuals are indifferent between the two locations, i.e.,

$$D(G) = z\,(\tilde{u}(1,1) - \tilde{u}(0,0) + \beta\,(V_C(H_2,1) - V_C(H_2,0)))\,.$$

Proof. The parental choices of the $H' = H_2$ group in each neighborhood are optimal because $T'(G) = 1 > \bar{T}$ and $T'(B) = 0 < \bar{T}$. Moreover, since utility is increasing in the local share of trusting individuals, each group prefers to reside in neighborhood G. However, the willingness to pay is highest for the H_3 group and lowest for the H_1 group. The specified rent ensures that the H_2 group is indifferent between the two locations, thereby clearing the market. □

The segregated equilibrium highlights the dual forces at play: parents aim to prepare their children for the future while also considering the local interactions they will experience. The original source of group differences stems from the higher return to trust for high-skill individuals. This initial difference is amplified by sorting and segregation, which reinforce the original disparities. In this case, it splits the middle group into two cultural subgroups based on their residential choices.

Additional equilibria may exist depending on the threshold $\bar{T}$, which determines the middle group's indifference between the two parenting styles. In particular, if this threshold is sufficiently low, the middle group could form its own subculture within neighborhood B by coordinating on permissive parenting. We label such equilibria partially segregated.

Proposition 6 (Partially segregated equilibrium). *If $\bar{T} < \frac{1}{3}$, there exists an additional equilibrium where all high-skill families $H' = H_3$ and half of mid-skill families $H' = H_2$ reside in neighborhood G, all parents in this neighborhood are permissive, $P = 0$, and all children are trusting $T' = 1$. All other families live in neighborhood B. Here all low-skill parents are authoritarian, $P = 1$, but all mid-skill individuals are permissive, $P = 0$, and hence the local fraction of trusting individuals is given by $T'(B) = \frac{1}{3}$. The rent in neighborhood B is zero, $D(B) = 0$, and the rent in the neighborhood G is such that mid-skill individuals are indifferent between the locations, i.e.:*

$$D(G) = z\left(\tilde{u}(1,1) - \tilde{u}\left(1, \frac{1}{3}\right)\right).$$

Proof. The parental choices of the $H' = H_2$ group are optimal because they constitute one-third of the population in the B neighborhood and, as assumed, $\bar{T} < \frac{1}{3}$. As in the fully segregated case, the willingness-to-pay for G is lowest for the H_1 group. The given rent ensures the group H_2 is indifferent and, therefore, clears the market. □

Notice that future returns no longer appear in the compensating differential that determines the rent, since mid-skill parents make the same decisions in both locations. Thus, the rent merely compensates for the direct effect of exposure to more distrusting individuals in local interactions in neighborhood B. Given that in this equilibrium both the H_2 and H_3 parents choose permissive parenting, the equilibrium rent in fact makes H_3 parents indifferent between the neighborhoods as well, so additional equilibria exist with different allocations of these two groups across the neighborhoods.

A parallel but welfare-lowering partial segregation equilibrium exists when $\bar{T}$ is close to one. In this case, mid-skill parents may fail to coordinate on permissive parenting even in neighborhood G.

5.3 Financial constraints and segregation

In our baseline model, the only force toward segregation comes from different perceived returns to trust across groups. More generally, this mechanism can interact with other forces that may push towards more or less segregation in society. To illustrate, consider the role of financial constraints. So far, we have not imposed that parents need to have sufficient funds to be able to pay rent in their chosen neighborhood; this is as if there is a financial market where the rent can be borrowed if necessary. Consider an alternative setting where parents can locate in neighborhood G only if they have sufficient income, $Y(H, T) \geq D(G)$ (rent will always be zero in neighborhood B). It then also matters how parental income $Y(H, T)$ correlates with the child's skill H', because some parents that would live in neighborhood G in the unconstrained equilibrium may not be able to afford to do so under the financial constraint.

So far, we have assumed that skill is perfectly correlated between parent and child, $H' = H$, so that the children with the highest skill also have the richest parents. More generally, a fraction of high-skill children may have parents with lower human capital and hence lower income. Consider the case where, in the group of high-skill children with $H' = H_3$, fraction $\mu < 0.5$ of parents are financially constrained, i.e., the parent's state variables are such that $Y(H, T) < D(G)$. Compared to the baseline case, the main new feature is that a fraction of families with high-skill children, $H' = H_3$, will now live in neighborhood B. Because these parents are always permissive, this will raise the fraction of trusting children in B. If there are sufficiently many such families, a segregated equilibrium is no longer possible, and instead all mid-skill parents in B will also be permissive and have trusting children.

Proposition 7 (Partially segregated equilibrium under financial constraints). *If $\mu \geq \frac{3\bar{T}}{2}$, there no longer exists a segregated equilibrium in which mid-skill children in neighborhood B are distrusting. The equilibrium, therefore, takes the form described in Proposition 6. Specifically, fraction $1 - \mu$ of high-skill families $H' = H_3$ and fraction $\frac{3-2(1-\mu)}{2}$ of mid-skill families $H' = H_2$ live in* *neighborhood G. All parents in this neighborhood are permissive, $P = 0$, and all children are trusting, $T' = 1$.*

All other families live in neighborhood B, where only parents with $H' = H_1$ are authoritarian, $P = 1$, whereas all other parents are permissive and their children are trusting. The share of trusting children in B is therefore $\frac{1}{3}$.

The rent in neighborhood B is zero, $D(B) = 0$, and the rent in neighborhood G is such that mid-skill individuals are indifferent between the locations, i.e.:

$$D(G) = z\left(\tilde{u}(1, 1) - \tilde{u}\left(1, \frac{1}{3}\right)\right).$$

Proof. The equilibrium outcome is as in Proposition 6; the segregated equilibrium does not exist because the presence of the $H' = H_3$ families in neighborhood B on its own is sufficient to induce all $H' = H_2$ parents to be permissive and have trusting children. □

The result suggests that social mobility, inequality, and residential segregation are self-reinforcing over time. In our baseline case with $H' = H$, parents with more human capital pass on this advantage to their children. As a result, sharp residential segregation arises, thereby further widening the gap between richer and poorer families. When initial differences across families are smaller, neighborhood disparities are also reduced, leading to lower inequality within the next generation.

5.4 Defensive parenting

Our model of trust and neighborhood sorting highlights how parental decisions regarding socialization are shaped by the local environment. In low-trust neighborhoods, parents adopt defensive parenting strategies to shield their children from negative peer influences, leading to a prevalence of authoritarian parenting. This mechanism aligns with empirical findings from Agostinelli et al. (2026), henceforth ADSZ, who investigate how parents intervene in their children's socialization choices, particularly regarding peer selection.

ADSZ analyze how both parental influence and peer interactions shape children's skill development during their high school years, using a dynamic rational choice framework. In their model, friendships are formed by mutual consent among children, but parents can intervene by steering their children away from academically weaker peers—a behavior the authors classify as authoritarian parenting. While this approach leads to an improvement in the average academic performance of a child's peer group, it comes at a cost by diminishing the overall effectiveness of skill formation. In their model, families do not choose the neighborhood in which they reside, which is exogenously given.

They analyze the theoretical mechanism and structurally estimate their model using data from the Add Health Study, a longitudinal survey tracking a cohort of US students throughout their high school years. The data set provides rich information on students' academic performance, family socioeconomic background, and parental control over peer selection. A key survey question asks children:

> *"Do your parents let you make your own decisions about the people you hang around with?"*

ADSZ classify parents who respond 'No' as authoritarian, meaning they restrict their children's choice of friends, while those who respond 'Yes' are classified as non-authoritarian. This empirical distinction allows them to examine the relationship between neighborhood environments and parenting styles.

Their study documents that authoritarian parenting is more prevalent when the average academic proficiency of the child's peer group is lower and when inequality within the peer group is high. This typically occurs in disadvantaged neighborhoods. This suggests that parents engage in defensive parenting not because of intrinsic authoritarian tendencies, but as a rational response to adverse local conditions. Their findings parallel the mechanism in our trust model, where parents in low-trust neighborhoods enforce strict control to protect their children from harmful influences.

Moreover, they find that authoritarian parenting is effective in improving peer quality: children whose parents interfere in their friendship choices subsequently interact with academically stronger peers. However, this comes at a cost: interfering in peer selection can weaken the parent-child relationship, potentially reducing children's responsiveness to other parental investments.[24]

Many of ADSZ's findings align with the framework developed in this section. In their model, authoritarian parenting is a defensive response to a hostile environment, just as, in our model, parents instill low trust in children growing up in poor neighborhoods. In both cases, parents intervene in peer selection when they perceive the social environment as harmful. A key innovation in our framework is the link between these parenting strategies and endogenous residential sorting.

5.5 Empirical evidence on parenting and neighborhoods from the WVS

We now return to the data from the WVS discussed in Section 4.4 to document new evidence on the relationship between parenting styles and neighborhood quality. Our model suggests that parents engage in defensive parenting when their children are exposed to potentially harmful influences in their local environment. Specifically, parental perceptions of an unsafe environment or of negative peer influences—such as crime or substance abuse—are associated

24 Agostinelli et al. (2022) extend and adapt the earlier framework to analyze the impact of the COVID-19 shock, focusing on the temporary shutdown of schools.

with a greater likelihood of adopting an authoritarian parenting style as a form of protection. By exerting stricter control over their children's interactions and activities, authoritarian parents aim to shield them from adverse social influences.

A direct implication of this mechanism is that families residing in high-risk neighborhoods should be more prone to authoritarian parenting. In contrast, in safer, high-trust communities, parents can afford to adopt a more permissive approach, allowing greater autonomy in their children's social interactions. This reasoning further implies that trust and neighborhood quality should be positively correlated: individuals living in safer neighborhoods, where cooperation is prevalent, are more likely to express trust in others. Conversely, in disadvantaged neighborhoods with lower social cohesion and greater exposure to crime, individuals may develop a more skeptical outlook, reinforcing a culture of distrust. If empirically confirmed, these patterns would provide further support for the role of local conditions in shaping both parenting styles and cultural attitudes toward trust.

Measuring neighborhood quality and trust

We proxy neighborhood quality in two ways. First, we use a question capturing whether a neighborhood is perceived as unsafe and prone to violence. The question asks: *"How frequently do the following things occur in your neighborhood? Street violence and fights."* We classify a neighborhood as 'High neighborhood quality' if the respondent answers 'Not Frequently' or 'Not at All Frequently' to this question. All other responses are categorized as 'Low neighborhood quality.'

Second, we use factor analysis to construct a measure of overall neighborhood quality. This approach extracts a common component that reflects overall neighborhood conditions, yielding a continuous quality score. While the question remains the same, we now consider the full range of related behaviors included in the WVS. In addition to street violence and fights, respondents are asked about the frequency of robberies, alcohol consumption in the streets, police or military interference in private life, racist behavior, drug sales in the streets, and sexual harassment. Each behavior is rated from 1 ('Very Frequently') to 4 ('Not at All Frequently'). We apply factor analysis to this set of variables and generate a continuous factor-based score labeled *Neighborhood quality (Factor)*. This score is standardized to have mean zero and standard deviation one, with higher values indicating better neighborhood quality. For regressions, we use the continuous score; for graphical analysis by parenting style, we split the distribution at the median to define 'high' and 'low' quality neighborhoods.

We follow a similar strategy to construct measures of trust. The WVS includes a general trust question: *"Generally speaking, would you say that most people can be trusted or that you need to be very careful in dealing with people?"* We define the variable *Trust in people* as an indicator equal to one if the respondent selects 'Most people can be trusted.' In addition, the WVS contains a battery of more detailed questions: *"I'd like to ask you how much you trust people from various groups. Could you tell me for each whether you trust people from this group completely, somewhat, not very much or not at all?"* Respondents rate their level of trust in various groups, including family, neighbors, people they know personally, people they meet for the first time, people of another religion, and people of another nationality. Each group is rated on a scale from 1 ('Trust Completely') to 4 ('Do Not Trust at All'). We adopt the perspective of parents and focus on generalized trust (*Trust in people*), along with trust in the two most relevant groups: people met for the first time and neighbors. Using factor analysis, we combine these measures into a continuous trust score, *Trust (Factor)*, standardized to have a mean of zero and a standard deviation of one. The factor-based score is reversed so that higher values correspond to higher trust. As with neighborhood quality, we use the continuous score in regressions and define 'high' versus 'low' trust by the median split in graphical analyses.

Neighborhood quality and trust

We begin by examining the relationship between neighborhood quality and trust. Ideally, we would use average trust levels measured at the neighborhood level. However, in the absence of such data, we rely on self-reported individual trust. This measure captures both local social attitudes and the respondent's personal disposition, making it an imperfect proxy. Nonetheless, it allows us to assess whether empirical patterns are consistent with the theoretical framework.

Fig. 4 presents the binscatter plot of the relationship between neighborhood quality and trust, using the factor-based measures described above. The figure reveals a strong positive correlation: individuals living in higher-quality neighborhoods exhibit higher levels of trust. This finding aligns with our theory, which suggests that trust formation is shaped by the local environment. In safer, more stable communities, social interactions are more predictable and cooperative norms are reinforced, fostering higher reciprocal trust. In contrast, trust tends to erode in lower-quality neighborhoods.

Parenting style across neighborhoods

We now turn to the relationship between neighborhood quality, trust, and parenting styles. Panel (a) of Fig. 5 compares parenting styles across low- and high-quality neighborhoods, based on the reported frequency of violence. Panel (b) employs the factor-based quality score and divides the sample according to its median value.

Both panels convey a compelling message. In lower-quality neighborhoods, i.e., higher exposure to violence, respondents are 18 pp more likely to adopt an authoritarian style. In contrast, in higher-quality neighborhoods, permissive and

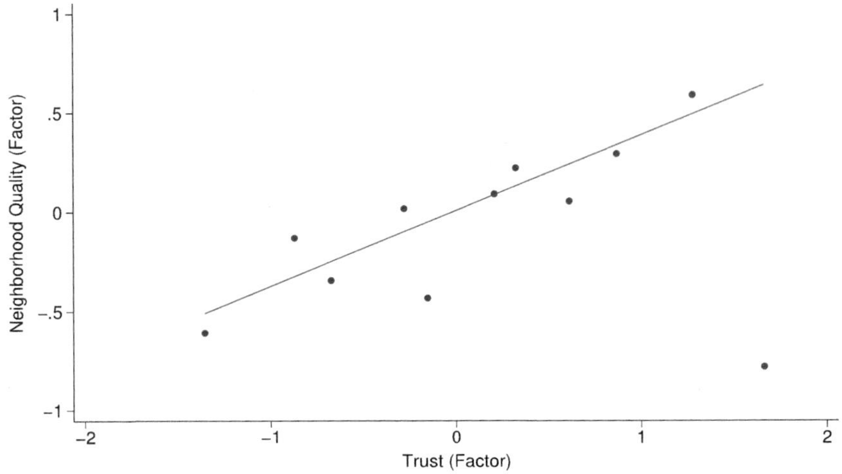

FIGURE 4 Neighborhood quality and trust.
Notes: This figure shows the relationship (binscatter) between neighborhood quality and trust in the sample. Neighborhood quality is derived from factor analysis based on responses to questions about the frequency of specific behaviors in the neighborhood. Trust is similarly measured using factor analysis based on responses to questions about trust in different groups of people. See the text for further details.

authoritative parenting styles are more common, each increasing by 9 pp. Using the factor-based score yields qualitatively similar results: moving from high to low neighborhood quality increases the likelihood of authoritarian parenting by 11 pp and decreases the probability of permissive and authoritative styles by 7 pp and 5 pp, respectively.[25]

Fig. 6 replicates this analysis using trust measures. Panel (a) distinguishes between high and low general trust in people; panel (b) uses the factor-based trust score. The results echo those for neighborhood quality. Respondents with low levels of trust are 13 pp more likely to be authoritarian than high-trust respondents, 7 pp less likely to be authoritative, and 6 pp less likely to be permissive. The factor-based measure in panel (b) yields similar findings. These patterns support the idea that individuals who express higher trust in their social environment are more likely to engage in less intensive forms of parenting.

Regression analysis

The regression analysis in Table 1 discussed above already includes controls for neighborhood quality and trust, serving a dual purpose. First, it allows us to test the robustness of the estimated effect of religiosity after accounting for

25 The effect size is smaller with the factor-based measure. This suggests that parents are especially responsive to visible threats such as violence, which may be perceived as the most salient risk.

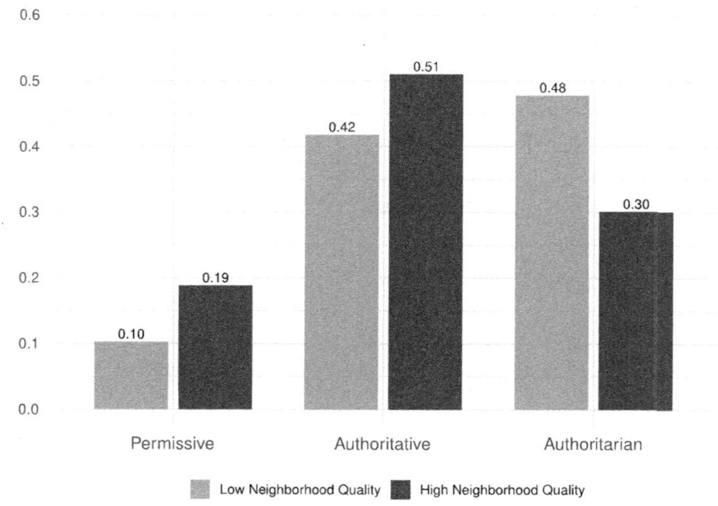

(a) Violent Episodes in the Neighborhood

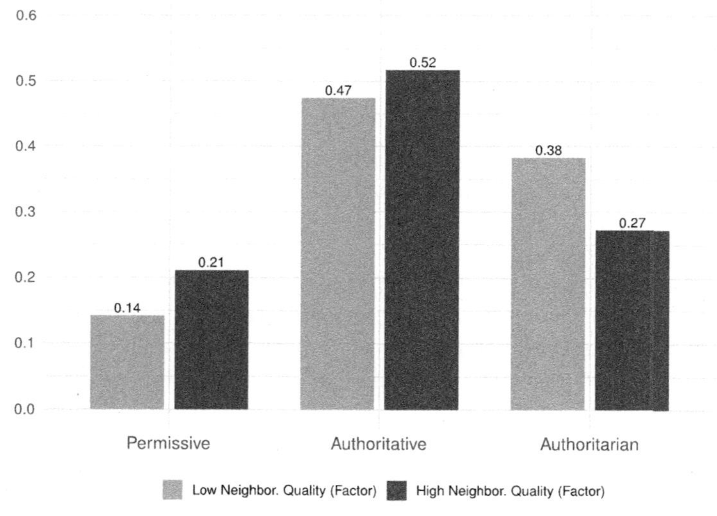

(b) Factor Analysis

FIGURE 5 Parenting style and neighborhood quality.
Notes: This figure shows the distribution of parenting styles by neighborhood quality. In panel (a), 'Low Neighborhood Quality' refers to respondents who answered 'Very frequently' or 'Quite frequently' to the question: *"How frequently do the following things occur in your neighborhood? Street violence and fights"*. All other respondents are classified as living in 'High Neighborhood Quality' neighborhoods. In panel (b), 'High Neighborhood Quality' refers to respondents with a neighborhood quality score above the median; 'Low Neighborhood Quality' refers to those with a score below the median. The neighborhood quality score is derived from factor analysis based on responses to questions about the frequency of specific behaviors in the neighborhood. See the text for further details.

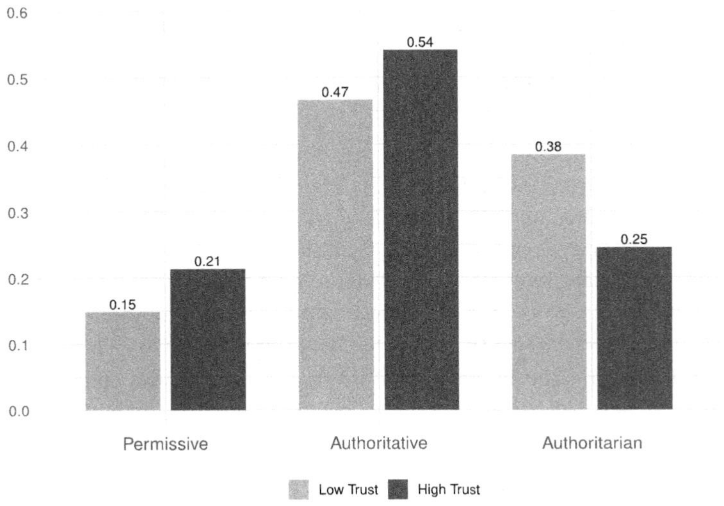

(a) Trust in People

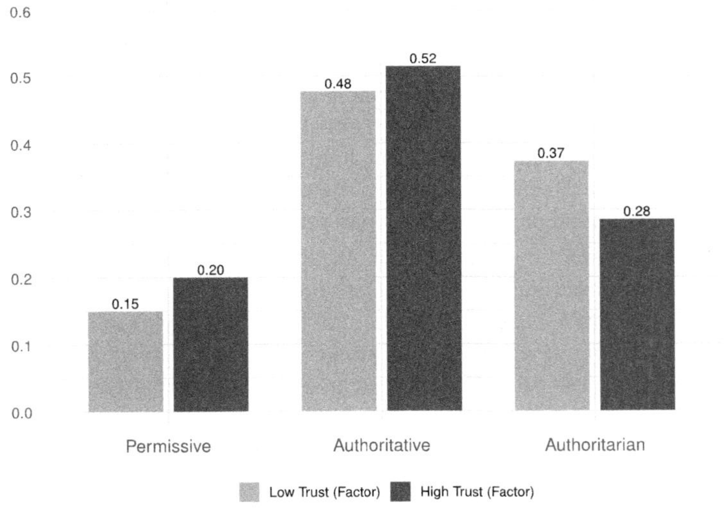

(b) Factor Analysis

FIGURE 6 Parenting style and trust.

Notes: This figure shows the distribution of parenting styles by level of trust. In panel (a), 'High Trust' refers to respondents who answered 'Most people can be trusted' to the question: *"Generally speaking, would you say that most people can be trusted or that you need to be very careful in dealing with people?"*. Respondents who answered 'Need to be very careful' are classified as 'Low Trust.' In panel (b), 'High Trust' refers to respondents with a trust score above the median; 'Low Trust' refers to those with a score below the median. The trust score is derived from factor analysis based on responses to questions about generalized trust and trust in different groups of people such as people met for the first time and neighbors. See the text for further details.

neighborhood- and trust-related factors. Second, it helps isolate the independent relationship between neighborhood quality, trust, and parenting styles, while controlling for individual characteristics—such as age, race, education, and religiosity—that are themselves associated with the propensity to adopt specific parenting styles.

As anticipated, we also include trust as a regressor, in line with our theoretical framework, which suggests that both the external environment (defensive parenting) and the local level of trust (strategic complementarity) influence the choice of parenting style. Specifically, high-risk environments may induce authoritarian parenting as a protective strategy to shield children from negative influences, whereas higher levels of individual or community trust may encourage more permissive or authoritative approaches.

Table 1 confirms the insights from the graphical analysis and provides additional evidence. As in previous analyses, we rely on both the direct and factor-based measures of neighborhood quality and trust. First, irrespective of the proxy used, higher neighborhood quality and trust are positively associated with permissive parenting and negatively associated with authoritarian parenting. Columns (8) and (9) confirm that parenting intensity decreases with neighborhood quality and trust. Second, although neighborhood quality and trust are correlated, their estimated effects are of similar magnitude and remain independently significant, suggesting that they capture distinct dimensions of the social environment. Third, the effects are economically meaningful. For example, the estimates in columns (2) and (5) suggest that moving from a low-trust respondent in a low-quality neighborhood to a high-trust respondent in a high-quality neighborhood increases the probability of permissive parenting by 10 pp and reduces the likelihood of authoritarian parenting by 14 pp.

Taken together, the data analysis in this section supports the central mechanism proposed in our theoretical model. The observed relationship between neighborhood quality, trust, and parenting styles aligns with the prediction that parents engage in defensive parenting in response to adverse environments. In low-trust, high-risk neighborhoods, parents are more likely to adopt an authoritarian style to shield their children from negative peer influences. Conversely, in safer, high-trust communities, parents have greater flexibility to adopt more permissive or authoritative approaches, fostering autonomy and social adaptability in their children.

The significant role of individual trust further highlights the complementarity between cultural attitudes and external conditions in shaping (and being shaped by) parenting decisions, which echoes the work of Hauk and Sáez Martí (2002), Sáez Martí and Zenou (2012), and Rohner et al. (2013) in different contexts. These results suggest that social capital and community trust are not merely outcomes of economic and social structures but also active forces driving the intergenerational transmission of cultural traits. Future research could examine how interventions aimed at improving neighborhood environments and strengthening trust might shift parenting strategies, thereby helping to mitigate the persistence of economic and cultural disparities across generations.

5.6 Relationship with the literature

This section builds on the vast literature on neighborhood effects, with a focus on social interactions and human capital formation. We offer a selective overview of the contributions most relevant to our analysis. A number of recent studies by Raj Chetty and Nathaniel Hendren (e.g., Chetty and Hendren, 2018a, 2018b) provide empirical evidence on the role of neighborhoods in intergenerational mobility. Using their estimates, Fogli et al. (2025) calibrate a general equilibrium model, showing how rising income inequality and residential segregation in the United States since the 1980s have mutually reinforced each other through parental neighborhood selection and educational investments.[26]

Another strand of research examines the effects of relocating children to better neighborhoods. Chetty et al. (2016) use data from a randomized housing intervention to show that moving from high- to low-poverty areas significantly improves children's long-term economic outcomes. Similarly, Chyn (2018) analyzes public housing demolitions in Chicago, where displaced low-income families relocated using housing vouchers. He finds that displaced children—especially those relocated at a young age—experience higher employment rates, higher wages, lower violent crime arrests, and reduced high school dropout rates. Agostinelli et al. (2026)—discussed in more detail above—use an estimated structural model to assess the scalability of these moving-to-opportunity policies. While their quantitative predictions align with previous findings, they show that scaling up the policy leads to significantly smaller positive effects, primarily due to the defensive reaction of parents in more affluent communities.[27] Our work is also related to the extensive literature on social interactions within neighborhoods (e.g., Brock and Durlauf, 2001a, 2001b, 2002, and Durlauf and Ioannides, 2010) and the associated empirical literature.[28]

A puzzle in the literature on cultural transmission and social interactions is why negative social phenomena like juvenile crime persist even though no parents (or at least no significant proportion of them) actively promote

[26] A large strand of the literature focused on the mechanism leading to residential segregation; see, for example, Schelling (1971), Benabou (1993), Durlauf (1996), Fernández and Rogerson (1996), Aliprantis and Carroll (2018), Eckert and Kleineberg (2021), and Chyn and Daruich (2022).

[27] A related literature examines the relationship between residential segregation, house price capitalization, and unequal access to high-quality public schools. See, for example, Black (1999), Epple and Sieg (1999), Bayer et al. (2007), and Agostinelli et al. (2024).

[28] See also, among others, Case and Katz (1991), Altonji and Mansfield (2018), Hoxby (2000), Zimmerman (2003), Calvó-Armengol et al. (2009), Sacerdote (2011), Arcidiacono et al. (2012), Carrell et al. (2013), Feld and Zölitz (2017), Boucher et al. (2023), and List et al. (2025).

them. Sáez Martí and Sjögren (2008) show that this can occur in models of cultural transmission where parents influence their children's values, but when transmission fails, children learn from peers. The persistence of such negative cultures is possible when the selection of different cultural variants within peer groups depends not only on their frequency but also on the intrinsic merit children assign to them. In other words, children may be attracted to certain types of juvenile behavior, which can grow and persist even in the face of concerted efforts by the surrounding adult community.

Finally, our work relates to the literature on the economic value of trust and social capital that was already mentioned in Section 4. Trust is deeply persistent, transmitted across generations, and linked to economic performance across countries. Durlauf (2006) highlights how neighborhood sorting and social interactions reinforce disparities in trust and economic mobility, while Alesina and La Ferrara (2002) show that trust declines in more unequal and ethnically fragmented societies. Dohmen et al. (2012) provide an empirical study of the transmission of risk and trust attitudes within families, documenting strong correlations between parents and children in these dimensions, in line with the theory outlined here.

5.7 Taking stock

In this section, we presented a stylized model in which parents may choose to dampen their children's natural inclination to trust others. We interpret this behavior as a form of defensive parenting. When parents perceive the local environment as a threat rather than a nurturing opportunity, they may prioritize protection over openness, discouraging interactions with the broader community. These defensive strategies shape local social norms and can give rise to persistent low-trust equilibria.

Much of the existing literature—including our own prior work—has examined the persistence of spatial inequality through mechanisms such as human capital investment and segregation dynamics, often with an eye toward policy interventions. Our analysis adds a new dimension by focusing on parenting and cultural transmission. We show how the intergenerational transmission of preferences and beliefs interacts with neighborhood choice and local peer effects, reinforcing patterns of inequality over time.

Trust plays a central role. In low-trust environments, parents may restrict their children's exposure to the surrounding community, limiting interactions outside the family or immediate circle. These choices reinforce residential sorting and deepen social divisions. Over time, this process becomes self-reinforcing: the resulting segregation and lack of trust shape the next generation's environment, prompting similar parenting responses. By embedding cultural transmission into models of neighborhood choice, education, and mobility, we offer a new perspective on how segregation sustains not only economic inequality, but also persistent differences in values, aspirations, and social norms, ultimately reinforcing social stratification.

6 Outlook and future research

The economic literature linking parenting and culture discussed in this chapter is still in its early stages. Existing work shows that the economic approach is fruitful and can account for a range of empirical regularities concerning the mutual interaction between economic conditions, parenting, cultural values, and social stratification. Much remains to be done to expand this approach to new areas, quantify the strength of its mechanisms, and derive policy implications.

A first challenge is that existing datasets provide a limited picture of the relationships posited by the economics of parenting. While there is evidence on how economic conditions relate to specific parenting choices and cultural values, the theories developed here rest on the idea that parents anticipate returns to instilling particular values and engaging in certain parenting strategies, based on expectations about their children's future economic success and well-being. The field would benefit from empirical research documenting parents' beliefs about the short- and long-term repercussions of their parenting choices and the values they aim to transmit. A nascent literature has begun to gather such evidence in the context of human capital accumulation (Attanasio et al., 2022; Boneva et al., 2022); these approaches could be extended to encompass the broader range of parenting choices and expected outcomes at the heart of the theories discussed here.

A second task is to assess the role of endogenous parenting responses in shaping culture, relative to other contributing forces. While the models presented in this chapter are conceptual, they are, in principle, amenable to quantification through calibration or structural estimation. ADSZ demonstrate this in the context of parental interventions in peer formation using a simulated method-of-moments estimation. Similar approaches could be employed to assess the role of parenting in the formation of culture, the emergence of social stratification, and broader patterns of social mobility.

A more specific challenge that the theoretical framework may help address is the persistence of differences in economic outcomes across social groups. This question was at the core of Max Weber's foundational work. While Weber's specific claim regarding the central role of Protestant ethics in economic success has since been debated, contemporary examples abound of social groups that achieve disproportionate economic success—such as Chinese immigrant communities in Southeast Asia, South Asians in the United States, and British Nigerians in the United Kingdom. Economists have traditionally shied away from considering preferences or cultural factors as an explanation for such patterns, instead treating preferences as given and focusing on other factors such as technology and institutions. The justification of this approach was that economics, as perceived at the time, had little to say about the origin of preferences. The approach described here moves beyond this perspective by conceiving preferences and cultural values themselves as outcomes of an economic process, as proposed originally by Stigler and Becker (1977) and developed further in the work described in this chapter. It would be fruitful to examine the mutual links between the economic conditions faced by particular groups in society, the cultural values that are formed in response to these conditions, and their role in the economic success of such groups.

A closely related issue is the long-term persistence of social status within families and low multi-generational social mobility (see, e.g., Clark, 2014 and Braun and Stuhler, 2018). It is now well documented that correlations in economic status across distant generations far exceed what would be predicted by simple extrapolations of one-generation mobility. Given the dilution of genetic endowments through marriage in each generation, it is unlikely that biological factors account for much of this correlation. Rather, the evidence points to the persistence of cultural values within families. The models discussed in this chapter offer promising tools for analyzing how such values are formed and transmitted within family dynasties.

Quantitative models are essential to bring these insights to bear on policy. This chapter has touched on topics central to public policy, including inequality, social mobility, education, and equal opportunity. While a large literature exists on these topics, relatively few studies incorporate endogenous parental responses. ADSZ show that interventions aimed at shaping peer environments—such as busing policies that mix children from different neighborhoods—can be considerably affected by how parents respond. A policy that appears promising in partial equilibrium, with parental behavior held fixed, may prove ineffective once implemented at scale, precisely because behavioral adjustments offset the intended effects. This logic likely extends to many other policy areas. If parents perceive the stakes to be high, they will respond. Understanding these responses is a critical challenge for future research.

Future work could also move beyond the household to examine how institutions, technologies, and media interact with parenting in shaping norms and preferences. For instance, digital environments and social networks may amplify or undermine parental influence, with potentially unequal effects across socioeconomic groups. This issue is particularly pressing in light of the widespread diffusion of smartphones, social media, and online gaming, which are transforming children's daily experiences and the ways in which they interact. Institutions beyond the family—such as schools, religious organizations, and workplaces—also interact with parenting choices in shaping cultural transmission. While we touched upon some of these institutional interactions, much remains to be understood about how they collectively shape cultural evolution over time.

Another promising direction involves studying how rising environmental risk—due to climate change, migration, or political instability—shapes parenting strategies and, in turn, affects broader societal dynamics. Incorporating the endogenous evolution of parenting norms into macro-level models could also shed light on how micro-level decisions compound to shape collective beliefs, trust, and institutional resilience over time. More broadly, it can help explain persistent differences in development trajectories, support for institutions, and the long-run effects of inequality in both high- and low-income countries.

Finally, the work described in this chapter builds on insights from the other social sciences. Social stratification and mobility are core concerns of sociology. While we have highlighted shared roots, notably in the work of Max Weber, this survey has mostly focused on contributions from economics and has not engaged in depth with current sociological research. We have also abstracted from important aspects such as affective bonds or identity formation, which are central in psychology and anthropology. Much could be gained by bridging these gaps more systematically—bringing new ideas into economics while demonstrating how models of purpose-driven parental behavior can fruitfully contribute to research in other social sciences.

7 Conclusion

This chapter examines how parental decisions shape the intergenerational transmission of preferences, values, and human capital in a broad economic and social context. Our discussion is guided by a framework in which parents are motivated by the desire to build a stairway to their children's success. They make decisions on parenting style, human-capital investment, and the transmission of specific cultural values based on the anticipated economic and cultural returns to particular traits and skills.

We apply this framework to both economic and non-economic value transmission. First, we analyze the transmission of work ethic, a value directly linked to economic success, and show how parenting choices interact with economic conditions, shaping cultural stratification and the endogenous formation of social classes. Second, as an example of a non-economic value, we examine the transmission of religion. Here, parents may transmit religious or secular worldviews not only for economic reasons, but also due to intrinsic normative beliefs. Third, we extend our analysis to social interactions and neighborhood choice, highlighting how residential sorting reinforces disparities in trust, human capital investment, and parenting practices. Parents' concerns about external influences—such as peers and institutions—shape their location decisions, further entrenching spatial inequality and cultural segmentation. These dynamics are mutually reinforcing: parenting strategies shape the social environment, which in turn influences future parenting decisions, creating a feedback loop that amplifies long-run inequality.

The theoretical predictions of the models we describe are supported by empirical evidence from the World Values Survey. First, we find that higher religiosity is associated with a greater likelihood of adopting an authoritarian parenting style, consistent with our model's implication that parents with strong normative convictions exert stricter control over their children's exposure to the outside environment. Second, we provide evidence of defensive parenting across communities: in disadvantaged neighborhoods, parents tend to shield their children from external influences, even if this means forgoing potential benefits. In environments marked by crime or juvenile delinquency, the perceived risks of openness outweigh its expected returns. Finally, trust in others is positively correlated with neighborhood quality, in line with our model's prediction that parents are more likely to foster trust when the surrounding environment is perceived as safe and supportive.

Understanding parenting strategies and the dynamics of cultural transmission provides insight into the persistence of inequality across generations and highlights potential policy levers for mitigating disparities. Policies that enhance access to high-quality education, reduce economic segregation, and foster social trust could weaken the self-reinforcing link between parental choices and persistent inequality.

Research on the mutual interactions between parenting decisions, cultural transmission, and economic outcomes is still in its early stages. For young researchers interested in parenting and culture, the field offers many promising and underexplored directions. We hope that many of the open research questions in this area will be taken up in the coming years.

Appendix A Proofs for propositions

Proof of Proposition 2. If $\rho \geq \tilde{\rho}$, parents with $A = 1$ will invest given the argument in the proof of Proposition 1, while others will not. The steady-state share s_1 of individuals with a work ethic $A = 1$ then satisfies:

$$s_1 = p_0 + s_1(p_1 - p_0),$$

implying that

$$s_1 = \frac{p_0}{1 + p_0 - p_1}.$$

Let $p_{M,1} = 1 - w_N/w_M + \rho$ denote the probability that an individual with a work ethic ($A = 1$) will choose to be a manager, with the corresponding probability for the other group given by $p_{M,0} = 1 - w_N/w_M$. Then, the probability for a child of a parent with work ethic to become a manager is $p_{CM,1} = p_1 p_{M,1} + (1 - p_1)p_{M,0}$, and, for other children, we have $p_{CM,0} = p_0 p_{M,1} + (1 - p_0)p_{M,0}$, where $p_{CM,1} > p_{CM,0}$. The shares of managers and laborers, respectively, who have a work ethic are given by:

$$s_{1,M} = \frac{s_1 p_{M,1}}{s_1 p_{M,1} + (1 - s_1)p_{M,0}},$$

$$s_{1,N} = \frac{s_1(1 - p_{M,1})}{s_1(1 - p_{M,1}) + (1 - s_1)(1 - p_{M,0})}.$$

Here, we have $s_{1,M} > s_{1,N}$ because having a work ethic makes it more likely to choose to be a manager. We can now write the transition matrix from the occupation of the parent to the occupation of the child as:

$$T = \begin{pmatrix} s_{1,M} p_{CM,1} + (1 - s_{1,M}) p_{CM,0} & s_{1,M}(1 - p_{CM,1}) + (1 - s_{1,M})(1 - p_{CM,0}) \\ s_{1,N} p_{CM,1} + (1 - s_{1,N}) p_{CM,0} & s_{1,N}(1 - p_{CM,1}) + (1 - s_{1,N})(1 - p_{CM,0}) \end{pmatrix}.$$

The first row contains the probabilities that a child of a manager will turn into a manager and a worker, respectively, and the second row contains the transition probabilities for workers. In each entry, the denominator reflects the composition of the parent's occupation in terms of $A = 1$ and $A = 0$ individuals. Consider now the difference Δ in the probability that the child will be a manager between a manager and a laborer parent, i.e., the difference between the entries in the first column of T. We have:

$$\begin{aligned} \Delta &= s_{1,M} p_{CM,1} + (1 - s_{1,M}) p_{CM,0} - (s_{1,N} p_{CM,1} + (1 - s_{1,N}) p_{CM,0}) \\ &= (s_{1,M} - s_{1,N}) p_{CM,1} - (s_{1,M} - s_{1,N}) p_{CM,0} \\ &= (s_{1,M} - s_{1,N})(p_{CM,1} - p_{CM,0}) \\ &> 0, \end{aligned}$$

where the last step follows because $p_{CM,1} > p_{CM,0}$ and $s_{1,M} > s_{1,N}$. Thus, there is persistence in occupation from generation to generation and, therefore, limited social mobility. Next, the difference in the share of managers and laborers who have a work ethic is given by:

$$\begin{aligned} s_{1,M} - s_{1,N} &= \frac{s_1 p_{M,1}}{s_1 p_{M,1} + (1 - s_1) p_{M,0}} - \frac{s_1(1 - p_{M,1})}{s_1(1 - p_{M,1}) + (1 - s_1)(1 - p_{M,0})} \\ &= \frac{s_1}{s_1 + (1 - s_1)\frac{p_{M,0}}{p_{M,1}}} - \frac{s_1}{s_1 + (1 - s_1)\frac{1 - p_{M,0}}{1 - p_{M,1}}}, \end{aligned}$$

which is increasing in $p_{M,1}$ and, hence, in ρ, given that $p_{M,1} = 1 - w_N / w_M + \rho$. An increase in ρ also increases the difference $p_{CM,1} - p_{CM,0}$ in the probability that a child will turn into a manager between parents with and without a work ethic, implying that an increase in ρ increases Δ and, hence, lowers social mobility in occupation. Lastly, when ρ rises, lower social mobility in occupation also translates into lower social mobility in terms of income, because managers earn more than laborers on average and an increase in ρ further increases the average earnings gap between the two occupations. □

Proof of Proposition 4. The parental decision problem implies that a parent with religion R and parenting cost ξ chooses to be authoritarian if:

$$z \mu_R \Delta p > \xi + z \beta \rho.$$

Here, the left-hand side is the benefit from authoritarian parenting, given by the paternalistic enjoyment of a greater probability of passing on one's beliefs, and the right-hand side is the cost, given by the cost of authoritarian parenting ξ plus the altruistic concern about the forgone return to independence for the child. The parent will, therefore, choose to be authoritarian if the condition:

$$\rho < \frac{\mu_R \Delta p - \xi z^{-1}}{\beta}$$

is satisfied. The first condition states that this condition holds even for the M parent with the highest cost of parenting $\xi = 1$ (recall that ξ is uniformly distributed on $[0, 1]$). The second condition implies that there is an interior cutoff for ξ such that M parents below the cutoff are authoritarian and those above are permissive. As ρ rises, the share of M parents below the cutoff declines, implying that a rising share of M parents are permissive, which raises the share of children who become secular. The third condition states that M parents with the lowest cost $\xi = 0$ are permissive, while F parents with the highest cost $\xi = 1$ remain authoritarian. Regarding the steady-state shares, in this last case, the steady-state distribution across types $\mathbf{s} = (s_F \ s_M \ s_S)'$ has to satisfy:

$$\mathbf{s} = \begin{pmatrix} p & \frac{1-p}{2} & \frac{1-p}{2} \\ \frac{1-p}{2} & \frac{1-p}{2} & \frac{1-p}{2} \\ \frac{1-p}{2} & p & p \end{pmatrix} \mathbf{s},$$

which yields:

$$\mathbf{s} = \begin{pmatrix} \frac{1}{3} \\ \frac{1-p}{2} \\ \frac{p}{2} + \frac{1}{6} \end{pmatrix}.$$

Regarding the impact of ρ on the income gap between secular and fervent individuals, there are two forces. First, a rise in ρ unambiguously raises the relative income of independent children who were subject to a permissive parenting style, and there are more such children among the secular than among the fervent. Second, a rise in ρ changes the composition of types in each group; in particular, if ρ is large, there are relatively more fervent individuals who were raised permissively, but (randomly) adopted fervent beliefs. The second channel disappears as p approaches one (where transmission becomes deterministic). Hence, for p sufficiently close to one the first channel dominates, and raising ρ unambiguously increases the income gap. □

Appendix B Additional tables

See next pages.

TABLE B.1 The determinants of parenting style—full set of controls.

	Permissive			Authoritarian			Intensity of parenting		
	(1)	(2)	(3)	(4)	(5)	(6)	(7)	(8)	(9)
Religious	−0.09***	−0.09***	−0.10***	0.10***	0.10***	0.11***	0.20***	0.19***	0.21***
	(0.02)	(0.02)	(0.02)	(0.02)	(0.02)	(0.02)	(0.03)	(0.03)	(0.03)
High neighbor. quality		0.06***			−0.07**			−0.12***	
		(0.02)			(0.03)			(0.04)	
Trust in people		0.04***			−0.07***			−0.12***	
		(0.02)			(0.02)			(0.03)	
Neighbor. quality (Factor)			0.02**			−0.02			−0.03**
			(0.01)			(0.01)			(0.02)
Trust (Factor)			0.02*			−0.03**			−0.05***
			(0.01)			(0.01)			(0.02)
High education	0.06***	0.04***	0.04**	−0.11***	−0.09***	−0.09***	−0.17***	−0.13***	−0.13***
	(0.02)	(0.02)	(0.02)	(0.02)	(0.02)	(0.02)	(0.03)	(0.03)	(0.03)
Black	−0.08***	−0.06***	−0.07***	0.37***	0.34***	0.36***	0.45***	0.40***	0.43***
	(0.02)	(0.02)	(0.02)	(0.04)	(0.04)	(0.04)	(0.05)	(0.05)	(0.05)
Hispanic	−0.04*	−0.03	−0.02	0.17***	0.16***	0.15***	0.21***	0.18***	0.18***
	(0.02)	(0.02)	(0.02)	(0.03)	(0.03)	(0.03)	(0.04)	(0.04)	(0.04)
Other	0.01	0.02	0.02	0.06*	0.05	0.06*	0.05	0.04	0.04
	(0.03)	(0.03)	(0.03)	(0.03)	(0.03)	(0.03)	(0.05)	(0.05)	(0.05)

continued on next page

TABLE B.1 *(continued)*

	Permissive			Authoritarian			Intensity of parenting		
	(1)	(2)	(3)	(4)	(5)	(6)	(7)	(8)	(9)
Female	0.03*	0.03**	0.03**	−0.06***	−0.07***	−0.07***	−0.09***	−0.10***	−0.10***
	(0.02)	(0.02)	(0.02)	(0.02)	(0.02)	(0.02)	(0.03)	(0.03)	(0.03)
Age	−0.00	0.00	0.00	−0.00	−0.01*	−0.01*	−0.00	−0.01	−0.01
	(0.00)	(0.00)	(0.00)	(0.00)	(0.00)	(0.00)	(0.00)	(0.00)	(0.00)
Age squared	0.00	−0.00	−0.00	0.00	0.00	0.00	0.00	0.00	0.00
	(0.00)	(0.00)	(0.00)	(0.00)	(0.00)	(0.00)	(0.00)	(0.00)	(0.00)
Observations	2,466	2,455	2,405	2,466	2,455	2,405	2,466	2,455	2,405

Notes: This table shows the relationship between religiosity, neighborhood quality, trust, and parenting style. The dependent variables are: an indicator for a permissive parenting style (columns 1–3); an indicator for an authoritarian parenting style (columns 4–6); and a measure of intensity of parenting, coded as 1 for permissive, 2 for authoritative, and 3 for authoritarian (columns 7–9). *High neighborhood quality* is an indicator for respondents who answer 'Not frequently' or 'Not at all frequently' to the question: *"How frequently do the following things occur in your neighborhood? Street violence and fights"*. *Trust in people* is an indicator for respondents who answer 'Most people can be trusted' to the question: *"Generally speaking, would you say that most people can be trusted or that you need to be very careful in dealing with people?"*. *Neighborhood quality (Factor)* is derived from factor analysis based on responses to questions about the frequency of specific behaviors at the neighborhood level. *Trust (Factor)* is derived from factor analysis based on responses to questions about trust in different groups of people. *High education* is an indicator for respondents with at least a bachelor's degree or equivalent education (ISCED 6). *White* is the omitted race. See the text for further details. Robust standard errors are reported in parentheses.
$^{*}p < 0.10$, $^{**}p < 0.05$, $^{***}p < 0.01$.

TABLE B.2 The determinants of parenting style—multinomial probit.

	Base outcome: Intensity of parenting = 1 (Permissive)					
	Intensity of parenting = 2 (Authoritative)			Intensity of parenting = 3 (Authoritarian)		
	(1)	(2)	(3)	(4)	(5)	(6)
Religious	0.35***	0.36***	0.37***	0.66***	0.66***	0.69***
	(0.09)	(0.09)	(0.09)	(0.09)	(0.09)	(0.09)
Marginal effect	[−0.01]	[−0.01]	[−0.01]	[0.10]	[0.10]	[0.11]
High neighbor. quality		−0.26*			−0.44***	
		(0.13)			(0.14)	
Marginal effect		[0.00]			[−0.06]	
Trust in people		−0.12			−0.39***	
		(0.09)			(0.09)	
Marginal effect		[0.03]			[−0.08]	
Neighbor. quality (Factor)			−0.08			−0.12**
			(0.05)			(0.05)
Marginal effect			[−0.00]			[−0.02]
Trust (Factor)			−0.06			−0.17***
			(0.06)			(0.06)
Marginal effect			[0.01]			[−0.03]

continued on next page

TABLE B.2 *(continued)*

	Base outcome: Intensity of parenting = 1 (Permissive)					
	Intensity of parenting = 2 (Authoritative)			Intensity of parenting = 3 (Authoritarian)		
	(1)	(2)	(3)	(4)	(5)	(6)
High education	−0.13	−0.09	−0.08	−0.53***	−0.41***	−0.42***
	(0.09)	(0.09)	(0.09)	(0.09)	(0.09)	(0.10)
Marginal effect	[0.06]	[0.05]	[0.05]	[−0.11]	[−0.09]	[−0.09]
Observations	2,466	2,455	2,405	2,466	2,455	2,405

Notes: This table shows the relationship between religiosity, neighborhood quality, trust, and parenting style using a multinomial probit regression analysis. The dependent variable is a measure of intensity of parenting, coded as 1 for permissive, 2 for authoritative, and 3 for authoritarian. Regression coefficients and marginal effects are reported with reference to the baseline outcome, which is the permissive parenting style. *High neighborhood quality* is an indicator for respondents who answer 'Not frequently' or 'Not at all frequently' to the question: *"How frequently do the following things occur in your neighborhood? Street violence and fights"*. *Trust in people* is an indicator for respondents who answer 'Most people can be trusted' to the question: *"Generally speaking, would you say that most people can be trusted or that you need to be very careful in dealing with people?"*. *Neighborhood quality (Factor)* is derived from factor analysis based on responses to questions about the frequency of specific behaviors at the neighborhood level. *Trust (Factor)* is derived from factor analysis based on responses to questions about trust in different groups of people. *High education* is an indicator for respondents with at least a bachelor's degree or equivalent education (ISCED 6). All regressions control for race, gender, age, and age squared. See the text for further details. Robust standard errors are reported in parentheses; marginal effects are reported in square brackets. $^{*}p < 0.10$, $^{**}p < 0.05$, $^{***}p < 0.01$.

Appendix C World Values Survey (Wave 7): list of countries

We provide below the list of countries in WVS Wave 7 for which it is possible to construct our measures of parenting styles and religiosity:

Andorra; Argentina; Australia; Bangladesh; Armenia; Bolivia; Brazil; Myanmar; Canada; Chile; China; Taiwan ROC; Colombia; Cyprus; Czechia; Ecuador; Ethiopia; Germany; Greece; Guatemala; Hong Kong SAR; Indonesia; Iran; Iraq; Japan; Kazakhstan; Jordan; Kenya; South Korea; Kyrgyzstan; Lebanon; Libya; Macau SAR; Malaysia; Maldives; Mexico; Mongolia; Morocco; Netherlands; New Zealand; Nicaragua; Nigeria; Pakistan; Peru; Philippines; Puerto Rico; Romania; Russia; Serbia; Singapore; Slovakia; Vietnam; Zimbabwe; Tajikistan; Thailand; Tunisia; Turkey; Ukraine; Egypt; Great Britain; United States; Uruguay; Venezuela; Northern Ireland.

References

Agostinelli, Francesco, Doepke, Matthias, Sorrenti, Giuseppe, Zilibotti, Fabrizio, 2022. When the great equalizer shuts down: schools, peers, and parents in pandemic times. Journal of Public Economics 206, 104574.

Agostinelli, Francesco, Doepke, Matthias, Sorrenti, Giuseppe, Zilibotti, Fabrizio, 2026. It takes a village: the economics of parenting with neighborhood and peer effects. Journal of Political Economy 134 (1), 313–365.

Agostinelli, Francesco, Luflade, Margaux, Martellini, Paolo, 2024. On the Spatial Determinants of Educational Access. NBER Working Paper 32246.

Alesina, Alberto, Fuchs-Schündeln, Nicola, 2007. Good-bye Lenin (or not?): the effect of communism on people's preferences. American Economic Review 97 (4), 1507–1528.

Alesina, Alberto, Giuliano, Paola, 2014. Family ties. In: Aghion, Philippe, Durlauf, Steven N. (Eds.), Handbook of Economic Growth, vol. 2A. Elsevier, pp. 177–215.

Alesina, Alberto, La Ferrara, Eliana, 2002. Who trusts others? Journal of Public Economics 85 (2), 207–234.

Algan, Yann, Cahuc, Pierre, 2010. Inherited trust and growth. American Economic Review 100 (5), 2060–2092.

Aliprantis, Dionissi, Carroll, Daniel R., 2018. Neighborhood dynamics and the distribution of opportunity. Quantitative Economics 9 (1), 247–303.

Altonji, Joseph G., Mansfield, Richard K., 2018. Estimating group effects using averages of observables to control for sorting on unobservables: school and neighborhood effects. American Economic Review 108 (10), 2902–2946.

Andersen, Thomas Barnebeck, Sinding Bentzen, Jeanet, Dalgaard, Carl-Johan, Sharp, Paul Richard, 2017. Pre-reformation roots of the protestant ethic. The Economic Journal 127 (604), 1756–1793.

Arcidiacono, Peter, Foster, Gigi, Goodpaster, Natalie, Kinsler, Josh, 2012. Estimating spillovers using panel data, with an application to the classroom. Quantitative Economics 3 (3), 421–470.

Attanasio, Orazio, 2015. The determinants of human capital formation during the early years of life: theory, measurement, and policies. Journal of the European Economic Association 13 (6), 949–997.

Attanasio, Orazio, Boneva, Teodora, Rauh, Christopher, 2022. Parental beliefs about returns to different types of investments in school children. Journal of Human Resources 57 (6), 1789–1825.

Barro, Robert J., McCleary, Rachel M., 2003. Religion and economic growth across countries. American Sociological Review 68 (5), 760–781.

Baumrind, Diana, 1967. Child care practices anteceding three patterns of preschool behavior. Genetic Psychology Monographs 75 (1), 43–88.
Bayer, Patrick, Ferreira, Fernando, McMillan, Robert, 2007. A unified framework for measuring preferences for schools and neighborhoods. Journal of Political Economy 115 (4), 588–638.
Becker, Gary S., 1981. A Treatise on the Family. Harvard University Press.
Becker, Gary S., Mulligan, Casey B., 1997. The endogenous determination of time preference. The Quarterly Journal of Economics 112 (3), 729–758.
Becker, Sascha O., Woessmann, Ludger, 2009. Was Weber wrong? A human capital theory of protestant economic history. The Quarterly Journal of Economics 124 (2), 531–596.
Becker, Sascha O., Woessmann, Ludger, 2013. Not the opium of the people: income and secularization in a panel of Prussian counties. American Economic Review 103 (3), 539–544.
Benabou, Roland, 1993. Workings of a city: location, education, and production. The Quarterly Journal of Economics 108 (3), 619–652.
Bisin, Alberto, Verdier, Thierry, 2000. Beyond the melting pot: cultural transmission, marriage, and the evolution of ethnic and religious traits. The Quarterly Journal of Economics 115 (3), 955–988.
Bisin, Alberto, Verdier, Thierry, 2001. The economics of cultural transmission and the dynamics of preferences. Journal of Economic Theory 97 (2), 298–319.
Bisin, Alberto, Verdier, Thierry, 2010. The economics of cultural transmission and socialization. In: Benhabib, Jess, Bisin, Alberto, Jackson, Matthew O. (Eds.), Handbook of Social Economics, vol. 1A. Elsevier, Amsterdam. Chapter 9.
Black, Sandra E., 1999. Do better schools matter? Parental valuation of elementary education. The Quarterly Journal of Economics 114 (2), 577–599.
Boneva, Teodora, Golin, Marta, Kaufmann, Katja, Rauh, Christopher, 2022. Beliefs about Maternal Labor Supply. IZA Discussion Paper No. 15788.
Botticini, Maristella, Eckstein, Zvi, 2005. Jewish occupational selection: education, restrictions, or minorities? Journal of Economic History 65 (4), 922–948.
Botticini, Maristella, Eckstein, Zvi, 2012. The Chosen Few: How Education Shaped Jewish History, 70–1492. Princeton University Press, Princeton, NJ.
Boucher, Vincent, Del Bello, Carlo L., Panebianco, Fabrizio, Verdier, Thierry, Zenou, Yves, 2023. Education transmission and network formation. Journal of Labor Economics 41 (1), 129–173.
Bourdieu, Pierre, 1986. The forms of capital. In: Richardson, J.G. (Ed.), Handbook of Theory and Research for the Sociology of Education. Greenwood Press, New York, pp. 241–258.
Braun, Sebastian Till, Stuhler, Jan, 2018. The transmission of inequality across multiple generations: testing recent theories with evidence from Germany. The Economic Journal 128 (609), 576–611.
Brock, William A., Durlauf, Steven N., 2001a. Discrete choice with social interactions. The Review of Economic Studies 68 (2), 235–260.
Brock, William A., Durlauf, Steven N., 2001b. Interactions-based models. In: Heckman, J.J., Leamer, E.E. (Eds.), Handbook of Econometrics, vol. 5. Elsevier, Amsterdam, pp. 3297–3380.
Brock, William A., Durlauf, Steven N., 2002. A multinomial-choice model of neighborhood effects. American Economic Review 92 (2), 298–303.
Calhoun, Craig, 2004. Gerhard Lenski, some false oppositions, and 'the religious factor'. Sociological Theory 22 (2), 194–204.
Calvó-Armengol, Antoni, Patacchini, Eleonora, Zenou, Yves, 2009. Peer effects and social networks in education. The Review of Economic Studies 76 (4), 1239–1267.
Cantoni, Davide, 2015. The economic effects of the protestant reformation: testing the Weber hypothesis in the German lands. Journal of the European Economic Association 13 (4), 561–598.
Carrell, Scott E., Sacerdote, Bruce I., West, James E., 2013. From natural variation to optimal policy? The importance of endogenous peer group formation. Econometrica 81 (3), 855–882.
Case, Anne, Katz, Lawrence F., 1991. The Company You Keep: The Effects of Family and Neighborhood on Disadvantaged Youths. NBER Working Paper 3705.

Chetty, Raj, Hendren, Nathaniel, 2018a. The impacts of neighborhoods on intergenerational mobility I: childhood exposure effects. The Quarterly Journal of Economics 133 (3), 1107–1162.

Chetty, Raj, Hendren, Nathaniel, 2018b. The impacts of neighborhoods on intergenerational mobility II: county-level estimates. The Quarterly Journal of Economics 133 (3), 1163–1228.

Chetty, Raj, Hendren, Nathaniel, Katz, Lawrence F., 2016. The effects of exposure to better neighborhoods on children: new evidence from the moving to opportunity experiment. American Economic Review 106 (4), 855–902.

Chyn, Eric, 2018. Moved to opportunity: the long-run effects of public housing demolition on children. American Economic Review 108 (10), 3028–3056.

Chyn, Eric, Daruich, Diego, 2022. An Equilibrium Analysis of the Effects of Neighborhood-based Interventions on Children. NBER Working Paper 29927.

Clark, Gregory, 2014. The Son Also Rises: Surnames and the History of Social Mobility. Princeton University Press.

Cobb-Clark, Deborah A., Salamanca, Nicolas, Zhu, Anna, 2019. Parenting style as an investment in human development. Journal of Population Economics 32 (4), 1315–1352.

Coleman, James S., 1988. Social capital in the creation of human capital. American Journal of Sociology 94 (Suppl.), S95–S120.

de la Croix, David, Doepke, Matthias, Mokyr, Joel, 2018. Clans, guilds, and markets: apprenticeship institutions and growth in the preindustrial economy. The Quarterly Journal of Economics 133 (1), 1–70.

de Vries, Jan, 2008. The Industrious Revolution: Consumer Behavior and the Household Economy, 1650 to the Present. Cambridge University Press, Cambridge, UK.

Doepke, Matthias, Klasing, Mariko, 2025. Preparing kids for capitalism: the effect of German reunification on the intergenerational transmission of preferences. London School of Economics. Unpublished manuscript.

Doepke, Matthias, Sorrenti, Giuseppe, Zilibotti, Fabrizio, 2019. The economics of parenting. Annual Review of Economics 11 (1), 55–84.

Doepke, Matthias, Zilibotti, Fabrizio, 2008. Occupational choice and the spirit of capitalism. The Quarterly Journal of Economics 123 (2), 747–793.

Doepke, Matthias, Zilibotti, Fabrizio, 2014. Culture, entrepreneurship, and growth. In: Aghion, Philippe, Durlauf, Steven N. (Eds.), Handbook of Economic Growth, vol. 2A. Elsevier, Amsterdam. Chapter 1.

Doepke, Matthias, Zilibotti, Fabrizio, 2017. Parenting with style: altruism and paternalism in intergenerational preference transmission. Econometrica 85 (5), 1331–1371.

Doepke, Matthias, Zilibotti, Fabrizio, 2019. Love, Money, and Parenting: How Economics Explains the Way We Raise Our Kids. Princeton University Press, Princeton, New Jersey.

Dohmen, Thomas, Falk, Armin, Huffman, David, Sunde, Uwe, 2012. The intergenerational transmission of risk and trust attitudes. The Review of Economic Studies 79 (2), 645–677.

Durlauf, Steven N., 1996. A theory of persistent income inequality. Journal of Economic Growth 1 (1), 75–93.

Durlauf, Steven N., 2006. Groups, social influences, and inequality. In: Bowles, Samuel, Durlauf, Steven N., Hoff, Karla (Eds.), Poverty Traps. Princeton University Press, Princeton, NJ, pp. 141–175. Chapter 6.

Durlauf, Steven N., Fafchamps, Marcel, 2004. Social Capital. Working Paper 10485. National Bureau of Economic Research.

Durlauf, Steven N., Ioannides, Yannis M., 2010. Social interactions. Annual Review of Economics 2 (1), 451–478.

Eckert, Fabian, Kleineberg, Tatjana, 2021. Saving the American Dream? Education Policies in Spatial General Equilibrium. Policy Research Working Paper 9574. World Bank.

Enke, Benjamin, 2019. Kinship, cooperation, and the evolution of moral systems. The Quarterly Journal of Economics 134 (2), 953–1019.

Epple, Dennis, Sieg, Holger, 1999. Estimating equilibrium models of local jurisdictions. Journal of Political Economy 107 (4), 645–681.

Feld, Jan, Zölitz, Ulf, 2017. Understanding peer effects: on the nature, estimation, and channels of peer effects. Journal of Labor Economics 35 (2), 387–428.

Fernández, Raquel, 2008. Culture and economics. In: Durlauf, Steven N., Blume, Lawrence E. (Eds.), New Palgrave Dictionary of Economics, second edition. Palgrave Macmillan, New York.

Fernández, Raquel, Fogli, Alessandra, 2009. Culture: an empirical investigation of beliefs, work, and fertility. American Economic Journal: Macroeconomics 1 (1), 146–177.

Fernández, Raquel, Rogerson, Richard, 1996. Income distribution, communities, and the quality of public education. The Quarterly Journal of Economics 111 (1), 135–164.

Fogli, Alessandra, Guerrieri, Veronica, Ponder, Mark, Prato, Marta, 2025. The End of the American Dream? Inequality and Segregation in US Cities. Institute Working Paper 111. Federal Reserve Bank of Minneapolis.

Giuliano, Paola, Nunn, Nathan, 2021. Understanding cultural persistence and change. The Review of Economic Studies 88 (4), 1541–1581.

Glaeser, Edward L., Laibson, David, Sacerdote, Bruce, 2002. An economic approach to social capital. Economic Journal 112 (483), F437–F458.

Gorodnichenko, Yuriy, Roland, Gérard, 2011. Individualism, innovation, and long-run growth. Proceedings of the National Academy of Sciences 108 (Suppl. 4), 21316–21319.

Gorodnichenko, Yuriy, Roland, Gérard, 2017. Culture, institutions, and the wealth of nations. Review of Economics and Statistics 99 (3), 402–416.

Greif, Avner, 1994. Cultural beliefs and the organization of society: a historical and theoretical reflection on collectivist and individualist societies. Journal of Political Economy 102 (5), 912–950.

Greif, Avner, 2006. Family structure, institutions, and growth: the origins and implications of western corporations. American Economic Review 96 (2), 308–312.

Greif, Avner, Tabellini, Guido, 2010. Cultural and institutional bifurcation: China and Europe compared. American Economic Review 100 (2), 135–140.

Guiso, Luigi, Sapienza, Paola, Zingales, Luigi, 2003. People's opium? Religion and economic attitudes. Journal of Monetary Economics 50 (1), 225–282.

Guiso, Luigi, Sapienza, Paola, Zingales, Luigi, 2004. The role of social capital in financial development. American Economic Review 94 (3), 526–556.

Guiso, Luigi, Sapienza, Paola, Zingales, Luigi, 2006. Does culture affect economic outcomes? Journal of Economic Perspectives 20 (2), 23–48.

Guiso, Luigi, Sapienza, Paola, Zingales, Luigi, 2016. Long-term persistence. Journal of the European Economic Association 14 (6), 1401–1436.

Haerpfer, Christian, Inglehart, Ronald, Moreno, Alejandro, Welzel, Christian, Kizilova, Kseniya, Diez-Medrano, Jaime, Lagos, Marta, Norris, Pippa, Ponarin, Eduard, Puranen, Bi, 2022. World Values Survey: Round Seven – Country-Pooled Datafile Version 5.0.0. JD Systems Institute and WVSA Secretariat, Madrid, Spain and Vienna, Austria.

Hanifan, Lyda J., 1916. The rural school community center. The Annals of the American Academy of Political and Social Science 67 (1), 130–138.

Hauk, Esther, Sáez Martí, María, 2002. On the cultural transmission of corruption. Journal of Economic Theory 107 (2), 311–335.

Heckman, James J., Mosso, Stefano, 2014. The economics of human development and social mobility. Annual Review of Economics 6 (1), 689–733.

Hoxby, Caroline, 2000. Peer Effects in the Classroom: Learning from Gender and Race Variation. NBER Working Paper 7867.

Inglehart, Ronald, 1990. Culture Shift in Advanced Industrial Society. Princeton University Press, Princeton, NJ.

Kant, Immanuel, 1785. Groundwork of the Metaphysics of Morals. Translated by Mary Gregor. Cambridge University Press, 1997.

Knack, Stephen, Keefer, Philip, 1997. Does social capital have an economic payoff? A cross-country investigation. The Quarterly Journal of Economics 112 (4), 1251–1288.

Lenski, Gerhard, 1961. The Religious Factor: A Sociological Study of Religion's Impact on Politics, Economics, and Family Life. Doubleday, Garden City, NY.

List, John, Momeni, Fatemeh, Vlassopoulos, Michael, Zenou, Yves, 2025. Neighborhood Spillover Effects of Early Childhood Interventions. Working Paper. University of Chicago.

Lizzeri, Alessandro, Siniscalchi, Marciano, 2008. Parental guidance and supervised learning. The Quarterly Journal of Economics 123 (3), 1161–1195.

Lundberg, Shelly, Romich, Jennifer L., Tsang, Kwok Ping, 2009. Decision-making by children. Review of Economics of the Household 7 (1), 1–30.

Maccoby, Eleanor E., Martin, John A., 1983. Socialization in the context of the family: parent-child interaction. In: Mussen, Paul H., Hetherington, Eileen M. (Eds.), Handbook of Child Psychology: Vol. 4. Socialization, Personality, and Social Development. Wiley, New York, pp. 1–101.

Marx, Karl, 1859. A Contribution to the Critique of Political Economy. Translated by S.W. Ryazanskaya. International Publishers, 1970.

McCleary, Rachel M., Barro, Robert J., 2019. The Wealth of Religions: The Political Economy of Believing and Belonging. Princeton University Press, Princeton, NJ.

Mokyr, Joel, 2018. A Culture of Growth: The Origins of the Modern Economy. Princeton University Press, Princeton, NJ.

Putnam, Robert D., 1993. Making Democracy Work: Civic Traditions in Modern Italy. Princeton University Press, Princeton, NJ.

Putnam, Robert D., 2000. Bowling Alone: The Collapse and Revival of American Community. Simon & Schuster, New York.

Rohner, Dominic, Thoenig, Mathias, Zilibotti, Fabrizio, 2013. War signals: a theory of trade, trust, and conflict. The Review of Economic Studies 80 (3), 1114–1147.

Sacerdote, Bruce, 2011. Peer effects in education: how might they work, how big are they and how much do we know thus far? In: Hanushek, Eric A., Machin, Stephen, Woessmann, Ludger (Eds.), Handbook of the Economics of Education, vol. 3. Elsevier, Amsterdam, pp. 249–277.

Sáez Martí, María, Sjögren, Anna, 2008. Peers and culture. Scandinavian Journal of Economics 110 (1), 73–92.

Sáez Martí, María, Zenou, Yves, 2012. Cultural transmission and discrimination. Journal of Urban Economics 72 (2–3), 137–146.

Sáez Martí, María, Zilibotti, Fabrizio, 2008. Preferences as human capital: rational choice theories of endogenous preferences and socioeconomic changes. Finnish Economic Papers 21 (2), 81–94.

Schelling, Thomas C., 1971. Dynamic models of segregation. Journal of Mathematical Sociology 1 (2), 143–186.

Stigler, George J., Becker, Gary S., 1977. De gustibus non est disputandum. American Economic Review 67 (2), 76–90.

Veblen, Thorstein, 1899. The Theory of the Leisure Class. Dover, New York, 1994.

Weber, Max, 1905. The Protestant Ethic and the Spirit of Capitalism. Translated by Talcott Parsons, with a foreword by R.H. Tawney. Charles Scribner's Sons, New York, 1958. Republished by Dover, New York, 2003.

Weber, Max, 1920. The Economic Ethics of the World Religions. Mohr Siebeck, Tübingen, Germany. Originally published as a series of essays between 1915 and 1920.

Zhang, Lin, Ikeda, Shinsuke, 2016. Welfare-enhancing parental altruism and children's habit formation. International Review of Economics 63, 281–303.

Zimmerman, David, 2003. Peer effects in academic outcomes: evidence from a natural experiment. Review of Economics and Statistics 85 (1), 9–23.

9780443471841